myeconlab®

Get Ahead of the Curve

Save Time.

Improve Results.

More than 3 million students have used a Pearson MyLab product to get a better grade.

MyEconLab is an all-in-one learning and testing environment for introductory economics. This easy-to-navigate site provides students with a variety of resources, including

- An interactive Pearson eText

- Personalized learning opportunities—YOU choose what, where, and when you want to study

- Self-assessment tests that create a personalized study plan to guide you on making the most efficient use of study time

- Dynamic resources including videos and animated graphs to enhance your learning experience

To take advantage of all that MyEconLab has to offer, you will need an access code. If you do not already have an access code, you can buy one online at **www.myeconlab.com.**

Personalized Learning

In MyEconLab you are treated as an individual with specific learning needs.

Auto-Graded Tests and Assignments

* MyEconLab comes with two pre-loaded sample tests for each chapter so you can self-assess your understanding of the material.

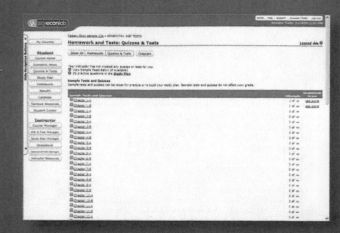

Personalized Study Plan

* A study plan is generated based on your results on sample tests and instructor assignments. You can clearly see which topics you have mastered and, more importantly, which topics you need to work on!

Practice Problems

* Use the study plan exercises to get practice where you need it. To check how you're doing, click "results" to get an overview of all your scores.

Save Time. Improve Results. www.myeconlab.com

Pearson eText

Pearson eText gives you access to the text wherever you can access the internet. eText pages look exactly like the printed text, offering powerful new functionality for students and instructors.

Users can create notes, highlight text in different colours, create bookmarks, zoom, click hyperlinked words and phrases to view definitions, and choose single-page or two-page view.

Pearson eText allows for quick navigation using a table of contents and provides full-text search. The eText may also offer links to associated media files, enabling users to access videos and animations.

Save Time. Improve Results. www.myeconlab.com

Economics Today

The Micro View

PEARSON

ALWAYS LEARNING

Miller • Abbott • Fefferman • Kessler • Sulyma

Economics Today

The Micro View

Third Custom Edition for Mohawk College

Taken from:
Economics Today: The Micro View, Fifth Canadian Edition
by Roger LeRoy Miller, Brenda Abbott, Sam Fefferman, Ronald K. Kessler,
and Terrence Sulyma

Cover Art: Courtesy of PhotoDisc, DigitalVision/Getty Images

Taken from:

Economics Today: The Micro View, Fifth Canadian Edition
by Roger LeRoy Miller, Brenda Abbott, Sam Fefferman, Ronald K. Kessler, and Terrence Sulyman
Copyright © 2012, 2009, 2005, 2002, 1999 by Pearson Education Canada, Inc.
Published by Addison-Wesley
Toronto, Ontario

This special edition published in cooperation with Pearson Learning Solutions.

All trademarks, service marks, registered trademarks, and registered service marks are the property of their respective owners and are used herein for identification purposes only.

Pearson Learning Solutions, 501 Boylston Street, Suite 900, Boston, MA 02116
A Pearson Education Company
www.pearsoned.com

Printed in Canada

1 2 3 4 5 6 7 8 9 10 V092 16 15 14 13 12 11

000200010270757717

MHB

ISBN 10: 1-256-31626-1
ISBN 13: 978-1-256-31626-8

My married name is Abbott, my maiden name is Novakowski. Two families united from different backgrounds: one from PEI, the other from Alberta; one English, one Ukrainian/Polish. A true multicultural family.

—B.A./B.N.

I would like to dedicate this book to Brenda, Tara, Amy, Shane, Kaitlyn, and Cohen. I am very fortunate to have the support of such a loving family.

—S.F.

For Lea, a lifesaver in the storms of my life.

—R.K.

To John and Mary Sulyma, for instilling in me a thirst for knowledge and love of learning. To Andrea, Drew, and Vanya for their love and support.

—T.S.

Brief Contents

Contents

Preface

From the Authors

In creating *Economics Today: The Micro View*, Fifth Canadian Edition, substantial revisions to the previous edition were made, based on the helpful suggestions and comments provided by adopters and reviewers. We were careful to ensure that any changes we made to the fifth edition would maintain the straightforward and approachable style that has made this book so popular in postsecondary institutions across Canada.

As instructors with extensive teaching experience in both college and university settings, we want to continue to present a text that students can relate to based on their personal, social, and career interests. We also hope that this book will encourage students to broaden their interests to include local, national, and global economic issues. Many of our students will not take subsequent economics courses; in that case, we want them to be ready for the world, and not just for intermediate economics courses.

The approach used in *Economics Today: The Micro View*, Fifth Canadian Edition, is based on the belief that students learn more when they are involved and engaged in the material they are studying. The presentation of issues and applications in a Canadian setting is a major strength of this text. Each chapter begins with an issue that introduces certain economic principles; those principles are presented throughout the chapter, and at the end of the chapter an Issues and Applications section explains how those principles can be applied to that issue. This section ends with For Critical Analysis questions, which help reinforce the theory at hand and encourage students to reflect on economics in the "real" world—their world.

In addition, each chapter contains numerous short Examples and Policy Examples that further illustrate the points being made in the text. Each of these examples is accompanied by For Critical Analysis questions, which encourage students to actively apply the economic principles presented in the chapter. Mindful of the importance of global events to Canada's economic well-being, we have used many examples and issues that connect Canada with the rest of the world. Suggested solutions to all of the For Critical Analysis questions are provided at the end of the text.

The text's emphasis on real world current socioeconomic issues provides for numerous engaging student assessment activities, including critical thinking exercises, Internet and paper-based research projects, student group debates, online discussions, blogs, and wikis. By encouraging each student to learn to analyze an issue from numerous viewpoints, the text helps develop critical analysis and advocacy skills that will prove invaluable in future employment situations.

For the Fifth Canadian Edition we have reorganized and consolidated chapter material, updated numerous Issues and Applications and Example boxes, included additional Canadian and international comparisons and examples, and added new end-of-chapter questions and exercises.

Below is a sample of some of the new issues and examples discussed in the Fifth Canadian Edition:

- Nice Guys Can Finish First (Example 1-4)
- Beware of "Free" Lecture Podcasts (Example 2-1)
- A Canadian Housing Bubble? (Chapter 3 Issues and Applications)
- The Great Global Recession of 2009 (Chapter 5 Issues and Applications)
- Is Ticketmaster in Cahoots with Scalpers? (Example 6-2)
- When Blogging Becomes a Competitive Business (Example 9-1)
- The High Cost of Staying Alive (Example 10-3)
- Wind Blows Down Canadian Wireless Prices (Example 11-5)

In addition, we have made several important changes to the chapter content.

As suggested by reviewers, we have removed the former Chapter 7, "Rents, Profit, and Financial Environment of Business," as this does not directly relate to the key microeconomic topics typically covered in a Principles of Microeconomics course.

The two labour chapters—Chapter 13 "Labour Demand and Supply" and Chapter 14 "Unions and Labour Market Monopoly Power"—have been combined into one chapter by streamlining the concepts covered.

A new chapter entitled "Market Efficiency and Market Failure" has been added, which follows the chapter covering elasticity. This new chapter introduces key concepts such as consumer surplus, producer surplus, and deadweight loss, which provides the option of more rigorously assessing the efficiency losses related to different types of market failure and government policies. In subsequent chapters new appendices have been added that apply these key concepts to situations of market failure and government policies covered in the main body of the chapter. **Those who wish to proceed to subsequent chapters without covering this new content can easily do so, without any loss of continuity.**

In the end, we believe that *Economics Today: The Micro View* and MyEconLab will provide students with a relevant and interesting resource—one that will present students with a "window to the world" that will help them in their personal lives as citizens and professionals. We hope that you will enjoy this book and begin to appreciate the many ways in which economics can be a part of your day-to-day activities.

Economic Principles in Practice

CHAPTER OPENING ISSUES. Each opening issue motivates student interest in the key chapter concepts. The issue presented is revisited in the Issues and Applications section at the culmination of the chapter.

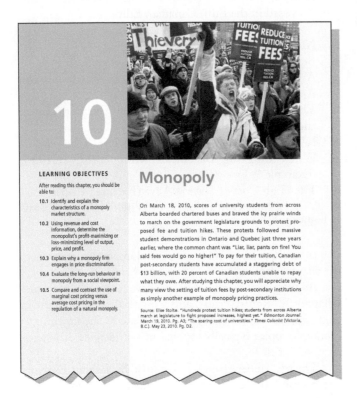

LEARNING OBJECTIVES

After reading this chapter, you should be able to:

10.1 Identify and explain the characteristics of a monopoly market structure.

10.2 Using revenue and cost information, determine the monopolist's profit-maximizing or loss-minimizing level of output, price, and profit.

10.3 Explain why a monopoly firm engages in price discrimination.

10.4 Evaluate the long-run behaviour of a monopoly from a social viewpoint.

10.5 Compare and contrast the use of marginal cost pricing versus average cost pricing in the regulation of a natural monopoly.

Monopoly

On March 18, 2010, scores of university students from across Alberta boarded chartered buses and braved the icy prairie winds to march on the government legislature grounds to protest proposed fee and tuition hikes. These protests followed massive student demonstrations in Ontario and Quebec just three years earlier, where the common chant was "Liar, liar, pants on fire! You said fees would go no higher!" To pay for their tuition, Canadian post-secondary students have accumulated a staggering debt of $13 billion, with 20 percent of Canadian students unable to repay what they owe. After studying this chapter, you will appreciate why many view the setting of tuition fees by post-secondary institutions as simply another example of monopoly pricing practices.

Source: Elise Stolte. "Hundreds protest tuition hikes; students from across Alberta march at legislature to fight proposed increases, highest yet." *Edmonton Journal.* March 19, 2010. Pg. A3; "The soaring cost of universities." *Times Colonist* (Victoria, B.C.). May 23, 2010. Pg. D2.

ISSUES AND APPLICATIONS. The Issues and Applications feature is designed to encourage students not just to apply economic concepts, but also to think critically about them. Each begins with the concepts being applied and is followed by For Critical Analysis questions that could be used to prompt in-class discussions. Suggested answers to these questions are given at the back of the text, as well as in the Instructor's Manual at the end of the appropriate chapter.

Media Concentration in Canada: A Public Concern?

Concepts Applied: Regulation, Competition Policy, Media Concentration and the Public Interest

CanWest Global's newspaper, the *National Post*, competes with Canada's only other major national newspaper, *The Globe and Mail*, owned by BCE. CanWest and BCE have substantial media holdings in Canada. Does media concentration threaten editorial diversity?

A Decade of Mega-Takeovers and Mergers

Over the past decade, Canada has experienced a significant increase in concentration in its various media industries, as noted below.

In mid 1996, Conrad Black, publisher of almost 650 newspapers worldwide, approached the Competition Bureau for approval of his plan to acquire 50.7 percent of Southam Incorporated, publisher of 32 Canadian daily papers. After the Bureau gave its consent, Mr. Black's company, Hollinger Inc., became the largest newspaper publisher in Canada. Subsequent to the acquisition, Hollinger owned 59 of the 105 daily newspapers in Canada, including all the dailies in Saskatchewan, Prince Edward Island, and Newfoundland. Shortly after, Mr. Black purchased the *Financial Post* and incorporated it in his new national newspaper, the *National Post*, which debuted on October 27, 1998.

On November 3, 2000, The Competition Bureau announced that it would not challenge the $3.2 billion acquisition by CanWest Global of the majority of Hollinger's Canadian media interests. As a result, on November 15, 2000, CanWest became the largest daily newspaper publisher in Canada and one of the country's leading international multimedia news, information, and entertainment providers. Immediately after its Hollinger purchase, CanWest owned English language assets in Canada as well as 120 ...

In addition to its newspaper holdings, CanWest Global owns Canada's Global Television Network, which broadcasts over the air via 11 television stations, licensed in eight provinces, and reaches 94 percent of English-speaking Canada. CanWest also owns Canada.com, which is one of Canada's largest Internet news sites.

In December 2000, the CRTC allowed BCE to buy the CTV network, a decision that created Canada's largest communications company—Bell Globemedia, later known as CTV Globemedia (CTVgm). The CTV purchase closely followed BCE's acquisition of *The Globe and Mail*. In securing the ownership of CTV, BCE promised the CRTC that it would pump over $200 million into Canadian broadcasting during the next seven years. The CRTC has stipulated that $140 million of these monies should go into drama and documentary production created by independent Canadian writers and producers.

On July 5, 2001, the CRTC approved Quebecor Inc.'s purchase of the TVA television network, the dominant firm in the Quebec television broadcasting market. Prior to the CRTC decision, Quebecor had already accumulated significant Canadian media assets including Videotron, the largest cable TV producer in Quebec, and Sun Media, the second-largest newspaper group in Canada, with eight metropolitan dailies, eight community dailies and 175 local weeklies and specialty publications. As in the BCE vision, the CRTC made the Qu ...

POLICY EXAMPLES. Many of the economic debates reported in the media involve important policy issues. Here, students are presented with various key policy questions on both the domestic and international fronts. Each Policy Example is followed by a For Critical Analysis question that encourages students to consider exactly what is involved in the discussion and what the further ramifications might be. Suggested solutions to these questions are provided at the back of the text and in the Instructor's Manual.

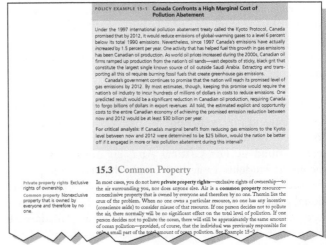

POLICY EXAMPLE 15-1   Canada Confronts a High Marginal Cost of Pollution Abatement

Under the 1997 international pollution abatement treaty called the Kyoto Protocol, Canada promised that by 2012, it would reduce emissions of global-warming gases to a level 6 percent below its total 1990 emissions. Nevertheless, since 1997 Canada's emissions have actually *increased* by 1.5 percent per year. One activity that has helped fuel this growth in gas emissions has been Canadian oil production. As world oil prices increased during the 2000s, Canadian oil firms ramped up production from the nation's oil sands—vast deposits of sticky, black grit that constitute the largest single known source of oil outside Saudi Arabia. Extracting and transporting all this oil requires burning fossil fuels that create greenhouse gas emissions.

Canada's government continues to promise that the nation will reach its promised level of gas emissions by 2012. By most estimates, though, keeping this promise would require the nation's oil industry to incur hundreds of millions of dollars in costs to reduce emissions. One predicted result would be a significant reduction in Canadian oil production, requiring Canada to forgo billions of dollars in export revenues. All told, the estimated explicit and opportunity costs to the entire Canadian economy of achieving the promised emission reduction between now and 2012 would be at least $30 billion per year.

For critical analysis: If Canada's marginal benefit from reducing gas emissions to the Kyoto level between now and 2012 were determined to be $25 billion, would the nation be better off if it engaged in more or less pollution abatement during this interval?

15.3 Common Property

Private property rights Exclusive rights of ownership.

Common property Nonexclusive property that is owned by everyone and therefore by no one.

In most cases, you do not have **private property rights**—exclusive rights of ownership—to the air surrounding you, nor does anyone else. Air is a **common property** resource—nonexclusive property that is owned by everyone and therefore by no one. Therein lies the crux of the problem. When no one owns a particular resource, no one has any incentive (conscience aside) to consider misuse of that resource. If one person decides not to pollute the air, there normally will be no significant effect on the total level of pollution. If one person decides not to pollute the ocean, there will still be approximately the same amount of ocean pollution—provided, of course, that the individual was previously responsible for only a small part of the total amount of ocean pollution. See Example 15-2.

EXAMPLES. Many thought-provoking and relevant examples highlight Canadian, as well as international, events and demonstrate economic principles. The For Critical Analysis questions that follow encourage students to apply the knowledge and information gained from the example. Possible answers to the questions are provided at the back of the text and in the Instructor's Manual.

EXAMPLE 8-3 **Economies of Scale at Dell**

In the mid-1990s, Dell Computer Corporation embarked on a plan to become the lowest-cost computer manufacturer in the world. Now, the company has factories that receive more than half of all customer orders via the Internet. These orders flow to a plant's "air-traffic control room," where procurement of parts, computer assembly, and shipping are managed.

At each point on the factory floor, which at some plants can be as large as 300 000 square feet, groups in charge of producing various computer components are linked via intranets, or internal computer networks. Each forklift truck contains a wireless computer that follows the paths of components to ensure that they reach the correct assembly points. Forklift trucks carrying completed computers are similarly equipped, to ensure that they reach the correct loading dock from among the dozens where trucks are waiting to be loaded.

In its newest and largest plants, Dell can produce more than 1000 computers per hour, which is almost twice as many as a typical plant could produce only half a dozen years ago. Even rival computer manufacturers agreed by the early 2000s that Dell had taken advantage of economies of scale to become the most cost-efficient manufacturer of personal computers.

For critical analysis: What has happened to Dell's short-run average cost curves as it has moved down along its long-run average cost curve?

Minimum Efficient Scale

Economists and statisticians have obtained actual data on the relationship between changes in all inputs and changes in average cost. It turns out that for many industries, the long-run average cost curve does not resemble that shown in part (b) of Figure 8-5. Rather, it more closely resembles Figure 8-7. What you observe there is a small portion of

FIGURE 8-7
Minimum Efficient Scale

This long-run average cost curve reaches a minimum point at A. After that point, long-run average costs remain horizontal, or constant, and then rise at some higher rate of output. Point A is called the minimum efficient scale for the firm because that is the point at which it reaches minimum costs. It is the lowest rate of output at which the average long-run costs are minimized.

BUSINESS APPLICATIONS. New to the Fifth Canadian Edition, a comprehensive business-related problem is presented at the end of each chapter. This pedagogical activity has two major purposes. Each problem applies chapter concepts to relevant real-life business situations. After a student has worked through a number of these business applications, he or she will begin to appreciate the broad range of business careers that are available in the functional areas of accounting, finance, marketing, and management.

BUSINESS APPLICATION

LO 5.2 Compare and contrast the effects that external benefits and external costs have on achieving allocative efficiency in a free market, laissez-faire environment.

Financial Management: External Benefits and Government Financial Support

One of the practical areas of business finance is concerned with finding creative ways to raise the funds needed to implement profitable business ventures. When a project results in significant *external benefits* to the local economy, the firm might be successful in acquiring financial support from the local government, as a way of capturing some of these external benefits. The following example describes how one can apply a commonly used financial math method called *present value of an annuity* to estimate the maximum amount of financial assistance that the firm can expect to receive from the government.

Example

Darin Keetz, the owner of the city's major league hockey team, is requesting taxpayer dollars to help finance a new downtown hockey arena. Based on economic analysis undertaken by the city's department of economic development, Darin estimates that the new arena will attract a massive amount of new downtown development in the form of new hotels with casinos, luxury condos, office towers, medical clinics and laboratories, and shopping malls that offer entertainment, restaurants, shopping outlets, and indoor swimming and waterslide facilities.

Darin's own finance department projects that the new downtown development will increase downtown property values to the point of increasing the revenue that the city receives from property taxes by $100 million a year over the next 10 years. This amount would be considered an external benefit related to the arena project. Determine the maximum

amount of financial support that Darin could seek from the local government to build the new hockey arena, assuming an interest rate of 9 percent.

Solution

Find the present value of an annuity consisting of 10 annual third-party benefits worth $100 million each, as described below. Note that R stands for periodic payment, n = number of payments, and i is the interest rate that money can be invested at over a long term.

The present value of an annuity formula is as follows:

$$PV = \$R\left(\frac{1-(1+i)^{-n}}{i}\right) = \$100 \text{ million} \times \left(\frac{1-(1+.09)^{-10}}{.09}\right)$$
$$= \$641.77 \text{ million}$$

Based on the above calculation, the maximum amount of financial assistance that Darin can expect to get from the government is $641.77 million.

Business Application Problem

A western Canadian city has approached Ridaway Rodeos in a bid to host the new North Pacific Championship Rodeo. Ridaway projects an annual external benefit of $3 840 000 for the city's economy caused by the new rodeo event. If the bid to host the rodeo is successful, it will stay in the city for the next 10 years. Determine the maximum amount of financial support that Ridaway could seek from the local government, based on the amount of the external benefit, assuming an interest rate of 10 percent.

Pedagogy With a Purpose: The *Micro View*

This Fifth Canadian Edition of *Economics Today: The Micro View* is loaded with the same highly regarded pedagogy of the previous edition. It helps students apply what they learn.

FOR CRITICAL ANALYSIS. At the end of each Example and Policy Example, students are asked to reflect on real-world problems by answering For Critical Analysis questions. The answers to the questions are found at the end of the student text and in the Instructor's Manual.

DID YOU KNOW THAT . . . ? Each chapter starts with a provocative question to engage students' interest and lead them into the content of the chapter.

LEARNING OBJECTIVES. On the first page of each chapter, several learning objectives are presented, giving purpose and focus to the chapter. These are then fully reviewed at the end of the chapter.

GRAPHS. Articulate and precise, the four-colour graphs illustrate key concepts.

KEY TERMS. Key terms are printed in **bold type** and are defined in the margin of the text the first time they appear. These terms are also reproduced alphabetically in the Glossary at the end of the text.

MYECONLAB SUMMARY CHART. Each chapter ends with a chart linking the learning objectives with the MyEconLab study plan. It identifies what students should know after reading each chapter and where to go when they need to practise.

PROBLEMS. A variety of problems support each chapter, with each problem linked to the appropriate learning objective in the chapter. Answers for all odd-numbered problems are provided at the back of the textbook. The complete set of problem answers (both even- and odd-numbered) appears in the Instructor's Manual.

Teaching/Learning Package

Instructor's Resource CD-ROM

This resource provides all of the following supplements in one convenient package.

■ **Instructor's Manual.** The Instructor's Manual has been adapted for this Fifth Canadian Edition of *Economics Today: The Micro View*. This extensive manual includes chapter overviews, objectives, and outlines; points to emphasize, including more theoretical issues for those who wish to stress theory; suggested questions for further class discussion; answers to the For Critical Analysis questions and end-of-chapter problems from the text; and selected references.

■ **Pearson Canada TestGen.** This software enables instructors to view and edit the existing test-bank questions, add new questions, and generate custom tests. It includes a minimum of 100 multiple-choice questions, 10 short-answer questions, and 5 essay questions per chapter.

■ **PowerPoint Presentations.** PowerPoint Presentations are available for each chapter of the text to highlight and illustrate important ideas.

MyEconLab

This text is fully integrated with MyEconLab, a robust online learning system featuring lots of practice exercises and study tools as well as a personalized study plan generated to suit your individual study needs. The site is available 24 hours a day so you can study where you want, how you want, and when you want.

MyEconLab is found at www.myeconlab.com. Follow the simple registration instructions on the Access Code card bound into every new copy of this text.

CourseSmart

CourseSmart is a new way for instructors and students to access textbooks online anytime from anywhere. With thousands of titles across hundreds of courses, CourseSmart helps instructors choose the best textbook for their class and give their students a new option for buying the assigned textbook as a lower cost eTextbook. For more information, visit www.coursesmart.com.

TECHNOLOGY SPECIALISTS. Pearson's Technology Specialists work with faculty and campus course designers to ensure that Pearson technology products, assessment tools, and online course materials are tailored to meet your specific needs. This highly qualified team is dedicated to helping schools take full advantage of a wide range of educational resources by assisting in the integration of a variety of instructional materials and media formats. Your local Pearson Canada sales representative can provide you with more details on this service program.

Acknowledgments

We could not have completed the Fifth Canadian Edition without the help of a terrific team of professionals at Pearson Canada. Thanks to Don Thompson, our Sponsoring Editor, for giving us this opportunity. Our Developmental Editor, Paul Donnelly, was a constant source of timely advice and encouragement. Avinash Chandra, Project Manager, and Leanne Rancourt, Production Editor, guided the book through the final stages with calm and sure hands. Our Copy Editor, Caroline Miller, juggled four authors and four different writing styles with great dexterity.

We would also like to thank the following professors who helped with the development of this text by offering us their insightful comments and constructive criticisms:

Sarah Arliss, Seneca College
Constantin Colonescu, Grant MacEwan University
Carl Graham, Assiniboine Community College
Moshe Lander, Northern Alberta Institute of Technology
Stephen Law, Mount Allison University
Joan McEachern, Kwantlen Polytechnic University
A. Gyasi Nimarko, Vanier College
John Pirrie, St. Lawrence College
Carl Weston, Mohawk College

In completing this work, we sincerely appreciate the support and patience we have received from each of our families.

Finally, we would like to thank our colleagues and students at Northern Alberta Institute of Technology and British Columbia Institute of Technology for their valuable advice and support during the writing of this book.

Brenda Abbott
Sam Fefferman

Ronald K. Kessler
Terrence Sulyma

1

The Nature of Economics

On March 11, 2010, thousands of students participated in events held at more than 60 university and college campuses across the country to stage Canada's first Bottled Water Free Day. Amid pledges to "kick the bottle" and get "back to the tap," the event organizers raised awareness regarding the wasteful and negative effects of consuming bottled water. To date in Canada, 76 municipalities, four municipal associations, eight school boards, five university campuses, and countless businesses have implemented restrictions on bottled water. Meanwhile, more than a billion people around the world are without safe drinking water. How are these events related? Why are they of interest to economists? Read on.

Source: "Thousands Mark Canada's First Bottled Water Free Day." *Canada NewsWire*. Ottawa. March 11, 2010.

LEARNING OBJECTIVES

After reading this chapter, you should be able to:

1.1 Explain the meaning of scarcity.

1.2 Define economics and distinguish between microeconomics and macroeconomics.

1.3 Describe how resource use decisions are affected by the rationality assumption, costs and benefits at the margin, and incentives.

1.4 Explain the three key processes involved in the scientific method.

1.5 Distinguish between positive and normative economics.

1.6 Describe the relationship among theories, policies, and socioeconomic goals.

MyEconLab helps you master each objective and study more efficiently. See end of chapter for details.

DID YOU KNOW THAT...?

Canadians reported that they spend more of their weekly leisure time using the Internet than watching TV for the first time ever, according to a study released in 2010. On average, Canadians are now spending more than 18 hours a week online, compared to 16.9 hours watching television. Overall, 89 percent of Canadians have Internet access, with the highest rates of access reported in Ontario, British Columbia, and Alberta. Across all age groups, males are spending more time online than females. The most frequent online activity is e-mail, followed by social networking; music downloading; online gaming; and completing homework and research for school, college, and university. The world around us continues to change rapidly, and much of that change stems from the decreasing cost and increasing convenience associated with information technology. As you will learn from this chapter, the increasing importance of the online world can be explained in terms of rational behaviour, an important premise that underlies the study of economics.

Sources: "Weekly internet usage overtakes television watching." News and Polls. Ipsos North America. March 22, 2010. http://www.ipsos-na.com/news-polls/pressrelease.aspx?id=4720; *The 2009 Canadian Internet Fact Guide*. Ipsos Canada. pg 2–3. http://www.ipsos.ca/reid/interactive/ifg.cfm

1.1 Scarcity

You can't have it all! You were probably first exposed to this very important economics lesson when you were a toddler and your parents denied your request to buy you a new toy at the supermarket. You undoubtedly experienced this same lesson many times over by the time you enrolled in this course. After you graduate, you may face such choices as buying a brand new car, putting a down payment on a condo, travelling to faraway places, or getting married and starting a family. As a senior member of your community, you may have to choose between spending tax dollars on building a new hospital and improving the education system for the next generation.

Whenever individuals or communities cannot obtain everything they desire, choices occur. Choices occur because of the fundamental economic problem of *scarcity*. Scarcity is the most basic concept in all of economics.

> **Scarcity** The condition that arises because wants always exceed what can be produced with limited resources.

Scarcity refers to the condition that arises because wants always exceed what can be produced with limited resources.

As a result of scarcity, we do not and cannot have enough income and wealth to satisfy our every desire.

Scarcity is not the same thing as poverty. Scarcity occurs among the rich as well as the poor. Even the richest person faces scarcity because available time is limited. Low income levels do not create more scarcity. High income levels do not create less scarcity.

Scarcity and Wants

Wants refer to the goods and services that we wish to consume as well as the goals that we seek to achieve. **Goods** are physical items that we as consumers are willing to pay for, such as meat, jeans, DVDs, and cars. **Services** are the tasks performed by others that we as consumers are willing to pay for, such as haircuts, education, and medical, dental, and legal services. The goals that we seek to achieve can be individual or social in nature. The important thing to note is that we are referring to goods, services, and goals that require the use of our limited resources.

> **Goods** The physical items that consumers are willing to pay for.
>
> **Services** The tasks performed by others that consumers are willing to pay for.

Scarcity and Resources

The scarcity concept arises from the fact that resources are insufficient to satisfy our every desire. Resources are the inputs used in the production of the things that we want. **Production** can be defined as virtually any activity that results in the conversion of resources into goods and services. Production includes the manufacturing, wholesaling, and retailing of goods as well as the delivery of services. The resources used in production are called *factors of production*, and some economists use the terms *resources* and *factors of*

> **Production** Any activity that results in the conversion of resources into goods and services.

production interchangeably. The total quantity of all resources that an economy has at any one time determines what that economy can produce.

Factors of production can be classified in many ways. Here is one such classification:

1. **Land** encompasses all the nonhuman gifts of nature, including timber, water, fish, minerals, and the original fertility of the land. It is often called the *natural resource.*
2. **Labour** is the human resource, which includes all productive contributions made by individuals who work, such as steelworkers, ballet dancers, and professional baseball players.
3. **Physical capital** consists of the factories and equipment used in production. It also includes improvements to natural resources, such as irrigation ditches.
4. **Human capital** is the economic characterization of the education and training of workers. How much the nation produces depends not only on how many hours people work but also on how productive they are, and that, in turn, depends in part on education and training. To become more educated, individuals have to devote time and resources, just as a business has to devote resources if it wants to increase its physical capital. Whenever a worker's skills increase, human capital has been improved.
5. **Entrepreneurship** is actually a subdivision of labour and involves human resources that perform the functions of risk taking, organizing, managing, and assembling the other factors of production to make business ventures. Entrepreneurship also encompasses taking risks that involve the possibility of losing large sums of wealth on new ventures. It includes new methods of doing common things, and generally experimenting with any type of new thinking that could lead to making more money income. Without entrepreneurship, virtually no business organization could operate.

When resources are used to produce goods and services, they earn income. The incomes earned by land, labour, capital, and entrepreneurship are referred to as **rent**, **wages**, **interest**, and **profit**, respectively.

1.2 Defining Economics

What is economics exactly? *Economics* is one of the social sciences and, as such, seeks explanations of real events. All social sciences analyze human behaviour. The physical sciences, on the other hand, generally analyze the behaviour of electrons, atoms, and other nonhuman phenomena.

Economics is a social science that studies how people allocate their limited resources to satisfy their wants. That is, economics is concerned with how individuals, groups, and societies respond to the economic problem of scarcity.

Resources are limited relative to wants. Consumers, managers, business owners, citizens, and politicians must continually make choices among alternative courses of action. For example, as a consumer, you choose how to spend your limited income on a vast array of goods and services. If you own a business or manage a government department, you will have to decide what resources to hire in order to best promote the goals of your organization, while working within a limited budget. As a citizen and potential politician, you make decisions that affect how limited tax dollars are used for the betterment of society. Economics helps us study how such choices can be made.

As Example 1–1 suggests, even a web page designer, who prefers to engage in artistic endeavours, must practise economics on a regular basis.

Land Nonhuman gifts of nature.

Labour Productive contributions made by individuals who work.

Physical capital Factories and equipment used in production.

Human capital The education and training of workers.

Entrepreneurship Human resources that perform the functions of risk taking, organizing, managing, and assembling other factors of production to make business ventures.

Rent Income earned by land.

Wages Income earned by labour.

Interest Income earned by capital.

Profit Income earned by the entrepreneur.

Economics A social science that studies how people allocate their limited resources to satisfy their wants.

EXAMPLE 1–1 The Economics of Web Page Design

As noted in this chapter's Did You Know That . . . ? section, Canadians are spending more time on the Web than watching television. During a typical month, Canadians spent more than 45 billion minutes on the Internet.

continued

Companies that want to sell their products realize that the explosive growth in Internet use suggests that advertisements posted on the Web can potentially reach very large audiences, in Canada and worldwide. These companies also know that when people access the Internet, their home pages are typically those of their Internet service provider, a popular search engine such as Yahoo!, or their favourite media website. Consequently, many companies advertise on these web pages. In 2009, Canadian online advertising ballooned to a record $1.82 billion, and it is projected to increase by 15 percent to $2.1 billion in 2010. In all but one of the past 10 years, online advertising has increased at double digit annual rates, making it the fastest growing media in terms of advertising revenues. Online advertising is now the third most frequent form of advertising behind television and newspaper advertising.

The owner of any web page that carries advertising faces the economic problem of scarcity. For example, advertisers widely consider the Yahoo! search engine home page "prime real estate" because so many people see it each day. But there is relatively little space on the computer screen to view the page without having to scroll farther down the screen. Thus, when Yahoo! allocates space to promote its own services and products, it gives up space that it could sell to advertisers. On the other hand, if Yahoo! fills up too much of its prime screen space with ads, some users will switch to a less cluttered search engine. Web designers try to minimize the space taken up by ads on prime screen space by using animations that cycle through a number of different ads in the same space on a web page. However, Net surfers are willing to spend only a limited amount of time viewing such animations. All these considerations make web design a crucial economic concern.

For critical analysis: What are the "unlimited wants" and "limited resources" that face a person in charge of designing a frequently visited web page?

Source: IAB Canada. *2009 Actual + 2010 Estimated Canadian Online Advertising Revenue Survey Detailed Report.* Ernst & Young. August 10, 2010. http://www.iabcanada.com/reports/IABCanada_2009Act2010Budg_CdnOnlineAdRev_FINAL.pdf. (Accessed September 11, 2010.)

How does the economic problem of scarcity apply to a web designer?

Microeconomics versus Macroeconomics

Economics is typically divided into two fields of study: *microeconomics* and *macroeconomics*.

Microeconomics studies decision making undertaken by individuals and by firms in specific parts of the economy. It is like looking through a microscope to focus on individual households, firms, industries, and occupations.

Macroeconomics studies the behaviour of the economy as a whole. It deals with economywide phenomena, such as changes in unemployment, the general price level, and national income.

Microeconomic analysis, for example, is concerned with the effects of changes in the price of natural gas relative to that of other energy sources. It examines the effects of new taxes on a specific product or industry. If price controls were to be reinstituted in Canada, how individual firms and consumers would react to them would be in the realm of microeconomics. The raising of wages by an effective union strike would also be analyzed using the tools of microeconomics.

By contrast, such issues as the rate of inflation, the amount of economywide unemployment, and the yearly growth in the output of goods and services in the nation all fall into the domain of macroeconomic analysis. In other words, macroeconomics deals with **aggregates**, or economywide measures, such as total output in an economy.

Microeconomics The study of decision making undertaken by individuals and by firms in specific parts of the economy.

Macroeconomics The study of the behaviour of the economy as a whole.

Aggregates Economywide measures.

The Power of Economic Analysis

Knowing that an economic problem of scarcity exists every time you make a decision is not enough. As you study economics, you will be encouraged to develop a framework of analysis that will allow you to effectively analyze possible solutions to each economic problem—whether you are a student trying to decide how much studying time you should devote to a course, a consumer making the choice between renting and owning your next home, a business owner interested in setting the most profitable price for your product, or a government leader searching for the policy that would most effectively create jobs in your province.

The remainder of this chapter is concerned with introducing you to a powerful framework of analysis that includes the *economic way of thinking*, the *scientific approach*, and *policy analysis* based on valued economic goals.

Indeed, just as taking an art or literature appreciation class increases the pleasure you receive when you view paintings or read novels, taking an economics course will increase your understanding when viewing news clips on the Internet, watching the news on TV, listening to newscasts on the radio, or reading newspapers.

1.3 Rational Decision Making

The **economic way of thinking** assumes that the typical response to an economic problem of scarcity is rational behaviour. That is, individuals behave as if they compare the costs and benefits of different possible choices when they make resource use decisions. They behave in this manner in order to further their own self-interest.

Economists presume that individuals act *as if* motivated by self-interest and respond predictably to opportunities for gain. This central insight of economics was first clearly articulated by Adam Smith in 1776. Smith wrote in his most famous book, *An Inquiry into the Nature and Causes of the Wealth of Nations*, that "it is not from the benevolence of the butcher, the brewer, or the baker that we expect our dinner, but from their regard to their own interest." Otherwise stated, the *typical* person about whom economists make behavioural predictions is assumed to look out for his or her own self-interest in a rational manner. The word *typical* is very important. Economists know that not all people respond in the same way when faced with the same circumstances. If offered a free trip to Hawaii for participating in a marketing experiment, for example, most people will take part. There inevitably will be some who do not want to go to Hawaii, perhaps because they do not like travelling, so they will not participate in the study. But, *on average*, the promised trip to Hawaii will be sufficient to attract participants because people behave in a predictably self-interested way.

> **Economic way of thinking** Assumes that the typical response to an economic problem of scarcity is rational behaviour.

The Rationality Assumption

The **rationality assumption** of economics, simply stated, is as follows:

> **An individual makes decisions based on maximizing his or her own self-interest.**

The distinction here is between what people may think—the realm of psychology and psychiatry and perhaps sociology—and what they do. Economics does *not* involve itself in analyzing individual or group thought processes. Economics looks at what people actually do in life with their limited resources. It does little good to criticize the rationality assumption by stating, "Nobody thinks that way" or "I never think that way" or "How unrealistic! That's as irrational as anyone can get!"

Take the example of driving. When you consider passing another car on a two-lane highway with oncoming traffic, you have to make very quick decisions: you must estimate the speed of the car you are going to pass, the speed of the oncoming cars, the distance between your car and the oncoming cars, and your car's potential rate of acceleration. If we were to apply a model to your behaviour, we would use the laws of calculus. In fact, you and most other drivers in such a situation do not actually think of using the laws of calculus, but we could predict your behaviour *as if* you did.

In practical terms, the rationality assumption implies that an individual will adopt a course of action if the action's relevant benefits exceed its relevant costs. Let us proceed to examine what we mean by *relevant* costs and benefits.

> **Rationality assumption** An individual makes decisions based on maximizing his or her own self-interest.

Opportunity Cost

The natural fact of scarcity implies that we must make choices. One of the most important results of this fact is that every choice made (or not made, for that matter) means that some opportunity had to be sacrificed. Every choice involves giving up another opportunity to do or use something else.

Consider a practical example. Every choice you make to study one more hour of economics requires that you give up the opportunity to do any of the following activities: study more of another subject, listen to music, sleep, browse at a local store, read a novel, or work out at the gym. Many more opportunities are forgone if you choose to study economics for an additional hour.

Because there were so many alternatives from which to choose, how could you determine the value of what you gave up to engage in that extra hour of studying economics? First of all, no one else can tell you the answer because only you can *subjectively* put a value on each alternative. Only you know the value of another hour of sleep or of an hour looking for the latest CDs. That means that only you can determine the highest-valued alternative that you had to sacrifice in order to study economics one more hour. It is you who must come up with the *subjective* estimate of the expected value of the best alternative.

The value of the best alternative that must be sacrificed to satisfy a want is called *opportunity cost*. The **opportunity cost** of any action is the value of what is given up—the highest-ranked alternative—because a choice was made. When you study one more hour, there may be many alternatives available for the use of that hour, but assume that you can do only one thing in that hour—your highest-ranked alternative. What is important is the choice that you would have made if you had not studied one more hour. Your opportunity cost is the *highest-ranked* alternative, not *all* alternatives.

In economics, cost is a forgone opportunity.

In this chapter's Issues and Applications we use the concept of *opportunity cost* to assess the value of allocating tens of billions of dollars a year of limited resources to the manufacture of bottled water products such as Aquafina and Dasani, which contribute to pollution and solid waste, despite the fact that we already have a much cheaper source of safe water flowing from our municipal water systems. The opportunity costs are that we forgo the option to have a healthier environment and we forgo allocating the invested resources to important causes such as providing drinking water to the more than one billion people around the world who don't have access to safe water.

In Example 1–2 we will examine how the relatively high opportunity cost of searching for a compatible romantic partner has helped create an industry based in cyberspace.

Opportunity cost The value of the best alternative that must be given up because a choice was made.

EXAMPLE 1–2 Is the Opportunity Cost of Finding a Mate Lower on the Internet?

For many single people looking for a companion, the biggest difficulty is not necessarily a lack of potential mates. The problem is that the time spent dating in search of "Ms. Right" or "Mr. Right" could otherwise be devoted to alternative activities. The highest-valued of these alternative activities is the opportunity cost of the time spent on each date.

This provides a fundamental rationale for the existence of such Internet-based companies as Match.com. For about $35 per month, a person looking for "that special someone" with desired characteristics, similar interests, and so on can enter personal information into a database and be matched, by computer, with someone else. According to the company's "director of flirting and dating," its business is all "about numbers, and it's also about time." In short, it is about the high opportunity cost of finding a compatible partner. For the really picky people who face especially high opportunity costs of screening candidate mates for very specific characteristics, there are special Internet services available, albeit at higher prices. Goodgenes.com is open to graduates of Ivy League universities and a select group of other top-notch colleges and universities. For Jewish men and women, there is JDate.com, and Matrimony.org helps link Islamic singles.

For critical analysis: Why do the prices charged by websites specializing in people who share very specific characteristics tend to be higher than the prices charged by general dating services, such as Match.com?

Why are individuals willing to pay for online dating services?

Making Decisions at the Margin

As you progress through this text, you will be reminded frequently that in order to rationally evaluate a possible course of action, you must compare the action's *marginal benefit* with its *marginal cost*. **Marginal benefit** refers to all the *extra* benefits that one receives in pursuing a course of action, while **marginal cost** refers to all the *extra* costs or sacrifices incurred. In order to ensure that you properly identify the marginal cost relevant to your decision at hand, you must be careful not to include *sunk costs*. **Sunk costs** refer to irreversible costs incurred prior to your decision.

As an example, suppose you are in the process of estimating the extra (marginal) transportation costs associated with a Nova Scotia vacation that you are planning to take. You own your car and you have paid the annual insurance and car licence fee long before contemplating this vacation. If you decide to use your own car for this trip, the annual licence fee and insurance are sunk costs that are not relevant to the decision of travelling to Nova Scotia. As such, you should not include these two costs in your estimate of the extra (marginal) transportation costs. To better understand the notion of marginal and sunk costs, we refer you to Example 1–3: "What Does a Year at College Really Cost?"

Making decisions at the margin will often reveal that there can be too much of a good thing! As an example, suppose that at a time when marijuana use is at an all-time low, one of the contenders for prime minister, in a federal election campaign, proposes a policy for eliminating all marijuana use in Canada. While this type of zero tolerance policy proposal can win votes, if implemented, it can result in the transfer of a massive amount of policing resources away from the prevention of serious violent crimes in order to achieve a very small reduction in marijuana use. In other words, the marginal cost of the zero tolerance policy far exceeds the marginal benefit!

Marginal benefit All the extra benefits that one receives in pursuing a course of action.

Marginal cost All the extra costs or sacrifices incurred.

Sunk costs Irreversible costs incurred prior to your decision.

EXAMPLE 1–3   What Does a Year at College Really Cost?

Jane Sanders is currently earning $2000 per month working full time in Hamilton, Ontario. She lives in a one-bedroom apartment and pays $700 per month in rent. Her monthly food, personal care, and entertainment expenses are $500 per month. Since she does not own a vehicle, she pays $65 per month for a bus pass.

Jane is in the process of estimating the extra cost related to the decision to enroll full time in the first year of a business program at a college in the Hamilton area. If she enrolls, she will give up her full-time job for the eight-month period of the first-year program. If Jane goes to college, she plans to continue to live in her one-bedroom apartment, take the bus to the college campus, and maintain her current lifestyle. Jane estimates that her decision to enroll in college for the first year (eight-month period) will cost $13 720, estimated as follows:

TABLE 1–1

Rent	$700 × 8 =	$ 5 600
Food, Personal Care, Entertainment	$500 × 8 =	$ 4 000
Public Transportation	$ 65 × 8 −	$ 520
Tuition, Books, College Fees		$ 3 600
Total Cost		**$13 720**

For critical analysis: Did Jane correctly determine the extra cost related to the decision to enroll in college full time for eight months? What else must Jane try to estimate in order to make a rational decision? Explain.

Responding to Incentives

If it is reasonable to assume that individuals make decisions by comparing marginal costs and benefits, then we are in a position to better understand and predict how people respond to incentives. We define an **incentive** as an inducement to take a particular action. The inducement can be a reward, or a "carrot," which would take the form of an increase in

Incentive Inducement to take a particular action.

benefit or a decrease in cost. Alternatively, the inducement can be a punishment, or a "stick," in the form of an increase in cost or a decrease in benefit. To the extent that a change in incentives implies a change in the relation between the marginal costs and benefits associated with various choices, individual decisions will change.

Indeed, much of human behaviour can be explained in terms of how individuals respond to changing incentives over time. School students are motivated to do better by a variety of incentive systems, ranging from gold stars and certificates of achievement when they are young to better grades with accompanying promises of a "better life" as they get older. The rapid growth in Internet use noted in this chapter's Did You Know That . . . ? section can be explained in terms of increased incentives due to the decline in cost and increase in convenience associated with information technology.

In Policy Example 1–1, you are asked to help governments reduce incentives to engage in smuggling and counterfeiting activities by identifying policies that either increase the marginal costs or decrease the marginal benefits related to these illegal actions.

POLICY EXAMPLE 1–1   International Smuggling and Counterfeiting

In order to develop a domestic, state-owned cigarette manufacturing monopoly industry, the Chinese government has pursued strategies to keep out foreign-made cigarettes. One such strategy is the imposition of tariffs (taxes) as high as 430 percent on cigarettes imported into China that are manufactured by large, multinational cigarette companies such as British American Tobacco (BAT). These high tax rates have encouraged the annual flow of tens of billions of dollars in contraband cigarettes.

One example of contraband is the smuggling of foreign-made cigarettes into China, which avoids the government-imposed tariffs. In 2006, it was discovered that BAT, one of the world's biggest tobacco companies, had restructured its operations to expand its own smuggling trade in China, where one-third of all the world's smokers reside.

A second example of contraband is the rapid growth in the Chinese manufacturing and trade of counterfeit brand-name cigarettes such as Marlboro and State Express 555. It is estimated that hundreds of illegal Chinese cigarette businesses manufacture approximately 400 billion fake brand-name cigarettes a year. These businesses operate illicit factories hidden in thickly forested mountain regions and in deep caves buried metres below ground. Over the past decade, the production of counterfeit cigarettes in China has increased eightfold!

Why has there been this tremendous growth in counterfeiting, given that the Chinese government employs over 50 000 special agents to reduce this criminal behaviour? The answer is that the returns on counterfeiting are so high that many agents are bribed to "look the other way."

Closer to home, on April 13, 2010, the Canadian federal government levied fines totalling $225 million on two large multinational cigarette companies—JTI–Macdonald Corp. and R.J. Reynolds—for their roles in smuggling cigarettes into Canada. These fines, combined with additional monies paid to settle civil lawsuits, will put a total of $550 million into the hands of the Canadian federal and provincial governments. The smuggling of cheap cigarettes into Canada is attributed to the relatively high tax rates that federal and provincial governments impose on legal cigarettes manufactured and sold in Canada.

For critical analysis: What actions can governments in China and Canada take to increase the marginal cost related to illegal smuggling and counterfeiting activities? Can you identify other policy actions that decrease the marginal benefit related to these illegal activities?

Sources: "Research reveals tobacco company's role in China's cigarette smuggling crisis." Tuesday, July 18, 2006. London School of Hygiene and Tropical Medicine Press; Te-Ping Chen. "China's Marlboro Country." June 28, 2009. Tobacco Underground. Organized Crime and Corruption Reporting Project. http://www.reportingproject.net/underground/index.php?option=com_content&view=article&id=9&Itemid=22; Tibbetts, Janice. "Record fines for smuggled smokes." Canwest News Service. Ottawa. *Edmonton Journal*. April 14, 2010. P. A5.

Defining Self-Interest

Self-interest does not always mean increasing one's wealth as measured in dollars and cents. We assume that individuals seek many goals, not just increased monetary wealth. Thus, the self-interest part of our economic-person assumption includes goals relating to prestige, friendship, love, power, helping others, creating works of art, and many other matters. As Example 1–4 illustrates, performing acts of kindness can go hand in hand with pursuing one's own self interest.

EXAMPLE 1–4   Nice Guys Can Finish First

An academic study published in 2010 discredits the popular myth that people who exhibit altruistic or generous behaviour are typically less attractive to potential romantic partners compared to "bad boys" or "selfish people."

This research study examined heterosexual men's and women's attraction to opposite sex photographs, which were matched with descriptions (profiles) that varied in the level of generosity portrayed. The research participants, whose mean age ranged from 19.15 to 20.10 years, each received a package consisting of four photographs and four descriptions. Each research participant saw a "neutral person" and a "generous person," each seeking a short-term relationship. The same research participant observed a "neutral person" and a "generous person," each seeking a long-term relationship. After viewing each picture with its description, the research participants rated how willing they were to associate with the person in different ways, including as a short-term romantic partner, as a long term romantic partner, as a fellow worker, and as a platonic friend.

An example of a "neutral person" would be a picture of a person of the opposite sex accompanied by a profile that did not reference any tendencies for generous acts and behaviour. The corresponding example of a "generous person" would be a picture of a person of the opposite sex accompanied by a profile that did reference tendencies for generous acts and behaviour, such as "I enjoy helping people" or "One of my hobbies is volunteering at the food bank."

All photographs were downloaded from an Internet site where each picture had already been rated by the opposite sex in terms of physical attractiveness. The pictures chosen for this study had been given neutral physical attractiveness ratings. This was done so that physical traits such as "good looks" or "unattractive appearance" would not affect the results of the study.

The findings of this study can be briefly summarized as follows. Research participants of both sexes rated people with generous tendencies as desirable for long-term relationships. Female research participants preferred the males that exhibited generous behaviour for short-term romantic relationships. However, male research participants tended to rate altruistic females as less desireable for short-term relationships.

For critical analysis: Based on this Example, critically evaluate this statement: "When individuals consistently engage in generous acts and behaviour, this contradicts the rationality assumption described in this chapter."

Source: Pat Barclay. "Altruism as a courtship display: Some effects of third party generosity on audience perceptions." *British Journal of Psychology*, February 2010, 101(1), 123–135.

1.4   The Scientific Method

Economics is a social science that makes use of the same kinds of methods used in other sciences, such as biology, physics, and chemistry. Similar to these other sciences, economics engages in key processes that include making assumptions, forming models or theories, and testing these models with real-world facts. Economic **models or theories** are simplified representations of the real world that we use to help us understand and predict economic

Models or theories Simplified representations of the real world used to understand and predict economic phenomena.

phenomena in the real world. There are, of course, differences among the sciences. The social sciences, especially economics, make little use of laboratory methods in which changes in variables can be explained under controlled conditions. Rather, social scientists, and especially economists, usually have to examine what has already happened in the real world to test their models.

Models and Realism

At the outset, it must be emphasized that no model in *any* science, and therefore no economic model, is complete in the sense that it captures *every* detail or interrelationship that exists. Indeed, a model, by definition, is an abstraction from reality. It is conceptually impossible to construct a perfectly complete, realistic model. For example, in physics, we cannot account for every molecule and its position, nor every atom and subparticle. Not only would such a model be prohibitively expensive to build, but also working with it would be impossibly complex.

The nature of scientific model building is such that the model should capture only the essential relationships that are sufficient to analyze the particular problem or answer the particular question with which we are concerned. *An economic model cannot be faulted as unrealistic simply because it does not represent every detail of the real world.* A map of a city that shows only major streets is not necessarily unrealistic if, in fact, all you need to know is how to navigate through the city using major streets. As long as a model is realistic in terms of shedding light on the *central* issue at hand or forces at work, it may be useful.

A map is a basic model. It is always a simplified representation, always unrealistic. But it is also useful in making (refutable) predictions about the world. If the model—the map—predicts that when you take Campus Avenue to the north, you always reach the campus, that is a (refutable) prediction. If our goal is to explain observed behaviour, the simplicity or complexity of the model we use is irrelevant. If a simple model can explain observed behaviour in repeated settings just as well as a complex one, the simple model has some value and is probably easier to use.

Assumptions

Every model, or theory, is based on a set of assumptions. Assumptions define the conditions under which a model is meant to apply. By eliminating detail that is not considered to be essential to the economic phenomena under investigation, assumptions help simplify a model.

In the theory of the firm, we assume that, typically, firms attempt to maximize profits when deciding how much of a product to produce in an industry. This assumption leads to an economic model of the firm that provides numerous predictions about how the firm will react to various events and incentives. As an example, one prediction would be that if a firm can sell its product at a higher price, it will tend to produce more of this product. Another prediction would be that if a major cost of producing this product increases, such as energy costs, the firm will likely reduce the level of production of this product. Finally, this model would predict that if the government lowered the taxes imposed on the firms in this industry, this would entice firms to increase their supply of this product.

While the owners of the firms in the industry under investigation may well have a variety of other motives for producing the product, the profit-maximizing assumption model is valid to the extent that it consistently provides accurate predictions of real-world behaviour.

THE CETERIS PARIBUS ASSUMPTION: ALL OTHER THINGS BEING EQUAL. Constructing a model typically involves making generalizations of how variables in our environment relate to each other. It would be impossible to isolate the effects of changes in one variable on another variable if we always had to worry about the many additional variables that might also enter the analysis. As in other sciences, economics uses the **ceteris paribus assumption**, which is the assumption that nothing changes except the factor or factors being studied. *Ceteris paribus* means "other things being constant" or "other things being equal."

Ceteris paribus [KAY-ter-us PEAR-uh-bus] assumption The assumption that nothing changes except the factor or factors being studied; "other things being constant," or "other things being equal."

Consider an example taken from economics. One of the most important determinants of how much of a particular product a family buys is the price of that product relative to other products. We know that in addition to relative prices, other factors influence decisions about making purchases. Some of them have to do with income, others with tastes, and yet others with custom and religious beliefs. Whatever these other factors are, we hold them constant when we look at the relationship between changes in prices and changes in how much of a given product people will purchase. As Example 1–5 illustrates, Canadian researchers applied the *ceteris paribus* assumption in designing a scientific study to test the effectiveness of a popular anti-cold formulation created in Canada.

EXAMPLE 1–5 The Science behind COLD-fX

On October 5, 2005, the *Canadian Medical Association Journal* published the results of a scientific study that showed COLD-fX, an anti-cold formulation, reduced the incidence and frequency of recurrent colds by more than half. COLD-fX also cut the duration of colds and significantly reduced their severity. Shortly after the research results were published, the stock price of CV Technologies, the company manufacturing COLD-fX, reached an all-time high of $4.74 per share, an increase of 166 percent over the previous year's stock price!

Research subjects for the COLD-fX study were required to be in good general health, to be between 18 and 65 years of age, and to have contracted at least two colds in the past year. Subjects were excluded if they had been vaccinated against influenza in the previous six months.

Volunteers who qualified for the study were randomly assigned to receive either the ginseng extract that makes up COLD-fX or a placebo, which was made to look exactly like the COLD-fX capsule except that the placebo did not contain any type of medication. All subjects were instructed to take two capsules per day for a period of six months following the onset of influenza season. They were instructed not to take any other cold medication while involved in the study. All observations and analyses were performed by a statistician under double-blind conditions. That is, the statistician did not know which subjects were actually taking COLD-fX or the placebo. Similarly, each subject did not know whether he or she was taking COLD-fX or the placebo.

For critical analysis: The COLD-fX study is interested in examining the relationship between which two variables? Explain how the study attempts to apply the *ceteris paribus* assumption.

Sources: "Interactive charts. CV technologies." CTVGlobemedia. http://www.globeinvestor.com. (Accessed May 12, 2007.); Gerald N. Predy, Vinti Goel, Ray Lovlin, Allan Donner, Larry Stitt, and Tapan K. Basu. "Efficacy of an extract of North American ginseng containing poly-furanosyl-pyranosyl-saccharides for preventing upper respiratory tract infections: a randomized controlled trial." *CMAJ*, October 25, 2005, 173(9). doi:10.1503/cmaj.1041470.

Testing Models

We generally do not attempt to determine the usefulness, or "goodness," of a model merely by evaluating how realistic its assumptions are. Rather, we consider a model good if it yields usable predictions and implications for the real world. In other words, can we use the model to predict what will happen in the world around us?

Once we have determined that the model does predict real-world phenomena, the scientific approach to the analysis of the world around us requires that we consider evidence. Evidence is used to test the usefulness of a model. This is why we call economics an *empirical* science, **empirical** meaning using real-world data to test the usefulness of a model. Economists are often engaged in empirically testing their models.

Empirical Using real-world data to test the usefulness of a model.

Consider two competing models for the way students act when doing complicated probability problems to choose the best gambles. One model predicts that, on the basis of the assumption of rational self-interest, students who are paid more for better performance will, in fact, perform better on average during the experiment. A competing model might be that students whose last names start with the letters A through L will do better than students with last names starting with M through Z, irrespective of how much they are paid. The model that consistently predicts more accurately is the model that we would normally choose. In this example, the "alphabet" model did not work well; the first letter of the last name of the students who actually did the experiment was irrelevant in predicting how well they would perform the mathematical calculations necessary to choose the correct gambles. The model based on rational self-interest predicted well, in contrast.

Models of Behaviour, Not Thought Processes

Take special note of the fact that economists' models do not relate to the way people *think*; they relate to the way people *act*, to what they do in life with their limited resources. Models tend to generalize human behaviour. Normally, the economist does not attempt to predict how people will think about a particular topic, such as a higher price of oil products, accelerated inflation, or higher taxes. Rather, the task at hand is to predict how people will act, which may be quite different from what they say they will do (much to the consternation of poll takers and market researchers). The people involved in examining thought processes are psychologists and psychiatrists, who are not usually economists.

Example 1–6 provides you with an economic model that is used to explain and predict criminal behaviour.

EXAMPLE 1-6   An Economic Model of Crime

What marginal benefits and costs relate to car theft?

As you may suspect, numerous sociological, cultural, psychological, and physiological theories are used to explain criminal behaviour. Traits such as deviance, abnormality, depravity, insanity, and genetics are used to characterize those who break the law. In this Example, we will present an economic model of crime, based on the rationality assumption. That is, in an economic model of criminal behaviour, individuals compare the marginal costs and marginal benefits of engaging in an illegal act (as opposed to a legal act). If the marginal benefits of engaging in a crime exceed its marginal costs, the individual will commit the crime.

What might be included in the marginal benefits of engaging in a crime? For many crimes, such as property theft, identity theft, financial fraud, drug trafficking, and tax evasion, part of the marginal benefit would be the extra monies received. Other marginal benefits might prove to be psychological in nature, such as the thrill of danger, peer approval, retribution, the need to feed an addiction, or even a sense of accomplishment.

What about the marginal costs of committing an illegal act? The costs would include material costs (equipment, guns, vehicles), psychological costs (guilt, anxiety, fear, aversion to risk), expected punishment costs, and opportunity costs.

The expected punishment costs are a combination of the probability of being "caught" (arrested and convicted) and the severity of the penalty when convicted. If there is a high probability of being caught and/or there is a large penalty when convicted, this results in a relatively large marginal cost of committing a crime.

The opportunity cost of committing a crime consists of the net benefit of the legal activity that is forgone while planning, performing, and concealing the criminal act. The lower an individual's income from legal activity, the lower the opportunity cost of committing a crime.

As with any scientific model, the validity of the economic model of crime depends on testing the model's predictions with real-world evidence. Numerous studies have found a clear negative association between high costs of punishment and crime rates. These studies suggest that the probability of getting caught is a stronger deterrent to criminal action than

continued

the severity of the penalty when convicted. Studies also indicate that individuals are more apt to engage in crimes when they earn low incomes in an environment of significant income inequality. In other words, one is more apt to commit a crime when there is a lot to gain and little to lose.

For critical analysis: Based on the economic model of crime, predict how each of the following would affect the crime rate: an increase in the unemployment rate, a decrease in conviction rates.

Source: E. Eide (1999). "Economics of criminal behaviour." *Handbook of Law and Economics*, 8100, 345–389. (Adobe Acrobat document - 145Kb) http://www-staff.lboro.ac.uk/~ecrs3/Econ%20of%20Criminology/media/Eide%20(1999).pdf.

The economic model of crime presented in Example 1–6 above can prove useful in identifying incentives that help to reduce specific crimes. As an example, the international cigarette smuggling and counterfeiting problem noted in Policy Example 1–1, could be reduced by decreasing the benefits derived from smuggling cigarettes. If the Chinese government reduced the taxes imposed on cigarettes legally sold in the country, this would reduce the price and profit that criminals would get from smuggling and counterfeiting cigarettes.

1.5 Positive versus Normative Economics

Economic theory uses *positive analysis*, a value-free approach to inquiry. No subjective or moral judgments enter into the analysis. Positive analysis relates to such statements as "If *A*, then *B*." For example, "If the price of gasoline goes up relative to all other prices, then the amount of it that people will buy will fall." That is a positive economic statement. It is a statement of *what is*, and its validity can be tested by observing the facts. It is not a statement of anyone's value judgment or subjective feelings. For many problems analyzed in the hard sciences, such as physics and chemistry, the analyses are considered to be virtually value-free. After all, how can someone's values enter into a theory of molecular behaviour? But economists face a different problem. They deal with the behaviour of individuals, not molecules. That makes it more difficult to stick to what we consider to be value-free or *positive economics* without reference to our feelings. **Positive economics** refers to analysis that can be tested by observing the facts.

Positive economics Analysis that can be tested by observing the facts.

When our values are interjected into the analysis, we enter the realm of *normative economics*, involving *normative analysis*. **Normative economics** refers to analysis based on value judgments made about what ought to be. A positive economic statement is, "If the price of gas rises, people will buy less." If we add to that analysis the statement, "so we should not allow the price to go up," we have entered the realm of normative economics— we have expressed a value judgment. In fact, any time you see the word *should*, you will know that values are entering into the discussion. Just remember that positive statements are concerned with *what is*, whereas normative statements are concerned with *what ought to be*.

Normative economics Analysis based on value judgments made about what ought to be.

In the last section of this chapter, we will introduce the important social and economic goals that governments try to achieve when they design economic policy. Normative analysis is often encountered when you examine the various goals that form the basis of policy. As an example, in this chapter's Issues and Applications, you will see that the proposal to tax bottled water is, in part, based on certain goals, such as "a pollution-free environment," which are normative in nature.

A Warning: Recognize Normative Analysis

It is easy to define positive economics. It is quite another matter to catch all unlabelled normative statements in a textbook such as this one (or any other), even though the authors go over the manuscript many times before it is printed. Therefore, do not get the impression that a textbook's authors will be able to keep all personal values out of the book. They will slip through. In fact, the very choice of which topics to include in an introductory textbook involves normative economics. There is no value-free, or objective, way to decide which topics to include in a textbook. The authors' values ultimately make a difference when choices have to be made. But from your own standpoint, you might want to be able to recognize when you are engaging in normative, as opposed to positive, economic analysis. Reading this text will help equip you for that task.

1.6 Economic Policy and Socioeconomic Goals

As we noted above, economic models will enhance your ability to understand and predict behaviour. In the chapters to come, we will illustrate how these models prove useful in formulating, assessing, and reacting to government policies that affect you as a consumer, an employee, an investor, a business owner, and a concerned citizen.

Policies Action plans designed to achieve goals.

Most government economic **policies** are action plans designed to achieve commonly accepted socioeconomic goals. The goals that are most frequently considered, when forming and evaluating economic policies, are described below.

1.   Full Employment: an economy in which people looking for work find jobs reasonably quickly.
2.   Efficiency: an economy in which resources are allocated to the production of goods and services in a way that achieves maximum benefit for society.
3.   Economic Growth: an economy with the ability to increase its rate of production over time to enhance society's well being.
4.   Price Stability: an economy in which prices remain relatively stable over time.
5.   Equity: an economy that moves closer toward some social consensus of fairness. An example often used as a basis of economic policy is the goal of a *more equitable distribution of income*, which aims to reduce the level of poverty in the economy.

Theory and Policy

Economic theory plays a useful role in helping us understand how existing and proposed policies relate to major socioeconomic goals. As you progress through this text, you may be surprised at the frequency with which a proposed policy is shown to conflict with the very goals it is meant to promote, once you employ the relevant economic model.

For example, a local politician may propose a rent control policy aimed at reducing apartment rents in order to make housing more affordable to the poor. That is, the rent control policy is aimed at promoting a more equitable distribution of income. However, once you become familiar with the demand-and-supply model presented in Chapter 4, you will see that this policy will more likely conflict with the goal of an equitable distribution of income because of the resulting shortages in livable accommodation. Moreover, this same policy will also conflict with the goal of full employment to the extent that construction workers are laid off as fewer new apartments are being built.

We hope that you will enjoy the challenge of using economic models to formulate superior alternative policies. A superior policy refers to a plan of action that promotes as many socioeconomic goals as possible with minimal goal conflict. In the rent control example, you may find that relevant economic theory suggests that a policy of increasing competition in the apartment construction and rental industries may prove to be the superior policy. By increasing the supply of affordable, quality housing units, the goals of full employment and equitable distribution can both be promoted!

ISSUES AND APPLICATIONS

Bottled Water: The Hummer of Beverages?

Concepts Applied: Economics, Microeconomics versus Macroeconomics, Scarcity, Opportunity Cost, Economic Way of Thinking, Incentives, Policy Analysis

In Canada, consumption of bottled water exceeds that of coffee, tea, apple juice, milk, and beer.

The Rapid Growth of the Bottled Water Industry

Everyone knows that water is an essential resource. Yet, more than a billion people around the world don't have access to safe, clean water. The worldwide demand for water is doubling every 20 years, to the point that two-thirds of the people on this planet may be facing severe water shortages by the year 2025.

Despite the fact that clean and safe tap water is available in developed nations such as Canada and the U.S., the bottled water market has been exploding in North America. Today, close to one-fifth of the population relies exclusively on bottled water for their daily hydration. In Canada, bottled water consumption exceeds coffee, tea, apple juice, milk, and beer consumption.

The global bottled water industry is dominated by four companies: Coca-Cola (Dasani), Pepsi (Aquafina), Nestlé (Perrier), and Danone (Evian). In response to growing interest in healthier lifestyles and declining demand for soft drinks, these companies have been promoting bottled water as a more desirable option than tap water. North Americans spend more than US$11 billion per year drinking over 8 billion gallons of bottled water. Currently, bottled water is the fastest growing and most profitable segment of the beverage industry in North America. Within the next ten years, industry analysts project that bottled water could overtake soft drinks as the leading beverage.

Critics of the bottled water industry argue that its rapid growth is not due to informed individual consumer choices but rather is in response to the deceptive and non-competitive practices of the large beverage companies. Moreover, these critics point to the significant resource costs and environmental degradation related to the bottled water industry. The specific arguments are explained below.

Concerns Related to the Bottled Water Industry

Consumers can be easily misled by the "pure," "crisp," "fresh," and "sparkling" glossy advertising of the leading brands of bottled water. The product has often been depicted as coming from pristine natural spring and glacier-like environments, when in fact the water comes from municipal water sources (the same as tap water) or from borehole ground water wells located near the bottling plants. In response to consumer demands, industry leader Aquafina (Pepsi) has agreed to print "Public Water Source" on Aquafina labels. To date, Coca-Cola (Dasani) has not followed suit, even though its water source is the same as tap water.

One might have legitimate health-related concerns over the fact that while cities such as Toronto test their water quality every few hours, bottled water plants are publicly inspected only once every three to six years. To date, companies such as Coca-Cola have refused to publicly report on the health and quality of their bottled water in ways required of public water systems.

Through the widespread use of exclusivity contracts with schools, colleges, and universities, Coca-Cola and Pepsi have conducted successful marketing campaigns aimed at weaning the younger generation off of tap water in favour of bottled water. The University of British Columbia (UBC) was the first university in Canada to sign an exclusivity contract with Coca-Cola in 1995. Under this contract, UBC was to receive $8.5 million dollars in return for giving Coca-Cola the exclusive right to sell its products on campus. This contract excluded all Coca-Cola competitors from selling their products at UBC. During the contract period it was reported that over 40 percent of water fountains were removed or disabled on the UBC campus. Needless to say, these exclusivity contracts set the stage for Coca-Cola to charge high prices for its bottled water products.

We must question whether the bottled water industry is squandering our limited resources in producing a product that is arguably no better than tap water, which is available at a much lower cost. A 1.5 litre bottle of Aquafina costs around $2.70, but the same amount of water taken from the Montreal municipal system costs 1/500th of a cent. The extra costs for the higher priced bottled water include what some might consider unnecessary "purifying" of already good quality water, creating plastic bottles, packaging, advertising, marketing, transportation, and a healthy profit. Globally, an estimated US$100 billion is spent every year on the purchase of bottled water. It is estimated that it would only take US$30 billion to halve the number of people who do not have ready access to clean, safe, drinking water, and achieve one of the Millennium Development Goals established by the United Nations (UN) in 2000.

Yet another concern has to do with bottled water's impact on the environment. The plastic bottles create carbon dioxide (CO_2) when they are made, trucked to the store, and later disposed of in a landfill or recycled. It is estimated that the energy required to manufacture a single plastic 1 litre bottle, fill it with water, truck it to a typical retail location, and then bury it in a landfill creates about .23 pounds of CO_2. That's equivalent to what an average car would emit in driving about half a kilometre.

A Tax on Bottled Water?

What types of policies might the government employ in order to reduce the degree to which our limited resources are used to produce bottled water? If we apply the economic way of thinking to those who manufacture and sell bottled water, any policy which reduces the marginal benefit or increases the marginal cost of supplying this product will reduce its production.

Starting January 1, 2008, Chicago began levying a tax of 5 cents per litre of bottled water sold in its city, thereby increasing the marginal cost of selling this product. In the latter part of 2007, Toronto City Council was reviewing a proposal to impose a tax of 5 cents per litre on water bottled in Ontario and 10 cents per litre for water bottled outside of the province.

The Industry Response to the Proposed Toronto Tax

The Canadian Bottled Water Association (CBWA), representing the major bottled water manufacturers, mounted a strong campaign opposing Toronto's proposed tax on the sale of bottled water. The CBWA argued that it is unfair and unwise to impose a discriminatory tax on a single grocery item, especially a healthy beverage alternative. The CBWA also noted that imposing a tax within Toronto would drive consumers to buy their food and beverage items outside the city limits, which could harm local businesses and create unemployment.

On November 27, 2007, Toronto City Council decided not to pursue a policy of taxing bottled water. Council members stated that this type of tax would be too costly to administer and that it may not even be legal.

Other Policies Aimed at Slowing the Growth in the Bottled Water Industry

On April 23, 2009, Vancouver City Council voted to eliminate the use of bottled water at all municipal facilities over the following few years. The move was meant to reduce environmental costs, cut solid waste, and battle greenhouse-gas emissions. City staff were directed to find alternative sources of drinking water on city properties, such as the increased use of tap water and water fountains.

To date in Canada, 76 municipalities, four municipal associations, eight school boards, five university campuses, and countless businesses have implemented restrictions on bottled water.

For critical analysis:

1. Explain how this issue relates to the concepts of scarcity, opportunity cost, and the meaning of economics.
2. This issue focuses on production and consumption related to one industry in Canada. Is this a microeconomic or macroeconomic focus? Explain.
3. How might the government affect the marginal benefit derived from supplying bottled water so as to reduce the amount of resources used in the production of bottled water?
4. How does this issue apply to policy analysis?

Sources: "November 21st campus day of action: update and results." *Inside the Bottle*. December 2, 2007. http://www.inside the bottle.org/november-21st-campus-day-action-update-and-results; Kelly Grant. "Toronto mulls bottled-water tax; several U.S. cities have adopted similar measure." *National Post*. November 21, 2007. pg A1; Polaris Institute. "Water royalties coming soon: Quebec eyes B.C. and Ontario models." November 27, 2007. http://www.polarisinstitute.org/water_royalties_coming_soon_quebec_eyes_b_c_and_ontario_models. Kelly Grant. "Bottled water tax will not be studied." *National Post*. National edition. November 27, 2007. Pg. A14; "Vancouver bans bottled water on city property." *CBC News*. Thursday, April 23, 2009. http://www.cbc.ca/canada/british-columbia/story/2009/04/23/bc-vancouver-bottled-water.html.

SUMMARY

Here is what you should know after reading this chapter. MyEconLab will help you identify what you know, and where to go when you need to practise. We suggest that as soon as you review one of the Learning Objective sections below, you then proceed to go through the related section in MyEconLab.

LEARNING OBJECTIVES	KEY TERMS	MYECONLAB PRACTICE
1.1 Scarcity. Scarcity refers to the condition that arises because human wants in terms of goods, services, and goals always exceed what can be produced with the available limited resources—land, labour, entrepreneurship, and physical and human capital. Economics is a social science that studies how people allocate limited resources to satisfy unlimited wants.	scarcity, 2 goods, 2 services, 2 production, 2 land, 3 labour, 3 physical capital, 3 human capital, 3 entrepreneurship, 3 rent, 3 wages, 3 interest, 3 profit, 3	• **MyEconLab** Study Plan 1.1
1.2 Defining Economics. Economics is usually divided into microeconomics, which is the study of individual decision making by households and firms, and macroeconomics, which is the study of economywide phenomena such as inflation, unemployment, and national income.	economics, 3 microeconomics, 4 macroeconomics, 4 aggregates, 5	• **MyEconLab** Study Plan 1.2
1.3 Rational Decision Making. Benefits at the Margin, Incentives, and Resource Use. Under the rationality assumption, the individual will employ resources in uses where the marginal benefit exceeds the marginal cost so as to maximize his or her own self-interest. Marginal cost is measured in terms of opportunity cost, which is the highest-valued alternative that must be sacrificed to satisfy a want. A change in marginal cost or marginal benefit will change the incentives that an individual faces and will lead to a change in resource use decisions.	economic way of thinking, 5 rationality assumption, 6 opportunity cost, 6 marginal benefit, 7 marginal cost, 7 sunk costs, 7 incentive, 8	• **MyEconLab** Study Plan 1.3
1.4 The Scientific Method. In using the scientific method, one makes assumptions, constructs models or theories, and tests these models with the facts. Models are simplified representations of the real world that make predictions that can be tested by the facts.	models or theories, 10 ceteris paribus assumption, 11 empirical, 12	• **MyEconLab** Study Plan 1.4

LEARNING OBJECTIVES	KEY TERMS	MYECONLAB PRACTICE
1.5 Positive versus Normative Economics. Positive economics deals with *what is*, whereas normative economics deals with what *ought to be*. Positive statements are of the "if . . . then" nature and are testable by facts. By contrast, normative statements are based on subjective value judgments.	positive economics, 14 normative economics, 14	• **MyEconLab** Study Plan 1.5
1.6 Economic Policy and Socioeconomic Goals. Theories can help us identify how various policies affect socioeconomic goals, such as full employment, efficiency, economic growth, price stability, and equity.	policies, 15	• **MyEconLab** Study Plan 1.6

PROBLEMS

(Answers to the odd-numbered problems appear at the back of the book.)

LO 1.1 Explain the meaning of scarcity.

1. Identify the factor of production that best relates to each of the following:
    a. a degree in engineering
    b. underground oil reserves
    c. the factor that earns profit
    d. a newly constructed pulp and paper mill
    e. the factor that earns wages

LO 1.2 Define economics and distinguish between microeconomics and macroeconomics.

2. According to Example 1–1, "The Economics of Web Page Design," what aspects of web design make it an "economic concern"?

3. Categorize the following issues as either a microeconomic issue or a macroeconomic issue.
    a. The national unemployment rate increases.
    b. The wage increases of nurses do not keep up with the wage increases of doctors.
    c. The price of cigarettes increases due to a tax imposed on cigarette manufacturers.
    d. The Canadian annual inflation rate exceeds the average annual increase in Canadian wages.
    e. The nation's total annual rate of production declines.

f. In response to strong competition, a Canadian retail corporation files for bankruptcy.

LO 1.3 Describe how resource use decisions are affected by the rationality assumption, costs and benefits at the margin, and incentives.

4. In order to spend a winter in Victoria, B.C., Paul Dafoe rents out his Montreal condo, as well as his car, to a married couple attending university. Paul estimates that the total cost associated with his decision to winter in Victoria for the eight-month period is $15 000. He calculates this total cost by adding the following costs: round trip airfare; eight months' rental fees for a Victoria condo; estimated total grocery, personal care, and entertainment expenses while staying in Victoria; and total rental car expenses incurred in Victoria. Is $15 000 the correct marginal cost associated with Paul's decision to winter in Victoria? Explain.

5. Jon Krechen is currently earning $3000 per month working full time as a computer technical support person for a college situated in Toronto. Jon lives in a one-bedroom apartment and pays $1000 per month in rent. Jon's monthly living expenses, including food, personal care, taxes, insurance, and entertainment amount to $1600 per month. Since Jon does not own a vehicle, he pays $75 per month for a bus pass.

Jon is in the process of estimating the marginal (extra) cost related to his decision to enroll full-time in an intensive two-month computer networking course in the Toronto area. While taking the computer course, Jon will be on a two-month leave without pay from the college where he works. Jon will continue to live in the same apartment and will travel by bus to the training centre offering the computer course. Jon estimates that his living expenses will be the same as if he were working. The tuition, books, and fees related to taking the computer course are $4500. Compute Jon's marginal cost of taking the two-month computer course.

6. Recent Canadian studies indicate that Canadians in the lower income brackets tend to donate more time, per year, to volunteer activities, compared to individuals who earn higher levels of income. Is this observation consistent with rational behaviour? Explain.

7. Your bank advertises that cash withdrawals from your bank machine are "free" if you always keep a minimum monthly balance of $5000 in your chequing account. In this case, are your cash withdrawals truly "free"? Explain.

8. According to Example 1–2, "The Opportunity Cost of Finding a Mate—Lower on the Internet?", what economic concept helps explain the popularity of online dating websites? Explain.

9. The mayor of a Canadian city justifies the construction of a beautiful new city hall on the basis of there being sufficient tax dollars available to pay for this project. Is the mayor's decision to construct the city hall a rational one? Explain.

10. Since health care is an essential service, all health-care services should be provided free of charge. Moreover, the government should continue to increase the resources to health care until all hospital waitlists across the nation disappear. Is this view consistent with making decisions at the margin? Explain.

LO 1.4 Explain the three key processes involved in the scientific method.

11. Give a refutable implication (one that can be tested by evidence from the real world) for each of the following models:
    a. The accident rate of drivers is inversely related to their age.
    b. The rate of inflation is directly related to the rate of change in the nation's money supply.
    c. The wages of professional basketball players are directly related to their high-school grade-point averages.

d. The rate at which bank employees are promoted is inversely related to their frequency of absenteeism.

12. Consider the following statements on the basis of positive economic analysis that assumes ceteris paribus. List one other thing that might change and thus alter the outcome stated.
    a. Increased demand for laptop computers will drive up their price.
    b. Falling gasoline prices will result in additional vacation travel.
    c. A reduction in corporate income tax rates will result in more people working.

LO 1.5 Distinguish between positive and normative economics.

13. Identify which of the following statements use positive economic analysis and which use normative analysis.
    a. Increasing the minimum wage will reduce employment opportunities for young people.
    b. A teacher should earn a higher salary than a hockey player, since the teacher's job is far more valuable to society.
    c. Everyone should enjoy free access to dental care.
    d. If the price of admission to each NHL hockey game is reduced, there will be an increase in ticket sales for each NHL game.

LO 1.6 Describe the relationship among theories, policies, and socioeconomic goals.

14. Identify which socioeconomic goal(s) may be promoted and which goal(s) may be conflicted with, for each policy listed below.
    a. Policy: In order to provide free public-health services, the government severely taxes Canadian corporation profits.
    b. Policy: The government raises the rate of income tax on all employees. The extra tax dollars raised are used to compensate upper-income investors who were swindled by fraud schemes.
    c. Policy: The government increases the monthly benefits (payments) to those collecting welfare. These people immediately spend the extra income on new goods and services.
    d. Policy: The government levies a special tax on all luxury goods. The taxes collected are used to keep college and university tuition fees relatively low.

BUSINESS APPLICATION

Finance: Fundamental Stock Investment Analysis

How might you go about determining whether to buy or sell a specific company stock?

Obviously, if you could predict the stock price, you would buy the stock if the price were predicted to increase in the near future, and possibly sell if the price were expected to fall. According to what is often called *fundamental stock analysis*, the single most important factor affecting a stock price is the expected profitability of the company that originally issued the stock. According to fundamental stock analysis, a company's stock price will increase if investors expect that the annual profit of this firm will increase significantly in the near future.

The expected profit of any corporation will be affected by both *macroeconomic* and *microeconomic* factors. Macroeconomic factors would include broad global and national events and trends. In formulating profit expectations, investors will also closely monitor microeconomic measures and trends at the specific industry and company level.

Business Application Problem

For each event and hypothetical company listed below, answer the following questions:

  i.   Is it a macroeconomic event or a microeconomic event?
  ii. Will it tend to increase or decrease the company's stock price? (Hint: predict how the event will affect the expected profit of the firm in question.)

a. *Event:* Due to the declining Canadian dollar (exchange rate), Canadian companies that export products to the U.S. experience a major increase in annual sales.
   Company: Timber Corp., a Canadian lumber company that exports 80 percent of its products.

b. *Event:* Special taxes are imposed on Canadian firms that manufacture cigarettes.
   Company: The Smoke Factory, a Canadian cigarette manufacturer.

c. *Event:* With global inflation escalating out of control, investors lose confidence in paper currency. As a result, there is a worldwide trend toward the purchase of items that investors feel will retain their value over time.
   Company: Bre-Y Mining Corp., a large, multi-national gold mining firm.

d. *Event:* As a result of new management, a department store is able to achieve the same annual sales as the previous year with much lower operating costs.
   Company: Wardwoods, a Canadian department store.

e. *Event*: Due to an upward trend in Canadian interest rates, investors sell stocks in all the major Canadian industries in order to purchase Canadian bonds.
   Company: Morgan Mutual Fund, a corporation that manages investor funds by buying blue chip stocks in a wide range of Canadian industries (on behalf of investors).

Reading and Working with Graphs

A graph is a visual representation of the relationship between variables. In this appendix, we will stick to just two variables: an **independent variable**, which can change freely in value, and a **dependent variable**, which changes only as a result of changes in the value of the independent variable. For example, if nothing else is changing in your life, your weight depends on the amount of food you eat. Food is the independent variable and weight the dependent variable.

A table is a list of numerical values showing the relationship between two (or more) variables. Any table can be converted into a graph, which is a visual representation of that list. Once you understand how a table can be converted to a graph, you will understand what graphs are and how to construct and use them.

Consider a practical example. A conservationist may try to convince you that driving at lower highway speeds will help you conserve gas. Table A–1 shows the relationship between speed—the independent variable—and the distance you can go on a litre of gas at that speed—the dependent variable. This table does show a pattern of sorts. As the data in the first column get larger in value, the data in the second column get smaller.

Independent variable A variable whose value is determined independently of, or outside, the equation under study.

Dependent variable A variable whose value changes according to changes in the value of one or more independent variables.

Kilometres per Hour	Kilometres per Litre
70	11
80	10
90	9
100	8
110	7
120	6
130	5

TABLE A–1

Gas Consumption as a Function of Driving Speed

Now, let us take a look at the different ways in which variables can be related.

Direct and Inverse Relationships

Two variables can be related in different ways, some simple, others more complex. For example, a person's weight and height are often related. If we measured the height and weight of thousands of people, we would surely find that taller people tend to weigh more than shorter people. That is, we would discover that there is a **direct relationship** between height and weight. By this, we simply mean that an increase in one variable is usually associated with an increase in the related variable. This can easily be seen in part (a) of Figure A–1.

Direct relationship A relationship between two variables that is positive, meaning that an increase in one variable is associated with an increase in the other, and a decrease in one variable is associated with a decrease in the other.

Part (a)
Direct Relationship

Height — / — Weight →

Part (b)
Inverse Relationship

Price — / — Quantity Purchased →

FIGURE A–1
Relationships

Inverse relationship A relationship between two variables that is negative, meaning that an increase in one variable is associated with a decrease in the other, and a decrease in one variable is associated with an increase in the other.

Let us look at another simple way in which two variables can be related. Much evidence indicates that as the price of a specific commodity rises, the amount purchased decreases—there is an **inverse relationship** between the variable's price per unit and quantity purchased. A table listing the data for this relationship would indicate that for higher and higher prices, smaller and smaller quantities would be purchased. We see this relationship in part (b) of Figure A–1.

Constructing a Graph

Let us now examine how to construct a graph to illustrate a relationship between two variables.

A Number Line

Number line A line that can be divided into segments of equal length, each associated with a number.

The first step is to become familiar with what is called a **number line**. One is shown in Figure A–2. There are two things that you should know about it.

1.   The points on the line divide the line into equal segments.
2.   The numbers associated with the points on the line increase in value from left to right; saying it the other way around, the numbers decrease in value from right to left. However you say it, what we are describing is formally called an *ordered set of points*.

FIGURE A–2

Horizontal Number Line

On the number line, we have shown the line segments—that is, the distance from 0 to 10 or the distance between 30 and 40. They all appear to be equal and, indeed, are equal to 13 mm. When we use a distance to represent a quantity, such as barrels of oil, graphically, we are scaling the number line. In the example shown, the distance between 0 and 10 might represent 10 barrels of oil, or the distance from 0 to 40 might represent 40 barrels. Of course, the scale may differ on different number lines. For example, a distance of 1 cm could represent 10 units on one number line but 5000 units on another. Note that on our number line, points to the left of 0 correspond to negative numbers and points to the right of 0 correspond to positive numbers.

Of course, we can also construct a vertical number line. Consider the one in Figure A–3. As we move up this vertical number line, the numbers increase in value; conversely, as we descend, they decrease in value. Below 0 the numbers are negative, and above 0 the numbers are positive. And as on the horizontal number line, all the line segments are equal. This line is divided into segments such that the distance between −2 and −1 is the same as the distance between 0 and 1.

Combining Vertical and Horizontal Number Lines

By drawing the horizontal and vertical lines on the same sheet of paper, we are able to express the relationships between variables graphically. We do this in Figure A–4.

We draw them so that they intersect at each other's 0 point, and so that they are perpendicular to each other. The result is a set of coordinate axes, where each line is called an axis. When we have two axes, they span a plane.

For one number line, you need only one number to specify any point on the line; equivalently, when you see a point on the line, you know that it represents one number or one value. With a coordinate value system, you need two numbers to specify a single point in the plane; when you see a single point on a graph, you know that it represents two numbers or two values.

y-axis The vertical axis in a graph.

x-axis The horizontal axis in a graph.

Origin The intersection of the y-axis and the x-axis in a graph.

The basic things that you should know about a coordinate number system are that the vertical number line is referred to as the **y-axis**, the horizontal number line is referred to as the **x-axis**, and the point of intersection of the two lines is referred to as the **origin**.

Any point such as A in Figure A–4 represents two numbers—a value of x and a value of y. But we know more than that; we also know that point A represents a positive value of y because it is above the x-axis, and we know that it represents a positive value of x because it is to the right of the y-axis.

Point A represents a "paired observation" of the variables x and y; in particular, in Figure A–4, A represents an observation of the pair of values $x = 10$ and $y = 1$. Every point in the coordinate system corresponds to a paired observation of x and y, which can be simply written (x, y)—the x-value is always specified first, then the y-value. When we give the values associated with the position of point A in the coordinate number system, we are, in effect, giving the coordinates of that point. A's coordinates are $x = 10$, $y = 1$, or $(10, 1)$.

Graphing Numbers in a Table

Consider Table A–2. Column 1 shows different prices for T-shirts, and column 2 gives the number of T-shirts purchased per week at these prices. Note the pattern of these numbers. As the price of a T-shirt falls, the number of T-shirts purchased per week increases. Therefore, an inverse relationship exists between these two variables, and as soon as we represent it on a graph, you will be able to see the relationship. We can graph this relationship using a coordinate number system—a vertical and a horizontal number line for each of these two variables. Such a graph is shown in part (b) of Figure A–5.

In economics, it is conventional to put dollar values on the y-axis. We therefore construct a vertical number line for price and a horizontal number line, the x-axis, for quantity of T-shirts purchased per week. The resulting coordinate system allows the plotting of each of the paired observation points; in part (a), we repeat Table A–2, with a column added expressing these points in paired-data (x, y) form. For example, point J is the paired observation $(30, 9)$. It indicates that when the price of a T-shirt is \$9, 30 will be purchased per week.

If it were possible to sell parts of a T-shirt ($\frac{1}{2}$ or $\frac{1}{20}$ shirt), we would have observations at every possible price. That is, we would be able to connect our paired observations, represented as lettered points. Let us assume that we can make T-shirts perfectly divisible. We would then have a line that connects these points, as shown in the graph in Figure A–6.

In short, we have now represented the data from the table in the form of a graph. Note that an inverse relationship between two variables shows up on a graph as a line or curve that slopes downward from left to right. (You might as well get used to the idea that economists call a straight line a "curve," even though it may not curve at all. Much of economists' data turn out to be curves, so they refer to everything represented graphically, even straight lines, as curves.)

FIGURE A–3
Vertical Number Line

FIGURE A–4
A Set of Coordinate Axes

TABLE A–2

T-Shirts Purchased

(1) Price per T-Shirt	(2) Number of T-Shirts Purchased per Week
$10	20
9	30
8	40
7	50
6	60
5	70

FIGURE A–5

Graphing the Relationship between T-Shirts Purchased and Price

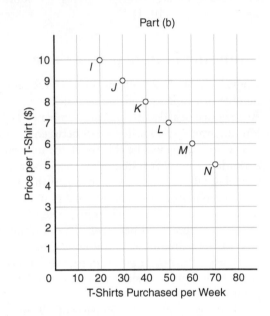

Part (b)

Part (a)

T-Shirts Purchased per Week	Price per T-Shirt	Point on Graph
20	$10	I (20, 10)
30	9	J (30, 9)
40	8	K (40, 8)
50	7	L (50, 7)
60	6	M (60, 6)
70	5	N (70, 5)

FIGURE A–6

Connecting the Observation Points

The Slope of a Line (A Linear Curve)

An important property of a curve represented on a graph is its *slope*. Consider Figure A–7, which represents the quantities of shoes per week that a seller is willing to offer at different prices. Note that in part (a) of Figure A–7, as in Figure A–5, we have expressed the coordinates of the points in parentheses in paired-data form.

The *slope* of a line is defined as the change in the y-values divided by the corresponding change in the x-values as we move along the line. Let us move from point E to point D in part (b) of Figure A–7. As we move, we note that the change in the y-values, which is

Part (a)

Pairs of Shoes Offered per Week	Price per Pair	Point on Graph
400	$100	A (400,100)
320	80	B (320, 80)
240	60	C (240, 60)
160	40	D (160, 40)
80	20	E (80, 20)

FIGURE A–7

A Positively Sloped Curve

the change in price, is +$20 because we have moved from a price of $20 to a price of $40 per pair. As we move from E to D, the change in the x-values is +80; the number of pairs of shoes willingly offered per week rises from 80 to 160 pairs. The slope calculated as a change in the y-values divided by the change in the x-values is, therefore,

$$\frac{20}{80} = \frac{1}{4}$$

It may be helpful for you to think of slope as a "rise" (movement in the vertical direction) over a "run" (movement in the horizontal direction). We show this abstractly in Figure A–8. The slope is measured by the amount of rise divided by the amount of run. In the example in Figure A–8, and of course in Figure A–7, the amount of rise is positive and so is the amount of run. That is because it is a direct relationship. We show an inverse relationship in Figure A–9. The slope is still equal to the rise divided by the run, but in

FIGURE A–8

Figuring Positive Slope

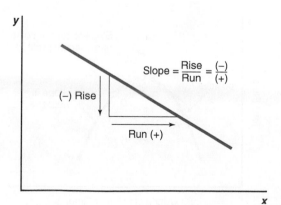

FIGURE A–9

Figuring Negative Slope

this case, the rise and the run have opposite signs because the curve slopes downward. That means that the slope will have to be negative and that we are dealing with an inverse relationship.

Now, let us calculate the slope for a different part of the curve in part (b) of Figure A–7. We will find the slope as we move from point B to point A. Again, we note that the slope, or rise over run, from B to A equals

$$\frac{20}{80} = \frac{1}{4}$$

A specific property of a straight line is that its slope is the same between any two points; in other words, the slope is constant at all points on a straight line in a graph.

We conclude that for our example in Figure A–7, the relationship between the price of a pair of shoes and the number of pairs of shoes willingly offered per week is linear, which simply means "in a straight line," and our calculations indicate a constant slope. Moreover, we calculate a direct relationship between these two variables, which turns out to be an upward-sloping (from left to right) curve. Upward-sloping curves have positive slopes—in this case, it is $+\frac{1}{4}$.

We know that an inverse relationship between two variables shows up as a downward-sloping curve—rise over run will be a negative slope because the rise and run have opposite signs as shown in Figure A–9. When we see a negative slope, we know that increases in one variable are associated with decreases in the other. Therefore, we say that downward-sloping curves have negative slopes. Can you verify that the slope of the graph representing the relationship between T-shirt prices and the quantity of T-shirts purchased per week in Figure A–6 is $-\frac{1}{10}$?

Slopes of Nonlinear Curves

The graph presented in Figure A–10 indicates a *nonlinear* relationship between two variables—total profits and output per unit of time. Inspection of this graph indicates that at first, increases in output lead to increases in total profits; that is, total profits rise as output increases. But beyond some output level, further increases in output cause decreases in total profits.

Can you see how this curve rises at first, reaches a peak at point C, and then falls? This curve relating total profits to output levels appears mountain-shaped.

Considering that this curve is nonlinear (it is obviously not a straight line), should we expect a constant slope when we compute changes in y divided by corresponding changes in x in moving from one point to another? A quick inspection, even without specific numbers, should lead us to conclude that the slopes of lines joining different points in this curve, such as between A and B, B and C, or C and D, will *not* be the same. The curve slopes upward (in a positive direction) for some values and downward (in a negative direction) for other values. In fact, the slope of the line between any two points on this curve will be different from the slope of the line between any two other points. Each slope will be different as we move along the curve.

FIGURE A–10

The Slope of a Nonlinear Curve

Instead of using a line between two points to discuss slope, mathematicians and economists prefer to discuss the slope *at a particular point*. The slope at a point on the curve, such as point *B* in the graph in Figure A–10, is the slope of a line *tangent* to that point. A tangent line is a straight line that touches a curve at only one point. For example, it might be helpful to think of the tangent at *B* as the straight line that just "kisses" the curve at point *B*.

To calculate the slope of a tangent line, you need to have some additional information besides the two values of the point of tangency. For example, in Figure A–10, if we knew that the point *R* also lay on the tangent line and we knew the two values of that point, we could calculate the slope of the tangent line. We could calculate rise over run between points *B* and *R*, and the result would be the slope of the line tangent to the one point *B* on the curve.

APPENDIX SUMMARY

1. Direct relationships involve a dependent variable changing in the same direction as the change in the independent variable.
2. Inverse relationships involve the dependent variable changing in the opposite direction of the change in the independent variable.
3. When we draw a graph showing the relationship between two economic variables, we are holding all other things constant (the Latin term for which is *ceteris paribus*).
4. We obtain a set of coordinates by putting vertical and horizontal number lines together. The vertical line is called the *y*-axis; the horizontal line, the *x*-axis.

5. The slope of any linear (straight-line) curve is the change in the *y*-values divided by the corresponding change in the *x*-values as we move along the line. Otherwise stated, the slope is calculated as the amount of rise over the amount of run, where rise is movement in the vertical direction and run is movement in the horizontal direction.
6. The slope of a nonlinear curve changes; it is positive when the curve is rising and negative when the curve is falling. At a maximum or minimum point, the slope of the nonlinear curve is zero.

APPENDIX PROBLEMS

(Answers to the odd-numbered problems appear at the back of the book.)

A-1. Explain which is the independent variable and which is the dependent variable in the following examples.

a. Once you determine the price of a notebook at your college bookstore, you will decide how many notebooks to buy.

b. You will decide how many credit hours to register for this semester once the university tells you how many work-study hours you will be assigned.

c. You are anxious to receive your Economics exam grade because you studied many hours in the weeks preceding the exam.

A-2. For the following items, state whether a direct or an indirect relationship exists.

a. the number of hours you study for an exam and your exam mark.

b. the price of pizza and the quantity purchased.

c. the number of games your college basketball team won last year and the number of season tickets sold this year.

A-3. Complete the table and plot the following function:

$y = 3x$

x	y
4	
3	
2	
1	
0	
−1	
−2	
−3	
−4	

A-4. Review Figure A–4, and then state whether the following paired observations are on, above, or below the *x*-axis and on, to the left of, or to the right of the *y*-axis.

a. (−10, 4)
b. (20, −2)
c. (10, 0)

A-5. Calculate the slope for the function you graphed in Problem A-3.

A-6. Complete the table and plot the following function:

$$y = x^2$$

x	y
4	
3	
2	
1	
0	
−1	
−2	
−3	
−4	

A-7. Indicate at each ordered pair whether the slope of the curve you plotted in Problem A-6 is positive, negative, or zero.

A-8. State whether the following functions imply a positive or negative relationship between x and y.

a. $y = 5x$

b. $y = 3 + x$

c. $y = -3x$

2

Production Possibilities and Economic Systems

Soaring Canadian car insurance rates created havoc for politicians and consumers alike in the first decade of the twenty-first century. The issue of skyrocketing auto insurance rates threatened the election campaigns of free-enterprise, conservative governments in New Brunswick, Ontario, and Alberta. In 2005, the Consumers' Association of Canada completed research involving 714 Canadian communities and close to 4 000 000 insurance quotes. Consistent with previous findings, car insurance rates tended to be significantly lower in provinces where this service is provided by government, rather than the private sector. However, in November 2008, the Fraser Institute released a study suggesting that government-run car insurance monopolies force consumers to purchase too much insurance protection. The concepts presented in this chapter will help you understand both the public benefits and costs related to delivering services, such as auto insurance, under different economic systems.

Source: Brett J. Skinner. "Three of four provinces with government auto insurance monopolies have highest rates in Canada." News Releases. Fraser Institute. November 18, 2008. http://www.fraserinstitute.org/researchnews/news/display.aspx?id=12720 (Accessed August 27, 2010.)

MyEconLab helps you master each objective and study more efficiently. See end of chapter for details.

LEARNING OBJECTIVES

After reading this chapter, you should be able to:

2.1 Define the production possibilities curve and identify its assumptions.

2.2 Use the production possibilities curve to illustrate the concepts of scarcity, trade-offs, unemployment, productive efficiency, allocative efficiency, increasing opportunity cost, and economic growth.

2.3 Use the production possibilities curve to explain the trade-off between consumption goods and capital goods.

2.4 Distinguish between absolute advantage and comparative advantage and use these concepts to explain how specialization and trade can increase production and consumption.

2.5 Explain the differences between the pure capitalist, pure command, and mixed economic systems.

2.6 Describe the features of pure capitalism and explain how capitalism answers the three basic economic questions.

DID YOU KNOW THAT...?

Identity theft is the fastest growing fraud in both Canada and the United States. The phone rings up to 1200 times a day at PhoneBusters, an antifraud call centre, but the dozen or so call-takers are so swamped that most victims hang up while they are waiting in the queue. In 2009, according to PhoneBusters, about 11 109 Canadian victims reported losses related to identify theft of $10.8 million. This amounts to an increase of over 68 percent over the losses of $6.4 million reported in 2007 in Canada. However, this figure falls dramatically short of the number of cases of identity theft that are suspected to occur in Canada.

One hard drive stolen from a computer at a Regina data management company contained the names, addresses, dates of birth, social insurance numbers, pension statements, personal records for workers' compensation, and personal applications for provincial government rebates of over 300 000 Canadians. In January 2007, it was reported that as many as 2 million credit cards were affected when computer hackers stole customer information from the U.S. parent company of Canadian retailers Winners and Home-Sense. Thieves use stolen information such as this to gain unlawful access to personal bank accounts and credit cards and to fraudulently apply for loans.

In economics, identity theft can be viewed as a form of capital investment undertaken by dishonest individuals, as explained in this chapter.

Sources: Canadian Anti-Fraud Centre Criminal Intelligence Analytical Unit. *Annual Statistical Report 2009: Mass Marketing Fraud and Identity Theft Activities.* PhoneBusters. Pg. 23. http://www.phonebusters.com/english/documents/AnnualStatisticalReport2009_001.pdf; *Public Advisory: Special Report for Consumers on Identity Theft.* May 21, 2003. The Department of the Solicitor General of Canada. http://www.sgc.gc.ca/publications/policing/Identity_Theft_Consumers_e.asp. (Accessed November 29, 2003); *Expositor.* "Identity theft in Canada." *The Leader-Post* (Regina, Sask.; Brantford, Ont.) Canadian Credit Centre. February 1, 2003.

2.1 The Production Possibilities Curve

We begin this chapter by introducing an economic model called the production possibilities curve. We will use this model to sharpen your understanding of concepts discussed in Chapter 1, such as scarcity, choice, opportunity cost, efficiency, full employment, and economic growth. As well, we will illustrate how production possibilities can be expanded through specialization and trade. Finally, we will complete this chapter by examining the different economic systems that nations and industries can use to determine production possibilities.

Production possibilities curve (PPC) A curve that represents all possible production combinations of two goods that can be produced.

The **production possibilities curve (PPC)** is a curve representing all possible production combinations of two goods that can be produced under the following assumptions:

1. The nation's resources—land, labour, capital, and entrepreneurship—are fully and efficiently employed producing just these two goods (or services).
2. The production is measured over a specific period of time—for example, one year.
3. The quantity and quality of resources used to produce these two goods are fixed over this period of time.
4. The technology is fixed over this period of time.

Technology Society's pool of applied knowledge concerning how goods and services can be produced.

Technology is defined as society's pool of applied knowledge concerning how goods and services can be produced by managers, workers, engineers, scientists, and craftspeople, using land and capital. You can think of technology as the formula (or recipe) used to combine factors of production. When better formulas are developed, more production can be obtained from the same amount of resources. The level of technology sets the limit on the amount and types of goods and services that we can derive from any given amount of resources. The production possibilities curve is drawn under the assumption that we use the best technology that we currently have available and that this technology does not change over the time period under study.

The Production Possibilities Curve: An Example

Figure 2–1 describes a production possibilities curve for Canada for two goods—automobiles and newsprint—for 2007 (the data in Figure 2–1 are hypothetical). We assume for the moment that automobiles and newsprint are the only two goods that can be produced in Canada.

Part (a) of Figure 2–1 shows the various production combinations of automobiles and newsprint, assuming full and efficient employment of resources and a fixed level of resources and technology. If all resources are devoted to automobile production (point *A*), 3 million autos can be produced per year. Instead, if Canada decides to devote all its resources to newsprint production (point *G*), 6 million tonnes of newsprint per year can be produced. In between are other alternative possible production combinations. All of these production combinations are plotted as points *A, B, C, D, E, F,* and *G* in part (b) of Figure 2–1. Once connecting these points with a smooth curve, constructs Canada's production possibilities.

Note that this production possibilities curve indicates the *maximum* quantity of one good that can be produced in 2007, given some quantity of the other good that is to be produced. Therefore, if we are given that 2 million autos are to be produced in 2007, then the maximum amount of newsprint that can be produced in 2007 is 4 million tonnes at point *E* on the curve.

2.2 Applications of the Production Possibilities Curve

We now turn to examine how we can apply the production possibilities curve model to better understand concepts introduced in Chapter 1.

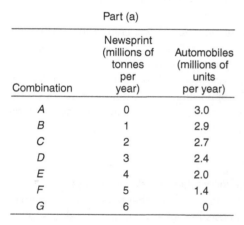

Part (a)

Combination	Newsprint (millions of tonnes per year)	Automobiles (millions of units per year)
A	0	3.0
B	1	2.9
C	2	2.7
D	3	2.4
E	4	2.0
F	5	1.4
G	6	0

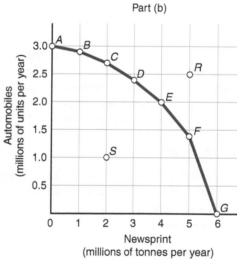

Part (b)

FIGURE 2–1

A Society's Trade-Off between Automobiles and Newsprint

The production of automobiles is measured in millions of units per year, while the production of newsprint is measured in millions of tonnes per year. The various combinations are given in part (a) and plotted in part (b). Connecting the points *A–G* with a relatively smooth line gives the production possibilities curve for automobiles and newsprint. Point *R* lies outside the production possibilities curve and is therefore unattainable at the point in time for which the graph is drawn. Point *S* lies inside the production possibilities curve and therefore represents an inefficient use of available resources or unemployment.

The Production Possibilities Curve, Scarcity, and Trade-Offs

Recall from the previous chapter that *scarcity* refers to the condition that arises because wants always exceed what can be produced with limited resources. The production possibilities curve in Figure 2–1 can be viewed as a boundary that separates the attainable production combinations, on or inside the curve, from the unattainable points outside of the curve (such as point *R* in Figure 2–1). That is, even though we are assuming that the resources are being fully and efficiently employed using the most up-to-date technology, Canada faces a *limit*, in terms of what it can produce, as portrayed by the production possibilities curve. The existence of this boundary, in the face of unlimited wants, gives us a vision of the economic problem of scarcity.

The fact that the production possibilities curve slopes downward to the right suggests that due to scarcity, society is forced to make choices that involve trade-offs. In Figure 2–1, you can clearly see that if Canada is currently at point *E* in the current year, and chooses to move to point *F*, next year, when it can produce additional tonnes of newsprint, Canada has to trade off some automobile production. Note that trade-offs will occur anywhere *on* the production possibilities curve.

As a student, you face the scarcity problem of using a limited amount of time to achieve both your academic and personal goals. Every time you attend a class or a study group session you trade off the opportunity to spend that time learning in a different manner or engaging in a work- or leisure-related activity. As Example 2–1 illustrates, new technologies are changing the nature of the trade-offs students face when they consider whether they will attend their next class or choose the best alternative use of their time.

What is the opportunity cost of replacing a face-to-face lecture with a podcast lecture?

EXAMPLE 2–1 Beware of "Free" Lecture Podcasts

At Simon Fraser University (SFU) in Vancouver, the class lectures for numerous university courses are recorded as podcasts that registered students can download to their computers or to portable devices such as iPods or iPhones. From 2008 to 2010, SFU created podcasts for 23 622 lectures in 1353 university courses. The lecture podcasts are available free of charge to students registered in the related courses. In this Example, we critically assess the increasingly frequent practice of using these podcasts as a reason to skip the corresponding face-to-face class sessions.

Every student has his or her own subjective estimate of the expected value of the next-best alternative to attending class. For each student, the value of an hour spent in class depends in part on what time of the day the class meets. SFU's lecture podcasts permit students to reallocate their time. For example, if a particular student would rather work a few additional hours on a part-time job that starts in the mid-afternoon or enjoy a sunny afternoon on the beach, she can miss afternoon classes. She can then listen to the class lectures later that evening, when the opportunity cost of that learning activity is lower.

Of course, there is still an opportunity cost associated with skipping the actual face-to-face class meeting. The student misses out on the opportunity to ask questions of her professor during the lecture and to interact with other class members. The student may also score poorly on a class participation mark.

For critical analysis:

1. What opportunity costs (sacrifices) might you incur when you skip your classes?
2. In classes where group discussion or group work is an essential feature of the learning process, who bears some of the additional costs of higher absenteeism rates resulting from posting lectures on the Web?

Source: "Podcasting @ SFU." Simon Fraser University website. http://cgi.sfu.ca/~lectures/pub_html_podcasts/cgi-bin/index.php.

The Production Possibilities Curve and Unemployment

Recall that full employment is one of the important socioeconomic goals identified in Chapter 1. Our simple production possibilities model helps us better understand the importance of this goal. Suppose, looking at Figure 2–1, that Canada failed to achieve the goal of full employment. Where, roughly speaking, would Canada's production combination be located—inside, on, or outside of the production possibilities curve? The answer would be somewhere *inside* the production possibilities curve, such as point *S*. When Canada is inside its production possibilities curve, a major cost of unemployment is that society forgoes some production of goods and services. That is, unemployment leads to a lower standard of living for society as a whole. If Canada were to eliminate this unemployment and move from point *S* to point *E*, would this involve a trade-off? The answer is no, as the extra production would be derived from putting unemployed workers back to work, allowing more of both goods to be produced.

The Production Possibilities Curve and Efficiency

The production possibilities curve can be used to define the notion of efficiency. Whenever the economy is operating on the PPC in Figure 2–1 at such points as *A*, *B*, *C*, or *D*, we say that its production is efficient. Such points as *S*, which lie below the production possibilities curve, are said to represent production situations that are not efficient.

PRODUCTIVE EFFICIENCY. Efficiency can mean many things to many people. Even within economics, there are different types of efficiency. Here, we are discussing efficiency in production, or **productive efficiency**, which occurs when a given output level is produced at minimal cost. Alternatively stated, productive efficiency occurs when a given level of inputs is used in a manner that produces the maximum output possible, given the level of technology.

Productive efficiency Occurs when a given output level is produced at minimal cost.

A simple, common-sense definition of productive efficiency is getting the most out of what we have as an economy. Clearly, we are not getting the most out of what we have if we are at point *S* in part (b) of Figure 2–1. We can move from point *S* to, say, point *C*, thereby increasing the total quantity of automobiles produced without any decrease in the total quantity of newsprint produced. We can move from point *S* to point *E*, for example, and have both more automobiles and more newsprint. Point *S* is called a **productively inefficient point**, which is defined as any point below the production possibilities curve, assuming resources are fully employed.

Productively inefficient point Any point below the production possibilities curve, assuming resources are fully employed.

Example 2–2 below describes a global initiative designed to educate children in the poorest regions of the world in a productively efficient (minimal cost) manner.

EXAMPLE 2-2   One Laptop per Child

Most of the nearly 2 billion children in the developing world are inadequately educated or uneducated. One in three does not complete grade five. Children are resigned to poverty and isolation, never knowing what the light of learning could mean to their lives. At the same time, their governments struggle to compete in a very dynamic, social, and global information economy.

Attempting to enhance the education of children living in the developing (poorer) nations using traditional "bricks and mortar" educational resources—building schools, hiring teachers, buying textbooks—seems to be too expensive a task, and hence unrealistic. As an example, in Canada, it costs on average over US$7500 per year for every student in the traditional education system. Given the resources that poor countries can reasonably allocate to education—sometimes less than $20 per year per pupil—a worldwide nonprofit association called "One Laptop per Child (OLPC)" is seeking to bring education to children (and their parents) in poorer nations through the creation of a laptop costing less than $100. OLPC has currently developed the XO laptop, a machine designed for "learning learning."

The XO laptop has been designed to provide the most engaging wireless network available at a cost of $100 per unit. The laptops are connected to each other and to the Internet. The children in the neighbourhood are thus permanently connected to chat, share information on the Web, gather by videoconference, make music together, edit texts, read ebooks, and enjoy the use of collaborative games online. As the children grow and pursue new ideas, the software, content, resources, and tools should be able to grow with them. The battery of the laptop can work for many hours and can be charged in special gang chargers in the school or by mechanical or solar power, so there is no need to have electricity. The unique XO display allows the use of the laptop under a bright sun, enabling the user to work outside, if need be.

What is the economic argument for using laptops to educate children in poorer nations?

As of the first quarter of 2010, 1.4 million XO laptops have been delivered to children in 35 countries, including Rwanda, Haiti, Afghanistan, Brazil, and Uruguay.

For critical analysis: Explain how the One Laptop per Child concept promotes productive efficiency.

continued

Sources: Peter Beaumont. "Rwanda's laptop revolution." *The Observer*. March 28, 2010. http://www.guardian.co.uk/technology/2010/mar/28/rwanda-laptop-revolution; "Mission." One Laptop per Child. http://www.laptop.org/en/vision/mission/index.shtml; "Laptop." One Laptop per Child. http://www.laptop.org/en/laptop/; "Annual expenditure on educational institutions per student for all services (2006). *Education at a Glance 2009: OECD Indicators*. September 2009. http://www.oecd.org/dataoecd/41/25/43636332.pdf. (Accessed August 25, 2010.)

Allocative efficiency Producing the mix of goods and services most valued by consumers.

ALLOCATIVE EFFICIENCY. The concept of **allocative efficiency** is concerned with producing the mix of goods and services most valued by consumers. While all the points along the production possibilities curve in Figure 2–1 are productively efficient, only one production combination on this curve will be allocatively efficient. Suppose that point *E* in part (b) of Figure 2–1 is the most highly valued combination. If Canada ends up producing this combination, it is being allocatively efficient.

Stated in terms of the concepts learned in Chapter 1, if society were to move away from point *E*, in either direction, the marginal benefit derived from this move would be less than the marginal cost associated with this move. In other words, the extra value derived from producing a different combination of cars and newsprint would be less than the value given up by departing from point *E*. If the firms that produce these goods make decisions on the basis of society's marginal benefits and marginal costs, rational behaviour has the potential to lead us to this allocatively efficient production combination.

In this chapter's Issues and Applications, the merits of providing auto insurance via privately owned companies is compared with the merits of having the government administer auto insurance in Canada. One of the advantages of private auto insurance is that each injured individual can take the necessary legal action to ensure that the dollar value of the compensation resulting from an accident claim (marginal benefit) is sufficient to cover the full marginal cost related to the individual's injuries and losses sustained from the accident. In this way, private auto insurance promotes allocative efficiency.

In contrast, under public auto insurance, the government dictates the maximum insurance payouts to injured parties for claims, such as those relating to the pain and suffering incurred in an accident. Since these maximum payouts are often set in a manner that attempts to reduce the total cost of these claims, the public insurance system may tend to underallocate resources in the payment of claims to injured individuals.

The Production Possibilities Curve and Opportunity Cost

We have re-created the curve in Figure 2–1 as Figure 2–2. Each combination, *A* through *G*, of automobiles and newsprint is represented on the production possibilities curve. Starting with the production of zero newsprint, Canada could produce 3 million automobiles with its available resources and technology. When we increase production of newsprint from zero to 1 million tonnes per year, we have to give up the automobile production represented by that first vertical arrow, *Aa*. From part (a) of Figure 2–1 you can see that this is 0.1 million autos a year (3.0 million – 2.9 million). Again, if we increase production of newsprint by 1 million tonnes per year, we go from *B* to *C*. In order to do so, we have to give up the vertical distance *Bb*, or 0.2 million automobiles a year. By the time we go from 5 million to 6 million tonnes of newsprint, to obtain that 1 million tonne increase we have to forgo the vertical distance *Ff*, or 1.4 million automobiles. In other words, the opportunity cost of the last 1 million tonnes of newsprint is 1.4 million autos, compared with 0.1 million autos, the opportunity cost for the first million tonnes of newsprint (starting at zero production).

Law of increasing relative cost When society takes more resources and applies them to the production of any specific good, the opportunity cost increases for each additional unit produced.

LAW OF INCREASING RELATIVE COST. What we are observing is called the **law of increasing relative cost**: when society takes more resources and applies them to the production of any specific good, the opportunity cost increases for each additional unit produced. The reason that, as a country, we face the law of increasing relative cost (which causes the production possibilities curve to bow outward) is that certain resources are better suited for producing some goods than they are for others. Resources are generally not

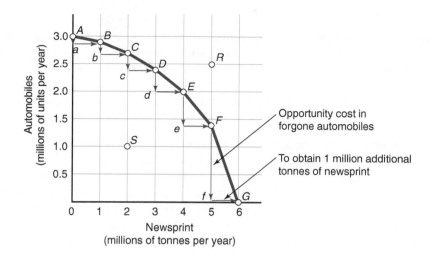

FIGURE 2–2

The Law of Increasing Relative Cost

Consider equal increments of newsprint production, as measured on the horizontal axis. All the horizontal arrows—*aB, bC,* and so on—are of equal length (1 million tonnes). The opportunity cost of going from 5 million tonnes of newsprint per year to 6 million *(Ff)* is much greater than going from zero tonnes to 1 million tonnes *(Aa).* The opportunity cost of each additional equal increase in newsprint production rises.

perfectly adaptable for alternative uses. When increasing the output of a particular good, producers must use less adaptable resources than those already used in order to produce the additional output. Hence the cost of producing the additional units increases. In our hypothetical example here, at first, the mechanical technicians in the automobile industry would shift over to producing newsprint. After a while, though, upholstery specialists and windshield installers would also be asked to help. Clearly, they would be less effective in making newsprint.

As a rule of thumb, *the more specialized the resources, the more bowed the production possibilities curve.* At the other extreme, if all resources are equally suitable for newsprint production or automobile production, the curves in Figures 2–1 and 2–2 would approach a straight line representing a constant opportunity cost situation.

Policy Example 2–1 describes recent policy decisions made by the government of British Columbia that affect the production combination of two highly valued types of goods: natural-wilderness-area-related goods and energy-related goods (oil and gas). This example encourages you to apply the concepts of opportunity cost and allocative efficiency to evaluate policies that affect the way in which our resources are used.

POLICY EXAMPLE 2–1   The Multi-Billion Dollar Park

In October 1997, the British Columbia New Democratic Party (NDP) government established the Muskwa-Kechika land-use area, a wilderness area larger than Switzerland, located in the northeast part of the province. In 2000, more land was added, bringing the total Muskwa-Kechika Management Area (M-KMA) to 6.3 million hectares, which made it the largest land-use decision of its kind in North America.

The management intent for the M-KMA is to maintain in perpetuity the wilderness quality, the diversity and abundance of wildlife, and the ecosystems on which the wildlife depends. One of the primary challenges is to be able to prevent corporate interests from exploiting the region's natural resources by engaging in logging, oil and gas drilling, and mining practices that would jeopardize the area's natural beauty and wildlife.

On June 25, 2003, the British Columbia Liberal government announced that it would allow exploration of extensive natural gas deposits, with a potential development value of $16 billion, in parts of the M-KMA.

According to the 2005–2006 M-KMA annual report to the premier and public, resource extraction for energy products such as oil and natural gas is permitted in 75 percent of the area, while 25 percent is designated under the provincial park system. This report noted that the intent is to use "best practices" to ensure that resource extraction occurs with minimal

continued

reduction in the quality of the natural wilderness area. For example, in extracting oil and gas for energy production, methods used to reduce negative impacts include building winter ice and snow roads that will be deactivated once the activity at well sites has been completed, conducting heliportable exploration drilling, timing activities so they are coordinated with other resource users such as guide outfitters, and coordinating resource road development with other industry companies.

For critical analysis: Sketch the appropriate two-good production possibilities curve, assuming the law of increasing relative cost and illustrating the trade-off indicated in this example. On this production possibilities curve, sketch the allocatively efficient point E, which we assume is halfway down the curve you sketched. Sketch another point F, which is on the curve but in the direction of more energy products (oil and gas) when compared to point E. What is the opportunity cost of moving from point E to point F? If British Columbia's economy moved from point E to point F, how would the marginal benefit of such a move compare with the marginal cost of such a move? Explain.

Source: "Muskwa-Kechika, BC's working wilderness, 2005–2006, Report to the Premier and the public." Muskwa-Kechika Management Area. Muskwa-Kechika Advisory Board. http://www.muskwa-kechika. com/pdf/2005-2006_annual_report.pdf.

The Production Possibilities Curve and Economic Growth

During any particular time period, a society cannot be outside the production possibilities curve. Over time, however, it is possible to have more of everything. This occurs through economic growth. Figure 2–3 shows the production possibilities curve for automobiles and newsprint shifting outward. The two additional curves represent new choices open to an economy that has experienced economic growth. Such economic growth occurs because of many things, including increases in the quantity of resources available, increases in the productivity of existing resources, and changes in technology.

Scarcity still exists, however, no matter how much economic growth there is. At any point in time, we will always be on some production possibilities curve; thus, we will always face trade-offs. The more we want of one thing, the less we can have of others.

If a country experiences economic growth, the production possibilities curve between automobiles and newsprint will move outward, as is shown in Figure 2–3. This takes time and does not occur automatically. One reason it will occur involves the choice about how much to consume today.

FIGURE 2–3

Economic Growth Allows for More of Everything

If the country experiences economic growth, the production possibilities curve between automobiles and newsprint will shift out, as shown. This takes time, however, and it does not occur automatically. This means, therefore, that we can have more automobiles and more newsprint only after a period of time during which we have experienced economic growth.

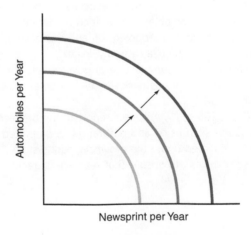

2.3 Consumption Goods versus Capital Goods

The production possibilities curve and economic growth can be used to examine the trade-off between present consumption and future consumption. **Consumption** is the use of goods and services for direct personal satisfaction. These goods and services are what we call consumption or consumer goods—food, clothes, and entertainment, for example. And we have already defined physical capital as the manufactured goods, such as machines and factories, used to make other goods and services.

Consumption The use of goods and services for direct personal satisfaction.

Why We Make Capital Goods

Why would we be willing to use productive resources to make things—capital goods—that we cannot consume directly? For one thing, capital goods enable us to produce larger quantities of consumer goods or to produce them less expensively than we otherwise could. Before fish are "produced" for the market, such equipment as fishing boats, nets, and poles are produced first. Imagine how expensive it would be to obtain fish for the market without using these capital goods. Catching fish with one's hands is not an easy task. The price per fish would be very high if capital goods were not used.

Forgoing Current Consumption

Whenever we use productive resources to make capital goods, we are implicitly forgoing current consumption. We are waiting until some time in the future to consume the fruits that will be reaped from the use of capital goods. In effect, when we forgo current consumption to invest in capital goods, we are engaging in an economic activity that is forward looking—we do not get instant utility or satisfaction from our activity.

At the start of this chapter, in the Did You Know That . . . ? section, we noted the rapid growth of identity theft in Canada. Even an individual contemplating a theft faces a choice between increased current consumption versus increased capital accumulation. That is, instead of breaking into a home to steal a consumer item, such as a TV or stereo, the identity thief uses sophisticated electronic devices to steal the identity of others. While securing the identity of others does not, in itself, provide immediate self-gratification in terms of current consumption, it does allow the sophisticated thief the ability to enhance his or her future consumption through the fraudulent use of credit cards and debit cards. Just as a new machine can reduce the costs of a legitimate business, identity theft lowers the cost of engaging in illegal activity by reducing the probability of being "caught in the act." That is, identity thieves often acquire the personal data of others, without ever having any direct contact with the victims. Indeed, identity theft can be viewed as a form of capital investment undertaken by dishonest individuals.

The Trade-Off between Consumption Goods and Capital Goods

To have more consumer goods in the future, we must accept fewer consumer goods today. In other words, an opportunity cost is involved here. Every time we make a choice for more goods today, we incur an opportunity cost of fewer goods tomorrow, and every time we make a choice of more goods in the future, we incur an opportunity cost of fewer goods today. With the resources that we do not use to produce consumer goods for today, we invest in capital goods that will produce more consumer goods for us later. The trade-off is shown in Figure 2–4. On the left in part (a), you can see this trade-off depicted as a production possibilities curve between capital goods and consumption goods.

Assume that we are willing to give up $1 billion worth of consumption today. We will be at point A in the left-hand diagram of part (a). This will allow the economy to grow. We will have more future consumption because we invested in more capital goods today. In the

FIGURE 2–4

Capital Goods and Growth

In part (a), the nation chooses not to consume $1 billion, so it invests that amount in capital goods. In part (b), it chooses even more capital goods. The PPC moves even farther to the right on the right-hand diagram in part (b) as a result.

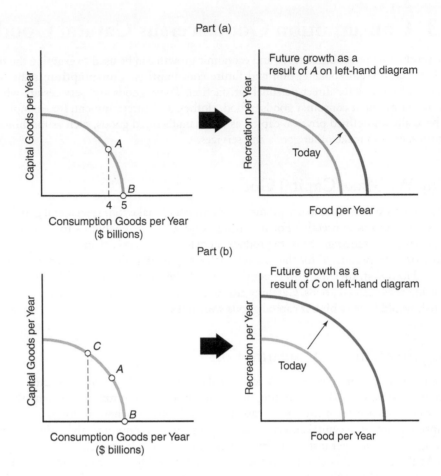

Part (a)

Part (b)

right-hand diagram of part (a), we see two goods represented: food and recreation. The production possibilities curve will move outward if we collectively decide to restrict consumption each year and invest in capital goods.

In part (b), we show the results of our willingness to forgo more current consumption. We move to point *C*, where we have much fewer consumer goods today, but produce a lot more capital goods. This leads to more future growth in this simplified model, and thus, the production possibilities curve in the right-hand side of part (b) shifts outward more than it did in the right-hand side of part (a).

In other words, the more we give up today, the more we can have tomorrow, provided, of course, that the capital goods are productive in future periods and that society desires the consumer goods produced by this additional capital.

At the individual consumer's level, the decision to enroll full time in a post-secondary educational institution entails a trade-off between additional capital goods and additional consumer goods. As we noted in Chapter 1, the decision to enroll in a college or university on a full-time basis entails the extra costs of lost employment income for eight months per year, as well as additional out-of-pocket costs, such as tuition, fees, and textbooks. These additional educational costs mean that the individual full-time student sacrifices some current consumption goods when enrolled in a post-secondary institution.

So, what does an individual gain when he or she purchases additional years of post-secondary education? Since post-secondary education is a form of human capital, the student should be more productive upon graduation and therefore should earn a higher income in future years. This means that the college or university graduate will be able to consume a greater quantity of consumer goods in the future. Example 2–3 examines whether the facts support the view that Canadian post-secondary education is a productive form of human capital.

EXAMPLE 2-3   Canadian Post-Secondary Education Pays Off Big Time!

Canadian college and university students can indeed look forward to a higher level of consumption upon graduation, and their future prospects continually improve as they accumulate even greater levels of post-secondary education, according to a report published by the C.D. Howe Institute on May 14, 2009.

Based on the C.D. Howe report, Table 2–1 presents annualized percentage rates of returns for Canadian males and females for each of the three Canadian post-secondary education achievement levels: bachelor's/undergraduate degree, master's degree, and Ph.D. degree. These rates of return are computed by utilizing a sophisticated compound interest formula to compare the extra annual income gained (marginal benefit) over one's lifetime with the extra annual costs (marginal cost), including the extra forgone income, tuition, fees, and textbook costs associated with each of the three levels of post-secondary education.

Highest Level of Education Achieved	Percentage Rate of Return for Male Graduates	Percentage Rate of Return for Female Graduates
Undergraduate/bachelor's degree	11.5%	14.1%
Master's degree	2.9%	5%
Ph.D. degree	<0	3.6%

Source: Karim Moussaly-Sergieh and François Vaillancourt. *Extra Earning Power: The Financial Returns to University Education in Canada.* C.D. Howe Institute. May 14, 2009. http://www.cdhowe.org/pdf/ebrief_79.pdf.

TABLE 2-1

Private Rates of Return for University Graduates by Sex and Type of Degree

As you can see from Table 2–1, for Canadian males, the annual percentage rates of return are 11.5 percent, 2.9 percent, and a negative return for a bachelor's degree, a master's degree, and a Ph.D. degree, respectively. The corresponding rates of return for female graduates appear to be significantly larger at 14.1 percent, 5 percent, and 3.6 percent, respectively.

The fact that each rate of return is positive (except the Ph.D. for males) implies that for each level of post-secondary education, the marginal benefit exceeds the marginal cost, making the investment a productive one.

What is perhaps even more impressive is that the undergraduate/bachelor's degree rate of return compares very favourably with other alternative investments available. In April 2010, a five-year term deposit at a typical Canadian chartered bank earned a mere 3 percent a year in interest. Clearly, an investment in post-secondary education in Canada pays off big time!

For critical analysis: Sketch two identical production possibilities curves for 2011 for post-secondary education and current consumption goods. On the first production possibilities curve, show point A that describes the production combination chosen by a 2011 high-school graduate who decides not to enroll in post-secondary education. On the second production possibilities curve, show point B that describes the production combination chosen by a 2011 high-school graduate who decides to seek and obtain a bachelor's degree. For each of the two production possibilities curves, roughly sketch the appropriate 2030 production possibilities curve.

2.4 Specialization and Greater Productivity

Individuals and societies have sought to increase their production possibilities through specialization. **Specialization** involves working at a relatively well-defined, limited endeavour, such as accounting or teaching. Individuals, regions, and nations produce a narrow range of products. Most people, in fact, do specialize. For example, you could probably change the oil in your car if you wanted to. Typically, though, you would take your car to a

Specialization Working at a relatively well-defined, limited endeavour; individuals, regions, and nations producing a narrow range of products.

garage and let the mechanic do it. You benefit by letting the garage mechanic specialize in changing the oil and in completing other repairs on your car. The specialist has all the proper equipment to do the work and will likely get the job finished sooner than you could. Specialization usually leads to greater productivity, not only for each individual but also for the country.

Absolute Advantage

Absolute advantage The ability to perform a task using the fewest number of labour hours.

Specialization occurs because different individuals and different nations have different skills. Sometimes, it seems that some individuals are better at doing everything than anyone else and are said to have an **absolute advantage**, the ability to perform a task using the fewest number of labour hours. A president of a large company might be able to type better than any of the typists, file better than any of the file clerks, and wash windows better than any of the window washers. The president has an absolute advantage in all these endeavours—by using fewer labour hours for each task than anyone else in the company. The president does not, however, spend time doing those other activities. Why not? Because a president is paid the most for undertaking managerial duties and specializes in that one particular task despite having an absolute advantage in all tasks. Indeed, absolute advantage is irrelevant in predicting how the president's time is spent; only *comparative advantage* matters.

Comparative Advantage

Comparative advantage The ability to perform an activity at the lowest opportunity cost.

Comparative advantage is the ability to perform an activity at the lowest opportunity cost. You have a comparative advantage in one activity whenever you have the lowest opportunity cost of performing that activity. Take the example of a lawyer and her secretary who can both review law cases and type legal opinions. Suppose the lawyer can review two law cases or type one legal opinion in one hour. At the same time, her secretary can review one law case or type one legal opinion in one hour. Here, the lawyer has an absolute advantage in reviewing law cases and seemingly is just as good as her secretary at typing legal opinions. Is there any reason for the lawyer and her secretary to "trade"? The answer is yes, because such trading will lead to higher output.

Consider the scenario of no trading. Assume that during each eight-hour day, the lawyer and her secretary devote half of their day to reviewing law cases and half to typing legal opinions. The lawyer would review eight law cases (4 hours × 2 per hour) and type four legal opinions (4 × 1). During that same period, the secretary would review four law cases (4 × 1) and type four legal opinions (4 × 1). Each day the combined output for the lawyer and her secretary would be 12 reviewed law cases and eight typed legal opinions.

If the lawyer specialized only in reviewing law cases and her secretary specialized only in typing legal opinions, their combined output would rise to 16 reviewed law cases (8 × 2) and eight typed legal opinions (8 × 1). Overall, production would increase by four law cases per day.

The lawyer has a comparative advantage in reviewing cases. In the time it takes her to review one case (one-half hour), she could have typed one-half of a legal opinion. Her opportunity cost of reviewing the law case is therefore one-half of a legal opinion. The secretary, however, gives up typing an entire legal opinion each time she reviews a case. Since the lawyer's opportunity cost of reviewing law cases is less than her secretary's, she has the comparative advantage in reviewing law cases. See if you can work out why the secretary has a comparative advantage in typing legal opinions.

You may be convinced that everybody can do everything better than you. In this extreme situation, do you still have a comparative advantage? The answer is yes. To discover your comparative advantage, you need to find a job in which your *disadvantage* relative to others is the smallest. You do not have to be a mathematical genius to figure this out. To determine your comparative advantage, simply find out which job maximizes your income.

The coaches of sports teams are constantly faced with determining each player's comparative advantage. Former Blue Jay Dave Winfield was originally one of the best pitchers in college baseball, winning the most valuable player award for pitching for the University of Minnesota Golden Bears in the 1973 College World Series. After he was drafted by the San Diego Padres, the coach decided to make him an outfielder, even though he was one of the best pitchers on the roster. The coach wanted Winfield to concentrate on his hitting. Good pitchers do not bring in as many fans as home-run kings. Dave Winfield's comparative advantage was clearly in hitting homers, rather than practising and developing his pitching game.

Scarcity, Self-Interest, and Specialization

In Chapter 1, you learned about the assumption of rational self-interest. It says that for the purposes of our analyses, we assume that individuals are rational in that they will do what is in their own self-interest. They will not consciously carry out actions that will make them worse off. In this chapter, you learned that scarcity requires people to make choices. We assume that they make choices based on their self-interest and attempt to maximize benefits net of opportunity cost. In so doing, individuals recognize their comparative advantage and end up specializing. Ultimately, when people specialize, they increase the money they make and become richer, as illustrated by Example 2–4.

EXAMPLE 2–4   Specializing in Providing Baggage-Free Business Trips

When Steve Zilinek was working as an investment adviser, he noticed something about travelling businesspeople. Although many of these individuals possess considerable financial resources, they must expend another key resource when they travel—namely, time that they could otherwise devote to other activities. Zilinek estimated that packing bags; waiting at airport check-in, security, and baggage stations; and laundering clothing takes about three hours per trip—time that could otherwise be devoted to alternative pursuits.

Zilinek decided that he might have a comparative advantage in providing baggage services to frequent travellers. He founded FlyLite, a company that specializes in storing, caring for, and shipping all the items that individuals desire to have with them on business trips, such as clothing and toiletries. FlyLite's customers send the items they regularly take on business trips to the company, which places them in storage. Before a trip, a client fills out and submits a Web form indicating which items she will require at her destination. FlyLite then arranges for the items to be shipped to her hotel. When her business trip concludes, the customer sends the items back to FlyLite, which dry cleans the clothing and then re-stores all items until her next trip. For FlyLite's clients, paying about $100 per trip for its services is the next-best alternative to devoting three hours to handling baggage on their own.

For critical analysis:
1. Use this example to explain how specialization based on comparative advantage increases the income for both the owner of FlyLite and the business traveller.
2. How do you suppose that an increase in the average amount of time that people must spend dealing with baggage at airports affects the number of people utilizing FlyLite's services?

Comparative Advantage and Trade among Nations

Though most of our analysis of absolute advantage, comparative advantage, and specialization has dealt with individuals or firms, it is equally applicable to countries. First, consider Canada. The Prairie provinces have a comparative advantage in the production of grains and other agricultural goods. Ontario and Quebec in Central Canada tend to specialize in industrialized production, such as automobiles and newsprint. Not surprisingly, grains are shipped from the Prairies to Central Canada, and automobiles are shipped in the reverse direction. Such specialization and trade allow for higher incomes and standards of living. If the Prairies and Central Canada were politically defined as separate countries, the same analysis would still hold, but we would call it international trade. Indeed, Europe is smaller than Canada in area, but instead of one nation, Europe has 15. What we call *interprovincial trade* in Canada is called *international trade* in Europe. There is no difference, however, in the economic results—both yield greater economic efficiency and higher average incomes.

Political problems that do not normally arise within a particular nation often do between nations. For example, if Nova Scotia crab fishers develop a cheaper method of harvesting crabs than fishers in British Columbia, British Columbia fishers will lose out. They cannot do much about the situation, except try to lower their own costs of production. If crab fishers in Alaska, however, develop a cheaper method, both Nova Scotia and British Columbia fishers can (and likely will) try to raise political barriers to prevent Alaskan fishers from freely selling their product in Canada. Canadian crab fishers will use such arguments as "unfair" competition and loss of Canadian jobs. In so doing, they are only partly right: crab-fishing jobs may decline in Canada, but jobs will not necessarily decline overall. If the argument of Canadian crab fishers had any validity, every time a region in Canada developed a better way to produce a product manufactured somewhere else in the country, employment in Canada would decline. That has never happened and never will.

When countries specialize where they have a comparative advantage and then trade with the rest of the world, the average standard of living in the world rises. In effect, international trade allows the world to move from inside the global production possibilities curve toward the curve itself, thereby improving worldwide economic efficiency.

The Division of Labour

Division of labour Individuals specializing in a subset of tasks related to a specific product.

In any firm that includes specialized human and nonhuman resources, there is a division of labour among those resources. **Division of labour** occurs when individuals specialize in a subset of tasks related to a specific product. The best-known example of all time comes from one of the earliest and perhaps most famous economists, Adam Smith, who, in his book *The Wealth of Nations* (1776), illustrated the benefits of a division of labour in the making of pins: "One man draws out the wire, another straightens it, a third cuts it, a fourth points it, a fifth grinds it at the top for receiving the head; to make the head requires two or three distinct operations; to put it on is a peculiar business, to whiten the pins is another; it is even a trade by itself to put them into the paper."

Making pins this way allowed 10 workers without very much skill to make almost 48 000 pins "of a middling size" in a day. One worker, toiling alone, could have made perhaps 20 pins a day; therefore, 10 workers could have produced 200. Division of labour allowed for an increase in the daily output of the pin factory from 200 to 48 000! (Smith did not attribute all of the gain to the division of labour according to talent but credited also the use of machinery and the fact that less time was spent shifting from task to task.)

What we are discussing here involves a division of the resource called labour into different kinds of labour. The different kinds of labour are organized in such a way as to increase the amount of output possible from the fixed resources available. We can, therefore, talk about an organized division of labour within a firm leading to increased output.

2.5 Economic Systems

Economic system The social arrangements or institutional means through which resources are used to satisfy human wants.

In the remainder of this chapter, we will study some of the established social arrangements that various nations use in choosing their production possibilities that, realistically, can include millions of goods and services being produced to satisfy the wants of millions of consumers.

At any point in time, every nation has its own **economic system**, which can be defined as the social arrangements or institutional means through which resources are used to satisfy human wants. No matter what institutional means—marketplace or government—a nation chooses to use, the following three basic economic questions must always be answered because of the economic problem of scarcity.

1. *What and how much will be produced?* Literally billions of different things could be produced with society's scarce resources, but not all at the same time. Some mechanism must exist that causes some things to be produced and others to remain as either inventors' pipe dreams or individuals' unfulfilled desires.
2. *How will it be produced?* There are many ways to produce a desired item. It is possible to use more labour and less capital or *vice versa*. It is possible to use more unskilled labour and fewer units of skilled labour. Somehow, in some way, a decision must be made as to the particular mix of inputs, the way they should be organized, and how they are brought together at a particular place.
3. *For whom will it be produced?* Once a commodity is produced, who should get it? In a modern economy, individuals and businesses purchase commodities with money income. The question then is what mechanism is there to distribute income, which then determines how commodities are distributed throughout the economy.

Not long ago, in response to the problem of scarcity, textbooks presented two extreme economic systems as possible polar alternatives for the industrialized nations to consider—the *pure command economy* versus the *pure capitalist economy*—in order to answer the three basic economic questions. Despite the fact that many countries have recently moved away from a command economy, it is appropriate to review both types of economic systems. This is because many informed citizens within Canada and other capitalist economies feel that elements of the command economy should prevail in the provision of important services, such as health care, education, and national security.

Pure Command Economy

Public (government) ownership of all property resources characterizes a pure command economy. A **pure command economy** is an economic system characterized by public ownership of all property resources. The three basic economic questions—What, How, For Whom—are answered in a very centralized manner by government or the "state." Detailed five-year plans are formulated by the central authorities in order to respond to the three basic economic questions.

> **Pure command economy** An economic system characterized by public ownership of all property resources.

Until recently, such nations as Russia and China used the pure command economy to make their resource-allocation decisions. In the past, this type of system has typically been associated with nations practising communism or socialism.

Pure Capitalist Economy

In contrast to the pure command economy, a **pure capitalist economy** is an economic system characterized by private ownership of all property resources. Households and firms interacting through a system of markets answer the three basic economic questions—What, How, For Whom—in a decentralized manner. The pure capitalist economy goes by other names, such as *capitalism, market economy,* or *price system.*

> **Pure capitalist economy** An economic system characterized by private ownership of all property resources.

Mixed Economic Systems

The pure command and the pure capitalist systems are extreme economic systems. Real-world economies, which typically fall somewhere between these two extreme systems, are called mixed economies. In **mixed economies**, decisions about how resources are used are made partly by the private sector and partly by the public sector. As an example, Canada is referred to as a mixed capitalist system. This is because, while the majority of products are produced in the private sector, there are other goods and services provided by the government.

> **Mixed economy** An economic system in which decisions about how resources are used are made partly by the private sector and partly by the public sector.

2.6 Capitalism in More Depth

Since there has been a global trend away from pure command economies toward capitalist economies, we will describe pure capitalism in more depth below.

Features of Capitalism

In elaborating on the pure capitalist economy, we will periodically refer to the Circular Flow Model presented in Figure 2–5.

Key features of pure capitalism include:

1. *Private ownership of resources:* Individual households and individual firms own the productive resources in pure capitalism. As described in Figure 2–5, households have two essential roles in capitalism—they supply resources to firms, and they demand goods and services with the income received from supplying resources. Firms, in turn, demand or hire resources in order to supply goods and services to households.

2. *Self-interest:* The primary motive underlying decisions made by households and firms in pure capitalism is the pursuit of self-interest. More specifically, firms attempt to maximize their own profit, when deciding what resources to demand or hire and what products to supply. Similarly, households are assumed to attempt to maximize individual wealth and other personal goals when deciding on where to supply their resources. When demanding goods and services, households attempt to maximize self-satisfaction or utility.

3. *Consumer sovereignty:* The pure capitalist system is to serve the household in its consumer role. Operationally, this means that capitalism is to produce the mix of goods and services that consumers desire, at the lowest possible prices.

4. *Markets and prices:* The Circular Flow Diagram in Figure 2–5 indicates the two broad types of markets that exist in pure capitalism—product markets and factor (resource) markets. When consumer demand changes or resource availability changes, this sets off changes in relative prices in affected product and factor markets. These price changes ultimately reallocate resources in line with the change in consumer demand or resource availability. While we will examine how prices are determined in individual markets in the chapters that follow, we will provide a simple example below.

Suppose that consumer demand for red wine increases and consumer demand for cigarettes decreases. Referring to the product markets in Figure 2–5, the price of red wine will increase, while the price of cigarettes will decrease. The higher price for red wine serves as a signal to firms that red wine is now relatively more profitable to produce than cigarettes.

Driven by the profit motive, the red wine firms will increase their demand to hire resources, while the cigarette firms will decrease their demand for resources, to reduce their losses. Prices will now change in the factor markets in Figure 2–5. Prices (i.e., wages) of resources (i.e., employees) that engage in the production of red wine will increase relative to the prices offered to resources in the cigarette industry. Resources,

FIGURE 2–5

Circular Flow Model

This model describes how households and firms interact through both product and factor markets in a pure capitalist economy. In the product markets, the households demand goods and services, while the firms supply the goods and services. In the factor markets, these roles are reversed. That is, households supply the resources, and the firms demand the resources.

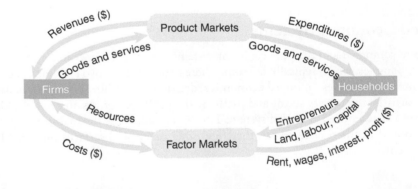

guided by self-interest, will move out of cigarette production and into the production of red wine. Eventually, red wine production will increase. Note how this system of markets and prices operates to reallocate resources in line with changes in consumer demand, thus promoting consumer sovereignty.

5. *Competition:* In order to ensure that the self-interests of firms and resources work to the best interests of consumers, it is necessary that many independent sellers and buyers compete in each market. This will be more fully explained in the subsequent chapters of this text.

6. *Limited government:* To the extent that competition exists in each market, the "invisible hand" of self-interest will serve to promote consumer sovereignty. Hence, allocating resources to meet changes in consumer demand does not require the "heavy hand" of government. The French have termed this feature of capitalism **"laissez-faire,"** which means that the government should leave it (the economy) alone or "let it be."

Laissez-faire French term for "leave it alone"; the government should leave it (the economy) alone or "let it be."

One way to remember some of the important attributes of the market economy is by thinking of capitalism's **Three Ps:** Private property, Profits, and Prices.

As Policy Example 2–2 outlines, political factors play a role in issues surrounding the use of alternate economic systems to allocate and distribute our limited economic resources, goods, and services.

Three Ps Private property, Profits, and Prices inherent in capitalism.

POLICY EXAMPLE 2–2   Canadian Politics: Right, Left, and Centre

Chapter 1 noted that Canadian government policies are, in part, based on economic theories applied to government efforts that attempt to achieve key socioeconomic goals. To more fully understand how policies are determined, it is important to recognize that political factors often play an important role. That is, policies are frequently guided by the principles of the political party of the government in power. In Canada, the three major political parties at both the federal and provincial levels are the Conservatives, the New Democrats, and the Liberals. The Conservative Party, often referred to as the right-wing party, seeks to move the economy more toward the pure capitalist model, with private ownership and competition, decentralized individual decision-making through free markets, and a laissez-faire approach to the economy. The New Democrats, who sit on the left side of the political landscape, place a high priority on serving the interests of labour and working families, promoting social justice, reducing poverty and inequality, protecting the rights of minorities, and ensuring public funding and provision of social programs and services. Often, the principles of the New Democrats tend to move various industries and services in the direction of a command system, with more government involvement. The Liberal Party, known as the centralists, supports a variety of policies from both the right and the left ends of the political spectrum, seemingly guided by public opinion as identified through political polls. The most recent federal Liberal Party emphasized the importance of balancing the government budget with providing affordable social programs. Liberals typically favour mixed economic systems. Voters who wish to avoid extreme shifts in policies often vote for the Liberals.

For critical analysis: State whether each of the following policies is more consistent with the principles of the Conservatives or New Democrats. Policy A: Waiting time for surgeries is reduced through the expansion of government-funded surgical units located in government-run hospitals. Policy B: Waiting time for surgeries is reduced through the provision of new surgical services through privately owned health-care clinics.

Sources: "Founding Principles. Getting things done for all of us." The Conservative Party of Canada. http://www.conservative.ca. (Accessed June 1, 2007.); "Issues. NDP." The NDP Party of Canada. http://www.ndp.ca/ (Accessed June 1, 2007.); "Vision. Liberal—Stronger Together." Liberal Party of Canada. http://www.liberal.ca/default_e.aspx. (Accessed June 1, 2007.)

TABLE 2-2

Production Costs for 100 Units of Product X

Technique A or B can be used to produce the same output. Obviously, B will be used because its total cost is less than A's. Using production technique B will generate a $2 savings for every 100 units produced.

Inputs	Input Unit Price	A Production Technique A (input units)	Cost	B Production Technique B (input units)	Cost
Labour	$10	5	$50	4	$40
Capital	8	4	32	5	40
Total cost of 100 units			82		80

Capitalism and the Three Economic Questions

Now that we have reviewed the essential features of pure capitalism, we can proceed to examine how this economic system operates to answer the three basic economic questions—What, How, and For Whom.

WHAT AND HOW MUCH WILL BE PRODUCED? Since firms can enhance profits by producing what consumers are willing to buy, we can see that consumer demand plays an important role in deciding what goods and services are produced. In more formal terms, the profit motive and competition lead firms to promote allocative efficiency—that is, firms will produce the mix of goods and services most wanted by society. However, we must keep in mind that if the highest price that consumers are willing to pay for a good is less than the lowest resource cost at which the good can be produced, no profit will result, and none of this good will be produced. In other words, resource availability also plays a role in determining what goods and services are produced.

HOW WILL IT BE PRODUCED? The question of how output will be produced in a pure capitalist system relates to the efficient use of scarce inputs. Consider the possibility of using only two types of resources: capital and labour. A firm may have the options given in Table 2–2. It can use various combinations of labour and capital to produce the same amount of output.

Two hypothetical combinations are given in Table 2–2. How then is it decided which combination will be used? Under pure capitalism, the least cost combination (technique B, in our example) will be chosen by firms because it will maximize profits. In other words, in pure capitalism, competition and the profit motive encourage firms to achieve productive efficiency.

FOR WHOM WILL IT BE PRODUCED? This last question involves how households share in the consumption of the goods and services produced. This, in turn, is based on the distribution of money incomes and wealth among households. Households with higher levels of income and wealth will get to purchase and consume a greater portion of the goods produced in the economy.

What determines the distribution of wealth and money income among different households? This distribution is based on the quantities, qualities, and types of the various human and nonhuman resources that different households own and supply to the marketplace. Households that own large quantities of resources that are highly in demand in the marketplace will earn high levels of income.

As Example 2–5 illustrates, the way in which a nation answers the economic question "For whom will it be produced?" will affect what and how much will be produced.

How can improved sanitation in India improve economic well being?

EXAMPLE 2-5   India Has More Cellphones Than Toilets

Since the early 1990s, India, the second most crowded country in the world, has moved significantly closer to becoming a capitalist economy. According to a report undertaken by United Nations University (UNU) in Tokyo, released in April 2010, India is now wealthy enough to have 45 percent of its population own a cellphone (545 million cellphones), yet only 31 percent of

continued

its population (366 million people) have access to clean toilet facilities. In other words, about 1.2 billion people in India do not have access to basic sanitation. The UNU report points out that there would be a return of between $3 and $4 for every additional dollar spent on improved sanitation due to reduced health and poverty related costs, as well as higher productivity.

Source: "Mobile telephones more common than toilets in India, UN report finds." UN News Centre. United Nations University. Tokyo. April 14, 2010. http://www.un.org/apps/news/story.asp?NewsID=34369&Cr=mdg&Cr1=

For critical analysis: Using this Example, explain how the way India answers the economic question "For whom will it be produced?" has affected what and how much will be produced. Since total wealth in India is increasing rapidly, can you suggest a government policy that could imiprove basic sanitation conditions? How will this policy pay for itself in the long run?

It should be noted that many current debates regarding economic systems apply to individual industries within a national economy. The central question posed in this chapter's Issues and Applications is, "What economic system should be used to best provide auto insurance in Canada?" As this Issues and Applications section points out, different economic systems are currently being used to provide auto insurance in Canada, depending on the province in which one resides.

ISSUES AND APPLICATIONS

Private or Public Auto Insurance: What Is Best for Canada?

Concepts Applied: Capitalist, Command, and Mixed Systems; Productive Efficiency; Allocative Efficiency; and Equity

How does establishing fault in accidents affect the cost of car insurance?

In response to public outrage over skyrocketing car insurance premiums, the Consumers' Association of Canada completed a comprehensive report on auto insurance rates in Canada in September 2003. In presenting the report, the association noted that government-owned, or public, auto insurance systems offer the lowest premiums for Canadian drivers.

Provincial Automobile Insurance Rates

Figure 2–6, taken from the report, compares the average annual auto insurance premiums among provinces, assuming the same insurance coverage, vehicle, driving record, and claims history. The average premiums are based on over 7000 rate quotes across Canada. All quotes assume an insurance

coverage of $2 million liability, $500 collision deductible, and $300 comprehensive deductible. As you can see from this figure, the annual car insurance premiums are significantly lower in the provinces of British Columbia, Saskatchewan, Manitoba, and Quebec, where the mandatory insurance is provided by a government monopoly.

The Consumers' Association of Canada's report also noted the differences in the annual rate of increase in premiums between the private and public insurance systems in 2003. While premiums were escalating by up to 70 percent per year in the six provinces where privately owned insurance companies operate, Manitoba's publicly run auto insurance system was increasing annual premiums by only 7.2 percent.

FIGURE 2–6

Comparison of Average Auto Insurance Rates by Province, 2003

Source: *Review of Automobile Insurance Rates*. Consumers' Association of Canada. September 2003, pg. 11. http://www.consumer.ca/pdfs/030910_report.pdf. Copyright Consumers' Association of Canada. (Accessed November 11, 2003).

To add fuel to the fire, in provinces offering private insurance, individuals can pay significantly higher premiums based on such criteria as age, gender, and marital status, regardless of the driving record or type of vehicle being insured. In New Brunswick, in 2003, older drivers who drove newer, much more expensive cars, and who had driving convictions, paid up to $2000 less for auto insurance compared to young drivers with clean driving records. A 2002 Ford Taurus SE was more than $7000 cheaper for an 18-year-old male with a clean driving record to insure in Saskatoon's public insurance system than in Toronto or St John's, where private insurance companies operate. In provinces with public auto insurance, where rates were not based on age or gender, a young driver with a clean record paid a lower premium than an older driver with driving convictions.

Follow-Up Study

On October 15, 2005, the Consumers' Association of Canada published a follow-up study comparing the automobile insurance rates in different provinces, keeping factors constant such as the driver's vehicle, driving record, claims history, deductibles and liability, and other types of coverage. As Figure 2–7 shows, similar to the 2003 study, the insurance rates continue to be significantly lower in British Columbia, Manitoba, and Saskatchewan, where the mandatory insurance is provided by a government monopoly.

To this date, the Consumers' Association of Canada has not yet conducted a more recent study of provincial auto insurance rates. As a result, in 2010 this author conducted a cursory examination of provincial rates using various online auto insurance rate calculators available on the Internet. A comparison was made for the annual insurance premium that a middle-aged male would have to make in 2010 in order to secure insurance coverage with $2 million liability, $500 collision deductible, and $300 comprehensive deductible in nine of the 10 Canadian provinces (data was not available for Newfoundland). Table 2–3 presents the results of this comparison. As you can see, the lowest annual premium is obtained in British Columbia, where auto insurance is provided by a government monopoly. The average annual premiums calculated for the three provinces that operate public auto insurance companies equals $927, which is lower than $1011, the average annual premiums calculated in the six provinces that operate "competitive" private insurance companies.

Providing Auto Insurance: Two Extreme Models

To better understand the significant differences in automobile premiums being charged across provinces and across customers within the same province, we will first contrast the two extreme economic systems that are possible in the provision of car insurance.

Under the pure capitalist or pure market model, privately owned, for-profit insurance companies sell the mandatory auto

TABLE 2–3

Comparison of Annual Auto Insurance Rates by Province, 2010

Province (City)	Annual Premium May 2, 2010, to May 1, 2011
Alberta (Edmonton)	$929
British Columbia (Vancouver/Burnaby)	$670
Saskatchewan (Saskatoon)	$921
Manitoba (Winnipeg)	$1190
Ontario (Toronto)	$1473
New Brunswick (Fredericton)	$810
Quebec (Montreal)	$744
Nova Scotia (Halifax)	$991
Prince Edward Island (Charlottetown)	$1117

Sources: "Insurance services." Rate Calculator. CAA. http://www.caa.ca/insurance/insurance-e.cfm; "Compare auto insurance quotes." Rate Calculator. Kanetix. http://www.kanetix.ca/auto-insurance.

insurance policies, and the claims are paid out according to a decentralized tort-based or fault-based system.

In a fault-based system, the injured party must first prove that the other party is at fault, and then the injured party can bring legal action for recovery of damages against the person who caused the accident. The claim for recovery of damages will typically include monies to replace lost wages, out-of-pocket expenses, medical expenses, damages to the vehicle, and an amount to compensate for the pain and suffering related to injuries sustained as a result of the accident. If the injured party and the party at fault cannot agree on the amount of the total claim, the matter will eventually go to court. The fault-based system awards damages in a very decentralized

manner, as the amount of each accident claim is assessed on the merits of each individual situation.

At the other extreme, auto insurance can be delivered in a manner resembling a pure command economic system. In this model, the one government-owned Crown corporation (public monopoly) provides all mandatory auto insurance for the entire province, and the claims are paid out on a pure no-fault basis.

In a pure no-fault system, one's own insurance company (or the government monopoly) pays for the damages that one incurs, regardless of fault. A comprehensive predetermined compensation schedule would dictate the maximum payment for specific types of losses, expenses, and injuries. In a pure no-fault system, one's individual right to sue for damages is eliminated.

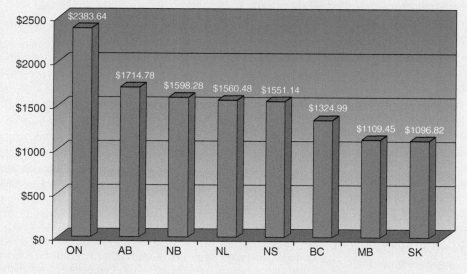

Average Auto Insurance Rates by Province
714 Communities, 3 985 162 Quotations

FIGURE 2–7

Comparison of Average Auto Insurance Rates by Province: October 2005

Source: *National Study of Automobile Insurance Rates: Third Release.* Consumer's Association of Canada. October 19, 2005. pg. 7. http://www.consumer.ca/pdfs/cac_auto_ins_atlantic_provinces_report-final1.pdf.

The Advantages of Using the Command Model

It is interesting to note that Manitoba, the province that charges the lowest average annual auto insurance premiums, according to the Consumers' Association of Canada's study, operates an insurance system that most closely resembles the pure command model. That is, Manitoba Public Insurance (MPI), a government-owned monopoly, provides the mandatory car insurance, and the claims are paid out on a no-fault basis.

So, how can a pure command system result in lower auto insurance premiums when compared with the pure capitalist model? First, there are factors inherent in the public system that make it more productively efficient. Due to its no-fault feature, the system does not have to employ the expensive legal and court-related resources to establish fault and to establish the extent of the legal damages experienced by each injured party in each accident. As well, the amount of benefits paid out per claim to compensate an injured

party for pain and suffering is significantly lower in the public system.

Since the government is the sole organization providing mandatory car insurance in the province, it does not have to employ resources to market its services to the customer. Moreover, as the sole provider, the public insurance organization is able to avoid the duplication in administrative resources that typically occurs when numerous private car insurance companies compete with each other in the same province. Because the public system can offer the same insurance coverage with minimal use of resources, it is able to keep its costs down and, in turn, charge low premiums.

A public insurance organization, such as Manitoba Public, does not have to raise premiums to a point where profits have to be earned on its operations, as is the case with privately run companies. Unlike the provincially owned public insurance providers, multinational private insurance corporations face the added pressure of raising premiums in order to recoup losses incurred in past global disasters, such as the September 11 terrorist attacks in the United States.

The Advantages of Using the Capitalist Model

In a series of recent studies, the Fraser Institute, a Canadian organization that promotes market-based policies, defends the use of the capitalist model in providing mandatory auto insurance. The Institute argues that a public auto insurance system results in more accidents and imposes greater burdens on the health-care system when compared with private insurance. After examining two private insurance provinces and three public insurance provinces, the Institute notes that the number of collisions and the number of collision related deaths, injuries, and hospital admissions is significantly higher, per 100 000 population or per vehicle kilometres travelled, in those provinces with public insurance. This difference is most pronounced for males between the ages of 16 and 25 years. The Institute suggests that since the public insurance system fails to charge higher premiums for certain high-risk classes, such as the younger male class, it encourages too many risky drivers to take to the road, and it shifts collision costs to other drivers—primarily female, safer, and older drivers. As well, the expensive lawsuits that accompany the fault system can provide incentives for safer driving.

Another benefit of the pure capitalist approach to auto insurance relates to the goal of allocative efficiency. A fault-based insurance system provides the opportunity for each injured individual to take the necessary legal action to ensure that the dollar value of the compensation resulting from an accident claim (marginal benefit) is sufficient to cover the full marginal cost related to the individual's injuries and losses sustained from the accident.

As an example, two individuals may suffer the same physical injury in an accident, but the pain and suffering experienced by one of the individuals would be significantly greater if that individual could no longer engage in his or her favourite hobby—playing the piano. The fault-based insurance system could enable the piano lover to receive a higher level of compensation based on the higher level of pain and suffering (i.e., the higher level of marginal cost). In contrast, the pure command model's no-fault system would likely pay out the same level of benefits to both injured individuals.

Using a Mixed System

Despite the potential benefits of using a pure capitalist approach in the provision of auto insurance, Canadians residing in the private insurance jurisdictions are putting political pressure on their provincial governments to play an active role in the auto insurance industry. Many of the private insurance provinces are moving toward a mixed economic system of providing auto insurance. While privately owned corporations continue to provide the car insurance in these provinces, the provincial governments are proposing to fix the premium rates and set maximum dollar limits for the payout of certain types of claims, such as pain and suffering. These governments have a difficult task ahead of them as they attempt to strike an acceptable balance between affordable premiums, public safety, equity, and their own political party's commitment to promote a capitalist provincial economy.

For critical analysis:

1. Explain how the pure command model of providing auto insurance can promote productive efficiency.
2. Explain how the pure capitalist model of providing auto insurance can promote the goals of public safety and allocative efficiency.
3. Explain what equity (fairness) trade-offs are involved when choosing the pure command model of providing auto insurance.
4. A provincial government freezes the premiums charged by private insurance companies but lets the fault system determine the payment of claims. What problems will likely occur with this mixed-system policy?

Sources: *Review of Automobile Insurance Rates. Consumers' Association of Canada*. September 2003, pg. 5. http://www.consumer.ca/pdfs/030910_report.pdf. (Accessed August 25, 2010.); *Auto Insurance Rate Comparison Study*—July 28, 2003. Consumers' Association of Canada. July 2003, pg. 3. http://www.cacbc.com/reports/July%2028,2003%20Report%20Auto%20NB.pdf. (Accessed November 11, 2003.); SGI 2003 Rate Comparison Profiles. http://www.sgi.sk.ca/sgi_internet/rates/2003_rate_profiles.html#. (Accessed November 11, 2003.); Mark, Mullins "Public auto insurance: a mortality warning for motorists." Fraser Institute, September 2003, pp. 1–4. http://www.fraserinstitute.org/research-news/display.aspx?id=13327. (Accessed August 25, 2010.)

SUMMARY

Here is what you should know after reading this chapter. MyEconLab will help you identify what you know, and where to go when you need to practise. We suggest that as soon as you review one of the Learning Objective sections below, you then proceed to go through the related section in MyEconLab.

LEARNING OBJECTIVES	KEY TERMS	MYECONLAB PRACTICE
2.1 The Production Possibilities Curve. The production possibilities curve describes all possible combinations of two goods that can be produced, assuming full and efficient employment of resources, a fixed time period, fixed quantity and quality of resources, and fixed technology.	production possibilities curve, 30 technology, 30	• **MyEconLab** Study Plan 2.1
2.2 Applications of the Production Possibilities Curve. The production possibilities curve illustrates the scarcity problem by acting as a production boundary in the face of unlimited wants. Its downward slope implies a trade-off—more of one good means less of another. An increasing opportunity cost situation is shown by a "bowed out" production possibilities curve. Unemployment is reflected by a point inside the curve, signifying lost production. Any production combination on the curve is productively efficient and the one combination that society values the most is allocatively efficient. Economic growth shifts the production possibilities curve outward over time.	productive efficiency, 33 productively inefficient point, 33 allocative efficiency, 34 law of increasing relative cost, 34	• **MyEconLab** Study Plan 2.2
2.3 Consumption Goods versus Capital Goods. A production possibilities curve that involves capital goods and consumption goods illustrates that when we use more of our resources to produce capital goods that enhance future consumption, we must forgo present consumption goods.	consumption, 37	• **MyEconLab** Study Plan 2.3
2.4 Specialization and Greater Productivity. Absolute advantage refers to the ability to produce one unit of a product at a lower labour cost than another producer. Comparative advantage refers to producing a unit of a product at a lower opportunity cost than another producer. According to the comparative advantage principle, the combined production of two producers can be increased if each producer specializes according to comparative advantage. The terms of trade principle states that each producer will gain from	specialization, 39 absolute advantage, 40 comparative advantage, 40 division of labour, 42	• **MyEconLab** Study Plan 2.4

LEARNING OBJECTIVES	KEY TERMS	MYECONLAB PRACTICE
specialization and trade, if the terms of trade are between each producer's opportunity cost of production.		
2.5 Economic Systems. In a pure command system, the government owns the resources and the three basic questions—What, How, For Whom—are answered in a centralized manner by government. In pure capitalism, resources are privately owned and the basic questions are answered in a decentralized manner by individual firms and households interacting in markets. In a mixed economic system, where there is both private and public ownership of resources, the basic questions are partly answered by government and partly by individual firms and households in markets.	economic system, 42 pure command economy, 43 pure capitalist economy, 43 mixed economy, 43	• **MyEconLab** Study Plan 2.5
2.6 Capitalism in More Depth. The key features of pure capitalism include private ownership of resources, self-interest motives, consumer sovereignty, markets and prices, competition, and limited government. Consumer demand and resource availability determine *what* goods and services will be produced; the least costly method will be chosen in deciding *how* the goods will be produced; the degree to which households own marketable resources will determine *for whom* goods are produced.	laissez-faire, 45 Three *Ps*, 45	• **MyEconLab** Study Plan 2.6

PROBLEMS

(Answers to the odd-numbered problems appear at the back of the book.)

LO 2.1, LO 2.2 Define the production possibilities curve and identify its assumptions; use the production possibilities curve to illustrate the concepts of scarcity, trade-offs, unemployment, productive efficiency, allocative efficiency, increasing opportunity cost, and economic growth.

1. The production possibilities curve for the nation of Epica for the two goods—factories and yachts—for 2008 is described in the accompanying graph.

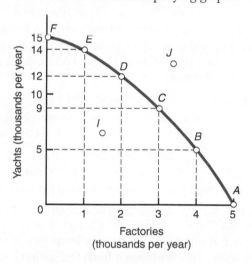

a. If Epica produces 12 000 yachts in 2008, what is the maximum number of factories that can be produced in 2008?
b. If Epica devotes all its resources to the production of factories, what is the maximum number of factories that can be produced in 2008?
c. What factors prevent Epica from producing the combination at point *J* in 2008?
d. If Epica is at point *I* in 2008, this situation could conflict with what two socioeconomic goals?
e. What is the opportunity cost of producing an additional factory when moving: (i) from point *E* to *D*? (ii) from point *C* to *B*?
f. What is the opportunity cost of producing an additional yacht when moving: (i) from point *A* to *B*? (ii) from point *E* to *F*?
g. What economic law is illustrated by your answers to parts (e) and (f) above?
h. If society values production combination *D* the most, but Epica is producing combination *C*, this situation conflicts with what socioeconomic goal?
i. How will economic growth affect Epica's production possibilities curve over time?

2. The production possibilities curve for the nation of Fantasia for the two goods, TVs and business machines, for 2007 is described in the accompanying graph.

a. If Fantasia produces 2000 machines in 2007, what is the maximum number of TVs that can be produced in 2007?
b. What factors prevent Fantasia from producing the combination at point *H* in 2007?
c. If Fantasia completely specializes in the production of TVs in 2007, what maximum number of TVs could it produce per year?
d. If Fantasia is at point *G* in 2007, this situation could conflict with what two socioeconomic goals?
e. What is the opportunity cost of producing an additional machine when moving from: (i) point *A* to point *B*? (ii) point *D* to point *E*?
f. What economic law is illustrated by your answers to part (e) above?
g. Which of the points *A, B, C, D, E, F, G,* and *H* are productively efficient?
h. If society values the production combination at point *D* the most, but Fantasia is currently producing at point *C*, this situation conflicts with what socioeconomic goal?
i. Which one of the two points *B* or *E* would lead to a greater rate of economic growth? Why? What important trade-off is illustrated here?
j. How will economic growth affect Fantasia's production possibilities curve over time?

3. The table on page 54 illustrates the marks a student can earn on examinations in economics and biology if the student uses all available hours for study.

Economics	Biology
100	40
90	50
80	60
70	70
60	80
50	90
40	100

Plot this student's production possibilities curve. Does this PPC illustrate increasing or constant opportunity costs?

4. The following sets of numbers represent hypothetical production possibilities for a country in 2008. Plot these points on graph paper.

Cheese	Apples
4	0
3	1.6
2	2.4
1	2.8
0	3.0

Does the law of increasing relative cost seem to hold? Why? On the same graph, plot and draw the production possibilities curve that will represent 10 percent economic growth.

5. Construct a production possibilities curve for a country facing increasing opportunity costs for producing food and video games. Show how the PPC changes given the following events:
   a. A new and better fertilizer is developed.
   b. There is a surge in labour that can be employed in both the agriculture sector and the video game sector.
   c. A new programming language is invented that is less costly to code and is more memory-efficient, enabling the use of smaller games cartridges.
   d. A heat wave and drought result in a decrease of 10 percent in usable farmland.

LO 2.3 Use the production possibilities curve to explain the trade-off between consumption goods and capital goods.

6. Two countries, Workland and Playland, have similar populations and identical production possibilities curves but different preferences. The production possibilities combinations are as follows:

Point	Capital Goods	Consumption Goods
A	0	20
B	1	19
C	2	17
D	3	14
E	4	10
F	5	5

Playland is located at point *B* on the PPC, and Workland is located at point *E*. Assume that this situation continues into the future and that all other things remain the same.
   a. What is Workland's opportunity cost of capital goods in terms of consumption goods?
   b. What is Playland's opportunity cost of capital goods in terms of consumption goods?
   c. How would the PPCs of Workland and Playland be expected to compare with each other 50 years in the future?

7. If, by going to college, you give up the chance to work in your mother's business for 35 hours per week at $7 per hour, what would be your opportunity cost of earning a two-year college diploma? What incentives exist to make you incur that opportunity cost? What are you giving up today in order to have more in the future? Assume that you will need to spend 60 weeks in college to earn a diploma.

LO 2.4 Distinguish between absolute advantage and comparative advantage and use these concepts to explain how specialization and trade can increase production and consumption.

8. Referring to Example 2–4: Specializing in Providing Baggage-Free Business Trips, why might one expect the businesspeople who earn the most per hour to be most interested in using this new type of baggage-free service?

9. You can wash, fold, and iron a basket of laundry in two hours and prepare a meal in one hour. Your roommate can wash, fold, and iron a basket of laundry in three hours and prepare a meal in one hour. Should you and your roommate specialize in particular tasks? Why? And if so, who should specialize in which task? Calculate how much labour time you save if you choose to "trade" an appropriate task with your roommate, as opposed to doing it yourself.

LO 2.5, 2.6 Explain the differences between the pure capitalist, pure command, and mixed economic systems; describe the features of pure capitalism and explain how capitalism answers the three basic economic questions.

10. Noah and Nora are partners in a fast-food submarine sandwich shop. In one hour, Noah can prepare 10 sandwiches and 30 pasta salads. In the same hour, Nora can prepare 10 sandwiches and 20 pasta salads.
    a. Who has the absolute advantage in preparing pasta salads?
    b. Who has the comparative advantage in preparing sandwiches?
    c. For each hour spent on specializing in preparing the items in which each partner has a comparative advantage, what will be the net gain in production?

11. Toby and Tony are partners in their popular downtown Italian eatery. In one hour, Toby can produce 10 gourmet pizzas and five lasagne supremes. In the same hour, Tony

can prepare five gourmet pizzas and five lasagne supremes.

   a. Who has the absolute advantage in producing pizzas?

   b. Who has the comparative advantage in producing the lasagne?

   c. For each hour spent on specializing in preparing the items in which each partner has a comparative advantage, what will be the net gain in production?

12. State whether each of the following policies is more consistent with the principles of the Conservative party or the New Democratic party.

   Policy A: The Canadian government provides tax cuts to parents of young children that amount to $100 per child.

   Policy B: The Canadian government expands day-care spaces through the expansion of government-owned and -operated day-care services.

13. What features of capitalism help explain how consumer sovereignty can be achieved with limited government involvement?

14. Briefly explain how capitalism answers the three basic economic questions.

15. The following table gives the production techniques and input prices for 100 units of product X.

Input	Input Unit Price	Production Technique A (units)	B (units)	C (units)
Labour	$10	6	5	4
Capital	8	5	6	7

   a. In a market system, which techniques will be used to produce 100 units of product X?

   b. If the market price of a unit of X is $1, which technique will lead to the greatest profit?

   c. The output of X is still 100 units, but the price of labour and capital changes so that labour is $8 and capital is $10. Which production technique will be used?

   d. Using the information in part (c), what is the potential profit of producing 100 units of X?

BUSINESS APPLICATION

LO 2.3 Use the production possibilities curve to explain the trade-off between consumption goods and capital goods.

Finance: Is Deficit Financing Always Undesirable?

Deficit financing refers to the practice of having to incur a new debt when purchasing a good. Understanding the difference between consumer and capital goods may shed some light on whether or not deficit financing is appropriate. In general, economists are more likely to suggest financing capital goods on a deficit basis than consumption goods. Since most of the benefits of a capital good accrue in future periods, it is rational to borrow funds and then gradually pay back the loan in the future when the benefits of the investment good accrue. This holds true for both private and public sector goods, as the following problem illustrates.

Business Application Problem

For each pair of goods listed below, indicate which good is better suited to deficit financing.

   a. Spending $30 000 on a "fully loaded" sports car or spending $30 000 obtaining a Bachelor of Commerce degree.

   b. Constructing a civic convention centre or constructing community leisure pools with waterslides.

   c. Constructing an exercise gym on a work site that is freely available to your employees or paying for trips to Mexico for your employees.

   d. An insurance salesman purchasing a season's pass to a posh golf course or a college instructor purchasing a season's pass to a posh golf course.

   e. Constructing an expensive, beautifully designed city hall or subsidizing the city's major-league sports team.

The Production Possibilities Curve and Comparative Advantage

The gains from specialization and trade can be effectively illustrated by the production possibilities curve model. Let us assume that two Canadian family farms, the Pulets and the Dowbys, can produce chicken and perogies on each of their farm operations. The Pulets can produce one kilogram of chicken per hour or one kilogram of perogies per hour. The Dowbys can produce two kilograms of chicken per hour or eight kilograms of perogies per hour. Armed with this productivity information, we can proceed to construct production possibilities for each family farm.

Before Specialization and Trade

We will construct a daily production possibilities curve for the two products, chicken and perogies, for each family farm, by assuming that each family works an eight-hour day.

The Pulets' production possibilities curve in Figure B–1 part (a) shows that in a typical day, if they devote all eight hours to producing perogies, they can produce eight kilograms of perogies per day, which is at point *A*. Alternatively, if the Pulets devote all of the eight hours to producing chicken, they can produce eight kilograms of chicken per day, which is at point *B* in Figure B–1 part (a). Currently, the Pulets are not specializing and trading, and so they are producing and consuming six kilograms of perogies and two kilograms of chicken on a daily basis, which is at point *C* in Figure B–1 part (a).

The Dowbys' production possibilities curve in Figure B–1 part (b) shows that in a typical day, if they devote all eight hours to producing perogies, they can produce 64 kilograms of perogies per day, which is at point *A*. Alternatively, if the Dowbys devote all of the eight hours to producing chicken, they can produce 16 kilograms of chicken per day, which is at point *B* in Figure B–1 part (b). Currently, the Dowbys are not specializing and trading, and so they are producing and consuming 48 kilograms of perogies and four kilograms of chicken on a daily basis, which is at point *C* in Figure B–1 part (b).

You will notice that both production possibilities curves are assumed to be straight lines. This implies that the opportunity cost of production will stay constant as each farm

FIGURE B–1

The Before-Specialization, Before-Trade Production Possibilities

In part (a), the Pulets have chosen to produce and consume two kilograms of chicken and six kilograms of perogies. In part (b), the Dowbys have chosen to produce and consume four kilograms of chicken and 48 kilograms of perogies.

Part (a)
Pulets' Production Possibilities Curve

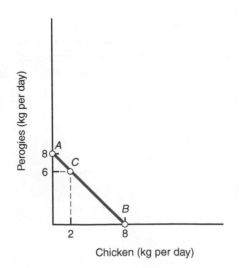

Part (b)
Dowbys' Production Possibilities Curve

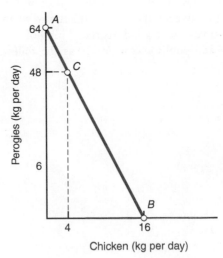

specializes in the production of one of its products. This assumption will simplify our production possibilities illustration of the gains from trade and specialization.

Figure B–1 illustrates that the Dowbys can produce more of both products, when compared to the Pulets, despite the fact that both family farms are employing the same level of total labour input on a daily basis. This implies that the Dowbys can produce a kilogram of each product at a lower labour cost than the Pulets. In other words, the Dowbys have the absolute advantage in the production of chicken and in the production of perogies.

Since the Dowbys have the absolute advantage in the production of each product, it may appear that there would be no incentive for the Dowbys to specialize and trade with the Pulets. However, as we will explain below, the Pulets do have the comparative advantage in the production of chicken, and therefore, the Dowbys can increase their consumption possibilities by specializing and trading with the Pulets.

After Specialization and before Trade

As noted in Chapter 2, we can identify the family farm that has the comparative advantage in each product by computing opportunity costs.

Opportunity Costs Incurred by the Pulets

According to Figure B–1 part (a), if the Pulets switch production possibilities from point A to point B, eight additional kilograms of chicken can be produced by giving up eight kilograms of perogies. Therefore, one additional kilogram of chicken has an opportunity cost or sacrifice of one kilogram of perogies on the Pulets' farm. If the Pulets switch production possibilities from point B to point A in Figure B–1 part (a), you can see that one additional kilogram of perogies has an opportunity cost of one kilogram of chicken. These opportunity costs are summarized in Table B–1.

Opportunity Costs Incurred by the Dowbys

According to Figure B–1 part (b), if the Dowbys switched production possibilities from point A to point B, 16 additional kilograms of chicken can be produced by giving up 64 kilograms of perogies. Therefore, one additional kilogram of chicken has an opportunity cost of four kilograms of perogies. If the Dowbys were to switch production possibilities from point B to point A in Figure B–1 part (b), you can see that one additional kilogram of perogies has an opportunity cost of one-quarter of a kilogram of chicken. These opportunity costs are summarized in Table B–1.

	Opportunity cost of 1 kg of chicken:	Opportunity cost of 1 kg of perogies:
Pulets	1 kg of perogies	1 kg of chicken
Dowbys	4 kg of perogies	1/4 = 0.25 kg of chicken

TABLE B–1

Opportunity Costs for Each Farm for Each Product

The Pulets can produce a kilogram of chicken at a lower opportunity cost than the Dowbys. The Dowbys can produce a kilogram of perogies at a lower opportunity cost than the Pulets.

Comparative Advantage Principle

Table B–1 indicates that the Pulets can produce an additional kilogram of chicken at a lower opportunity cost, one kilogram of perogies, than the Dowbys' opportunity cost of four kilograms of perogies. This implies that the Dowbys can produce an additional kilogram of the other product, perogies, at a lower opportunity cost than the Pulets (0.25 kilograms versus one kilogram of chicken). In other words, the Pulets have the comparative advantage in the production of chicken, and the Dowbys have the comparative advantage in the production of perogies.

The **Comparative Advantage Principle** states that the combined production of two producers can be enhanced if each producer specializes in the product in which it has the comparative advantage. According to this principle, the combined daily production of both family farms can be increased by having the Pulets specialize in the production of chicken and the Dowbys specialize in the production of perogies.

Comparative Advantage Principle States that the combined production of two producers can be enhanced if each producer specializes in the product in which it has the comparative advantage.

Figure B–1 part (a) reminds us that before specialization, the Pulets were producing two kilograms of chicken and six kilograms of perogies. Figure B–1 part (b) indicates that before specialization, the Dowbys were producing four kilograms of chicken and 48 kilograms of perogies. Therefore, the combined family farm production before specialization was $2 + 4 = 6$ kilograms of chicken and was $6 + 48 = 54$ kilograms of perogies.

According to Figure B–1 part (a), if the Pulets specialized in the production of chicken, they would switch production possibilities to point B and produce eight kilograms of chicken and zero kilograms of perogies per day. Figure B–1 part (b) indicates that if the Dowbys specialized in perogies, they would switch production possibilities to point A and produce 64 kilograms of perogies and zero kilograms of chicken per day. Note that by specializing according to comparative advantage, the combined family farm production of chicken has increased from six kilograms to eight kilograms per day. Similarly, the combined family farm production of perogies has increased from 54 kilograms to 64 kilograms per day.

After Specialization and after Trade

With each family farm specializing according to comparative advantage, the need will arise to trade the surplus production between family farms. Under specialization, the only way the Pulets can obtain perogies is by trading off some chicken. Similarly, the Dowbys will have to trade some of their perogies in order to consume some chicken. In trading with each other, the question now becomes, how much of one product should each farm trade away in order to get an additional kilogram of the other product?

The Terms of Trade Principle

Terms of trade The amount of one product that must be traded in order to obtain an additional unit of another product.

Terms of Trade Principle Each producer will gain from specialization and trade if the terms of trade is between the producers' opportunity costs of production.

The **terms of trade** for chicken is the amount of the other product, perogies, that must be traded in order to obtain one additional kilogram of chicken. The **Terms of Trade Principle** states that each producer will gain from specialization and trade if the terms of trade is between the producers' opportunity costs of production.

As an example, a mutually beneficial terms of trade for one kilogram of chicken would be anywhere between one kilogram of perogies (opportunity cost at the Pulets farm) and four kilograms of perogies (opportunity cost at the Dowbys farm). Thus, one acceptable terms of trade for one kilogram of chicken would be two kilograms of perogies. Assuming these terms of trade and assuming that the Pulets end up trading five kilograms of their chicken in exchange for 10 kilograms of perogies with the Dowbys, Table B–2 illustrates how both family farms can increase their consumption possibilities.

THE PULETS' GAIN FROM TRADE. According to Table B–2, if the Pulets specialize and produce eight kilograms of chicken and then trade away five kilograms of chicken for 10 kilograms of perogies, they end up consuming $8 - 5 = 3$ kilograms of chicken and $0 + 10 = 10$ kilograms of perogies, after specialization and after trade. On the basis of point C of Figure B–1, the Pulets produced and consumed only two kilograms of chicken and six kilograms of perogies, before specialization and trade. In other words, specialization and trade increased the Pulets' consumption of chicken and perogies by one kilogram and four kilograms per day, respectively.

Figure B–2 part (a) describes the Pulets' gain as a rightward shift from point C on the Pulets' production possibilities curve to point $C1$ on the Pulets' new consumption possibilities curve. Note that the slope of the Pulets' new consumption possibilities curve is 2, which is based on the terms of trade for one kilogram of chicken.

THE DOWBYS' GAIN FROM TRADE. Table B–2 also describes how the Dowbys can enhance their consumption possibilities with the terms of trade of two kilograms of perogies for one kilogram of chicken. Before trade and specialization, the Dowbys produced and consumed four kilograms of chicken and 48 kilograms of perogies (point C in Figure B–1 part (b)). After trade and specialization, the Dowbys can consume five kilograms of chicken and 54 kilograms of perogies. Specialization and trade increased the Dowbys' consumption of chicken and perogies by one kilogram and six kilograms per day, respectively.

Farm	(1) Production Before Specialization	(2) Production After Specialization	(3) Trade: Sells (−) Buys (+)	(4) = (2) + (3) Consumption After Specialization and Trade	(5) = (4) − (1) Gains from Specialization and Trade
Pulets					
Chicken	2 kg	8 kg	−5 kg	8 − 5 = 3 kg	3 − 2 = +1 kg
Perogies	6 kg	0 kg	+10 kg	0 + 10 = 10 kg	10 − 6 = +4 kg
Dowbys					
Chicken	4 kg	0 kg	+5 kg	0 + 5 = 5 kg	5 − 4 = +1 kg
Perogies	48 kg	64 kg	−10 kg	64 − 10 = 54 kg	54 − 48 = +6 kg

TABLE B–2

Gains from Specialization and Trade

After specialization and trade, the Pulets gain one kilogram of chicken and four kilograms of perogies. The Dowbys gain one kilogram of chicken and six kilograms of perogies.

Figure B–2 part (b) describes the Dowbys' gain as a rightward shift from point *C* on the Dowbys' production possibilities curve to point *C1* on the Dowbys' new consumption possibilities curve. Again, note that the slope of the Dowbys' new consumption possibilities curve is 2, which is based on the terms of trade for one kilogram of chicken.

In summary, we have just shown how the Dowbys can benefit by specializing and trading with the Pulets, despite the fact that the Dowbys have the absolute advantage in both products. This is because the opportunity costs of production differ between both family farms. In other words, *the gains from specialization and trade are based on comparative advantage and not absolute advantage.*

Part (a)
Pulets' After-Specialization, After-Trade
Consumption Possibilities Curve

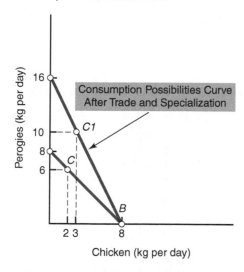

Part (b)
Dowbys' After-Specialization, After-Trade
Consumption Possibilities Curve

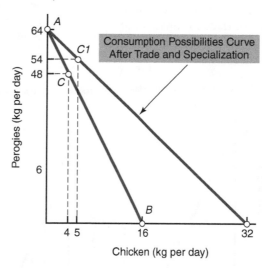

FIGURE B–2

After-Specialization, After-Trade Consumption Possibilities

In part (a) and part (b), specialization and trade allow both the Pulets and the Dowbys to increase their consumption possibilities beyond their production possibilities.

APPENDIX SUMMARY

1. Absolute advantage refers to the ability to produce one unit of a product at a lower labour cost than another producer. Comparative advantage refers to the ability to produce a unit of a product at a lower opportunity cost than another producer.

2. According to the Comparative Advantage Principle, the combined production of two producers can be increased if each producer specializes according to comparative advantage. This principle applies even in those cases where one producer has the absolute advantage in both product areas.

3. The terms of trade for one product, *A*, is the amount of the other product, *B*, that must be traded in order to obtain one additional unit of *A*.

4. The Terms of Trade Principle states that each producer will gain from specialization and trade if the terms of trade is between the producers' opportunity costs of production. In this case, consumption possibilities can exceed production possibilities.

APPENDIX PROBLEMS

(Answers to the odd-numbered problems appear at the back of the book.)

B-1. Answer each of the following questions on the basis of the before-specialization and trade production possibilities for the Martin and the Richard families described in the accompanying two graphs. Before specialization and trade, each family is producing and consuming production combination *C*.

   a. Which family has the absolute advantage in the production of each product?

   b. Compute the opportunity cost of producing one litre of beer for each family.

   c. Which family has the comparative advantage in the production of each product?

   d. Before specialization, each family is producing combination *C* on its respective production possibilities curve. Assuming that each family decides to specialize in its area of comparative advantage, compute the gains in total combined production for each product.

   e. In order for both families to share the gains from specialization, the terms of trade for one litre of beer should be somewhere between ___ and ___ litres of wine.

B-2. Answer each of the following questions on the basis of the before-specialization and trade production possibilities for the nations of Mazland and Attica for the two products, cellphones and digital cameras, as shown in the accompanying graphs. Before specialization and trade, each nation is producing and consuming production combination *C*.

   a. Which nation has the absolute advantage in the production of each product?

   b. Compute the opportunity cost of producing one camera for each nation.

   c. Which nation has the comparative advantage in the production of each product?

   d. Before specialization, both nations are producing combination *C* on their respective production possibilities curve. Assuming that each nation decides to specialize in its area of comparative advantage, compute the gains in total combined production for each product.

   e. In order for both nations to share the gains from specialization, the terms of trade for one camera should be somewhere between ___ and ___ phones.

Martin's Production Possibilities

Richard's Production Possibilities

Mazland's Production Possibilities

Attica's Production Possibilities

Demand and Supply

Canadian home sales totaled 111 110 units in the first quarter of 2010, which is the third highest level on record for that time of year. While the annual Canadian inflation rate rose only 1.4 percent, the average price of Canadian owner-occupied dwellings escalated at an annual rate of 18 percent. During this same period, Canadian household debt reached a record level of $1.41 trillion, with each Canadian owing $41 740 on average. At the start of 2010, Canada ranked first in terms of debt to financial assets among the 20 most developed nations.

Is Canada experiencing a housing bubble similar to the one recently experienced in the United States? The theory in this chapter will provide you with the tools needed to predict the future direction of prices in any market, including the Canadian housing market.

LEARNING OBJECTIVES

After reading this chapter, you should be able to:

3.1 Explain the law of demand.

3.2 Distinguish between a change in quantity demanded and a change in demand.

3.3 Explain the law of supply.

3.4 Distinguish between a change in quantity supplied and a change in supply.

3.5 Explain how the forces of demand and supply interact to determine equilibrium price and quantity.

3.6 Describe how changes in demand and supply can change equilibrium price and quantity.

MyEconLab helps you master each objective and study more efficiently. See end of chapter for details.

DID YOU KNOW THAT...?

How do your household's spending habits compare to the typical household in Canada? According to Statistics Canada's Survey of Household Spending, released on December 18, 2009, each Canadian household spends an average monthly amount of $1217 on personal taxes: income tax, UI and CPP deductions, and property taxes; $1625 on shelter: rent or mortgage, utilities, supplies, equipment, and furnishings; $810 on transportation: auto-related and public transportation; $620 on food ($155 per week); $340 on recreation ($85 per week); $335 per month on personal insurance payments and pension contributions; $269 on health and personal care; $238 on clothing; $140 on gifts and charitable contributions; $147 on tobacco, alcohol, and games of chance; $98 on education; $90 on miscellaneous items; and $21 on reading materials and printed matter.

The poorest 25 percent of Canadians spend over 52 percent of their total spending on the basics—food, shelter, and clothing. The richest 25 percent of Canadian households spend only 28 percent of their budgets on these three basic items.

Eighty-six percent of households reported owning a DVD player; 79.4 percent own a computer; 73.2 percent own a cellphone; 65.5 percent and 23.7 percent subscribe to cable and satellite TV respectively. Household spending on reading materials—books, magazines, and newspapers—decreased 2.7 percent over the previous year.

The contents of this chapter will help you identify the various factors that both explain and predict the composition of household consumer expenditures.

Source: "Survey of household spending." *The Daily.* Statistics Canada. Dec. 18, 2009. http://www.statcan.gc.ca/daily-quotidien/091218/dq091218b-eng.htm.

3.1 The Law of Demand

Demand The quantities of a specific good or service that individuals are willing to purchase at various possible prices, other things being constant.

Law of demand The observation that there is an inverse relationship between the price of any good and its quantity demanded, holding other factors equal.

Demand has a special meaning in economics. It refers to the quantities of specific goods or services that individuals, either singly or as a group, will purchase at various possible prices, other things being constant. We can, therefore, talk about the demand for microprocessor chips, french fries, CD players, and health care.

Associated with the concept of demand is the **law of demand**, which can be stated as follows:

> **When the price of a good goes up, people buy less of it, other things being equal. When the price of a good goes down, people buy more of it, other things being equal.**

The law of demand tells us that the quantity demanded of any commodity is inversely related to its price, other things being equal. In an inverse relationship, one variable moves up in value when the other moves down. The law of demand states that a change in price causes the quantity demanded to change in the *opposite* direction.

Note that we tacked onto the end of the law of demand the statement "other things being equal." We referred to this in Chapter 1 as the *ceteris paribus* assumption. It means, for example, that when we predict that people will buy fewer CD players if their price goes up, we are holding constant the price of all other goods in the economy as well as people's incomes. Implicitly, therefore, if we are assuming that no other prices change when we examine the price behaviour of CD players, we are looking at the *relative* price of CD players.

The law of demand is supported by millions of observations of how people behave in the marketplace. Theoretically, it can be derived from an economic model based on rational behaviour, as was discussed in Chapter 1. Basically, if nothing else changes and the price of a good falls, the lower price induces us to buy more over a certain period of time. This is because we can enjoy additional net gains that were unavailable at the higher price. For the most part, if you examine your own purchasing behaviour, you will see that it generally follows the law of demand.

Relative Prices versus Money Prices

Relative price Any commodity's price in terms of another commodity.

The **relative price** of any commodity is its price in terms of another commodity. The actual price that you pay in dollars and cents for any good or service at any point in time is called its **money price**. Consider an example that you might hear quite often around older friends or relatives. "When I bought my first new car, it cost only $1500." The implication, of course, is that the price of cars today is outrageously high because the average new car might cost $20 000. But that is not an accurate comparison. What was the price of the average house during that same year? Perhaps it was only $12 000. By comparison, then, given that houses today average about $200 000, the current price of a new car does not sound so far out of line, does it?

The point is that comparing money prices during different time periods does not tell you much. You have to find out relative prices. Consider a simplified example of the price comparison of prerecorded DVDs versus prerecorded videocassettes between last year and this year. In Table 3–1, we show the money prices of DVDs and videocassettes for two years during which time both have gone up. That means that we have to pay more for DVDs and more for videocassettes in today's dollars. If we look, though, at the relative prices of DVDs and videocassettes, we find that last year, DVDs were twice as expensive as videocassettes, whereas this year they are only 1.5 times as expensive. Conversely, if we compare videocassettes to DVDs, last year they cost only half as much as DVDs, but today they cost about 67 percent as much. In the one-year period, though both prices have gone up in money terms, the relative price of DVDs has fallen (and equivalently, the relative price of videocassettes has risen).

When evaluating the effects of price changes, we must always compare prices per *constant-quality unit*. Sometimes, relative price changes occur because the quality of a product improves, thereby bringing about a decrease in the item's effective price per constant-quality unit.

Money price The actual price that you pay in dollars and cents for any good or service at any point in time.

	Money Price		Relative Price	
	Last Year	This Year	Last Year	This Year
DVDs	$20	$24	$20 / $10 = 2.0	$24 / $16 = 1.5
Videocassettes	$10	$16	$10 / $20 = 0.5	$16 / $24 = 0.67

TABLE 3–1

Money Price versus Relative Price

The money prices of both DVDs and videocassettes have risen. But the relative price of DVDs has fallen (or conversely, the relative price of videocassettes has risen).

The Demand Schedule

Let us take a hypothetical demand situation to see how the inverse relationship between the price and the quantity demanded looks (holding other things equal). We will consider the quantity of rewriteable DVDs demanded *per year* by one person. Without stating the *time dimension*, we could not make sense out of this demand relationship because the numbers would be different if we were talking about the quantity demanded per month or the quantity demanded per decade.

In addition to implicitly or explicitly stating a time dimension for a demand relationship, we are also implicitly referring to constant-quality units of the good or service in question. Prices are always expressed in constant-quality units in order to avoid the problem of comparing commodities that are, in fact, not truly comparable.

In part (a) of Figure 3–1, we see that if the price were $1 per DVD, 50 of them would be bought each year by our representative individual, but if the price were $5 per DVD, only 10 would be bought each year. This reflects the law of demand. Part (a) is also simply called *demand*, or a *demand schedule*, because it gives a schedule of alternative quantities demanded per year at different possible prices.

The Demand Curve

Tables expressing relationships between two variables can be represented in graphical terms. To do this, we need only construct a graph that has the price per constant-quality DVD on the vertical axis, and the quantity measured in constant-quality DVDs per year on the horizontal axis. All we have to do is take combinations *A* through *E* from part (a) of Figure 3–1 and plot those points in part (b). Now we connect the points with a smooth

FIGURE 3–1

The Individual Demand Schedule and the Individual Demand Curve

In part (a), we show combinations A through E of the quantities of DVDs demanded, measured in constant-quality units at prices ranging from $5 down to $1 per DVD. In part (b), we plot combinations A through E on a grid. The result is the individual demand curve for DVDs.

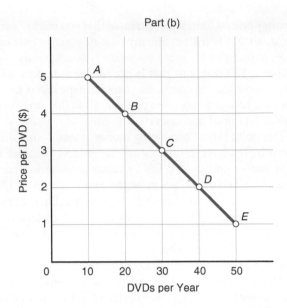

Part (a)

Combination	Price per Constant-Quality DVD	Quantity of Constant-Quality DVDs per Year
A	$5	10
B	4	20
C	3	30
D	2	40
E	1	50

Demand curve A graphical representation of the law of demand.

Market All of the arrangements that individuals have for exchanging with one another.

Market demand Determined by adding the individual demand at each price for all the consumers in the market.

line, and *voila*, we have a *demand curve*.[1] It is downward-sloping (from left to right) to indicate the inverse relationship between the price of DVDs and the quantity demanded per year. Our presentation of demand schedules and curves applies equally well to all commodities, including toothpicks, hamburgers, textbooks, credit, and labour services. Remember, the **demand curve** is simply a graphical representation of the law of demand.

Individual versus Market Demand Curves

The demand schedule shown in part (a) of Figure 3–1 and the resulting demand curve shown in part (b) are both given for one individual. As we shall see, determining price in the **market** (all of the arrangements that individuals have for exchanging with one another) depends on, among other things, the *market demand* for a particular commodity. The way in which we measure a **market demand** schedule and derive a market demand curve for DVDs or any other commodity is by adding the individual demand at each price for all consumers in the market. Suppose that the market for DVDs consists of only two buyers: buyer 1, for whom we have already shown the demand schedule in Figure 3–1, and buyer 2, whose demand schedule is displayed in Figure 3–2, part (a), column 3. Column 1 of Figure 3–2, part (a) shows the price, and column 2 gives the quantity demanded by buyer 1 (data taken directly from Figure 3–1). Column 4 states the total quantity demanded at each price, obtained by adding columns 2 and 3. Graphically, in part (d) of Figure 3–2, we add the demand curves of buyer 1 (part (b)) and buyer 2 (part (c)) to derive the market demand curve.

There are, of course, millions of potential consumers for DVDs. We will assume that the summation of all of the consumers in the market results in a demand schedule, given in part (a) of Figure 3–3, and a demand curve, given in part (b). The quantity demanded is now measured in millions of units per year. Remember, part (b) in Figure 3–3 shows the market demand curve for the millions of users of DVDs. The "market" demand curve that we derived in Figure 3–2 assumed that there were only two buyers in the entire market. This is why that demand curve is not a smooth line—whereas the true market demand curve in part (b) of Figure 3–3 is—and has no kinks.

You have likely heard about the increased interest in using technology such as radio frequency identification tags (RFID tags) to track items such as manufacturing, wholesale, and retail merchandise; precious jewellery and art; and library books at all times in their life cycle. As Example 3–1 implies, the increased use of RFID tags can be illustrated graphically as a downward movement along the demand curve for RFID tags.

---

[1]Even though we call them "curves," for the purposes of exposition, we often draw straight lines. In many real-world situations, demand and supply curves will, in fact, be lines that do curve. To connect the points in part (b) with a line, we assume that for all prices in between the ones shown, the quantities demanded will be found along that line.

FIGURE 3–2

The Horizontal Summation of Two Demand Schedules

Part (a) shows how to sum the demand schedule for one buyer with that of another buyer. Column 2 shows the quantity demanded by buyer 1, taken from part (a) of Figure 3–1. Column 4 is the sum of columns 2 and 3. We plot the demand curve for buyer 1 in part (b) and the demand curve for buyer 2 in part (c). When we add those two demand curves horizontally, we get the market demand curve for two buyers, shown in part (d).

Part (a)

(1) Price per DVD	(2) Buyer 1 Quantity Demanded	(3) Buyer 2 Quantity Demanded	(4) = (2) + (3) Combined Quantity Demanded per Year
$5	10	10	20
4	20	20	40
3	30	40	70
2	40	50	90
1	50	60	110

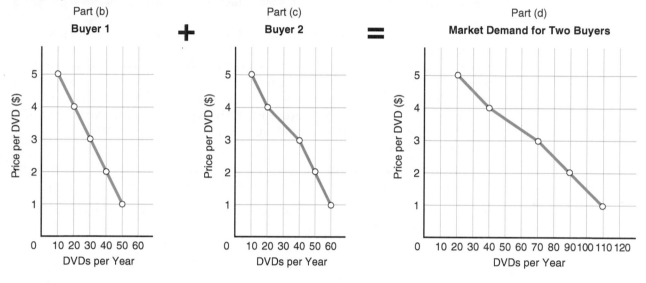

FIGURE 3–3

The Market Demand Schedule for DVDs

In part (a), we add up the millions of existing demand schedules for DVDs. In part (b), we plot the quantities from part (a) on a grid; connecting them produces the market demand curve for DVDs.

Part (a)

Price per Constant-Quality DVD	Total Quantity Demanded of Constant-Quality DVDs per Year (millions)
$5	20
4	40
3	60
2	80
1	100

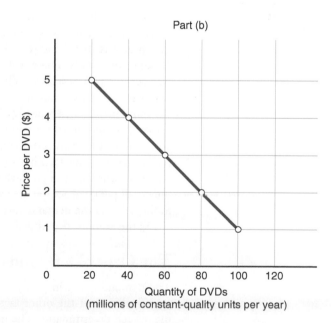

EXAMPLE 3-1 **Why RFID Tags Are Catching On Fast**

An RFID tag contains a tiny microchip and a radio antenna, and it emits a unique signal that a computer-operated reader can use to track any item to which the tag is attached. In principle, any tagged item can be tracked as it travels in planes, trucks, or ships through ports and warehouses, onto retailers shelves, through checkout lines, and into homes and offices.

Just a couple of years ago, the price of an RFID tag was about 30 cents. In 2010, it dropped to between 7 and 15 cents per tag, and in just a few more years the price is likely to decline to less than a nickel per tag. Given this trend in RFID prices, an increasing number of tags have been put to use by retailers, hospitals, trucking firms, airlines, railroads and shipping lines.

Staples Business Depot piloted RFID tagging with four suppliers and one retail location in Toronto. Suppliers placed RFID tags on pallets and cases bound for Staples, and when they were delivered, the company found that the time to process each pallet was reduced from nearly 18 minutes to less than three minutes, significantly reducing the cost of handling. It is estimated that Wal-Mart and other large retailers saved nearly $100 million by adopting RFID. The European Central Bank, which already embeds RFID tags in the largest denomination euro notes to help deter theft and counterfeiting, is now contemplating placing tags in smaller denomination notes.

Sources: "Frequently asked questions: the cost of RFID equipment." *RFID Journal*. http://www.rfidjournal.com/faq/20. Ken Hunt. "Are you reading me?" *The Globe and Mail*. April 12, 2007. Pg. 28.

For critical analysis: What economic principle (law) explains why there is an increase in the practice of RFID tagging?

3.2 Shifts in Demand

Assume that the federal government gives every student registered in a Canadian college, university, or technical school a personal computer that uses DVDs. The demand curve shown in part (b) of Figure 3–3 is no longer an accurate representation of the total market demand for DVDs. There will now be an increase in the number of DVDs demanded *at each and every possible price*. What we have to do is shift the curve outward, or to the right, to represent the rise in demand. The demand curve in Figure 3–4 will shift from D_1 to D_2. Take any price, say, $3 per DVD. Originally, before the federal government giveaway of personal computers, the amount demanded at $3 was 60 million DVDs per year. After the government giveaway, however, the quantity demanded at $3 is 100 million DVDs per year. What we have seen is a shift in the demand for DVDs.

The shift can also go in the opposite direction. What if colleges uniformly outlawed the use of personal computers by students? Such a regulation would cause a shift inward—to the left—of the demand curve for DVDs. In Figure 3–4, the demand curve would shift to D_3; the amount demanded would now be less at each and every possible price.

The Other Determinants of Demand

The demand curve in part (b) of Figure 3–3 is drawn with other things held constant, specifically all of the other factors that determine how much will be bought. There are many such determinants. The major ones are income; tastes and preferences; the prices of related goods; expectations regarding future prices, future incomes, and future product availability; and population (market size). Let us examine each determinant more closely.

INCOME. For most goods, an increase in income will lead to an increase in demand. The phrase *increase in demand* always refers to a comparison between two different demand curves. Thus, for most goods, an increase in income will lead to a rightward shift in the

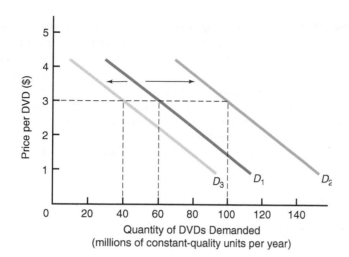

FIGURE 3–4

A Shift in the Demand Curve

If some factor other than price changes, the only way we can show its effect is by moving the entire demand curve, say, from D_1 to D_2. We have assumed in our example that the move was precipitated by the government's giving a free personal computer to every registered post-secondary student in Canada. That meant that at all prices, a larger number of DVDs would be demanded than before. Curve D_3 represents reduced demand compared to curve D_1, caused by a law prohibiting computers on campus.

Normal goods Goods for which demand rises as income rises.

Inferior goods Goods for which demand falls as income rises.

position of the demand curve from, say, D_1 to D_2 in Figure 3–4. You can avoid confusion about shifts in curves by always relating a rise in demand to a rightward shift in the demand curve and a fall in demand to a leftward shift in the demand curve.

Goods for which the demand rises when income rises are called **normal goods**. Most goods, such as shoes, computers, and CDs, are "normal goods." For some goods, however, demand *falls* as income rises. These are called **inferior goods**. Beans might be an example. As households get richer, they tend to spend less and less on beans and more and more on meat. (The terms *normal* and *inferior* are merely part of the economist's terminology; no value judgments are implied by or associated with them.)

Remember, a shift to the left in the demand curve represents a fall, or decrease, in demand, and a shift to the right represents a rise, or increase, in demand.

Example 3–2 illustrates how an economic recession (downturn) can have quite different effects on consumer demand, depending on whether the product being consumed is a normal or an inferior good.

EXAMPLE 3–2   A Recession Tale of Two Macs

During the 2008–2009 global recession, sales in Apple retail stores experienced significant declines. Between December 2008 and December 2009, the number of visitors per Apple retail outlet dropped 1.8 percent, while same-store sales dropped 17.4 percent. Overall, Mac computer shipments decreased an average of 17.5 percent.

The global recession appeared to be much kinder to the other "Mac"—the McDonald's fast-food chain. In February 2009, McDonald's Corp. recorded a whopping 7.1 percent rise in global January sales at restaurants open at least 13 months. McDonald's and other fast-food restaurants have benefited as declining household incomes have encouraged restaurant customers to seek lower-priced menus.

For Critical Analysis:

1. Based on the data provided in this example, would you classify Mac computers as a normal or an inferior good? Explain. Sketch a graph showing how the demand for Mac computers has been affected by the global recession.

2. Would you classify a meal from McDonald's as a normal or an inferior good? Sketch a graph showing how the demand for McDonald's meals has been affected by the global recession.

Sources: "Recession hitting Apple retail stores hard." Hot Stories. Macnn News. January 28, 2009. http://www.macnn.com/articles/09/01/28/needham.on.apple.stores/; "McDonald's thrives in downturn." Business Browser. *Edmonton Journal*. February 10, 2009. Pg. E2.

TASTES AND PREFERENCES. A change in consumer tastes in favour of a good can shift its demand curve outward to the right. When Frisbees became the rage, the demand curve for them shifted outward to the right; when the rage died out, the demand curve shifted inward to the left. Fashions depend to a large extent on people's tastes and preferences. Economists have little to say about the determination of tastes; they have no "good" theories of taste determination or why people buy one brand of a product rather than others. Advertisers, however, do have various theories that they use in trying to make consumers prefer their products to those of competitors.

Example 3–3 illustrates how taste-related factors have recently affected the demand for hair dye.

EXAMPLE 3–3　Brunettes Now Have More Fun

In the 1960s, manufacturers of hair dye aired television and radio commercials claiming that "Blondes Have More Fun" and that "Gentlemen Prefer Blondes." For years thereafter, purchases of blonde hair colourings were a significantly higher share of total U.S. expenditures on hair dyes.

Women's tastes in hair colour began to change in the mid-2000s, however. More of the top female stars of stage and screen are brunettes, such as Sandra Bullock, Demi Moore, Penelope Cruz, and Rihanna. In addition, there has been an increase in U.S. populations of Hispanic, Asian, and Arabic women, whose natural hair shades tend to be brunette colours. Finally, greying women from the baby boom generation born between the mid-1940s and the late 1950s have found that darker shades better cover grey and require less maintenance.

For critical analysis: Explain how various taste-related factors have shifted the demand curve for brunette hair dyes.

PRICES OF RELATED GOODS: SUBSTITUTES AND COMPLEMENTS. Demand schedules are always drawn with the prices of all other commodities held constant. In other words, when deriving a given demand curve, we assume that only the price of the good under study changes. For example, when we draw the demand curve for butter, we assume that the price of margarine is held constant. When we draw the demand curve for stereo speakers, we assume that the price of stereo amplifiers is held constant. When we refer to *related goods*, we are talking about goods for which demand is interdependent. If a change in the price of one good shifts the demand for another good, those two goods are related. There are two types of related goods: *substitutes* and *complements*. We can define and distinguish between substitutes and complements in terms of how the change in price of one commodity affects the demand for its related commodity.

Substitutes Two goods are substitutes when either one can be used to satisfy a similar want.

Two goods are **substitutes** when either one can be used to satisfy a similar want. Butter and margarine are substitutes. Let us assume that each originally cost $4 per kilogram. If the price of butter remains the same and the price of margarine falls from $4 to $2 per kilogram, people will buy more margarine and less butter. The demand curve for butter will shift inward to the left. If, conversely, the price of margarine rises from $4 to $6 per kilogram, people will buy more butter and less margarine. The demand curve for butter will shift outward to the right. An increase in the price of margarine will lead to an increase in the demand for butter, and an increase in the price of butter will lead to an increase in the demand for margarine. For substitutes, a price change in the substitute will cause a change in demand *in the same direction*.

Complements Two goods are complements if both are used together for consumption or enjoyment.

Two goods are **complements** if both are used together for consumption or enjoyment. For complements, the situation is reversed. Consider stereo speakers and stereo amplifiers. We draw the demand curve for speakers with the price of amplifiers held constant. If the price per constant-quality unit of stereo amplifiers decreases from, say, $500 to $200, that will encourage more people to purchase component stereo systems. They will now buy more speakers than before at any given price. The demand curve for speakers will shift outward to the right. If, by contrast, the price of amplifiers increases from $200 to $500, fewer people will purchase component stereo systems. The demand curve for speakers will shift inward to the left. To summarize, a decrease in the price of amplifiers leads to an increase in the demand for speakers. An increase in the price of amplifiers leads to a decrease in the demand for speakers. Thus, for complements, a price change in a product will cause a change in demand *in the opposite direction*.

EXPECTATIONS. Consumers' expectations regarding future prices, future incomes, and future availability may prompt them to buy more or less of a particular good without a change in its current money price. For example, consumers getting wind of a scheduled 100 percent price increase in DVDs next month may buy more of them today at today's prices. Today's demand curve for DVDs will shift from D_1 to D_2 in Figure 3–4 on page 67. The opposite would occur if a decrease in the price of DVDs were scheduled for next month.

Expectations of a rise in income may cause consumers to want to purchase more of everything today at today's prices. Again, such a change in expectations of higher future income will cause a shift in the demand curve from D_1 to D_2 in Figure 3–4. Finally, expectations that goods will not be available at any price will induce consumers to stock up now, increasing current demand.

POPULATION. An increase in the population in an economy (holding per-capita income constant) often shifts the market demand outward for most products. This is because an increase in population means an increase in the number of buyers in the market. Conversely, a reduction in the population will shift most market demand curves inward because of the reduction in the number of buyers in the market.

The rapid growth of Canadian Internet pharmacies selling prescription drugs to American consumers can be explained in terms of some of the nonprice determinants mentioned above. That is, the higher prices of substitute products, such as prescription drugs sold by American pharmacies, have resulted in a significant increase in American consumer demand for the cheaper Canadian prescription drugs. As well, Internet and fax technology has made it very easy to promote and sell Canadian prescription drugs to virtually any location in the United States. This, in turn, has increased the population or number of American buyers wishing to purchase prescription drugs from Canadian online pharmacies. As a result of these changes in nonprice determinants, the market demand curve for prescription drugs sold by Canadian Internet pharmacies has been shifting to the right.

Changes in Demand versus Changes in Quantity Demanded

We have made repeated references to demand and to quantity demanded. It is important to realize that there is a difference between a *change in demand* and a *change in quantity demanded*.

Demand refers to a schedule of planned rates of purchase and depends on a great many nonprice determinants. Whenever there is a change in a nonprice determinant, there will be a change in demand—a shift in the entire demand curve to the right or to the left.

Quantity demanded is a specific quantity at a specific price, represented by a single point on a demand curve. When price changes, quantity demanded changes according to the law of demand, and there will be a movement from one point to another along the same demand curve. Look at Figure 3–5. At a price of $3 per DVD, 60 million DVDs per year are demanded. If the price falls to $1, quantity demanded increases to 100 million per year. This movement occurs because the current market price for the product changes. In Figure 3–5, you can see the arrow pointing down the given demand curve D.

When you think of demand, think of the entire curve. Quantity demanded, in contrast, is represented by a single point on the demand curve.

A change or shift in demand causes the *entire* curve to move. The *only* thing that can cause the entire curve to move is a change in a determinant *other than its own price*.

If the price of iPods goes down, what will happen to the demand for amplified speaker systems for iPods?

In economic analysis, we cannot emphasize too much the following distinction that must constantly be made:

> **A change in a good's own price leads to a change in quantity demanded, for any given demand curve, other things held constant. This is a movement *along* the curve.**

A change in any other determinant of demand leads to a change in demand. This causes a shift *of* the curve.

As Example 3–4 explains, knowing the difference between a change in quantity demanded and a change in demand will help you understand the effects that a used or secondary market has on the market for a new good.

EXAMPLE 3-4   Garth Brooks, Used CDs, and the Law of Demand

A few years ago, country singer Garth Brooks tried to prevent his latest album from being sold to any retail chain or store that also sold used CDs. His argument was that the used-CD market deprived labels and artists of earnings. His announcement came after a giant American retailer started selling used CDs side by side with new releases, at half the price. Brooks, along with the distribution arms of Sony, Warner Music, Capitol-EMI, and MCA were trying to quash the used-CD market. This shows that none of these parties understood the law of demand.

Let us say the price of a new CD is $15. The existence of a secondary used-CD market means that to people who choose to resell their CDs for $5, the net cost of a new CD is, in fact, only $10. Because we know that quantity demanded is inversely related to price, more copies of a new CD will be sold at a price of $10 than of the same CD at a price of $15. Taking only this force into account, eliminating the used-CD market will reduce the sales of new CDs.

But there is another force at work here, too. Used CDs are substitutes for new CDs. If used CDs are not available, some people who would have purchased them will instead purchase new CDs. If this second effect outweighs the incentive to buy less because of the higher effective price, then Brooks' attempt to suppress the used-CD market is correct. ·

For critical analysis: Sketch a demand curve for the product "new music CDs." On this same graph, describe the various effects that the used-CD market has on the "quantity demanded" and the "demand" for "new music CDs."

3.3 The Law of Supply

The other side of the market for a product involves the quantities of goods and services that *firms* are prepared to *supply* to the market. The **supply** of any good or service is the amount that firms are willing to sell at various possible prices, other things being constant. The relationship between price and quantity supplied, called the **law of supply**, can be summarized as follows:

> **At higher prices, a larger quantity will generally be supplied than at lower prices, all other things held constant. At lower prices, a smaller quantity will generally be supplied than at higher prices, all other things held constant.**

There is generally a direct relationship between quantity supplied and price. Producers are normally willing to produce and sell more of their product at a higher price than at a lower price, other things being constant. At $5 per DVD, 3M, Sony, Maxell, Fuji, and other manufacturers would almost certainly be willing to supply a larger quantity than at $1 per unit, assuming, of course, that no other prices in the economy had changed.

As with the law of demand, millions of instances in the real world have given us confidence in the law of supply. On a theoretical level, the law of supply is based on a model in which producers and sellers seek to make the most gain possible from their activities. For example, as a DVD manufacturer attempts to produce more and more DVDs over the same time period, it will eventually have to hire more workers and overutilize its machines. Only if offered a higher price per DVD will the manufacturer be willing to incur these extra costs. That is why the law of supply implies a direct relationship between price and quantity supplied.

Supply The quantities of a specific good or service that firms are willing to sell at various possible prices, other things being constant.

Law of supply The observation that there is a direct relationship between the price of any good and its quantity supplied, holding other factors constant.

The Supply Schedule

Just as we were able to construct a demand schedule, we can construct a *supply schedule*, which is a table relating prices to the quantity supplied at each price. A supply schedule can also be referred to simply as *supply*. It is a set of planned production rates that depends on the price of the product. We show the individual supply schedule for a hypothetical producer in part (a) of Figure 3–6. At $1 per DVD, for example, this producer will supply 200 000 DVDs per year; at $5, it will supply 550 000 DVDs per year.

The Supply Curve

We can convert the supply schedule in part (a) of Figure 3–6 into a *supply curve*, just as we created a demand curve in Figure 3–1. All we do is take the price–quantity combinations from part (a) of Figure 3–6 and plot them in part (b). We have labelled these combinations *F* through *J*. Connecting these points, we obtain the **supply curve**, an upward-sloping curve that shows the typically direct relationship between price and quantity supplied. Again, we have to remember that we are talking about quantity supplied *per year*, measured in constant-quality units.

Supply curve An upward-sloping curve that shows the typically direct relationship between price and quantity supplied.

The Market Supply Curve

Just as we had to add the individual demand curves to get the market demand curve, we need to add the individual producers' supply curves to get the market supply curve. Look at Figure 3–7, in which we horizontally sum two typical DVD manufacturers' supply curves. Supplier 1's data are taken from Figure 3–6; supplier 2 is added. The numbers are presented in part (a). The graphical representation of supplier 1 is in part (b), of supplier 2 in part (c), and of the summation in part (d). The result, then, is the supply curve for DVDs for suppliers 1 and 2.

There are many more suppliers of DVDs, however. The total market supply schedule and total market supply curve for DVDs are represented in Figure 3–8, with the curve in part (b) obtained by adding all of the supply curves, such as those shown in parts (b) and (c) of Figure 3–7. Note the difference between the market supply curve with only two

FIGURE 3–6

The Individual Producer's Supply Schedule and Supply Curve for DVDs

Part (a) shows that at higher prices, a hypothetical supplier will be willing to provide a greater quantity of DVDs. We plot the various price-quantity combinations in part (a) on the grid in part (b). When we connect these points, we find the individual supply curve for DVDs. It is positively sloped.

Part (a)

Combination	Price per Constant-Quality DVD	Quantity of DVDs Supplied (thousands of constant-quality units per year)
F	$5	550
G	4	400
H	3	350
I	2	250
J	1	200

Part (b)

FIGURE 3–7

Horizontal Summation of Supply Curves

In part (a), we show the data for two individual suppliers of DVDs. Adding how much each is willing to supply at different prices, we arrive at the combined quantities supplied in column 4. When we plot the values in columns 2 and 3 on grids in parts (b) and (c) and add them horizontally, we obtain the combined supply curve for the two suppliers in question, shown in part (d).

Part (a)

(1) Price per DVD	(2) Supplier 1 Quantity Supplied (thousands)	(3) Supplier 2 Quantity Supplied (thousands)	(4) = (2) + (3) Combined Quantity Supplied per Year (thousands)
$5	550	350	900
4	400	300	700
3	350	200	550
2	250	150	400
1	200	100	300

suppliers in Figure 3–7 and the one with a large number of suppliers—the entire true market—in part (b) of Figure 3–8. There are no kinks in the true total market supply curve because there are so many suppliers.

Observe what happens at the market level when price changes. If the price is $3, the quantity supplied is 60 million DVDs. If the price goes up to $4, the quantity supplied increases to 80 million per year. If the price falls to $2, the quantity supplied decreases to 40 million DVDs per year. Changes in quantity supplied are represented by movements along the supply curve in part (b) of Figure 3–8.

FIGURE 3-8

The Market Supply Schedule and the Market Supply Curve for DVDs

In part (a), we show the summation of all the individual producers' supply schedules; in part (b), we graph the resulting supply curve. It represents the market supply curve for DVDs and is upward sloping.

Part (a)

Price per Constant-Quality DVD	Quantity of DVDs Supplied (millions of constant-quality units per year)
$5	100
4	80
3	60
2	40
1	20

Part (b)

3.4 Shifts in Supply

When we looked at demand, we found out that any change in anything relevant other than the price of the good or service caused the demand curve to shift inward or outward. The same is true for the supply curve. If something relevant changes apart from the price of the product or service being supplied, we will see the entire supply curve shift.

Consider an example. A new method of putting magnetic material on DVDs has been invented. It reduces the cost of producing a DVD by 50 percent. In this situation, DVD producers will supply more of their product at all prices because their cost of so doing has fallen dramatically. Competition among DVD manufacturers to produce more at every price will shift the supply schedule of DVDs outward to the right from S_1 to S_2 in Figure 3–9. At a price of $3, the quantity supplied was originally 60 million DVDs per year, but now the quantity supplied (after the reduction in the costs of production) at $3 a DVD will be 90 million DVDs a year. (This is similar to what has happened to the supply curve of personal computers and fax machines in recent years as the price of the computer memory chip has fallen.)

Now, consider the opposite case. If the cost of the magnetic material needed for making DVDs doubles, the supply curve in Figure 3–9 will shift from S_1 to S_3. At each price, the number of DVDs supplied will fall due to the increase in the price of raw materials.

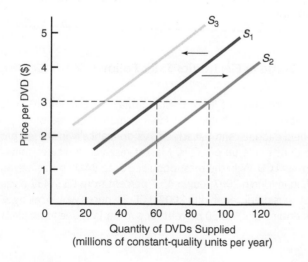

FIGURE 3-9

A Shift in the Supply Curve

If the cost of producing DVDs were to fall dramatically, the supply curve would shift rightward from S_1 to S_2 such that at all prices, a larger quantity would be forthcoming from suppliers. Conversely, if the cost of production rose, the supply curve would shift leftward to S_3.

The Other Determinants of Supply

When supply curves are drawn, only the price of the good in question changes, and it is assumed that other things remain constant. The other things assumed constant are the costs of resources (inputs) used to produce the product, technology and productivity, taxes and subsidies, producers' price expectations, and the number of firms in the industry. These are the major nonprice determinants of supply. If any of them changes, there will be a shift in the supply curve.

COST OF INPUTS USED TO PRODUCE THE PRODUCT. If one or more input prices fall, the supply curve will shift outward to the right; that is, more will be supplied at each price. The opposite will be true if one or more inputs become more expensive. For example, when we draw the supply curve of new cars, we are holding the cost of steel (and other inputs) constant. If the price of steel decreases, the supply curve for new cars will shift *outward to the right*. When we draw the supply curve of blue jeans, we are holding the cost of cotton fixed. The supply curve for blue jeans will shift inward to the left if the price of cotton *increases*.

TECHNOLOGY AND PRODUCTIVITY. Supply curves are drawn by assuming a given technology, or "state of the art." When the available production techniques change, the supply curve will shift. For example, when a better, cheaper, production technique for DVDs becomes available, the supply curve will shift to the right. A larger quantity will be forthcoming at every price because the cost of production is lower.

TAXES AND SUBSIDIES. Certain taxes, such as a per-unit tax, are effectively an addition to production costs and therefore reduce the supply. If the supply curve were S_1 in Figure 3–9, a per-unit tax increase would shift it to S_3. A subsidy would do the opposite; it would shift the curve to S_2. Every producer would receive from the government a "gift" of a few cents for each unit produced.

PRICE EXPECTATIONS. A change in the expectation of a future relative price of a product can affect a producer's current willingness to supply, just as price expectations affect a consumer's current willingness to purchase. For example, DVD suppliers may withhold part of their current supply from the market if they anticipate higher prices in the future. The current amount supplied at all prices will decrease.

NUMBER OF FIRMS IN THE INDUSTRY. In the short run, when firms can only change the number of employees they use, we hold the number of firms in the industry constant. In the long run, the number of firms (or the size of some existing firms) may change. If the number of firms increases, the supply curve will shift outward to the right. If the number of firms decreases, it will shift inward to the left.

Example 3–5 describes how some of the determinants of supply, noted above, have affected the markets relating to popular electronic products. Indeed, the current trends in supply may help us predict whether Plasma or LCD will dominate the flat screen TV markets in the future.

Why have sales of LCD TVs grown rapidly?

EXAMPLE 3–5   Surge in Electronics Sales Follows Dramatic Drop in LCD Prices

Beginning in 2004, the prices of liquid crystal displays (LCDs), which are key components in many electronic devices, plummeted. Worldwide, manufacturers of cellphones, computers, electronic hand-held gadgets, and flat screen TVs dramatically increased production—particularly for those brands made up of LCDs. Market research indicates that the average North American price of an LCD TV in the most popular 30- to 34-inch size averaged US$780 in the first quarter ending in March 2007, down 45.7 percent from US$1437 a year earlier.

Industry observers predicted that in 2007, LCD TV prices would fall by 30 percent or more, compared with a decline of 15 to 20 percent for plasma TVs, due to ample LCD panel supplies.

continued

They forecast that the plasma TV market would start shrinking in 2009 after hitting $24 billion in 2008, while they saw LCD TV demand reaching $75 billion in 2008 and $93 billion in 2010. Large corporations such as Sony and Taiwan's Chunghwa Picture Tubes have already made decisions to halt production of plasma TVs in order to increase their focus on LCD flat screens. About 80 percent of global flat screen research and development spending is being allocated to LCD panels, with the remaining 20 percent to plasma and some other technologies.

In 2009, new technology embodied in LCD TVs began to close the gap between the picture quality produced by LCD TVs and that produced by plasma sets. Major manufacturers started replacing LCD backlighting from cold cathode fluorescent lamps (CCFL) with light-emitting diodes (LEDs). With LED backlighting, LCD TVs can now independently turn off clusters of lights to create deeper black levels and produce a picture quality equal to, if not surpassing, plasma high-definition TVs (HDTVs).

For critical analysis: With the aid of a diagram explain what has been happening to the market supply curve for LCD flat screen TVs and why. In a separate diagram, sketch the predicted effects on the supply curve for plasma TVs in 2009 and after.

Sources: Tom Katsiroubas. "LCD pic catches up with plasmas; with LED backlighting, black levels and colours on LCD sets are now comparable to plasmas." *Toronto Star*. November 26, 2009. Pg. L9.; Kiyoshi Takenaka. "Shift to big-screen TVs favours LCD over plasma: Quality rising as price gap narrows." *Calgary Herald*. Final edition. December 4, 2006. Pg. B7; "TV sales enhance Best Buy picture; same-store sales up 14% in Canada." *Calgary Herald*. Final edition. April 5, 2007. Pg. D10.

Changes in Supply versus Changes in Quantity Supplied

We cannot overstress the importance of distinguishing between a movement along the supply curve—which occurs only when the product's price changes—and a shift in the supply curve—which occurs only with changes in other nonprice factors. A change in price always brings about a change in quantity supplied along a given supply curve. We move from one point to another along the same supply curve. This is specifically called a *change in quantity supplied*.

When you think of *supply*, think of the entire curve. Quantity supplied is represented by a single point on the curve.

> **A change in supply causes the entire curve to shift.** The *only* thing that can cause the entire curve to shift is a change in a determinant *other than price*.

Consequently,

> **A change in the price leads to a change in the quantity supplied, other things being constant.** This is a *movement along* the curve.

> **A change in any other determinant of supply leads to a change in supply.** This causes a *shift of* the curve.

3.5 Putting Demand and Supply Together

In the sections on supply and demand, we tried to confine each discussion to supply or demand only. But you have probably already realized that we cannot view the world just from the supply side or just from the demand side. There is an interaction between the two. In this section, we will discuss how they interact and how that interaction determines the prices that prevail in our economy. Understanding how demand and supply interact is essential to understanding how prices are determined in our economy and other economies in which the forces of supply and demand are allowed to work.

Let us first combine the demand and supply schedules and then combine the curves.

Demand and Supply Schedules Combined

Let us place part (a) from Figure 3–3 (the market demand schedule) and part (a) from Figure 3–8 (the market supply schedule) together in part (a) of Figure 3–10. Column 1 shows the price; column 2, the quantity supplied per year at any given price; and column 3, the quantity demanded. Column 4 is merely the difference between columns 2 and 3, or the difference between the quantity supplied and the quantity demanded. In column 5, we label those differences as either excess quantity supplied (a **surplus**), or excess quantity demanded (a **shortage**). For example, at a price of $2, only 40 million DVDs would be supplied, but the quantity demanded would be 80 million. The difference is 40 million, which we label as excess quantity demanded (a shortage). At the other end of the scale, a price of $5 per DVD would elicit 100 million in quantity supplied, but quantity demanded would drop to 20 million. This leaves a difference of 80 million units, which we call excess quantity supplied (a surplus).

What do you notice about the price of $3? At that price, the quantity supplied and the quantity demanded per year are both 60 million. The difference, then, is zero. There is neither excess quantity demanded (shortage) nor excess quantity supplied (surplus). Hence the price of $3 is very special. It is called the **market clearing price** or **equilibrium price**—

Surplus A situation in which quantity supplied is greater than quantity demanded at a price above the market clearing price.

Shortage A situation in which the quantity demanded exceeds the quantity supplied at a price below the market clearing price.

Market clearing price or **equilibrium price** The price at which market quantity demanded equals market quantity supplied.

Part (a)

(1) Price per Constant-Quality DVD	(2) Quantity Supplied (DVDs per year)	(3) Quantity Demanded (DVDs per year)	(4) Difference (2) – (3) (DVDs per year)	(5) Condition
$5	100 million	20 million	80 million	Excess quantity supplied (surplus)
4	80 million	40 million	40 million	Excess quantity supplied (surplus)
3	60 million	60 million	0	Market clearing price—equilibrium (no surplus, no shortage)
2	40 million	80 million	–40 million	Excess quantity demanded (shortage)
1	20 million	100 million	–80 million	Excess quantity demanded (shortage)

Part (b)

FIGURE 3-10

Putting Demand and Supply Together

In part (a), we see that at the price of $3, the quantity supplied and the quantity demanded are equal, resulting in neither an excess in the quantity demanded nor an excess in the quantity supplied. We call this price the equilibrium, or market clearing, price. In part (b), the intersection of the supply and demand curves is at *E*, at a price of $3 per constant-quality DVD and a quantity of 60 million per year. At point *E*, there is neither an excess in the quantity demanded nor an excess in the quantity supplied. At a price of $1, the quantity supplied will be only

20 million DVDs per year, but the quantity demanded will be 100 million. The difference is excess quantity demanded at a price of $1. The price will rise, and so we will move from point *A* up the supply curve and point *B* up the demand curve to point *E*. At the other extreme, $5 elicits a quantity supplied of 100 million but a quantity demanded of only 20 million. The difference is excess quantity supplied at a price of $5. The price will fall, and so we will move down the demand curve and the supply curve to the equilibrium price, $3 per DVD.

the price at which market quantity demanded equals market quantity supplied. The market clearing price of $3 clears the market of all excess supply or excess demand. We refer to this price as the equilibrium price, in the sense that this is the price at which there is no tendency for change. At this price, consumers are able to buy all that they wish to purchase and suppliers are able to sell all that they wish to supply.

We can define **equilibrium** in general as a point from which there tends to be no movement unless demand or supply changes. Any movement away from this point will set in motion certain forces that will cause movement back to it. Therefore, equilibrium is a stable point. Any point that is not at equilibrium is unstable and cannot be maintained.

Equilibrium A point from which there tends to be no movement unless demand or supply changes.

Demand and Supply Curves Combined

The equilibrium point occurs where supply and demand intersect. Part (b) from Figure 3–3 and part (b) from Figure 3–8 are combined as part (b) in Figure 3–10. The only difference now is that the horizontal axis measures both the quantity supplied and the quantity demanded per year. Everything else is the same. The demand curve is labelled *D*, the supply curve *S*. We have labelled the intersection of the two curves as point *E*, for equilibrium. That corresponds to a market clearing price of $3, at which both the quantity supplied and the quantity demanded are 60 million units per year. There is neither a surplus nor a shortage. Point *E*, the equilibrium point, always occurs at the intersection of the supply and demand curves. This is the price toward which the market price will automatically tend to gravitate.

Shortages

The demand and supply curves in Figure 3–10 represent a situation of equilibrium. But a non–market-clearing, or disequilibrium, price will bring into play forces that cause the price to change and move toward the market clearing price. Then, equilibrium is again sustained. Look once more at part (b) in Figure 3–10. Suppose that instead of being at the market clearing price of $3 per DVD, for some reason the market price is $1 per DVD. At this price, the quantity demanded (100 million), exceeds the quantity supplied (20 million). We have a situation of excess quantity demanded at the price of $1. This is usually called a shortage. Consumers of DVDs would find that they could not buy all that they wished at $1 apiece. But forces will cause the price to rise: Competing consumers will bid up the price, and suppliers will raise the price and increase output, whether explicitly or implicitly. (Remember, some buyers would pay $5 or more, rather than do without DVDs. They do not want to be left out.) We would move from points *A* and *B* toward point *E*. The process would stop when the price again reached $3 per DVD.

Surpluses

Now, let us repeat the experiment with the market price at $5 per DVD, rather than at the market clearing price of $3. Clearly, the quantity supplied will exceed the quantity demanded at that price. The result will be an excess quantity supplied at $5 per unit. This is often called a surplus, a situation in which quantity supplied is greater than quantity demanded at a price above the market clearing price. Given the curves in part (b) in Figure 3–10, however, there will be forces pushing the price back down toward $3 per DVD. Competing suppliers will attempt to reduce their inventories by cutting prices and reducing output, and consumers will offer to purchase more at lower prices. Suppliers will want to reduce inventories, which will be above their optimal level; that is, there will be an excess over what each seller believes to be the most profitable stock of DVDs. After all, inventories are costly to hold. But consumers may find out about such excess inventories and see the possibility of obtaining increased quantities of DVDs at a decreased price. It benefits consumers to attempt to obtain a good at a lower price, and they will therefore try to do so. If the two forces of supply and demand are unrestricted, they will bring the price back to $3 per DVD.

3.6 Changes in Equilibrium

Shifts in Demand or Supply

When a nonprice determinant of demand or supply changes, this will result in a shift in the demand or the supply curve for the product under study. In turn, this will cause the product's equilibrium price and equilibrium quantity to change. In certain situations, it is possible to predict in which direction the equilibrium price and equilibrium quantity will change. Specifically, whenever one curve is stable while the other curve shifts, we can tell what will happen to price and quantity. Consider the four possibilities in Figure 3–11. Each possibility starts with the equilibrium price of DVDs equal to $3 ($P_1$) and the equilibrium quantity equal to 60 million DVDs (Q_1).

INCREASE IN DEMAND. In Figure 3–11 part (a), the supply curve remains stable but *demand increases* from D_1 to D_2. Note that the result is both *an increase in the equilibrium price* of DVDs from P_1 to P_2 and an *increase in equilibrium quantity* from Q_1 to Q_2 ($Pe\uparrow Qe\uparrow$).

Nonprice determinants that can cause an increase in demand include an increase in income with DVDs being a normal good; an increase in the price of a substitute good for DVDs; a decrease in the price of a complement good for DVDs; an increase in population or number of buyers; a change in tastes that favours DVDs; and expectations that DVD prices will increase in the future.

Example 3–6 shows how increased incomes in large nations such as China and taste factors such as the perceived health benefits of eating dark chocolate have caused an increase in demand for chocolate. According to Figure 3–11(a), this increase in demand helps to explain why chocolate prices increased in 2007.

FIGURE 3–11

Shifts in Demand or Supply

In part (a), the supply curve is stable at S. The demand curve shifts outward, or increases, from D_1 to D_2. The equilibrium price P_e increases from P_1 to P_2 and the equilibrium quantity Q_e increases from Q_1 to Q_2. In part (b), with the supply curve stable, the demand curve shifts to the left or decreases. In this case, the equilibrium price decreases from P_1 to P_3, while the equilibrium quantity decreases from Q_1 to Q_3. In part (c), the demand curve is stable at D. Now the supply curve shifts to the right or increases. This results in a decrease in the equilibrium price from P_1 to P_2 but an increase in equilibrium quantity from Q_1 to Q_2. In part (d), with the demand curve stable at D, there is a leftward shift, or a decrease in the supply. While this causes the equilibrium price to increase from P_1 to P_3, the equilibrium quantity decreases from Q_1 to Q_3.

Part (a) An increase in demand: $P_e \uparrow Q_e \uparrow$

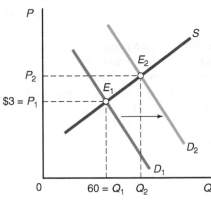

Part (b) A decrease in demand: $P_e \downarrow Q_e \downarrow$

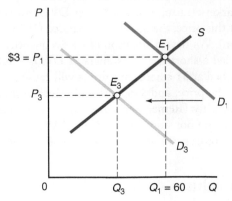

Part (c) An increase in supply: $P_e \downarrow Q_e \uparrow$

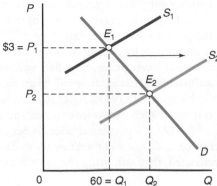

Part (d) A decrease in supply: $P_e \uparrow Q_e \downarrow$

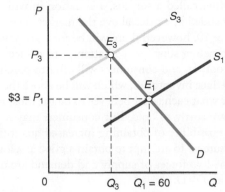

DECREASE IN DEMAND. In Figure 3–11 part (b), the supply curve remains stable but *demand decreases* from D_1 to D_3. Note that the result is both a *decrease in the equilibrium price* of DVDs from P_1 to P_3 and a *decrease in equilibrium quantity* from Q_1 to Q_3 $(P_e\downarrow Q_e\downarrow)$.

INCREASE IN SUPPLY. In Figure 3–11 part (c), the demand curve remains stable but supply increases from S_1 to S_2. Note that the result is a decrease in the equilibrium price of DVDs from P_1 to P_2 and an increase in equilibrium quantity from Q_1 to Q_2 $(P_e\downarrow Q_e\uparrow)$.

Nonprice determinants that can cause an increase in supply include a decline in the costs of inputs used to manufacture DVDs; a technological change increasing the productivity of manufacturing DVDs; a reduction in taxes imposed on DVD manufacturers; an increase in the subsidies enjoyed by DVD manufacturers; and an increase in the number of firms manufacturing DVDs.

Example 3–5 on pages 74–75 shows how the increase in supply of LCD flat screen TVs has increased significantly due to the decline in a key cost of input—LCD panels. Figure 3–11 part (c) explains how this increase in supply has led to a decline in the price of LCD flat screen TVs relative to comparable plasma TVs. Even though in 2007 the prices of LCD TVs were still typically higher than for the same size plasma TVs, the price gap had significantly narrowed.

DECREASE IN SUPPLY. In Figure 3–11 part (d), the demand curve remains stable but supply decreases from S_1 to S_3. Note that the result is both an increase in the equilibrium price of DVDs from P_1 to P_3 and a decrease in equilibrium quantity from Q_1 to Q_3 $(P_e\uparrow Q_e\downarrow)$.

In addition to the demand factors noted above, supply shifts also help to explain the rising chocolate bar prices described in Example 3–6 "Chocoholics Beware." Government policies aimed at increasing the supply of the alternative, environment-friendly fuel source ethanol are driving up the prices of corn, sugar, cattle feed, and therefore milk. This rise is causing the costs of key inputs in the production of chocolate to increase. Figure 3–11 part (d) explains how this translates into higher chocolate prices by shifting the supply curve of chocolate to the left.

The principles of supply and demand presented above are powerful tools that will allow you to predict the future effects that current events will have on markets that affect you, as Example 3–6 illustrates. Presumably, you will be able to react to these predictions in a manner that promotes your self-interest.

What is causing price increases in global chocolate bar markets?

EXAMPLE 3–6   Chocoholics Beware

In December 2009, the price of cocoa, a key ingredient in chocolate, reached a 33-year high. This followed hikes in prices for chocolate bars made by large, multinational chocolate manufacturers such as Mars, Hershey, Cadbury, and Nestlé, who had recently been charged with price-fixing. In 2010, industry observers predicted that consumers could expect the price of chocolate bars to increase significantly in the near future.

Higher incomes in developing countries like China, as well as the perceived cancer-fighting antioxidant health benefits of dark chocolate, are enhancing the long-term demand for chocolate bars.

The chocolate manufacturers are also being affected by the same input cost pressures as other food suppliers. Escalating world oil prices and the desire of countries such as the U.S. and China to be more energy self-sufficient have caused an increasing amount of sugar and corn—key ingredients in chocolate bars—to be used in the production of environment-friendly fuels, such as ethanol, instead of serving as inputs to food and candy products.

continued

Latest data released on cocoa output from the world's leading cocoa growers—the Ivory Coast and Ghana—show that 2010 cocoa production levels are well below those of the previous year. Ivory Coast officials have said the spread of swollen shoot disease among plantations is likely to impact the country's full-year harvest. Meanwhile, Indonesia, the third largest global producer of cocoa, implemented an export tax on cocoa starting on April 1, 2010. This tax encourages more domestic processing of cocoa beans but reduces the amount of cocoa supplied to international chocolate manufacturers.

For Critical Analysis:

Identify two factors noted in this Example that are shifting the demand curve for chocolate bars. Sketch a graph to show how the demand curve for chocolate bars is shifting and how this affects the equilibrium price of chocolate bars.

Sources: Dana Flavelle. "Cocoa finds its sweet spot; as prices for the flavourful beans soar on global markets, it may be time to stock up on chocolate." *Toronto Star*. Ontario edition. April 6, 2007. Pg. F1; "Cocoa supplies likely to be down on last year, report." Confectionary News. April 22, 2010. http://www.confectionerynews.com/The-Big-Picture/Cocoa-supplies-likely-to-be-down-on-last-year-report.

When Both Demand and Supply Shift

Each example given in Figure 3–11 shows a predictable outcome for equilibrium price and quantity based on a shift in either the demand curve holding the supply curve constant or the supply curve holding the demand curve constant. Often, we want to predict the changes in equilibrium price and quantity in market situations where *multiple nonprice determinants* are changing at the same time, resulting in shifts in *both* demand and supply. As you will see below, unless you know the full extent of each individual shift in demand and supply, the overall outcome will be *indeterminate* for *either* equilibrium price *or* equilibrium quantity.

INCREASE IN DEMAND AND INCREASE IN SUPPLY. Suppose the price of CDs, a substitute for DVDs, significantly increases, causing an *increase in demand* for DVDs. At the same time, new technology reduces the cost of manufacturing DVDs, resulting in an *increase in supply* of DVDs. To predict the overall effect on the equilibrium price and quantity of DVDs, we suggest that you begin by analyzing the effect of *each individual shift* on equilibrium price and quantity using the appropriate part in Figure 3–11.

According to part (a) in Figure 3–11, an *increase in demand* for DVDs will cause the *equilibrium price to increase* and the *equilibrium quantity to increase* ($Pe\uparrow Qe\downarrow$). Similarly, part (c) in Figure 3.11 suggests that *an increase in supply* will cause *the equilibrium price to decrease* and the *equilibrium quantity to increase* ($P_e\downarrow Qe\uparrow$).

If you now combine the effects of both shifts, you can conclude that the *equilibrium quantity will certainly increase*, but the overall effect on equilibrium price is *indeterminate*, meaning that it could go up or down or stay the same, depending on the extent of the shift in both curves. Figure 3–12 describes a situation where the supply shifts by a larger amount than the demand shifts, resulting in an overall decrease in the equilibrium price of DVDs.

Consider another similar example. Cellphone prices have been declining despite the fact that the demand for cellphones has been significantly increasing worldwide. Now that you have been exposed to the tools of demand and supply, you are in a better position to understand these trends in the cellular phone industry.

The smaller computer chips that have been invented have reduced the size and increased the portability of cellphones, resulting in an increase in demand for these phones. As well, the concern for personal safety has increased the demand for cellphones. At the same time, new technology has significantly reduced the cost of the computer chips used in the manufacture of cellphones, and this has increased the supply of cellphones. Since you know that the price of cellphones has been declining, you can conclude that the increase in supply has exceeded the increase in demand in the cellphone industry. The graph describing the relative shifts in demand and supply for cellphones will look similar to Figure 3–12.

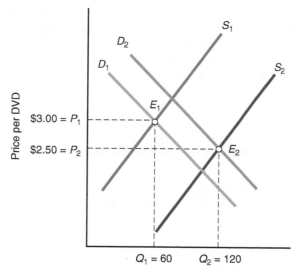

FIGURE 3–12

An Increase in Demand and Supply

The original equilibrium price is $3.00 per DVD, and the original equilibrium quantity is 60 million DVDs, which is determined by the intersection of D_1 and S_1. With an increase in demand and supply, the new demand curve is D_2, and the new supply curve is S_2. The new equilibrium price and quantity, located at the intersection of D_2 and S_2, is $2.50 and 120 million DVDs, respectively. The overall result is that the equilibrium price decreases and the equilibrium quantity increases significantly.

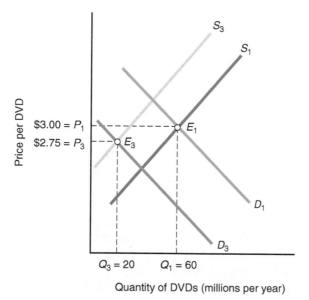

FIGURE 3–13

A Decrease in Demand and Supply

The original equilibrium price is $3.00 per DVD, and the original equilibrium quantity is 60 million DVDs, which is determined by the intersection of D_1 and S_1. With a decrease in demand and supply, the new demand curve is D_3, and the new supply curve is S_3. The new equilibrium price and quantity, located at the intersection of D_3 and S_3, is $2.75 and 20 million DVDs, respectively. The overall result is that the equilibrium price decreases and the equilibrium quantity decreases significantly.

DECREASE IN DEMAND AND DECREASE IN SUPPLY. Suppose the average household income declines, causing a *decrease in demand* for DVDs. At the same time, the number of firms manufacturing DVDs declines, resulting in *a decrease in supply* of DVDs. On the basis of parts (b) and (d) of Figure 3–11, you can conclude that the *equilibrium quantity will certainly decrease,* but the overall *effect on equilibrium price is indeterminate.* If after further investigation, you determine that the decrease in demand (pulling the price down) far exceeds the decrease in supply (pushing the price up), you can predict that the equilibrium price will decline, as illustrated in Figure 3–13.

INCREASE IN DEMAND AND DECREASE IN SUPPLY. Suppose consumers, expecting the prices of DVDs to skyrocket in the future, increase their demand for DVDs in the current period. At the same time, the government imposes a new tax on DVD manufacturers, causing a *decrease in supply* of DVDs. On the basis of parts (a) and (d) of Figure 3–11, you can conclude that the *equilibrium price will certainly increase,* but the overall *effect on equilibrium quantity is indeterminate.*

DECREASE IN DEMAND AND INCREASE IN SUPPLY. Suppose the price of DVD players, a complement of DVDs, significantly increases, causing a decrease in demand for DVDs. At the same time, the government provides subsidies to Canadian DVD manufacturers, resulting in an increase in supply of DVDs. On the basis of parts (b) and (c) of Figure 3–11, you can conclude that the *equilibrium price will certainly decrease*, but the overall *effect on equilibrium quantity is indeterminate*.

As Example 3–7 explains, industry supply and demand trends can have a significant impact on the fortunes or misfortunes of Canadian provincial governments.

EXAMPLE 3-7 Shale Natural Gas: A Game Changer for Alberta?

Canada, and particularly Alberta, has traditionally been a major producer (supplier) of natural gas in the continental North American market. Between the summer of 2008 and December 2009, natural gas prices dropped significantly from $12 per GJ to $4 per GJ, a 67 percent decrease.

This decrease in natural gas prices was attributed to a number of factors. The global recession of 2008–2009 significantly reduced the level of global production, which has a negative impact on the demand for natural gas. As well, the winter of 2009 was relatively mild (compared to previous winters), further reducing the need for natural gas for heating.

Recently, new technology has enhanced the efficiency of extracting natural gas from shale, a type of rock with low permeability. This new technology has been responsible for dramatic increases in U.S. natural gas production, which is considerably more cost efficient than the conventional processes used for extracting natural gas in Alberta. Thus, while North American supplies of natural gas have increased substantially, Canadian production declined 8 percent in 2009, with a 44 percent drop in Canadian drilling activity.

The steep drop in natural gas prices, production, and drilling activity has significantly reduced the royalty revenue that the Alberta government collects from the natural gas industry. In the 2009–2010 budget year, revenue from natural gas royalties declined by $4.1 billion, a 70 percent drop from the previous fiscal year. As a result, the Alberta government has not run fiscal surpluses in subsequent budget years. Indeed for the 2010–2011 fiscal year, the Alberta government plans to freeze or cut spending in various program areas.

Because of the historically high natural gas inventory levels, Canadian natural gas prices and production are not expected to show any significant boost until 2011 or 2012. In the longer run, energy observers predict a rebound in natural gas prices. Natural gas, relatively more environment-friendly than other fossil fuels, is quickly replacing coal in the generation of electricity. As well, there is renewed interest in designing vehicles that run on natural gas in order to meet more stringent laws governing vehicle emission standards.

Sources: Government of Alberta. *Budget 2010: Striking the Right Balance. 2010–13 Fiscal Plan: Revenue Outlook.* pg. 48. http://www.finance.alberta.ca/publications/budget/budget2010/fiscal-plan-revenue.pdf; "North American natural gas-heating season and winter update." Natural Resources Canada. http://www.nrcan.gc.ca/eneene/sources/natnat/shocou-eng.php.

For critical analysis: Identify three factors noted in this example that contributed to the decrease in natural gas prices between 2008 and 2009. Sketch a graph of the North American natural gas market and show how demand and supply changed in that period.

A Canadian Housing Bubble?

Concepts Applied: Changes in Demand and Supply, Changes in Equilibrium Price, Opportunity Cost, Rational Decision Making, Consumption vs. Investment

Record-low interest rates increased the demand for home ownership in Canada in the first quarter of 2010.

During the first quarter of 2010, actual home sales in Canada numbered 111 110 units. That was the third highest level on record for the first quarter period in Canadian housing history. Average Canadian home prices escalated at rapid annual rates from 2009 to 2010, as indicated in Table 1.

TABLE 1

Average Canadian Home Prices

Region	March 2010	March 2009	Annual % Change
Canada	$340 920	$289 881	18%
British Columbia	$516 970	$425 708	21%
Alberta	$362 231	$328 538	10%
Saskatchewan	$239 716	$227 526	5%
Manitoba	$219 046	$204 663	7%
Ontario	$349 405	$292 276	20%
Quebec	$241 556	$217 862	11%
New Brunswick	$155 110	$152 415	2%
Nova Scotia	$211 172	$188 651	12%
Prince Edward Island	$139 938	$147 682	–5%
Newfoundland	$234 403	$198 057	18%

Source: "MLS® statistics." Canadian Real Estate Association. http://www.crea.ca/public/news_stats/statistics.htm#

Given that the one-year rise in Canadian home prices (18 percent) significantly exceeded the annual rate of Canadian inflation (only 1.4 percent), a key question on the minds of Canadian households, investors, economists, and politicians has been, "Is Canada experiencing a housing bubble similar to the one experienced in the United States that preceded, and possibly caused, the great recession of 2008–2009?" In order to address this question, we must first review some basic terms and concepts that relate to a homeowner's decision to purchase a home.

Financing a Home Purchase

Given that a Canadian home can cost hundreds of thousands of dollars, most homeowners finance this large purchase by making an initial down payment and incurring a mortgage loan.

DOWN PAYMENT To purchase a home, the household must be able to put down a minimum cash down payment equal to 5 percent of the purchase price. As an example, the average price of a detached home in Hamilton was $331 523 in February 2010. The minimum down payment required to buy this type of home would be. 05 x $331 523 = $16 576.15. In cases where the down payment is less than 20 percent of the purchase price, the purchaser has to purchase mortgage insurance from the Canada Mortgage and Housing Corporation (CMHC), which typically increases the monthly mortgage payment.

MORTGAGE LOAN A home mortgage loan is a loan that one incurs to purchase the remainder owing on a property, where the loan is backed by the value of the home. Once the home is purchased with this type of loan, the purchaser has an obligation to make regular monthly payments over a period of time.

As an example, suppose that Cidnee Gerard, a resident of Hamilton, purchases a $331 523 home by putting down a 20 percent down payment equal to $66 304.60. She finances the remainder of the purchase price by incurring a mortgage loan with a principal amount equal to $331 523 – $66 304.60 = $265 218.40.

MONTHLY MORTGAGE PAYMENT The home purchaser must pay off the mortgage loan by making regular monthly or biweekly payments. A portion of each regular payment goes towards interest to the borrower and the remainder goes towards paying back the principal amount borrowed. Once the principal amount of the mortgage loan is paid off, the borrower owns the home outright and the regular payments come to an end.

The size of each regular payment depends on a number of factors, including the principal amount borrowed, the life or amortization period of the mortgage loan, the interest rate, and the interest rate term.

In our example, let us assume that Cidnee signed a mortgage loan with a principal amount of $265 218.40 with an amortization period of 25 years and a five-year fixed interest rate of 4.7 percent. The amortization period of 25 years means that Cidnee plans to pay off the entire principal amount in 25 years, at which time she will own the home outright and will cease making monthly payments. The five-year fixed interest rate of 4.7 percent means that the interest rate will stay fixed at 4.7 percent for the next five years, which will fix the monthly payments for the five-year period. In this example, the payments will be $1497.54 each month for the next five years. Note that you can easily calculate the monthly payment using a mortgage calculator at the one of the Canadian bank websites.

If Cidnee wanted to reduce her monthly payments on the same $265 218.40 loan, she could increase the amortization principal to, say, 35 years and she could choose a one-year fixed-rate mortgage at 2.9 percent. This means that she will take 35 years to pay off the mortgage loan, and her current monthly payment would be $1003.40. This monthly payment will only stay fixed for one year. After that, it could increase depending on the market rate of interest in the economy. As an example, if rates go up by 3 percentage points in the next year, the monthly payment will go up to $1481.87.

QUALIFYING FOR A MORTGAGE LOAN   The Canadian government tightened the mortgage lending rules as of April 19, 2010, as follows. All borrowers must meet the standards for a five-year fixed-rate mortgage even if they choose a mortgage with a lower interest rate and shorter interest-rate term. The standards typically consist of two affordability rules imposed by the lending bank. The first affordability rule, called the Gross Debt Service (GDS) ratio, is that your monthly housing expenses—mortgage payment, property taxes, and heating costs—should not be more than 32 percent of your gross household monthly income. The second affordability rule, known as the Total Debt Service (TDS) ratio, is that your entire monthly debt expenses—including mortgage, car, and credit card payments—should not be more than 40 percent of your gross monthly income.

Renting vs. Owning Your Home

MARGINAL COST OF HOME OWNERSHIP   The decision to own rather than rent your home depends on both financial and non-financial considerations. Table 2 below compares the financial costs related to two alternatives facing Cidnee Gerard. In the first alternative, Cidnee rents a three-bedroom apartment in Hamilton and pays $1022 in rent per month, which is the average monthly rent in Hamilton in the last quarter of 2009. If Cidnee rents the apartment, she must put down a $1000 damage deposit, which she expects to get back when she leaves the apartment. Therefore the only sacrifice (opportunity cost) related to the damage deposit is the interest that the down

payment could have earned if invested in a bank GIC earning 2 percent interest per year.

In the second alternative, Cidnee purchases a $331 523 home with a 20 percent down payment equal to $66 304.60 and a mortgage loan of $265 218.40 with the following terms: an amortization period of 25 years and a five-year fixed interest rate of 4.7 percent. The costs of owning the home include the down payment; the interest that the down payment could have earned if invested in a bank GIC earning 2 percent interest per year; property taxes; home insurance; closing and transaction costs, including inspection and appraisal fees and the legal costs of securing the home; and maintenance costs related to the upkeep of the home. When computing the costs over the three years between renting and owning a home, Cidnee assumes that the home price stays fixed at $331 523.

Note that monthly utility costs are not shown in Table 2 because these would be incurred in either alternative, so they have been cancelled out.

TABLE 2

Costs of Renting vs. Owning a Home

	Amount Per Year	Total Over Next 3 Years
Cost of Renting		
Rent ($1022 per month)	$12 264	$36 792
Opportunity Cost of Damage Deposit: 2% × $1000 = $20 forgone interest each year	$20	$60
Total Cost of Renting	**$12 284**	**$36 852**
Cost of Owning		
Mortgage Payment ($1497.54 per month)	$17 970.48	$53 911.44
Down Payment of $66 304.60 (incurred in the first year only)	$66 304.60	$66 304.60
Opportunity Cost of Down Payment: 2% × $66 304.60 = $1326.09 forgone interest each year	$1326.09	$3978.28
Property Taxes = $2500 per year	$2500	$7500
Home Insurance = $600 per year	$600	$1800
Transaction and Closing Costs (incurred in the first year only)	$3,500	$3500
Home Maintenance Expenses = $1500 per year	$1500	$4500
Total Cost of Owning	**$93 701.17**	**$141 494.32**

Based on the financial considerations in Table 2, the marginal cost of owning a home (vs. renting) over a three year period equals $141 494.32 − $36 852 = $104 642.32. Depending on Cidnee's personal values, there may be additional sacrifices related to owning a home. If Cidnee rents a home, she can easily move to another location to quickly exploit a new opportunity. If Cidnee owns a home, she may not be able to sell the home at a desirable price in order to be able to move to another location quickly. As well, as a homeowner, Cidnee has the added responsibility of maintaining her home, which takes time and may be stressful.

MARGINAL BENEFIT OF HOME OWNERSHIP In making a rational decision to own rather than rent a home, one must compare the marginal benefit with the marginal cost of home ownership. In terms of financial considerations, one potential benefit of owning a home is the accumulation of personal equity (wealth). As you likely realize, if you rent a home, all your rent payments go to the landlord, and at the end of the day, you have nothing to show for incurring all those monthly rental expenses.

In Cidnee's example, if her home price stays the same over the next three years, she will accumulate equity equal to the $66 304.60 down payment she incurred in the first year as well as the portion of her monthly mortgage payments that paid off the principal amount borrowed, which equals $18 072.05. In total, she will accumulate $84 376.65, which would be part of the marginal benefit related to owning her home.

The marginal benefit of owning her home could be significantly higher if Cidnee's home increases in value over the three-year period under study. As an example, if Cidnee's original home value of $331 523 increases by 5 percent in each of the three years, the home will be valued at $383 779.31. This amounts to an additional capital (equity) gain of $52 256.31. In this situation, the marginal benefit associated with home ownership would be $84 376.65 + $52 256.31 = $136 632.96. The $136 632.96 marginal benefit exceeds the $104 642.32 marginal cost, making the decision to become a homeowner a rational one.

It should be noted that the marginal benefit of owning a home (based on financial considerations) depends crucially on the future direction of home prices. If over the three-year period of study the value of Cidnee's home decreases, this will reduce the amount of personal equity accumulated and the marginal benefit of home ownership will be significantly less than its marginal cost.

Depending again on Cidnee's personal values, additional benefits related to owning a home may include privacy; pride of ownership; tenure of home ownership—nobody can ask her to leave once her home is paid for; freedom to have pets; and freedom to renovate and landscape to suit her own preferences.

Factors Affecting Canadian Housing Prices in 2009 and 2010

After reviewing home ownership fundamentals, we can now return to the question of whether the sharp increase in home prices witnessed in 2010 constitutes a Canadian housing bubble. If the factors that caused the increases in Canadian home prices are temporary, once they run their course, the bubble will burst and Canadian home prices would drastically decline, causing significant hardship to individual homeowners, as well as to the Canadian economy as a whole. In this section, we will examine key factors that affected the Canadian housing market in 2009 and 2010.

CANADIAN INTEREST RATES In order to stimulate the Canadian economy during the 2008–2009 recession, the Bank of Canada, a policy arm of the federal government, pursued policies that resulted in record low Canadian interest rates. This significantly reduced home mortgage interest rates, lowering the costs (monthly payments) related to purchasing homes. Between 1986 and 2009, the average five-year mortgage rate in Canada was 8.23 percent. In the first quarter of 2010, the five-year rate was below 5 percent, and variable rate mortgages were just above 2 percent.

When the Canadian recession appeared to subside in the last quarter of 2009, the Bank of Canada made public statements suggesting that Canadian interest rates would likely start to increase in the middle of 2010.

TIGHTER MORTGAGE LENDING RULES As noted above, on February 16, 2010, the federal government announced its intentions to institute policies starting April 19, 2010, that would make it more difficult for some Canadians to qualify for home mortgage loans.

HARMONIZED SALES TAX In 2009, the Ontario and B.C. governments announced a major overhaul of sales taxes in their provinces. Starting in July 2010, the goods and services tax (GST) and provincial sales taxes were replaced by one tax called the harmonized sales tax (HST). One effect of the tax was to increase costs related to buying a home over $400 000. If households purchased their homes before July 2010, they could avoid these additional taxes. It is not surprising that, according to Table 1 above, Ontario and B.C. experienced the largest annual increase in home prices between March 2009 and March 2010.

HIGH UNEMPLOYMENT RATES For the years 2001 and 2011, the Canadian unemployment rate is predicted to hover around 8 percent, which is significantly above historical rates. High unemployment rates tend to reduce many households' willingness and ability to purchase homes. When job security is low, consumers are reluctant to make long-term purchase commitments involving hundreds of thousands of dollars.

AFFORDABILITY During the first quarter of 2010, as average Canadian housing prices increased by 18 percent, the average weekly earnings (including overtime) of Canadians rose by only 2.8 percent. Put another way, the increase in average consumer income is significantly below the increase in Canadian home prices. This trend reduces the affordability of Canadian homes.

RECORD NUMBER OF RETIREES A key demographic trend expected to impact home prices is Canada's aging population, whereby a much greater portion of the population will consist of seniors and retirees. This trend is expected to favour the purchase of condos and leasing of rental units over owner-occupied single detached homes.

HIGH DEBT TO ASSET RATIO One key factor that affects the ability of Canadian households to purchase big-ticket items, such as homes and cars, is the household debt-to-asset ratio. Household assets refer to the total wealth, or assets or equity, of a household, which includes physical assets such as homes and financial assets such as stocks, bonds, and bank accounts. Household debt includes the value of mortgage loans, personal lines of credit, and credit card debt. When the household debt-to-asset ratio increases, Canadians are less able to maintain the same level of household spending.

A report published in May 2010 by the Certified General Accountants Association of Canada presented data indicating that Canadian household debt is at a record level of $1.41 trillion. This implies that each Canadian individual (on average) owed more than $41 740 in December 2009, more than 2.5 times the amount owed per person in 1986. Canada ranks first in terms of debt to financial assets among the 20 developed nations that are members of the Organisation for Economic Co-operation and Development (OECD). The debt-to-income ratio of the typical Canadian reached 144 percent by the end of 2009.

ESCALATING HOUSING STARTS Housing starts refer to the number of new homes constructed over a specified period of time. This adds to the stock or supply of homes. During the first quarter of 2010, urban housing starts were up 50.4 percent compared to the same period in 2009.

INCREASED RESALE LISTINGS Resale Listings refer to the number of used homes that are put up for sale. These listings affect the supply of available housing. During the first three months of 2010 the total Canadian listings increased by 14.1% compared to the same period in 2009.

Owner-Occupied Homes: Investment or Consumption Goods?

For most Canadian households, an owner-occupied home can be considered both an investment and a consumption good. This implies that a decision to own a home can be rational, even if it appears to be an inferior investment. A recent study examined the annual compound rate of return on residential real estate in 12 Canadian cities over a 25-year period. Toronto provided the best rate of return at 5.75 percent per year. This rate of return fell significantly below the annual increase in the Toronto Stock Exchange (TSE) over the same 25-year period, which was 8.64 percent.

Even in situations where home prices "bubble to a boil," households can derive a significant amount of personal satisfaction from home ownership. As was already noted, there are many benefits to home ownership beyond the financial ones.

Owning your own home can also enhance the enjoyment you derive from shopping for home-related items such as home furnishings, tools, and pictures.

Sources: "Government of Canada takes action to strengthen housing financing." Department of Finance Canada. February 16, 2010. http://www.fin.gc.ca/n10/10-011-eng.asp; "Canadian mortgage rates 1986–2009." ByTheOwner.com. http://blog.bytheowner.com/2009/11/05/canadian-mortgage-rates-1986-2009. (Accessed May 15, 2010); "Global forecast update." Global Economic Research. Scotiabank Group. May 5, 2010. http://www.scotiacapital.com/English/bns_econ/forecast.pdf; "Payroll employment, earnings and hours." *The Daily*. Statistics Canada. February 2010 (preliminary) http://www.statcan.gc.ca/daily-quotidien/100429/dq100429a-eng.htm; *Where Is the Money Now: The State of Canadian Household Debt as Conditions for Economic Recovery Emerge*. Certified General Accountants Association of Canada. May 2010. http://www.cga-canada.org/ en-ca/ResearchAndAdvocacy/AreasofInterest/DebtandConsumption/Pages/ca_debt_report.aspx; "Housing now Canada." Canadian Mortgage and Housing Corporation. April 2010. http://www03.cmhc-schl.gc.ca/catalog/productDetail.cfm?lang=en&cat=70&itm=1&sid=590cba09284e431bba99e89594e44ba7&fr=1273943928140; Joe Castaldo. "Why buying a house is a bad investment." *Canadian Business Magazine*. March 15, 2010. Pg. 28.

For critical analysis:

1. Identify three factors noted in this Issues and Applications that contributed to a temporary increase in demand (housing bubble) for Canadian homes in late 2009 and early 2010. Sketch a demand and supply graph for Canadian owner-occupied homes, and show how these factors have affected the Canadian housing market as well as the equilibrium price of Canadian homes.

2. Identify three factors noted in this Issues and Applications that have the potential to burst the Canadian housing bubble by decreasing the demand for Canadian owner-occupied homes. Sketch a demand and supply graph for Canadian owner-occupied homes, and show how these factors have affected the Canadian housing market as well as the equilibrium price of Canadian homes.

3. What two factors noted in this Issues and Applications have the effect of reducing Canadian home prices by shifting the supply curve for owner-occupied Canadian homes?

4. Briefly explain how one's decision to purchase a home can be a rational decision even if the home turns out to be a poor investment.

SUMMARY

Here is what you should know after reading this chapter. MyEconLab will help you identify what you know, and where to go when you need to practise. We suggest that as soon as you review one of the Learning Objective sections below, you then proceed to go through the related section in MyEconLab.

myeconlab

LEARNING OBJECTIVES	KEY TERMS	MYECONLAB PRACTICE
3.1 The Law of Demand. According to the law of demand, other things being equal, households will purchase fewer units of a good at a higher price and more units of a good at a lower price. This law is described by a downward-sloping demand curve.	demand, 62 law of demand, 62 relative price, 62 money price, 63 demand curve, 64 market, 64 market demand, 64	• **MyEconLab** Study Plan 3.1
3.2 Shifts in Demand. A change in the good's own price causes a change in quantity demanded, which is a movement along the same demand curve. A change in demand is described as a shift in the entire demand curve caused by a change in a nonprice determinant, such as income, tastes, prices of related goods, expectations, and number of buyers. An increase in demand means that the demand curve shifts rightward, while a decrease in demand implies a leftward shift.	normal goods, 67 inferior goods, 67 substitutes, 68 complements, 68	• **MyEconLab** Study Plan 3.2
3.3 The Law of Supply. According to the law of supply, firms will produce and offer for sale more units of a good at a higher price and fewer units of a good at a lower price. This law is described by an upward-sloping supply curve.	supply, 71 law of supply, 71 supply curve, 71	• **MyEconLab** Study Plan 3.3
3.4 Shifts in Supply. A change in the good's own price causes a change in quantity supplied, which is a movement along the same supply curve. A change in supply is described as a shift in the entire supply curve caused by a change in a nonprice determinant such as input prices, technology and productivity, taxes and subsidies, price expectations, and number of sellers. An increase in supply means that the supply curve shifts rightward, while a decrease in supply implies a leftward shift.		• **MyEconLab** Study Plan 3.4

LEARNING OBJECTIVES	KEY TERMS	MYECONLAB PRACTICE
3.5 Putting Demand and Supply Together. The equilibrium price and equilibrium quantity occur where market demand equals market supply. Graphically, equilibrium occurs where the market demand curve intersects the market supply curve. At this point, the plans of sellers and buyers match, meaning that shortages and surpluses are eliminated.	surplus, 76 shortage, 76 market clearing price or equilibrium price, 76 equilibrium, 77	• **MyEconLab** Study Plan 3.5
3.6 Changes in Equilibrium. An increase in demand will cause equilibrium price and quantity to increase, whereas a decrease in demand will cause equilibrium price and quantity to decrease. An increase in supply will cause equilibrium price to decrease and equilibrium quantity to increase, while a decrease in supply will cause equilibrium price to increase and equilibrium quantity to decrease. When both demand and supply change in the same direction, the equilibrium quantity will also change in the same direction, but the equilibrium price might increase, decrease, or remain the same. When both demand and supply change in opposite directions, the equilibrium price will change in the same direction as demand, but the equilibrium quantity might increase, decrease, or remain the same.		• **MyEconLab** Study Plan 3.6

PROBLEMS

(Answers to the odd-numbered problems appear at the back of the book.)

LO 3.1, 3.2 Explain the law of demand; distinguish between a change in quantity demanded and a change in demand.

1. Examine the following table, and then answer the questions.

	Price per Unit Last Year	Price per Unit Today
Heating oil	$1.00	$2.00
Natural gas	$0.80	$3.20

What has happened to the absolute price of heating oil? Of natural gas? What has happened to the price of heating oil relative to the price of natural gas? What has happened to the relative price of natural gas? Will consumers, through time, change their relative purchases? If so, how?

2. Give an example of a complement and a substitute in consumption for each of the following items:
   a. bacon
   b. coffee
   c. automobiles

3. Consider the market for Canadian beef. Explain whether each of the following events would cause an increase in demand, a decrease in demand, an increase in quantity demanded, or a decrease in quantity demanded. Also describe how each event will affect the demand curve for Canadian beef.
   a. The price of chicken decreases.
   b. Household income increases, and beef is a normal good.
   c. The price of Canadian beef decreases.
   d. A Canadian cow is found to have mad cow disease.
   e. The Canadian government raises the price of Canadian beef.

LO 3.3, 3.4 Explain the law of supply; distinguish between a change in quantity supplied and a change in supply.

4. Consider the market for newly constructed bungalow homes in Canada. Explain whether each of the following events would cause an increase in supply, a decrease in supply, an increase in quantity supplied, or a decrease in quantity supplied. Also describe how each event will affect the supply curve for new Canadian bungalow homes.
   a. The price of lumber skyrockets in Canada.
   b. The Canadian government lowers the price of new bungalow homes in Canada.
   c. New technology is developed that significantly reduces the cost of building new bungalows.
   d. The Canadian government provides subsidies to builders of new Canadian bungalows.
   e. The price of Canadian bungalows increases.

LO 3.5, 3.6 Explain how the forces of demand and supply interact to determine equilibrium price and quantity; describe how changes in demand and supply can change equilibrium price and quantity.

5. Suppose that, in a recent market period, an industry-wide survey determined the following relationship between the price of rock music CDs and the quantity supplied and demanded.

Price	Quantity Demanded	Quantity Supplied
$ 9	100 million	40 million
$10	90 million	60 million
$11	80 million	80 million
$12	70 million	100 million
$13	60 million	120 million

   a. What is the equilibrium price and equilibrium quantity?
   b. If the industry price is $13, is there a shortage or a surplus of CDs? How much is the shortage or surplus? Will the price stay at $13? Explain.
   c. If the industry price is $10, is there a shortage or a surplus of CDs? How much is the shortage or surplus? Will the price stay at $10? Explain.

6. Refer to Example 3–6, "Chocoholics Beware," and use a demand and supply diagram (for chocolate bars) to describe the changes in supply that have occurred in the chocolate bar market in 2009–2010. Show graphically how these changes in supply will affect the equilibrium price of chocolate bars.

7. Suppose that a survey for a later market period indicates that the quantities supplied in the table in Problem 5 are unchanged. The quantity demanded, however, has increased by 30 million at each price. Construct the resulting demand curve in the illustration you made for Problem 5. Is this an increase or a decrease in demand? What is the new equilibrium quantity and the new market price? Give two examples that might cause such a change.

8. Example 3–7, "Shale Natural Gas: A Game Changer for Alberta" noted that concern over the environment will likely have some positive effects for the producers of natural gas in the long run. Identify and briefly explain specific factors related to the environment that will affect the market for natural gas. Sketch a demand and supply diagram, and explain how these factors will affect the graph and the equilibrium price for natural gas.

9. In the market for rock music CDs, explain whether the following events would cause an increase or decrease in demand or an increase or decrease in the quantity demanded. Also explain what happens to the equilibrium quantity and the equilibrium price.
   a. The price of CD packaging material declines.
   b. The price of CD players declines.
   c. The price of cassette tapes increases dramatically.
   d. A booming economy increases the income of the typical CD buyer.
   e. Many rock fans suddenly develop a fondness for country music.

10. Consider the market for laptop computers. Explain whether the following events would cause an increase or decrease in supply or an increase or decrease in the quantity supplied. Illustrate each, and show what would happen to the equilibrium market price, given a typical downward-sloping demand curve.
    a. The price of memory chips used in laptop computers declines.
    b. The price of memory chips used in desktop personal computers declines.
    c. The number of manufacturers of laptop computers increases.
    d. The prices of computer peripherals, printers, fax–modems, and scanners decrease.

11. The following diagram describes the hypothetical monthly demand and supply conditions for eggs in a small provincial market.
    a. If the price in the egg market above were initially at $1.40 per dozen, there would be a (surplus or shortage) equal to ___ thousands of dozens of eggs per week. Will the price stay at $1.40?

b. If the price in the egg market above were initially at $0.80 per dozen, there would be a (surplus or shortage) equal to ___ thousands of dozens of eggs per week. Will the price stay at $0.80?

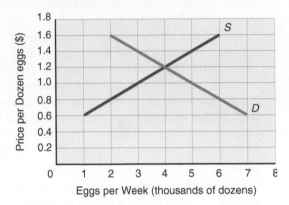

c. Determine the equilibrium price and equilibrium quantity in the egg market described above.
d. In the egg market described above, explain whether each of the following events would cause an increase or decrease in demand or supply. Also explain what happens to the equilibrium price and quantity.
 i. Studies show that daily use of eggs reduces the risk of getting serious diseases.
 ii. The cost of feeding chickens significantly increases.
 iii. Average consumer income increases, and eggs are an inferior good.
 iv. The government provides a subsidy to egg producers. A subsidy is a situation where the government pays the egg producers a set amount per dozen produced.

12. Airline routes are typically controlled by imposing a quota on the number of airline companies that may use the route and the number of flights on the route. Consequently, the government restricts the number of round-trip seats available on these flight routes. Suppose that the following table describes the daily demand and supply schedules for seats on round-trip flights between Toronto and Vancouver.

Price per seat	Quantity Demanded (number of seats)	Quantity Supplied (number of seats)
($)200	2000	1200
300	1800	1400
400	1600	1600
500	1400	1800
600	1200	2000

a. What is the equilibrium price and quantity for the Toronto-to-Vancouver airline seats? How much, in total dollars, do passengers spend on this route each day?

b. Suppose the government limits the daily number of round-trip seats to ensure that only 1200 seats can be made available on the Toronto-to-Vancouver route. What will be the new price per round-trip seat on this route? With the quota policy, do passengers end up spending more or less each day on this same route in total dollars? Can you think of how this quota policy might actually benefit the passengers (consumers) in the longer run?

13. The following diagram describes the hypothetical monthly demand and supply for one-bedroom apartments in a small college town.

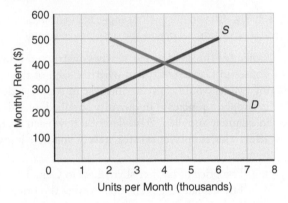

a. What is the equilibrium monthly rent (price) and equilibrium monthly quantity?
b. Suppose that the mayor of this town decides to make housing more affordable for the local college students by imposing a rent control that holds the price of a one-bedroom apartment to $300 per month.
 This rent control policy will result in a (shortage or surplus) of _____ units per month.
c. What will this rent control policy do to the market for two-bedroom apartments that are not regulated by the government? What will happen to the equilibrium price and quantity for the unregulated two-bedroom apartments?

14. In May 2000, the Canadian government imposed a tax on bicycles imported from Taiwan and China. Show how this tax affects the market for Taiwanese and Chinese bicycles, shifting the appropriate curve and indicating a new market equilibrium quantity and price. In a separate graph, show the effect of the tax on Canadian-made bicycles, shifting the appropriate curve and indicating the new market equilibrium and price.

15. The following diagram describes the market for Canadian red wine. Explain how each of the following sets of events will affect the equilibrium price and equilibrium quantity of Canadian red wine. Note that in some cases, your answer will be "indeterminate," meaning that with the given information, you cannot predict the direction of change.

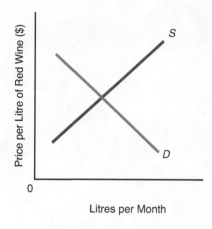

a. Studies indicate that Canadian red wine reduces the risk of heart disease. At the same time, the cost of the grapes used to produce red wine decreases.

b. Frost destroys a significant amount of the red grapes used to produce Canadian red wine. At the same time, the price of California red wine, a key substitute for Canadian red wine, increases.

c. New technology significantly lowers the cost of producing wine. At the same time, the price of Canadian white wine decreases.

BUSINESS APPLICATION

LO 3.2 Distinguish between a change in quantity demanded and a change in demand.

Marketing: Market Segmentation— The Aging Population

A typical first-year economics text tends to focus on a market at the product (or resource) level. However, in order to gain a better understanding of consumer demand, the marketing staff of a company will often segment (subdivide) a product market in order to identify a potentially profitable target market or market niche. In short, a market segment (target market) consists of a group of consumers who respond in a similar way to a given set of marketing efforts.

A very useful basis of market segmentation starting in the early 2000s was the age-related demographic trends in the Canadian population. Due to Canada's relatively low fertility rates and long life expectancy, Canada's population is aging.

The baby boom generation, born between 1946 and 1964, was aged between 46 and 64 in 2010 and is considered to be the consumer group with the most buying power. In 2010, the fastest growing age group (amongst the boomers) consisted of individuals aged 55 to 64, who are just starting to retire. As the baby boom generation begins to reach age 65 by 2011, we will experience a marked acceleration in the number and proportional population of seniors. Projections suggest that by 2021, there will be almost 7 million people over 65, who will make up 19 percent of the total population, and by 2041, seniors will represent approximately 25 percent of the population.

In the 1970s, for every person aged 55 to 64 years, there were 2.3 individuals in the 15- to 24-year-old age group. By 2010, this ratio had fallen to close to 1.0. Beginning in 2011, seniors will make up a greater percentage of the total population than dependent children.

Sources: "2006 Census: age and sex." *The Daily.* Statistics Canada. July 17, 2007. http://www.statcan.ca/Daily/English/070717/d070717a.htm; *Growing Up: The Social and Economic Implications of an Aging Population.* Certified General Accountants Association of Canada. January 26, 2005. pp. 17–20. http://www.cga-canada.org/en-ca/ResearchAndAdvocacy/AreasofInterest/AgingPopulation/Pages/ca_aging_report.aspx.

Business Application Problem

Contrast the effects that the aging population will have on the demand for each of the following sets of items.

a. tennis vs. golf
b. Diet Coke vs. Pepsi
c. urban condominiums vs. suburban homes
d. minivans vs. recreational vehicles
e. red meat vs. chicken

4

LEARNING OBJECTIVES

After reading this chapter, you should be able to:

4.1 Define price elasticity of demand and calculate it using two different methods.

4.2 Define the three price elasticity ranges and explain their effects on total revenues.

4.3 Discuss the three factors that determine the price elasticity of demand.

4.4 Describe the effects of substitutes, complements, and income on elasticity of demand.

4.5 Define price elasticity of supply and the four determinants of elasticity of supply.

Elasticity

Cigarette smoking is unhealthy, which is one reason that governments tax cigarettes. Cigarette consumption is relatively insensitive to price changes, however, and so higher cigarette taxes only moderately reduce cigarette purchases. Beer consumption tends to be more responsive to price changes. Thus, if beer drinking and cigarette smoking are complementary activities, boosting taxes on beer might do more to reduce cigarette consumption. How can we measure the responsiveness of consumption to a change in price? How can we determine whether cigarettes and beer are complements? In this chapter, you will learn the answers to these questions.

EconLab helps you master each objective and study more efficiently. See end of chapter for details

DID YOU KNOW THAT...?

A fall in the price of beer might lead to an increase in campus violence. The law of demand indicates that a decline in the price of beer increases consumption. Economists have found that a 10 percent reduction in the price of beer is associated with an increase in the incidence of campus violence of just over 3.5 percent.

College officials are not alone in having to worry about how individuals respond to lower prices. Businesses must constantly take into account consumer response to changing prices. If McDonald's lowers its prices by 10 percent, will fast-food consumers respond by buying so many more Big Macs

that the company's revenues will rise? At the other end of the spectrum, can Rolls Royce dealers "get away with" a 2 percent increase in prices? In other words, will Rolls-Royce purchasers respond so little to the relatively small increase in price that the total revenues received for Rolls-Royce sales will not fall and may actually rise? The only way to answer these questions is to know how responsive people in the real world will be to changes in prices. Economists have a special name for price responsiveness—elasticity, which is the subject of this chapter.

4.1 Price Elasticity

To begin to understand what elasticity is all about, just keep in mind that it means "responsiveness" or "sensitivity." Here, we are concerned with the price elasticity of demand and the price elasticity of supply. We wish to know the extent to which a change in the price of, say, petroleum products will cause the quantity demanded and the quantity supplied to change, other things held constant. Let us restrict our discussion at first to the demand side.

Price Elasticity of Demand

Price elasticity of demand (E_p) is the relative amount by which the quantity demanded will change in response to a change in the price of a particular good.

We will formally define price elasticity of demand, which we will label E_p, as follows:

What impact would a tax on beer have on consumption?

$$E_p = \frac{\text{Percentage change in quantity demanded}}{\text{Percentage change in price}}$$

Consider an example in which a 10 percent rise in the price of oil leads to a reduction in quantity demanded of only 1 percent. Putting these numbers into the formula, we find that the price elasticity of demand for oil, in this case, equals the percentage change in quantity demanded divided by the percentage change in price, or

$$E_p = \frac{-1\%}{+10\%} = -0.1$$

An elasticity of −0.1 means that a 1 percent *increase* in the price would lead to a mere 0.1 percent *decrease* in the quantity demanded. If you were now told, in contrast, that the price elasticity of demand for oil was −2, you would know that a 1 percent increase in the price of oil would lead to a 2 percent decrease in the quantity demanded.

Price elasticity of demand (E_p)
The relative amount by which the quantity demanded will change in response to a change in the price of a particular good.

RELATIVE QUANTITIES ONLY. Note that in our elasticity formula, we talk about *percentage* changes in quantity demanded divided by *percentage* changes in price. We are, therefore, not interested in the absolute changes, only in relative amounts. This means that it does not matter if we measure price changes in terms of cents, dollars, or hundreds of dollars. It also does not matter whether we measure quantity changes in bushels, grams, or litres. The percentage change will be independent of the units chosen. So, a $1 increase in a cup of coffee has more of an impact than a $1 increase in the price of a car.

ALWAYS NEGATIVE. The law of demand states that quantity demanded is *inversely* related to the relative price. An increase in the price of a good leads to a decrease in the quantity demanded. If a decrease in the relative price of a good should occur, the quantity demanded would increase by a certain percentage. The point is that price elasticity of demand will always be negative. By convention, *we will ignore the minus sign in our discussion from this point on.*

Basically, the greater the *absolute* price elasticity of demand (disregarding sign), the greater is the demand responsiveness to relative price changes—a small change in price has a great impact on quantity demanded. The smaller the absolute price elasticity of demand, the smaller is the demand responsiveness to relative price changes—a large change in price has little effect on quantity demanded. See Example 4–1 for further insight.

EXAMPLE 4–1　"If They Doubled the Price, We'd Still Drink Coffee"

Every time there is frost in Brazil, the price of coffee beans rises, and everyone fears a big rise in the price of coffee. Members of the media interview coffee drinkers and ask how they will respond to the higher prices. Not surprisingly, even when coffee prices soared 150 percent a few years ago, some interviewees said they had to have their cup of coffee, no matter what. But if that were true for all coffee drinkers, why don't coffee prices rise as much as bean prices? If what coffee drinkers tell us were really true, their price elasticity of demand would be zero, and the retail price of coffee could skyrocket. But it never does. The truth is, interviewing coffee drinkers (or other consumers) about intentions tells us little. We need to examine the change in total market quantity demanded after an increase in price. The data make it clear: at least some people drink less coffee when the relative price goes up.

For critical analysis: Would the same be true for gas prices?

Calculating Elasticity

To calculate the price elasticity of demand, we have to compute percentage changes in quantity demanded and in price. To find the percentage change in quantity demanded, we divide the change in the quantity demanded by the original quantity demanded:

$$\frac{\text{Change in quantity demanded}}{\text{Original quantity demanded}}$$

To find the percentage change in price, we divide the change in price by the original price:

$$\frac{\text{Change in price}}{\text{Original price}}$$

There is an arithmetic problem, though, when we calculate percentage changes in this manner. The percentage change, say, from 2 to 3—50 percent—is not the same as the percentage change from 3 to 2—33⅓ percent. In other words, you obtain a different value for the elasticity depending on whether you look at the change in demand when the price increased or when the price decreased.

To compute the average price elasticity of demand, we need to deal with the average change in quantity demanded caused by the average change in price. That means that we take the average of the two prices and the two quantities over the range we are considering and compare the change with these averages. For relatively small changes in price, the formula for computing the price elasticity of demand then becomes

$$E_p = \frac{\text{Change in quantity}}{\text{Sum of quantities}/2} \div \frac{\text{Change in price}}{\text{Sum of prices}/2}$$

We can rewrite this more simply if we do two things: (1) We can let Q_1 and Q_2 equal the two different quantities demanded before and after the price change and let P_1 and P_2 equal the two different prices. (2) Because we will be dividing a percentage by a percentage, we simply use the ratio, or the decimal form, of the percentages. Therefore,

$$E_p = \frac{\Delta Q}{(Q_1 + Q_2)/2} \div \frac{\Delta P}{(P_1 + P_2)/2}$$

where the Greek letter Δ stands for "change in." Example 4–2 provides a real-life example.

EXAMPLE 4–2 The Price Elasticity of Demand for Gasoline

During the week following the Gulf Coast devastation wrought by Hurricane Katrina in September 2005, the nationwide price of gasoline in the United States rose from $2.61 to $3.07. The total quantity of gasoline consumed declined from 9.42 million barrels to 9.04 million barrels.

We can calculate the price elasticity of the demand for gasoline by U.S. consumers using the formula presented earlier (under the assumption, of course, that all other things, such as bus fares, were constant):

$$E_p = \frac{\text{change in Q}}{\text{sum of quantities}/2} \div \frac{\text{change in P}}{\text{sum of prices}/2}$$

$$= \frac{9.42 \text{ million} - 9.04 \text{ million}}{(9.42 \text{ million} + 9.04 \text{ million})/2} \div \frac{\$3.07 - \$2.61}{(\$3.07 + \$2.61)/2}$$

$$= \frac{0.38 \text{ million}}{18.46 \text{ million}/2} \div \frac{\$0.46}{\$5.68/2} = 0.25.$$

The price elasticity of 0.25 means that a 1 percent increase in price generated a 0.25 percent decrease in the quantity of gasoline demanded.

For critical analysis: Would the estimated price elasticity of demand for gasoline have been different if we had not used the average-values formula? How?

4.2 Price Elasticity Ranges

We have names for the varying ranges of price elasticities, depending on whether a 1 percent change in price elicits more or less than a 1 percent change in the quantity demanded.

1. **Elastic demand** is a demand relationship in which a given percentage change in price will result in a larger percentage change in quantity demanded. We say that a good has an elastic demand whenever the price elasticity of demand is greater than 1. A 1 percent change in price causes a change of more than 1 percent in the quantity demanded.
2. **Unit elasticity of demand** is a demand relationship in which the quantity demanded changes exactly in proportion to the changes in price. In a situation of unit elasticity of demand, a 1 percent change in price causes a response of exactly a 1 percent change in the quantity demanded.

Elastic demand A demand relationship in which a given percentage change in price will result in a larger percentage change in quantity demanded.

Unit elasticity of demand A demand relationship in which the quantity demanded changes exactly in proportion to the changes in price.

Inelastic demand A demand relationship in which a given percentage change in price will result in a less than proportionate percentage change in the quantity demanded.

3. **Inelastic demand** is a demand relationship in which a given percentage change in price will result in a less than proportionate percentage change in the quantity demanded. In a situation of inelastic demand, a 1 percent change in price causes a response of less than a 1 percent change in the quantity demanded.

When we say a commodity's demand is elastic, we are indicating that consumers are relatively responsive to changes in price. When we say that a commodity's demand is inelastic, we are indicating that its consumers are relatively unresponsive to price changes. When economists say that demand is inelastic, it does not mean that quantity demanded is totally unresponsive to price changes. Remember, the law of demand suggests that there will be some responsiveness in quantity demanded to a price change. The question is how much. That is what elasticity attempts to determine. As you can see from Policy Example 4–1, who actually pays when a tax is imposed depends on whether the demand for the product is elastic or inelastic. So, if you are a smoker and a tax is imposed, are you going to pay most of that tax or will the producer absorb the tax?

POLICY EXAMPLE 4–1   Who Pays Higher Cigarette Taxes?

Governments impose cigarette taxes, which are assessed as a flat amount per pack sold. These taxes are paid by sellers of cigarettes from the revenues they earn from their total sales. Thus, to receive the same effective price for selling a given quantity, a cigarette seller would have to receive a price that is higher by exactly the amount of the tax. As shown in part (a) of Figure 4–1, this means that imposing a cigarette tax shifts the supply curve upward by the amount of the tax. Sellers supply a given quantity of cigarettes at a price that is higher by the amount of the tax that they will transmit to the government.

Who *truly* pays the tax depends on the price elasticity of demand, however. Take a look at part (b) of Figure 4–1, which illustrates what would happen to the market price in the case of perfectly inelastic demand for cigarettes. In this instance, the market price rises by the full amount that the supply curve shifts upward. This amount, of course, is the amount of the tax. Consequently, if cigarette consumers were to have a perfectly inelastic demand for cigarettes, they would effectively pay the entire tax in the form of higher prices. Part (c) illustrates the opposite case, in which the demand for cigarettes happens to be perfectly elastic. In this situation, the

continued

FIGURE 4–1

Price Elasticity and a Cigarette Tax

Placing a per-pack tax on cigarettes causes the supply curve to shift upward by the amount of the tax, as illustrated in part (a), in order for sellers to receive the same effective price for any given quantity of cigarettes they sell. If the demand for cigarettes were perfectly inelastic, as depicted in part (b), imposing the tax would cause the market price of cigarettes to rise by the amount of the tax, so that cigarette consumers would effectively pay all the tax. Conversely, if the demand for cigarettes were perfectly elastic, as shown in part (c), the market price would not change, and sellers would pay all the tax. The quantity demanded would fall to Q_2.

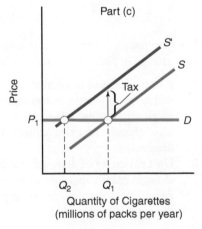

market price is unresponsive to a tax-induced shift in the supply curve, so sellers must pay all the tax.

   Realistically, the price elasticity of demand for cigarettes is relatively low—most cigarette price elasticity estimates indicate values of 0.2 to 0.4. Thus, the burden of cigarette taxes falls mainly on cigarette consumers.

For critical analysis: Based on the information in this example, if taxes on cigarettes increase by 10 percent, by what range of percentages may desired cigarette purchases decline?

Extreme Elasticities

There are two extremes in price elasticities of demand. One extreme represents total unresponsiveness of quantity demanded to price changes, which is referred to as **perfectly inelastic demand**, or zero elasticity—a demand that exhibits zero responsiveness to price changes. The other represents total responsiveness, which is referred to as infinitely elastic demand, or **perfectly elastic demand**—even the slightest increase in price will lead to zero quantity demanded.

   We show perfect inelasticity in part (a) of Figure 4–2. Note that the quantity demanded per year is 8 million units, no matter what the price. Hence, for any percentage price change, the quantity demanded will remain the same, and thus, the change in the quantity demanded will be zero. Look back at our formula for computing elasticity. If the change in the quantity demanded is zero, the numerator is also zero, and a nonzero number divided into zero results in an answer of zero, too. Hence, there is perfect inelasticity.

Perfectly inelastic demand A demand that exhibits zero responsiveness to price changes.

Perfectly elastic demand A demand that has the characteristic that even the slightest increase in price will lead to zero quantity demanded.

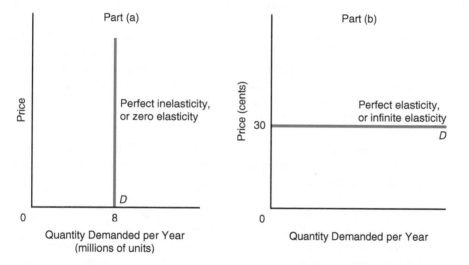

FIGURE 4–2

Extreme Price Elasticities

In part (a), we show complete price unresponsiveness. The demand curve is vertical at the quantity of 8 million units per year. This means that the price elasticity of demand is zero. In part (b), we show complete price responsiveness. At a price of 30 cents, in this example, consumers will demand an unlimited quantity of the particular good in question. This is a case of infinite price elasticity of demand.

At the opposite extreme is the situation depicted in part (b) of Figure 4–2. Here, we show that at a price of 30 cents, an unlimited quantity will be demanded. At a price that is only slightly above 30 cents, no quantity will be demanded. There is complete, or infinite, responsiveness here, and hence, we call the demand schedule in part (b) infinitely elastic or perfectly elastic.

Elasticity and Total Revenues

Suppose that you are in charge of the pricing decision for a cellphone service company. How would you know when it is best to raise or not to raise prices? The answer depends, in part, on the effect of your pricing decision on total revenues, or the total receipts of your company. (The rest of the equation is, of course, your cost structure, a subject we examine later.) It is commonly thought that the way to increase total receipts is to increase price per unit. But is this always the case? Is it possible that a rise in price per unit could lead to a decrease in total revenues? The answers to these questions depend on the price elasticity of demand.

Let us look at Figure 4–3. In part (a), column 1 shows the price of cellphone service in dollars per minute, and column 2 represents billions of minutes demanded per year. In column 3, we multiply column 1 by column 2 to derive total revenue because total revenue is always equal to the number of units (quantity) sold times the price per unit. In column 4, we calculate values of elasticity. Note what happens to total revenues throughout the schedule. They rise steadily as the price rises from 10 cents to 50 cents per minute; but when the price rises further to 60 cents per minute, total revenues remain constant at $3 billion. At prices per minute higher than 60 cents, total revenues fall as price increases. Indeed, if prices are above 60 cents per minute, total revenues can be increased only by *cutting* prices, not by raising them.

Labelling Elasticity

The relationship between price and quantity on the demand schedule is given in columns 1 and 2 of part (a) in Figure 4–3. Part (b) shows the demand curve, *D*, representing that schedule. Part (c) shows the total revenue curve representing the data in column 3. Note, first, the level of these curves at small quantities. The demand curve is at a maximum height, but total revenue is zero, which makes sense according to this demand schedule— at a price of $1.10 and above, no units will be purchased, and therefore, total revenue will be zero. As the price is lowered, we travel down the demand curve, and total revenues increase until the price is 60 cents per minute, remain constant from 60 cents to 50 cents per minute, and then fall at lower unit prices. Corresponding to those three sections, demand is elastic, unit-elastic, and inelastic. Hence, we have three relationships among the three types of price elasticity and total revenues.

1. *Elastic demand.* For some products, consumers are very price sensitive. If the price is lowered, total revenues will rise when the firm faces demand that is elastic, and if it raises the price, total revenues will fall. Consider another example. If the price of Diet Coke were raised by 25 percent and the price of all other soft drinks remained constant, the quantity demanded of Diet Coke would probably fall dramatically. The decrease in quantity demanded due to the increase in the price of Diet Coke would lead, in this example, to a reduction in the total revenues of the Coca-Cola Company. Therefore, if demand is elastic, price and total revenues will move in *opposite* directions.

2. *Unit-elastic demand.* When the firm is facing demand that is unit-elastic, if it increases the price, total revenues will not change. If it decreases the price, total revenues will not change either. If demand is unit-elastic, changes in price do not change total revenues.

3. *Inelastic demand.* For some products, consumers are not sensitive to price changes. When the firm is facing demand that is inelastic, if it raises the price, total revenues will go up; if it lowers the price, total revenues will fall. Consider another example. You have just invented a cure for the common cold, and the medication has been approved by Health Canada for sale to the public. You are not sure what price you should charge, and so you start out with a price of $1 per pill. You sell 20 million pills at that price over a year. The next year, you decide to raise the price by 25 percent, to $1.25. The number of pills you sell drops to 18 million per year. The price increase of 25 percent has led to a 10 percent decrease in quantity demanded. Your total revenues, however, will rise to $22.5 million because of the price increase. We therefore conclude that if demand is inelastic, price and total revenues move in the *same* direction.

The elastic, unit-elastic, and inelastic areas of the demand curve are shown in Figure 4–3. For prices from $1.10 per minute of cellphone time to 60 cents per minute, as the price decreases, total revenues rise from zero to $3 billion. Demand is price-elastic. When the price changes from 60 cents to 50 cents, however, total revenues remain constant at $3 billion; demand is unit-elastic. Finally, when the price falls from 50 cents to 10 cents, total revenues decrease from $3 billion to $1 billion; demand is inelastic. In parts (b) and (c) of Figure 4–3,

FIGURE 4–3

The Relationship between Price Elasticity of Demand and Total Revenues for Cellphone Service

In part (a), we show the elastic, unit-elastic, and inelastic sections of the demand schedule according to whether a reduction in price increases total revenues, causes them to remain constant, or causes them to decrease, respectively. In part (b), we show these regions graphically on the demand curve. In part (c), we show them on the total revenue curve.

Part (a)

(1) Price, P, per Minute of Cellphone Service	(2) Quantity Demanded, D (billions of minutes)	(3) Total Revenue ($ billions) = (1) X (2)	(4) Elasticity, $E_p =$ $\dfrac{\text{Change in Q}}{(Q_1 + Q_2)/2}$ $\div$ $\dfrac{\text{Change in P}}{(P_1 + P_2)/2}$
$1.10	0	0	
1.00	1	1.0	21.000 ⎫
0.90	2	1.8	6.330 ⎪
0.80	3	2.4	3.400 ⎬ Elastic
0.70	4	2.8	2.143 ⎪
0.60	5	3.0	1.444 ⎭
0.50	6	3.0	1.000 } Unit-elastic
0.40	7	2.8	0.692 ⎫
0.30	8	2.4	0.467 ⎬ Inelastic
0.20	9	1.8	0.294 ⎪
0.10	10	1.0	0.158 ⎭

Part (b)

Legend:
■ Elastic ($E_p > 1$)
■ Unit-elastic ($E_p = 1$)
■ Inelastic ($E_p < 1$)

Demand, or average revenue, curve

Price per Minute ($) vs. Quantity per Period (billions of minutes)

Part (c)

Legend:
■ Elastic
■ Unit-elastic
■ Inelastic

Total revenue curve

Total Revenue ($ billions) vs. Quantity per Period (billions of minutes)

Price Elasticity of Demand		Effect of Price Change on Total Revenues (TR)	
		Price Decrease	Price Increase
Inelastic	$(E_p < 1)$	TR ↓	TR ↑
Unit-elastic	$(E_p = 1)$	No change in TR	No change in TR
Elastic	$(E_p > 1)$	TR ↑	TR ↓

we have labelled the sections of the demand curve accordingly, and we have also shown how total revenues first rise, then remain constant, and finally fall.

The relationship between price elasticity of demand and total revenues brings together some important microeconomic concepts. Total revenues, as we have noted, are the product of price per unit times number of units sold. The law of demand states that along a given demand curve, price and quantity changes will move in opposite directions: One increases as the other decreases. Consequently, what happens to the product of price times quantity depends on which of the opposing changes exerts a greater force on total revenues. But this is just what price elasticity of demand is designed to measure—responsiveness of quantity demanded to a change in price. The relationship between price elasticity of demand and total revenues is summarized in Table 4–1.

4.3   Determinants of the Price Elasticity of Demand

We have learned how to calculate the price elasticity of demand. We know that, theoretically, it ranges numerically from zero (completely inelastic) to infinity (completely elastic). What we would like to do now is come up with a list of the determinants of the price elasticity of demand. The price elasticity of demand for a particular commodity at any price depends, at a minimum, on the following nonprice determinants:

1.   the existence, number, and quality of substitutes
2.   the percentage of a consumer's total budget devoted to purchases of that commodity
3.   the length of time allowed for adjustment to changes in the price of the commodity

Existence of Substitutes

The closer the substitutes for a particular commodity and the more substitutes there are, the greater will be its price elasticity of demand. At the limit, if there is a perfect substitute, the elasticity of demand for the commodity will be infinite. Thus, even the slightest increase in the commodity's price will cause an enormous reduction in the quantity demanded; quantity demanded will fall to zero. We are really talking about two goods that the consumer believes are exactly alike and equally desirable, like five-dollar bills whose only difference is serial numbers. When we talk about less extreme examples, we can only speak in terms of the number and the similarity of substitutes that are available. Thus, we will find that the more narrowly we define a good, the closer and greater will be the number of substitutes available. For example, the demand for Diet Coke may be highly elastic because consumers can switch to Diet Pepsi. The demand for diet drinks in general, however, is relatively less elastic because there are fewer substitutes.

Share of Budget

We know that the greater the percentage of a person's total budget spent on a commodity, the greater that person's price elasticity of demand for that commodity. The demand for pepper is thought to be very inelastic merely because individuals spend so little on it relative to their total budgets. In contrast, the demand for such things as transportation and housing is thought to be far more elastic because they occupy a large part of people's budgets. Changes in their prices cannot be ignored so easily without sacrificing a lot of other alternative goods that could be purchased.

Consider a numerical example. A household earns $40 000 per year. It spends $4 on pepper per year and $4000 on transportation services. Now, consider the spending power of this family when the price of pepper and the price of transportation both go up by 100 percent. If the household buys the same amount of pepper, it will now spend $8. It will thus have to reduce other expenditures by $4. This $4 represents only 0.01 percent of the entire household budget. By contrast, a doubling of transportation costs requires that the family spend $8000 on transportation, if it is to purchase the same quantity. That increased expenditure on transportation of $4000 represents 10 percent of total expenditures that must be switched from other purchases. We would therefore predict that the household will react differently to the doubling of prices for pepper than it will for transportation. It will buy almost the same amount of pepper but will spend significantly less on transportation.

Time for Adjustment

When the price of a commodity changes and that price change persists, more people will learn about it. Further, consumers will be better able to revise their consumption patterns when they have more time to do so. In fact, the longer they do take, the less costly it will be for them to engage in this revision of consumption patterns. Consider a price decrease. The longer the price decrease persists, the greater will be the number of new uses that consumers will discover for the particular commodity, and the greater will be the number of new users of that particular commodity.

The longer any price change persists, the greater is the elasticity of demand, if other things hold constant. Elasticity of demand is greater in the long run than in the short run.

Let us take an example. Suppose that the price of electricity goes up by 50 percent. How do you adjust in the short run? You can turn the lights off more often, you can stop using the stereo as much as you do, and so on. Otherwise it is very difficult to cut back on your consumption of electricity. In the long run, though, you can devise methods to reduce your consumption. Instead of using electric heating, the next time you have a house built, you might install solar heating. Instead of using an electric stove, the next time you move, you might have a gas stove installed. You might purchase fluorescent bulbs because they use less electricity. The more time you have to think about it, the more ways you will find to cut your electricity consumption. We would expect, therefore, that the short-run demand curve for electricity would be relatively inelastic (in the price range around P_e), as demonstrated by D_1 in Figure 4–4. However, the long-run demand curve may exhibit

Why might the price for elasticity of demand for transportation be greater than the price elasticity of demand for, say, salt?

Quantity Demanded per Period

FIGURE 4–4

Short-Run and Long-Run Price Elasticity of Demand

Consider an equilibrium situation in which the market price is P_e and the quantity demanded is Q_e. Then, there is a price increase to P_1. In the short run, as evidenced by the demand curve D_1, we move from equilibrium quantity demanded, Q_e, to Q_1. After more time is allowed for adjustment, the demand curve rotates at original price P_e to D_2. Quantity demanded falls again, now to Q_2. After even more time is allowed for adjustment, the demand curve rotates at price P_e to D_3. At the higher price P_1, in the long run, the quantity demanded falls all the way to Q_3.

much more elasticity (in the neighbourhood of P_e), as demonstrated by D_3. Indeed, we can think of an entire family of demand curves, such as those depicted in that figure. The short-run demand curve is for the period when there is no time for adjustment. As more time is allowed, the demand curve goes first to D_2 and then all the way to D_3. Thus, in the neighbourhood of P_e, elasticity differs for each of these curves. It is greater for the less steep curves (but slope alone does not measure elasticity for the entire curve).

Example 4–3 clearly shows that long-run price elasticities of demand tend to exceed the short-run elasticities.

HOW TO DEFINE THE SHORT RUN AND THE LONG RUN. We have mentioned the short run and the long run. Is the short run one week, two weeks, one month, or two months? Is the long run three years, four years, or five years? The answer is that there is no single answer. What we mean by the long run is the period of time necessary for consumers to make a full adjustment to a given price change, all other things held constant. In the case of the demand for electricity, the long run will be however long it takes consumers to switch over to cheaper sources of heating, to buy houses that are more energy efficient, to purchase appliances that are more energy efficient, and so on. The long-run elasticity of demand for electricity, therefore, relates to a period of at least several years. The short run—by default—is any period less than the long run.

Does the addition of solar panels to a newly built house represent a short-run or a long-run response to an increase in the price of electricity?

EXAMPLE 4–3   What Do Real-World Price Elasticities of Demand Look Like?

In Table 4–2, we present demand elasticities for selected goods. None of them is zero, and the largest is 4.6. Remember that even though we are leaving off the negative sign, there is an inverse relationship between price and quantity demanded, and the minus sign is understood. Also remember that these elasticities represent averages over given price ranges. Choosing different price ranges could yield different elasticity estimates for these goods.

Economists have consistently found that estimated price elasticities of demand are greater in the long run than in the short run, as seen in Table 4–2. There you see that all available estimates indicate that the long-run price elasticity of demand for vacation air travel is 2.7, whereas the estimate for the short run is 1.1. Throughout the table, you see that all estimates of long-run price elasticities of demand exceed their short-run counterparts.

TABLE 4–2

Price Elasticity of Demand for Selected Goods

Here are estimated demand elasticities for selected goods. All of them are negative, although we omit the minus sign. We have given some estimates of the long-run price elasticities of demand. The long run is associated with the time necessary for consumers to adjust fully to any given price change. (Note: "N.A." indicates that no estimate is available.)

	Estimated Elasticity	
Category	Short Run	Long Run
Air travel (business)	0.4	1.2
Air travel (vacation)	1.1	2.7
Beef	0.6	N.A.
Cheese	0.3	N.A.
Electricity	0.1	1.7
Fresh tomatoes	4.6	N.A.
Gasoline	0.2	0.5
Intercity bus service	0.6	2.2
Private education	1.1	1.9
Restaurant meals	2.3	N.A.
Tires	0.9	1.2

For critical analysis: Explain the intuitive reasoning behind the difference between long-run and short-run price elasticity of demand.

4.4 Cross-Elasticity of Demand

In an earlier chapter, we discussed the effect of a change in the price of one good on the demand for a related good. We defined substitutes and complements in terms of whether a reduction in the price of one caused a decrease or an increase in the demand for the other. If the price of compact discs (CDs) is held constant, the amount of CDs demanded (at any price) will certainly be influenced by the price of a close substitute, such as MP3 players. If the price of stereo speakers is held constant, the amount of stereo speakers demanded (at any price) will certainly be affected by changes in the price of stereo amplifiers.

What we now need to do is come up with a numerical measure of the price responsiveness of demand to the prices of related goods. This is called the **cross-elasticity of demand (E_{xy})**, which is defined as the percentage change in the quantity demanded of one good (holding its price constant) divided by the percentage change in the price of the related good. In equation form, the cross-elasticity of demand for good X with respect to good Y is

$$E_{xy} = \frac{\text{Percentage change in quantity demanded of good X}}{\text{Percentage change in price of good Y}}$$

Cross-elasticity of demand (E_{xy}) The percentage change in the quantity demanded of one good (holding its price constant) divided by the percentage change in the price of a related good.

When two goods are substitutes, the cross-elasticity of demand will be positive. For example, when the price of margarine goes up, the demand for butter will rise as consumers shift away from the now relatively more expensive margarine to butter. A producer of margarine could benefit from a numerical estimate of the cross-elasticity of demand between butter and margarine. For example, if the price of butter went up by 10 percent and the margarine producer knew that the cross-elasticity of demand was 1, the margarine producer could estimate that the demand for margarine would also go up by 10 percent at any given price. Plans for increasing margarine production could then be made.

When two related goods are complements, the cross-elasticity of demand will be negative (and we will not disregard the minus sign). For example, when the price of stereo amplifiers goes up, the demand for stereo speakers will fall. This is because as prices of amplifiers increase, the quantity of amplifiers demanded will naturally decrease. Because amplifiers and stereo speakers are often used together, the demand for speakers is likely to fall. Any manufacturer of stereo speakers must take this into account in making production plans. In this chapter's Issues and Applications, we look at whether increasing taxes on beer would lead to a decrease in cigarette consumption. If beer and cigarettes are complements, then the cross-elasticity of demand will be negative, and when the price of beer goes up the demand for cigarettes will fall.

If goods are completely unrelated, their cross-elasticity of demand will be zero. Read Policy Example 4–2 for further discussion of cross-elasticity.

POLICY EXAMPLE 4–2   **Do People Substitute Wireless Phone Services for Wired Services?**

If people regard cellphones as a form of communication that they use mainly on the go and traditional land-wired phone service as a means of communication from their homes, then the two types of services are not substitutes. In contrast, if people respond to higher prices of land-wired phone service by consuming more wireless phone services instead—and perhaps using only wireless services—then they are substitute services.

Recently, two economists, Allan Ingraham and J. Gregory Sidak, estimated that the cross-elasticity of demand between wireless and wired phone services is about 0.02. This estimate implies that a 10 percent increase in the price of land-wired phone services induces a 0.2 percent increase in the quantity of wireless phone services demanded. The two types of phone services are substitutes, but the degree of substitution is very slight.

For critical analysis: As younger people, who tend to use cellphones more than land-line phones, gradually replace their elders, what is likely to happen to the cross-elasticity of demand for the two types of telecommunications services?

Income Elasticity of Demand

In Chapter 3, we discussed the determinants of demand. One of those determinants was income. Briefly, we can apply our understanding of elasticity to the relationship between changes in income and changes in demand. We measure the responsiveness of quantity demanded to income changes by the *income elasticity of demand* (E_i), holding relative price constant:

$$E_i = \frac{\text{Percentage change in quantity demanded}}{\text{Percentage change in income}}$$

Income elasticity of demand A horizontal shift in the demand curve in response to changes in income.

Price elasticity of demand A movement along the curve in response to price changes.

Income elasticity of demand refers to a *horizontal shift* in the demand curve in response to changes in income, whereas **price elasticity of demand** refers to a movement *along* the curve in response to price changes. Thus, income elasticity of demand is calculated at a given price, and price elasticity of demand is calculated at a given income.

A simple example will demonstrate how income elasticity of demand can be computed. Table 4–3 gives the relevant data. The product in question is DVDs. We assume that the price of DVDs remains constant relative to other prices. In period 1, six DVDs per month are purchased. Income per month is $400. In period 2, monthly income increases to $600, and the quantity of DVDs demanded per month increases to eight. Using the same mid-point formula that we used in computing the price elasticity of demand, we get:

$$E_i = \frac{(8-6)/7}{(600-400)/500} = \frac{2/7}{2/5} = \frac{5}{7} = 0.714$$

Note that the sign of the income elasticity of demand is positive. That is because as income rises, the quantity of DVDs demanded also increases. In Chapter 3, we defined this kind of good as a "normal" good—one that we want more of as our income increases. An "inferior" good is one that we want less of as our income increases. The sign of the income elasticity of demand for an inferior good will therefore be negative, since quantity demanded will decrease as income increases. It is important to retain the negative sign on the income elasticity of demand for an inferior good, since the sign tells us whether the good is, in fact, normal or inferior.

You have just been introduced to three types of elasticities. Two of them—the price elasticity of demand (E_p), and income elasticity (E_i)—are the two most important factors in influencing the quantity demanded for most goods. Reasonably accurate estimates of these can go a long way toward making accurate forecasts of demand for goods or services. For an illustration of income elasticity, see Example 4–4. Should Canadian Tire "Money" be considered income, just like frequent flyer points?

TABLE 4–3

How Income Affects Quantity of DVDs Demanded

Period	Number of DVDs Demanded per Month	Income per Month
1	6	$400
2	8	600

EXAMPLE 4–4 **Frequent Flyer Miles as Income**

For the past 20 years, airlines have been discovering that consumers measure their income in more than one way. Most airlines now offer frequent flyer points for air travel, and many are affiliated with other businesses as well. For example, Air Canada gives frequent flyer points for renting cars from Budget and for staying in any number of hotels. Travellers can also apply for a Visa card that gives them one frequent flyer mile for every dollar charged. Airlines have found the demand for their services is increasing. It appears that air travellers count their frequent flyer miles as part of their incomes and, thus, they demand more air travel as their incomes increase. As anyone who has ever shopped at Canadian Tire knows, Canadian Tire money can add up quickly. Some of the older Canadian Tire money is even traded on eBay.

continued

For critical analysis: The federal government has decided that the value of flights paid for with frequent flyer miles earned while travelling on business should be considered part of an individual's income—and thus subject to income tax. What effect will this have on the income elasticity of demand for air travel?

4.5 Elasticity of Supply

The **price elasticity of supply (E_s)** is defined similarly to the price elasticity of demand— the responsiveness of the quantity supplied of a commodity to a change in its price. Supply elasticities are generally positive. This is because at higher prices, larger quantities will generally be forthcoming from suppliers. The formula for the price elasticity of supply is as follows:

$$E_s = \frac{\text{Percentage change in quantity supplied}}{\text{Percentage change in price}}$$

Price elasticity of supply (E_s) The responsiveness of the quantity supplied of a commodity to a change in its price.

Classifying Supply Elasticities

Just as with demand, there are different types of supply elasticities. They are similar to the types of demand elasticities.

If a 1 percent increase in price elicits a greater than 1 percent increase in the quantity supplied, we say that at the particular price in question on the supply schedule, *supply is elastic.* The most extreme elastic supply is called **perfectly elastic supply**—the slightest reduction in price will cause quantity supplied to fall to zero.

If, conversely, a 1 percent increase in price elicits a less than 1 percent increase in the quantity supplied, we refer to that as an *inelastic supply.* The most extreme inelastic supply is called **perfectly inelastic supply**—no matter what the price, the quantity supplied remains the same.

If the percentage change in the quantity supplied is equal to the percentage change in the price, we call this *unit-elastic supply.*

We show in Figure 4–5 two supply schedules, *S* and *S'.* You can tell at a glance, without reading the labels, which one is perfectly elastic and which one is perfectly inelastic. As you might expect, most supply schedules exhibit elasticities that are somewhere between zero and infinity.

Perfectly elastic supply When the slightest reduction in price will cause quantity supplied to fall to zero.

Perfectly inelastic supply When no matter what the price, the quantity supplied remains the same.

Determinants of the Elasticity of Supply

1. SHORT- AND LONG-RUN ELASTICITIES OF SUPPLY   We pointed out earlier that the longer the time period allowed for adjustment, the greater the price elasticity of

Quantity Supplied per Period

FIGURE 4–5

The Extremes in Supply Curves

Here, we have drawn two extremes of supply schedules: *S* is a perfectly elastic supply curve; *S'* is a perfectly inelastic one. In the former, an unlimited quantity will be supplied at price P_1. In the latter, no matter what the price, the quantity supplied will be Q_1. An example of *S'* might be the supply curve for fresh fish on the morning the boats come in.

demand. It turns out that the same proposition applies to supply. The longer the time for adjustment, the more elastic is the supply curve. Consider why this is true:

> **The longer the time allowed for adjustment, the more firms are able to figure out ways to increase (or decrease) production in an industry.**

> **The longer the time allowed for adjustment, the more resources can flow into (or out of) an industry through expansion (or contraction) of existing firms.**

We therefore talk about short-run and long-run price elasticities of supply. The short run is defined as the time period during which full adjustment has not yet taken place. The long run is the time period during which firms have been able to adjust fully to the change in price.

Consider an increase in the price of housing. In the very short run, when there is no time allowed for adjustment, the amount of housing offered for rent or for sale is relatively inelastic. However, as more time is allowed for adjustment, current owners of the housing stock can find ways to increase the amount of housing they will offer for rent from given buildings. The owner of a large house can decide, for example, to have two children move into one room so that a "new" extra bedroom can be rented out. This can also be done by the owner of a large house who decides to move into an apartment and rent each floor of the house to a separate family. Thus, the quantity of housing supplied will increase. With more time, landlords will find it profitable to build new rental units.

We can show a whole set of supply curves similar to the ones we generated for demand. As Figure 4–6 shows, when nothing can be done in the short run, the supply curve is vertical, S_1. As more time is allowed for adjustment, the supply curve rotates to S_2 and then to S_3, becoming more elastic as it rotates.

2. AVAILABILITY OF RAW MATERIALS If the supply of raw materials, such as oil, is limited and non-renewable, a change in production may be hard for firms, making supply inelastic. If producers can increase their output without a rise in costs, then supply is elastic.

3. COMPLEXITY OF PRODUCTION If the production process is relatively easy and labour is unskilled and mobile, supply is elastic. If the production process is more complex and not as mobile, supply is inelastic.

4. EXCESS CAPACITY AND INVENTORIES If the supplier has excess capacity, it is easier to increase supply to the market. A producer who has a ready supply of the product can quickly increase its supply to the market.

FIGURE 4–6

Short-Run and Long-Run Price Elasticity of Supply

Consider a situation in which the price is P_e and the quantity supplied is Q_e. In the short run, we hypothesize a vertical supply curve, S_1. With the price increase to P_1, therefore, there will be no change in the short run in quantity supplied; it will remain at Q_e. Given some time for adjustment, the supply curve will rotate to S_2. The new amount supplied will increase to Q_1. The long-run supply curve is shown by S_3. The amount supplied again increases to Q_2.

ISSUES AND APPLICATIONS

To Combat Cigarette Consumption, Should the Government Raise Taxes on Beer?

Concepts Applied: Price Elasticity of Demand, Cross-Elasticity of Demand

Smoking and drinking seem to go hand in hand.

According to the National Cancer Institute, cigarette smoking and other forms of tobacco use are directly responsible for at least one-third of all cancer deaths each year. Cigarette smoking contributes to the development of cancers of the lungs, head and neck, and throat. In addition, cigarette smoking contributes to cardiovascular disease and significantly raises the chance a heart attack. Smoking also poses problems for fetuses. Women who smoke during pregnancy are more likely to give birth to babies with below-average weights.

The Price Elasticity of Demand for Cigarettes

Why do so many people continue to smoke? One reason is that the average price of a cigarette sold in Canada is not much more than 40 cents. Among bad habits that people can pick up, smoking remains one of the least expensive.

In addition, cigarettes contain nicotine, which is a very addictive substance. This undoubtedly helps explain why the price elasticity of cigarette demand is approximately 0.3. Because the demand for cigarettes is relatively inelastic, relatively large price increases would be required to bring about a significant decline in cigarette consumption.

Taxation Policies to Combat Cigarette Consumption

Both the provincial and the federal governments levy taxes on cigarettes. Because the demand for cigarettes is inelastic, the market price of cigarettes reflects most of these taxes. Consequently, consumers pay the bulk of cigarette taxes, which account for about 77 percent of the average after-tax price of a pack of cigarettes.

Critics of the cigarette tax policy contend that in light of the relatively low price elasticity of demand for cigarettes, much higher taxes would be required to generate a significant drop in cigarette consumption. Canada raised taxes and found that teenage smoking fell from 42 percent to 16 percent, but smuggling of cigarettes increased.

Reducing Cigarette Consumption via Taxation of Alcohol?

Recently, some economists have proposed raising taxes on alcohol as another means of discouraging cigarette consumption. Their idea originates from the observation that bars are often smoke filled, which suggests that many people who drink regard alcoholic beverages as complements to cigarette smoking. Heavier taxes on alcohol would push up the price of alcoholic beverages, thereby generating a reduction in cigarette consumption.

Estimates indicate that the cross-elasticity of demand for cigarettes is approximately −0.2; each 10 percent increase in the price of beer thereby reduces cigarette demand by about 2 percent, and so cigarette smokers do indeed regard beer as a complement to cigarette consumption. Significant increases in taxes on beer could potentially supplement the use of cigarette taxes as a means of discouraging cigarette consumption.

Higher alcohol taxes would also help discourage the excessive use of alcohol, which imposes its own public health costs. The price elasticity of the demand for beer is only slightly less than 1, meaning that the demand for beer is nearly unit-elastic. This implies that a significant percentage increase in the price of beer due to higher taxes on beer would generate a nearly equal percentage reduction in beer consumption. In principle, therefore, higher taxes on beer and other alcoholic beverages could contribute to improved public health by reducing consumption of both cigarettes and alcohol.

For critical analysis:

1. On the basis of the information given here, would you expect that beer consumers pay a higher portion of the total tax on each unit of beer, compared with the fraction of the total tax that cigarette consumers pay on each pack of cigarettes? Why?

2. If a beer producer and a cigarette producer both raise their prices, which is more likely to experience an increase in total revenues? Explain.

SUMMARY

Here is what you should know after reading this chapter. MyEconLab will help you identify what you know, and where to go when you need to practise. We suggest that as soon as you review one of the Learning Objective sections below, you then proceed to go through the related section in MyEconLab.

LEARNING OBJECTIVES	KEY TERMS	MYECONLAB PRACTICE
4.1 Price Elasticity of Demand. Price elasticity of demand is a measure of the percentage change in quantity demanded relative to the percentage change in price, given income, the prices of other goods, and time. Because of the law of demand, price elasticity of demand is always negative.	price elasticity of demand (E_p), 93	• **MyEconLab** Study Plan 4.1
4.2 Price Elasticity Ranges. We classify demand as *elastic* if a 1 percent change in price leads to a more than 1 percent change in quantity demanded, *unit-elastic* if it leads to exactly a 1 percent change in quantity demanded, and *inelastic* if it leads to less than a 1 percent change in quantity demanded. When facing a perfectly elastic demand, the slightest increase in price leads to zero quantity demanded; when facing a perfectly inelastic demand, no matter what the price, the quantity demanded remains unchanged. Perfect inelasticity means absolutely no price responsiveness. Price elasticity of demand falls as we move down a straight-line demand curve. It goes from infinity to zero. Elasticity and slope are not equivalent; for example, the slope of a straight-line curve is always constant, whereas elasticity changes as we move along a linear curve. A vertical demand curve is perfectly inelastic; a horizontal demand curve is perfectly elastic.	elastic demand, 95 unit elasticity of demand, 95 inelastic demand, 96 perfectly inelastic demand, 96 perfectly elastic demand, 96	• **MyEconLab** Study Plan 4.2

LEARNING OBJECTIVES	KEY TERMS	myeconlab MYECONLAB PRACTICE
4.3 Determinants of the Price Elasticity of Demand. Price elasticity of demand depends on (a) the existence, number, and quality of substitutes, (b) the share of total budget accounted for by the commodity, and (c) the length of time allowed for adjustment to changes in the price of the commodity.		• **MyEconLab** Study Plan 4.3
4.4 Cross-Elasticity of Demand. Cross-elasticity of demand measures the responsiveness of the demand for one product, either a substitute or a complement, to changes in the price of another product. When the cross-elasticity of demand is negative, the two commodities under study are complements; when the cross-elasticity of demand is positive, they are substitutes. Income elasticity of demand is given by the percentage change in quantity demanded divided by the percentage change in income, given the relative price. When the income elasticity of demand is positive, the good in question is a normal good; when the income elasticity of demand is negative, the good is an inferior good.	cross-elasticity of demand, (E_{xy}) 103 income elasticity of demand, 104 price elasticity of demand, 104	• **MyEconLab** Study Plan 4.4
4.5 Price Elasticity of Supply. Price elasticity of supply is given by the percentage change in quantity supplied divided by the percentage change in price. The greater the time allowed for adjustment, the availability of raw materials, the complexity of production, and the inventories, the greater the price elasticity of supply.	price elasticity of supply (E_s), 105 perfectly elastic supply, 105 perfectly inelastic supply, 105	• **MyEconLab** Study Plan 4.5

PROBLEMS

(Answers to the odd-numbered problems appear at the back of the book.)

LO 4.1 Define price elasticity of demand and calculate it using two different methods.

1. Use the following hypothetical demand schedule for tea to answer the questions.

Quantity Demanded per Week (kilograms)	Price per Kilogram	Elasticity
1000	$ 5	
800	10	
600	15	
400	20	
200	25	

   a. Using the mid-point formula, determine the elasticity of demand for each price change. (Example: When price changes from $5 to $10, quantity demanded changes from 1000 to 800 kilograms, so the elasticity of demand, using average values, is $1/3$ or 0.33.)
   b. Could coffee be considered a substitute for tea?
   c. Would you consider this commodity a luxury or a necessity?

2. Calculate the price elasticity of demand for the product in the table below using average values for the prices and quantities in your formula. Over the price range in question, is this demand schedule inelastic, unit-elastic, or elastic? Is total revenue greater at the lower price or the higher price?

Price per Unit	Quantity Demanded
$4	22
6	18

3. A new mobile home park charges nothing for water used by its inhabitants. Consumption is 100 000 litres per month. The decision is then made to charge according to how much each mobile home owner uses, at a rate of $10 per 1000 litres. Consumption declines to 50 000 litres per month. What is the difficulty here in accurately estimating the price elasticity of the demand for water by these residents?

4. Suppose that the price of salt rises from 15 cents to 17 cents a kilogram. The quantity demanded decreases from 525 kilograms to 475 kilograms per month, and the quantity supplied increases from 525 kilograms to 600 kilograms per month. (Use averages in calculating elasticities.)
   a. Calculate the price elasticity of demand (E_p) for salt.
   b. Is the demand for salt price-elastic or price-inelastic?

5. Suppose that an automobile dealer cuts his car prices by 15 percent. He then finds that his car sales have increased by 20 percent.
   a. What can you say about the price elasticity of demand for cars?
   b. What will happen to the dealer's total revenue?

6. The diagram below depicts the demand curve for "miniburgers" purchased from Joe's Campus Grill. Use the information in this diagram to answer the following questions.
   a. What is the price elasticity of demand along the range of the demand curve between a price of $0.20 per miniburger and a price of $0.40 per miniburger? Is demand elastic or inelastic over this range?
   b. What is the price elasticity of demand along the range of the demand curve between a price of $0.80 per miniburger and a price of $1.20 per miniburger? Is demand elastic or inelastic over this range?

   c. What is the price elasticity of demand along the range of the demand curve between a price of $1.60 per miniburger and a price of $1.80 per miniburger? Is demand elastic or inelastic over this range?

LO 4.2 Define the three price elasticity ranges and explain their effects on total revenues.

7. Can any demand curve possibly be perfectly inelastic ($E_p = 0$)? Explain.

LO 4.3 Discuss the three factors that determine the price elasticity of demand.

8. Given each example, determine whether price elasticity will tend to be elastic or inelastic.
   a. a 45-cent box of salt you buy once a year
   b. a type of high-powered ski boat you can rent from any number of rental agencies
   c. a 75-cent guitar pick for the lead guitarist of a major rock band

For Example 4–3, "What Do Real-World Price Elasticities of Demand Look Like?", cheese has a price elasticity of demand of around 0.3. Does the quality of substitutes affect this elasticity?

LO 4.4 Describe the effects of substitutes, complements, and income on elasticity of demand.

9. Calculate the income elasticity of demand for the product in the following table, using average values for incomes and quantities.

Quantity of DVD Players per Year	Per Capita Annual Group Income
1000	$15 000
2000	20 000

   a. Is the demand for this product income-elastic or income-inelastic?

   b. Would you consider this commodity a luxury or a necessity?

10. Which of the following cross-elasticities of demand would you expect to be positive and which to be negative?

   a. tennis balls and tennis racquets

   b. tennis balls and golf balls

   c. dental services and toothpaste

   d. dental services and candy

   e. soft drinks and ice cubes

   f. soft drinks and fruit juices

LO 4.5 Define price elasticity of supply and describe the difference between the long-run and short-run supply schedules.

11. Suppose that the price of salt rises from 15 cents to 17 cents a kilogram. The quantity demanded decreases from 525 kilograms to 475 kilograms per month, and the quantity supplied increases from 525 kilograms to 600 kilograms per month. (Use averages in calculating elasticities.)

   a. Calculate the elasticity of supply (E_s) for salt.

   b. Is the supply of salt price-elastic or price-inelastic?

12. From Issues and Applications, "To Combat Cigarette Consumption, Should the Government Raise Taxes on Beer?", we found out that smokers regard beer as a complement. If taxes are increased on beer, what will happen to cigarette consumption?

BUSINESS APPLICATION

LO 4.1 Define price elasticity of demand and calculate it using two different methods.

Finance: Why Have Pharmaceutical Companies Been Profitable Investments?

The following graph shows a comparison of stock index performance (annualized percent rate of return) for pharmaceutical companies and the Dow Jones industrials.

Business Application Problem

Use the concept of *price elasticity of demand* to explain why pharmaceutical companies have been good stock investments compared to the performance of the stock market as a whole.

6

LEARNING OBJECTIVES

After reading this chapter, you should be able to:

6.1 Explain the role of markets, intermediaries, and prices in the price system.

6.2 Compare and contrast price ceiling and price floor policies.

6.3 Compare and contrast the offer-to-purchase and the marketing board price support policies.

6.4 Describe the various types of quantity restrictions that governments can impose on markets.

6.5 Explain how price elasticity governs the effects that a per-unit excise tax has on tax incidence, resource allocation, and government tax revenue collected.

Extensions of Demand, Supply, and Elasticity

Hospital and bed closures, crowded emergency rooms, health-care worker strikes, physician emigration to the United States, and growing waitlists for a variety of medical treatments have all become part of the daily news across Canada. Politicians, academics, and concerned citizens are debating the merits of using market incentives to address these reported problems. Michael Moore's blockbuster movie documentary *Sicko* urges a movement away from the practice of "for-profit" health care but some politicians consider privatization the best way to improve services.

The concepts presented in this chapter will enhance your ability to understand and evaluate the problems and proposed solutions relating to Canada's health-care system.

MyEconLab helps you master each objective and study more efficiently. See end of chapter for details.

DID YOU KNOW THAT...?

In 2009, about 4.8 million Canadians, representing roughly 17 percent of the population aged 15 years and older, were smokers. Approximately 19 percent of men aged 15 years and older were smokers, compared to 16 percent of women. Daily smokers consumed an average of 13.3 cigarettes per day, a significant decrease from the 15.0 cigarettes per day reported during the same period in 2008. Of the daily smokers, men continued to smoke more cigarettes than women—14.2 cigarettes per day for males, 12.2 cigarettes for females. Young adults aged 20–24 years reported the highest smoking rate, at 21 percent, compared to the 28 percent rate reported in 2008. In the 20–24 years age group, there was a significant decrease in the smoking rate among males; it fell to 25 percent from 32 percent in 2008. The 2009 smoking rate of 18 percent for female young adults was not considered to be significantly lower than the 23 percent reported in 2008. The current smoking rate among youth aged 15–19 years is 14 percent, the lowest rate on record since Health Canada first started reporting for this group.

Sources: "Canadian Tobacco Use Monitoring Survey (CTUMS): CTUMS 2009 Wave 1 survey results. "Health Canada. http://www.hc-sc.gc.ca/hc-ps/tobac-tabac/research-recherche/stat/_ctums-esutc_2009/w-p-1_sum-som-eng.php. (Accessed February 15, 2010.)

6.1 The Price System

A **price system**, otherwise known as a *market system*, is one in which relative prices are constantly changing to reflect changes in supply and demand for different commodities. The prices of those commodities are the signals to everyone within the system as to what is relatively scarce and what is relatively abundant. Indeed, it is the *signalling* aspect of the price system that provides the information to buyers and sellers about what should be bought and what should be produced. In a price system, there is a clear-cut chain of events in which any changes in demand and supply cause changes in prices. Those price changes, in turn, affect the opportunities that businesses and individuals have for profit and personal gain. Such changes influence our use of resources.

Price system An economic system in which relative prices are constantly changing to reflect changes in supply and demand for different commodities.

Exchange and Markets

The price system features **voluntary exchange**, acts of trading between individuals that make both parties to the trade subjectively better off. The **terms of exchange**—the prices we pay for the desired items—are determined by the interaction of the forces underlying supply and demand. In our economy, the majority of exchanges takes place voluntarily in markets. A market encompasses the exchange arrangements of both buyers and sellers that underlie the forces of supply and demand. Indeed, one definition of a market is a low-cost institution for facilitating exchange. A market in essence increases incomes by helping resources move to their highest-valued uses by means of prices. Prices are the providers of information.

Voluntary exchange Acts of trading between individuals that make both parties to the trade subjectively better off.

Terms of exchange The prices we pay for the desired items.

Transaction Costs

Individuals turn to markets because markets reduce the cost of exchanges. These costs are sometimes referred to as **transaction costs**, which are broadly defined as the costs associated with finding out exactly what is being exchanged as well as the cost of enforcing contracts. If you were Robinson Crusoe and lived alone on an island, you would never incur a transaction cost. For everyone else, transaction costs are just as real as the costs of production. High-speed, large-scale computers have allowed us to reduce transaction costs by increasing our ability to process information and keep records.

Consider some simple examples of transaction costs. The supermarket reduces transaction costs relative to your having to go to numerous specialty stores to obtain the items you desire. Organized stock exchanges, such as the Toronto Stock Exchange (TSX), have reduced transaction costs of buying and selling shares and bonds. In general, the more organized the market, the lower are the transaction costs. One group of individuals who constantly attempt to lower transaction costs are intermediaries.

Transaction costs The costs associated with finding out exactly what is being exchanged as well as the cost of enforcing contracts.

The Role of the Intermediary

As long as there are costs to bringing together buyers and sellers, there will be an incentive for intermediaries, often called middlemen, to lower those costs. This means that intermediaries specialize in lowering transaction costs. Whenever producers do not sell their products directly to the final consumer, there are, by definition, one or more intermediaries involved. Farmers typically sell their output to distributors, who are usually called wholesalers, who then sell those products to the retailers, or grocery stores.

Recently, technology has reduced the need, and hence the job prospects, for intermediaries in the travel agent business, as seen in Example 6–1.

EXAMPLE 6–1 Booking Your Airline Flight—An Agent? Or the Web?

For decades, most airline travellers bought their tickets from an independent travel agent, not from the airline itself. On August 27, 2001, Air Canada announced plans to slash the maximum commission it paid to travel agents by half—from 10 percent to 5 percent. In 2002, Air Canada discontinued paying commissions to travel agents for tickets issued in Canada, claiming that this was necessary to remain competitive with other North American airlines, such as American, Continental, and Delta. The purpose of these moves by North American airlines was to encourage consumers to book their flights directly from the airlines' websites.

Topaz International, a leading provider of consultant and audit services to the corporate global travel industry, conducts yearly comparative studies of corporate travel airfares booked through travel agencies and various public Internet sites, including airline websites and travel sites such as Orbitz, Expedia, and Travelocity. Using the results from 2008, Topaz found that business travel itineraries booked through a designated corporate travel agency cost an average of $61 less than the same itinerary booked on an airline's website or other travel website. Moreover, for over 91 percent of the itineraries studied, the travel agency booking resulted in the same or lower fares. This was the eighth consecutive annual study conducted by Topaz International that has confirmed the cost savings that travellers realize when using the services of a professional travel agency.

It is interesting to note that Air Canada resumed paying commissions to travel agents in June 2009.

For critical analysis: List a number of reasons why travellers might benefit from booking their air travel through travel agents rather than directly from the airline websites. Why might they have an even greater preference of booking through agents rather than through hotel websites when they are making accommodation plans?

Sources: CBC News Online Staff. "Travel agents sue over commission cuts." March 5, 2003; Buyers beat web fares, Topaz audits show." Topaz International. http://www.etopaz.com/assets/pdf/internet_audit.pdf; "Air Canada Resumes Paying Travel Agents." *Calgary Herald*. June 5, 2009. Pg. D1.

The Rationing Function of Prices

A shortage creates a situation that forces price to rise toward a market clearing, or equilibrium, level. A surplus brings into play forces that cause the price of a product to fall toward its market clearing level. The synchronization of decisions by buyers and sellers that creates a situation of equilibrium is called the *rationing function of prices*. Prices are indicators of relative scarcity.

An equilibrium price clears the market. The plans of buyers and sellers, given the price, are not frustrated.[1] It is the free interaction of buyers and sellers that sets the price

---

[1]There is a difference between frustration and unhappiness. You may be unhappy because you cannot buy a Rolls-Royce, but if you had sufficient income, you would not be frustrated in your attempt to purchase one at the current market price. By contrast, you would be frustrated if you went to your local supermarket and could get only two cans of your favourite soft drink when you had wanted to purchase a dozen and had the necessary income.

that eventually clears the market. Price, in effect, rations a commodity to demanders who are willing and able to pay the highest price. Whenever the rationing function of prices is frustrated by government-enforced price ceilings that set prices below the market clearing level, a prolonged shortage situation is not allowed to be corrected by the upward adjustment of the price.

You should note that if prices are not allowed to ration goods, services, or resources, other forms of rationing will have to be used. Admission to universities and colleges is often rationed not by tuition (a dollars-and-cents-price) but by grade point average. The highest "bidders" for admission—those with the highest GPAs—are accepted.

There are other ways to ration goods. *First-come, first-served* is one method. *Political power* is another. *Physical force* is yet another. Cultural, religious, and physical differences have been and are used as rationing devices throughout the world.

Consider first-come, first-served as a rationing device. In countries that do not allow prices to reflect true relative scarcity, first-come, first-served has become a way of life. We call this *rationing by queues,* where *queue* means "line." Whoever is willing to wait in line the longest obtains meat that is being sold at less than the market clearing price. All who wait in line are paying a higher *total* price than the money price paid for the meat. Personal time has an opportunity cost. To calculate the total price of the meat, we must add up the money price plus the opportunity cost of the time spent waiting.

In this chapter's Issues and Applications, it is noted that Canada's current medicare system prohibits using prices to ration the services provided by doctors and hospitals. That is, patients are not allowed to pay a price or user fee to gain immediate access to the medical, diagnostic, or surgical services provided by specialist physicians. As a result, rationing by queues has become prevalent in the Canadian health-care system. Indeed, it is estimated that in 2009, Canadians waited an average of 26.1 weeks from the time they received a referral from their general practitioner to the time they received treatment from a medical specialist.

Lotteries are another way to ration goods. You may have been involved in a rationing-by-lottery scheme during your first year in college when you were assigned a parking pass for campus lots. Selling raffle tickets for popular college sweatshirts is also a method of rationing by lottery.

Rationing by *coupons* has also been used, particularly during wartime. In Canada, during World War II, families were allotted coupons that allowed them to purchase specified quantities of rationed goods, such as meat and gasoline. To purchase these goods, you had to pay a specified price *and* give up a coupon.

The Essential Role of Rationing

In a world of scarcity, there is, by definition, competition for what is scarce. After all, any resources that are not scarce can be had by everyone at a zero price in as large a quantity as everyone wants, such as air to burn in internal combustion engines. Once scarcity arises, there has to be some method to ration the available resources, goods, and services. The price system is one form of rationing; the others that we mentioned are alternatives. Economists cannot say which system of rationing is the best. They can, however, say that rationing via the price system leads to the most efficient use of available resources. This means that generally in a price system, further trades could not occur without making somebody worse off. In other words, in a freely functioning price system, all of the gains from mutually beneficial trade will be exhausted.

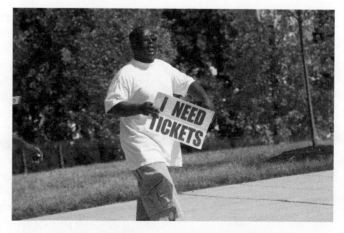

TICKET SCALPING. The issue of using the price system to ration a limited good often arises when the media publicizes the practice of ticket scalping. If you have ever tried to purchase sold-out tickets to a major league playoff game or a superstar's rock concert, you probably know about the practice of ticket scalping.

What economic goal can be served by ticket scalpers?

No matter what the ticket price, the available total quantity of tickets is at Q_1, which is the stadium capacity. The Heritage Classic tickets were originally offered for sale at the "face value" of $135. Just days before the event, the quantity demanded at the ticket price of $135 is Q_2. Without ticket scalpers, there would be a shortage ($Q_2 - Q_1$). If ticket scalping occurs, the ticket price can increase to the equilibrium price of $2500.

For many of these venues, ticket prices are initially set below the equilibrium price so that long lineups develop at ticket counters. These queues increase the media hype surrounding the event. As the day of the big event approaches, scalpers who paid the original price, or "face value," for the tickets end up selling those tickets at a much higher price, either online or just outside the gates, netting a handsome profit.

For example, when tickets were first issued for the 2003 Heritage Classic, the NHL's first outdoor game and star-studded hall-of-famers' match, good seats were selling for $135 each. At this price, the event planners reported that they could have sold 700 000 seats, more than 10 times the capacity of Edmonton's Commonwealth Stadium, where the games were to be played. Just days before the event, online scalpers were asking up to $2500 a ticket—almost 20 times the original price!

Figure 6–1 describes the market conditions for the Heritage Classic just before game day. If there had been no scalping of tickets, the price of each ticket would have remained at the face value of $135, with a shortage of tickets equal to ($Q_2 - Q_1$). However, according to Figure 6–1, there were potential ticket buyers who were willing to pay up to $2500 per ticket to be part of a moment that might come only once in a lifetime. Ticket scalpers were intermediaries who eliminated the shortage situation by getting the Heritage Classic tickets into the hands of consumers who tended to value the tickets the most (i.e., at a price of $2500).

EXAMPLE 6–2   Is Ticketmaster in Cahoots with Scalpers?

In a number of Canadian provinces, ticket scalping is illegal. As result, in February 2009, Canadian ticket purchasers launched a $500-million class action against Ticketmaster. The suit alleges that the popular ticket seller is encouraging scalping of its tickets by limiting the original sale of tickets at face value on its main website and encouraging customers to buy scalped tickets at much higher prices at its subsidiary website, TicketsNow.com. For example, Ticketmaster came under fire for the way it handled ticket sales for Leonard Cohen's Canadian tour. On February 25, 2009, the tickets sold out the minute they officially went on sale at a face value of $99. However, some fans were able to buy these same tickets two days earlier via TicketsNow at the inflated price of $568 each.

A similar lawsuit was launched in the United States. Ticketmaster was charged with redirecting fans unable to buy tickets at face value, seconds after the tickets went on sale, to TicketsNow, where the tickets were selling for hundreds and even thousands of dollars above face value. Ticketmaster earns a lucrative commission for each ticket scalped at TicketsNow.com.

continued

For many economists, anti-scalping laws seem unwarranted. The buying and selling of scalped tickets is purely voluntary. This implies that both the buyer and the seller expect to gain from the exchange, or it would not occur. In other words, ticket scalping is simply the price system's way of efficiently rationing a scarce commodity.

For critical analysis: Sketch a graph showing Leonard Cohen tickets that have a face value of $99 being scalped for $568.

Sources: "Ticketmaster facing $500-million class-action lawsuit." CanWest News. Don Mills, ON.: February 9, 2009; Linda Nguyen. "Ontario begins probe of *Ticketmaster* sales practices; Ticket outlet served with $500-million lawsuit in province." *Vancouver Sun.* March 3, 2009. Pg. C6.

6.2 Price Ceilings and Price Floors

The rationing function of prices is often not allowed to operate when governments impose price controls. **Price controls**—government-mandated minimum or maximum prices that may be charged for goods and services—typically involve setting a **price ceiling**—the maximum price that may be allowed in an exchange. The world has had a long history of price ceilings applied to some goods, wages, rents, and interest rates, among other things. Occasionally, a government will set a **price floor**—a minimum price below which a good or service may not be sold. These have most often been applied to wages and agricultural products. Let us consider price controls in terms of price ceilings.

Price Ceilings: Rent Controls

In order to understand and evaluate a price-ceiling situation, we will use the example of a rent control policy. **Rent control** refers to the placement of a price ceiling or maximum price on rents.

Figure 6–2 describes a hypothetical market situation relating to two-bedroom apartment units in a Canadian city. If there is no government intervention, the equilibrium monthly rental price of a two-bedroom unit is $800 per month. At this price, 60 000 quality two-bedroom units are being supplied and demanded for rental purposes each month.

In response to pressure due to public complaints that apartment rents are excessive, the provincial government decides to implement a price ceiling policy for two-bedroom apartment units. This rent control policy consists of legislating a maximum rental price of $650 per month. Any landlord who charges a monthly rent more than $650 for two-bedroom units would face large fines. The intent of the rent controls is to promote a

Price controls Government-mandated minimum or maximum prices that may be charged for goods and services.

Price ceiling The maximum price that may be allowed in an exchange.

Price floor A minimum price below which a good or service may not be sold.

Rent control The placement of a price ceiling or maximum price on rents.

FIGURE 6–2

Price Ceiling Policy: Rent Controls on Two-Bedroom Apartments

If there is no government intervention in this apartment market, the equilibrium monthly rent will be $800 per month and the equilibrium quantity will be 60 000 units per month. Under rent controls, with a price ceiling of $650 per month, landlords will wish to supply only 50 000 quality two-bedroom rental units per month, while tenants will demand 70 000 units per month. A shortage of 20 000 units per month will eventually emerge. Moreover, once the quantity supplied is reduced to 50 000 units per month, according to the demand curve, there will be consumers who will pay a black market price up to $1000 per month.

more equitable distribution of income or simply "equity." That is, the government hopes to use the price ceiling policy as a means of ensuring that quality two-bedroom units remain affordable to lower-income families. By reducing the monthly rent charged, there will be a transfer of income from higher-income landlords to lower-income tenants (consumers).

What can we predict about the effects of the rent control policy, on the basis of the theory of supply and demand? In Figure 6–2, the price or rent of each two-bedroom unit is now set at $650 per month, which is below the equilibrium price. As is the case with any effective price ceiling policy, the maximum price will only replace the free market price if it is set below the equilibrium. As Figure 6–2 illustrates, at a monthly rent of $650 per month, 50 000 quality two-bedroom units will tend to be supplied per month (in the long run), while 70 000 apartment units would be demanded per month. A shortage of 20 000 units per month will result in the long run.

Nonprice-rationing devices Methods used to ration scarce goods that are price controlled.

The price ceiling policy leads to fewer exchanges and **nonprice-rationing devices**, which are methods used to ration scarce goods that are price controlled. With the rent controls imposed, the price system is no longer allowed to eliminate the shortage of apartment units. In other words, the available supply of apartment units is rationed according to nonprice criteria, such as first-come, first-served, or "rent only to friends," or "rent to desirable-looking people," and so forth. Typically, queuing or long line-ups develop, which means that many of those potential tenants wishing to rent two-bedroom apartments may have a lengthy wait before a rental unit becomes vacant.

Black market A market in which the price-controlled good is sold at an illegally high price through various under-the-table methods.

Typically, an effective price ceiling policy leads to a black market. A **black market** is a market in which the price-controlled good is sold at an illegally high price through various under-the-table methods. In our rental apartment example, landlords may charge "key money," which can be a relatively large lump-sum illegal cash payment that must be made before a tenant is allowed to obtain the keys for the apartment. If the illegal key money is included in determining the actual monthly rent, we would call this monthly amount the black market price. As the demand curve in Figure 6–2 indicates, after the rent controls are imposed and a reduced supply of 50 000 units occurs, there will be tenants who will be willing to pay a black market price of up to $1000 per month. In other words, the actual monthly rent that is being charged (with the key money included) is more than the free market price of $800 per month!

It should be noted that black market behaviour is not limited to apartment units. In any market where price ceilings are imposed, there is the potential for black markets. If, due to an energy crisis, the price of gasoline is controlled, a hidden cash payment to the gas attendant may be required to gas up one's car. If beef shortages develop due to ceiling prices on beef, the butcher may give special service to a customer who offers the butcher free tickets for great seats at an upcoming rock concert. Indeed, the number of ways in which the true, implicit price of a price-controlled good or service can be increased is infinite, limited only by the imagination.

RENT CONTROLS AND EFFICIENCY. Let us return to the example of rent controls in order to describe how a price ceiling policy can result in an inefficient allocation of scarce resources. In housing markets, equilibrium rental prices can promote allocative efficiency by serving three functions: (1) to promote the construction of new housing in response to increased consumer demand, (2) to promote the efficient maintenance of the existing supply of housing, and (3) to ration the current supply of housing to the highest-valued uses.

Rent controls have discouraged the construction of new rental units. Rents are the most important long-term determinant of profitability, and rent controls have artificially depressed them. Consider some examples. Halifax, with less than 15 percent of the population of Toronto, built proportionally more rental units than Toronto in 1995. This, in spite of a 7.2 percent vacancy rate in Halifax, compared with a 1.2 percent vacancy rate in Toronto. The major difference? There were no rent controls in Halifax, while rent increases were strictly controlled in Toronto. In the same year, Vancouver, with 70 percent of the population of Toronto, saw the construction of 11 000 rental units; only 4000 were built in Toronto. Again, the difference was that there were no rent controls in Vancouver.

Due to growing concerns over the negative impact that rent controls can have on the construction of new apartments, the Manitoba government changed its rent ceiling policy in 2004 so as to exempt newly constructed apartment buildings from the controls for a period of 15 years.

When rental rates are held below equilibrium levels, property owners cannot use higher rents to recover the cost of maintenance, repairs, and capital improvements. Hence, they curtail these activities. In the extreme situation, taxes, utilities, and the expenses of basic repairs exceed rental receipts. The result is abandoned and/or deteriorating buildings. In situations where landlords do maintain their apartment buildings, they often decide to sell these units as condominiums and recoup their investment that way. This has the effect of severely reducing the supply of rental housing, thus making the housing shortage even worse.

Like any other price, rents ration output: in this case, the allocation of apartments among prospective tenants. When the rent is held at an arbitrarily low level, the number of prospective tenants increases, and excess demand develops. Students, for example, who might otherwise live with their families, decide they can afford to live on their own. In this situation, rationing of the available supply of rental housing is achieved through nonprice mechanisms, such as queuing or making under-the-table payments to landlords.

ATTEMPTS AT EVADING RENT CONTROLS. The distortions produced by rent controls lead to efforts by both landlords and tenants to evade the rules. This, in turn, leads to the growth of expensive government bureaucracies whose job it is to make sure that those rules are, indeed, followed. In 1995, the Ontario government spent about $1.8 million administering its *Residential Rent Regulation Act*.

In the 1980s, Ontario landlords had an incentive to speculate on the real estate market. They bought and sold apartment buildings, driving up prices and financing costs. Then, they applied for rent increases to cover the rising costs. Tenants, for their part, routinely tried to sublet all or part of their rent-controlled apartments at fees substantially above the rent they paid to the owner. They pocketed the difference, perhaps to help pay for a more expensive apartment.

RENT CONTROLS AND EQUITY. The big losers from rent controls are clearly landlords. But there is another group of losers—low-income individuals, especially single mothers, trying to find their first apartment. Some observers now believe that rent controls have worsened the problem of homeless people in such cities as Toronto.

Poor individuals cannot afford a hefty key money payment, nor can they assure the landlord that they will pay their rents on time or even regularly. Because controlled rents are usually below market clearing levels, there is little incentive for apartment owners to take any risk on low-income individuals as tenants. As a result, economists question whether rent ceilings actually promote equity, especially in the long run.

Who benefits from rent control? Ample evidence indicates that upper-income professionals benefit the most. These are the people who can use their mastery of the bureaucracy and their large network of friends and connections to exploit the rent control system. These are also the people who can easily afford to pay key money or to pay an agency to locate an apartment for them.

Because the private sector was unwilling to finance construction of new rental units in an environment of rent controls, the Ontario government had to spend up to $3.5 billion per year subsidizing the building of non-profit housing. Rents might have been controlled at lower-than-market levels, but renters and homeowners alike paid higher than necessary taxes to fund the government's subsidies.

Policy Example 6–1 provides an example of a price ceiling policy recently applied in Canada to the services of people engaged in assisted human reproduction.

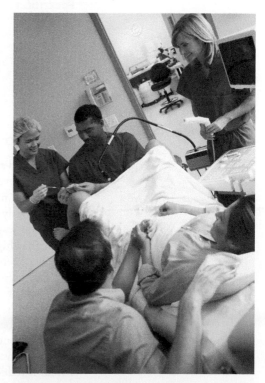

Why are more Canadians travelling to other countries for assisted human reproduction?

POLICY EXAMPLE 6–1   Assisted Human Reproduction Not for Sale in Canada?

In an attempt to regulate and control reproductive technologies, the Canadian government passed the *Assisted Human Reproduction Act* in 2004. Among other things, this legislation bans human cloning and prohibits Canadian infertility clinics from offering monetary payments to sperm and egg donors.

Critics of this act have warned that it will significantly reduce hope for numerous infertile couples residing in Canada, especially those who fall in the lower income brackets. Before the passage of this law, many U.S. companies were involved in matching U.S. women willing to sell their eggs with Canadian couples planning to undergo in vitro fertilization (IVF) at a cost of up to US$6000. These U.S. companies arranged for the donor to travel to a Canadian clinic, where her eggs were retrieved in a surgical procedure performed by a Canadian doctor. Under the *Assisted Human Reproduction Act,* this process becomes illegal, because the donor is getting paid. In economic terms, the act imposes a price ceiling of zero dollars for the act of donating eggs for fertilization within Canada.

Under this legislation, many Canadian couples have now found it much more expensive to undergo IVF because they must travel to the United States (or another country) to have the procedure done. In 2009, it was reported that Canadian couples were paying US$30 000 for egg donation and IVF in Seattle clinics. Since many Canadians cannot afford to complete an IVF treatment cycle in another country, these couples go "underground," finding donors online and paying them under the table. To date, there is much concern that this legislation threatens the health and welfare of Canadians because it encourages Canadian couples to find their own doctors, clinics, and donors underground or in an unregulated market in a foreign country.

In 2008, the Quebec Court of Appeal ruled that large parts of the legislation, including those related to regulating the treatment of infertility, fall under provincial jurisdiction and are therefore unconstitutional. As of 2010, the case was awaiting decision from the Supreme Court of Canada.

For critical analysis: Sketch a graph of the demand and supply of the services of egg donors in Canada. Illustrate how the *Assisted Human Reproduction Act* affects this graph.

Sources: Heather Sokoloff. "Fertility tourists expected to flock to U.S. clinics." *National Post*. October 31, 2000; Kathryn Blaze Carlson. "Baby by stealth; Reproduction law forcing 'dangerous alternatives.'" *National Post*. March 13, 2010. Pg. A1.

Price Floors: Minimum Wage

Minimum wage The lowest hourly wage rate that firms may legally pay their workers.

As we noted above, price controls can take the form of price floors, where a minimum price is fixed above the equilibrium price. An example of price floors currently in force in Canada are minimum wages set by provincial governments. The **minimum wage** is the lowest hourly wage rate that firms may legally pay their workers. Proponents want higher minimum wages to ensure low-income workers a "decent" standard of living. Opponents claim that higher minimum wages cause increased unemployment, particularly among unskilled teenagers.

Every province in Canada has a minimum wage. Figure 6–3 sets out the hourly minimum wage for each province.

What happens when the government passes legislation setting a floor on wages? The effects can be seen in Figure 6–4. We start off in equilibrium with the equilibrium wage rate of W_e and the equilibrium quantity of labour demanded and supplied equal to Q_e. A minimum wage, W_m, higher than W_e, is imposed. At W_m, the quantity demanded for labour is reduced to Q_d, and some workers now become unemployed. Note that the reduction in employment from Q_e to Q_d, or the distance from B to A, is less than the excess quantity of labour supplied at wage rate W_m. This excess quantity supplied is the distance between A and C, or the distance between Q_d and Q_s. The reason the reduction in

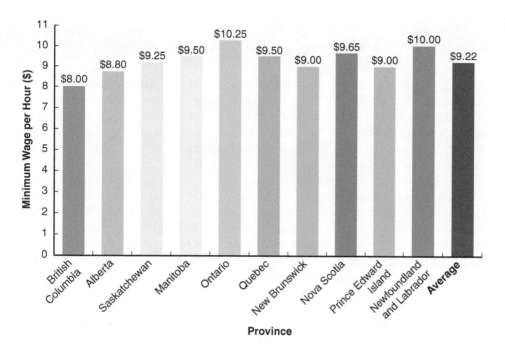

FIGURE 6–3

Provincial Minimum Wage Rates per Hour

Every province in Canada legislates a minimum wage rate per hour. As of October 2010, the rate varied from $8.00 to $10.25 per hour. The average minimum wage was $9.22 per hour.

"Minimum wage rates across Canada, 2007–11." Wages. Backgrounder. April 8, 2010. Province of Manitoba website. http://news.gov.mb.ca/news/index.html?archive=2010-04-01&item=8124. (Accessed August 30, 2010.)

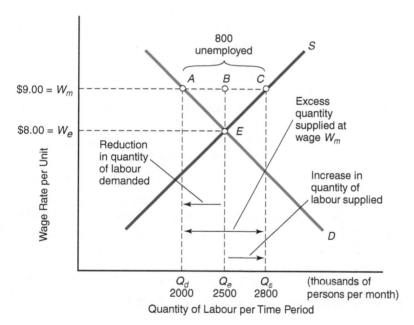

FIGURE 6–4

The Effect of Minimum Wages

The market clearing wage rate is $W_e = \$8.00$. The market clearing quantity of employment is $Q_e = 2500$, determined by the intersection of supply and demand at point E. A minimum wage equal to $W_m = \$9$ is established. The quantity of labour demanded is reduced to $Q_d = 2000$; the reduction in employment from $Q_e = 2500$ to Q_d is equal to the distance between B and A. That distance is smaller than the excess quantity of labour supplied at wage rate W_m. The distance between B and C is the increase in the quantity of labour supplied that results from the higher minimum wage rate.

employment is smaller than the excess supply of labour at the minimum wage is that the latter also includes a second component, consisting of the additional workers who would like to work more hours at the new, higher minimum wage. Some workers may become unemployed as a result of the minimum wage, but others will move to sectors where minimum wage laws do not apply; wages will be pushed down in these uncovered sectors.

In the long run (a time period that is long enough to allow for adjustment by workers and firms), some of the reduction in labour demanded will result from a reduction in the number of firms, and some will result from changes in the number of workers employed by each firm. Economists estimate that a 10 percent increase in the real minimum wage decreases total employment of those affected by 3 to 20 percent.[2] Policy Example 6-2 questions whether minimum wage rates provide a net benefit to Canadian workers.

---

[2]Because we are referring to a long-run analysis here, the reduction in labour demanded would be demonstrated by an eventual shift inward to the left of the short-run demand curve, D, in Figure 6–4.

POLICY EXAMPLE 6–2   Do Minimum Wage Rates Benefit Canadian Workers?

Not that long ago, British Columbia consistently posted the highest minimum wage of all 10 provinces. But as of May 2010, B.C.'s minimum wage rate of $8 per hour was the lowest in Canada. Moreover, B.C. has not raised its minimum wage rate for over six years, despite increases in the province's cost of living. Why has B.C. changed its view regarding the effectiveness of minimum wage policy, especially when it is being pressured by powerful union groups to raise the rate to $10 per hour?

Economic observers suggest that two key events help to explain B.C.'s recent stance on minimum wage rate policy. First, the left-leaning, pro-labour New Democrat government was replaced by a pro-business Liberal government. Second, in January 2009, the Fraser Institute, a right-wing economic think tank that has the ear of the B.C. Liberal government, published a labour market study entitled *The Economic Effects of Increasing British Columbia's Minimum Wage*. This report concluded that raising the minimum wage rate in B.C. would result in a greater marginal cost than marginal benefit.

In its study, the Fraser Institute assessed the marginal benefit of a higher minimum wage to discover how much this policy would reduce the poverty rate. Since only 3 to 4 percent of B.C. workers are currently earning a minimum wage, the policy of raising the rate would affect a very small percentage of B.C. families. After examining the characteristics of those B.C. workers that would typically directly benefit from an increased minimum wage, the study found that the majority of these individuals (56 percent) were between 15 and 24 years of age, still going to school, and living at home with their parents.

Therefore, minimum wage increases would have a negligible effect on adults, generally, and those supporting families, specifically.

On the other hand, the study found significant marginal costs related to raising the minimum wage rate from $8 to $10 per hour. Based on other research conducted in Canada and the U.S., the Fraser Institute estimated that raising the minimum wage rate would result in the loss of between 10 898 and 52 200 jobs. Moreover, the research suggests that higher minimum wages have other negative effects, including fewer employee benefits and less training for workers.

For critical analysis: Sketch a demand and supply diagram for unskilled workers in B.C., assuming an equilibrium wage rate of $8 per hour and a minimum wage rate of $10 per hour. Use this diagram to explain the effects of a policy that would raise the B.C. minimum wage from $8 to $10 per hour.

Source: Keith Godin and Niels Veldhuis. *The Economic Effects of Increasing British Columbia's Minimum Wage*. Studies in the Labour Market. Fraser Institute. January 2009. Pg. 3–5. http://www.fraserinstitute.org/commerce.web/product_files/EconomicEffectsBCMinimumWage.pdf.

6.3 Price Supports: Offer to Purchase and Marketing Boards

Throughout the 20th century, governments around the world have implemented a variety of policies in support of farmers. Typically, the government initiatives have been in response to two well-publicized problems that plague the farm sector.

In the short run, on a year-to-year basis, a farmer's annual income can vary significantly due to uncontrollable supply factors, such as weather conditions and the uncoordinated production plans of the farmer's vast number of competitors. From a long-term viewpoint, due to high productivity and low income elasticity of demand, the increase in the supply of farm goods has significantly exceeded the increase in the demand for these same farm products, especially in the more developed nations. Therefore, the average annual income of farmers has lagged behind average incomes earned in nonfarm occupations. In response to the problems outlined above, governments have implemented policies in order to promote equity from the farmer's perspective.

In this section, we will apply the theory of demand, supply, and elasticity to understand and evaluate common types of farm **price support policies**, which aim to help the farmers by enhancing the prices they receive for the farm products they supply.

Price support policies Policies that aim to help the farmers by enhancing the prices they receive for the farm products they supply.

Offer-to-Purchase Policy

One type of price support policy used to enhance farm income is the **offer-to-purchase policy**, which is a price floor policy reinforced by the purchase of surplus output by the government. Figure 6–5 describes a hypothetical market for apples in a Canadian province. Note that without government intervention, an equilibrium price of $500 per tonne and an equilibrium of 15 000 tonnes (per year) would prevail. Annual total revenue for all the apple growers in the province would be $500 × 15 000 = $7 500 000.

In order to promote the goal of a more equitable distribution of income for the apple farmers, the provincial government sets a minimum price floor of $700 per tonne. Since this price exceeds the equilibrium price, an annual surplus equal to (17 000 – 14 000) or 3000 tonnes results, as indicated in Figure 6–5. In order to maintain the price at $700 per tonne, the government will also have to purchase this surplus at a total taxpayer cost of $700 × 3000 tonnes = $2 100 000. The apple growers' total revenue increases to $700 × 17 000 tonnes = $11 900 000. This means an increase in revenue of $11 900 000 – $7 500 000 = $4 400 000 for the apple growers!

While the offer-to-purchase policy described above does increase the total revenues of the apple growers, it accomplishes this at the expense of the consumer and the taxpayer. The consumer pays a higher price of $700 per tonne, compared with an equilibrium price of $500 per tonne. As well, taxpayers pay a total of $2 100 000 per year to purchase the surplus, which often rots in government storage bins. This policy results in allocative inefficiency due to the surplus output. Politically, the government becomes very unpopular if the voters find out that they are paying higher prices for apples that are rotting in storage. Finally, since the offer-to-purchase policy helps the farmers by securing a higher price per unit (per tonne), the largest, most affluent farms get the greatest benefit from the price supports.

Offer-to-purchase policy A price floor policy reinforced by the purchase of surplus output by the government.

Marketing Board Policy

Due to some of the problems related to the offer-to-purchase policy, provincial governments in Canada have preferred to aid the farmers by allowing them to form producer **marketing boards**—a policy that allows producers to band together to restrict total

Marketing boards A policy that allows producers to band together to restrict total quantity supplied by using quotas.

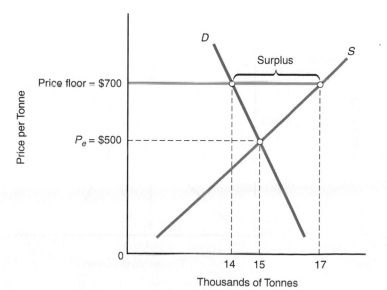

FIGURE 6–5

The Offer-to-Purchase Price Support

If the government does not intervene in the apple market, all the apple growers in the province will sell 15 000 tonnes a year at an equilibrium price of $500 per tonne. In order to support the apple farmers' incomes, the government sets a price floor equal to $700 per tonne. A surplus of (17 000 – 14 000) or 3000 tonnes per year will result. In order to keep the apple price at $700 per tonne, the government will have to purchase the surplus of 3000 tonnes, paying $700 per tonne of surplus.

quantity supplied by using quotas. Returning to the apple growers example, if the majority of the apple growers agree to form a marketing board, the board will typically use quotas to restrict the quantity of apples sold to a level below the equilibrium quantity. This, in turn, will increase the price per tonne above the equilibrium price. If demand for apples is inelastic, the higher price will result in an increase in total revenue.

Figure 6–6 describes how a marketing board can increase the apple growers' total revenue. We again note that without government intervention, the equilibrium price will be $500 per tonne and the equilibrium quantity will be 15 000 tonnes. Under a laissez-faire policy, the apple growers' total revenue will be $500 × 15 000 tonnes = $7 500 000. The provincial government, not wanting to use taxpayer dollars to purchase surplus apples, decides to let the apple growers form a marketing board. The marketing board sets a quota on each of the apple growers, which results in a lower total quantity of 14 000 tonnes being sold to the consumer. Since the quantity sold is reduced, the price increases to $700 per tonne. With the marketing board, the total revenue for the apple growers is now $700 × 14 000 tonnes = $9 800 000. Despite a reduced quantity sold, the farmers' total revenue increases because demand is inelastic!

Over one-half of Canadian farmers' total sales are regulated by agricultural marketing boards. Chickens, turkeys, eggs, milk, butter, tobacco, grapes, and mushrooms are all sold through marketing boards that restrict the supply of these products to the marketplace.

WHO LOSES WHEN MARKETING BOARDS REGULATE SUPPLY? The consumer pays more for the regulated goods than necessary and is therefore the biggest loser. One estimate suggests that the average Canadian family pays $200 to $400 per year more than it would if all farm produce were sold at unregulated prices.

Prospective farmers lose, too. When quotas were first established, they were given to existing producers. New producers, however, have to purchase quotas from other farmers or from the appropriate marketing board. Some quotas have become prohibitively expensive. A minimum-size quota for a chicken farm today would cost $1 million; a minimum-size quota for a dairy farm in the Fraser Valley of British Columbia would cost $3 million. And that is not counting the cost of the land and the livestock.

Another loser is the foreign farmer who would like to export farm products to Canada. The government restricts entry of foreign produce because the additional supply would reduce prices. Canada used to keep out foreign produce with import quotas, but the GATT (General Agreement on Tariffs and Trade) in its latest round of talks banned import quotas on agricultural goods. Thus, the federal government now uses import duties (i.e., taxes on imported produce) to restrict supply of foreign goods. The tariff on butter from the United States, for example, is 351 percent.

FIGURE 6–6

Marketing Board Policy

If there is no government policy, the equilibrium price of $500 and the equilibrium quantity of 15 000 tonnes will prevail. The total farm revenue will be $500 × 15 000 = $7 500 000. If a marketing board is allowed to be established, the board will impose quotas on each of its apple grower members. As a result, the total quantity supplied will be fixed at 14 000 tonnes. At this quantity, the price per tonne will increase to $700, and total farm revenue will increase to $700 × 14 000 = $9 800 000.

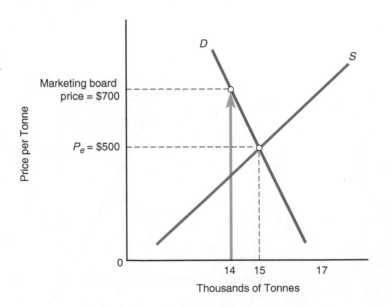

WHO WINS WHEN MARKETING BOARDS REGULATE SUPPLY? Existing farmers are clearly the major winners. The boards do stabilize their incomes, and so they can plan from one year to the next. To the extent that marketing boards restrict the supply of inelastic demand products, the total revenue of the existing farmers will increase. Supporters of marketing boards also point out that by guaranteeing a living for Canadian farmers, we are providing ourselves with a made-at-home food supply—something much more valuable than the costs associated with supply management. In addition, we are helping preserve a way of life that is disappearing elsewhere—the family farm.

Some farmers object to being regulated by marketing boards. They believe that they, as entrepreneurs, will be better salespeople for their products than a government bureaucracy. This is happening most clearly in the wheat and barley industry, where a special form of marketing board exists. Policy Example 6–3 explains this policy.

POLICY EXAMPLE 6–3   **The Beginning of the End for the Canadian Wheat Board?**

The Canadian government has been involved in guaranteeing prices for wheat farmers since World War I. In 1917, to regulate the supply of wheat to troops in Europe and to Canadians at home, and to guarantee grain farmers a reasonable living, the government set up the Board of Grain Supervisors. After the war, the Board's name was changed to the Canadian Wheat Board. It still operates today.

The Canadian Wheat Board buys all the wheat a farmer produces and sells it on world markets. Farmers cannot sell their wheat independently. The Board advances 75 percent of the expected price to farmers in the spring, and then settles up with them after the wheat is sold in the fall. Farmers never receive less than the expected price, so if the world price is lower than predicted, the Wheat Board suffers a loss. But if the price is higher, farmers are paid more. This has the effect of reducing fluctuations in farm income by putting a floor under the price farmers receive.

Recently, some grain growers have been objecting to being forced to sell to the Wheat Board. They claim that by selling directly to the United States, they would earn $2 to $3 per bushel more, a significant price difference. But other farmers want the Wheat Board to remain. They fear that, as individual farmers, they would not have the leverage to stand up against major wheat buyers and demand a high price. They fear that, in the end, their incomes would fall.

The federal Conservative government, consistent with its laissez-faire views, had set August 1, 2008, as the date when western Canadian farmers had the choice to bypass the Wheat Board and sell their barley on the open market. This date was delayed due to court battles between the Canadian Wheat Board and the federal government. In January 2010, the federal government won the legal battle and were able to pass legislation that would allow board members to vote to bypass the Wheat Board when selling barley. This means that the Canadian Wheat Board will just have a monopoly over the sale of wheat produced in western Canada. Many feel that it is only a matter of time before the wheat monopoly will also be eliminated, which would spell the end of the Canadian Wheat Board.

For critical analysis: Using a market demand and supply diagram for barley, describe how the price will change when more and more farmers bypass the Canadian Wheat Board (marketing board) to sell their barley. If demand for barley is inelastic, what will happen to the farmers' total revenue?

Sources: "Tories on iffy ground on wheat monopoly," *Leader-Post* (Regina). Final edition. June 23, 2007. Pg. D1.FRO.; "Ottawa eyes end to wheat board's monopoly on barley." *Dawson Creek Daily News* (Dawson Creek, B.C.). March 4, 2010. Pg. A3.

6.4 Quantity Restrictions

Governments can impose quantity restrictions on a market. The most obvious restriction is an outright ban on the ownership or trading of a good. It is currently illegal to buy and sell human organs as well as certain psychoactive drugs such as cocaine and heroin. It is also illegal to open a new chartered bank without obtaining a government charter. This requirement effectively restricts the number of chartered banks in Canada. Policy Example 6–4 explains how an outright ban can create illegal markets that continue to supply the product.

POLICY EXAMPLE 6–4   Could Legalizing Marijuana Reduce Mexican Drug Violence?

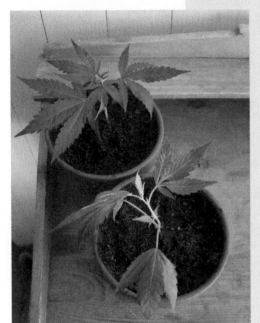

How might the policy of legalizing marijuana in California promote the public's interest?

As evidenced in the media, Mexico is currently plagued by a violent drug trade controlled by the Mexican drug mafia cartels. In 2009, there were 6500 drug-related killings, and as of mid-March 2010, more than 2000 people had died in drug-related homicides. That amounts to more than one death per hour. The majority of the drugs peddled by the Mexican mafia are sold in the United States, where drugs such as marijuana are illegal to buy and sell, except for medicinal purposes.

What these figures illustrate is that, while governments can enact laws that ban products such as marijuana, they cannot prevent the illegal demand and supply for marijuana in underground or black markets, often with ties to organized crime. Typically, the demand and supply curves differ when marijuana is banned compared to when it is legally available. The suppliers of the banned substance face higher costs due to the risk of getting caught and being convicted. Since the consumers also face the risk of being caught and convicted, demand decreases compared to the legal situation.

In November 2010, California residents voted on a policy proposal to legalize marijuana. The new policy would make it legal for anyone 21 years and older to possess an ounce of marijuana. It would also allow cities and counties to permit marijuana to be grown and sold locally, and for state and local governments to impose taxes on marijuana production and sales.

One reason for this policy proposal is to bring in new tax revenue to help reduce the state of California's US$20 billion government deficit. As well, there would be a large decrease in demand for marijuana supplied by the Mexican drug lords, since the 39 million Californians will have access to the drug at lower prices, from legal, regulated, domestic producers. As the profits of the Mexican drug dealers are reduced, they will be less able to afford the military might that encourages the drug-related violence already witnessed.

A major concern related to the legalization of marijuana is that the increased supply of this substance may encourage greater drug abuse and addiction in California.

For critical analysis: Sketch a demand and supply diagram illustrating the equilibrium price and quantity of marijuana when it is banned (i.e., sold on the black market). In the same diagram, show what happens to demand and supply when marijuana is legalized, based on the contents of this Example. What will happen to the equilibrium price and quantity of marijuana when it is legalized? Explain.

Sources: Steve Chapman. "An unconventional cure for Mexico's drug violence." *Chicago Tribune*. March 28, 2010. http://articles.chicagotribune.com/2010-03-28/news/ct-oped-0328-chapman-md-20100328_1_drug-cartels-drug-related-killings-drug-trade; Robert Mackey. "Move to legalize marijuana in California sparks fears about drop in prices." *New York Times*. March 23, 2010.

Some of the most common quantity restrictions exist in the area of international trade. The Canadian government and many foreign governments impose import quotas on a variety of goods. An **import quota** is a supply restriction that prohibits the importation of more than a specified quantity of a particular good in a one-year period. Canada has had import quotas on cotton textiles, shoes, and immigrant labour. For many years, there were import quotas on dairy products coming into Canada from the United States. These quotas were recently removed and replaced by tariffs, but the effect is still to limit the amount of dairy products that we import. There are also "voluntary" import quotas on certain goods. Japanese car makers, for example, have agreed since 1981 "voluntarily" to restrict the number of cars they send to Canada.

In many cases, import quotas are designed to increase the total amount spent by Canadians on domestically produced goods. However, if the Canadian demand for the foreign good being restricted is price inelastic, Canadian consumers may end up spending more dollars on the foreign product, resulting in a decrease in demand for the made-in-Canada good.

Import quota A supply restriction that prohibits the importation of more than a specified quantity of a particular good in a one-year period.

6.5 Elasticity and Excise Taxes

Canadian governments at both the federal and provincial levels can levy various taxes in order to affect market outcomes. One example is the **excise tax**, which is a tax imposed on a particular commodity or service, such as cigarettes, alcohol, gasoline, CDs, MP3 players, or hotel services. In the following section, we will apply the theory of demand, supply, and elasticity to predict the effects of a per-unit tax imposed on the firms manufacturing and supplying cigarettes in a Canadian province.

Excise tax A tax imposed on a particular commodity or service.

The Effects of a Per-Unit Tax on Market Supply

Suppose the federal government imposes an excise tax of $15 per carton of cigarettes on the firms manufacturing and supplying cigarettes in Ontario. To simplify the situation, we will assume that the manufacturers sell directly to cigarette consumers. In Figure 6–7, the pretax market supply and demand is S_1 and D_1.

Since the per-unit tax imposes an extra cost on the cigarette manufacturers at each price, this will cause a decrease in the supply of cigarettes.

> **Graphically, the market supply curve will shift up vertically, at each quantity, by the amount of the per unit tax.**

In Figure 6–7, this means that the supply curve will shift upward by a vertical amount of $15 (the per-unit tax) to form S_2, the new after-tax supply curve. This shift can be explained as follows.

According to S_1, the pretax supply curve, the manufacturers will be willing to supply 5 million cartons per month if they receive $50 per carton. In order to supply 6 million cartons of cigarettes per month, the manufacturers will have to receive $55 per carton.

After a new tax of $15 per carton is imposed on the manufacturers, they will be willing to supply 5 million cartons per month only if the price charged to the consumers is now $65 per carton, which is based on the new supply curve, S_2. If the manufacturers charge the consumers $65, they will receive the $50 they require, after remitting to the government $15 for each carton sold.

Similarly, after the tax, the manufacturers will be willing to supply 6 million cartons per month only if the price charged to the consumers is now $70 (on S_2). By charging $70 per carton, the manufacturers will be able to receive the necessary $55, after paying to the government a tax of $15 per carton. On the basis of this example, we can conclude that for each possible quantity, the after-tax supply curve will shift upward by $15, the amount of the per-unit tax.

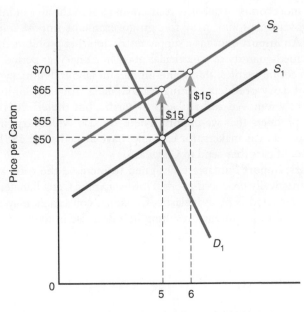

Quantity of Cartons per Month (millions)

Tax incidence The division of the burden of a tax between the buyer and the seller.

Tax Incidence

When the government imposes a per-unit excise tax, who bears the brunt of the tax—the buyer or the seller? This is a question relating to **tax incidence**, which is the division of the burden of a tax between the buyer and the seller. In our cigarette example above, the government imposes the tax on the manufacturers (sellers). However, the sellers can shift at least part of the tax to the buyers (consumers), to the extent that they can increase the equilibrium price charged for a carton of cigarettes.

> **In general, the buyer's portion of the tax burden equals the increase in equilibrium price that results from the tax. The seller's portion of the tax burden equals the per-unit tax minus the buyer's tax burden.**

In Figure 6–8, the per-unit tax imposed on the cigarette manufacturers shifts the supply curve upward by $15 (the tax per unit). This decrease in supply causes the equilibrium price to increase from $50 per carton to $62 per carton. The tax incidence can now be established as follows: The buyer's portion of the tax burden equals the increase in equilibrium price, which is $62 − $50 = $12 per carton. The seller's tax burden is the difference between the per-unit tax and the buyer's tax burden, which is $15 − $12 = $3 per carton.

The seller's tax burden of $3 per carton can be further explained by referring to Figure 6–8. Before the tax, the sellers received the equilibrium price of $50. After the tax, the sellers receive the new equilibrium price minus the per-unit tax that they have to remit to the government, which is $62 − $15 = $47. The sellers end up receiving $50 − $47 = $3 less per carton after the tax.

Elasticity and Tax Incidence

Elasticity of demand and supply affects the degree to which the burden of an excise tax is shared between the buyers and the sellers of the product being taxed. If demand is relatively elastic, buyers can easily escape the burden of a tax imposed on product A, by switching their consumption to close substitutes for product A. In this situation, sellers will be careful not to increase the equilibrium price too much for fear of scaring away the consumers of their product. Therefore, when demand is elastic, sellers will bear a greater portion of the tax burden.

On the other hand, if demand for product A is relatively inelastic, sellers can shift a larger portion of the tax burden to consumers by significantly increasing the price, as the

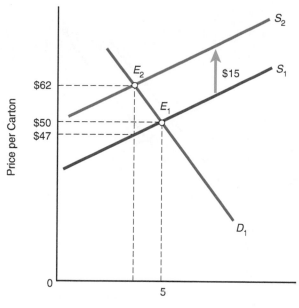

FIGURE 6–8

The Tax Incidence Related to a $15 Per-Carton Excise Tax

The before-tax equilibrium price equals $50 per carton, based on the intersection of D_1 and S_1. The $15 per-unit tax shifts the supply curve by $15 to S_2. The new after-tax equilibrium price is now $62 per carton, based on the intersection of D_1 and S_2. The buyer's portion of the tax burden equals the increase in equilibrium price, which is $62 − $50 = $12 per carton. The seller's portion of the tax burden is the per-unit tax minus the buyer's tax burden, which is $15 − $12 = $3 per carton. In other words, the seller receives $50 − $47 = $3 less for each carton sold, after the tax.

consumers have few alternative goods to switch to. In Figure 6–8, the demand for cigarettes is relatively inelastic, which explains why the consumer's tax burden of $12 significantly exceeds the seller's tax burden of $3 per carton.

Elasticity of supply can also affect tax incidence. If supply is relatively elastic, sellers can easily escape the burden of a tax imposed on product A, by switching their production and supply to alternative products that are not taxed. As many sellers leave the market for product A, the price of A will increase significantly, shifting a large portion of the tax burden to consumers of product A. Therefore, when supply is elastic, buyers will bear a greater portion of the tax burden.

If the supply for product A is relatively inelastic, this means that the sellers cannot easily switch to producing and supplying other nontaxed products. In this situation, sellers will continue to supply a significant amount of product A, even if faced with a large tax burden. In Figure 6–9, the supply of cigarettes is relatively inelastic. Under these market conditions, the same $15 per-carton tax causes the equilibrium price to go up to $54 per carton. The buyer's tax burden equals the increase in equilibrium price, which is $54 − $50 = $4 per carton. The seller's burden is the per-unit tax minus the buyer's burden, which is $15 − $4 = $11 per carton. You can see that when supply is relatively inelastic, the seller bears the greater portion of the tax burden.

In general, the tax burden falls more heavily on the side of the market that is relatively more inelastic.

Elasticity and Resource Allocation

In many situations, an excise tax is imposed in order to discourage the production and consumption of a particular product that the government feels is detrimental to society. As an example, both the federal and provincial governments have imposed heavy excise taxes on cigarettes, which helps explain the significant decline in Canadian tobacco use noted in this chapter's Did You Know That . . . ? section. Under what elasticity conditions will the government be relatively successful in discouraging cigarette production and consumption?

When demand and/or supply is relatively elastic, a per-unit excise tax will significantly reduce the equilibrium quantity of cigarettes, thereby effectively reducing the amount of resources being used to produce this undesirable product.

The before-tax equilibrium price equals $50 per carton, based on the intersection of D_1 and S_1. The $15 per-unit tax shifts the supply curve up by $15 to S_2. The new after-tax equilibrium price is now $54 per carton, based on the intersection of D_1 and S_2. The buyer's portion of the tax burden equals the increase in equilibrium price, which is $54 − $50 = $4 per carton. The seller's portion of the tax burden is the per-unit tax minus the buyer's tax burden, which is $15 − $4 = $11 per carton. In other words, the seller receives $50 − $39 = $11 less for each carton sold, after the tax.

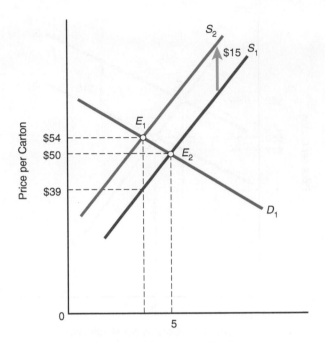

Quantity of Cartons per Month (millions)

Elasticity and Government Tax Revenue

Excise taxes provide tax revenues to both the federal and provincial governments in Canada. Elasticity affects the total amount of tax revenues that can be raised through these types of taxes.

A per-unit excise tax will generate greater total tax revenues when the demand and/or supply of the taxed product is relatively inelastic.

In these situations, the equilibrium quantity of the taxed product will not significantly decrease in response to a per-unit tax. If the after-tax equilibrium quantity remains relatively large, the total tax revenue generated will also be relatively large.

Policy Example 6–5 describes the private copying levies that the Canadian government uses to discourage the widespread downloading of music from the Internet and through the burning of CDs. The proceeds from these levies are used to compensate the Canadian music industry for the piracy of copyrighted music. By viewing each levy as a per-unit excise tax, you can use the theory of elasticity to evaluate this government policy.

POLICY EXAMPLE 6–5 **An Excise Tax on Music Piracy?**

In Canada, sales of music CDs, music DVDs, and other "physical" music formats declined by 12 percent from 2005 to 2006. In the first quarter of 2007, these sales plummeted an unprecedented 35 percent! This is consistent with the long-term decline in global music sales since 1999, which industry analysts attribute to widespread illegal Internet file-sharing and pre-recorded CD and DVD counterfeiting (copying).

In the December 2008 *Supplement Canada Gazette*, The Copyright Board of Canada announced the tariffs to be imposed on the sale of blank audio recording media until the end of 2009. The tariffs amount to per-unit taxes described as follows: $0.24 on audio cassette tapes of 40 minutes or longer; $0.29 on CD-Rs and CD-RWs; and $0.29 on CD-R Audio, CD-RW Audio, and minidiscs. These levies (taxes) represent the Canadian government's response to the flurry of free copying of copyrighted music through Internet downloads and CD burning. The proceeds from the levies on private copying are to be distributed to music performers, songwriters, and music producers, as partial compensation for the loss of sales due to piracy.

continued

For critical analysis: Explain how the price elasticity of demand and supply for blank media will affect the total amount collected from the levies on private copying. How will elasticity affect the degree to which these levies discourage the copying of copyrighted music? Under what circumstances would consumers be unfairly "taxed" by these private-copying levies?

Sources: "Canada's music sales fall 35% in first quarter." News. The Canadian Recording Industry Association. Toronto, April 26, 2007. http://www.cria.ca/news/250407_n.php. (Accessed July 14, 2007.); "Introduction. Copying For Private Use." *Copyright Act*, Subsection 83(8). Copyright Board Of Canada. p. 1. Ottawa. May 11, 2007; "Tariff of levies to be collected by CPCC in 2008 and 2009 on the sale, in Canada, of blank audio recording media." *Supplement Canada Gazette*. Copyright Board of Canada. December 6, 2008. http://www.cb-cda.gc.ca/tariffs-tarifs/certified-homologues/2008/20081206-c-b.pdf.

ISSUES AND APPLICATIONS

For-Profit Health Care in Canada?

Concepts Applied: Market versus Command Systems, Rationing Function of Prices, Price Ceilings, Allocative Efficiency, Productive Efficiency, and Equity

Is for-profit health care the way to reduce scenes like this?

In 2009, Ipsos Reid conducted a national study relating to the amount of time that Canadians typically wait to undergo a medical treatment or procedure performed by a medical specialist. Some of the results from this study are summarized in Table 6–1 on page 152. Canadians waited an average of 26.1 weeks from the time they received a referral from their general practitioner to the time they received treatment from a medical specialist. This represents an increase of over 180 percent from 1993, when the typical waiting time was 9.3 weeks. In research involving 23 OECD (developed) nations, published on November 2009, Canada ranked near the bottom: 20th, with 2.18 doctors per 1000 people. Despite the apparent shortage of medical services in Canada, provincial governments have recently been spending an increasing portion of their budgets on health care.

These disturbing trends and statistics have renewed a debate over which type of system best suits the provision of health-care services—a market system or a command system. To appreciate the differing views, we will begin by examining Canada's existing system of providing health-care services.

Canadian Medicare

Canada has a predominantly publicly financed, privately delivered health-care system that consists of 10 provincial (and three territorial) government health insurance plans. This mixed system of providing health-care services is frequently referred to as medicare.

The federal government's role in health care involves using financial incentives to ensure that each province provides equal access to universal, comprehensive coverage for medically necessary hospital, in-patient, and outpatient physician services.

TABLE 6–1

Canadian Patient Waiting
Times for Medical
Treatment or Procedures
Performed by Medical
Specialists

Type of Medical Condition or Procedure	Median # Weeks From GP Referral to Procedure or Treatment	# Procedures or Treatments
Radiation oncology	33 weeks	160
Nuclear medicine	19 weeks	21
Psychiatry	5.7 weeks	340
Gastroenterology	18.6 weeks	70
Orthopaedics	41.1 weeks	151
Plastic surgery	24.7 weeks	185
Obstetricians and gynaecologists	27.6 weeks	588
Ophthalmology	64.3 weeks	95
Weighted average median time	26.1 weeks	

Source: *National Physician Diary Study 2009: Wait Time Results by National Specialty Society*. Ipsos Reid. Pg. 3–16. http://www.waittimealliance.ca/June2009/WTA-Physician-Diary-Study-June2009_e.pdf.

Typically, each province makes each of its working residents pay into the medicare insurance fund through compulsory taxation (or compulsory monthly premiums). When a Canadian consumer (patient) visits a physician (or hospital), monies from the medicare fund pay for the visit. This means that the patient does not incur any additional out-of-pocket expense each time he or she makes another visit to a physician or hospital.

In the Canadian medicare system, physicians typically operate their own private practices and are compensated from the medicare insurance fund on a fee-for-service basis. Since the majority of acute-care Canadian hospitals are operated by the public sector on a nonprofit basis, the only pressure to contain hospital costs is the annual hospital budget determined by government authorities.

A Market-Oriented Health-Care Model?

Those who support market solutions for our health-care system criticize Canadian medicare for its price ceiling policy for medical services. Under this policy, the federal government commands that a maximum price of zero be charged for both doctor and hospital visits. Figure 6–10 illustrates this view.

According to the market supporters, medicare's zero price ceiling policy has caused shortages, resulting in Canadian patients waiting long periods before receiving treatment or surgery. A zero price encourages many individuals to frequently visit doctors and hospitals, and take diagnostic tests for the most trivial reasons, resulting in an excess demand for medical services. As a result, patients experiencing really serious health problems are forced to wait a long time before receiving the badly needed treatment.

A second problem with Canadian medicare, according to market advocates, is that it essentially results in government-owned monopolies providing health insurance and hospital services in each province. The lack of competition and the absence of the profit incentive helps contribute to medical shortages, productive inefficiency, and escalating health-care costs.

The market system supporters propose that Canada adopt a number of market incentives currently present in the American health-care system. In the United States, health-care services are predominantly provided in the for-profit private sector. As Table 6–2 indicates, public expenditures constitute a much smaller portion of total health expenditures in the United States compared with Canada.

FIGURE 6–10

Zero Price Ceiling under
Medicare

Since there is no additional charge per visit, there is a zero price ceiling policy under medicare. This results in a shortage, where the quantity of visits demanded exceeds the quantity of visits supplied. The shortage is reflected in significant waiting times before Canadian patients receive health-care services.

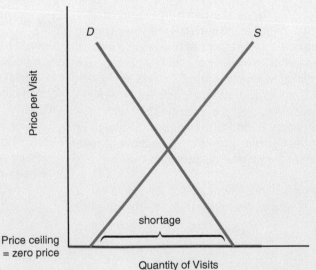

Expenditure as a Percentage	Canada 2004	Canada 2008	U.S. 2004	U.S. 2008
Total expenditure on health as a percentage of gross domestic product (GDP)	9.8%	10.1%	15.4%	15.7%
Public (government) expenditures on health as a percentage of total health expenditures	69.8%	70.0%	44.7%	45.5%

TABLE 6–2

Annual National Health Expenditures: Canada and the United States, 2004 and 2008

Sources: "Core health indicators." WHO Statistical Information System (WHOSIS). World Health Organization. http://www.who.int/whosis/database/core/core_select.cfm; *World Health Statistics 2010: Part II: Global Health Indicators.* Table 7. World Health Organization. http://www.who.int/whosis/whostat/EN_WHS10_Part2.pdf.

In order to finance their health-care costs, many American consumers voluntarily pay monthly premiums to private health insurance companies. In addition, consumers may have to pay a co-payment or user fee each time they visit a physician or hospital. Some private insurance plans may involve an experience rating, which is a situation where those who make more frequent visits to physicians may end up paying higher insurance premiums. According to market supporters, the user fees and experience ratings help eliminate waiting periods and ensure that those patients who value the medical services the most will be the ones visiting the health-care providers. The user fee will discourage frivolous use of scarce medical resources.

In the United States, large, private, for-profit health maintenance organizations (HMOs) operate hospitals, run diagnostic services, and hire physicians and nurses. In theory, one would expect to see a given quality of health care provided with minimal resource use in the United States, as it is in the interests of HMOs to contain the costs of providing health care, in order to enhance profits and stave off competition.

Evaluation of the Market-Based Solutions

Those who defend Canadian medicare argue that one cannot use the market model to analyze health care, which many consumers view as an extreme-necessity (highly inelastic) good. Consumers of health care (patients) lack the knowledge necessary to evaluate whether a contemplated visit to the doctor is trivial or not. Moreover, after the first visit to the general practitioner, it is typically the doctor who makes the decision, on behalf of the patient, to consume additional health-care resources. In this situation, it is meaningless to suggest that

user fees paid by the patients will ensure a more efficient use of medical resources. Indeed, user fees and experience ratings will unfairly penalize the poor and the chronically ill.

The view that private for-profit corporations will be more efficient than the government in providing health-care services can be challenged by comparing recent Canadian and American statistics. The data presented in Tables 6–2 and 6–3 indicate that although Canada spends a smaller percentage of GDP (national income) on health care than the United States, Canada manages to achieve a higher level of health achievement in terms of life expectancy, life expectancy adjusted for time spent in poor health, and infant mortality rates. It seems that a much larger portion of every dollar spent on health care in the United States is spent on activities not directly related to patient health care, such as administration, marketing, and earning corporate profits.

In November 2002, the Romanow Report presented the findings and recommendations of the Commission on the Future of Health Care in Canada. The Commission rejected the notion of using additional market incentives to improve Canada's health-care system. The Commission attributes the recent shortcomings of various health-care services in Canada to a number of factors not related to medicare—a long-term decline in federal government cash transfers to the provinces for health-care spending; provincial budget cutbacks made during the early 1990s; the aging population; and the high income elasticity of demand for health care in Canada. The Commission recommended that Canada's health-care system be improved through an expanded public health sector financed by substantial increases in federal government cash transfers to the provinces.

Health Achievement	Canada 2004	Canada 2008	U.S. 2004	U.S. 2008
Life expectancy at birth—females	83	83	80	81
Life expectancy at birth—males	78	79	75	76
Healthy life expectancy at birth—females: life expectancy at birth adjusted for time spent in poor health	74	75	71	72
Healthy life expectancy at birth—males: life expectancy at birth adjusted for time spent in poor health	70	71	67	68
Probability of dying (per 1000 live births) under five years of age (under-five mortality rate)	6	—	8	

TABLE 6–3

Health Achievement Levels: Canada and the United States, 2004 and 2008

Sources: "Core health indicators." WHO Statistical Information System (WHOSIS). World Health Organization. http://www.who.int/whosis/database/core/core_select.cfm. (Accessed July 9, 2007.); *World Health Statistics 2010: Part II: Global Health Indicators.* Tables 1 and 7. World Health Organization. http://www.who.int/whosis/whostat/EN_WHS10_Part2.pdf.

For critical analysis:

1. According to those who promote market solutions in health care, what aspects of Canadian medicare encourage allocative inefficiency? Explain briefly.

2. According to those who promote market solutions in health care, what features of the American health-care system promote (a) allocative efficiency, and (b) productive efficiency?

3. According to the medicare supporters, why will user fees fail to promote allocative efficiency?

4. Explain how user fees for health-care services can conflict with equity.

5. Explain why it appears that the Canadian health-care system is more productively efficient than the American system.

Sources: Nadeem Esmail and Michael Walker. "How good is Canadian health care?" August 2002. Fraser Institute. http://www.fraserinstitute.ca/shared/readmore.asp?sNav=pb&id=394. (Accessed December 27, 2003.); Nadeem Esmail and Michael Walker. "*Waiting Your Turn: Hospital Waiting Lists In Canada.*" 13th Edition. October 2003. Fraser Institute. http://www.fraserinstitute.ca/shared/readmore.asp?sNav=pb&id=587. (Accessed December 27, 2003.); Roy Romanow, Commissioner. "Building on values: the future of health care in Canada." November 2002. pp. 100–106. http://www.hc-sc.gc.ca/english/pdf/care/romanow_e.pdf. (Accessed December 28, 2003.); Nadeem Esmail and Michael Walker. *Waiting Your Turn*, 16th Edition. October 2006. The Fraser Institute. http://www.fraserinstitute.ca/shared/readmore.asp?sNav=pb&id=863; Nadeem Esmail and Michael Walker. "How good is canadian health care? 2006 report: an international comparison of health care systems." December 2006. The Fraser Institute. http://www.fraserinstitute.ca/shared/readmore.asp?sNav=pb&id=877; "Practising physicians" OECD iLibrary. November 12, 2009. http://www.oecd-ilibrary.org/oecd/content/tablecollection/20758480.

SUMMARY

Here is what you should know after reading this chapter. MyEconLab will help you identify what you know, and where to go when you need to practise. We suggest that as soon as you review one of the Learning Objective sections below, you then proceed to go through the related section in MyEconLab.

LEARNING OBJECTIVES	KEY TERMS	MYECONLAB PRACTICE
6.1 The Price System. Markets and intermediaries reduce the costs of mutually beneficial exchanges between buyers and sellers. Equilibrium prices ensure that resources and goods are allocated to the highest-valued uses, and all the gains from mutually beneficial trades are exhausted.	price system, 133 voluntary exchange, 133 terms of exchange, 133 transaction costs, 133	• **MyEconLab** Study Plan 6.1
6.2 Price Ceilings and Price Floors. Price ceilings, such as rent controls, set a maximum legal price below the equilibrium price. Ceilings lead to shortages, inefficient nonprice-rationing devices, and black markets. Price floors, such as minimum wages, set a minimum legal price above the equilibrium price that results in surpluses.	price controls, 137 price ceiling, 137 price floor, 137 rent control, 137 nonprice-rationing devices, 137 black market, 138 minimum wage, 140	• **MyEconLab** Study Plan 6.2

LEARNING OBJECTIVES	KEY TERMS	MYECONLAB PRACTICE
6.3 Price Supports: Offer to Purchase and Marketing Boards. Offer-to-purchase and marketing board policies provide support to low and unstable farm incomes by establishing farm product prices at levels that exceed equilibrium prices. The offer-to-purchase policy is a floor price policy in which the resulting surpluses are purchased by the government. The policy provides the greatest support to the largest farm operators at the expense of consumers and taxpayers. Marketing boards typically restrict the quantity supplied of farm products in order to support farm prices. When demand is inelastic, this strategy will increase total farm revenues at the expense of consumers and prospective farmers.	price support policies, 143 offer-to-purchase policy, 143 marketing boards, 143	• **MyEconLab** Study Plan 6.3
6.4 Quantity Restrictions. Examples of quantity restrictions include direct government bans, licensing restrictions, and quotas. Consumers may end up spending more dollars on the restricted goods if demand is price inelastic.	import quota, 147	• **MyEconLab** Study Plan 6.4
6.5 Elasticity and Excise Taxes. A per-unit excise tax typically increases the equilibrium price and decreases the equilibrium quantity of the taxed good or service. In terms of tax incidence, the buyer's portion of the tax burden equals the equilibrium price increase, while the seller's portion equals the per-unit tax minus the buyer's portion of the tax burden. The excise tax burden falls more heavily on the side of the market that is relatively more inelastic. The resource allocation effects of an excise tax, in terms of a reduction in the quantity produced, will be greatest when demand and/or supply is relatively price elastic. The government will collect a larger amount of tax revenue when the demand and/or supply of the taxed product is relatively price inelastic.	excise tax, 147 tax incidence, 148	• **MyEconLab** Study Plan 6.5

PROBLEMS

(Answers to the odd-numbered problems appear at the back of the book.)

LO 6.1 Explain the role of markets, intermediaries, and prices in the price system.

1. Based on Example 6-2, "Is Ticketmaster in Cahoots with Scalpers," explain the economic role that ticket scalpers play in the market for a sold-out event.

2. Under Canadian medicare, how are the diagnostic, medical, and surgical services of specialist physicians being rationed?

LO 6.2 Compare and contrast price ceiling and price floor policies.

3. Below is the market demand-and-supply schedule for lettuce in a Canadian city.

Price per Crate	Quantity Demanded (crates per year)	Quantity Supplied (crates per year)
$1	10 million	0 million
2	9	1
3	8	4
4	7	7
5	6	8
6	4	9

a. Assuming no government intervention, what price and quantity would result in the lettuce market?

b. Suppose that the price of lettuce in part (a) was considered excessive. Consequently, the government legislated a maximum price of $3 per crate. At this maximum price, a (shortage or surplus) of ____ million crates would develop. This policy is an example of a (price ceiling or price floor) policy.

c. Assuming the policy in part (b) above, what would be the maximum black market price?

d. Suppose that the price of lettuce in part (a) above was considered to be too low for lettuce farmers to make a decent living. Consequently, the government legislated a minimum price of $5 per crate. At this minimum price, a (shortage or surplus) of ____ million crates would develop. This policy is an example of a (price ceiling or price floor) policy.

4. Policy Example 6-1, "Assisted Human Reproduction Not for Sale in Canada" noted that under the *Assisted Human Reproduction Act*, couples go underground, where they turn to donors they find online and pay under the table. Based on the theory of demand and supply and price ceilings, would the amount paid under the table to an egg donor be the same or more than the equilibrium price? Explain.

5. This is a graph of the monthly demand for and supply of milk in a Canadian province.

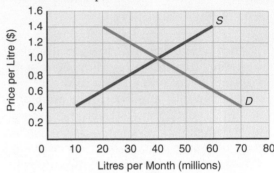

a. If the government did not intervene in the milk market, what price and quantity would result?

b. If the government imposed a maximum price policy of $0.80 per litre, this would result in a (shortage or surplus) of ____ millions of litres of milk per month. This would be called a (price floor or price ceiling) policy.

c. For the policy described in part (b) above, what would be the black market price?

d. If the government imposed a minimum price policy of $1.40 per litre, this would result in a (shortage or surplus) of ____ millions of litres of milk per month. This would be called a (price floor or price ceiling) policy.

6. "It is questionable whether a policy of rent controls promotes equity, despite leading to an inefficient allocation of resources." Fully explain the previous statement.

LO 6.3 Compare and contrast the offer-to-purchase and the marketing board price support policies.

7. For this problem, refer to the demand and supply schedules for lettuce provided in Problem 3 above.

a. Assuming that the market sets the price and quantity for lettuce, compute the total revenue received by the lettuce farmers.

b. If the government were to implement an offer-to-purchase policy to support the price of lettuce at $5 per crate, there would be a (shortage or surplus) equal to ____ million crates per year. Compute the total revenue received by the lettuce farmers under this policy. What would be the total taxpayer cost associated with this policy?

c. Suppose that the government decided to support the price of lettuce by allowing a marketing board to develop and restrict the quantity of lettuce supplied to 6 million crates per year. What price per crate would develop? Compute the total revenue received by the lettuce farmers under this policy. Is the price elasticity of demand elastic or inelastic in the $4 to $5 price range? Explain.

8. Identify and explain both the short-run and long-run problems facing Canadian farmers.

9. For this problem, refer to the demand and supply curves for milk provided in Problem 5.

   a. Assuming that the market sets the price and quantity for milk, compute the total revenue received by the milk farmers.

   b. If the government were to implement an offer-to-purchase policy to support the price of milk at $1.20 per litre, there would be a (shortage or surplus) equal to ____ million litres per month. Compute the total revenue received by the milk farmers under this policy. What would be the total taxpayer cost associated with this policy?

   c. Suppose that the government decided to support the price of milk by allowing a marketing board to develop and restrict the quantity of milk supplied to 30 million litres per month. What price per litre would develop? What would be the total revenue received by the milk farmers under this marketing board policy? Is the price elasticity of demand elastic or inelastic in the $1.00 to $1.20 per litre price range? Explain.

LO 6.4 Describe the various types of quantity restrictions that governments can impose on markets.

10. Suppose the Canadian government imposes an import quota on California wines, with the goal of increasing the total dollar amount that Canadian consumers spend on Canadian wines. Sketch a demand and supply graph for California wines and use this graph to illustrate an import quota policy. (Hint: assume that this policy operates in the same way as a marketing board crop-restriction, policy.)

11. If the Canadian demand for California wines is inelastic, will the quota policy in question 10 increase or decrease the total dollar amount that Canadians spend on California wines? Explain.

12. The Canadian Liberal Party has introduced legislation a number of times to legalize the practice of possessing small amounts of marijuana. In the same proposed legislation, the policy increases the penalty for those caught trafficking or producing marijuana. Using a demand and supply graph for marijuana, show how this type of proposed legislation would affect the market demand, supply, and equilibrium price of marijuana. Under what conditions would the equilibrium quantity bought and sold increase, as a result of this legislation?

LO 6.5 Explain how price elasticity governs the effects that a per-unit excise tax has on tax incidence, resource allocation, and government tax revenue collected.

13. The market demand and the before-tax market supply for gasoline sold in a Canadian province are described in the following table.

Price (per litre)	Market Demand (millions of litres per day)	Before-Tax Market Supply (millions of litres per day)	After-Tax Market Supply (millions of litres per day)
$0.70	20	80	
0.60	30	70	
0.50	40	60	
0.40	50	50	
0.30	60	40	
0.20	70	30	

If the government imposes an excise tax of $0.20 per litre on the suppliers of gasoline in this market, answer the following:

   a. In the above table, fill in the after-tax market supply, at each price per litre.

   b. Determine the after-tax equilibrium gas price and quantity.

   c. Determine the tax incidence related to this $0.20 per litre excise tax.

   d. Determine the total daily tax revenue that the government will receive from this gas excise tax.

   e. Under what conditions will the tax revenue computed in part (d) increase—when the demand for gasoline becomes more elastic or less elastic? Explain.

   f. Under what conditions will the excise tax more effectively reduce gas consumption—when the demand for gasoline becomes more elastic or less elastic?

14. Suppose the government imposes a per-litre excise tax on all the firms supplying vodka in Canada. For each of the following, pick the market conditions that would tend to increase the buyer's portion of the tax burden:

   a. Buyers have very few vodka substitutes available versus lots of good vodka substitutes available.

   b. Vodka makes up a large portion of each buyer's total monthly expenditures versus it makes up a very small portion of each buyer's total monthly expenditures.

   c. Buyers consider vodka to be a necessity item versus a luxury item.

   d. The firms supplying vodka can easily switch to supplying other products versus they cannot easily switch to supplying other products.

15. In order to raise funds for Canadian musicians, the Canadian government imposes a per-unit excise tax on all firms supplying blank recordable CDs in Canada. The accompanying graph describes the market demand, before-tax market supply, and after-tax market supply curves for the blank recordable CD market in Canada.

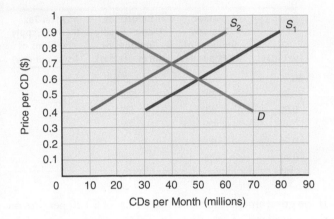

Use the above graph to answer each of the following:

a. What is the before-tax equilibrium price and quantity?

b. What is the amount of the CD excise tax on a per-CD basis?

c. What is the after-tax equilibrium price and quantity?

d. Determine the tax incidence.

e. Determine the total monthly tax revenue that the Canadian government will receive from this CD excise tax.

f. Under what conditions will the tax revenue computed in part (e) increase—when the supply for CDs becomes more elastic or less elastic? Explain.

g. Under what conditions will the CD excise tax more effectively discourage the use of CDs for illegal music downloads—when the supply for CDs becomes more elastic or less elastic?

16. Suppose a provincial government imposes an excise tax on all firms supplying beer in the province. Determine the tax incidence, under each of the following market conditions:

a. The demand for beer is perfectly elastic.

b. The demand for beer is perfectly inelastic.

c. The supply of beer is perfectly elastic.

d. The supply of beer is perfectly inelastic.

BUSINESS APPLICATION

LO 6.4 Describe the various types of quantity restrictions that governments can impose on markets.

Concepts: Policies Aimed at Affecting Demand and Supply: Quantity Restriction Policies

Small Business/Management: Industry Outlook and Strategies

Demand and supply trends can be applied to develop an industry outlook, which is invaluable to a small business owner or upper-level corporate manager making strategic decisions about expansion plans or marketing strategies. One such strategy is a quantity restriction policy. To illustrate this application, consider the following hypothetical graph, which focuses on the market for dentist services.

Market for Dentist Services

Business Application Problems

1. For each of the following events, determine whether the event will increase or decrease the demand or the supply of dentist services. Also, for each event, predict whether the event will tend to cause an increase or decrease in the fee (price) that dentists can charge per unit of service.

a. **EVENT:** The widespread use of fluorides has reduced tooth decay.

b. **EVENT:** There has been a significant trend toward preventative practices, such as flossing and regular teeth cleaning.

c. **EVENT:** More para-professionals, such as dental nurses, are performing standard dental procedures, such as fillings.

d. **EVENT:** Compared to previous years, now fillings, crowns, and bridges are being made with more durable, longer-lasting materials.

e. **EVENT:** Schools of dentistry across the nation are producing graduates at a much faster rate than the growth in the population.

2. From an existing dentist's point of view, do the trends in demand and supply (described in part (a), above) suggest a positive or negative industry outlook?

3. One advantage of trying to predict the industry outlook is that the business owner and/or corporate manager may be able to change that outlook, through strategies to change the industry demand and/or supply. For each of the following business strategies, determine whether

the strategy will increase or decrease the demand or the supply of dentist services. Also, for each event, predict whether the event will tend to cause an increase or decrease in the fee (price) that dentists can charge per unit of service.

a. **STRATEGY:** The National Association of Dentists requires a higher grade for a student to qualify for dental school.

b. **STRATEGY:** The National Association of Dentists increases the standards that foreign dentists must meet in order to practice dentistry in the country.

c. **STRATEGY:** The National Association of Dentists successfully lobbies the government to provide subsidized dental care to seniors and those on welfare.

d. **STRATEGY:** Through anaesthetics, "laughing gas," and hypnosis, dentists are increasingly making the visit to the dentist chair more relaxed and virtually pain free.

e. **STRATEGY:** Dental secretaries contact patients to remind them to attend their regular six-month checkup.

4. As president of your provincial dental association, you are examining the possibility of implementing a quantity restriction policy similar to that used by farmer marketing boards. You have just conducted statistical analysis on the nature of supply and demand for key services provided by dentists in your province. As an example, the graph below describes the current state of market demand and supply for crowns in your province.

a. If you pursue a laissez-faire policy and let the current market conditions prevail, what will be the equilibrium price per crown?

Market for Crowns in Province

Quantity of Crowns per Year (thousands)

b. Under the laissez-faire policy, what will be the annual total revenue collected by the dentists from the provision of crowns in your province?

c. Suppose you decide to convince your fellow dentists to pursue a marketing-board–type policy where the annual supply of crowns would be fixed at 11 000. This would be, in part, achieved by restricting the degree to which foreign dentists could practice in your province, as well as increasing the passing averages in your school of dentistry. Under this marketing board policy, what will be the annual total revenue collected by the dentists from the provision of crowns in your province?

d. Is the demand for the crown services elastic or inelastic in the $600 to $800 price range? Explain.

The Deadweight Loss Due to Government Market Intervention

Chapter 6 noted that government policies such as price ceilings and price floors typically conflict with the goal of allocative efficiency. As noted in earlier chapters, allocative efficiency is concerned with producing the right mix or quantities of goods to maximize economic value or well being, given limited resources. This Appendix illustrates how the concepts of consumer and producer surplus can be used to estimate the total dollar loss in economic value resulting from government market intervention policies, such as price controls. These concepts can similarly be applied to estimate the efficiency loss related to other forms of government market intervention, such as marketing boards and excise taxes. Before proceeding, we will briefly review how a laissez-faire policy promotes allocative efficiency, as illustrated in Chapter 5.

Market Equilibrium and Allocative Efficiency

In a laissez-faire (unregulated) market situation, production and consumption takes place to the point where market demand equals market supply, or where the marginal benefit received from the last unit consumed equals its marginal cost. At this market equilibrium, the sum of consumer and producer surplus is maximized, which means that allocative efficiency is achieved. This assumes that there are no forms of market failure present.

For example, consider Figure C-1, which describes the market for two-bedroom apartments in a Canadian city. Under a laissez-faire policy, the equilibrium price of $600 per unit and the equilibrium quantity of 60 000 units will prevail, where the marginal benefit of the last rental unit consumed ($600) just equals its marginal cost of production ($600). At this equilibrium point, the sum of consumer and producer surplus is maximized. For the equilibrium quantity of 60 000 units, the consumer surplus is the area under the demand curve and over the $600 price line, which equals the area of the blue triangle: .5 × base × height = .5 × 60 000 units × $700 per unit = $21 000 000. The producer surplus is the area above the supply curve and under the $600 price line, which

FIGURE C–1

Allocative Efficiency in an Apartment Rental Market

Allocative efficiency is achieved at the market equilibrium price of $600 per unit and quantity of 60 000 units. This is because the sum of consumer and producer surplus is maximized at this equilibrium point. For the equilibrium quantity of 60 000 units, the consumer surplus is the area under the demand curve and over the $600 price line, which equals the area of the blue triangle: .5 × base × height = .5 × 60 000 units × $700 per unit = $21 000 000. The producer surplus is the area above the supply curve and under the $600 price line, which equals the area of the red triangle: .5 × base × height = .5 × 60 000 units × $600 per unit = $18 000 000.

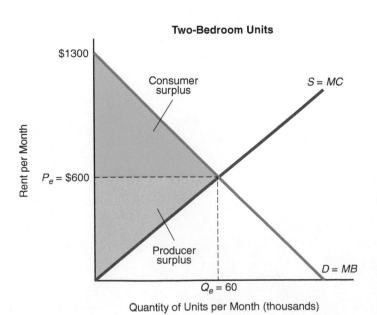

Two-Bedroom Units

equals the area of the red triangle: $.5 \times$ base $\times$ height $= .5 \times 60\ 000$ units $\times \$600$ per unit $= \$18\ 000\ 000$. In this two-bedroom rental market, the maximum consumer and producer surplus that is possible occurs at the market equilibrium and equals $\$21\ 000\ 000 + \$18\ 000\ 000 = \$39\ 000\ 000$. This $\$39$ million represents the net benefit (net value) that buyers and sellers derive from participating in this apartment rental market and is maximized at this equilibrium point.

Price Ceiling Policies and Allocative Inefficiency

In Chapter 6 we studied a price ceiling policy where, in a specific market, the government sets the price below the equilibrium price. We saw how this policy causes a shortage for the product that is being price controlled.

Figure C–2 describes a price ceiling policy that is being imposed on a two-bedroom apartment rental market. The ceiling price, P_c, of $\$400$ per unit is below the equilibrium price, P_e, of $\$600$ per unit. At the ceiling price, the number of rental units supplied will eventually decrease from 60 000 units per month at Q_e to 40 000 units per month at Q_c. At $Q_e = 40\ 000$ units, the consumer surplus and producer surplus will be reduced by triangular areas M and N, respectively, indicating a situation of allocative inefficiency.

At the ceiling policy quantity of 40 000 units, the marginal cost of supplying the next rental unit is approximately $\$400$ (height of the supply curve at $Q_c = 40\ 000$), while the marginal benefit of the next rental unit is approximately $\$850$ (height of the demand curve at $Q_c = 40,000$).

If one more rental unit is supplied, the extra $\$850$ value gained will exceed the $\$400$ value of lost production in the next-best product area. From society's view, there will be a net gain in value of approximately $\$450$ by renting out this additional two-bedroom unit. By not producing more than 40 000 rental units, this extra net gain in value is lost, and society is *underproducing* two-bedroom rental units.

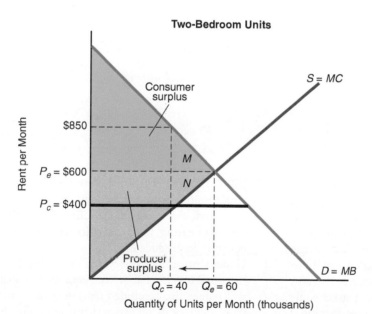

Two-Bedroom Units

Quantity of Units per Month (thousands)

FIGURE C–2

Rent Ceiling Policy and Allocative Inefficiency

With the price ceiling set at $400 per unit, the quantity supplied will decrease from 60 000 units to 40 000 units. This reduces the consumer and producer surpluses by the triangular areas of *M* and *N*, respectively, resulting in allocative inefficiency.

Price Floor Policies and Allocative Inefficiency

In Chapter 6, we studied a price floor policy where, in a specific market, the government sets the price above the equilibrium price. We saw how this policy causes a surplus for the product that is being price controlled.

Figure C–3 describes a price floor policy being implemented in the wheat market. The floor price, P_f, of $\$6$ per bushel is above the equilibrium price, P_e, of $\$5$ per bushel. At the floor price, the quantity of wheat supplied will eventually increase from 3 million bushels per month at Q_e to 4 million bushels per month at Q_f. At Q_f = 4 million bushels, the consumer surplus and producer surplus will be reduced by triangular areas S and R, respectively, indicating a situation of allocative inefficiency.

At the floor policy quantity of 4 million bushels, the marginal cost of supplying the last bushel of wheat is approximately $6 (height of the supply curve at Q_f = 4 million), while the marginal benefit of the last bushel of wheat is approximately $4 (height of the demand curve at Q_f = 4 million).

If one fewer bushel of wheat is supplied, the $4 value lost to wheat consumers (marginal benefit) will be less than $6 value (marginal cost) gained by reallocating resources to the next-best product area (say, barley). From society's view, there will be a net gain in value of approximately $2 by producing one fewer bushel of wheat and one more bushel of another product (barley). In other words, a price floor policy results in society *overproducing* the price-controlled good.

FIGURE C–3

Price Floor Policy and Allocative Inefficiency

With the price floor set at $6 per bushel, the quantity supplied will increase from 3 million bushels to 4 million bushels. This reduces the consumer and producer surpluses by the triangular areas of S and R, respectively, resulting in allocative inefficiency.

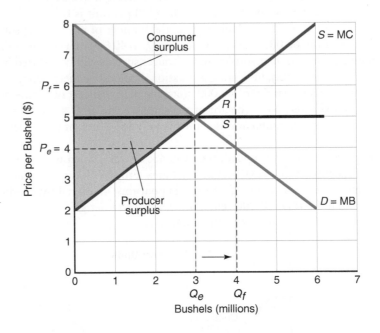

APPENDIX SUMMARY

1. Allocative efficiency is concerned with producing the appropriate mix or quantities of goods so as to maximize economic value or well being, given our limited resources. In a laissez-faire (unregulated) market situation, production and consumption take place to the point where market demand equals market supply or where the marginal benefit received from the last unit consumed equals its marginal cost. At this market equilibrium, the sum of consumer and producer surplus is maximized, which means that allocative efficiency is achieved.

2. Under a price ceiling policy, the quantity supplied will be reduced to a level below equilibrium quantity. This will reduce the combined consumer and producer surplus, resulting in allocative inefficiency. For the last unit produced, the marginal benefit exceeds the marginal cost, indicating that the price-controlled product is being underproduced.

3. Under a price floor policy, the quantity supplied will be increased to a level above the equilibrium quantity. This will reduce the combined consumer and producer surplus, resulting in allocative inefficiency. For the last unit produced, the marginal benefit will be less than the marginal cost, indicating that the price controlled product is being overproduced.

APPENDIX PROBLEMS

C-1. Refer to Figure C-4, which describes the regular gasoline market for a large Canadian city.

    a. Under a laissez-faire market policy, calculate the sum of the consumer and producer surplus.

    b. Suppose the government imposed a price ceiling of $.90 per litre. Calculate the change in consumer and producer surplus due to this policy. How does this policy affect the goal of allocative efficiency?

    c. Does this price ceiling policy result in an over-production or under-production of regular gasoline? Explain.

C-2. Refer to Figure C-4, which describes the regular gasoline market for a large Canadian city.

    a. Suppose the government imposed a price floor of $1.60 per litre. Calculate the change in consumer and producer surplus due to this policy. How does this policy affect the goal of allocative efficiency?

    b. Does this price floor policy result in an overproduction or underproduction of regular gasoline? Explain.

FIGURE C–4

Market for Regular Gasoline

7

LEARNING OBJECTIVES

After reading this chapter, you should be able to:

7.1 Describe the utility theory and how it impacts the decisions of consumers.

7.2 Define the law of diminishing marginal utility and how it relates to consumer optimum.

Consumer Choice

In Canada, even if you live in a city, you can surely appreciate the existence of Banff National Park, the Rocky Mountains, and the great wilderness areas in the North and other parts of the country. And even if you have never seen a whale, you may receive some satisfaction from knowing that whales have not been made extinct. Therefore, you may feel a certain loss when an environmental disaster, such as a huge oil spill, occurs. Should your feelings of loss be taken into account when government officials attempt to determine the policy response to environmental damage? To answer this question, you need to know how consumers make choices and what values they place on those choices.

MyEconLab helps you master each objective and study more efficiently. See end of chapter for details.

DID YOU KNOW THAT...?

In a typical year, a Canadian family spends about 15 percent of its income on food and about the same on housing. Within individual families, however, these relative percentages may be quite different. Some families devote a much higher percentage of their income to housing than do others. What determines how much each family spends on different items in its budget? One explanation is, simply, individual tastes—the values that family members place on different items on which they can spend their income. The saying "you can't argue with tastes" suggests that individuals have different preferences about how to allocate their limited incomes. Although there is no real theory about what determines people's tastes, we can examine some of the behaviour that underlies how consumers react to changes in the prices of the goods and services that they purchase. Recall that people generally purchase less at higher prices than at lower prices. This is called the law of demand.

Because the law of demand is important, its derivation is useful as it allows us to arrange the relevant variables, such as price, income, and tastes, in a way that lets us understand the real world better and even perhaps generate predictions about it. One way of deriving the law of demand involves an analysis of the logic of consumer choice in a world of limited resources. In this chapter, therefore, we discuss what is called utility analysis.

7.1 Utility Theory

When you buy something, you do so because of the satisfaction you expect to receive from having and using that good. For everything that you like to have, the more you have of it, the higher the level of satisfaction you receive. Another term that can be used for satisfaction is **utility**, or want-satisfying power of a good or service. This property is common to all goods that are desired. The concept of utility is purely subjective, however. There is no way that we can measure the amount of utility that a consumer might be able to obtain from a particular good, for utility does not imply "useful" or "utilitarian" or "practical." For this reason, there can be no accurate, scientific assessment of the utility that someone might receive by consuming a frozen dinner or viewing a movie relative to the utility that another person might receive from that same good or service. Nevertheless, we can infer whether a person receives more utility from consuming one good versus another by that person's behaviour. For example, if an individual buys more coffee than tea (when both tea and coffee are priced equally), we are able to say that the individual receives more utility from consuming coffee than from consuming tea.

The utility that individuals receive from consuming a good depends on their tastes and preferences. These tastes and preferences are normally assumed to be given and stable for a particular individual. It is tastes that determine how much utility that individual derives from consuming a good, and this, in turn, determines how that individual allocates income. People spend a greater proportion of their incomes on goods they like. But we cannot explain why tastes are different among individuals. For example, we cannot explain why some people like yogurt but others do not.

We can analyze in terms of utility the way consumers decide what to buy, just as physicists have analyzed some of their questions about what they call "force." No physicist has ever seen a unit of force, and no economist has ever seen a unit of utility. In both cases, however, these concepts have proven useful for analysis.

Throughout this chapter, we will be discussing **utility analysis**, which is the analysis of consumer decision making based on utility maximization.

Utility The want-satisfying power of a good or service.

What are some of the determinants of this consumer's decision to buy a new cellphone?

Utility analysis The analysis of consumer decision making based on utility maximization.

Utility and Utils

Economists once believed that utility could be measured. In fact, there is a school of thought based on utility theory called *utilitarianism*, developed by the English philosopher Jeremy Bentham (1748–1832). Bentham held that society should seek the greatest happiness for the greatest number. He sought to apply an arithmetic formula for

Util A representative unit by which utility is measured.

measuring happiness. He and his followers developed the notion of measurable utility and invented the **util** to measure it. For the moment, we will also assume that we can measure satisfaction using this representative unit. Our assumption will allow us to quantify the way we examine consumer behaviour.[1] Thus, the first chocolate bar that you eat might yield you four utils of satisfaction; the first peanut cluster, six utils; and so on. Today, no one really believes that we can actually measure utils, but the ideas forthcoming from such analysis will prove useful in our understanding of the way in which consumers choose among alternatives.

Total and Marginal Utility

Consider the satisfaction, or utility, that you receive each time that you rent and watch a video. To make the example straightforward, let us say that there are hundreds of videos to choose from each year and that each of them is of the same quality. Let us say that you normally rent one video per week. You could, of course, rent two, or three, or four per week. Presumably, each time you rent another video per week, you will get additional satisfaction, or utility. The question, though, that we must ask is, given that you are already renting one per week, will the next one rented that week give you the same amount of additional utility?

Marginal utility The change in total utility divided by the change in the number of units consumed.

That additional, or incremental, utility is called **marginal utility**, the change in total utility divided by the change in the number of units consumed, where *marginal*, as before, means "incremental" or "additional." (Marginal changes also refer to decreases, in which cases we talk about *decremental* changes.) The concept of marginality is important in economics because we make decisions at the margin. At any particular point, we compare additional (marginal) benefits with additional (marginal) costs.

Applying Marginal Analysis to Utility

The specific example presented in Figure 7–1 will clarify the distinction between total utility and marginal utility. The table in part (a) shows the total utility and the marginal utility of watching videos each week. Marginal utility is the difference between total utility derived from one level of consumption and total utility derived from another level of consumption. A simple formula for marginal utility is this:

$$\text{Marginal utility} = \frac{\text{Change in total utility}}{\text{Change in number of units consumed}}$$

In our example, when a person has already watched two videos in one week and then watches another, total utility increases from 16 utils to 19. Therefore, the marginal utility (of watching one more video after already having watched two in one week) is equal to three utils.

Graphic Analysis

We can transfer the information in part (a) of Figure 7–1 onto a graph, as we do in parts (b) and (c). Total utility, which is represented in column 2 of part (a), is transferred to part (b).

---

[1]What follows is typically called *cardinal utility analysis* by economists. It requires cardinal measurement. Numbers such as 1, 2, and 3 are cardinal numbers. We know that 2 is exactly twice as many as 1 and that 3 is exactly three times as many as 1. You will see in Appendix D at the end of this chapter a type of consumer behaviour analysis that requires only *ordinal* measurement of utility, meaning ranked or ordered. *First, second,* and *third* are ordinal numbers; nothing can be said about their exact size relationships. We can only talk about their importance relative to each other. Temperature, for example, is an ordinal ranking. One hundred degrees Celsius is not twice as warm as 50 degrees Celsius. All we can say is that 100 degrees Celsius is warmer than 50 degrees Celsius.

FIGURE 7–1

Total and Marginal Utility of Watching Videos

If we were able to assign specific values to the utility derived from watching videos each week, we could obtain a marginal utility schedule similar in pattern to the one shown in part (a). In column 1 is the number of videos watched per week; in column 2, the total utility derived from each quantity; and in column 3, the marginal utility derived from each additional quantity, which is defined as the change in total utility due to a change of one unit of watching videos per week. Total utility from part (a) is plotted in part (b). Marginal utility is plotted in part (c), where you see that it reaches zero where total utility hits its maximum at between four and five units.

Part (a)

(1) Number of Videos Watched per Week	(2) Total Utility (utils per week)	(3) Marginal Utility (utils per week)
0	0	
1	10	10 (10 − 0)
2	16	6 (16 − 10)
3	19	3 (19 − 16)
4	20	1 (20 − 19)
5	20	0 (20 − 20)
6	18	−2 (18 − 20)

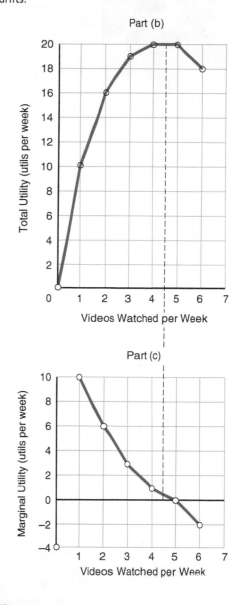

Part (b)

Part (c)

Total utility continues to rise until four videos are watched per week. This measure of utility remains at 20 utils through the fifth video, and at the sixth video per week it falls to 18 utils; we assume that at some quantity consumed per unit time period, boredom sets in. This is shown in part (b).

Marginal Utility

If you look carefully at parts (b) and (c) of Figure 7–1, the notion of marginal utility becomes very clear. In economics, the term *marginal* always refers to a change in the total. The marginal utility of watching three videos per week instead of two videos per week is the increment in total utility and is equal to three utils per week. All of the points in part (c) are taken from column 3 of the table in part (a). Note that marginal utility falls

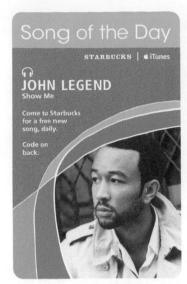

How does marginal utility derived from a music download influence the quantity of music downloads consumed?

Diminishing marginal utility The principle that as an individual consumes more of a particular commodity, the total level of utility, or satisfaction, derived from that consumption usually increases. Eventually, however, the rate at which it increases diminishes as more is consumed.

throughout the graph. A special point occurs after four videos are watched per week because the total utility curve in part (b) is unchanged after the consumption of the fourth video. That means that the consumer receives no additional (marginal) utility from watching the fifth video. This is shown in part (c) as *zero* marginal utility. After that point, marginal utility becomes negative.

In our example, when marginal utility becomes negative, it means that the consumer is fed up with watching videos and would require some form of compensation to watch any more. When marginal utility is negative, an additional unit consumed actually lowers total utility by becoming a nuisance. Rarely does a consumer face a situation of negative marginal utility. Whenever this point is reached, goods become, in effect, "bads." A rational consumer will stop consuming at the point at which marginal utility becomes negative, even if the good is free.

7.2 Diminishing Marginal Utility

Note that in part (c) of Figure 7–1, marginal utility is continuously declining. This property has been named *the principle of diminishing marginal utility*. It is not a concept that can be proven, but economists and others have believed in it for years and it has even been called a law. This supposed law concerns a psychological, or subjective, utility that you receive as you consume more and more of a particular good. Stated formally, the law of **diminishing marginal utility** is as follows:

> **As an individual consumes more of a particular commodity, the total level of utility, or satisfaction, derived from that consumption usually increases. Eventually, however, the rate at which it increases diminishes as more is consumed.**

Take a hungry individual at a dinner table. The first serving is greatly appreciated, and the individual derives a substantial amount of utility from it. The second serving does not have quite as much impact as the first one, and the third serving is likely to be even less satisfying. This individual experiences diminishing marginal utility of food and stops eating. This is true for most people. All-you-can-eat restaurants count on this fact; a second helping of ribs may provide some marginal utility, but the third helping would have only a little or even negative marginal utility. The fall in the marginal utility of other goods is even more dramatic. See, for instance, Example 7–1. Why are candy vending machines different from newspaper vending machines?

EXAMPLE 7–1 Newspaper Vending Machines versus Candy Vending Machines

Have you ever noticed that newspaper vending machines nearly everywhere in Canada allow you to put in the correct change—the cost of one newspaper—lift up the door, and take as many newspapers as you want? Contrast this type of vending machine with candy machines. They are completely locked at all times. You must designate the candy that you wish, normally by using some type of keypad. The candy then drops down to a place where you reach to retrieve it but from which you cannot grab any other candy. The difference between these two types of vending machines is explained by diminishing marginal utility. Newspaper companies dispense newspapers from coin-operated boxes that allow dishonest people to take more copies than they pay for. What would a dishonest person do with more than one copy of a newspaper, however? The marginal utility of a second newspaper is normally zero. The benefit of storing excessive newspapers is usually nil because yesterday's news has no value. But the same analysis does not hold for candy. The marginal utility of a second candy bar is certainly less than the first, but it is normally not zero. Moreover, one can store candy for relatively long periods of time at relatively low cost. Consequently, food vending machine companies have to worry about dishonest users of their machines and must make their machines much more theft-proof than newspaper companies do.

For critical analysis: Can you think of a circumstance under which there would be no diminished marginal utility to newspaper purchasers so that they might be inclined to take more than one newspaper out of a vending machine?

Consider for a moment the opposite possibility—increasing marginal utility. Under such a situation, the marginal utility after consuming, say, one hamburger would increase. The second hamburger would be more valuable to you, and the third would be even more valuable yet. If increasing marginal utility existed, each of us would consume only one good or service! Rather than observing that "variety is the spice of life," we would see that monotony in consumption was preferred. We do not observe this, and therefore, we have great confidence in the concept of diminishing marginal utility.

Optimizing Consumption Choices

Every consumer has a limited income. Choices must be made. When a consumer has made all choices about what to buy and in what quantities, and when the total level of satisfaction, or utility, from that set of choices is as great as it can be, we say that the consumer has *optimized*. When the consumer has attained an optimum consumption set of goods and services, we say that this individual has reached **consumer optimum**.[2]

Consider a simple two-good example. The consumer has to choose between spending income on the rental of videos at $5 each and on purchasing deluxe hamburgers at $3 each. Let us say that the last dollar spent on hamburgers yields three utils of utility, but the last dollar spent on video rentals yields 10 utils. Wouldn't this consumer increase total utility if some dollars were taken away from hamburger consumption and allocated to video rentals? The answer is yes. Given diminishing marginal utility, more dollars spent on video rentals will reduce marginal utility per last dollar spent, whereas fewer dollars spent on hamburger consumption will increase marginal utility per last dollar spent. The optimum—where total utility is maximized—might occur when the satisfaction per last dollar spent on both hamburgers and video rentals per week is equal for the two goods. Thus, the amount of goods consumed depends on the prices of the goods, the income of the consumers, and the marginal utility derived from each good.

Table 7–1 presents information on utility derived from consuming various quantities of videos and hamburgers. Columns 4 and 8 show the marginal utility per dollar spent on videos and hamburgers, respectively. If the prices of both goods are zero, individuals will consume each as long as their respective marginal utility is positive (at least five units of each and probably much more). It is also true that a consumer with infinite income will continue consuming goods until the marginal utility of each is equal to zero. When the price is zero or the consumer's income is infinite, there is no effective constraint on consumption.

Consumer optimum is attained when the marginal utility of the last dollar spent on each good is the same and income is completely exhausted. The individual's income is $26. From columns 4 and 8 of Table 7–1, maximum equal marginal utilities per dollar occur at the consumption level of four videos and two hamburgers (the marginal utility per dollar spent equals 7.3). Note that the marginal utility per dollar spent for both goods is also (approximately) equal at the consumption level of three videos and one hamburger, but here, total income is not completely exhausted. Likewise, the marginal utility per dollar spent is (approximately) equal at five videos and three hamburgers, but the expenditures necessary for that level of consumption exceed the individual's income.

Table 7–2 shows the steps taken to arrive at consumer optimum. The first video would yield a marginal utility per dollar of 10.0, while the first hamburger would yield a marginal utility of only 8.3 per dollar. Because it yields the higher marginal utility per dollar, the video is purchased. This leaves $21 of income. The second video yields a higher marginal utility per dollar (9.0, versus 8.3 for hamburgers), and so it is also purchased, leaving an unspent income of $16. At the third purchase, the first hamburger now yields a higher marginal utility per dollar than the next video (8.3 versus 8.0), and so the first hamburger is purchased. This leaves income of $13 to spend. The process continues until all income is exhausted and the marginal utility per dollar spent is equal for both goods.

Consumer optimum Reached when the consumer has attained an optimum consumption set of goods and services.

---

[2]Optimization typically refers to individual decision-making processes. When we deal with many individuals interacting in the marketplace, we talk in terms of an equilibrium in the marketplace. Generally speaking, equilibrium is a property of markets rather than of individual decision making.

TABLE 7–1

Total and Marginal Utility from Consuming Videos and Hamburgers on an Income of $26

(1) Videos per Period	(2) Total Utility of Videos per Period (utils)	(3) Marginal Utility (utils) MU_v	(4) Marginal Utility per Dollar Spent (MU_v/P_v) (price = $5)	(5) Hamburgers per Period	(6) Total Utility of Hamburgers per Period (utils)	(7) Marginal Utility (utils) MU_h	(8) Marginal Utility per Dollar Spent (MU_h/P_h) (price = $3)
0	0.0	–	–	0	0	–	–
1	50.0	50.0	10.0	1	25	25	8.3
2	95.0	45.0	9.0	2	47	22	7.3
3	135.0	40.0	8.0	3	65	18	6.0
4	171.5	36.5	7.3	4	80	15	5.0
5	200.0	28.5	5.7	5	89	9	3.0

TABLE 7–2

Steps to Consumer Optimum

In each purchase situation described here, the consumer always purchases the good with the higher marginal utility per dollar spent (*MU/P*). For example, at the time of the third purchase, the marginal utility per last dollar spent on videos is 8.0, but it is 8.3 for hamburgers, and $16 of income remains, and so the next purchase will be a hamburger. Here, $P_v = \$5$ and $P_h = \$3$.

	Choices					
	Videos		Hamburgers			
Purchase	Unit	(MU_v/P_v)	Unit	(MU_h/P_h)	Buying Decision	Remaining Income
1	First	10.0	First	8.3	First video	$26 – $5 = $21
2	Second	9.0	First	8.3	Second video	$21 – $5 = $16
3	Third	8.0	First	8.3	First hamburger	$16 – $3 = $13
4	Third	8.0	Second	7.3	Third video	$13 – $5 = $ 8
5	Fourth	7.3	Second	7.3	Fourth video and second hamburger	$ 8 – $5 = $ 3 $ 3 – $3 = $ 0

To restate, consumer optimum requires the following:

A consumer's money income should be allocated so that the last dollar spent on each good purchased yields the same amount of marginal utility (when all income is spent).

A Little Math

We can state the rule of consumer optimum in algebraic terms by examining the ratio of marginal utilities and prices of individual products. This is sometimes called the *utility maximization rule*.

The rule simply states that a consumer maximizes personal satisfaction when allocating money income in such a way that the last dollars spent on good A, good B, good C, and so on, yield equal amounts of marginal utility. Marginal utility (*MU*) from good A is indicated by *MU* of good A. For good B, it is *MU* of good B.

Our algebraic formulation of this rule, therefore, becomes

$$\frac{MU \text{ of good A}}{\text{Price of good A}} = \frac{MU \text{ of good B}}{\text{Price of good B}} = \cdots = \frac{MU \text{ of good Z}}{\text{Price of good Z}}$$

The letters A, B, . . . , Z indicate the various goods and services that the consumer might purchase.

We know, then, that the marginal utility of good A divided by the price of good A must equal the marginal utility of any other good divided by its price in order for the consumer to maximize utility. Note, though, that the application of the utility maximization rule is not an explicit or conscious act on the part of consumers. Rather, this is a model of consumer optimum.

How a Price Change Affects Consumer Optimum

Consumption decisions are summarized in the law of demand, which states that the amount purchased is inversely related to price. We can now see why by using the law of diminishing marginal utility.

Purchase decisions are made such that the value of the marginal utility of the last unit purchased and consumed is just equal to the price that had to be paid. No consumer will, when optimizing, buy 10 units of a good per time period when the personal valuation placed on the tenth unit is less than the price of the tenth unit.

If we start out at consumer optimum and then observe a price decrease, we can predict that consumers will respond to the price decrease by consuming more. Now, with a lower price, it is possible to consume more than before and still not have the marginal utility be less than the price because the price has fallen. If the law of diminishing marginal utility holds, the purchase and consumption of additional units will cause marginal utility to fall. Eventually it will fall to the point at which it is equal to the price of the final good consumed. The limit to this increase in consumption is given by the law of diminishing marginal utility.

A hypothetical demand curve for video rentals per week for a typical consumer is presented in Figure 7–2. Because of the law of diminishing marginal utility, with the consumption of more videos, the marginal utility of the last unit of these additional videos is lower. What has happened is that at a lower price, the number of video rentals per week increased from two to three; marginal utility must have fallen. At a higher consumption rate, the marginal utility falls to meet the lower price for video rentals per week.

The Demand Curve Revisited

Linking the "law" of diminishing marginal utility and the utility maximization rule gives us a negative relationship between the quantity demanded of a good or service and its price. As the relative price of video rentals goes up, for example, the quantity demanded will fall; and as the relative price of video rentals goes down, the quantity demanded will rise. Figure 7–2 shows this demand curve for video rentals. As the price

FIGURE 7–2

Video Rental Prices and Marginal Utility

A reduction in price from $5 to $4 per video rental causes consumers to increase consumption until marginal utility falls (because of the law of diminishing marginal utility).

of video rentals falls, the consumer can maximize total utility only by renting more videos and vice versa. In other words, the relationship between price and quantity desired is simply a downward-sloping demand curve. Note, though, that this downward-sloping demand curve (the law of demand) is derived under the assumption of constant tastes and incomes. You must remember that we are keeping these important determining variables constant when we simply look at the relationship between price and quantity demanded.

Marginal Utility, Total Utility, and the Diamond–Water Paradox

Even though water is essential to life and diamonds are not, water is cheap and diamonds are dear. The economist Adam Smith in 1776 called this the "diamond–water paradox." The paradox is easily understood when we realize that the supply of water is abundant relative to demand and therefore carries a low price. Diamonds, however, are scarce relative to demand and therefore carry a high price. To better understand this, we must make the distinction between total utility and marginal utility. The total utility of water greatly exceeds the total utility derived from diamonds. What determines the price, though, is what happens on the margin. We have relatively few diamonds, and so the marginal utility of the last diamond consumed is high. The opposite is true for water. Total utility does not determine what people are willing to pay for a unit of a particular commodity; marginal utility does. Look at the situation presented graphically in Figure 7–3. We show the demand curve for diamonds, labelled $D_{diamonds}$. The demand curve for water is labelled D_{water}. We plot quantity in terms of kilograms per unit time period on the horizontal axis. On the vertical axis, we plot price in dollars per kilogram. We use kilograms as our common unit of measurement for water and for diamonds. We could just as well have used gallons, acre-feet, or litres.

Note that the demand for water is many, many times the demand for diamonds. We draw the supply curve of water as S_1 at a quantity of Q_{water}. The supply curve for diamonds is given as S_2 at quantity $Q_{diamonds}$. At the intersection of the supply curve of water with the demand curve of water, the price per kilogram is P_{water}. The intersection of the supply curve of diamonds with the demand curve of diamonds is at $P_{diamonds}$. Note that $P_{diamonds}$ exceeds P_{water}. Diamonds sell at a higher price than water. See Example 7–2 for an illustration of the diamond–water paradox.

FIGURE 7–3

The Diamond–Water Paradox

We pick kilograms as a common unit of measurement for both water and diamonds. To demonstrate that the demand for and supply of water are immense, we have put a break in the horizontal quantity axis. Although the demand for water is much greater than the demand for diamonds, the marginal valuation of water is given by the marginal value placed on the last unit of water consumed. To find that, we must know the supply of water, which is given as S_1. At that supply, the price of water is P_{water}. But the supply for diamonds is given by S_2. At that supply, the price of diamonds is $P_{diamonds}$. The total valuation that consumers place on water is tremendous relative to the total valuation consumers place on diamonds. What is important for price determination, however, is the marginal valuation, or the marginal utility received.

EXAMPLE 7-2 The Price of Water in Saudi Arabia

The diamond–water paradox deals with the situation in which water, although necessary for life, may be much cheaper than some luxury items. In Saudi Arabia, as you might expect, the contrary can be true. A litre of water costs five times as much as a litre of gasoline, whereas a pair of custom-made British wool dress pants costs only $25. These relative prices are quite different from what we are used to seeing in Canada. Water costs next to nothing, a litre of gas costs about $1.10, and custom-made wool pants cost at least $200. To understand what has happened in Saudi Arabia, simply substitute gasoline for water and water for diamonds in Figure 7–3.

For critical analysis: List some of the effects on human behaviour that such a high relative price of water would cause.

Behavioural Economics and Consumer Choice Theory

Utility analysis has long been appealing to economists because it makes clear predictions about how individuals will adjust their consumption of different goods and services based on the prices of those items and their incomes. Traditionally, another attraction of utility analysis to many economists has been its reliance on the assumption that consumers behave *rationally*, or that they do not intentionally make decisions that would leave them worse off. As we discussed in Chapter 1, proponents of behavioural economics have doubts about the rationality assumption, which causes them to question the utility-based theory of consumer choice.

DOES BEHAVIOURAL ECONOMICS BETTER PREDICT CONSUMER CHOICES?
Advocates of behavioural economics question whether utility theory is supported by the facts, which they argue are better explained by applying the assumption of *bounded rationality*. Recall from Chapter 1 that this assumption states that human limitations prevent people from examining every possible choice available to them and thereby thwart their efforts to effectively pursue long-term personal interests.

For evidence supporting the bounded rationality assumption, proponents of behavioural economics point to real-world examples that they claim violate rationality-based utility theory. For instance, economists have found that when purchasing electric appliances such as refrigerators, people sometimes buy the lowest-priced, energy-inefficient models, even though the initial savings often fail to compensate for higher future energy costs. There is also evidence that people who live in earthquake- or flood-prone regions commonly fail to purchase sufficient insurance against these events. In addition, experiments have shown that when people are placed in situations in which strong emotions come into play, they may be willing to pay different amounts for items than they would pay in calmer settings.

These and other observed behaviours, behavioural economists suggest, indicate that consumers do not behave rationally. If the rationality assumption does not apply to actual behaviour, they argue, it follows that utility-based consumer choice theory cannot either.

Can behavioural economics explain why people who enjoy shopping for its own sake might later regret the purchases they make?

CONSUMER CHOICE THEORY REMAINS ALIVE AND WELL. In spite of the doubts expressed by proponents of behavioural economics, most economists continue to apply the assumption that people behave *as if* they act rationally with an aim to maximize utility. These economists continue to apply utility theory because of a fundamental strength of this approach: it yields clear-cut predictions regarding consumer choices.

In contrast, if the rationality assumption is rejected, any number of possible human behaviours might be considered. To proponents of behavioural economics, ambiguities

Do people behave rationally when making purchases?

about actual outcomes make the bounded rationality approach to consumer choice more realistic than utility-based consumer choice theory. Nevertheless, a major drawback is that no clearly testable predictions emerge from the many alternative behaviours that people might exhibit if they fail to behave *as if* they are rational.

Certainly, arguments among economists about the "reasonableness" of rational consumers maximizing utility are likely to continue. So far, however, the use of utility-based consumer choice theory has allowed economists to make a wide array of predictions about how consumers respond to changes in prices, incomes, and other factors. By and large, these key predictions continue to be supported by the actual choices that consumers make.

ISSUES AND APPLICATIONS

Contingent Valuation: Pricing the "Priceless"

Concepts Applied: Utility, Total Utility, Demand Curve

How much are we willing to pay to keep our national parks clean?

It is difficult to estimate the dollar amount an average citizen is willing to pay to keep Banff National Park's air clean. One way economists attempt to derive the demand for pristine wilderness is to use contingent valuation.

Obviously, not everything has a price. That is because not everything is bought and sold in the marketplace. Much of what occurs in the environment is outside the marketplace. A wilderness area so remote that hardly anyone visits it certainly has a value, but what is it? The fact that few people visit does not mean it has little worth. If the wilderness were privately owned and the owner received virtually no income from occasional visitors, that does not mean that it would have virtually no value.

When Disaster Occurs

When the wilderness area with few visitors is harmed by some disaster of human origin, such as an oil spill, what has been lost? If your house is burned down, you can get a pretty accurate idea of what the insurance company will give you by looking at the housing market for an alternative. Such is not the case with an oil-blighted wilderness area in the far reaches of the North. Even though the BP oil spill in April 2010 occurred

far out in the Gulf of Mexico, the oil still made it onto the beaches and affected the wildlife both in the ocean and on land.

Nonuse Values

Even people who never use the wilderness area may place a value on it. They may place a value on the opportunity to preserve the wilderness for their grandchildren and on the mere knowledge that such a pristine wilderness area exists. The question, then, is how do we get an accurate valuation of these nonuse values?

Contingent Valuation

Some economists believe that they can obtain an estimate of the demand curve for a wilderness area, for example, that includes nonuse values by conducting opinion polls. In this technique, called *contingent valuation*, people are asked what they are willing to pay for a particular benefit or what they would accept as compensation for its loss. This technique was used in developing multibillion-dollar damage claims against Exxon after its oil tanker, the *Exxon Valdez*, ran aground in

Alaska in 1989. In essence, these contingent valuation surveys asked people *not* living in Alaska to place a value on the utility they lost by virtue of the fact that a part of Alaska's pristine beauty was harmed.

Criticisms of Opinion Data

Many economists are critical of opinion surveys conducted to estimate utility. They point out that such estimates of supposed willingness to pay are without strong meaning if individuals do not actually have to make the payments. One opinion survey estimated the average individual's willingness to pay to prevent the extinction of the whooping crane at $200 per year. That comes to almost $3 billion per year for all Canadian adults. Given that there are fewer than 170 whooping cranes in existence, this total represents about $23.6 million per bird *per year*. There are literally thousands of species that might be protected. Even if households' average willingness to pay is only $10 per year per endangered species, summing that amount over all environmental "goods" would exceed the average family's yearly income many times.

The way in which opinion survey questions are phrased also reveals their weaknesses. In one study, the people interviewed said they would be willing to pay $90 a year to preserve clean air in Banff National Park. In a follow-up survey, when they were asked about paying for competing claims of cleaner air in Toronto and in the eastern provinces as well, they were willing to spend only $16 a year to preserve clean air in Banff National Park.

Finally, when people are asked about their willingness to accept money in exchange for a harm to a resource, rather than their willingness to pay to prevent that very same harm, the dollar values they cite are substantially higher.

For critical analysis:

1. Why can't opinion polls be used effectively to estimate demand curves?
2. How do individuals normally express their perceived level of satisfaction for a good or a service in the marketplace?

SUMMARY

Here is what you should know after reading this chapter. MyEconLab will help you identify what you know and where to go when you need to practise. We suggest that as soon as you review one of the Learning Objective sections below, you then proceed to go through the related section in MyEconLab.

LEARNING OBJECTIVES	KEY TERMS	MYECONLAB PRACTICE
7.1 Utility Theory. As an individual consumes more of a particular commodity, the total level of utility, or satisfaction, derived from that consumption increases. However, the rate at which it increases diminishes as more is consumed. This is known as the law of diminishing marginal utility.	utility, 165 utility analysis, 165 util, 166 marginal utility, 166	• **MyEconLab** Study Plan 7.1
7.2 Diminishing Marginal Utility. An individual reaches consumer optimum when the marginal utility per last dollar spent on each commodity consumed is equal to the marginal utility per dollar spent on every other good. When the price of a particular commodity goes up, to get back into an optimum position, the consumer must reduce consumption of the now relatively more expensive commodity. As this consumer moves back up the marginal utility curve, marginal utility increases. It is possible to derive a downward-sloping demand curve by using the principle of diminishing marginal utility.	diminishing marginal utility, 168 consumer optimum, 169	• **MyEconLab** Study Plan 7.2

PROBLEMS

(Answers to the odd-numbered problems appear at the back of the book.)

LO 7.1 Describe the utility theory and how it impacts the decisions of consumers.

1. Suppose that you are standing in the checkout line of a grocery store. You have 5 kilograms of oranges and three ears of corn. A kilogram of oranges costs 30 cents; so does an ear of corn. You have $2.40 to spend. You are satisfied that you have reached the highest level of satisfaction, or total utility. A friend comes along and tries to convince you that you have to put some of the corn back and replace it with oranges. From what you know about utility analysis, how would you explain this disagreement?

2. The campus pizzeria sells a single pizza for $12. If you order a second pizza, however, its price is only $5. Explain how this relates to marginal utility.

3. Assume that Alice Warfield's marginal utility is 100 utils for the last hamburger she consumed. If the price of hamburgers is $1 apiece, what is Warfield's marginal utility per dollar's worth of hamburger? What is her marginal utility per dollar's worth if the price is 50 cents per hamburger? If the price is $2? How do we calculate marginal utility per dollar's worth of specific commodities?

4. Where possible, complete the missing cells in the following table.

Number of Cheese-burgers	Total Utility of Cheese-burgers	Marginal Utility of Cheese-burgers	Boxes of French Fries	Total Utility of French Fries	Marginal Utility of French Fries
0	0	—	0	0	—
1	20	—	1	—	10
2	36	—	2	—	8
3	—	12	3	—	2
4	—	8	4	21	—
5	—	4	5	21	—

5. From the data in Problem 4, if the price of a cheeseburger is $2, the price of a box of fries is $1, and you have $6 to spend (and you spend all of it), what is the utility-maximizing combination of cheeseburgers and fries?

6. Return to Problem 5. Suppose that the price of cheeseburgers falls to $1. Determine the new utility-maximizing combination of cheeseburgers and french fries.

LO 7.2 Define the law of diminishing marginal utility and how it relates to consumer optimum.

7. A fall in the price of one good leads to more of that good being consumed, other things remaining constant. How might this increase in consumption be broken down?

8. Consider the table at the bottom of this page. Following the utility maximization rule, how much of each good will be consumed?

9. If total utility is increasing as more is consumed, what is happening to marginal utility?

10. Yesterday, you were consuming four eggs and two strips of bacon. Today, you are consuming three eggs and three strips of bacon. Your tastes did not change overnight. What might have caused this change? Are you better or worse off?

11. Complete the missing cells in the table below.

Number of Cheese-burgers	Total Utility of Cheese-burgers	Marginal Utility of Cheese-burgers	Boxes of French Fries	Total Utility of French Fries	Marginal Utility of French Fries
0	0	—	0	0	—
1	20	—	1	—	8
2	36	—	2	—	6
3	—	12	3	—	4
4	—	8	4	20	—
5	—	4	5	20	—

12. From the data in Problem 11, if the price of a cheeseburger is $2 and the price of a box of french fries is $1, and you have $6 to spend (and you spend all of it), what is the utility-maximizing combination of cheeseburgers and french fries?

13. In Example 7–1, "Newspaper Vending Machines versus Candy Vending Machines," newspaper vendors allow people to access more than one paper at a time. Similarly, in Prince Edward Island, you will see potatoes left by the roadside for people to buy, on their honour. Farmers say they more than come out ahead at the end of the day. What does this say about the diminishing marginal utility of potatoes?

Quantity of Good A	Marginal Utility of Good A	Price of Good A	Quantity of Good B	Marginal Utility of Good B	Price of Good B
100	15	$4.51	9	7	$1.69
101	12	4.51	10	5	1.69
102	8	4.51	11	3	1.69
103	6	4.51	12	2	1.69

BUSINESS APPLICATION

LO 1 and LO 2 Describe the utility theory and how it impacts the decisions of consumers; define the law of diminishing marginal utility and how it relates to consumer optimum.

Management: The Equi-Marginal Principle and Managing Resources Efficiently

Recall that a rational consumer will maximize utility (a goal) if the last dollar spent on each good consumed yields the same marginal utility. Similarly, the rational manager (or administrator) will maximize the achievement of the organization's goal(s) if the last budget dollar spent on hiring each resource yields the same marginal contribution to the organization's goal(s).

Business Application Problem

The general manager of a municipal police force has just been presented with an economic study showing that for the budget year just completed,

- Marginal dollar reduction in theft for the last dollar spent on hiring new beat police officers = $5

- Marginal dollar reduction in theft for the last dollar spent on renting new police cars = $9

Theoretically speaking, if next year's budget stays the same, should the general manager consider re-allocating resources in order to maximize the dollar reduction in theft?

More Advanced Consumer Choice Theory

It is possible to analyze consumer choice verbally, as we did for the most part in Chapter 7. The theory of diminishing marginal utility can be fairly well accepted on intuitive grounds and by introspection. If we want to be more formal and perhaps more elegant in our theorizing, however, we can translate our discussion into a graphic analysis with what we call indifference curves and the budget constraint. Here, we discuss these terms and their relationship and demonstrate consumer equilibrium in geometric form.

On Being Indifferent

What does it mean to be indifferent? It usually means that you do not care one way or the other about something—you are equally disposed to either of two alternatives. With this interpretation in mind, we will turn to two choices, video rentals and restaurant meals. In part (a) of Figure D–1, we show several combinations of video rentals and restaurant meals per week that a representative consumer considers equally satisfactory. That is to say, for each combination, *A, B, C,* and *D*, this consumer will have exactly the same level of total utility.

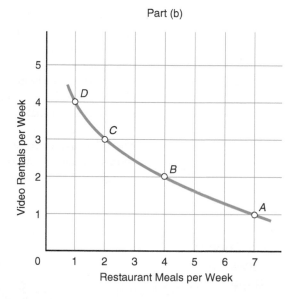

Part (a)

Combination	Video Rentals per Week	Restaurant Meals per Week
A	1	7
B	2	4
C	3	2
D	4	1

FIGURE D–1

Combinations That Yield Equal Levels of Satisfaction

A, B, C, and *D* represent combinations of video rentals and restaurant meals per week that give an equal level of satisfaction to this consumer. In other words, the consumer is indifferent among these four combinations.

The simple numerical example that we have used happens to concern video rentals and restaurant meals per week. This example is used to illustrate general features of indifference curves and related analytical tools that are necessary for deriving the demand curve. Obviously, we could have used any two commodities. Just remember that we are using a *specific* example to illustrate a *general* analysis.

We can plot these combinations graphically in part (b) of Figure D–1, with restaurant meals per week on the horizontal axis and video rentals per week on the vertical axis. These are our consumer's indifference combinations—the consumer finds each combination as acceptable as the others. When we connect these combinations with a smooth curve, we obtain what is called the consumer's *indifference curve.* Along the **indifference curve**, every combination of the two goods in question yields the same level of satisfaction. Every point along the indifference curve is equally desirable to the consumer. For

Indifference curve A curve where every combination of the two goods in question yields the same level of satisfaction.

example, four video rentals per week and one restaurant meal per week will give our representative consumer exactly the same total satisfaction as two video rentals per week and four restaurant meals per week.

Properties of Indifference Curves

Indifference curves have special properties relating to their slope and shape.

Downward Slope

The indifference curve shown in part (b) of Figure D–1 slopes downward; that is, it has a negative slope. Now, consider Figure D–2. Here, we show two points, A and B. Point A represents four video rentals per week and two restaurant meals per week. Point B represents five video rentals per week and six restaurant meals per week. Clearly, B is always preferred to A because B represents more of everything. If B is always preferred to A, it is impossible for points A and B to be on the same indifference curve because the definition of the indifference curve is a set of combinations of two goods that are equally preferred.

Curvature

The indifference curve that we have drawn in part (b) of Figure D–1 is special. Note that it is curved. Why didn't we just draw a straight line, as we have usually done for a demand curve? To find out why we do not posit straight-line indifference curves, consider the implications. We show such a straight-line indifference curve in Figure D–3. Start at point A. The consumer has no restaurant meals and five video rentals per week. Now the consumer wishes to go to point B. He or she is willing to give up only one video rental in order to get one restaurant meal. Now, let us assume that the consumer is at point C, consuming one video rental and four restaurant meals per week. If the consumer wants to go to point D, he or she is again willing to give up one video rental in order to get one more restaurant meal per week.

In other words, no matter how many videos the consumer rents, he or she is willing to give up one video rental to get one restaurant meal per week—which does not seem plausible. Doesn't it make sense to hypothesize that the more videos the consumer rents per week, the less he or she will value an *additional* video rental? Presumably, when the consumer has five video rentals and no restaurant meals per week, he or she should be willing to give up more than one video rental in order to get one restaurant meal. Therefore, a straight-line indifference curve as shown in Figure D–3 no longer seems plausible.

FIGURE D–2

Indifference Curves: Impossibility of an Upward Slope

Point B represents a consumption of more video rentals per week and more restaurant meals per week than point A. B is always preferred to A. Therefore, A and B cannot be on the same indifference curve, which is positively sloped, because an indifference curve shows equally preferred combinations of the two goods.

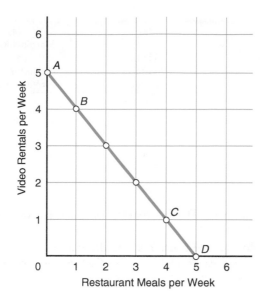

Implications of a Straight-Line Indifference Curve

If the indifference curve is a straight line, the consumer will be willing to give up the same number of video rentals (one for one in this simple example) to get one more restaurant meal per week, whether the consumer has no restaurant meals or a lot of restaurant meals per week. For example, the consumer at point *A* has five video rentals and no restaurant meals per week. He or she is willing to give up one video rental in order to get one restaurant meal per week. At point *C*, however, the consumer has only one video rental and four restaurant meals per week. Because of the straight-line indifference curve, this consumer is willing to give up the last video rental in order to get one more restaurant meal per week, even though he or she already has four.

In mathematical language, an indifference curve is convex with respect to the origin. Let us look at this in part (a) of Figure D–1. Starting with combination *A*, the consumer has one video rental but seven restaurant meals per week. To remain indifferent, the consumer would have to be willing to give up three restaurant meals to obtain one more video rental (as shown in combination *B*). However, to go from combination *C* to combination *D*, note that the consumer would have to be willing to give up only one restaurant meal for an additional video rental per week. The quantity of the substitute considered acceptable changes as the rate of consumption of the original item changes.

Consequently, the indifference curve in part (b) of Figure D–1 will be convex when viewed from the origin.

The Marginal Rate of Substitution

Instead of using marginal utility, we can talk in terms of the marginal rate of substitution between restaurant meals and video rentals per week. We can formally define the consumer's marginal rate of substitution as follows:

> **The marginal rate of substitution is equal to the change in the quantity of one good that just offsets a one-unit change in the consumption of another good, such that total satisfaction remains constant.**

We can see numerically what happens to the marginal rate of substitution in our example if we rearrange part (a) of Figure D–1 into Table D–1. Here, we show restaurant meals in the second column and video rentals in the third. Now we ask the question "What change in the consumption of video rentals per week will just compensate for a three-unit change in the consumption of restaurant meals per week and leave the consumer's total utility constant?" The movement from *A* to *B* increases video rental consumption by 1. Here, the marginal rate of substitution is 3:1—a three-unit decrease in restaurant meals requires an increase of one video rental to leave the consumer's total utility unaltered. Thus, the consumer values the three restaurant meals as the equivalent of one video rental. We do this for the rest of the table and find that as restaurant meals decrease further, the marginal rate of substitution goes from 3:1 to 1:1. The marginal rate of substitution of restaurant meals for video rentals per week falls as the consumer obtains more video rentals. That is, the consumer values successive units of video rentals less and less in terms of restaurant meals. The first video rental is valued at three restaurant meals; the last (fourth) video

TABLE D–1

Calculating the Marginal Rate of Substitution

As we move from combination A to combination B, we are still on the same indifference curve. To stay on that curve, the number of restaurant meals decreases by three and the number of video rentals increases by one. The marginal rate of substitution is 3:1. A three-unit decrease in restaurant meals requires an increase of one video rental to leave the consumer's total utility unaltered.

Combination	(1)	(2) Restaurant Meals per Week	(3) Video Rentals per Week	(4) Marginal Rate of Substitution of Restaurant Meals for Video Rentals
A		7	1	
B		4	2	3:1
C		2	3	2:1
D		1	4	1:1

rental is valued at only one restaurant meal. The fact that the marginal rate of substitution falls is sometimes called the *law of substitution*.

In geometric language, the slope of the consumer's indifference curve (actually, the negative of the slope) measures the consumer's marginal rate of substitution. Note that this marginal rate of substitution is purely subjective or psychological.

The Indifference Map

Let us now consider the possibility of having both more video rentals *and* more restaurant meals per week. When we do this, we can no longer stay on the same indifference curve that we drew in Figure D–1. That indifference curve was drawn for equally satisfying combinations of video rentals and restaurant meals per week. If the individual can now attain more of both, a new indifference curve will have to be drawn, above and to the right of the one shown in part (b) of Figure D–1. Alternatively, if the individual faces the possibility of having less of both video rentals and restaurant meals per week, an indifference curve will have to be drawn below and to the left of the one in part (b) of Figure D–1. We can map out a whole set of indifference curves corresponding to these possibilities.

Figure D–4 shows three possible indifference curves. Indifference curves that are higher than others necessarily imply that for every given quantity of one good, more of the other good can be obtained on a higher indifference curve. Looked at another way, if one goes from curve I_1 to I_2, it is possible to consume the same number of restaurant meals *and* be able to rent more videos per week. This is shown as a movement from point A to point B in Figure D–4. We could do it the other way. When we move from a lower to a higher indifference curve, it is possible to rent the same number of videos *and* to consume more restaurant meals per week. Thus, the higher a consumer is on the indifference map, the greater is that consumer's total level of satisfaction.

FIGURE D–4

A Set of Indifference Curves

An infinite number of indifference curves can be drawn. We show three possible ones. Realize that a higher indifference curve represents the possibility of higher rates of consumption of both goods. Hence, a higher indifference curve is preferred to a lower one because more is preferred to less. Look at points A and B. Point B represents more video rentals than point A; therefore, bundles on indifference curve I_2 have to be preferred over bundles on I_1 because the number of restaurant meals per week is the same at points A and B.

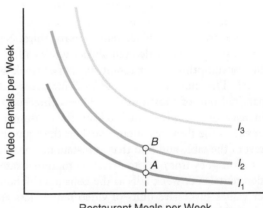

The Budget Constraint

Our problem here is to find out how to maximize consumer satisfaction. To do so, we must consult not only our *preferences*—given by indifference curves—but also our *market opportunities*—given by our available income and prices, called our **budget constraint** (all of the possible combinations of goods that can be purchased [at fixed prices] with a specific budget). We might want more of everything, but for any given budget constraint, we have to make choices, or trade-offs, among possible goods. Everyone has a budget constraint; that is, everyone faces a limited consumption potential. How do we show this graphically? We must find the prices of the goods in question and determine the maximum consumption of each allowed by our budget. For example, let us assume that videos rent for $10 apiece and restaurant meals cost $20. Let us also assume that our representative consumer has a total budget of $60 per week. What is the maximum number of videos the consumer can rent? Six. And the maximum number of restaurant meals per week he or she can consume? Three. So, now, as shown in Figure D–5, we have two points on our budget line, which is sometimes called the *consumption possibilities curve*. These anchor points of the budget line are obtained by dividing money income by the price of each product. The first point is at *b* on the vertical axis; the second, at *b'* on the horizontal axis. The budget line is linear because prices are given.

Any combination along line *bb'* is possible; in fact, any combination in the coloured area is possible. We will assume, however, that the individual consumer completely uses up the available budget, and we will consider as possible only those points along *bb'*.

Slope of the Budget Constraint

The budget constraint is a line that slopes downward from left to right. The slope of that line has a special meaning. Look carefully at the budget line in Figure D–5. Remember in the discussion of graphs in Appendix A that we measure a negative slope by the ratio of the fall in Y over the run in X. In this case, Y is video rentals per week and X is restaurant meals per week. In Figure D–5, the fall in Y is −2 video rentals per week (a drop from 4 to 2) for a run in X of one restaurant meal per week (an increase from 1 to 2); therefore, the slope of the budget constraint is $-\frac{2}{1}$ or −2. This slope of the budget constraint represents the rate of exchange between video rentals and restaurant meals; it is the realistic rate of exchange, given their prices.

Now we are ready to determine how the consumer achieves the optimum consumption rate.

Consumers will try to attain the highest level of total utility possible, given their budget constraints. How can this be shown graphically? We draw a set of indifference

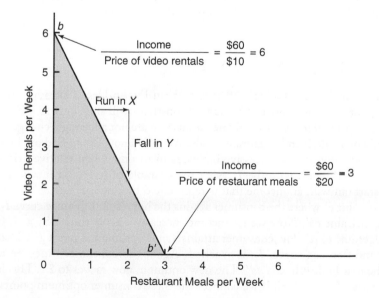

FIGURE D–5

The Budget Constraint

The line *bb'* represents this individual's budget constraint. Assuming that video rentals cost $10 each, restaurant meals cost $20 each, and the individual has a budget of $60 per week, a maximum of six video rentals or three restaurant meals can be bought each week. These two extreme points are connected to form the budget constraint. All combinations within the coloured area and on the budget constraint line are feasible.

curves similar to those in Figure D–4, and we bring in reality—the budget constraint *bb'*. Both are drawn in Figure D–6. Because a higher level of total satisfaction is represented by a higher indifference curve, we know that the consumer will strive to be on the highest indifference curve possible. However, the consumer cannot get to indifference curve I_3 because the budget will be exhausted before any combination of video rentals and restaurant meals represented on indifference curve I_3 is attained. This consumer can maximize total utility, subject to the budget constraint, only by being at point E on indifference curve I_2 because here the consumer's income is just being exhausted. Mathematically, point E is called the tangency point of the curve I_2 to the straight line *bb'*.

FIGURE D–6

Consumer Optimum

A consumer reaches an optimum when he or she ends up on the highest indifference curve possible, given a limited budget. This occurs at the tangency between an indifference curve and the budget constraint. In this diagram, the tangency is at *E*.

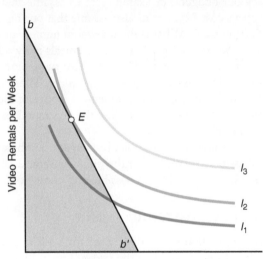

Restaurant Meals per Week

Consumer Optimum Revisited

Consumer optimum is achieved when the marginal rate of substitution (which is subjective) is just equal to the feasible, or realistic, rate of exchange between video rentals and restaurant meals. This realistic rate is the ratio of the two prices of the goods involved. It is represented by the absolute value of the slope of the budget constraint. At point E, the point of tangency between indifference curve I_2 and budget constraint *bb'*, the rate at which the consumer wishes to substitute video rentals for restaurant meals (the numerical value of slope of the indifference curve) is just equal to the rate at which the consumer *can* substitute video rentals for restaurant meals (the slope of the budget line).

Effects of Changes in Income

A change in income will shift the budget constraint *bb'* in Figure D–6. Consider only increases in income, not changes in price. The budget constraint will shift outward. Each new budget line will be parallel to the original one because we are not allowing a change in the relative prices of video rentals and restaurant meals. We would now like to find out how an individual consumer responds to successive increases in income when relative prices remain constant. We do this in Figure D–7, using the example of fast-food meals and movie tickets. We start out with an income that is represented by a budget line *bb'*. Consumer optimum is at point E, where the consumer attains the highest indifference curve I_1, given the budget constraint *bb'*. Now we let income increase. This is shown by a shift outward in the budget line to *cc'*. The consumer attains a new optimum at point E'. That is where a higher indifference curve, I_2, is reached. Again the consumer's income is increased so that the new budget line is *dd'*. The new optimum now moves to E''. This is where indifference curve I_3 is reached. If we connect the three consumer optimum points,

E, E', and E'', we have what is called an income-consumption curve. The **income-consumption curve** shows the optimum consumption points that would occur if income for that consumer were increased continuously, holding the prices of fast-food meals and movie tickets constant.

Income-consumption curve The set of optimal consumption points that would occur if income were increased, relative prices remaining constant.

FIGURE D-7

Income-Consumption Curve

We start off with income sufficient to yield budget constraint bb'. The highest attainable indifference curve is I_1, which is just tangent to bb' at E. Next we increase income. The budget line moves outward to cc', which is parallel to bb'. The new highest indifference curve is I_2, which is just tangent to cc' at E'. We increase income again, which is represented by a shift in the budget line to dd'. The new tangency point of the highest indifference curve, I_3, with dd' is at point E''. When we connect these three points, we obtain the income-consumption curve.

The Price-Consumption Curve

In Figure D-8, we hold income and the price of fast-food meals constant while we lower the price of tickets to movies. As we keep lowering the price of movie tickets, the quantity of tickets that could be purchased if all income were spent on viewing movies increases; thus, the extreme points for the budget constraint keep moving outward to the right as the price of movie tickets falls. In other words, the budget line rotates outward from bb' to bb'' and bb''. Each time the price of movie tickets falls, a new budget line is formed. There has to be a new optimum point. We find it by locating on each new budget line the highest attainable indifference curve. This is shown at points E, E', and E''. We see that as price decreases for movie tickets, the consumer views more movies per week. We call the line connecting points E, E', and E'' the **price-consumption curve** in Figure D-8. It connects the tangency points of the budget constraints and indifference curves, thus showing the amounts of two goods that a consumer will buy when money income and the price of one commodity are held constant while the price of the remaining good changes.

Price-consumption curve The set of consumer-optimum combinations of two goods that the consumer would choose as the price of one good changes while money income and the price of the other good remain constant.

FIGURE D-8

Price-Consumption Curve

As we lower the price of movie tickets, income measured in terms of movie tickets per week increases. We show this by rotating the budget constraint from bb' to bb'' and finally to bb'''. We then find the highest indifference curve that is attainable for each successive budget constraint. For budget constraint bb', the highest indifference curve is I_1, which is tangent to bb' at point E. We do this for the next two budget constraints. When we connect the optimum points, E, E', and E'' we derive the price-consumption curve, which shows the combinations of the two commodities that a consumer will purchase when money income and the price of one commodity remain constant while the other commodity's price changes.

Deriving the Demand Curve

We are now in a position to derive the demand curve using indifference curve analysis. In panel (a) of Figure D–9, we show what happens when the price of tickets to movies decreases, holding both the price of meals at fast-food restaurants and income constant. If the price of movie tickets decreases, the budget line rotates from *bb'* to *bb"*. The two optimum points are given by the tangency at the highest indifference curve that just touches those two budget lines. This is at *E* and *E'*. But those two points give us two price-quantity pairs. At point *E*, the price of movie tickets is $10; the quantity demanded is 2. Thus, we have one point that we can transfer to panel (b) of Figure D–9. At point *E'*, we have another price-quantity pair. The price has fallen to $5; the quantity demanded has increased to 5. We therefore transfer this other point to panel (b). When we connect these two points (and all the others in between), we derive the demand curve for tickets to movies, which slopes downward.

FIGURE D–9

Deriving the Demand Curve

In panel (a), we show the effects of a decrease in the price of movie tickets from $10 to $5. At $10, the highest indifference curve touches the budget line *bb'* at point *E*. The number of movies viewed is two. We transfer this combination—price, $10; quantity demanded, 2—down to panel (b). Next we decrease the price of movie tickets to $5. This generates a new budget line, or constraint, which is *bb"*. Consumer optimum is now at *E'*. The optimum quantity of movie tickets demanded at a price of $5 is five. We transfer this point—price, $5; quantity demanded, 5—down to panel (b). When we connect these two points, we have a demand curve, *D*, for tickets to movies.

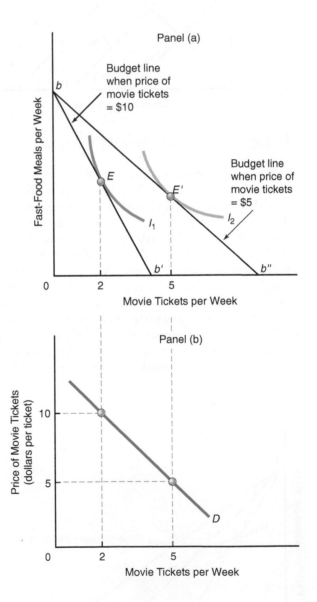

APPENDIX SUMMARY

1. Along an indifference curve, the consumer experiences equal levels of satisfaction. That is to say, along any indifference curve, every combination of the two goods in question yields exactly the same level of satisfaction.
2. Indifference curves typically slope downward and are usually convex to the origin.
3. To measure the marginal rate of substitution, we find out how much of one good has to be given up in order to allow the consumer to consume one more unit of the other good while still remaining on the same indifference curve. The marginal rate of substitution falls as one moves down an indifference curve.
4. Indifference curves represent preferences. A budget constraint represents opportunities—how much can be purchased with a given level of income. Consumer optimum is obtained when the highest feasible indifference curve is just tangent to the budget constraint line; at that point, the consumer reaches the highest feasible indifference curve.
5. An increase in income will shift the budget constraints outward.
6. The price-consumption curve connects the tangency points of the budget constraints and indifference curves, thus showing the amounts of two goods that a consumer will buy when money income and the price of one commodity are held constant while the price of the remaining good changes.

APPENDIX PROBLEMS

(Answers to the odd-numbered problems appear at the back of the book.)

D-1. Suppose that a consumer prefers A to B and B to C but insists that she also prefers C to A. Explain the logical problem here.

D-2. Suppose that you are indifferent among the following three combinations of food (f) and drink (d): $1f$ and $10d$, $2f$ and $7d$, $3f$ and $2d$. Calculate the marginal rate of substitution in consumption between the two goods. Does the substitution of the third f imply a greater sacrifice of d than the second did?

D-3. Construct a budget line from the following information: nominal income of $100 per week; price of beef, P_b, $2 per pound; price of shelter, P_s, $20 per week; all income is spent on beef and shelter. Suppose that your money income remains constant, the price of beef doubles to $4 per pound, and the price of shelter falls to $10 per week. Draw the new budget line. Are you now better off or worse off? What do you need to know before deciding?

D-4. Given the following three combinations of goods, $A = 3x + 4y$, $B = 4x + 6y$, and $C = 5x + 4y$, answer the following questions:
   a. Is any one bundle preferred to the other two?
   b. Could a consumer possibly find B and C to be equally acceptable? How about A and C?

D-5. Calculate the marginal rate of substitution of burritos for yogurt for the following consumer's indifference schedule:

Servings of Yogurt per Week	Burritos per Week
10	1
6	2
3	3
1	4

D-6. Assume that you are consuming only yogurt (Y) and gymnasium exercise (G). Each serving of yogurt costs $4, and each visit to the gym costs $8. Given your food and exercise budget, you consume 15 servings of yogurt and five visits to the gym each week. One day, the price of yogurt falls to $3 per serving and the price of gym visits increases to $10. Now you buy 20 servings of yogurt and four gym visits per week.
   a. Draw the old and new budget constraints, and show the two equilibrium bundles of yogurt servings and visits to the gym.
   b. What is your weekly budget for food and exercise?

D-7. Explain why each of the following statements is or is not consistent with our assumptions about consumer preferences:
   a. I cannot decide whether to go abroad this summer or to stay at home.
   b. That is mine. You cannot have it. There is nothing you can do to make me change my mind.
   c. I love hot pretzels with mustard at football games. If I had my way, I would never stop eating them.

8

LEARNING OBJECTIVES

After reading this chapter, you should be able to:

8.1 Distinguish between accounting profits and economic profits.

8.2 Understand the short-run production function and diminishing marginal returns.

8.3 Calculate the various costs for the firm in the short run.

8.4 Explain the important relationships of the cost curves.

8.5 Understand the long-run cost curve.

The Firm: Cost and Output Determination

You drive to work by the same route every day and wonder why that one restaurant changes every six months. It has gone from a Chinese restaurant to a vegetarian one, and has now morphed into an Irish pub. Other businesses in the area seem to be stable, but that one does not appear to be a good investment.

What could all of those previous owners have done wrong? This chapter will start you thinking about how knowledge of supply and demand needs to be supplemented with knowledge about the costs of doing business.

MyEconLab helps you master each objective and study more efficiently. See end of chapter for details.

DID YOU KNOW THAT...?

There are more than 25 steps in the process of manufacturing a simple lead pencil. In the production of an automobile, there are thousands. At each step, the manufacturer can have the job done by workers or machines or some combination of the two. The manufacturer must also figure out how much to produce each month. Should a new machine that can replace 10 workers be bought? Should more workers be hired, or should the existing workers be paid overtime? If the price of aluminum is rising, should the company try to make do with plastic? What you will learn about in this chapter is how producers can select the best combination of inputs for any given output that is desired.

8.1 The Profits of a Firm

Most people think of a firm's profit as the difference between the amount of revenues the firm takes in and the amount it spends for wages, materials, and so on. In a bookkeeping sense, the following formula could be used:

$$\text{Accounting profit} = \text{Total revenue} - \text{Explicit costs}$$

where **explicit costs** are expenses that business managers must take account of because they must actually be paid out by the firm. This definition of profit is known as **accounting profit**, total revenue minus total explicit costs. It is appropriate when used by accountants to determine a firm's taxable income. Economists are more interested in how firm managers react not just to changes in explicit costs but also to changes in **implicit costs**, defined as expenses that business managers do not have to pay out of pocket but are costs to the firm nonetheless because they represent an opportunity cost. They do not involve any direct cash outlay by the firm and must therefore be measured by the *alternative cost principle*. That is to say, they are measured by what the resources (land, capital) currently used in producing a particular good or service could earn in other uses. Economists use the full opportunity cost of all resources (including both explicit and implicit costs) as the figure to subtract from revenues to obtain a definition of profit. Another definition of implicit cost is therefore the opportunity cost of using factors that a producer does not buy or hire but already owns.

How can the manufacturing process for pencils be made more efficient?

Explicit costs Expenses that business managers must take account of because they must actually be paid out by the firm.

Accounting profit Total revenue minus total explicit costs.

Implicit costs Expenses that business managers do not have to pay out of pocket.

Opportunity Cost of Capital

Firms enter or remain in an industry if they earn, at minimum, a **normal rate of return**—the amount that must be paid to an investor to induce investment in a business. People will not invest their wealth in a business unless they obtain a positive normal (competitive) rate of return—that is, unless their invested wealth pays off. Any business wishing to attract capital must expect to pay at least the same rate of return on that capital as all other businesses (of similar risk) are willing to pay. Put another way, when a firm requires the use of a resource in producing a particular product, it must bid against alternative users of that resource. Thus, the firm must offer a price that is at least as much as other potential users are offering to pay. For example, if individuals can invest their wealth in almost any publishing firm and get a rate of return of 10 percent per year, each firm in the publishing industry must *expect* to pay 10 percent as the normal rate of return to present and future investors. This 10 percent is a *cost to the firm*, the opportunity cost of capital. The **opportunity cost of capital** is the amount of income, or yield, that could have been earned by investing in the next-best alternative. Capital will not stay in firms or industries in which the expected rate of return falls below its opportunity cost, that is, what could be earned elsewhere. If a firm owns some capital equipment, it can either use it or lease it and earn a return. If the firm uses the equipment for production, part of the cost of using that equipment is the forgone revenue that the firm could have earned had it leased out that equipment.

Normal rate of return The amount that must be paid to an investor to induce investment in a business.

Opportunity cost of capital The amount of income, or yield, that could have been earned by investing in the next-best alternative.

Opportunity Cost of Owner-Provided Labour and Capital

Single-owner proprietorships often grossly exaggerate their profit rates because they understate the opportunity cost of the labour that the proprietor provides to the business. Here, we are referring to the opportunity cost of labour. Take, for example, people who run a small grocery store. These people will sit down at the end of the year and figure out what their "profits" are. They will add up all their sales and subtract what they had to pay to other workers, to their suppliers, in taxes, and so on. The end result they will call "profit." They normally will not, however, have figured into their costs the salary that they could have made if they had worked for somebody else in a similar type of job. By working for themselves, they become residual claimants—they receive what is left after all explicit costs have been accounted for. Part of the costs, however, should include the salary the owner-operator could have received working for someone else.

Consider a simple example of a skilled auto mechanic working 14 hours a day at his own service station, six days a week. Compare this situation with how much he could earn as a trucking company mechanic working 84 hours a week. This self-employed auto mechanic might have an opportunity cost of about $20 an hour. For his 84-hour week in his own service station, he is forfeiting $1680. Unless his service station shows accounting profits of more than that per week, he is incurring losses in an economic sense.

Another way of looking at the opportunity cost of running a business is that opportunity cost consists of all explicit and implicit costs. Accountants only take account of explicit costs. Therefore, accounting profit ends up being the residual after only explicit costs are subtracted from total revenues.

This same analysis can apply to owner-provided capital, such as land or buildings. The fact that the owner owns the building or the land with which he or she operates a business does not mean that it is "free." Rather, use of the building and land still has an opportunity cost—the value of the next-best alternative use for those assets.

Some firms are nonprofit enterprises. Nevertheless, they face the same incentive to generate sufficient revenues or, in some cases, sufficient donations, to cover the opportunity cost of equipment and other capital resources.

POLICY EXAMPLE 8–1   Nonprofit Firms Join in the Quest for Profits

The American Medical Association and other leading medical societies are nonprofit organizations. This entitles them to special exemptions from taxes faced by for-profit companies.

The National Geographic Society now operates National Geographic Ventures, Inc., a for-profit firm that produces video documentaries, operates a mapping service, and manages retail outlets. The American Cancer Society earns millions of dollars each year in royalties from for-profit companies that it grants the right to use its name in for-profit marketing.

Profits earned by nonprofit organizations allow them to enlarge and facilitate their streams of cash inflows. This helps ensure that they cover the opportunity cost of capital. Nevertheless, profit-earning activities by nonprofit organizations are raising red flags. Are some of these organizations "nonprofit" only in name?

For critical analysis: Must nonprofit firms earn a normal rate of return?

Accounting Profits versus Economic Profits

The term "profits" in economics means the income that entrepreneurs earn, over and above all costs including their own opportunity cost of time, plus the opportunity cost of the capital they have invested in their business. Profits can be regarded as total revenues minus total costs—which is how accountants think of them—but we must now include *all* costs. Our definition of **economic profits** will be the following:

Economic profits = Total revenues − Total opportunity cost of all inputs used

or

Economic profits = Total revenues − (Explicit + Implicit costs)

Remember that implicit costs include a normal rate of return on invested capital. We show this relationship in Figure 8–1.

Economic profits Total revenues minus total opportunity costs of all inputs used, or total revenues minus the total of all implicit and explicit costs.

The Goal of the Firm: Profit Maximization

When we examined the theory of consumer demand, utility (or satisfaction) maximization by the individual provided the basis for the analysis. In the theory of the firm and production, *profit maximization* is the underlying hypothesis of our predictive theory. The goal of the firm is to maximize economic profits, and the firm is expected to try to make the positive difference between total revenues and total costs as large as it can.

Our justification for assuming profit maximization by firms is similar to our belief in utility maximization by individuals. To obtain labour, capital, and other resources required to produce commodities, firms must first obtain financing from investors. In general, investors are indifferent about the details of how a firm uses the funds they provide. They are most interested in the earnings on these funds and the risk of obtaining lower returns or losing the funds they have invested. Firms that can provide relatively higher risk-corrected returns will therefore have an advantage in obtaining the financing needed to continue or expand production. Over time, we would expect a policy of profit maximization to become the dominant mode of behaviour for firms that survive.

FIGURE 8–1

Simplified View of Economic and Accounting Profit

We see in the right column that accounting profit is the difference between total revenues and total explicit accounting costs. Conversely, we see in the left column that economic profit is equal to total revenues minus economic costs. Economic costs equal explicit accounting costs plus all implicit costs, including a normal rate of return on invested capital.

8.2 Short Run versus Long Run

The Firm

We define a business, or **firm**, as follows:

A firm is an organization that brings together factors of production—labour, land, physical capital, human capital, and entrepreneurial skill—to produce a product or service that it hopes can be sold at a profit.

Firm An organization that brings together factors of production—labour, land, physical capital, human capital, and entrepreneurial skill—to produce a product or service that it hopes can be sold at a profit.

A typical firm will have an organizational structure consisting of an entrepreneur, managers, and workers. The entrepreneur is the person who takes the risks, mainly of losing personal wealth. In compensation, the entrepreneur will get any profits that are made. Entrepreneurs take the initiative in combining land, labour, and capital to produce a good or a service. Entrepreneurs are the ones who innovate in the form of new production and new products. The entrepreneur also decides whom to hire to manage the firm. Some economists maintain that the true quality of an entrepreneur becomes evident through the selection of managers. Managers, in turn, decide who should be hired or fired and how the business generally should be set up. The workers ultimately use the other inputs to produce the products or services that are being sold by the firm. Workers and managers are paid contractual wages. They receive a specified amount of income for a specified time period. Entrepreneurs are not paid contractual wages. They receive no reward specified in advance. The entrepreneurs make profits, if there are any, for profits accrue to those who are willing to take risks. Because the entrepreneur gets only what is left over after all expenses are paid, that individual is often referred to as a *residual claimant*. The entrepreneur lays claim to the residual—whatever is left.

We have discussed short-run and long-run price elasticities of supply and demand. For consumers, the long run meant the time period during which all adjustments to a change in price could be made, and anything shorter than that was considered the short run. For suppliers, the long run was the time in which all adjustments could be made, and anything shorter than that was the short run.

Now that we are discussing firms only, we will maintain a similar distinction between the short and the long run, but we will be more specific. In the theory of the firm, the **short run** is defined as any time period that is so short that there is at least one input, such as current **plant size** (the physical size of the factories that a firm owns and operates to produce its output), that the firm cannot alter.[1] In other words, during the short run, a firm makes do with whatever big machines and factory size it already has, no matter how much more it wants to produce because of increased demand for its product. We consider the plant and heavy equipment, the size or amount of which cannot be varied in the short run, as fixed resources. In agriculture and in some other businesses, land may be a fixed resource.

There are, of course, variable resources that the firm can alter when it wants to change its rate of production. These are called *variable inputs* or *variable factors of production*. Typically, the variable inputs of a firm are its labour and its purchases of raw materials. In the short run, in response to changes in demand, the firm can, by definition, vary only its variable inputs.

The **long run** can now be considered the period of time in which *all* inputs can be varied. Specifically, in the long run, the firm can alter its plant size. How long is the long run? That depends on each individual industry. For Wendy's or McDonald's, the long run may be four or five months because that is the time it takes to add new franchises. For a steel company, the long run may be several years because that is how long it takes to plan and build a new plant. An electric utility might need over a decade to build a new dam, for example.

Short run and *long run* in our discussion are, in fact, management planning terms that apply to decisions made by managers. The firm can operate only in the short run in the sense that decisions must be made in the present. The same analysis applies to your own behaviour. You may have many long-run plans about graduate school, vacations, and the like, but you always operate in the short run—you make decisions every day about what you do every day.

The Relationship between Output and Inputs

A firm takes numerous inputs, combines them using a technological production process, and ends up with an output. There are, of course, a great many factors of production, or

---

Short run Any time period that is so short that there is at least one input that the firm cannot alter.

Plant size The physical size of the factories that a firm owns and operates to produce its output.

Long run The period of time in which all inputs can be varied.

---

[1]There can be many short runs but only one long run. For ease of analysis, in this section we simplify the case to one short run and talk about short-run costs.

inputs. We classify production inputs in two broad categories (ignoring land)—labour and capital. The relationship between output and these two inputs is as follows:

Output per time period = Some function of capital and labour inputs

Mathematically, the production relationship can be written $Q = f(K, L)$, where Q = Output per time period, K = Capital, and L = Labour. What mix of capital and labour is used for production depends on many factors, as you can see from Example 8–1.

EXAMPLE 8–1   China's Increasing Labour Costs

China has seen its labour costs increase as more companies build factories there. International companies are moving their factories to China to take advantage of the lower labour costs, but as more factories are built, the demand for skilled workers is exceeding the supply, thereby increasing wages.

Salaries have surged by 40 percent to $160 per month. Companies are seeing a decline in profits because of the rising costs. For an emerging economy like China, a balance between capital investments and worker training is necessary so they can maintain their economic advantage over countries in Europe and North America.

For critical analysis: Should a company only consider labour costs when determining where to build a new factory?

Source: "How rising wages are changing the game in China." *Bloomberg Businessweek*. http://www.businessweek.com/magazine/content/06_13/b3977049.htm.

Can China continue to keep labour costs low?

We have used the word *production* but have not defined it. **Production** is any process by which resources are transformed into goods or services. Production includes not only making things, but also transporting them, retailing, repackaging them, and so on. Note that if we know that production occurs, we do not necessarily know the value of the output. The production relationship tells nothing about the worth or value of the inputs or the output.

Production Any process by which resources are transformed into goods or services.

The Production Function: A Numerical Example

The relationship between the amount of physical output the firm can produce and the quantity of capital and labour used to produce it can be called a **production function**. The production function specifies the maximum possible output that can be produced with a given amount of inputs. It also specifies the minimum amount of inputs necessary to produce a given level of output. Firms that are inefficient or wasteful in their use of capital and labour will obtain less output than the production function in theory will show.

Production function The relationship between the amount of physical output the firm can produce and the quantity of capital and labour used to produce it.

However, no firm can obtain more output than the production function shows. Since the production function is a technological relationship between inputs and output, it follows that an improvement in technology that allows the firm to produce more output with the same amount of inputs (or the same output with fewer inputs) results in a new production function.

Look at part (a) of Figure 8–2. It shows a production function relating the total output of pocket calculators in column 2 to the quantity of labour measured in workers in column 1. When there are zero workers, there is zero output. When there are five workers per hour of input (given the capital stock), there is a total output of 62 calculators per hour. (Ignore for the moment the rest of that part.) Part (b) of Figure 8–2 shows this particular production function graphically. Note again that it relates to the short run and that it is for an individual firm.

FIGURE 8-2

Diminishing Returns, the Production Function, and Marginal Product: A Hypothetical Case of Pocket Calculator Production

Marginal product is the addition to the total product that results when one additional worker is hired. Thus, the marginal product of the fourth worker is 13 pocket calculators. With four workers, 52 calculators are produced, but with three workers, only 39 are produced; the difference is 13. In part (b), we plot the numbers from columns 1 and 2 of part (a). In part (c), we plot the numbers from columns

1 and 4 of part (a). When we go from zero workers to one, marginal product is eight. When we go from one worker to two, marginal product increases to 16. After two workers, marginal product declines, but it is still positive. Total product (output) reaches its peak at seven workers, so after seven workers marginal product becomes –5 calculators per hour.

Part (a)

(1)	(2)	(3)	(4)
		Average Physical Product	**Marginal Physical Product**
Labour (number of workers per hour)	**Total Product** (output in number of calculators per hour)	(Total product ÷ Number of workers per hour) (calculators per hour)	(Change in total product ÷ Change in number of workers) (calculators per hour)
0	0	—	
1	8	8.0	8
2	24	12.0	16
3	39	13.0	15
4	52	13.0	13
5	62	12.4	10
6	68	11.3	6
7	69	9.9	1
8	64	8.0	–5

Part (b)

Part (c)

Part (b) shows a total physical product curve, or the maximum amount of physical output that is possible when we add successive equal-sized units of labour while holding all other inputs constant. The graph of the production function in part (b) is not a straight line. In fact, it peaks at seven workers per hour and then starts to go down. To understand why it starts to go down with an individual firm in the short run, we have to analyze in detail the **law of diminishing (marginal) returns**—the observation that after some point, successive equal-sized increases in a variable factor of production, such as labour, added to fixed factors of production, will result in smaller increases in output.

But before that, let us examine the meaning of columns 3 and 4 of part (a) of Figure 8–2—that is, average and marginal physical product.

Law of diminishing (marginal) returns The observation that after some point, successive equal-sized increases in a variable factor of production, such as labour, added to fixed factors of production, will result in smaller increases in output.

Average and Marginal Physical Product

The **average physical product** of labour is the total product divided by the number of workers expressed in output per hour. You can see in column 3 of part (a) of Figure 8–2 that the average physical product of labour first rises and then steadily falls after four workers are hired.

Remember that *marginal* means "additional." Hence, the *marginal physical product* of labour (column 4 of part (a)) is the change in total product that occurs when a worker joins an existing production process. (The term *physical* here emphasizes the fact that we are measuring in terms of physical units of production, not in dollar terms.) It is also the *change* in total product that occurs when that worker quits or is laid off an existing production process. The **marginal physical product** of labour therefore refers to the *change in output caused by a one-unit change in the labour input.* (Marginal physical product is also referred to as *marginal productivity* and *marginal return.*)

Average physical product The total product divided by the number of workers expressed in output per hour.

Marginal physical product The change in output caused by a one-unit change in the labour input.

Diminishing Marginal Returns

The concept of diminishing marginal returns—also known as diminishing marginal product—applies to many situations. If you put a seat belt across your lap, a certain amount of safety is obtained. If you add another seat belt over your shoulder, some additional safety is obtained, but less than when the first belt was secured. When you add a third seat belt over the other shoulder, the amount of *additional* safety obtained is even smaller.

The same analysis holds for firms in their use of productive inputs. When the returns from hiring more workers are diminishing, it does not necessarily mean that more workers will not be hired. In fact, workers will be hired until the returns, in terms of the *value* of the *extra* output produced, are equal to the additional wages that have to be paid for those workers to produce the extra output. Before we get into that decision-making process, let us demonstrate that diminishing returns can be represented graphically and can be used in our analysis of the firm.

Measuring Diminishing Returns

How do we measure diminishing returns? First, we limit the analysis to only one variable factor of production (or input)—let us say the factor is labour. Every other factor of production, such as machines, must be held constant. Only in this way can we calculate the marginal returns from using more workers and know when we reach the point of diminishing marginal returns.

The marginal productivity of labour may increase rapidly at the very beginning. A firm starts with no workers, only machines. The firm then hires one worker, who finds it difficult to get the work started. But when the firm hires more workers, each is able to specialize, and the marginal productivity of those additional workers may actually be greater than it was with the previous few workers. Beyond some point, however, diminishing returns must set in, not because new workers are less qualified, but because each worker has (on average) fewer machines to work with (remember, all other inputs are fixed). In fact, eventually the firm will become so crowded that workers will start to get in each other's way. At that point, total production declines and marginal physical product becomes negative.

Using these ideas, we can define the law of diminishing returns as follows:

As successive equal increases in a variable factor of production are added to fixed factors of production, there will be a point beyond which the extra, or marginal, product that can be attributed to each additional unit of the variable factor of production will decline.

Note that the law of diminishing returns is a statement about the *physical* relationships between inputs and outputs that we have observed in many firms. If the law of diminishing returns were not a fairly accurate statement about the world, what would stop firms from hiring additional workers forever?

An Example of the Law of Diminishing Returns

Look again at Figure 8–2. The numbers in part (a) illustrate the law of diminishing marginal returns and are presented graphically in part (c). Marginal productivity (returns from adding more workers) first increases, then decreases, and finally becomes negative.

When one worker is hired, total output goes from 0 to 8. Thus, marginal physical product is eight calculators per hour. When the second worker is hired, total product goes from 8 to 24 calculators per hour. Marginal physical product therefore increases to 16 calculators per hour. When a third worker is hired, total product again increases, from 24 to 39 calculators per hour. This represents a marginal physical product of only 15 calculators per hour. Therefore, the point of diminishing marginal returns occurs after two workers are hired.

Note that after seven workers per hour, marginal physical product becomes negative. That means that the hiring of an eighth worker would create a situation that reduces total product. Sometimes, this is called the *point of saturation*, indicating that given the amount of fixed inputs, there is no further positive use for more of the variable input. We have entered the region of negative marginal returns.

8.3 Short-Run Costs to the Firm

You will see that costs are the extension of the production ideas just presented. Let us consider the costs the firm faces in the short run. To keep our example simple, assume that there are only two factors of production—capital and labour. Our definition of the short run will be the time during which capital is fixed but labour is variable.

Total costs The sum of all costs incurred.

In the short run, a firm incurs certain types of costs. We label the sum of all costs incurred **total costs**. Then, we break total costs down into total fixed costs and total variable costs, which we will explain shortly. Therefore,

$$\text{Total costs (TC)} = \text{Total fixed costs (TFC)} + \text{Total variable costs (TVC)}$$

Remember that these total costs include both explicit and implicit costs, including the normal rate of return on investment.

After we have looked at the elements of total costs, we will find out how to compute average and marginal costs.

Total Fixed Costs

Let us look at an ongoing business, such as Chrysler Canada Inc. The decision makers in that corporate giant can look around and see big machines, thousands of parts, huge buildings, and a multitude of other components of plant and equipment that have already been bought and are in place. Chrysler Canada has to take into account the technological obsolescence of this equipment, no matter how many vehicles it produces. The payments on the loans taken out to buy the equipment will all be exactly the same. The opportunity costs of any land that Chrysler Canada owns will all be exactly the same. These costs are more or less the same for the auto manufacturer, no matter how many automobiles it produces.

Fixed costs All costs that do not vary—that is, all costs that do not depend on the rate of production.

The opportunity cost (or normal rate of return) of capital must be included along with other costs. Remember that we are dealing in the short run, during which capital is fixed. If investors in Chrysler Canada Inc. have already put $100 million into a new factory addition, the opportunity cost of that capital invested is now, in essence, a *fixed cost*. Why? Because in the short run, nothing can be done about that cost; the investment has already been made. This leads us to a very straightforward definition of fixed costs: All costs that do not vary—that is, all costs that do not depend on the rate of production—are called **fixed costs**.

Let us now take as an example the fixed costs incurred by our producer of pocket calculators. This firm's total fixed costs will equal the cost of the rent on its equipment and the insurance it has to pay. We see in part (a) of Figure 8–3 that total fixed costs per hour are $10.

In part (b), these total fixed costs are represented by the horizontal line at $10 per hour. They are invariant to changes in the output of calculators per hour—no matter how many are produced, fixed costs will remain at $10 per hour.

Total Variable Costs

Total **variable costs** are costs whose magnitude varies with the rate of production. One obvious variable cost is wages. The more the firm produces, the more labour it has to hire; therefore, the more wages it has to pay. Another variable cost is parts. In the assembly of calculators, for example, microchips must be bought. The more calculators that are made, the more chips must be bought. Part of the rate of depreciation (the rate of wear and tear) on machines that are used in the assembly process can also be considered a variable cost if depreciation depends partly on how long and how intensively the machines are used. Total variable costs are given in part (a) of Figure 8–3 in column 3. These costs are translated into the total variable cost curve in part (b). Note that the total variable cost curve lies below the total cost curve by the vertical distance of $10. This vertical distance represents, of course, total fixed costs.

Variable costs Costs whose magnitude varies with the rate of production.

Short-Run Average Cost Curves

In part (b) of Figure 8–3, we see total costs, total variable costs, and total fixed costs. Now we want to look at average cost. The average cost concept is one in which we are measuring cost per unit of output. It is a matter of arithmetic to figure the averages of these three cost concepts. We can define them as follows:

$$\text{Average total costs (ATC)} = \frac{\text{Total costs (TC)}}{\text{Output } (Q)}$$

$$\text{Average variable costs (AVC)} = \frac{\text{Total variable costs (TVC)}}{\text{Output } (Q)}$$

$$\text{Average fixed costs (AFC)} = \frac{\text{Total fixed costs (TFC)}}{\text{Output } (Q)}$$

The arithmetic is done in columns 5, 6, and 7 in part (a) of Figure 8–3. The numerical results are translated into a graphical format in part (c). Because total costs (TC) equal variable costs (TVC) plus fixed costs (TFC), the difference between average total costs (ATC) and average variable costs (AVC) will always be identical to average fixed costs (AFC). That means that average total costs and average variable costs move together as output expands.

Now let us see what we can observe about the three average cost curves in Figure 8–3.

AVERAGE FIXED COSTS (AFC). **Average fixed costs**—total fixed costs divided by the number of units produced—continue to fall throughout the output range. In fact, if we were to continue the diagram farther to the right, we would find that average fixed costs would get closer and closer to the horizontal axis. That is because total fixed costs remain constant. As we divide this fixed number by a larger and larger number of units of output, the resulting AFC has to become smaller and smaller. In business, this is called "spreading the overhead."

Average fixed costs Total fixed costs divided by the number of units produced.

AVERAGE VARIABLE COSTS (AVC). The **average variable cost**—total variable costs divided by the number of units produced—curve takes a form that is U-shaped: first it falls; then it starts to rise. It is possible for the AVC curve to take other shapes in the long run.

Average variable costs Total variable costs divided by the number of units produced.

AVERAGE TOTAL COSTS (ATC). **Average total costs** are total costs divided by the number of units produced; sometimes called per-unit total costs. This curve has a shape similar to that of the AVC curve. However, it falls even more dramatically in the beginning and rises more slowly after it has reached a minimum point. It falls and then rises because average total costs are the summation of the AFC curve and the AVC curve. Thus, when AFC and AVC are both falling, ATC must fall, too. At some point, however, AVC starts to increase, while AFC continues to fall. Once the increase in the AVC curve outweighs the decrease in the AFC curve, the ATC curve will start to increase and will develop its familiar U-shape.

Average total costs Total costs divided by the number of units produced; sometimes called per-unit total costs.

FIGURE 8-3

Costs of Production: A Hypothetical Case of Pocket Calculator Production

In part (a), the derivation of columns 4 through 9 are given in parentheses in each column heading. For example, column 6, average variable costs, is derived by dividing column 3, total variable costs, by column 1, total output per hour. Note that

marginal cost (MC) in part (c) intersects average variable costs (AVC) at the latter's minimum point. Also, MC intersects average total costs (ATC) at the latter's minimum point.

Part (a)

(1) Total Output (Q/hour)	(2) Total Fixed Costs (TFC)	(3) Total Variable Costs (TVC)	(4) Total Costs (TC) (4) = (2) + (3)	(5) Average Fixed Costs (AFC) (5) = (2) ÷ (1)	(6) Average Variable Costs (AVC) (6) = (3) ÷ (1)	(7) Average Total Costs (ATC) (7) = (4) ÷ (1)	(8) Total Costs (TC) (4)	(9) Marginal Costs (MC) $(9) = \frac{\text{Change in (8)}}{\text{Change in (1)}}$
0	$10	$ 0	$10	—	—	—	$10	
1	10	5	15	$10.00	$5.00	$15.00	15	$5
2	10	8	18	5.00	4.00	9.00	18	3
3	10	10	20	3.33	3.33	6.67	20	2
4	10	11	21	2.50	2.75	5.25	21	1
5	10	13	23	2.00	2.60	4.60	23	2
6	10	16	26	1.67	2.67	4.33	26	3
7	10	20	30	1.43	2.86	4.28	30	4
8	10	25	35	1.25	3.13	4.38	35	5
9	10	31	41	1.11	3.44	4.56	41	6
10	10	38	48	1.00	3.80	4.80	48	7
11	10	46	56	0.91	4.18	5.09	56	8

Part (b)

Part (c)

Marginal Cost

We have stated repeatedly that the basis of decisions is always on the margin—decisions in economics are determined at the margin. This dictum also holds true within the firm. Firms, according to the analysis we use to predict their behaviour, are very interested in their *marginal costs*. Because the term *marginal* means "additional" or "incremental" (or "decremental") here, **marginal costs** refer to costs that result from a one-unit change in the production rate. For example, if the production of 10 calculators per hour costs a firm $48, and the production of 11 calculators costs it $56 per hour, the marginal cost of producing the eleventh calculator is $8.

Marginal costs Costs that result from a one-unit change in the production rate.

$$\text{Marginal cost} = \frac{\text{Change in total cost}}{\text{Change in output}}$$

We show the marginal costs of calculator production per hour in column 9 of part (a) in Figure 8–3, calculated according to the formula just given. A good example of the different costs is illustrated in Example 8–2 on page 200.

This marginal cost schedule is shown graphically in part (c) of Figure 8–3. Just like average variable costs and average total costs, marginal costs first fall and then rise. The U-shape of the marginal cost curve is a result of increasing and then diminishing marginal returns. At lower levels of output, the marginal cost curve declines. The reasoning is that as marginal physical product increases with each addition of output, the marginal cost of this last unit of output must fall. Conversely, when diminishing marginal returns set in, marginal physical product decreases (and eventually becomes negative); it follows that the marginal cost of the last unit must rise. These relationships are clearly reflected in the geometry of parts (b) and (c) of Figure 8–3.

In summary:

> **As long as marginal physical product rises, marginal cost will fall, and when marginal physical product starts to fall (after reaching the point of diminishing marginal returns), marginal cost will begin to rise.**

The Relationship between Average and Marginal Costs

Let us now look at the relationship between average costs and marginal costs. There is always a definite relationship between averages and marginals. Consider your grade point average (GPA). Say your GPA is currently a B. If you take an economics course and earn an A, what will happen to your GPA? It must increase. When your grade in a marginal course (the economics course) is higher than (above) your GPA, it pulls your average up. If you subsequently take an accounting course and earn a C, your GPA will fall.

Can the marginal cost of computer printers decline forever?

There is a similar relationship between average variable costs and marginal costs. When marginal costs are less than average costs, the latter must fall. Conversely, when marginal costs are greater than average costs, the latter must rise. When you think about it, the relationship makes sense. The only way for average variable costs to fall is for the extra cost of the marginal unit produced to be less than the average variable cost of all the preceding units. For example, if the average variable cost for two calculators is $4, the only way the average variable cost of three calculators can be less than that of two is for the variable costs attributable to the last calculator—the marginal cost—to be less than the average of the previously produced calculators. In this particular case, if average variable cost falls to $3.33 per calculator, total variable cost for the three calculators would be 3 × $3.33, or almost exactly $10. Total variable costs for two calculators is 2 × $4, or $8. The marginal cost is therefore $10 − $8 = $2, which is less than the average variable cost of $3.33.

A similar type of computation can be carried out for rising average variable costs. The only way for average variable costs to rise is for the cost of additional units to be more than that for units already produced. But the incremental cost is the marginal cost. In this particular case, the marginal costs have to be higher than the average variable costs.

There is also a relationship between marginal costs and average total costs. Remember that average total cost is equal to total cost divided by the number of units produced. Remember also that marginal cost does not include any fixed costs. Fixed costs are, by definition, fixed and cannot influence marginal costs. Our example can therefore be repeated substituting average total cost for average variable cost.

These rising and falling relationships can be seen in Figure 8–3 part (c), where MC intersects AVC and ATC at their respective minimum points.

Minimum Cost Points

At what rate of output of calculators per hour does our producer experience the minimum average total costs? Column 7 in part (a) of Figure 8–3 shows that the minimum average total cost is $4.28, which occurs at an output rate of seven calculators per hour. We can also find this minimum cost by finding the point in part (c) of Figure 8–3 at which the marginal cost curve intersects the average total cost curve. This should not be surprising. When marginal cost is below average total cost, average total cost falls. When marginal cost is above average total cost, average total cost rises. At the point where average total cost is neither falling nor rising, marginal cost must then be equal to average total cost. When we represent this graphically, the marginal cost curve will intersect the average total cost curve at the latter's minimum.

The same analysis applies to the intersection of the marginal cost curve and the average variable cost curve. When are average variable costs at a minimum? According to part (a) of Figure 8–3, average variable costs are at a minimum of $2.60 at an output rate of five calculators per hour. This is where the marginal cost curve intersects the average variable cost curve in part (c) of Figure 8–3. A good example of the relationship of costs is shown in Example 8–2.

EXAMPLE 8–2 The Cost of Driving a Car

Each year, the Canadian Automobile Association publishes a study on the annual cost of owning and driving an automobile. The 2008 study found that driving a new 2008 Cobalt LTZ involved the following:

Costs per kilometre
Fuel: 6.79 cents
Maintenance: 2.36 cents
Tires: 1.55 cents
Annual costs
Insurance: $1780
Licence and registration: $111
Financing charges: $768
Depreciation: $3857

On the basis of an average annual driving distance of 18 000 kilometres, total costs amounted to $8441.25 per year.

However, the average cost of driving a car varied depending on distance driven. At 18 000 kilometres per year, the cost was 46.9 cents per kilometre; at 24 000 kilometres per year, it was 38.4 cents; and at 32 000 kilometres per year, the cost was 32.1 cents per kilometre. (Depreciation was not factored into these numbers.)

For critical analysis: Which costs are total fixed costs, total variable costs, average total costs, and marginal costs?

8.4 The Relationship between Diminishing Marginal Returns and Cost Curves

There is a unique relationship between output and the shape of the various cost curves we have drawn. Let us consider specifically the relationship between marginal cost and the example of diminishing marginal physical returns in part (a) of Figure 8–4. It turns out that if wage rates are constant, the shape of the marginal cost curve in part (d) of Figure 8–4 is both a reflection of and a consequence of the law of diminishing returns. Let us assume that each unit of labour can be purchased at a constant price. Further assume that labour is the only variable input. We see that as more workers are hired, marginal physical product first rises and then falls after the point at which diminishing returns are encountered. Thus, the marginal cost of each extra unit of output will first fall as long as marginal physical product is rising, and then it will rise as long as marginal physical product is falling. Recall that marginal cost is defined as:

$$\text{MC} = \frac{\text{Change in total cost}}{\text{Change in output}}$$

Because the price of labour is assumed to be constant, the change in total cost is simply the constant price of labour, W (we are increasing labour by only one unit). The change in output is simply the marginal physical product (MPP) of the one-unit increase in labour. Therefore, we see that:

$$\text{Marginal cost} = \frac{W}{\text{MPP}}$$

This means that initially, when there are increasing returns, marginal cost falls (we are dividing W by increasingly larger numbers), and later, when diminishing returns set in and marginal physical product is falling, marginal cost must increase (we are dividing W by smaller numbers). As marginal physical product increases, marginal cost decreases, and as marginal physical product decreases, marginal cost must increase. Thus, when marginal physical product reaches its maximum, marginal cost necessarily reaches its minimum. To illustrate this, let us return to Figure 8–4. Assume that a worker at our pocket calculator factory is paid $5 per hour. When we go from zero labour input to one unit, output increases by eight calculators. Each of those eight calculators has a marginal cost of 63 cents. Now, the second unit of labour is hired, and it too costs $5 per hour. Output increases by 16. Thus, the marginal cost is $5 ÷ 16 = 31 cents. We continue the experiment. We see that the next unit of labour yields only 15 additional calculators, and so marginal cost starts to rise to 33 cents. The following unit of labour increases marginal physical product by only 13, so marginal cost becomes $5 ÷ 13 = 38 cents.

All of the foregoing can be restated in relatively straightforward terms:

Firms' short-run cost curves are a reflection of the law of diminishing marginal returns. Given any constant price of the variable input, marginal costs decline as long as the marginal product of the variable resource is rising. At the point at which diminishing marginal returns begin, marginal costs begin to rise as the marginal product of the variable input begins to decline.

The result is a marginal cost curve that slopes down, hits a minimum, and then slopes up. The average total cost curve and average variable cost curve are of course affected. They will have their familiar U-shape in the short run. Again, to see this, recall that:

$$\text{AVC} = \frac{\text{Total variable costs}}{\text{Total output}}$$

As we move from zero labour input to one unit in part (a) of Figure 8–4, output increases from zero to eight calculators. The total variable costs are the price per worker, W ($5), times the number of workers (1). Because the average product of one worker

FIGURE 8-4

The Relationship between Physical Output and Costs

As the number of workers increases, the total number of calculators produced rises, as shown in parts (a) and (b). In part (c), marginal product (MPP) first rises and then falls. Average physical product (APP) follows. The mirror image of part (c) is shown in part (d), in which MC and AVC first fall and then rise.

Part (a)

(1) Labour	(2) Total Product (number of calculators per hour)	(3) Average Physical Product (calculators per worker per hour) (3) = (2) ÷ (1)	(4) Marginal Physical Product (4) = Change in (2) ÷ Change in (1)	(5) Average Variable Cost (5) = (W = \$5) ÷ (3)	(6) Marginal Cost (6) = (W = \$5) ÷ (4)
0	0	—	—	—	—
1	8	8.0	8	\$0.63	\$0.63
2	24	12.0	16	0.42	0.31
3	39	13.0	15	0.38	0.33
4	52	13.0	13	0.38	0.38
5	62	12.4	10	0.40	0.50
6	68	11.3	6	0.44	0.83
7	69	9.9	1	0.55	5.00

Part (b)

Part (c)

Part (d)

(column 3) is eight, we can write the total product, eight, as the average product, eight, times the number of workers, one. Thus we see that:

$$AVC = \frac{\$5 \times 1}{8 \times 1} = \frac{\$5}{8} = \frac{W}{APP}$$

From column 3 in part (a) of Figure 8–4, we see that the average product increases, reaches a maximum, and then declines. Because $AVC = W/APP$, average variable cost decreases as average product increases and increases as average product decreases. AVC reaches its minimum when average product reaches its maximum. Furthermore, because $ATC = AVC + AFC$, the average total cost curve inherits the relationship between the average variable cost and diminishing returns.

Breakeven Analysis

A very useful analysis that firms use is **breakeven**, the output that a firm must produce to reach the point where its profits are zero. The breakeven point will cover all fixed and variable costs. It helps managers make better decisions about what quantity has to be produced so that profits can be realized. Breakeven quantity (BQ) is the total fixed costs divided by the selling price minus the average variable costs.

$$BQ = \frac{TFC}{\text{Selling price} - AVC}$$

If a firm wants a specific profit, it can add the desired profit to the total fixed cost and then divide by the selling price minus the average variable costs.

Breakeven The output that a firm must produce to reach the point where its profits are zero.

8.5 Long-Run Cost Curves

The long run is defined as a time period during which full adjustment can be made to any change in the economic environment. Long-run curves are sometimes called *planning curves*, and the long run, during which all inputs are variable, is sometimes called the **planning horizon**. We start out our analysis of long-run cost curves by considering a single firm contemplating the construction of a single plant. The firm has three alternative plant sizes from which to choose on the planning horizon. Each particular plant size generates its own short-run average total cost curve. Now that we are talking about the difference between long-run and short-run cost curves, we will label all short-run curves with an S and long-run curves with an L; short-run average (total) costs will be labelled SAC, and long-run average cost curves will be labelled LAC.

Planning horizon The long run, during which all inputs are variable.

Part (a) of Figure 8–5 shows three short-run average cost curves for three successively larger plants. Which is the optimal size to build? That depends on the anticipated normal, sustained (permanent) rate of output per time period. Assume for a moment that the anticipated normal, sustained rate is Q_1. If a plant of size 1 is built, the average costs will be C_1. If a plant of size 2 is built, we see on SAC$_2$ that the average costs will be C_2, which is greater than C_1. Thus, if the anticipated rate of output is Q_1, the appropriate plant size is the one from which SAC$_1$ was derived.

However, if the anticipated permanent rate of output per time period goes from Q_1 to Q_2 and a plant of size 1 had been decided on, average costs would be C_4. If a plant of size 2 had been decided on, average costs would be C_3, which is clearly less than C_4.

In choosing the appropriate plant size for a single-plant firm during the planning horizon, the firm will pick the size whose short-run average cost curve generates an average cost that is lowest for the expected rate of output.

Long-Run Average Cost Curve

If we now assume that the entrepreneur faces an infinite number of choices of plant sizes in the long run, we can conceive of an infinite number of SAC curves similar to the three

FIGURE 8–5

Preferable Plant Size and the Long-Run Average Cost Curve

If the anticipated permanent rate of output per unit time period is Q_1, the optimal plant to build would be the one corresponding to SAC_1 in part (a) because average costs are lower. However, if the permanent rate of output increases to Q_2, it will be more profitable to have a plant size corresponding to SAC_2. Unit costs fall to C_3.

If we draw all the possible short-run average cost curves that correspond to different plant sizes and then draw the envelope (a curve tangent to each member of a set of curves) to these various curves, SAC_1 to SAC_8, we obtain the long-run average cost curve, or the planning curve, as shown in part (b).

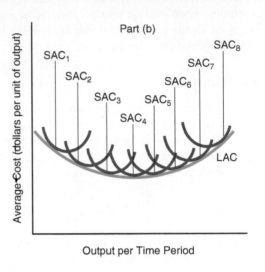

Long-run average cost curve The locus (path) of points representing the minimum unit cost of producing any given rate of output, given current technology and resource prices.

Planning curve The curve that represents the various average costs attainable at the planning stage of the firm's decision making.

in part (a) of Figure 8–5. We are not able, of course, to draw an infinite number; we have drawn quite a few, however, in part (b) of Figure 8–5. We then draw the "envelope" to all these various short-run average cost curves. The resulting envelope is the **long-run average cost curve**, which is the locus (path) of points representing the minimum unit cost of producing any given rate of output, given current technology and resource prices. This long-run average cost curve is sometimes called the **planning curve**, for it represents the various average costs attainable at the planning stage of the firm's decision making. It represents the locus of points giving the least unit cost of producing any given rate of output. Note that the LAC curve is *not* tangent to each individual SAC curve at the latter's minimum points. This is true only at the minimum point of the LAC curve. Then and only then are minimum long-run average costs equal to minimum short-run average costs.

Why the Long-Run Average Cost Curve Is U-Shaped

Note that the long-run average cost curve, LAC in part (b) of Figure 8–5, is U-shaped, similar to the U-shape of the short-run average cost curve developed earlier in this chapter. The reason behind the U-shape of the two curves is not the same, however. The short-run average cost curve is U-shaped because of the law of diminishing marginal returns. But the law cannot apply to the long run because in the long run, all factors of production are variable; there is no point of diminishing marginal returns because there is no fixed factor of production. Why, then, do we see the U-shape in the long-run average cost curve? The reason has to do with **economies of scale** (decreases in long-run average costs resulting from increases in output), **constant returns to scale** (no change in long-run average costs when output increases), and **diseconomies of scale** (increases in long-run average costs that occur as output increases). When the firm is experiencing economies of scale, the long-run average cost curve slopes downward—an increase in scale and production leads to a fall in unit costs. When the firm is experiencing constant returns to scale, the long-run average cost curve is at its minimum point such that an increase in scale and production does not change unit costs. When the firm is experiencing diseconomies of scale, the long-run average cost curve slopes upward—an increase in scale and production increases

Economies of scale Decreases in long-run average costs resulting from increases in output.

Constant returns to scale No change in long-run average costs when output increases.

Diseconomies of scale Increases in long-run average costs that occur as output increases.

FIGURE 8–6

Economies of Scale, Constant Returns to Scale, and Diseconomies of Scale Shown with the Long-Run Average Cost Curve

Long-run average cost curves will fall when there are economies of scale, as shown in part (a). They will be constant (flat) when the firm is experiencing constant returns to scale, as shown in part (b). They will rise when the firm is experiencing diseconomies of scale, as shown in part (c).

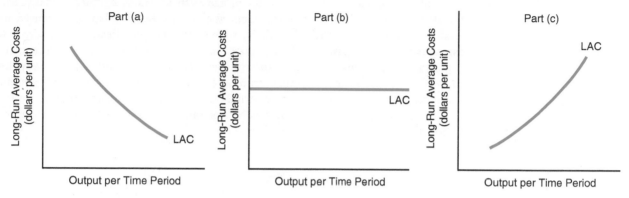

unit costs. These three sections of the long-run average cost curves are broken up into parts (a), (b), and (c) in Figure 8–6.

Reasons for Economies of Scale

We shall examine three of the many reasons a firm might be expected to experience economies of scale: specialization, the dimensional factor, and improved productive equipment.

SPECIALIZATION. As a firm's scale of operation increases, the opportunities for specialization in the use of resource inputs also increase. This is sometimes called *increased division of tasks* or *operations*. Gains from such division of labour or increased specialization are well known. When we consider managerial staff, we also find that larger enterprises may be able to put together more highly specialized staff.

DIMENSIONAL FACTOR. Large-scale firms often require proportionately less input per unit of output simply because certain inputs do not have to be physically doubled in order to double the output. Consider the cost of storage of oil. The cost of storage is basically related to the cost of steel that goes into building the storage container; however, the amount of steel required goes up less than in proportion to the volume (storage capacity) of the container (because the volume of a container increases more than proportionately with its surface area).

IMPROVED PRODUCTIVE EQUIPMENT. The larger the scale of the enterprise, the more the firm is able to take advantage of larger-volume (output capacity) types of machinery. Small-scale operations may not be able profitably to use large-volume machines that can be more efficient per unit of output. Also, smaller firms often cannot use technologically more advanced machinery because they are unable to spread out the high cost of such sophisticated equipment over a large output.

For any of these reasons, the firm may experience economies of scale, which means that equal percentage increases in output result in a decrease in average cost. Thus, output can double, but total costs will less than double; hence average cost falls. Note that the factors listed for causing economies of scale are all *internal* to the firm; they do not depend on what other firms are doing or what is happening in the economy.

Why a Firm Might Experience Diseconomies of Scale

One of the basic reasons a firm can expect to run into diseconomies of scale is that there are limits to the efficient functioning of management. Moreover, as more workers are hired, a more than proportionate increase in managers and staff people may be needed, and this could cause increased costs per unit. This is so because larger levels of output imply successively larger *plant* size, which, in turn, implies successively larger *firm* size. Thus, as the level of output increases, more people must be hired, and the firm gets bigger. However, as this happens, the support, supervisory and administrative staff, and the general paperwork of the firm, increase. As the layers of supervision grow, the costs of information and communication grow more than proportionately; hence the average unit cost will start to increase.

Some observers of corporate giants claim that many of them are experiencing some diseconomies of scale today. Witness the problems that General Motors and IBM had in the 2000s. Some analysts say that the financial problems that they have experienced are at least partly a function of their size relative to their smaller, more flexible competitors, who can make decisions faster and then take more rapid advantage of changing market conditions. This seems to be particularly true with IBM. It apparently adapted very slowly to the fact that the large mainframe computer business was declining as micro- and mini-computers became more and more powerful. Such companies as Dell, Oracle, and eBay all enjoy economies of scale because of standardized products. Example 8–3 is a great example of how Dell accomplished economies of scale.

EXAMPLE 8–3 Economies of Scale at Dell

In the mid-1990s, Dell Computer Corporation embarked on a plan to become the lowest-cost computer manufacturer in the world. Now, the company has factories that receive more than half of all customer orders via the Internet. These orders flow to a plant's "air-traffic control room," where procurement of parts, computer assembly, and shipping are managed.

At each point on the factory floor, which at some plants can be as large as 300 000 square feet, groups in charge of producing various computer components are linked via intranets, or internal computer networks. Each forklift truck contains a wireless computer that follows the paths of components to ensure that they reach the correct assembly points. Forklift trucks carrying completed computers are similarly equipped, to ensure that they reach the correct loading dock from among the dozens where trucks are waiting to be loaded.

In its newest and largest plants, Dell can produce more than 1000 computers per hour, which is almost twice as many as a typical plant could produce only half a dozen years ago. Even rival computer manufacturers agreed by the early 2000s that Dell had taken advantage of economies of scale to become the most cost-efficient manufacturer of personal computers.

For critical analysis: What has happened to Dell's short-run average cost curves as it has moved down along its long-run average cost curve?

Minimum Efficient Scale

Economists and statisticians have obtained actual data on the relationship between changes in all inputs and changes in average cost. It turns out that for many industries, the long-run average cost curve does not resemble that shown in part (b) of Figure 8–5. Rather, it more closely resembles Figure 8–7. What you observe there is a small portion of

FIGURE 8–7

Minimum Efficient Scale

This long-run average cost curve reaches a minimum point at *A*. After that point, long-run average costs remain horizontal, or constant, and then rise at some higher rate of output. Point *A* is called the minimum efficient scale for the firm because that is the point at which it reaches minimum costs. It is the lowest rate of output at which the average long-run costs are minimized.

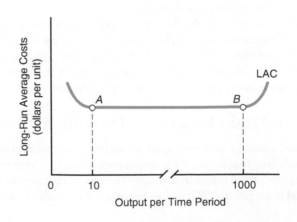

declining long-run average costs (economies of scale) and then a wide range of outputs over which the firm experiences relatively constant economies of scale. At the output rate when economies of scale end and constant economies of scale start, the **minimum efficient scale (MES)** for the firm is encountered. It occurs at point *A*. (The point is, of course, approximate. The more smoothly the curve declines into its flat portion, the more approximate will be our estimate of the MES.) The minimum efficient scale will always be the lowest rate of output at which long-run average costs are minimized. In any industry with a long-run average cost curve similar to the one in Figure 8–7, larger firms will have no cost-saving advantage over smaller firms as long as the smaller firms have at least obtained the minimum efficient scale at point *A*.

> **Minimum efficient scale (MES)** The output rate when economies of scale end and constant economies of scale start.

Among its uses, the minimum efficient scale gives us a rough measure of the degree of competition in an industry. If the MES is small relative to industry demand, the degree of competition in that industry is likely to be high because there is room for many efficiently sized plants. Conversely, when the MES is large relative to industry demand, the degree of competition is likely to be small because there is room for a relatively small number of efficiently sized plants or firms. Looked at another way, if it takes a very large scale of plant to obtain minimum long-run average cost, the output of just a few of these very large firms can fully satisfy total market demand. This means that there is no room for a large number of smaller plants if maximum efficiency is to be obtained in the industry.

ISSUES AND APPLICATIONS

Businesses Look Toward Costs To Determine Viability

Concepts Applied: Economic vs. Accounting Costs, Variable Costs, Fixed Costs, Long Run

Overproduction of books is a common practice since the marginal cost of printing additional copies is relatively low.

The reason that corner restaurant is constantly changing ownership could be because few small businesses take *all* costs into consideration when starting a business. As you can see from this chapter, there are many types of costs that need to be considered.

One of the first costs that a person must consider before opening up a business is the lost wages that he or she will suffer. Giving up a job that pays $50 000 per year to open up a business is an economic cost, not an accounting cost, but it will affect that person's ability to open up a business.

Next, if the person requests a loan, the bank will want to know what the fixed costs, such as rent, will be so it can take them into consideration. Variable costs are much harder to determine, especially in the long run. In a restaurant, for example, how much produce will be thrown out each

week because it is not used? What are the average costs per plate of spaghetti? What are the yearly costs of having staff available when few customers are coming into the restaurant?

A restaurant owner will also have to know how many plates of spaghetti he or she needs to sell every week to just break even. Too many small business owners start a business thinking they will succeed just because they have a unique product to offer, only to fail because they miscalculated the costs of production.

For critical analysis:

Why should a business owner calculate his or her costs per unit? If you were starting a business, would you look at the economic costs associated with your business, or just the accounting costs?

SUMMARY

Here is what you should know after reading this chapter. MyEconLab will help you identify what you know, and where to go when you need to practise. We suggest that as soon as you review one of the Learning Objective sections below, you then proceed to go through the related section in MyEconLab.

LEARNING OBJECTIVES	KEY TERMS	MYECONLAB PRACTICE
8.1 The Profits of a Firm. Accounting profits differ from economic profits. Economic profits are defined as total revenues minus total costs, where costs include the full opportunity cost of all factors of production plus all other implicit costs. The full opportunity cost of capital invested in a business is generally not included as a cost when accounting profits often overstate economic profits. We assume throughout that the goal of the firm is to maximize profits.	explicit costs, 189 accounting profit, 189 implicit costs, 189 normal rate of return, 189 opportunity cost of capital, 189 economic profits, 191	• **MyEconLab** Study Plan 8.1
8.2 Short Run versus Long Run. The short run for the firm is defined as the period during which plant size cannot be altered. The long run is the period during which all factors of production can be varied.	firm, 191 short run, 192 plant size, 192 long run, 192 production, 193 production function, 193 law of diminishing (marginal) returns, 194 average physical product, 195 marginal physical product, 195	• **MyEconLab** Study Plan 8.2
8.3 Short-Run Costs to the Firm. Fixed costs are costs that cannot be altered in the short run. Fixed costs are associated with assets that the firm owns that cannot be profitably transferred to another use. Variable costs are associated with input costs that vary as the rate of output varies. There are definitional relationships among average, total, and marginal costs. Total costs equal total fixed costs plus total variable costs. Fixed costs do not vary with the rate of production. Variable costs do vary with the rate of production. Average total cost equals total cost divided by quantity. Average variable cost equals total variable cost divided by quantity. Average fixed cost equals total fixed cost divided by quantity.	total costs, 196 fixed costs, 196 variable costs, 197 average fixed costs, 197 average variable costs, 197 average total costs, 197 marginal costs, 199	• **MyEconLab** Study Plan 8.3

LEARNING OBJECTIVES	KEY TERMS	MYECONLAB PRACTICE
8.4 The Relationship between Diminishing Marginal Returns and Cost Curves. Marginal cost equals the change in total cost divided by the change in quantity. Firms are also interested in how much they need to produce to break even. Breakeven quantity equals the total fixed cost divided by selling price minus average variable cost.	breakeven, 203	• **MyEconLab** Study Plan 8.4
8.5 Long-Run Cost Curves. Average total cost (ATC) equals the sum of average fixed cost (AFC) and average variable cost (AVC). The AFC curve continuously drops; the AVC curve falls during the early output stages but eventually AVC rises. So, ATC initially falls and then rises after the point of diminishing marginal returns, causing the long run ATC to appear to be U-shaped.	planning horizon, 203 long-run average cost curve, 204 planning curve, 204 economies of scale, 204 constant returns to scale, 204 diseconomies of scale, 204 minimum efficient scale (MES), 207	• **MyEconLab** Study Plan 8.5

PROBLEMS

(Answers to the odd-numbered problems appear at the back of the book.)

LO 8.1 Distinguish between accounting profits and economic profits.

1. After graduation, you face a choice. One option is to work for a multinational consulting firm and earn a starting salary (benefits included) of $40 000. The other option is to use $5000 in savings to start your own consulting firm. You could have earned an interest return of 5 percent on your savings. You choose to start your own consulting firm. At the end of the first year, you add up all of your expenses and revenues. Your total includes $12 000 in rent, $1000 in office supplies, $20 000 for office staff, and $4000 in telephone expenses. What are your total explicit costs and total implicit costs?

2. Suppose, as in Problem 1, that you choose to start your own consulting firm upon graduation. At the end of the first year, your total revenues are $77 250. On the basis of the information in Problem 1, what is the accounting profit, and what is your economic profit?

3. An individual leaves a college faculty, where she was earning $40 000 a year, to begin a new venture. She invests her savings of $10 000, which were earning 10 percent annually. She then spends $20 000 on office equipment, hires two students at $30 000 a year each, rents office space for $12 000, and has other variable expenses of $40 000. At the end of the year, her revenues are $200 000. What are her accounting profit and her economic profit for the year?

LO 8.2 Understand the short-run production function and diminishing marginal returns.

4. The short-run production function for a manufacturer of DVD drives is as follows:

Input of Labour (workers per week)	Total Output of DVD Drives
0	0
1	25
2	60
3	85
4	105
5	115
6	120

On the basis of this information, calculate the average physical product at each quantity of labour.

5. Using the information provided in Problem 4, calculate the marginal physical product of labour at each quantity of labour.

6. Define long-run average total cost. In light of the fact that businesses are operated day to day in the short run, of what use is the concept of long-run average total cost to the entrepreneur?

LO 8.3 Calculate the various costs for the firm in the short run.

7. Your school's basketball team had a foul-shooting average of 0.800 (80 out of 100) before last night's game, during which they shot 5 for 10 at the foul line.
   a. What was their marginal performance last night?
   b. What happened to the team's foul-shooting average?
   c. Suppose that their foul shooting in the next game is 6 for 10. What is happening to their marginal performance? Now what is the team average foul-shooting percentage?

8. The cost structure of a manufacturer of cable modems is described in the following table:

Output (units)	Average Fixed Cost	Total Cost
0	—	$200
5	$40	300
10	20	380
20	10	420
40	5	520

   a. Find the average variable cost at each level of production.
   b. What is the marginal cost of increasing output from 10 to 20 units? From 20 to 40 units?
   c. Find the average total cost at each level of production.

9. At the end of the year, a firm produced 10 000 laptop computers. Its total costs were $5 million, and its fixed costs were $2 million. What are the average variable costs of this firm?

10. The cost structure of a manufacturer of microchips is described in the following table. The firm's fixed costs equal $10 000 per day. Calculate the average variable cost, average fixed cost, and average total cost at each output level.

Output (microchips per day)	Total Cost of Output ($ thousands)
0	10
25	60
50	95
75	150
100	220
125	325
150	465

11. A watch manufacturer finds that at 1000 units of output, its marginal costs are below average total costs. If it produces an additional watch, will its average total costs rise, fall, or stay the same?

12. At its current short-run level of production, a firm's average variable costs equal $20 per unit, and its average fixed costs equal $30 per unit. Its total costs at this production level equal $2500.
   a. What is the firm's current output level?
   b. What are its total variable costs at this output level?
   c. What are its total fixed costs?

LO 8.4 Explain the important relationships of the cost curves.

13. You are given the following graph:

   a. At what output level is AVC at a minimum?
   b. At what output level is ATC at a minimum?
   c. At what output level is MC at a minimum?
   d. At what output level do the AVC and MC curves intersect?
   e. At what output level do the ATC and MC curves intersect?

14. The diagram below displays short-run cost curves for a facility that produces LCD screens for cellphones:

   a. What are the daily total fixed costs of producing LCD screens?

b. What are the total variable costs of producing 100 LCD screens per day?

c. What are the total costs of producing 100 LCD screens per day?

d. What is the marginal cost of producing the hundredth LCD screen? (Hint: To answer this question, you must first determine the total costs—or, alternatively, the total variable costs—of producing 99 LCD screens.)

LO 8.5 Understand the long-run cost curve.

15. A manufacturing firm with a single plant is contemplating changing its plant size. It must choose from among seven alternative plant sizes. In the following table plant size A is the smallest it might build, and size G is the largest. Currently, the firm's plant size is B.

Plant Size	Average Total Cost
A (smallest)	$5000
B	4000
C	3500
D	3100
E	3000
F	3250
G (largest)	4100

a. Is this firm currently experiencing economies of scale or diseconomies of scale?

b. What is the firm's minimum efficient scale?

BUSINESS APPLICATION

LO 8.1 and 8.3 Distinguish between accounting profits and economic profits; calculate the various costs for the firm in the short run.

Cost Accounting and Management: How Much Should Management Reimburse Employees for Use of Their Personal Car for Work Purposes?

Copy Corporation is currently embroiled in a labour dispute over the appropriate level of compensation for a union employee who used his personal vehicle to travel 500 kilometres on company business. Copy Corporation reimbursed the employee an amount that covered just the total gas cost of the trip.

Both the union and the employer agreed that the employee had made his car purchase decision prior to working for Copy Corporation. The union and the employer also agreed to use the following set of cost figures published by the Canadian Automobile Association (CAA) to settle the dispute. Note that the following costs are based on travelling 18 000 km per year (a typical year of driving).

Variable Costs		Annual Fixed Costs	
Fuel (and Oil)	$1074.60	Insurance	$1183.00
Maintenance	$437.40	Licence and Registration	$120.48
Tires	$216.00	Depreciation	$3729.13
		Finance Expense (Loan)	$709.00

Source: *1998 Driving Costs*, Canadian Automobile Association, 1998

Business Application Problem

Based on CAA's cost figures above, answer the following questions.

a. Find the average fuel cost (per kilometre). Calculate the employee's reimbursement for the 500 km business trip based on the average fuel cost.

b. Find the average variable cost (per kilometre). Calculate the employee's reimbursement for the 500 km business trip based on the average variable cost.

c. Find the average total cost (per kilometre) Calculate the employee's reimbursement for the 500 km business trip based on the average total cost.

d. Based on the situation outlined above, which cost criteria would be most appropriate as a basis for reimbursement: average gas cost, average variable cost, or average total cost? Why?

9

LEARNING OBJECTIVES

After reading this chapter, you should be able to:

9.1 Identify and explain the characteristics of a perfectly competitive market structure.

9.2 Using revenue and cost information, determine the firm's short-run profit-maximizing or loss-minimizing level of output and profit.

9.3 Derive the firm's short-run supply curve and explain how the short-run equilibrium price is determined in a perfectly competitive market.

9.4 Explain the features and long-run adjustments associated with long-run equilibrium in perfect competition.

9.5 Explain the three different long-run industry supply curve situations that are possible in perfect competition.

9.6 From a social viewpoint, evaluate the long-run behaviour in perfect competition.

Perfect Competition

If you want to watch new-release or best-seller movies regularly in the comfort of your own home, you face just one problem: How should you pay for this? Should you remit extra monthly fees to your cable company to access video on demand? Should you buy DVD movies from a supermarket or big box retailer? Should you pay a fixed monthly subscription rate that will allow you to rent as many DVDs as you want over the Internet? Should you join an online video club by promising to buy so many DVDs per year? With all these options available, would you still consider visiting your local video store? An understanding of the model of perfect competition will help you appreciate the changing nature of the home video movie industry.

MyEconLab helps you master each objective and study more efficiently. See end of chapter for details.

DID YOU KNOW THAT...?

According to a major study entitled "Competitive Alternatives 2010," Canada is the least costly place to locate a business in nine of the most industrialized nations in the world. The study compared set-up and operating costs—26 cost components in all—of firms competing in 17 industries. In 2010, on average, Canadian businesses enjoyed a 5 percent cost advantage over similar firms in the United States. For each of the regions examined, the study identified the following as cities where businesses can operate at lowest unit cost: for the New England/Atlantic Canada region: Moncton,

New Brunswick; for the Northeast U.S./Canada region: Sherbrooke, Quebec; for the Midwest U.S./Western Canada region: Winnipeg, Manitoba; and for the Pacific U.S./Canada region: Prince George, B.C.

As this chapter explains, for industries that resemble perfect competition, low costs become the primary factor contributing to business success, if not survival.

Source: "Competitive alternatives—highlights." 2010. KPMG. http://www.competitivealternatives.com/highlights/default.aspx

9.1 The Characteristics of Perfect Competition

Four Market Structures

In order to better understand and predict the behaviour of firms in our economy, we need to study the types of industry environments or market structures that businesses typically operate within. **Market structure** refers to characteristics of an industry—such as the number of sellers, the ease of entry of new firms, each firm's ability to set the price, and the degree to which each firm's product differs from its competitor's.

In the next three chapters, we will study four distinct market structures—perfect competition, monopoly, monopolistic competition, and oligopoly. The vast majority of Canadian industries can be classified as one of these four types of market structures. As you will see, market structure affects a firm's market behaviour—price, profit, and nonprice competitive behaviour. In turn, for each of the four market structures studied, we will examine how the firm's market behaviour affects public interest, which we call the firm's market performance.

Table 9–1 provides an overview of the four types of market structures we will study in the next three chapters.

> **Market structure** Characteristics of an industry—such as the number of sellers, the ease of entry of new firms, each firm's ability to set the price, and the degree to which each firm's product differs from its competitor's.

The Perfectly Competitive Market Structure

In this chapter, we are interested in studying how a firm acting within a perfectly competitive market structure makes decisions about how much to produce. In a situation of **perfect competition**, each firm is such a small part of the industry that it cannot affect the price of the product in question. That means that each perfectly competitive firm in the industry is a **price taker**—the firm takes price as a given, something determined *outside* the individual firm.

> **Perfect competition** A market structure in which each firm is such a small part of the industry that it cannot affect the price of the product in question.
>
> **Price taker** A competitive firm that takes price as a given, something determined outside the individual firm.

TABLE 9–1

Comparing Market Structures

Market Structure	Number of Sellers	Unrestricted Entry and Exit	Ability to Set Price	Long-Run Economic Profits Possible	Product Differentiation	Nonprice Competition	Examples
Perfect competition	Numerous	Yes	None	No	None	None	Agriculture, coal
Monopolistic competition	Many	Yes	Some	Not for most	Considerable	Yes	Restaurants, motels, retail trade
Oligopoly	Few	Partial	Some	Yes	Frequent	Yes	Cigarettes, steel, banks
Pure monopoly	One	No (for entry)	Considerable	Yes	None (product is unique)	Yes	Electric company, provincial telephone company, medicare

This definition of a competitive firm is obviously idealized, for in one sense, the individual firm *has* to set prices. How can we ever have a situation in which firms regard prices as set by forces outside their control? The answer is that even though every firm sets its own prices, a firm in a perfectly competitive situation will find that it will eventually have no customers at all if it sets its price above the competitive price. The best example is in agriculture. Although the individual farmer can set any price for a bushel of carrots, if that price does not coincide with the market price of a bushel of similar-quality carrots, no one will purchase the carrots at a higher price; nor would the farmer be inclined to reduce revenues by selling below the market price.

The following characteristics of perfect competition help us understand why a perfectly competitive firm is a price taker.

1. *Large numbers.* There must be a large number of buyers and sellers. When this is the case, no one buyer or one seller has any influence on price.
2. *Homogeneous product.* The product sold by each firm in the industry must be a perfect substitute for the product sold by another firm. Buyers must be able to choose from a large number of sellers of a product that the buyers believe to be the same.
3. *Easy entry and exit.* Firms in a competitive industry cannot be hampered in their ability to get resources or relocate resources. They move labour and capital in pursuit of profit-making opportunities to whatever business venture gives them their highest expected rate of return on their investment. New firms can easily enter the industry.
4. *Perfect market information.* Consumers are able to find out about lower prices charged by competing firms. Firms are able to find out about cost-saving innovations in order to lower production costs and prices, and they are able to learn about profitable opportunities in other industries.

In this chapter's Issues and Applications, it is noted that the Canadian home video movie industry that supplies new releases and best-seller movies closely resembles perfect competition. In a typical Canadian city, there are large numbers of video stores that rent an identical product—new releases and best-sellers. There are numerous close substitutes in the form of online movie rental firms, video on demand, and mass retailers who sell home-movie DVDs. It is relatively easy for a firm to enter or exit this industry. As Example 9–1 illustrates, blogging has provided novel ways to start up competitive businesses supplying online advertising space.

What features of perfect competition apply to a blogging business?

EXAMPLE 9–1   When Blogging Becomes a Competitive Business

There are an estimated 60 million weblogs (blogs) in existence. Most of them are personal diaries that happen to be online, have tiny audiences, and earn not a single penny in revenues. Nevertheless, a few blogs have emerged as essentially niche magazines run as businesses and published in an online format by companies such as Gawker Media; Weblogs, Inc.; and Engadget. Increasingly, others are also entering the blogging business. With today's low-cost computers and software in hand, bloggers face one main impediment to entering the blogging market: the opportunity cost of the time they devote to their blogs. Once bloggers attract a sufficient readership, they sell online ad space and begin generating revenues. Many, such as Heather Armstrong, author of a blog called Dooce, are now earning sufficient profits to account for the bulk of their family incomes. Effectively, Armstrong and other bloggers who have entered this market operate small proprietorships.

Surveys indicate that about 7 percent of bloggers post their blogs in hope of earning revenues. With some 60 million bloggers on the Web, this implies that more than 4 million people are competing to operate blogs as profitable businesses.

For critical analysis: Why is entry into the blogging market not entirely "free"?

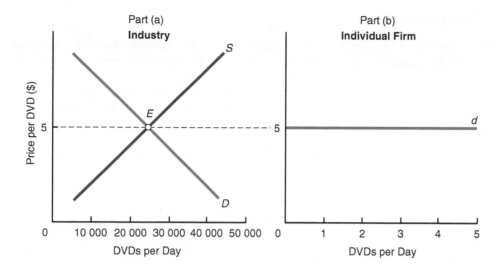

FIGURE 9–1

The Demand Curve for a DVD Producer

At $5—where market demand, *D*, and market supply, *S*, intersect—the individual firm faces a perfectly elastic demand curve, *d*. If it raises its price even one penny, it will sell no DVDs at all. Note the difference in the quantities of DVDs represented on the horizontal axes of parts (a) and (b).

The Demand Curve of the Perfect Competitor

When we discussed substitutes in Chapter 4, we pointed out that the more substitutes there were and the more similar they were to the commodity in question, the greater was the price elasticity of demand. Here, we assume for the perfectly competitive firm that it is producing a commodity that has perfect substitutes. That means that if the individual firm raises its price by one penny, it will lose all of its business. This, then, is how we characterize the demand schedule for a perfectly competitive firm: it is the going market price as determined by the forces of market supply and market demand—that is, where the market demand curve intersects the market supply curve. The single-firm demand curve in a perfectly competitive industry is perfectly elastic at the going market price. Remember that with a perfectly elastic demand curve, any increase in price leads to zero quantity demanded.

We show the market demand and supply curves in part (a) of Figure 9–1. Their intersection occurs at the price of $5. The commodity in question is recordable DVDs, and we assume for the purposes of this exposition that all DVDs are perfect substitutes for all others. At the going market price of $5 apiece, a hypothetical individual demand curve for a DVD producer who sells a very, very small part of total industry production is shown in part (b). At the market price, this firm can sell all the output it wants. At the market price of $5 each, which is where the demand curve for the individual producer lies, consumer demand for the DVDs of that one producer is perfectly elastic. This can be seen by noting that if the firm raises its price, consumers, who are assumed to know that this supplier is charging more than other producers, will buy elsewhere, and the producer in question will have no sales at all. Thus, the demand curve for that producer is perfectly elastic. We label the individual producer's demand curve *d*, whereas the *market* demand curve is always labelled *D*.

9.2 Determining Output and Profit in the Short Run

As we have shown, a perfect competitor has to accept the price of the product as a "given." If the firm raises its price, it sells nothing; if it lowers its price, it makes less money per unit sold than it otherwise could. The firm has one decision left: How much should it produce? We will apply our model of the firm to this question to come up with an answer. We will use the *profit-maximization model*, which assumes that firms attempt to maximize their total profits—the positive difference between total revenues and total costs.

Total Revenues

Total revenues The quantity sold multiplied by the price.

Every firm has to consider its *total revenues,* or TR. **Total revenues** are defined as the quantity sold multiplied by the price. (They are the same as total receipts from the sale of output.) The perfect competitor must take the price as a given.

Look at Figure 9–2. Columns 1 and 2 show total output and sales per day and the total cost of producing that output. Column 3 is the market price, *P,* of $5 per DVD, which is also equal to average revenue (AR) because:

$$AR = \frac{TR}{Q} = \frac{PQ}{Q} = P$$

FIGURE 9–2

Profit Maximization

Given the firm's costs and the market price of $5, the daily quantity that results in the largest profit is seven DVDs per day. In the table in part (a), the profit-maximizing quantity (rate of production) occurs where (TR – TC) = $5.53, which is the maximum profit. Theoretically, this profit-maximizing quantity occurs where MR = MC. In part (b), we find the maximum profit at the quantity level, where the TR curve exceeds the TC curve by the largest vertical amount, at seven DVDs per day. In part (c), we find the maximum profit at the quantity level, where the MR curve intersects the MC curve, at seven DVDs per day.

Part (a)

(1) Total Output per Day (Q)	(2) Total Costs (TC)	(3) Market Price (P)	(4) Total Revenues (TR) = (3) × (1)	(5) Total Profit (TR – TC) = (4) – (2)	(6) Average Total Cost (ATC) = (2) ÷ (1)	(7) Average Variable Cost (AVC)	(8) Marginal Cost (MC) = $\frac{\text{Change (2)}}{\text{Change (1)}}$	(9) Marginal Revenue (MR) = $\frac{\text{Change (4)}}{\text{Change (1)}}$
0	$10.00	$5	$ 0	–$10.00				
1	14.00	5	5	–9.00	$14.00	$4.00	$ 4.00	$5.00
2	17.00	5	10	–7.00	8.50	3.50	3.00	5.00
3	19.00	5	15	–4.00	6.33	3.00	2.00	5.00
4	20.00	5	20	0.00	5.00	2.50	1.00	5.00
5	21.50	5	25	3.50	4.30	2.30	1.50	5.00
6	24.48	5	30	5.52	4.08	2.41	2.98	5.00
7	29.47	5	35	5.53	4.21	2.78	4.99	5.00
8	37.47	5	40	2.53	4.68	3.43	8.00	5.00
9	49.47	5	45	–4.47	5.50	4.39	12.00	5.00
10	66.47	5	50	–16.47	6.65	5.65	17.00	5.00

where Q stands for quantity. If we assume that all units sell for the same price, it becomes apparent that another name for the demand curve is the *average revenue curve* (this is true regardless of the type of market structure under consideration).

Column 4 shows the total revenues, or TR, as equal to the market price, P, times the total output in sales per day, or Q. Thus, $TR = PQ$. We are assuming that the market supply and demand schedules intersect at a price of \$5 and that this price holds for all the firm's production. We are also assuming that because our DVD maker is a small part of the market, it can sell all that it produces at that price. Thus, part (b) of Figure 9–2 shows the total revenue curve as a straight line. For every unit of sales, total revenue is increased by \$5.

Comparing Total Costs with Total Revenues

Total costs are also plotted in part (b). Remember, the firm's costs always include a normal rate of return on investment. So, whenever we refer to total costs, we are not talking about accounting costs but about economic costs. When the total cost curve is above the total revenue curve, the firm is experiencing economic losses. When it is below the total revenue curve, the firm is making economic profits.

By comparing total costs with total revenues, we can calculate the number of DVDs the individual competitive firm should produce per day. Our analysis rests on the assumption that the firm will attempt to maximize total profits. In part (a) of Figure 9–2, we see that total profits reach a maximum of \$5.53 at a production rate of seven DVDs per day. We can see this graphically in part (b) of the figure. The firm will maximize profits where the total revenue curve exceeds the total cost curve by the greatest amount. That occurs at a rate of output and sales of seven DVDs per day; this rate is called the **profit-maximizing rate of production**—the rate of production that maximizes total profits, or the difference between total revenues and total costs; also, the rate of production at which marginal revenue equals marginal cost.

We can also find this profit-maximizing rate of production for the individual competitive firm by looking at marginal revenues and marginal costs.

Profit-maximizing rate of production The rate of production that maximizes total profits, or the difference between total revenues and total costs; also, the rate of production at which marginal revenue equals marginal cost.

Using Marginal Analysis to Determine the Profit-Maximizing Rate of Production

It is possible—indeed, preferable—to use marginal analysis to determine the profit-maximizing rate of production. We end up with the same results derived in a different manner, one that focuses more on where decisions are really made—on the margin. Managers examine changes in costs and relate them to changes in revenues. In fact, we almost always compare changes in cost with changes in benefits, where change is occurring at the margin, whether it be with respect to how much more or less to produce, how many more workers to hire or fire, or how much more to study or not study.

Marginal revenue represents the change in total revenues attributable to changing production by one unit of the product in question. Hence, a more formal definition of marginal revenue is:

Marginal revenue The change in total revenues attributable to changing production by one unit of the product in question.

$$\text{Marginal revenue} = \frac{\text{Change in total revenues}}{\text{Change in output}}$$

In a perfectly competitive market, the marginal revenue curve is exactly equivalent to the price line or the individual firm's demand curve, because the firm can sell all of its output (production) at the market price. Thus, in Figure 9–1, the demand curve, d, for the individual producer is at a price of \$5—the price line is coincident with the demand curve. But so is the marginal revenue curve, for marginal revenue, in this case, also equals \$5.

The marginal revenue curve for our competitive DVD producer is shown as a line at \$5 in part (c) of Figure 9–2. Note, again, that the marginal revenue curve is equal to the price line, which is equal to the individual firm's demand, or average revenue, curve, d.

When Are Profits Maximized?

Now, we add the marginal cost curve, MC, taken from column 8 in part (a) of Figure 9–2. As shown in part (c) of that figure, the marginal cost curve first falls and then starts to rise because of the law of diminishing returns, eventually intersecting the marginal revenue curve and then rising above it. Note that column 8 in part (a) of Figure 9–2 indicates that the marginal cost of the first unit of output is $4; the second unit of output is $3; and so forth.

In part (c), the marginal cost curve intersects the marginal revenue curve at seven DVDs per day. The firm has an incentive to produce and sell until the amount of the additional revenue received from selling one more DVD just equals the additional costs incurred for producing and selling that DVD. This is how the firm maximizes profit. Whenever marginal cost is less than marginal revenue, the firm will always make more profit by increasing production.

Now, consider the possibility of producing at an output rate of eight DVDs per day. The marginal cost curve at that output rate is higher than the marginal revenue curve (or d). The firm would be spending more to produce that additional output than it would be receiving in revenues; it would be foolish to continue producing at this rate.

But how much should it produce? It should produce at point E in Figure 9–2 part (c), where the marginal cost curve intersects the marginal revenue curve from below.[1] The firm should continue production until the cost of increasing output by one more unit is just equal to the revenues obtainable from that extra unit. This is a fundamental rule in economics:

Profit maximization normally occurs at the rate of output at which marginal revenue equals marginal cost.

For a perfectly competitive firm, this is at the intersection of the demand schedule, d, and the marginal cost curve, MC. When MR exceeds MC, each additional unit of output adds more to total revenues than to total costs, causing losses to decrease or profits to increase. When MC is greater than MR, each unit produced adds more to total cost than to total revenues, causing profits to decrease or losses to increase. Therefore, profit maximization occurs when MC equals MR. In our particular example, our profit-maximizing, perfectly competitive DVD producer will produce at a rate of seven DVDs a day.

In the mid-2000s, the Canadian government faced significant public pressure to implement policies that would restore international confidence in Canadian beef, due to the discovery of "mad cow disease" in Canada. Policy Example 9–1 encourages you to use marginal analysis to evaluate a policy proposal that would have every cow destined for Asia tested for "mad cow disease."

POLICY EXAMPLE 9-1   Quelling Fears of "Mad Cow Disease" in Asia

The Canada Beef Export Federation (CBEF) is an independent, nonprofit organization committed to improving export results for the perfectly competitive Canadian cattle and beef industry. In the year ending 2002, according to the CBEF, the three key export markets for Canadian beef were the United States, Mexico, and East Asia—purchasing 72 percent, 15 percent, and 10 percent, respectively, of all Canadian beef exports.

On the basis of current market and profit trends, the CBEF has established a marketing plan that would significantly increase Canadian beef exports to East Asia. According to this plan, East Asia will purchase over 30 percent of Canadian beef exports, the United States 45 percent, with the remaining 25 percent going to Mexico and other nations. East Asia is an attractive market to target because its consumers eat nonprime beef cuts, such as tripe, that

continued

[1]The marginal cost curve, MC, also cuts the marginal revenue curve, d, from above at an output rate of less than 1 in this example. This intersection should be ignored because it is irrelevant to the firm's decisions.

North Americans generally shun. That means that a carcass processed for Asia is worth up to $200 more than one killed for the North American market.

When two cases of bovine spongiform encephalopathy (BSE) or "mad cow disease" were discovered in cows raised in Canada in 2003, many nations around the world closed their borders to Canadian beef and cattle. As of the first quarter of 2009, two major Asian countries—South Korea and Mainland China—still prohibited the import of Canadian beef. According to statistics collected by the CBEF, in 2009, only 8.5 percent of Canadian beef exports were sold to Asian markets. This is far short of the federation's previous marketing plan.

In the past, Asian nations have suggested that if Canada were to test all cattle slaughtered for BSE, they would reconsider importing Canadian beef. Canada has so far resisted this demand, but some industry observers have suggested a policy of testing all animals destined for Asian consumption.

Source: "Canadian beef and veal product exports." Trade Statistics. Canada Beef Export Federation. http://www.cbef.com/PDF/Stats_1990-2010.pdf. (Accessed February 22, 2004); "Trade statistics 1990–2015." Newsletters and Statistics. Canadian Beef Export Federation. http://www.cbef.com. (Accessed May 29, 2010.)

For critical analysis: What maximum amount, per animal slaughtered, would Canadian beef producers be willing to pay, to ensure that all animals destined for the Asian markets are tested for BSE? Explain.

Short-Run Profits

To find what our competitive individual DVD producer is making in terms of profits in the short run, we have to add the average total cost curve to part (c) of Figure 9–2. That is, we take the information from column 6 in part (a) of Figure 9–2 and add it to part (c) of Figure 9–2 to get Figure 9–3.

In Figure 9–3, assuming a price of $5 per DVD, the profit-maximizing rate of output is seven DVDs per day, where marginal revenue equals marginal cost. At this output of seven DVDs, total revenue will equal price multiplied by quantity, which is $5 × 7 or $35 per day. Total cost, at an output level of seven DVDs, will be average total cost multiplied by the profit-maximizing rate of output, which is $4.21 × 7 = $29.47 per day. Total profit will then be total revenue minus total cost, or $35 − $29.47 = $5.53 per day.

As Figure 9–3 illustrates, the maximum total profit of $5.53 per day can be shown geometrically as the area of the shaded rectangle *abcd*. Recall that the area of a rectangle is the height multiplied by the length of the rectangle. The height of rectangle *abcd* equals the distance *dc*, which is the difference between the price ($5) and the average total

FIGURE 9–3

Measuring Total Short-Run Profits

To determine the profits graphically, first find the profit-maximizing quantity = $Q = 7$ DVDs per day. This is where MR = MC. The maximum total profit = $(P - ATC) \times Q$, where $Q = 7$ DVDs, P = given price = $5 and ATC = $4.21 at $Q = 7$ DVDs. Therefore, maximum total profit = ($5 − $4.21) × (7) = $5.53 = shaded area of rectangle *abcd*.

cost ($4.21). That is, the height of the shaded rectangle *abcd* is $5 – $4.21 = $0.79, which represents the *profit per unit* earned by the profit-maximizing firm. The length of rectangle *abcd* equals the profit-maximizing quantity of seven DVDs per day. Therefore, the area of the shaded rectangle, *abcd*, is the height multiplied by the length, or the profit per unit ($0.79) multiplied by the number of units sold (seven DVDs), which equals the total profit of $5.53 a day. Note that we are talking about an *economic profit* of $5.53 per day because a normal rate of return on investment is included in the average total cost curve, ATC.

Minimizing Losses

It is certainly possible for the competitive firm to incur losses in the short run. We give an example in Figure 9–4, where the going market price has fallen from $5 to $3 per DVD because of changes in market demand or supply conditions (or both). The firm will always do the best it can by producing where marginal revenue equals marginal cost, assuming it continues to operate (a point explained below).

We see in part (b) of Figure 9–4 that the marginal revenue curve is intersected (from below) by the marginal cost curve at an output rate of six DVDs per day. The firm is no longer making an economic profit as its average total cost of $4.08 per DVD exceeds the $3 price it can charge. The firm's minimum loss is equal to the loss per unit of $1.08 ($4.08 – $3) multiplied by the quantity of six DVDs, which equals a total loss of $6.48 per day.

Part (a)

(1) Total Output per Day (Q)	(2) Total Costs (TC)	(3) Market Price (P)	(4) Total Revenues (TR) = (3) × (1)	(5) Total Profit (TR – TC) = (4) – (2)	(6) Average Total Cost (ATC) = (2) ÷ (1)	(7) Average Variable Cost (AVC)	(8) Marginal Cost (MC) = Change (2) / Change (1)	(9) Marginal Revenue (MR) = Change (4) / Change (1)
0	$10.00	$3	$ 0	–$10.00				
1	14.00	3	3	–11.00	$14.00	$4.00	$4.00	$3
2	17.00	3	6	–11.00	8.50	3.50	3.00	3
3	19.00	3	9	–10.00	6.33	3.00	2.00	3
4	20.00	3	12	–8.00	5.00	2.50	1.00	3
5	21.50	3	15	–6.50	4.30	2.30	1.50	3
6	24.48	3	18	–6.48	4.08	2.41	2.98	3
7	29.47	3	21	–8.47	4.21	2.78	4.99	3
8	37.47	3	24	–13.47	4.68	3.43	8.00	3
9	49.47	3	27	–22.47	5.50	4.39	12.00	3
10	66.47	3	30	–36.47	6.65	5.65	17.00	3

FIGURE 9–4

Minimization of Short-Run Losses

To determine the losses graphically, first find the loss-minimizing quantity = Q = 6 DVDs per day. This is where MR = MC. The maximum total profit = (P – ATC) × Q, where Q = 6 DVDs, P = given price = $3 and ATC = $4.08 at Q = 6 DVDs. Therefore, total profit = ($3 – $4.08) × 6 = $–6.48. This minimum total loss of $6.48 equals the shaded area of rectangle abcd.

Part (b)

Should this firm go out of business when it faces a loss of $6.48 per day? At this point, we should note that we are assuming a short-run situation, where the firm is stuck with meeting some of its fixed obligations, such as paying its monthly rent due to a lease agreement, or monthly interest on funds already borrowed from the bank. Also, in the short run, the firm is optimistic that the price will increase in the near future so that an economic profit can be earned during some of the days of the month. Therefore, we are assuming that the firm intends to stay in business in the short run.

Should this firm opt for a *shutdown*, with a loss of $6.48 per day? By **shutdown** we mean that the firm stays in business but temporarily produces at a zero quantity level. If the firm were to shut down, it avoids incurring variable costs, but it would still have to pay for its total fixed costs. According to column 2 in part (a) of Figure 9–4, if the firm operates at a zero quantity level, it will still incur a total cost of $10 per day. This means that its total fixed costs are $10 per day. If the firm were to shut down in the short run, its total revenue would equal zero and its total costs would equal $10, leaving a total loss of $10 per day.

If, instead, the firm operates at an output rate of six DVDs per day, it minimizes its losses at $6.48 per day, as described in Figure 9–4. As you can see, at a price of $3 per DVD, this firm should not shut down.

In general, how do we know when it is best *not* to shut down in the face of economic losses? A firm should operate at a positive quantity level whenever the extra revenue it gets exceeds the extra costs incurred when operating at a positive quantity level, which are its *variable* costs. On a per-unit basis, as long as it is possible for the price of the product to exceed the firm's average variable cost, the firm should operate at a positive quantity level.

In the DVD example, at a quantity level of six DVDs per day, we can see that the price of $3 per DVD exceeds the average variable cost of $2.41 per DVD. By selling six DVDs per day, the firm gets a positive contribution toward recovering some of its fixed costs. Therefore, the firm should not shut down.

> **As long as the price per unit sold exceeds the average variable cost per unit produced, the firm will be recovering part of the opportunity cost of its investment in the business—that is, part of its fixed costs.**

Once you appreciate the importance of having price exceed average variable cost in the short run, you can appreciate why big discounts are frequently offered in businesses that face a large amount of fixed costs, as Example 9–2 explains.

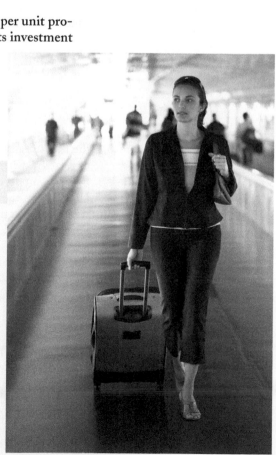

Shutdown A short-run situation where the firm stays in business but temporarily produces at a zero quantity level.

EXAMPLE 9–2 High Sunk Costs Can Mean Deep Discounts

Have you ever wondered why airline "standby" rates are so cheap? Or why you can pay half price to stay at a three-star hotel off-season? Or why restaurants frequently offer two-for-one entrees? Or why golf courses offer cheaper green fees during the quiet times of day or week? The answer to all of these questions is the same.

Whenever the production or sale of a product or service entails high sunk (fixed) costs and low variable costs, the marginal cost of supplying additional units of the service is very close to zero. This being the case, the firm can get some contribution toward its sunk costs by selling its service at deep discounts, as long as the discounted price more than covers the variable cost per unit. In other words, the firm will continue to provide units of the service as long as the marginal revenue exceeds the marginal cost. In this way, the firm can minimize its losses in the short run. Remember, if the firm shuts down in the short run, it is stuck with paying those large fixed monthly costs, which is why they are called sunk costs.

Why do airlines provide discounts for last minute bookings?

continued

Consider the operation of a three-star hotel in a popular ski resort area during the off-season. Most of the costs incurred by the hotel's owners relate to the fixed monthly mortgage payment associated with the hotel's land, building, fixtures, and facilities. As well, the costs of furnishing each hotel room and bathroom are fixed. The variable costs of renting out additional rooms would include such expenses as paying additional staff to clean the rooms and the extra laundry, which would result in a relatively low variable cost per room. In the off-season, when room vacancies become more common, the hotel owners can attract hotel guests by offering deep discounts, as long as the discounted daily room charge more than covers the relatively low variable cost per room.

For critical analysis: Suppose there is available seating on a popular jet flight between Vancouver and Toronto, moments before take-off. What is the marginal cost of allowing a passenger to fill one of these vacant seats? How large a discount can the airline give to this passenger? Explain.

Calculating the Short-Run Breakeven Price

Short-run breakeven price The price at which a firm's total revenues equal its total costs.

Look at demand curve d_1 in Figure 9–5. It just touches the minimum point of the average total cost curve, which is exactly where the marginal cost curve intersects the average total cost curve. At that price, which is about $4, the firm will be making exactly zero short-run economic profits. That price, the **short-run breakeven price**, is the price at which a firm's total revenues equal its total costs. At the breakeven price, the firm is just making a normal rate of return on its capital investment. (It is covering its explicit and implicit costs.) Point E_1, therefore, occurs at the short-run breakeven price for a competitive firm. It is the point at which marginal revenue, marginal cost, and average total cost are all equal (that is, at which $P = MC$ and $P = ATC$). The breakeven price is the one that yields zero short-run economic profits or losses.

Calculating the Short-Run Shutdown Price

Short-run shutdown price The price that just equals minimum average variable cost.

To calculate the firm's shutdown price, we must introduce the average variable cost (AVC) to our graph. In Figure 9–5, we have plotted the AVC values from column 7 in part (a) of Figure 9–2. For the moment, consider two possible demand curves, d_1 and d_2, which are also the firm's respective marginal revenue curves. Therefore, if demand is d_1, the firm will produce at E_1, where that curve intersects the marginal cost curve. If demand falls to d_2, the firm will produce at E_2. The special feature of the hypothetical demand curve, d_2, is that it just touches the average variable cost curve at the latter's minimum point, which is also where the marginal cost curve intersects it. This price is the **short-run shutdown price**, which just equals minimum average variable cost. Why? Below this price, the firm would be

FIGURE 9–5

Short-Run Breakeven Point versus Short-Run Shutdown Point

The short-run breakeven point occurs when the price (P_1) just equals minimum average total cost. Graphically, this occurs where the Price line is just tangent to the ATC curve at point E_1. At this point, the best the firm can do is "break even," which means that it earns "zero economic profit" or "normal profits." The short-run shutdown point occurs when the price (P_2) just equals minimum average variable cost. Graphically, this occurs where the Price line is just tangent to the AVC curve at point E_2. If the price goes below P_2, the firm is better off shutting down in the short run.

paying out more in variable costs than it is receiving in revenues from the sale of its product. Each unit it sold would add to its losses. Clearly, the way to avoid incurring these additional losses, if price falls below the shutdown point, is, in fact, to shut down operations.

As an example, suppose the price per DVD dropped to $2. As Table 9–2 indicates, the price is now below the average variable cost at every quantity. This indicates that the firm is better off shutting down in the short run. With this decision, the firm's total loss equals its total fixed costs of $10, which is the minimum loss displayed in Table 9–2. If, alternatively, the firm was to produce one DVD per day, the price of $2 would be $2 less than the average variable cost of $4 per DVD. In addition to the fixed costs of $10, the firm would lose an extra $2. Therefore, total losses would be $12 at an output of one DVD per day.

The Meaning of Zero Economic Profits

The fact that we labelled point E_1 in Figure 9–5 the breakeven point may have puzzled you. At point E_1, price is just equal to average total cost. If this is the case, why would a firm continue to produce if it were making no profits whatsoever? If we again make the distinction between accounting profits and economic profits, then at that price the firm has zero economic profits but positive accounting profits. Recall that accounting profits are total revenues minus total explicit costs. What is ignored in such accounting is the reward offered to investors—the opportunity cost of capital—plus all other implicit costs.

In economic analysis, the average total cost curve includes the full opportunity cost of capital. Indeed, the average total cost curve includes the opportunity cost of *all* factors of production used in the production process. At the short-run breakeven price, economic profits are, by definition, zero. Accounting profits at that price are not, however, equal to zero; they are positive. Consider an example. A clock manufacturer sells clocks at some price. The owners of the firm have supplied all the funds in the business. They have borrowed no money from anyone else, and they explicitly pay the full opportunity cost to all factors of production, including any managerial labour that they themselves contribute to the business. Their salaries show up as a cost in the books and are equal to what they could have earned in the best alternative occupation. At the end of the year, the owners find that after they subtract all explicit costs from total revenues, they have earned $100 000. Let us say that their investment was $1 million. Thus, the rate of return on that investment is 10 percent per year. We will assume that this turns out to be equal to the rate of return that, on average, all other clock manufacturers make in the industry.

This $100 000, or 10 percent rate of return, is actually, then, a competitive, or normal, rate of return on invested capital in that industry or in other industries with similar risks. If the owners had made only $50 000, or 5 percent on their investment, they would have been

TABLE 9–2

Short-Run Shutdown Example: Price = $2.00, or Below Minimum Average Variable Cost

(1) Total Output per Day (Q)	(2) Total Costs (TC)	(3) Market Price (P)	(4) Total Revenues (TR) = (3) × (1)	(5) Total Profit (TR − TC) = (4) − (2)	(6) Average Total Cost (ATC) = (2) ÷ (1)	(7) Average Variable Cost (AVC)	(8) Marginal Cost (MC) = Change (2) / Change (1)	(9) Marginal Revenue (MR) = Change (4) / Change (1)
0	$10.00	$2	$ 0	−$10.00				
1	14.00	2	2	−12.00	$14.00	$4.00	$ 4.00	$2.00
2	17.00	2	4	−13.00	8.50	3.50	3.00	2.00
3	19.00	2	6	−13.00	6.33	3.00	2.00	2.00
4	20.00	2	8	−12.00	5.00	2.50	1.00	2.00
5	21.50	2	10	−11.50	4.30	2.30	1.50	2.00
6	24.48	2	12	−12.48	4.08	2.41	2.98	2.00
7	29.47	2	14	−15.47	4.21	2.78	4.99	2.00
8	37.47	2	16	−21.47	4.68	3.43	8.00	2.00
9	49.47	2	18	−31.47	5.50	4.39	12.00	2.00
10	66.47	2	20	−46.47	6.65	5.65	17.00	2.00

able to make higher profits by leaving the industry. The 10 percent rate of return is the opportunity cost of capital. Accountants show it as a profit; economists call it a cost. We include that cost in the average total cost curve, similar to the one shown in Figure 9–5. At the short-run breakeven price, average total cost, including this opportunity cost of capital, will just equal that price. The firm will be making zero economic profits or a 10 percent *accounting* rate of return called "normal profits."

9.3 Short-Run Supply and Equilibrium

What does the supply curve for the individual firm in perfect competition look like? Actually, we have been looking at it all along. We know that when the price of DVDs is $5, the firm will supply seven of them per day. If the price falls to $3, the firm will supply six DVDs per day. And if the price falls to $2, the firm will shut down in the short run. Hence, in Figure 9–6, the firm's supply curve is the marginal cost curve above the short-run shutdown point. This is shown as the solid part of the marginal cost curve.

> The definition, then, of the individual firm's supply curve in a competitive industry is its marginal cost curve equal to and above minimum average variable cost.

The Short-Run Industry Supply Curve

In Chapter 3, we indicated that the market supply curve was the summation of individual supply curves. At the beginning of this chapter, we drew a market supply curve in Figure 9–1. Now, we want to derive more precisely a market, or industry, supply curve to reflect individual producer behaviour in that industry. First, we must ask: "What is an industry?" It is merely a collection of firms producing a particular product. Therefore, we have a way to figure out the total supply curve of any industry: We add the quantities that each firm will supply at every possible price. In other words, we sum the individual supply curves of all the competitive firms *horizontally*. The individual supply curves, as we just saw, are simply the marginal cost curves of each firm.

Consider doing this for a hypothetical world in which there are only two DVD producers in the industry, firm A and firm B. These two firms' marginal cost curves are given in parts (a) and (b) of Figure 9–7. The marginal cost curves for the two separate firms are presented as MC_A in part (a) and MC_B in part (b). Those two marginal cost curves are drawn only for prices above the minimum average variable cost for each firm. Hence, we are not including any of the marginal cost curves below minimum average variable cost. In part (a), for firm A, at $5, the quantity supplied would be seven. At $10, the quantity supplied would be nine. In part (b), we see the two different quantities that would be

FIGURE 9–6

Individual Firm's Short-Run Supply Curve

In general, the firm's supply curve indicates what quantity the firm will supply at different prices. In this figure, we can see that at different possible prices, the firm will supply that quantity that maximizes profit or minimizes losses. That is, when the price is above minimum average variable cost, the firm will supply that quantity where P = MC or MR = MC. Therefore, the firm's supply curve is the portion of its marginal cost curve that is above minimum average variable cost.

FIGURE 9-7

Deriving the Industry Supply Curve

Marginal cost curves above minimum average variable cost are presented in parts (a) and (b) for firms A and B. We horizontally sum the two quantities supplied, 7 and 10, at $5. This gives us point *F* in part (c). We do the same thing for the quantities at $10. This gives us point *G*. When we connect those points, we have the industry supply curve, *S*, which is the horizontal summation of the firms' marginal cost curves above their respective minimum average variable costs.

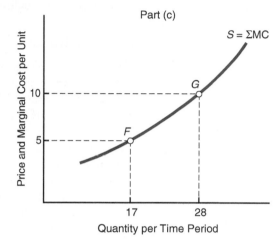

supplied by firm B corresponding to those two prices. In part (c), for the $5 price, we add horizontally the quantities 7 and 10. This gives us one point, *F*, for our short-run **industry supply curve**, *S*—the locus of points showing the minimum prices at which given quantities will be forthcoming from the industry; also called the market supply curve. We obtain the other point, *G*, by doing the same horizontal adding of quantities at $10. When we connect points *F* and *G*, we obtain industry supply curve *S*, which is also marked ΣMC, indicating that it is the horizontal summation of the marginal cost curves (above the respective minimum average variable cost of each firm).[2]

> **Industry supply curve** The locus of points showing the minimum prices at which given quantities will be forthcoming from the industry; also called the market supply curve.

> Because the law of diminishing returns makes marginal cost curves rise, the short-run supply curve of a perfectly competitive industry must be upward sloping.

Factors That Influence the Industry Supply Curve

As you have just seen, the industry supply curve is the horizontal summation of all of the individual firms' marginal cost curves above their respective minimum average variable cost points. This means that anything that affects the marginal cost curves of the firm will influence the industry supply curve. Therefore, the individual factors that will influence the supply schedule in a competitive industry can be summarized as the factors that cause the *variable costs* of production to change. These are factors that affect the individual marginal cost curves, such as changes in the individual firm's productivity, in factor costs (wages paid to labour, prices of raw materials, and so on), in taxes, and in anything else that would influence the individual firm's marginal cost curve.

All of these are *ceteris paribus* conditions of supply. Because they affect the position of the marginal cost curve for the individual firm, they affect the position of the industry supply curve. A change in any of these will shift the market supply curve.

---

[2]The capital Greek sigma, Σ, is the symbol for summation.

Short-Run Equilibrium

How is the market, or "going," price established in the short run in perfect competition? The short-run equilibrium price will occur where the short-run industry or market supply just equals the industry or market demand. We have just seen how the industry supply curve is the horizontal sum of the individual firms' marginal cost curves, assuming that firms maximize profits or minimize losses. This suggests that although no one single firm can affect the price, the supply plans of all the firms, combined, does play an important role in determining the industry price.

Short-Run Equilibrium for the Industry

Table 9–3 illustrates the process by which the competitive industry price is determined for the DVD market, on the basis of the following assumptions. The DVD industry comprises 100 identical perfectly competitive firms. Each firm has the total and per-units costs described in Figure 9–2. The industry or market demand schedule is given in column 4 in Table 9–3. While we will not attempt to derive the industry demand schedule, you may recall that it is the "horizontal sum" of all individual demand schedules for DVDs. Each individual demand schedule is based on the assumption that the consumer maximizes his or her utility when responding to price.

To determine the short-run industry equilibrium price in Table 9–3, we must first determine the individual firm's quantity supplied in column 2 of Table 9–3. To do this, we compare each price in column 1 of Table 9–3 with the marginal costs described in Figure 9–2. For example, at the price of $12 per DVD, the firm will maximize its profits if it supplies nine DVDs per day, where the marginal revenue of $12 just equals the marginal cost of $12. If the price falls to $8 per DVD, the firm will instead supply eight DVDs per day, where marginal revenue equals marginal cost.

After determining the individual firm's quantity supplied for all of the prices in Table 9–3, you are ready to derive the short-run industry supply schedule in column 3 of Table 9–3. At each price, the industry supply is simply 100 multiplied by the individual firm's quantity supplied at that same price. Once the industry supply schedule is determined for all prices in Table 9–3, you can see that the industry quantity supplied equals the industry quantity demanded at $5 per DVD. In other words, the short-run equilibrium industry price is $5 per DVD, and the short-run equilibrium industry quantity is 700 DVDs per day.

Part (a) of Figure 9–8 provides a sketch of the graph of the short-run equilibrium in the DVD industry, on the basis of the industry demand in Table 9–3, and assuming that the industry comprises 100 identical firms. Each firm faces the total and per-unit costs described in Figure 9–2. Note that part (a) in Figure 9–8 shows how the short-run industry supply, made up of the horizontal sum of 100 identical marginal cost curves, interacts with the industry demand curve to establish an equilibrium price of $5 per DVD and an equilibrium industry quantity of 700 DVDs per day.

Short-Run Equilibrium for the Firm

Where will each individual DVD firm settle at in the short run? The individual firm's *equilibrium quantity* will be the quantity that maximizes profits or minimizes losses, given the industry equilibrium price. As part (b) of Figure 9–8 illustrates, the firm will maximize its profit at an output level of seven DVDs per day, where the industry equilibrium

TABLE 9–3

Short-Run Equilibrium in the DVD Industry

(1) Price per DVD	(2) Quantity Supplied by Individual Firms	(3) Quantity Supplied by Industry (100 Firms)	(4) Quantity Demanded of Industry (all consumers)
$12	9	900	200
8	8	800	500
5	7	700	700
3	6	600	800

FIGURE 9-8

Short-Run Equilibrium for the DVD Industry and Firm

In part (a), the horizontal sum of the 100 identical firm marginal cost curves determines the short-run industry supply curve. This short-run industry supply curve interacts with the industry demand curve, D, to establish an equilibrium industry price of $5 per DVD and an industry equilibrium quantity of 700 DVDs. In part (b), at the industry price of $5, each individual firm's equilibrium quantity will be seven DVDs per day with an economic profit of $5.53, which is equal to the shaded area.

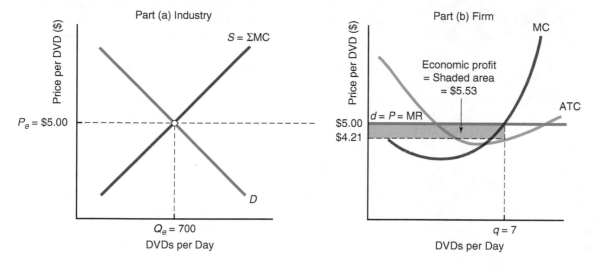

price of $5 per DVD is equal to the firm's marginal cost. Therefore, with an equilibrium industry price of $5 per DVD, the firm's equilibrium quantity is seven DVDs per day. As Figure 9–8 reveals, the firm's short-run total economic profit will be equal to its price minus average total cost multiplied by its equilibrium quantity, which equals ($5 – $4.21) × 7 = $5.53 per day.

In Figure 9–8, each firm earns a positive economic profit because at the firm's short-run equilibrium output level, price exceeds average total cost. If the industry demand for DVDs decreases so that the equilibrium price falls to a level equal to each firm's minimum average total cost, as described by point E_1 in Figure 9–5, then zero economic profits will prevail in short-run equilibrium. Further declines in industry demand will reduce the DVD price level below each firm's minimum average total cost. In these situations, each firm will operate at a loss or shut down with a loss, depending on whether price is above or below minimum average variable costs, as explained in Figures 9–4 and 9–5.

Canadian lumber firms manufacturing two-by-fours compete with lumber firms in the United States, South America, and Russia in a global market resembling perfect competition. Example 9–3 illustrates the importance that the U.S. economy and U.S. government policy have on the financial success of the Canadian lumber industry.

EXAMPLE 9-3   U.S. Recession Takes Its Toll on Canadian Lumber Firms

On May 29, 2009, Canfor Corporation, a Canadian lumber company, announced that it was going to indefinitely shut down three sawmills in the B.C. Interior, laying off 570 workers at mills in the towns of Vavenby, Radium, and Prince George. Canfor had already shut down sawmills at Mackenzie and Chetwynd and cut back shifts at others to reduce its lumber capacity. The shutdowns that took place during the summer of 2009 reduced Canfor's lumber production to about 2.5 billion board feet a year, half the company's estimated capacity.

Between January 2006 and March 2009, lumber prices plummeted from US$365 to US$140 per 1000 board feet of two-by-four spruce (which is below the breakeven point). For

continued

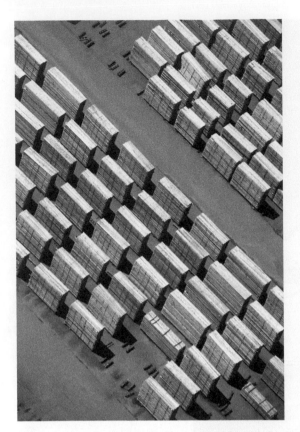

Why are Canadian lumber mills shutting down?

the year ending December 31, 2009, the company's net loss was $70.5 million ($0.50 per share), compared to a net loss of $345.2 million ($2.42 per share) reported for 2008. Canfor responded to this loss by putting pressure on suppliers and unions to reduce material and labour costs.

The Canadian lumber firms' woes can be explained by a number of demand and supply factors in the global lumber market. There was a serious slowdown in U.S. housing starts due to the sub-prime mortgage crisis and the great global recession. The increasing interest rates and very high unemployment levels in the U.S. economy meant that a significant number of homeowners were unable to meet their monthly mortgage payments, resulting in an estimated record 4 million home mortgage foreclosure filings in the U.S. in 2009.

The higher Canadian exchange rate has dampened foreign demand for Canadian lumber. The U.S. imposed tariffs on Canadian lumber in response to trade disputes and a recessionary economy. As well, significant increases in supply from foreign competitors in South America and Russia have dampened global lumber prices.

For critical analysis: Assuming perfect competition, construct both an industry and individual firm diagram relating to the Canadian lumber industry. In the industry diagram, describe the recent demand and supply shifts that have affected Canadian lumber prices. In the related firm diagram, sketch the price (US$140), marginal cost, and average total cost curves of the typical Canfor sawmill that has been shut down, assuming that the firm is maximizing its profits (or minimizing its losses). In the firm diagram, illustrate Canfor's total profits or losses.

Sources: Gordon Hamilton. "Canfor shuts three sawmills, laying off 570 workers; Vavenby, Radium and Prince George lose out." *Vancouver Sun*. May 29, 2009. pg. C1; "Lumber." Quotes and News. Wikinvest. May 28, 2010. http://www.wikinvest.com/commodity/Lumber; "Canfor reports net loss of $17.0 million for last quarter of 2009: Q4 lumber markets were weak, pulp markets continued to improve." News Release. Canfor. http://www.canfor.ca/_resources/news/2010/NR100210_Canfor_Reports_Net_Loss_of_$17_Million_for_Q4_2009.pdf; Adler, Lynn. "Foreclosures at record high in first half 2009 despite aid." Reuters (New York). July 16, 2009. http://www.reuters.com/article/idUSTRE56F0XK20090716.

9.4 Long-Run Equilibrium

We have just seen that a competitive firm can be in short-run equilibrium earning positive economic profits, or negative economic profits, or just breaking even, depending on the price. Only *one* situation, the breakeven, is possible in the long run, after sufficient time has passed to allow firms to change plant sizes and enter or exit the industry. This one situation is called *long-run equilibrium* and is explained below, using our DVD industry example.

Long-run equilibrium, as described in Figure 9–9, refers to the best situation that a competitive firm can look forward to in the long run. That is, in the long run, the industry supply, S_2, in conjunction with the industry demand, D, sets a price of $P_2 = \$3$ per DVD in part (a) of Figure 9–9. At this price, the firm's profit-maximizing quantity is q_2, where price equals marginal cost, in part (b) of Figure 9–9. At q_2, the typical firm is operating at minimum short-run and long-run average total cost, earning zero economic profits, as price equals average total cost.

Adjustments to Long-Run Equilibrium

Why does the typical firm in perfect competition end up in long-run equilibrium, as described in Figure 9–9? Suppose the initial industry supply is S_1 in part (a) of Figure 9–9, and the typical firm's plant size has a short-run average total cost equal to SAC_1 in part (b) of Figure 9–9. With the industry demand, D, the initial equilibrium price is $5. At the

FIGURE 9-9

Long-Run Equilibrium in Perfect Competition

In general, long-run equilibrium occurs when the industry equilibrium price just equals the typical firm's minimum long-run average total cost. This occurs when the industry supply curve is S_2 and the equilibrium price is $3 per DVD in part (a). At the $3 price, the typical firm in part (b) will maximize profit at q_2, where marginal revenue equals marginal cost. At q_2, the typical firm is operating at minimum short-run and long-run average total cost, earning zero economic profits, as price just equals average total cost.

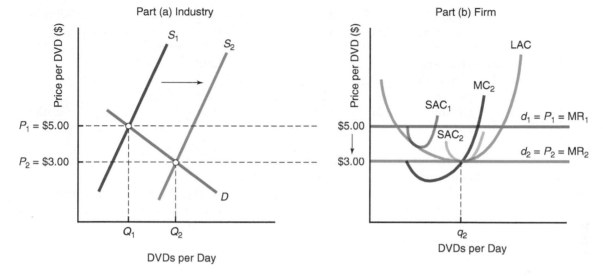

price of $5, the typical firm will be making positive economic profits, in short-run equilibrium (where the $5 price will exceed SAC_1).

Due to the competitive characteristics of easy entry, large number of firms, and homogeneous product, the industry will not stay at the $5 price in the long run. The positive economic profits earned by the typical competitive firm at the $5 price will attract new firms to the DVD industry. As new firms enter, the short-run industry supply curve will increase or shift from S_1 toward S_2 in part (a) of Figure 9–9. As the industry supply increases, the industry price will decrease.

How do existing firms react to the increased competitive pressures stemming from the new entrants? Since their product is homogeneous, they cannot differentiate their product from their competitors'. Therefore, existing firms must attempt to lower costs per unit by adopting more efficient plant sizes. In part (b) of Figure 9–9, the existing firms are able to lower unit costs by changing the typical plant size from one with unit costs of SAC_1 to the larger plant size associated with SAC_2. As plant sizes expand, the short-run industry supply will continue to increase, leading to further declines in industry price. The price will continue to decrease until each firm earns zero economic profit (a normal profit) and each firm can no longer gain efficiencies by changing plant sizes. This occurs in long-run equilibrium, when the industry price falls to a level equal to the typical firm's minimum long-run average total cost, which is $3 in Figure 9–9.

Note that our explanation of long-run equilibrium began with the typical firm earning positive economic profit in the short run. What if, in the short run, the typical firm was facing economic losses? In this case, some firms will leave the industry in the long run, causing a decrease in short-run industry supply. As a result, the industry price will increase to a level where the price will just equal minimum long-run average total cost. That is, the same long-run equilibrium situation will result.

It should be evident that perfectly competitive firms have no choice but to seek the most cost-efficient methods of operation in the long run. They do not have the luxury of controlling prices or differentiating their product. This implies that in the long run, competitive firms will seek to locate in geographical areas that minimize their production costs per unit. According to the Did You Know That . . . ? section of this chapter, this may result in a more rapid rate of economic growth for Canada in the future. In 2010, Canada was found to be the least costly place to locate a business, when one compares the setup and operating costs of firms competing in 17 major industrial sectors in nine of the most industrialized nations in the world. On average, Canadian businesses enjoyed a 5 percent cost advantage over similar firms situated in the United States.

9.5 Long-Run Industry Supply Curves

In part (a) of Figure 9–8, we drew the summation of all the portions of the individual firms' marginal cost curves, above each firm's respective minimum average variable costs, as the upward-sloping short-run supply curve for the competitive industry. We should be aware that a relatively steep upward-sloping supply curve might be appropriate only in the short run. In the long run, in perfect competition, further adjustments in quantity supplied will result, as firms adjust their plant size and enter or exit the industry.

The **long-run industry supply curve** is a market supply curve showing the relationship between quantities supplied by the entire industry and prices, after sufficient time has passed to allow firms to change plant sizes and enter or exit the industry. In other words, the long-run supply curve describes the industry response to a change in prices, after long-run equilibrium has been re-established.

The long-run industry supply curve can take one of three shapes, depending on whether the input costs stay constant, increase, or decrease, as the size of the industry changes.

Constant-Cost Industries

In principle, there are small enough industries that use such a small percentage of the total supply of inputs necessary for their production that the industry can expand without affecting input prices. In such a situation, we are dealing with a **constant-cost industry**. Since long-run per-unit costs stay constant, as the industry expands, the long-run industry supply curve is horizontal and is represented by S_L in part (a) of Figure 9–10.

We can work through the case in which constant costs prevail. We start out in part (a) with demand curve D_1 and supply curve S_1. The equilibrium price is P_1. Market demand shifts rightward to D_2. In the short run, the equilibrium price rises to P_2. This generates positive economic profits for existing firms in the industry. Such economic profits induce resources to flow into the industry. The existing firms expand and/or new firms enter. The short-run supply curve shifts outward to S_2. The new intersection with the new demand curve is at E_3. The new equilibrium price is again P_1. The long-run supply curve is obtained by connecting the intersections of the corresponding pairs of demand and supply curves, E_1 and E_3. Labelled S_L, it is horizontal; its slope is zero. In a constant-cost industry, long-run supply is perfectly elastic. Any shift in demand is eventually met by an equal shift in supply so that the long-run price is constant at P_1.

Retail trade is often given as an example of such an industry because output can be expanded or contracted without affecting input prices.

Increasing-Cost Industries

In an **increasing-cost industry**, expansion by existing firms and the addition of new firms cause the price of inputs specialized within that industry to be bid up. As costs of production rise, the ATC curve and the firms' MC curve shift upward, causing short-run supply curves (each firm's marginal cost curve) to shift upward. The result is a long-run industry supply curve that slopes upward, as represented by S_L in part (b) of Figure 9–10. Examples are residential construction and coal mining—both use specialized inputs that cannot be obtained in ever-increasing quantities without causing their prices to rise.

Decreasing-Cost Industries

In a **decreasing-cost industry**, an expansion in the number of firms in an industry can lead to a reduction in input prices and a downward shift in the ATC and MC curves. When this occurs, the long-run industry supply curve will slope downward. This is described in part (c) of Figure 9–10. Examples are computers and long-distance phone service.

Long-run industry supply curve A market supply curve showing the relationship between quantities supplied by the entire industry and prices, after sufficient time has passed to allow firms to change plant sizes and enter or exit the industry.

Constant-cost industry An industry that can increase its output in the long run, without affecting input prices.

Increasing-cost industry A situation where input prices increase as the industry expands in the long run.

Decreasing-cost industry A situation where input prices decrease as the industry expands in the long run.

FIGURE 9–10

Constant Cost, Increasing Cost, and Decreasing Cost Industries

In part (a), we show a situation in which the demand curve shifts from D_1 to D_2. Price increases from P_1 to P_2; however, in time, the short-run supply curve shifts outward because positive profits are being earned, and the equilibrium shifts from E_2 to E_3. The market clearing price is again P_1. If we connect such points as E_1 and E_3, we come up with the long-run supply curve S_L. This is a constant-cost industry. In part

(b), unit costs are increasing for the industry, and therefore, the long-run supply curve slopes upward and long-run prices rise from P_1 to P_2. In part (c), unit costs are decreasing for the industry as it expands, and therefore, the long-run supply curve slopes downward such that long-run prices decline from P_1 to P_2.

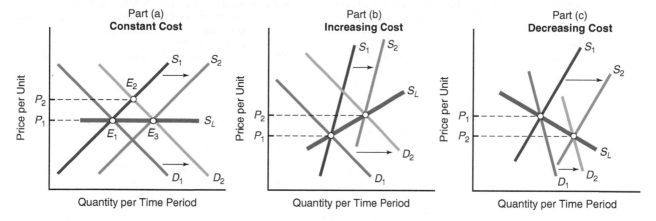

According to this chapter's Issues and Applications, the home-video movie industry is a good example of a decreasing-cost industry. As this industry has grown, the widespread use of DVDs has lowered the cost per unit of supplying these movies. Looking into the near future, the cost of supplying this product will continue to decrease, as the practice of downloading movies from the Internet becomes acceptable.

Not long ago, firms that provided digital photo printing services, such as discount department stores and pharmacies, charged as much as 50 cents per printed photo. Today, many consumers pay little more than a dime to have digital photos printed. Example 9–4 explains how this significant decrease in price can be explained by the long-run behaviour in a competitive industry.

EXAMPLE 9–4   The Big Rush to Provide Digital Snaps in a Snap

The North American digital photographic sector brings in over $85 billion in revenues each year. Since 2000, the majority of those revenues have been earned from the sale of digital cameras and related digital photography products and services. A rapidly growing segment of this sector has been the market for digital photo printing services. The growth of this market can be explained in terms of both short-run and long-run adjustments.

Early entrants in the digital photo printing industry were retailers who for years had provided developing and printing services for old-style photography that utilized film instead of digital imaging technologies. Part (a) of the accompanying figure depicts the short-run adjustments that occurred as the demand for photo printing services increased. The movement from E_1 to E_2 represents the increase in quantity supplied by the existing firms in the industry as they begin to earn positive economic profits.

In the long run, new firms entered the photo printing industry, attracted by the positive economic profits. Entrepreneurs quickly determined that the only impediment to entry into the business of printing digital photos was the few thousand dollars required to purchase a small booth, called a kiosk, with photo printing software and hardware. These kiosks were located in shopping malls, hospitals, and college campuses. Within a few more months, large corporations including Sony, Eastman Kodak, Fuji Photo Film, Staples, Best Buy, and Future Shop started to offer in-store and online digital photo printing services. In part (b) of Figure 9–11, the

continued

relatively large shift in supply from S_1 to S_2 reflects the long-run adjustment that has taken place as a result of the explosion of new entrants into the market. In the long run, the typical price per photo print has decreased from $0.15 to $0.12 per print.

FIGURE 9–11

Short-Run and Long-Run Adjustments in the Digital Photo Printing Industry

Part (a) shows that when the demand for digital photo printing services increased in the early 2000s, the market clearing price rose from about 15 cents per photo at point E_1 to about 19 cents per photo at point E_2. The equilibrium quantity of services also increased. Part (b) displays the long-run adjustments that took place as numerous firms entered the industry, causing market supply to increase. The equilibrium quantity of digital photo printing services continued to rise, but the market clearing price declined, from 19 cents per photo at point E_2 to about 12 cents per photo at point E_3.

For critical analysis: Sketch part (b) and create the long-run supply curve based on your sketch. According to your sketch, is the digital photo printing industry a constant cost, increasing cost, or decreasing cost industry? What is happening to each firm's average total cost curve as the industry expands?

Long-Run Adjustments to Technological Change

In the previous section, we examined how perfect competition responds to changes in demand and prices in the long run. We now turn to examine the long-run adjustments that a competitive industry will incur, when faced with a cost-saving technological change.

Suppose new technology that lowers the per-unit cost of producing DVDs has just been discovered. In order to benefit from the new technology, new plants must be constructed, which implies a long-run response on the part of the DVD firms. As soon as some firms complete this new construction, their short-run and long-run average cost and marginal cost curves will shift downward and to the right. This implies that at the same DVD price, these firms can now supply a larger rate of output. Firms that adopt this new technology will make short-run positive economic profits, as average total cost slips below the industry price. These economic profits will induce new firms to enter the DVD industry.

As the new technology spreads throughout the DVD industry, the short-run market supply curve will increase, causing the industry price to decline. Eventually, the industry will reach a new long-run equilibrium, when the industry price falls to a level equal to the reduced minimum long-run average total cost curve. While the DVD firms will no longer enjoy positive economic profits, consumers will derive a long-term benefit in the form of lower DVD prices.

9.6 Social Evaluation of Perfect Competition

As we shall study in a subsequent chapter, the Canadian government has passed laws that encourage various industries to adopt a market structure and behaviour that more closely resemble perfect competition. This suggests that perfect competition must promote important socioeconomic goals. This is particularly the case when we focus on perfect competition in long-run equilibrium.

Perfect Competition and Productive Efficiency

Look again at Figure 9–9 part (b). In long-run equilibrium, the perfectly competitive firm finds itself producing at output rate q_2. At that rate of output, the price is just equal to the minimum long-run average cost as well as the minimum short-run average cost. In this sense, perfect competition results in the production of goods and services using the least costly combination of resources. This is called *productive efficiency*. This is an important attribute of a perfectly competitive long-run equilibrium, particularly when we wish to compare perfect competition with other market structures. We will examine these other market structures in later chapters.

Perfect Competition and Allocative Efficiency

You may recall that allocative efficiency is concerned with producing the mix of goods and services that maximizes consumer satisfaction. Due to scarcity, it is crucial that economic resources are allocated to those uses that are most highly valued by consumers. In this section, we will explain how perfect competition promotes the goal of allocative efficiency.

We have seen that, in perfect competition, production takes place to the point where price just equals marginal cost. This is called **marginal cost pricing**, which is a system where the price charged to the consumer is equal to the opportunity cost to society of producing the last unit of the good in question. As we will explain below, marginal cost pricing promotes allocative efficiency.

ALLOCATIVE EFFICIENCY: A GRAPHIC ILLUSTRATION. In Figure 9–12, we illustrate how marginal cost pricing in the DVD industry promotes allocative efficiency. In this figure, we assume that the competitive industry is in long-run equilibrium with an equilibrium price of $3 per DVD and an equilibrium output of 800 DVDs per day.

At this point, it is appropriate to focus on the useful information that an industry demand curve provides us with. At any given quantity level, the height of the industry demand curve describes the maximum price that consumers are willing to pay for the last unit of output. As an example, in Figure 9–12, consumers are willing to pay a maximum

Marginal cost pricing A system where the price charged to the consumer is equal to the opportunity cost to society of producing the last unit of good in question.

FIGURE 9–12

Allocative Efficiency in the DVD Industry

In perfect competition, production takes place at the equilibrium level of 800 DVDs per day. At this equilibrium level, allocative efficiency is achieved as the marginal benefit of the last DVD (800th DVD) produced, $3, just equals the marginal cost of the last DVD produced. If, instead, 700 DVDs were produced per day, resources would be underallocated to the DVD industry as the marginal benefit of the 700th DVD produced, $5, exceeds its marginal cost of $2.

price of $3 for the 800th DVD produced, as this is the height of the demand curve at the 800 DVD output level. This suggests that the marginal benefit or extra value that the household derives from consuming the 800th DVD is also $3. Once we appreciate that the demand curve provides us with price and marginal benefit information, we can proceed to examine how a perfectly competitive industry promotes allocative efficiency. As Figure 9–12 illustrates, the competitive DVD industry will end up at an equilibrium quantity of 800 DVDs per day. At this output, we have industry demand equal to industry supply. But industry demand reflects price and marginal benefit, and industry supply reflects marginal cost. Therefore, we can see that in a competitive industry, production takes place to the point where *price just equals marginal cost or, more significantly, marginal benefit just equals marginal cost.*

In our DVD example, this means that just the "right" quantity of DVDs is being produced, from society's viewpoint. The consumer value for the last DVD produced, $3, just equals the extra cost to society of producing this last DVD (800th DVD). This extra cost, or marginal cost, reflects the value of the output in other industries that is sacrificed (opportunity cost), when additional resources are used to produce the 800th DVD.

ALLOCATIVE INEFFICIENCY: A GRAPHIC ILLUSTRATION. To better explain how a competitive equilibrium situation promotes allocative efficiency, we will use Figure 9–12 to illustrate why an alternative situation results in allocative inefficiency.

Suppose the competitive industry produces 700 DVDs per day, which is not an equilibrium situation, according to Figure 9–12. At this quantity, the marginal benefit of the 700th DVD is $5 (height of the demand curve), while its marginal cost to society is $2 per DVD (height of the supply curve). This represents a situation where there is an underallocation of resources to the production of DVDs and an overallocation of resources to other industries, as far as society is concerned. If resources are taken away from producing goods in other industries and used to produce one additional DVD, the extra $5 value gained by the DVD consumer (marginal benefit) will exceed the $2 value of lost production in the other industries (marginal cost). From society's view, there will be a net gain in value of $3 by allocating more resources to the DVD industry. Clearly, allocative efficiency is not achieved when 700 DVDs are produced.

Perfect Competition and a Normal Profit

In long-run equilibrium, each firm operates at a quantity level where price equals average total cost. In other words, perfectly competitive firms earn zero economic or "normal" profits in the long run. This is due to the easy-entry feature of this market structure. One could look at this normal profit result as promoting an equitable distribution of income to the extent that corporate share ownership is concentrated in the hands of upper-income individuals. In other words, the shareholders are earning a rate of profit that is just necessary to maintain the current level of investment and output—no more and no less.

Possible Shortcomings of Perfect Competition

PERFECT COMPETITION AND MARKET FAILURE. Situations arise when competitive markets either overallocate or underallocate resources to a good or service. These situations are instances of **market failure**. One example is when the production of a product entails external costs.

External costs refer to situations where the marginal social costs of producing a product exceed the marginal private costs of production. In these cases, some of the costs resulting from the production of the product spill over to affect third parties. Third parties refer to individuals or organizations other than the buyer and seller of the product.

An example of an external cost situation would be when the production of DVDs results in air pollution that causes health problems for those individuals who are not directly involved as buyers or sellers of DVDs. The firms who manufacture the DVDs typically do not have to pay for these extra spillover costs. In this situation, the DVD firms' marginal cost curves do not include the extra spillover pollution costs borne by others. In fact, the true marginal social cost curves would be somewhat higher than the private

Market failure A situation in which perfect competition either overallocates or underallocates resources to a good or service.

External costs Situations where the marginal social costs of producing a product exceed the marginal private costs of production.

marginal cost curves that govern the actual maximum profit production levels. Perfectly competitive firms would tend to overproduce DVDs relative to the socially desired production level.

Sometimes the production of a product results in **external benefits**, where the marginal social benefits from producing a product exceed the marginal private benefits. The production of the product results in spillover benefits to third parties. An example would be the discovery and production of a vaccine that prevents the spread of a contagious disease. The price that is charged to the consumers of this product does not reflect the extra spillover benefits. In this case, competitive marginal cost pricing will tend to underallocate resources to the product, from society's viewpoint.

External benefits A situation where the marginal social benefits from producing a product exceed the marginal private benefits.

Perfect Competition and Innovation

The rate of innovation and technological advance undertaken by perfectly competitive firms may prove to be socially sub-optimal. Activities related to such innovation as research and development are very expensive and entail significant risk. Since, in the long run, perfectly competitive firms can expect only normal profits, these firms may lack both the incentive and the level of funds necessary to engage in a socially desirable level of innovation.

ISSUES AND APPLICATIONS

Does Your Local Video Store Have a Future?

Concepts Applied: Characteristics of Perfect Competition, Shutdown Price, Long-Run Equilibrium, Long-Run Supply Curve

Is the bricks-and-mortar video store here to stay?

The Bricks-and-Mortar Video Rental Stores

Fifteen years ago, the Canadian home-video rental industry was quite easy to describe. The movies rented for home viewing were typically in VHS tape format. The VHS tapes were rented primarily from numerous independent and chain video stores, which we will call the "bricks-and-mortar" video stores.

Today, the consumer wishing to watch new-release or best-seller movies at home faces many choices. Video rentals are still primarily supplied through many independent and chain bricks-and-mortar video stores. As an example, as of June 2010, the Yellow Pages listed over 300 movie rental outlets operating in Toronto, Ontario.

Competition from Internet-Ordered, Mail-Delivered Movie Rentals

Consumers in both Canada and the U.S. now have the option of viewing, choosing, and ordering (for rent) new-release and best-seller movies over the Internet. The company taking these orders uses the mail to deliver the movies, for rent, to their customers' homes. In Canada, as of June, 2010, Zip.ca provides consumers with a number of monthly rental plans. As an example, you can rent two movies at a time, with no limit per month, for only $18.95 per month. Since the average member rents about eight DVDs per month, the typical cost is under $2.50 per rented DVD. DVD requests are sent to customers via

Canada Post first class mail. Other companies, such as Netflix, offer similar services.

Due to the growing popularity of Internet-ordered, mail-delivered movie rentals, companies such as Blockbuster, Rogers Video, and Movie Gallery have been facing declining in-store rental sales. In September 2009, it was revealed that Blockbuster planned to close up to 960 retail store locations by the end of 2010. This would bring Blockbuster's grand total of video rental store closures to over 20 percent of all its stores in operation.

On February 2, 2010, Movie Gallery, Inc. filed for bankruptcy protection for the second time in three years. As the operator of the Hollywood Video rental chain, Movie Gallery stated that it planned to close 805 poorly performing U.S. stores after falling sales and mounting losses. Its Movie Gallery Canada, Inc. affiliate was not part of the filing.

Considering that as of September 2009 Blockbuster's stock price was hovering at about $1.40, while Netflix's price was over $44 per share, it is not surprising that companies such as Blockbuster and Rogers Video are now providing Internet-ordered, mail-delivered movie rentals.

Competition from Large Retail Chains Selling DVDs

Another source of competition for the bricks-and-mortar video stores comes from the option to purchase DVDs. Attracted by a $3.5 billion Canadian home entertainment market—US$20 billion for North America—big box retailers, department stores, supermarkets, and large music chains provide Canadian consumers with the alternative to buy DVD movies. Walmart, Best Buy, Costco, Future Shop, The Bay, Zellers, Real Canadian Superstore, HMV Canada, and A&B Sound are all examples of large retailers selling (not renting) movie DVDs. Typically, one has the option of buying DVD movies from these companies either in-store or online.

Retail prices for DVDs have been declining, prompting many consumers to buy movies at a rate that far outpaces videotapes during their peak. The average DVD buy rate in 2003 was 17 discs per machine, almost three times average VHS tape purchases in the mid-1990s.

There are a number of reasons why mass retailers can sell DVDs at relatively low prices. Since each of these large retailers purchases new-release and best-seller DVDs in large quantities, one would expect that they would be eligible to receive significant volume discounts from DVD suppliers.

The large retail chains, such as Walmart, Best Buy, Costco, and Future Shop, carry many products other than DVDs. They can afford to set low prices and earn low profit margins on items such as DVDs because of the profits earned on such other diverse items sold as computers, TVs, stereo systems, cameras, camcorders, phones, office products, and appliances. The low DVD prices can serve a promotional purpose for the large diversified retailer. It can be a way to increase in-store

customer traffic on a regular basis. Consumers will set out to purchase small-ticket items, such as DVDs, on a more frequent basis, than big-ticket items. Marketers call this type of pricing strategy "promotional pricing." If prices are set at a level below average total cost, the practice is called "loss leader" pricing.

Other Competitive Threats

The bricks-and-mortar video rental stores must now compete with cable and satellite TV companies that provide movie channels, pay-TV movies, and video on demand to home subscribers. The video rental stores' ability to compete with the movie services of the cable and satellite TV companies depends, in part, on policies set by the movie studio executives in Hollywood. Currently, these studio executives have set the pecking order for new-release movies in favour of the bricks-and-mortar video rental stores. That is, the video stores get new movie releases before the cable and satellite TV companies.

The Changing Nature of Bricks-and-Mortar Video Rental Stores

How are the bricks-and-mortar video rental stores responding to all this competition? Many video rental outlets are now selling DVDs. Indeed, the rental stores have a lock on sales of previously viewed movies, which appeal to customers who appreciate the lower prices. So far, mass retailers have refrained from selling previously viewed movies.

Video stores are beginning to offer other products and services to its customers. In some of its video outlets, Rogers Video is selling its other products such as mobile phones, mobile phone service, cable services, and Internet services. Many video stores rent video games for systems such as Microsoft's Xbox, Sony's PlayStation, and Nintendo Wii.

Some industry observers feel that video rental stores will survive, despite the intense competition. No matter what the price, most consumers have a limit on the number of DVDs they wish to own. Currently, video on demand does not offer anywhere near the selection of titles found in a typical video store. As noted above, video stores are able to rent the new movie releases before they become available through video on demand.

Other analysts are not so optimistic about the bricks-and-mortar video stores. In the U.S., a number of video rental suppliers, such as Netflix, and more recently Blockbuster on Demand, are increasing their offerings of online streaming video downloads that you can instantly watch on a TV, a computer, or on your favorite mobile device at a very low rental price.

On September 23, 2010, Blockbuster Inc. filed for bankruptcy protection in the United States in an attempt to refinance and cut its debt load. This occurred just months after the bankruptcy filing of Movie Gallery, the second largest video and game rental company (behind Blockbuster) in the U.S.

For critical analysis:

1. What characteristics of perfect competition relate to the industry that currently supplies new-release and best-seller home-video movies in a typical Canadian city?

2. In this Issues and Applications, the practice of "loss leader" pricing was mentioned. Does it make economic sense to price a DVD movie at a level below average total cost?

3. If a firm specializes in renting new-release and best-seller movie videos, what amount of economic profit will it likely earn in the long run, and why?

4. What type of long-run supply curve best relates to the home-video movie industry?

Sources: Peter Brieger. "Video stores: evolve or die." *Financial Post.* January 28, 2004; "Zip.ca provides the best service of any online or store-based video service in Canada." Best Service. Learn More. zip.ca. http://www.zip.ca/SignUp/ learnservice.aspx; Vito Pilieci and Sabine Vollmer. "Video rental stores lose as customers go online." *The News & Observer*, June 30, 2007. Copyright © 2007 by The News & Observer Pub. Co; Jonathan Stempel. "Movie Gallery files bankruptcy, to shut 805 stores." Reuters. February 3, 2010. http://www.reuters.com/article/ idUSTRE61232U20100203; Don Reisinger. "Blockbuster to shutter up to 960 stores." CNET News. September 15, 2009. http://news.cnet.com/ 8301-13506_3-10353762-17.html.

SUMMARY

Here is what you should know after reading this chapter. MyEconLab will help you identify what you know, and where to go when you need to practise. We suggest that as soon as you review one of the Learning Objective sections below, you then proceed to go through the related section in MyEconLab.

LEARNING OBJECTIVES	KEY TERMS	MYECONLAB PRACTICE
9.1 The Characteristics of Perfect Competition. The four fundamental characteristics of perfect competition are: (1) a large number of buyers and sellers, (2) a homogeneous product, (3) easy exit from and entry into the industry, and (4) perfect market information in the hands of both buyers and sellers. A perfectly competitive firm is a price taker, meaning that the firm takes the price as given and outside of its control. The individual firm's demand curve is perfectly elastic (horizontal), which implies that the firm can sell all it wants at the given industry price, so price equals marginal revenue.	market structure, 213 perfect competition, 213 price taker, 213	• **MyEconLab** Study Plan 9.1
9.2 Determining Output and Profit in the Short Run. Profit is maximized at the rate of output where the positive difference between total revenue and total cost is the greatest. Losses are minimized where the negative difference between total revenue and total cost is the smallest. We assume that each firm chooses that rate of output that maximizes	total revenues, 216 profit-maximizing rate of production, 217 marginal revenue, 217 shutdown, 221 short-run breakeven price, 222 short-run shutdown price, 222	• **MyEconLab** Study Plan 9.2

LEARNING OBJECTIVES	KEY TERMS	MYECONLAB PRACTICE

profits or minimizes losses. This rate of output is called the firm's short-run equilibrium output level.

If the industry price is below the firm's minimum average variable cost, the firm will minimize its losses by shutting down, and will earn a negative economic profit (loss) equal to its total fixed costs. Graphically, the firm's shutdown point is where the price line is tangent to the minimum point on the average variable cost curve.

When the industry price exceeds the firm's minimum average variable cost, the firm will maximize profits (minimize losses) by operating at the rate of output where marginal revenue or price equals marginal cost. The total amount of economic profit earned will depend on the following relation between price and average total cost at this rate of output: Total Profit $= (P - ATC) \times Q$. If price exceeds average total cost, the firm will earn a positive economic profit. If price is less than average total cost, the firm will earn a negative economic profit. If the price just equals average total cost, the firm will earn a zero economic profit (break even). Graphically, the firm's breakeven point is where the price line is tangent to the minimum point of the average total cost curve.

| **9.3 Short-Run Supply and Equilibrium.** The firm's short-run supply curve is the portion of its marginal cost curve at and above its minimum average variable cost. The industry short-run supply curve, which is the horizontal sum of the individual firms' supply curves, interacts with the industry demand curve to set the industry equilibrium price. | industry supply curve, 225 | • MyEconLab Study Plan 9.3 |

LEARNING OBJECTIVES	KEY TERMS	MYECONLAB PRACTICE
9.4 Long-Run Equilibrium. In long-run equilibrium, the industry supply adjusts to a level that sets an equilibrium price just equal to each firm's minimum long-run and short-run average total cost. Each firm produces an output level where the equilibrium price equals marginal cost and earns a zero economic profit. Long-run adjustments, such as changes in plant size and entry and exit of firms, bring about long-run equilibrium. If the typical firm is earning short-run economic profits, new firms will enter, driving the price down to equal minimum average total cost (normal profit). If the typical firm is earning short-run economic losses, existing firms will leave, driving the price up to equal minimum average total cost.		• **MyEconLab** Study Plan 9.4
9.5 Long-Run Industry Supply Curves. The three different long-run supply situations are constant cost, increasing cost, and decreasing cost. In a constant cost industry, the long-run supply curve is horizontal (perfectly elastic) because input prices do not change as the industry expands. In an increasing cost industry, the long-run supply curve is upward sloping because input prices increase as the industry expands. In a decreasing cost industry, the long-run supply curve is downward sloping because input costs decrease as the industry expands.	long-run industry supply curve, 230 constant-cost industry, 230 increasing-cost industry, 230 decreasing-cost industry, 230	• **MyEconLab** Study Plan 9.5
9.6 Social Evaluation of Perfect Competition. In long-run equilibrium, perfect competition promotes the socioeconomic goals of productive efficiency (minimum ATC), allocative efficiency (P = MC), and an equitable distribution of income (normal economic profit). Possible shortcomings of perfect competition include market failure and a sub-optimal rate of innovation.	marginal cost pricing, 233 market failure, 234 external costs, 234 external benefits, 235	• **MyEconLab** Study Plan 9.6

PROBLEMS

(Answers to the odd-numbered problems appear at the back of the book.)

LO 9.1 Identify and explain the characteristics of a perfectly competitive market structure.

1. Explain why each of the following examples is not a perfectly competitive industry:

   a. The industry consists of one large firm and thousands of smaller firms, each selling an identical product. The large firm sets the price, and the remaining firms take this price as a given. Firms can easily enter or exit the industry.

   b. There are many buyers and sellers in the industry. Consumers and firms have perfect information about the prices of each competitor's product, which differ in quality from firm to firm.

   c. There are many independently owned taxicabs that compete in a city. The city's government requires all taxicabs to provide identical service. All taxicabs operate the identical automobile model, with identical options. All drivers must wear a designated uniform. Through licensing, the government limits the number of taxicab companies that can operate within the city's boundaries.

2. Refer to Example 9-1, "When Blogging Becomes a Competitive Business." Suppose you have established a blog that generates 100 000 visits (hits) per month. You currently charge advertisers $50 per month for each 125 pixel × 125 pixel button in the sidebar of your blog. You estimate that if you raise the price above $50, even by a penny, you will lose all your advertiser customers. Sketch the demand curve for hosting a 125 pixel × 125 pixel button placed on the sidebar of your blog. Are you a price taker? Briefly explain.

3. Answer the following:

   a. Sketch a graph of both the industry and the firm to illustrate the following situations in the market for video rentals, which is perfectly competitive. The industry supply and demand sets an equilibrium price of $4 per video rental per day. Illustrate the demand curve that a single independent video rental store faces, assuming the $4 price. Illustrate how a decrease in industry demand for video rentals results in a new equilibrium price of $3 and a new demand curve for the firm.

   b. In general, explain the difference between the industry's demand curve and the firm's demand curve in perfect competition.

LO 9.2 Using revenue and cost information, determine the firm's short-run profit-maximizing or loss-minimizing level of output and profit.

4. Refer to the video rental example in Problem 3 above. Fill in the daily total, average, and marginal revenue table, below, assuming a price of $3 per video.

Daily Quantity (# of videos)	1	2	3	4	5
Total revenue	——	——	——	——	——
Average revenue	——	——	——	——	——
Marginal revenue	——	——	——	——	——

5. The accompanying table represents the hourly output and cost structure for a local pizza outlet, which operates in perfect competition. Total fixed costs are $3 per hour.

Hourly Quantity (# pizzas)	0	1	2	3	4	5	6	7	8	9	10
Total Variable Costs per Hour ($)	0	6	8	9	11	15	21	29	40	54	71
Total Costs per Hour ($)	3	9	11	12	14	18	24	32	43	57	74

   a. If the price is $10 per pizza, compute the hourly total profit for each of the quantity levels in the accompanying table. What is the profit-maximizing (or loss-minimizing) quantity level? What is the maximum profit or minimum loss?

   b. Rework part (a) above assuming that the price drops to $3 per pizza.

   c. Rework part (a) above assuming that the price drops to $2 per pizza.

6. Refer to Example 9–2, "High Sunk Costs Can Mean Deep Discounts." Suppose that you own a restaurant that currently offers meals in the evening. If you decide to open your restaurant during lunch hours, identify the relevant fixed and variable costs. If you offered two-for-one lunch coupons, you would have to ensure that the average price per meal exceeded what amount?

7. In the accompanying table, we list the per-unit costs for a perfectly competitive firm manufacturing and selling a standard-sized bookcase unit.

Output (units per hour)	Average Fixed Cost (AFC)	Average Variable Cost (AVC)	Average Total Cost (ATC)	Marginal Cost (MC)
1	$102.00	$40	$142.00	
2	51.00	35	86.00	$30
3	34.00	40	74.00	50
4	25.50	45	70.50	60
5	20.40	50	70.40	70
6	17.00	55	72.00	80
7	14.57	60	74.57	90

a. If the price per unit is $81, determine the profit-maximizing quantity level and the maximum profit.

b. If the price per unit is $61, determine the profit-maximizing quantity level and the maximum profit. Should the firm shut down at this price, in the short run?

c. If the price per unit is $31, determine the profit-maximizing quantity level and the maximum profit.

d. The short-run breakeven point occurs at approximately what price?

e. The short-run shutdown point occurs at approximately what price?

8. Consider the accompanying graph. Then answer the questions.

Quantity per Time Period

a. Which demand curve indicates that the firm is earning normal profits?

b. Which demand curve indicates that the firm is earning abnormal profits?

c. Which demand curve indicates that the firm is indifferent between shutting down and producing?

d. Which curve is the firm's supply curve?

e. Below which price will the firm shut down?

9. The accompanying graph is for firm J. Study it, then answer the questions.

Output (units)

a. How many units will firm J sell in order to maximize profits?

b. What is firm J's total profit from selling the amount of output in part (a)?

c. At what price will firm J shut down in the short run?

d. If the cost curves shown represent production at the optimal long-run plant size, predict the long-run price.

10. Consider the following diagram. It applies to a perfectly competitive firm, which at present faces a market clearing price of $20 per unit and produces 10 000 units of output per week.

a. What is the firm's current average revenue per unit?

b. What are the present economic profits of this firm? Is the firm maximizing economic profits? Explain.

c. If the market clearing price drops to $12.50 per unit, should this firm continue to produce in the short run if it wishes to maximize its economic profits (or minimize its economic losses)? Explain.

d. If the market clearing price drops to $7.50 per unit, should this firm continue to produce in the short run if it wishes to maximize its economic profits (or minimize its economic losses)? Explain.

Output (thousands of units per week)

11. The accompanying diagram describes the short-run per-unit costs of Patio Pete's, which is a perfectly competitive firm manufacturing a standard white plastic patio chair.

a. Suppose that the market sets the price at $5 per chair. What would be Patio Pete's daily profit-maximizing quantity? Find the firm's maximum daily total profit at this price.

b. Suppose, on another day, the price changed to $3 per chair. At this price, at best, would Patio Pete's be earning a positive or a negative economic profit? Explain.

c. Referring to question b above, should Patio Pete shut down or operate in the short run? Explain.

d. If, on another day, the price per chair were $1, should Patio Pete's operate or shut down in the short run? Explain.

LO 9.3 Derive the firm's short-run supply curve and explain how the short-run equilibrium price is determined in a perfectly competitive market.

12. The accompanying graph describes the marginal and average variable cost curves for a typical firm operating in a perfectly competitive industry. Assuming that the industry consists of 100 identical firms, use the graph information to fill in the accompanying short-run supply table. What will be the short-run equilibrium price?

Price per Unit	Individual Quantity Supplied	Industry Supply	Industry Demand
$8	_____	_____	400
6	_____	_____	600
4	_____	_____	800
2	_____	_____	1000

13. Use the perfectly competitive firm's per-unit cost data in Problem 7 to fill in the accompanying short-run supply table. Assume that the industry consists of 1000 firms identical to the firm in Problem 7.

Price per Unit	Individual Quantity Supplied	Industry Supply (1000 firms)	Industry Demand
$91	_____	_____	5000
81	_____	_____	6000
51	_____	_____	8000
31	_____	_____	9000

a. On the basis of the information in the accompanying table, what will be the short-run equilibrium price?

b. At the short-run equilibrium price, what will be the typical firm's short-run equilibrium quantity? Determine the amount of total profit earned by the typical firm in equilibrium.

LO 9.4 Explain the features and long-run adjustments associated with long-run equilibrium in perfect competition.

14. Refer to the per-unit cost curves in Problem 9. Suppose that these costs relate to each firm's optimum long-run plant size. What will be the long-run equilibrium price in this industry?

15. Refer to the per-unit costs in Problem 7. Suppose that these costs relate to each firm's optimum long-run plant size.

a. Suppose the current price is $81 per unit. Will this be the long-run equilibrium price? Why, or why not?

b. What will be the long-run equilibrium price in this industry?

16. A firm in a perfectly competitive industry has total revenue of $200 000 per year, when producing 2000 units of output per year.

a. Find the firm's average revenue or price.

b. Find the firm's marginal revenue.

c. Assuming that the firm is maximizing profits, what is the firm's marginal cost?

d. If the firm is at long-run equilibrium, what is its average total cost?

LO 9.5 Explain the three different long-run industry supply curve situations that are possible in perfect competition.

17. What long-run supply situation best relates to each of the following? For each of the following situations, what will the long-run supply curve look like?
    a. As the number of active oil drilling rigs doubles, the extraction cost per barrel of oil increases.
    b. As the cellphone industry explodes in size, the per-unit cost of manufacturing cellphones decreases.

LO 9.6 From a social viewpoint, evaluate the long-run behaviour in perfect competition.

18. Explain the social benefits associated with each of the following long-run equilibrium conditions:
    a. The typical firm operates at a quantity level where price equals average total cost.
    b. Production takes place to the point where price equals marginal cost.
    c. The typical firm operates at minimum average total cost.

19. For each of the following, explain whether a competitive industry in long-run equilibrium will tend to overallocate or underallocate resources to the product it produces.
    a. Competitive research firms discover and supply a new drug that prevents the spread of a serious type of influenza.
    b. Competitive pulp producers pollute rivers and lakes, which increases the water treatment costs of nearby communities.

20. Identify and explain two reasons why a perfectly competitive industry environment may not foster innovation and technological advances.

BUSINESS APPLICATION

LO 9.2 Using revenue and cost information, determine the firm's short-run profit-maximizing or loss-minimizing level of output and profit.

Accounting: Short Run Analysis: Tools of a Cost Accountant

Monique's is a purely competitive firm that manufactures pulp in Quebec. The price of pulp is determined on a world-wide market in response to demand and supply forces.

At the end of every month, Ted Baxter, the cost accountant at Monique's, compares the projected pulp price with the company's short-run unit costs in order to determine the optimum production level for the next month. Once the optimum production schedule is determined, other important decisions can be made, such as the number of shifts to operate, hours of labour to employ, and the amount of raw materials to purchase. As well, the monthly profit or loss can be projected, which is important from a cash flow point of view.

Given the current plant facility and related commitments, the total monthly fixed cost is $250 000. The other relevant costs depend on the monthly production level and are described in the table below. Note that in the table below, the full capacity of the plant is 6000 tonnes per month.

Monthly Production Rate in tonnes (Q)	Total Variable Cost (TVC)	Average Variable Cost (AVC)	Marginal Cost per tonne (MC)	Average Total Cost (ATC)
0	$0			
1000	$124 000			
2000	$240 000			
3000	$375 000			
4000	$540 000			
5000	$750 000			
6000	$1 020 000			

Business Application Problem

1. a. Complete the accompanying table
   b. Due to a major union strike at competitive plants in the U.S., Ted projects that the price of pulp will increase to $230 per tonne in September. Based on this projection and the cost information provided, determine the profit maximizing (or loss minimizing) level of production and the total monthly profit in dollars.
   c. In October, the U.S. labour dispute was settled. As well, new competitive pulp plants started operation. As a result, the projected October price for pulp is only $140 per tonne. Based on this projected price and the cost information provided, determine the profit-maximizing (or loss-minimizing) October production rate, in tonnes. At this production rate, calculate the total monthly profit (or loss) in dollars.
   d. In November, the Asian economies—major buyers of Monique's pulp—went into a recession. As a result, the November price dropped to $118 per tonne. Based on the $118 price and the cost information provided, determine the profit-maximizing (or loss-minimizing) November production rate in tonnes. At this production rate, calculate the total monthly profit (or loss) in dollars.
   e. In general, in the short run, is the best production rate always going to be where Monique's achieves the lowest cost per tonne of pulp? Explain.
   f. In general, in the short run, should Ted always shut down the plant when he projects a loss? Explain.

10

LEARNING OBJECTIVES

After reading this chapter, you should be able to:

10.1 Identify and explain the characteristics of a monopoly market structure.

10.2 Using revenue and cost information, determine the monopolist's profit-maximizing or loss-minimizing level of output, price, and profit.

10.3 Explain why a monopoly firm engages in price discrimination.

10.4 Evaluate the long-run behaviour in monopoly from a social viewpoint.

10.5 Compare and contrast the use of marginal cost pricing versus average cost pricing in the regulation of a natural monopoly.

Monopoly

On March 18, 2010, scores of university students from across Alberta boarded chartered buses and braved the icy prairie winds to march on the government legislature grounds to protest proposed fee and tuition hikes. These protests followed massive student demonstrations in Ontario and Quebec just three years earlier, where the common chant was "Liar, liar, pants on fire! You said fees would go no higher!" To pay for their tuition, Canadian post-secondary students have accumulated a staggering debt of $13 billion, with 20 percent of Canadian students unable to repay what they owe. After studying this chapter, you will appreciate why many view the setting of tuition fees by post-secondary institutions as simply another example of monopoly pricing practices.

Source: Elise Stolte. "Hundreds protest tuition hikes; students from across Alberta march at legislature to fight proposed increases, highest yet." *Edmonton Journal*. March 19, 2010. Pg. A3; "The soaring cost of universities." *Times Colonist* (Victoria, B.C.). May 23, 2010. Pg. D2.

MyEconLab helps you master each objective and study more efficiently. See end of chapter for details.

DID YOU KNOW THAT...?

Single sellers of goods and services exist all around you. The company that equips your labs with new computers has probably been granted the exclusive right to do so by your college or university. The ski resort that offers you food at the top of the mountain does not allow anyone else to open a restaurant next to it. Just one drug manufacturer will typically supply the new prescription drug that you are eager to buy. If you book your wedding reception at a popular hotel ballroom, you will likely have to promise to use the hotel's expensive menu and wine list for this momentous occasion. No doubt, you will pay a high price if you want to enjoy your favourite beverage and snack while watching your home team play at the local stadium. In this chapter, you will learn more about situations where competition is restricted to one supplier. We call such situations *monopoly*.

10.1 The Characteristics of Monopoly

The word *monopoly* probably brings to mind notions of large, corrupt business organizations that gouge the consumer. But if we are to succeed in analyzing and predicting the behaviour of a firm operating in a monopoly environment, we must be more objective in our description of this type of market structure. Whether applied to large or small businesses, monopoly situations typically have the following characteristics in common.

1. *A monopoly firm is a single seller.* That is, we can define a **monopolist** as the single supplier of a good or service for which there are no close substitutes.
2. *A monopolist is a price searcher.* A **price searcher** is a firm that must determine the price–output combination that maximizes profit because it faces a downward-sloping demand curve. In a monopoly market structure, the firm and the industry are one and the same. Therefore, the firm's demand curve, *d*, is the same as the industry demand curve, *D*. Since the typical industry demand curve is downward sloping, the monopolist's demand curve is also downward sloping. When the monopoly firm increases its output sold per time period, this will decrease the price of the product. In contrast to perfect competition, where the price is given, in a monopoly the firm must "search" or determine the profit-maximizing price and output combination.
3. *Barriers to entry must exist in monopoly.* Since new businesses are started daily in Canada, there must be some reason why new firms are not successful in entering a monopoly industry. The types of barriers to entry may include exclusive ownership of resources; problems in raising adequate capital; economies of scale; legal or government restrictions; and, possibly, predatory tactics of the monopolist.

Monopolist A single supplier of a good or service for which there are no close substitutes.

Price searcher A firm that must determine the price–output combination that maximizes profit because it faces a downward-sloping demand curve.

What are some common examples of monopoly industries? In many large cities, there is often just one firm supplying all the natural gas, one utility firm selling electricity, and one firm providing local phone service. If one resides in a small city, one may regularly read the city's only daily newspaper, travel on the one available airline carrier to the nearest provincial capital, or stay at home and enjoy frequent visits to a local ski resort or a golf course owned by a monopolist.

Barriers to Entry

For any amount of monopoly power to continue to exist in the long run, the market must be closed to entry in some way. Either legal means or certain aspects of the industry's technical or cost structure may prevent entry. We will discuss several of the barriers to entry that have allowed firms to reap monopoly profits in the long run.

OWNERSHIP OF RESOURCES WITHOUT CLOSE SUBSTITUTES. Preventing a newcomer from entering an industry is often difficult. Indeed, some economists contend that no monopoly acting without government support has been able to prevent entry into the industry unless that monopoly has had the control of some essential natural resource. Consider the possibility of one firm's owning the entire supply of a raw material input that is essential to the production of a particular commodity. The exclusive ownership of such a vital resource serves as a barrier to entry until an alternative source of the raw material input is found or an alternative technology not requiring the raw material in question is developed. A good example of control over a vital input is the Aluminum Company of America, a firm that prior to World War II controlled the world's bauxite, which is the essential raw material in the production of aluminum. Such a situation is rare, though, and is usually temporary.

PROBLEMS IN RAISING ADEQUATE CAPITAL. Businesses in certain industries require a large initial capital investment. The firms already in the industry can, according to some economists, obtain monopoly profits in the long run because no competitors can raise the large amount of capital needed to enter the industry. This is called the "imperfect" capital market argument and is used to explain long-run, relatively high rates of return in certain industries. These industries are generally ones in which large fixed costs must be incurred merely to start production. Their fixed costs are generally for expensive machines necessary to the production process. Examples include industries that supply electricity, natural gas heating, cable TV, and local phone service using phone lines.

ECONOMIES OF SCALE. Sometimes it is not profitable for more than one firm to exist in an industry. This is so if, in order to realize lower unit costs, one firm would have to produce such a large quantity that there would be insufficient demand to warrant a second producer of the same product. Such a situation may arise because of a phenomenon we discussed in Chapter 8, economies of scale. When economies of scale exist, total costs increase less than proportionately to the increase in output. That is, proportional increases in output yield proportionately smaller increases in total costs, and per-unit costs drop. The advantage in economies of scale lies in the fact that larger firms (with larger output) have lower per-unit costs that enable them to charge lower prices, and that drives smaller firms out of business.

When long-run average costs decline as the scale of operation increases, a *natural monopoly* may develop. The **natural monopoly** is the firm that first takes advantage of economies of scale in order to establish a monopoly position. The natural monopolist is able to underprice its competitors and eventually force all of them out of the market.

In Figure 10–1, we have drawn a downward sloping long-run average cost curve (LAC). Recall that when average costs are falling, marginal costs are less than average costs. We can apply the same analysis in the long run. When the long-run average cost curve (LAC) is falling, the long-run marginal cost curve (LMC) will be below the LAC.

In our example, long-run average costs are falling over such a large range of production rates that we would expect only one firm to survive in such an industry. That firm would be the natural monopolist. It would be the first one to take advantage of the decreasing average costs; that is, it would construct the large-scale facilities first. As its average costs fell, it would lower prices and get an increasingly larger share of the market. Once that firm had driven all other firms out of the industry, it would set its price to maximize profits.

Natural monopoly The firm that first takes advantage of economies of scale in order to establish a monopoly position.

FIGURE 10–1

The Cost Curves That Might Lead to a Natural Monopoly: The Case of Electricity

Whenever long-run average costs are falling, so, too, will be long-run marginal costs. Also, long-run marginal costs (LMC) will always be below long-run average costs (LAC). A natural monopoly might arise in such a situation. The first firm to establish the low unit-cost capacity would be able to take advantage of the lower average total cost curve. This firm would drive out all rivals by charging a lower price than the others could sustain at their higher average costs.

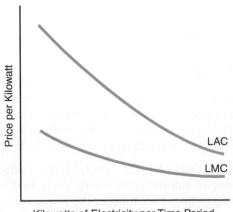

PREDATORY BEHAVIOUR. It should be noted that a firm may establish a monopoly position in a market by engaging in behaviour that has already eliminated its competition and/or that has the effect of deterring new entrants to its industry. In some countries, such behaviour is considered to be illegal. For example, a criminal sanction against predatory pricing has been part of Canada's competition law for over 50 years.

The concept of predatory pricing is best illustrated by a dominant firm in a market setting its prices so low, over a long enough period of time, that it may drive one or more of its competitors from the market, deter other companies from entering the market, or both. Following the exit of competitors from the market, the predator is expected to raise prices significantly in an attempt to recover the profit lost during the period of predatory pricing. Example 10–1 provides examples of how Microsoft has gained near-monopoly positions in a number of different markets by engaging in predatory behaviour.

EXAMPLE 10–1   Microsoft's Abuse of Monopoly

How has Microsoft attempted to "lock in" a large share of the internet browser market?

On November 12, 2002, the U.S. Court of Appeals for the District of Columbia Circuit found Microsoft guilty of engaging in a series of exclusionary, anticompetitive, and predatory acts to maintain its monopoly power in the operating system software industry. At the time of the court decision, Microsoft's share of the worldwide market for Intel-compatible PC operating systems exceeded 90 percent.

On the basis of the dominance of its Windows operating system, Microsoft was in a position to unfairly dominate other industries, such as the Web browser market. In the early 1990s, Netscape Navigator controlled 70 percent of the Web browser market. Threatened by Netscape's dominance of the Internet, Microsoft created Internet Explorer and gave this new software away for free to Internet service providers and computer makers. Microsoft "packaged" Explorer as an integral part of Windows, which prevented computer manufacturers from modifying or deleting this browser software. Microsoft entered into agreements with computer manufacturers and Internet providers that restricted the distribution of competing software. Partly as a result of this predatory behaviour, the use of Internet Explorer has grown to the point of dominating the Web browser market worldwide.

Despite the fact that the Court of Appeals ruling in November 2002 prohibits Microsoft from engaging in predatory behaviour, it appears that it continues to employ similar tactics in other markets. On March 25, 2004, the European Union (EU) fined Microsoft $606 million for using its near monopoly in operating systems to dominate the markets for Internet media software, server software, and the software that will run next generation computing devices. As an example, the EU's investigations support the view that Microsoft's Media Player has been bundled and sold with Windows in a way that has unfairly restricted the growth of rival software, such as RealNetworks Inc.'s Real Player and Apple Computer's QuickTime player. On March 1, 2007, the EU threatened Microsoft with a $4 million daily fine. It accused Microsoft of protecting its own interests by setting excessive prices for the documentation that competitors need to build products that interoperate with Windows PCs and servers.

In January 2009, the European Commission filed more charges against Microsoft. It claimed that company's plans to install Internet Explorer as part of the new Windows 7 operating system would severely reduce competition in the Internet browser market and give Microsoft an unfair, monopoly-like advantage in this industry. In December 2009, in order to prevent additional fines, Microsoft announced that it would create a version of Windows 7 for the European market that would, at the startup/installation stage, display a pop-up screen asking customers to pick one or more of 12 web browsers to download and install. Déjà vu!

For critical analysis: Using this example, explain the various ways that Microsoft has engaged in predatory behaviour.

Sources: "United States of America, plaintiff, v. Microsoft Corporation, defendant. United States District Court for the District of Columbia. November 12, 2002. United States Department of Justice. http://www. microsoft-antitrust.gov/pdf/Nov1202981232FinalJudgment.pdf; David Lawsky. "Microsoft ordered to strip Windows." *Financial Post*. March 25, 2004. Pg. FP4; "EU threatens Microsoft with new penalties." *Calgary Herald*. March 2, 2007. Pg. E8; Aoife White. "Microsoft, EU end current antitrust fight with deal to give European users more browser choice." The Canadian Press. Toronto. December 16, 2009.

LEGAL OR GOVERNMENTAL RESTRICTIONS. The federal and provincial governments can also erect barriers to entry. These include public franchises, licences, patents, tariffs, and specific regulations that tend to limit entry.

In many industries, it is illegal to enter without a government *licence*. For example, you could not start a medical practice in Canada without first obtaining a licence from the Canadian College of Physicians and Surgeons. Standards are closely monitored by the government to protect the health and safety of consumers. By restricting entry to the profession and by agreeing to a common fee structure, doctors maintain a relatively high earnings level.

A *public franchise* is necessary to enter some markets, such as in the provision of cable television service. The Canadian Radio-television and Telecommunications Commission (CRTC) must approve all applications for entry and, in many cases, grants local, or geographical, monopolies to cable TV providers. Because these franchises are restricted, long-run monopoly profits might be earned by such firms as Rogers Cablesystems, which are already in the industry.

In some cases, government might license itself to be the sole provider of some product or service. In some Canadian provinces, liquor is sold only through government-owned retail outlets.

A *patent* is issued to an inventor to provide protection from having the invention copied or stolen for a period of 20 years. Suppose that engineers working for Northern Telecom (Nortel) discover a way to build fibre-optic cable that requires half the amount of inputs of regular cable, and transmits data twice as fast. If Nortel is successful in obtaining a patent on this discovery, it can (in principle) prevent others from copying it. The patent holder has a monopoly.

Tariffs are special taxes that are imposed on certain imported goods. They have the effect of making imports relatively more expensive than their domestic counterparts so that consumers switch to the relatively cheaper domestically made products. If the tariffs are high enough, imports become overpriced, and domestic producers gain monopoly advantage as the sole suppliers. Many countries have tried this protectionist strategy by using high tariffs to shut out foreign competitors.

> **Tariffs** Special taxes that are imposed on certain imported goods.

Price and Revenue Behaviour under Monopoly

In this section, we will examine how price and revenue typically behave as a monopoly firm expands its production or quantity sold per time period. This will give you a better understanding of how the monopolist determines its profit-maximizing output level.

THE MONOPOLIST'S MARGINAL REVENUE: LESS THAN PRICE. A monopolist is the sole supplier of one product, good, or service. This means that the monopoly firm faces the same demand curve as the overall industry demand curve. As the industry demand curve, D, is typically downward sloping, we can deduce that the monopoly firm's demand curve, d, is also downward sloping. In order for the monopoly firm to increase its quantity sold per time period, the firm will have to decrease the price of its product.

How is marginal revenue related to price under a monopoly situation? Consider an egg farmer who is the sole supplier of eggs to an entire city. If on Monday the monopoly farmer decides to hold back daily output sold to just seven dozen eggs, the farmer can command a high price of, say, \$10 per dozen. Monday's total revenue will be \$10 × 7 dozen eggs = \$70. If the monopolist farmer wishes to increase the daily quantity sold on Tuesday to eight dozen eggs, the farmer will have to lower the price of each dozen sold on Tuesday to \$9 per dozen. This means that Tuesday's total revenue is \$9 × 8 = \$72. What is the marginal revenue of the eighth or last dozen of eggs sold on Tuesday? We will compute this marginal revenue in two different ways.

First, the marginal revenue refers to the change in total revenue in selling one more unit. If we compare Monday's with Tuesday's total revenue, we can see that the eighth unit (dozen) sold changes total revenue from \$70 to \$72. The marginal revenue of the last or eighth dozen of eggs sold on Tuesday is \$72 − \$70 = \$2. Note that while the price of the last or eighth unit (dozen) sold is \$9, the marginal revenue of this last unit is only \$2. Marginal revenue is less than the price for the eighth unit sold. In fact, if the same egg farmer were to reduce the price of the eggs even further on Wednesday, we would again

Monopoly: Price Searcher

FIGURE 10–2

Demand and Marginal Revenue Curves: Monopoly

For the monopolist, marginal revenue is less than price at each quantity level.

find that the marginal revenue of the last dozen sold on Wednesday would again be lower than Wednesday's price.

Figure 10–2 graphs the behaviour of price and marginal revenue for the monopoly egg farmer at different daily quantities sold. Note that in general, at each possible output level, marginal revenue is less than price.

Why is marginal revenue less than price in monopoly? Let us examine another way of computing the marginal revenue the monopoly farmer received from selling the last unit (eighth dozen eggs) on Tuesday. When the price per dozen was reduced from $10 on Monday to $9 on Tuesday, the farmer gained an extra $9 from selling one more dozen eggs (eighth dozen) when compared with Monday. However, in comparing both days, the farmer sold each of the first seven dozen eggs on Tuesday at $9 (compared to $10 on Monday). Therefore, on Tuesday, the farmer received $1 less for each of the first seven dozen eggs sold, or $7 less. If we combine the $9 gain from selling the eighth unit of eggs with the $7 loss incurred on the first seven dozen eggs sold, we also arrive at a marginal revenue of $9 − $7 = $2 for the eighth unit sold on Tuesday. Figure 10–3 uses a graph to illustrate this second way of determining the marginal revenue of the eighth unit of eggs sold.

MR = Area *A* − Area *B* = $9 − $7 = $2

FIGURE 10–3

Marginal Revenue Less Than Price

In going from selling seven to eight units per day, the firm incurs a gain and a loss. The gain from selling the eighth unit equals $9 × 1 = $9 = Area *A*. The loss equals the loss of $1 on each of the first seven units = $1 × 7 = $7 = Area *B*. The net gain equals the marginal revenue of selling the eighth unit which equals Area *A* − Area *B* = 9 − 7 = $2. The marginal revenue of $2 is less than $9, which is the price of the eighth unit sold.

Elasticity and Monopoly

The monopolist faces a downward-sloping demand curve (its average revenue curve). That means that it cannot charge just *any* price it wishes (a common misconception) because, depending on the price charged, a different quantity will be demanded.

Earlier we defined a monopolist as the single seller of a well-defined good or service with no *close* substitute. This does not mean, however, that the demand curve for a monopoly is vertical or exhibits zero price elasticity of demand. After all, consumers have limited incomes and alternative wants. The downward slope of a monopolist's demand curve occurs because individuals compare the marginal satisfaction they will receive with the cost of the commodity to be purchased. Take the example of telephone service. Even if there were absolutely no substitute whatsoever for telephone service, the market demand curve would still slope downward. At lower prices, people will add more phones and separate lines for different family members.

Furthermore, the demand curve for telephone service slopes downward because there are at least several *imperfect* substitutes, such as e-mail, letters, telegrams, in-person conversations, and CB and VHF-FM radios. Thus, even though we defined a monopolist as a single seller of a commodity with no *close* substitute, we can talk about the range of *imperfect* substitutes. The more such imperfect substitutes there are, the more elastic will be the monopolist's demand curve, all other things held constant.

Over time, the price elasticity of demand for the services provided by Canada Post, a legal monopoly, has changed, as explained by Policy Example 10–1.

POLICY EXAMPLE 10–1   Should Canada Post Remain a Monopoly—Or Does it Matter?

The *Canada Post Corporation Act*, created by the federal government, confers an exclusive monopoly on Canada Post in terms of the delivery within Canada of "letters" not weighing more than 500 grams. One reason that Canada Post has a legal monopoly is that it is subject to a Universal Service Obligation (USO), which typically requires Canada Post to provide mail service at uniform rates and minimal quality standards to all regions of Canada.

The rationale for a USO is to promote economic development by reducing one of the costs of settling in remote or underdeveloped areas of the country and promoting national unity by enhancing social communication and cohesiveness. Granting a monopoly allows Canada Post to make enough profit in the highly populated regions to finance the losses that occur in providing postal services in the remote rural areas.

Any monopoly power that Canada Post once had with respect to parcel delivery, however, has been whittled away by the growth of private couriers, such as United Parcel Service (UPS), Federal Express (FedEx), and Purolator. Over the last decade, technology has rendered the most fatal blow to Canada Post's position. Typically, a fax machine is faster than mailing a letter domestically or internationally. Now that fax modems are routinely installed or packaged with new personal computers, faxing is becoming ubiquitous. So too, is the use of the Internet and e-mail. According to the 2010 Canadian Internet Fact Guide, in 2010, 97 percent of Canadians aged 18 to 34 and 94 percent of Canadians aged 35 to 54 had Internet access at home. The most frequent Internet activities included e-mailing and social networking, cheap substitutes for mailing a letter anywhere in the world.

For critical analysis:

1. According to this example, what has happened to the price elasticity of demand for services provided by Canada Post, such as letter services and parcel deliveries? Explain. In what ways might Canada Post attempt to slow down the erosion of its monopoly position?

2. What would likely happen to postal service in the remote rural areas of Canada if Canada Post were to lose its legal monopoly?

Sources: E. Iacobucci, M. Trebilcock, and Tracey D. Epps. "Rerouting the mail: why Canada Post is due for reform." C.D. Howe Institute. http://www.cdhowe.org. February 2007; *The 2010 Canadian Internet Fact Guide*. Ipsos Reid. Pg. 2–3. http://www.ipsos.ca/reid/interactive/ifg.cfm.

10.2 Determining Output, Price, and Profit in Monopoly

To find out the rate of output at which the perfect competitor would maximize profits, we had to add cost data. We will do the same thing now for the monopolist. We assume that profit maximization is the goal of the pure monopolist, just as for the perfect competitor. The perfect competitor, however, has only to decide on the profit-maximizing rate of output because price was given. The competitor is a price taker. For the pure monopolist, we must seek a profit-maximizing *price–output combination* because the monopolist is a price searcher. We can determine this profit-maximizing price–output combination with either of two equivalent approaches—by looking at total revenues and total costs or by looking at marginal revenues and marginal costs. We shall examine both approaches.

The Total Revenues–Total Costs Approach

We show hypothetical demand (rate of output and price per unit), revenues, costs, and other data in part (a) of Figure 10–4. In column 3, we see total revenues for our hypothetical monopolist, and in column 4, we see total costs. We can transfer these two columns to part (b). The difference between the total revenue and total cost diagram in part (b) and the one we showed for a perfect competitor in Chapter 9 is that the total revenue line is no longer straight. Rather, it curves. For any given demand curve, in order to sell more, the monopolist must lower the price. Thus, the basic difference between a monopolist and a perfect competitor has to do with the demand curve for the two types of firms. Monopoly market power is derived from facing a downward-sloping demand curve.

Profit maximization involves maximizing the positive difference between total revenues and total costs. This occurs at an output rate of nine units where the maximum profit equals $12.50.

The Marginal Revenue–Marginal Cost Approach

Profit maximization will also occur where marginal revenue equals marginal cost. This is as true for a monopolist as it is for a perfect competitor (but the monopolist will charge a higher price). When we transfer marginal cost and marginal revenue information from columns 6 and 7 in part (a) of Figure 10–4 to part (c), we see that marginal revenue approximately equals marginal cost at an output rate of nine units. Remember that a marginal cost of $3.70 refers to the extra cost of producing the ninth unit of output; a marginal revenue of $3.75 refers to the extra revenue earned by selling the ninth unit of output. Therefore, the monopolist will continue to add to profit by producing the ninth unit. Profit maximization occurs at nine units of output, which is the same output as in part (b).

WHY PRODUCE WHERE MARGINAL REVENUE EQUALS MARGINAL COST? If the monopolist goes past the point where marginal revenue equals marginal cost, marginal cost will exceed marginal revenue. That is, the incremental cost of producing any more units will exceed the incremental revenue. It just would not be worthwhile, as was true also in perfect competition. But if the monopolist produces less than that, it is also not making maximum profits. Look at an output rate of seven units in Figure 10–4. Here, the monopolist's marginal revenue is $4.75, but marginal cost is only $2.90. The monopolist would be foolish to stop at seven units of output because if output is expanded, marginal revenue will still exceed marginal cost, and therefore, total profits will rise. In fact, the profit-maximizing monopolist will continue to expand output and sales until marginal revenue approximately equals marginal cost, which is at nine units of output.

The monopolist will not produce at an output rate of 10 because here, as we see, marginal cost is $4.20 and marginal revenue is $3.25. The difference of $0.95 represents the *reduction* in total profits from producing the tenth unit. Total profits will rise as the monopolist reduces its rate of output back toward nine units of output.

FIGURE 10–4

Monopoly Costs, Revenues, and Profits

In part (a), we give hypothetical demand (rate of output and price per unit), revenues, and costs. As shown in part (b), the monopolist's maximum profit of $12.50 is where the positive difference between TR and TC is the greatest, at nine units. As part (c) indicates, this maximum profit occurs where MR = MC with a price of $5.75 per unit.

Part (a)

(1) Output (units)	(2) Price per Unit	(3) Total Revenues (TR) = (2) × (1)	(4) Total Costs (TC)	(5) Total Profit (TR − TC) = (3) − (4)	(6) Marginal Cost (MC)	(7) Marginal Revenue (MR) = Change in (3) Change in (1)	(8) Average Total Cost (ATC) = (4) ÷ (1)
0	$8.00	$ 0.00	$10.00	−$10.00			
1	7.75	7.75	14.00	−6.25	$ 4.00	$7.75	$14.00
2	7.50	15.00	17.50	−2.50	3.50	7.25	8.75
3	7.25	21.75	20.75	1.00	3.25	6.75	6.92
4	7.00	28.00	23.80	4.20	3.05	6.25	5.95
5	6.75	33.75	26.70	7.05	2.90	5.75	5.34
6	6.50	39.00	29.50	9.50	2.80	5.25	4.92
7	6.25	43.75	32.40	11.35	2.90	4.75	4.63
8	6.00	48.00	35.55	12.45	3.15	4.25	4.44
9	5.75	51.75	39.25	12.50	3.70	3.75	4.36
10	5.50	55.00	43.45	11.55	4.20	3.25	4.35
11	5.25	57.75	48.55	9.20	5.10	2.75	4.41
12	5.00	60.00	54.85	5.15	6.30	2.25	4.57
13	4.75	61.75	62.65	−0.90	7.80	1.75	4.82
14	4.50	63.00	72.25	−9.25	9.60	1.25	5.16
15	4.25	63.75	83.95	−20.20	11.70	0.75	5.60

What Price to Charge for Output?

How does the monopolist set prices? We know the quantity is set at the point at which marginal revenue equals marginal cost. The monopolist then finds out how much can be charged—how much the market will bear—for that particular quantity. We know that the demand curve is defined as showing the *maximum* price for which a given quantity can be sold. That means that our monopolist knows that to sell nine units, it can charge only $5.75 because that is the price at which that specific quantity is demanded according to Figure 10–4 part (c). This price is found by drawing a vertical line from the quantity to the market demand curve. Where that line hits the market demand curve, the price is determined. We find that price by drawing a horizontal line from the demand curve over to the price axis; that gives us the profit-maximizing price of $5.75, as described in Figure 10–4 part (c).

The basic procedure for finding the profit-maximizing short-run price–quantity combination for the monopolist is first to determine the profit-maximizing rate of output, by either the total revenue–total cost method or the marginal revenue–marginal cost method, and then to determine by use of the demand curve, D, the maximum price that can be charged to sell that output.

Do not get the impression that just because we are able to draw an exact demand curve in Figure 10–4, real-world monopolists have such perfect information. The process of price searching by a less than perfect competitor is just that—a process. A monopolist can only estimate the actual demand curve and therefore can only make an educated guess when it sets its profit-maximizing price. This is not a problem for the perfect competitor because price is given already by the intersection of market demand and market supply. The monopolist, in contrast, reaches the profit-maximizing output–price combination by trial and error.

Calculating Monopoly Profit

We have talked about the monopolist's profit, but we have yet to indicate how much profit the monopolist makes. We have actually shown total profits in column 5 of part (a) in Figure 10–4. We can also find total profits by adding an average total cost curve to part (c) of that figure. We do that in Figure 10–5. When we add the average total cost curve, we find that the profit that a monopolist makes is equal to the shaded area, which is $(P_m - \text{ATC}_m) \times Q_m$ or ($5.75 − $4.36) × 9 = $12.51. Given the demand curve and a uniform pricing system (i.e., all units sold at the same price), there is no way for a monopolist to make greater profits than those shown by the shaded area.

It is possible for a monopoly firm to make positive economic profits in the long run. This is due to the existence of barriers to entry that prevents new firms from entering and eroding the monopolist's "excess" profit. The monopolist earns these positive economic profits by charging "excessive" prices—prices that exceed average total cost in the long run.

FIGURE 10–5

Monopoly Profit

In this figure, with per-unit dollar amounts measured on the vertical axis, we determine the maximum profit of a monopolist as follows. We first find the profit maximum quantity at $Q_m = 9$; the demand curve shows that the price = $P_m = \$5.75$ per unit. The average total cost curve shows that $\text{ATC}_m = \$4.36$ at $Q = 9$ units. Total profit is given as: $(P_m - \text{ATC}_m) \times Q_m$, which is ($5.75 − $4.36) × 9 units = $12.51 = Shaded area.

The Did You Know That . . . ? section of this chapter provides examples of monopoly situations where one can expect to pay relatively high prices. Suppose a large computer manufacturer donates funds toward the construction of a new building on campus on the basis of an agreement that the university will purchase all of its computer equipment from this one manufacturer. In this situation, the university can expect to pay "top dollar" for all the computer equipment it purchases, as it faces a monopoly situation. Similarly, in order for you to book your wedding reception at your favourite hotel ballroom, you will likely have to promise to use the hotel's menu and wine list for this joyous event. Since you face a monopoly in terms of planning for the food and beverages for your wedding, you will pay high prices for these refreshments.

NO GUARANTEE OF PROFITS. The term *monopoly* conjures up the notion of a greedy firm ripping off the public and making exorbitant profits. However, the mere existence of a monopoly does not guarantee high profits. Numerous monopolies have gone bankrupt. Figure 10–6 shows the monopolist's demand curve as D and the resultant marginal revenue curve as MR. It does not matter at what rate of output this particular monopolist operates; total costs cannot be covered. Look at the position of the average total cost curve. It lies everywhere above D (the average revenue curve). Thus, there is no price–output combination that will allow the monopolist even to cover costs, much less earn profits. This monopolist will, in the short run, suffer economic losses as shown by the shaded area. The graph in Figure 10–6 depicts a situation for millions of typical monopolies that exist; they are called inventions. The owner of a patented invention or discovery has a pure legal monopoly, but the demand and cost curves may be such that production is not profitable. Every year at inventors' conventions, one can see many inventions that have never been put into production because they were deemed "uneconomic" by potential producers and users.

FIGURE 10–6

Monopolies: Not Always Profitable

Some monopolists face the situation shown here. The average total cost curve, ATC, is everywhere above the average revenue, or demand, curve, D. In the short run, the monopolist will produce where MC = MR at point E. Output Q_m will be sold at price P_m, but cost per unit is C_1. Losses are the shaded rectangle. Eventually, the monopolist will go out of business.

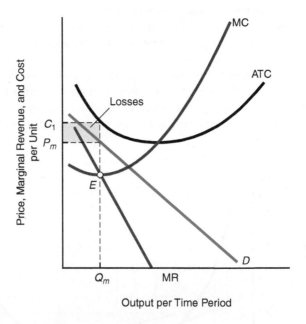

10.3 On Making Higher Profits: Price Discrimination

In a perfectly competitive market, each buyer is charged the same price for every unit of the particular commodity (corrected for differential transportation charges). Because the product is homogeneous and we also assume full knowledge on the part of the buyers, a difference in price cannot exist. Any seller of the product who tried to charge a price higher than the going market price would find that no one would purchase it from that seller.

In this chapter we have assumed until now that the monopolist charged all consumers the same price for all units. A monopolist, however, may be able to charge different people different prices or different prices for successive units sought by a given buyer. **Price discrimination** refers to the practice of charging different prices for units of the same product, not justified by cost differences. A firm will engage in price discrimination whenever feasible to increase profits.

Price discrimination The practice of charging different prices for units of the same product, not justified by cost differences.

Different Prices for Different Units of the Same Product

A negatively sloped demand curve suggests that consumers are willing to pay different amounts for different units of the same product. If a monopoly firm is able to charge the maximum amount that consumers are willing to pay for different units of the same product, the firm will enjoy a higher level of profit. Returning to Figure 10–4, you will recall that when our hypothetical monopolist charges a single price of $5.75 per unit, the firm earns an economic profit of $12.50. What amount of profit could be earned if this monopoly firm were to price discriminate?

A price-discriminating monopolist would, in the extreme, charge a different price for each unit of output according to the demand for its product. Thus, it would sell the first unit for $7.75, the second for $7.50, the third for $7.25 and so on, until the price it could charge for the next unit of output just equalled the marginal cost of producing it. In our example, therefore, the price discriminator would sell 11 units of output, with the eleventh unit selling for $5.25, just equal to its marginal cost. How much extra profit would it make? Total revenue would be $71.50—the sum of all of the prices charged for the 11 units sold ($7.75 + $7.50 + $7.25 + $7 + $6.75 + $6.50 + $6.25 + $6 + $5.75 + $5.50 + $5.25). Total cost would be unchanged at $48.55, and the resulting profit would be $22.95. Figure 10–7 reproduces Figure 10–4 and highlights the extra revenues that accrue to the price-discriminating monopolist. Distributing units of a product by auction, based on sealed bids, is one way to approximate the practice of perfect price discrimination, as described in Policy Example 10–2.

POLICY EXAMPLE 10–2 **Forcing Individuals to Reveal How Much They Are Willing to Pay**

Shanghai is a bustling city of more than 16 million people that is growing rapidly. Nevertheless, the city government strictly limits the number of available auto licence plates according to a mathematical formula that takes into account the number of recently scrapped cars and recent auto sales. In a typical year, this means that only 6000 new licence plates will be available for purchase, even though at least 20 000 people would like to obtain plates. To determine how much people are willing to pay for the restricted number of plates, the government conducts a monthly sealed auction. Those willing to pay the most for a licence plate often pay amounts exceeding the equivalent of $4000 to obtain the right to drive. In this way, Shanghai's government seeks to make economic profits from its control over licence plates.

How is Shanghai attempting to reduce traffic jams?

For critical analysis:

1. As a monopoly provider of vehicle licence plates, what type of pricing practice is the Shanghai government pursuing and why?

2. Can you think of any benefits accruing to the citizens of Shanghai as a result of this type of licence plate pricing policy?

Source: "Dubious license plate auctions stay for now." *China Daily News*. http://www.chinadaily.com.cn/english/doc/2004-05/25/content_333681.htm.

FIGURE 10–7

Additional Profits from Perfect Price Discrimination: Part (a)

Under perfect price discrimination, the firm charges the maximum that consumers are willing to pay for each unit sold. This increases total revenue at each output level. Put differently, marginal revenue is now equal to price under discrimination. The maximum profit quantity is now equal to 11 units, where price is just about equal to MC. The total maximum profit is now $22.95. This is higher than the total profit of $12.50 under the single-price monopoly.

(1) Output (units)	(2) Price per Unit (P)	(3) Total Revenue: Perfect Discrimination (TRd)	(4) Total Costs (TC)	(5) Total Profit: Perfect Discrimination	(6) Marginal Cost (MC)	(7) Marginal Revenue with Perfect Discrimination P = MR
0	$8.00	$ 0.00	$10.00	−$10.00		
1	7.75	7.75	14.00	−6.25	$ 4.00	$7.75
2	7.50	15.25	17.50	−2.25	3.50	7.50
3	7.25	22.50	20.75	1.75	3.25	7.25
4	7.00	29.50	23.80	5.70	3.05	7.00
5	6.75	36.25	26.70	9.55	2.90	6.75
6	6.50	42.75	29.50	13.25	2.80	6.50
7	6.25	49.00	32.40	16.60	2.90	6.25
8	6.00	55.00	35.55	19.45	3.15	6.00
9	5.75	60.75	39.25	21.50	3.70	5.75
10	5.50	66.25	43.45	22.80	4.20	5.50
11	5.25	71.50	48.55	22.95	5.10	5.25
12	5.00	76.50	54.85	21.65	6.30	5.00
13	4.75	81.25	62.65	18.60	7.80	4.75
14	4.50	85.75	72.25	13.50	9.60	4.50
15	4.25	90.00	83.95	6.05	11.70	4.25

Part (b)

The single-price monopoly will sell $Q_s = 9$ units of output at a price of $5.75 per unit. The single-price monopoly has a total revenue of $5.75 × 9 = $51.75 = light shaded area. The price discriminating monopoly will sell $Q_d = 11$ units and will charge the maximum price for each of these units. Under price discrimination, the total revenue will be equal to the total revenue of the single-price monopolist (light shaded area + dark shaded areas). Hence, for any cost structure, the price discriminator will earn a higher total revenue than the single-price monopoly.

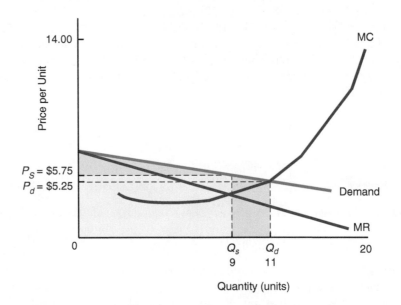

It is interesting to note that a monopolist that can price discriminate will usually produce a greater amount of output than a single-price monopoly. In fact, if the monopolist can perfectly price discriminate as in the above example, it will produce where price equals marginal cost—the perfectly competitive output.

Most monopolies, however, cannot charge a separate price for each unit of output. Instead, they sell blocks of output for different prices. For example, in some jurisdictions, electricity utility companies charge more for the first block of electricity consumed than for subsequent blocks used in the same month. For many years, when monopoly firms provided long-distance telephone service, consumers were charged a higher rate for the first minute of a long-distance telephone conversation compared with that for subsequent minutes. These practices reflect the fact that consumers typically place a higher marginal benefit on the first block of output than on subsequent blocks of output.

Different Prices for Different Groups of Buyers of the Same Product

Price discrimination is often found in situations where the consumers of a product (or service) can be separated into subgroups that exhibit different price elasticities of demand. In general, the monopoly firm can increase its profit by charging a higher price in the more inelastic market(s) and a lower price in the more elastic market(s).

For example, higher airfares are frequently charged to business travellers who, out of necessity, have to book a specific return flight. In contrast, leisure travellers, who do not have to travel on any specific flight, pay a lower airfare by agreeing to stay over a Saturday night before returning home. In this case, the business traveller constitutes an inelastic demand situation, while the leisure traveller is more price elastic.

People who go to see movie matinees are very price conscious (elastic demand) and therefore enjoy lower admission fees than those who go to the movies in the evenings. Similarly, people who carry around coupons will pay a lower rate per litre of gas compared with those consumers who never use coupons (inelastic users).

Example 10–2 illustrates how Shaw Communications sets different prices for its high-speed Internet service for different groups of customers.

EXAMPLE 10–2   Pricing Internet Service to Maximize Profit

In many Canadian cities and towns, high-speed Internet service is provided under a monopoly or close to a monopoly situation. In these cases, you will typically find that the Internet provider charges different prices to personal versus business users. This is because the elasticity of demand for high-speed Internet differs between personal and business users. The following table compares the rates that Shaw Communications charged to personal and business users for the same Internet service in a Canadian city in 2010.

TABLE 10–1

Personal vs. Business High-Speed Internet Rates

Features of Service	High-Speed: Personal User	High-Speed: Business User
Price per month	$35.00	$52.95
Connection speed	7.5 Mbps download	7.5 Mbps download
E-mail accounts	10	5

One of the graphs in Figure 10–8 describes the high-speed Internet market for the personal user, while the other graph describes the business market. For simplicity, we assume that the marginal cost of serving each additional user is constant.

FIGURE 10–8

The High-Speed Internet Market

continued

For critical analysis:

1. Which market is the business market, and why?

2. What factors explain why the elasticity of demand for the business market differs from the personal market?

3. Why does the price charged to business users exceed the price charged to personal users?

Sources: High-Speed [Internet] Package. Business Products and Services. Shaw Communications. http://www.shaw.ca/en-ca/ProductsServices/Business/Internet/HighSpeedPackage.htm; High Speed Internet. Internet. Products and Services. Shaw Communications. http://www.shaw.ca/en-ca/ProductsServices/Internet/High-Speed. (Accessed on June 2, 2010.)

Necessary Conditions for Price Discrimination

Four conditions are necessary for price discrimination to exist:

1. *The firm must face a downward-sloping demand curve.* In order to charge different consumers different prices, the firm must have some control over price setting.

2. *The firm must be able to separate markets at a reasonable cost.* The monopoly must be able to determine in a relatively simple manner which consumers are willing to pay high prices and which are not. If the cost of segregating the market is high, it will offset the extra profit gained from price discrimination.

3. *The buyers in the various markets must have different price elasticities of demand.* Buyers who are willing to pay high prices typically have fewer substitutes to choose from; hence, their demand is relatively price inelastic. Consumers with more elastic demands usually are less willing to pay high prices for goods and services.

4. *The firm must be able to prevent resale of the product or service.* If the purchaser of the monopoly's product can resell it to a higher-price buyer, then the low-price purchaser, and not the firm, captures the profit that accrues from price discrimination.

For example, charging students a lower price for a movie can be done relatively easily. The cost of checking student IDs is apparently not significant. Also, it is fairly easy to make sure that students do not resell their tickets to nonstudents.

As noted in this chapter's Issues and Applications, "Is it Fair to Practise Price Discrimination in Higher Education?", the practice of price discrimination may promote certain goals such as equity and allocative efficiency. That is, charging richer students higher tuition fees provides funds to help lower-income students attend top quality universities.

It must be made clear at the outset that charging different prices to different people or for different units that reflect differences in the cost of service to those particular people does not amount to price discrimination. If bus fares in the evening are higher than daytime fares because it is more costly to operate evening bus service, this is not price discrimination.

10.4 Social Evaluation of Monopoly

In Canada, there are instances where monopoly situations are considered illegal. This, in itself, suggests that many monopoly firms may act against the public interest. To better understand the "evils" of monopoly, we should note that we are evaluating the long-run behaviour that may occur in a monopoly market structure.

Monopoly and Allocative Efficiency

Let us run a little experiment. We will start with a purely competitive industry that has numerous firms, each unable to affect the price of its product. The supply curve of the industry is equal to the horizontal sum of the marginal cost curves of the individual producers above their respective minimum average variable costs. In part (a) of Figure 10–9,

FIGURE 10-9

The Effects of Monopolizing an Industry

In part (a), we show a competitive situation in which equilibrium is established at the intersection of D and S at point E. The equilibrium price would be P_e, and the equilibrium quantity would be Q_e. Each individual competitive producer faces a demand curve that is a horizontal line at the market clearing price, P_e. What happens if the industry is suddenly monopolized? We assume that the costs stay the same; the only thing that changes is that the monopolist now faces the entire downward-sloping demand curve. In part (b), we draw the marginal revenue curve. Marginal cost is S because that is the horizontal summation of all the individual marginal cost curves. The monopolist therefore produces at Q_m and charges price P_m. P_m in part (b) is higher than P_e in part (a), and Q_m is less than Q_e. We see, then, that a monopolist charges a higher price and produces less than an industry in a competitive situation.

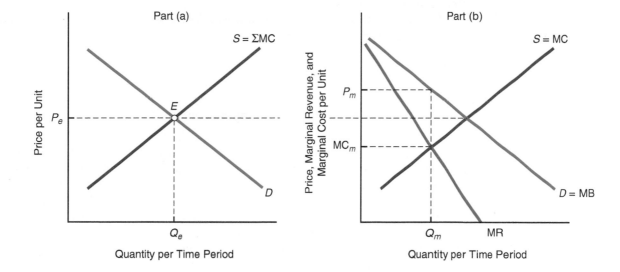

Part (a) — Price per Unit, Quantity per Time Period; $S = \Sigma MC$, E, P_e, D, Q_e

Part (b) — Price, Marginal Revenue, and Marginal Cost per Unit, Quantity per Time Period; $S = MC$, P_m, MC_m, $D = MB$, Q_m, MR

we show the market demand curve and the market supply curve in a perfectly competitive situation. The competitive price in equilibrium is equal to P_e, and the equilibrium quantity at that price is equal to Q_e. Each individual competitor faces a demand curve (not shown) that is coincident with the price line P_e. No individual supplier faces the market demand curve, D.

Now, let us assume that a monopolist comes in and buys up every single competitor in the industry. In so doing, we will assume that the monopolist does not affect any of the marginal cost curves or demand. We can therefore redraw D and S in part (b) of Figure 10–9 exactly the same as in part (a).

How does this monopolist decide how much to charge and how much to produce? If the monopolist is maximizing profit, it is going to look at the marginal revenue curve and produce at the output where marginal revenue equals marginal cost. But what is the marginal cost curve in part (b) of Figure 10–9? It is merely S because we said that S was equal to the horizontal summation of the portions of the individual marginal cost curves above each firm's respective minimum average variable cost. The monopolist therefore produces quantity Q_m and sells it at price P_m. Note that Q_m is less than Q_e and that P_m is greater than P_e. A monopolist therefore produces a smaller quantity and sells it at a higher price. This is the reason usually given when economists criticize monopolists. Monopolists raise the price and restrict production compared with a competitive situation. For a monopolist's product, consumers are forced to pay a price that exceeds the marginal cost of production. Resources are misallocated in such a situation—too few resources are being used in the monopolist's industry and too many are used elsewhere.

Note from Figure 10–9 that by setting MR = MC, the monopolist produces at a rate of output, Q_m, where the price exceeds marginal cost (compare P_m with MC_m). Suppose that $Q_m = 700$ units, $P_m = \$5$ per unit, and $MC_m = \$2$ per unit. The marginal cost of $\$2$ per unit reflects the value of the output in other industries that is sacrificed (opportunity cost), when additional resources are used to produce the last unit or 700th unit in this monopoly industry. Price, by contrast, represents the marginal benefit that buyers derive from the last unit produced. Thus, society places a $5 value on the last unit (700th unit) produced in this monopoly industry.

The monopoly outcome of $P > \text{MC}$ means that the value to society of the last unit produced is greater than its additional cost; hence not enough of the good is produced. In our example, if one more unit of the monopoly good is produced, the extra $5 value gained in the monopoly industry will exceed the $2 value of lost production in other industries (marginal cost). From society's point of view, there will be a net gain in value of approximately $3 by allocating more resources to the monopoly industry. Clearly, monopoly conflicts with allocative efficiency, which is concerned with producing the mix of goods and services most valued by society.

As Example 10–3 indicates, the competitive price can sometimes be a very small fraction of the monopoly price.

EXAMPLE 10–3   The High Cost of Staying Alive

Thalidomide is perhaps best known as a drug with a notorious past. In the 1950s and 1960s, it was given to pregnant women to treat nausea but tragically caused birth defects: thousands of children were born without arms or legs. The drug was ultimately banned around the world.

Remarkably, research findings published in the *New England Journal of Medicine* (*NEJM*) in 1999 indicated that thalidomide effectively treats diseases such as leprosy, childhood leukemia, and multiple myeloma (a life-threatening cancer). Subsequently, Celgene, a pharmaceutical company, was granted a new patent for thalidomide and was allowed to sell the drug to government-approved patients. Between 1999 and 2005, Celgene raised the price of thalidomide from $400 for a month's supply to $3600—a 900 percent increase! This compares to a monthly cost of $108 in Mexico and $168 in India, as posted in 2008.

In 2009, an Ontario resident was diagnosed with multiple myeloma. This person was successfully treated and the cancer went into remission. To prevent a relapse, his doctor prescribed thalidomide. Unfortunately, the man could not afford to pay the approximate cost of $4000 per month and so, to date, he is not able to take this drug. Celgene defends the high price as being necessary to cover the very high risks and costs associated with drug's research and development expenses. Celgene's claim appears to be backed by the president of the association that represents pharmaceutical companies in Canada, who estimates that it costs over a billion dollars to discover and develop a typical pharmaceutical drug.

Recent evidence suggests that multinational drug companies grossly overstate the true costs of developing pharmaceuticals. One study undertaken at the University of Medicine and Dentistry of New Jersey School concluded that 84 percent of drug research money around the world comes from public and charitable sources, not from the pockets of private drug companies. Dr. Marcia Angell, the former Editor in Chief of the prestigious *NEJM* estimates that the research and development costs per new drug are closer to $100 million, implying that the high drug prices charged by pharmaceutical companies result in excess profits. According to recently published data, the top pharmaceutical companies enjoy an average profit margin of 20 percent, compared to the 8 percent mean return earned by the 2000 companies studied. It is interesting to note that Celgene's profit margin rose from 16 percent in 2007 to 29 percent in 2009.

For critical analysis: Explain how Celgene's behaviour, as described in this example, is consistent with the theory of monopoly. In your answer, comment on how the nature of the price elasticity of demand for thalidomide affects Celgene's pricing behaviour.

Source: W5 Staff. "W5 investigates: pills, patients and profits." CTV News Video. W5. March 27, 2010. http://www.ctv.ca/servlet/ArticleNews/story/CTVNews/20100326/w5_pills_100326/20100327?s_name=W5.

Monopoly and Productive Efficiency

In theory, in long-run equilibrium, a perfectly competitive firm operates at minimum long-run average total cost. Being a price taker under intense competition, the perfectly competitive firm can survive only by being productively efficient.

Since a monopolist produces a product for which there is no close substitute, the firm can survive without having to operate at minimum average total cost. In cases where a monopolist is a very large corporation, the managers may pursue goals other than cost minimization. A manager may seek to enlarge the resources employed in his or her department as a way of obtaining a higher level of status and salary.

Monopoly and Long-Run Excess Profit

Due to barriers to entry, a monopoly firm can earn annual profits in excess of a normal profit. The excessive monopoly prices charged can be viewed as a "tax" on poorer consumers. To the extent that the shares of these monopoly firm(s) are concentrated in the hands of upper-income individuals, the proceeds of this "tax" are shared among affluent shareholders. In short, the existence of monopoly firms can result in a more inequitable distribution of income in our society.

One key area of the Canadian economy plagued by monopoly industries is the food sector. You may recall from a previous chapter how the Canadian federal and provincial governments have supported farm incomes by allowing various farming groups to form marketing boards that determine the quantity and price of their products. Each marketing board can be viewed as a monopoly supplier of the product it sells.

When a group of farmers supplying a specific product in a Canadian province decides to switch from competing independently to forming a marketing board, farm incomes are enhanced (as illustrated in Figure 10–9). Essentially, the marketing board imposes production quotas on each farmer to restrict quantity to Q_m (see Part (b)), and the price rises to P_m, so as to maximize profits. In order to keep the quantity sold in the province at the restricted level, trade barriers must be imposed to keep out similar products that are produced out of province and out of country.

The social costs of allowing legal monopolies in the form of farm marketing boards is discussed in Policy Example 10–3.

POLICY EXAMPLE 10–3 **Monopolies are Milking Canadian Food Consumers**

In April 2010, the C.D. Howe Institute, an economic think tank, published a study entitled *Freeing Up Food: The Ongoing Cost, and Potential Reform, of Supply Management*. In this study, "supply management" essentially refers to the policy of allowing marketing boards (monopolies) to control or manage the supply (sale) of specific agricultural products. The report authors estimate that Canadian marketing boards that operate in just the three areas—eggs, dairy, and poultry products—are responsible for about 20 percent of annual agricultural sales.

Between 1995 and 2009, while the Canadian consumer price index increased by 32 percent, the prices for poultry, dairy, and eggs rose 61 percent, 51 percent, and 54 percent, respectively. Canadian milk prices are more than twice as high as in the U.S. The high food prices have a negative effect on consumers as well as on other industries, such as food processors and restaurants, which are forced to restrain the production of their products and services (due to the higher costs).

According to the C.D. Howe Institute study, the aggregated value of all the production quotas in the Canadian egg, dairy, and poultry industries is approximately $28 billion. This translates to above-normal profits somewhere between $1.1 billion and $1.6 billion a year being earned by producers in these three industries.

Under these policies, the marketing board farmers are protected from competition from outside of the province and country. Resources are "wasted" on unproductive activities such as lobbying to maintain the marketing boards, as well enforcement of trade barriers that keep

continued

products from being imported from other provinces or countries. These unproductive activities unnecessarily raise the cost of producing the farm products and divert efforts to make farm operations more efficient.

A major conclusion of the C.D. Howe Report is that Canadian supply management policies are hindering entrepreneurship and economic growth in the Canadian food sector. Since marketing boards tend to restrict the entry of new farmers, innovative business that produce products such as raw milk, free-range eggs, and uncaged chickens are slow to expand. Canada will not be allowed to join international trade treaties such as the Trans-Pacific Partnership unless the supply management policies are abandoned. These treaties are considered important in terms of gaining access to the fast-growing Asian and Pacific markets.

For critical analysis: Based on this example, identify and explain the various social costs related to permitting monopolies in the form of farm marketing boards.

Sources: William B.P. Robson and Colin Busby. *Freeing up Food: The Ongoing Cost, and Potential Reform, of Supply Management.* Backgrounder. C.D. Howe Institute. April 2010. Pg. 1–6. http://www.cdhowe.org/pdf/backgrounder_128.pdf; "Another reason to take on Big Milk" *National Post.* April 16, 2010. Pg. A14.

Should All Monopolies Be Eliminated?

Before we leave the topic of the social cost of monopoly, we should recognize that some monopoly situations may benefit society as a whole. If large economies of scale exist in the monopoly industry, the monopolist can promote productive efficiency. If the government were to intervene to break up this one large efficient company into many smaller firms, average cost per unit may rise. Indeed, the consumers may end up paying more for the product under a more competitive structure! If the government were to try to eliminate a monopoly cable TV station in a small city by encouraging a second cable company to serve the city, think of the duplication of costs that could occur. As a start, two sets of cables would have to be laid throughout the city!

Monopolies created by patents may be socially desirable, to the extent that the promise of a monopoly encourages valuable inventions. Multinational drug companies have consistently argued that the lure of long-run "excess" profits, based on patent protection, serves as an excellent incentive to develop new and better prescription drugs.

As indicated in Policy Example 10–3 "The High Cost of Staying Alive," recent evidence suggests that the multinational drug companies may be grossly overstating the true cost of the research and development costs that they actually incur, so that a large portion of the excessive profits earned end up as profits for the shareholders of pharmaceutical corporations. As well, it appears that a significant portion of drug research money around the world comes from public and charitable sources, not from the pockets of private drug companies.

Governments around the world bestow monopoly rights called *copyright* to those who originate, create, or produce various works, performances, and broadcasts. From an economics viewpoint, copyright means that authors, artists, and musicians have the right to collect royalties (monies) from any form of reproduction and sale of their works. Because a monopoly is granted to the originators, they are able to restrict the distribution of their works in order to exact a higher price and maximize profits. In this way, copyright serves as an incentive to create high-quality literary, dramatic, artistic, and musical works that contribute to the enrichment and diversity of our culture, our freedom of expression, and our overall personal well-being. In Canada, the monopoly right related to copyright is bestowed for a term of the life of the originator and 50 years following his or her death.

Under copyright law, it is illegal for any person to reproduce the works of others, without the consent of the owner of the copyright. This type of illegal behaviour constitutes an *infringement of copyright*. As Policy Example 10–4 notes, the widespread practice of freely downloading music through the Internet is a form of copyright infringement that threatens the livelihoods of many artists and companies that record and distribute music.

POLICY EXAMPLE 10–4   Swapping Songs on the Internet: Is It Really Free?

The practice of music file sharing has presented significant challenges to the music industry globally, as well as to the economies of many nations. On June 1, 2010, the Recording Industry Association of America (RIAA) reported that in the U.S. alone, global music piracy costs $12.5 billion of economic losses every year, 71 060 U.S. jobs, $2.7 billion in workers' earnings, and $422 million in tax revenues. On its website, the Canadian Recording Industry Association (CRIA) reported that retail music sales in Canada have declined by more than half since the advent of widespread online music downloading just over a decade ago. Recorded music sales in Canada saw one of the sharpest drops among the world's top 10 music markets between 1999 and 2009 due to piracy. The remainder of this Policy Example provides a brief history of key events that have occurred over the past decade that have shaped government policy regarding music piracy.

On December 19, 2003, the Dutch Supreme Court ruled that companies like Kazaa cannot be prosecuted for copyright infringement of music and movies downloaded using its software. The file-sharing software makers (Kazaa, Grokster, and StreamCast Networks) have used two key arguments in their defence. The first is the Betamax doctrine, which states that products and services used for piracy are deemed legal if they are capable of substantial non-infringing uses.

What are the social costs related to the practice of downloading songs for free?

The second source of defence for the software makers is that file-sharing software, such as Kazaa, Grokster, and Morpheus (different from Napster), does not require a central company server. It is peer-to-peer software that allows users to search each other's hard drives for files they want. The files are downloaded right from each user's hard drive. This second line of defence prompted the Canadian Recording Industry Association (CRIA) to go to court to try to force Canadian Internet service providers to turn over the names of 29 large-volume file sharers. On March 31, 2004, a Canadian federal court denied the CRIA's request, stating that the actions of file sharers were no different from that of libraries that place copying machines in a room full of copyrighted books. It is expected that the court ruling will be appealed.

On June 25, 2005, the U.S. Supreme Court ruled that companies that build businesses with the active intent of encouraging copyright infringement should be held liable for their customers' illegal actions. This ruling gave the recording industry the ammunition to file lawsuits against companies creating file-sharing software as well as individuals freely swapping music on the Internet.

On July 27, 2006, Kazaa agreed to pay a substantial sum in compensation to the record companies for the illegal swapping of music. In 2007, the RIAA sent pre-litigation letters to 36 American universities to warn them of forthcoming lawsuits against students and staff for illegal music downloading. Prior to this action, RIAA had successfully sued almost 1000 students for damages ranging anywhere from $750 to $150 000.

On May 12, 2010, a U.S. Federal Court ruled that LimeWire, one of the largest remaining peer-to-peer service providers, will be liable for encouraging widespread copyright theft (music piracy). The Court found that LimeWire had intentionally encouraged direct infringements by its users, as 93 percent of the files available through LimeWire are protected by copyright. On October 26, 2010, a U.S. federal court judge granted the music industry's request to shut down LimeWire.

For critical analysis: Who really "pays" for the actions of those who freely upload music files over the Internet?

Sources: "The free music myth." The Canadian Recording Industry Association. http://www.cria.ca/fmm.html. (Accessed March 20, 2004). CBC News Online. "Canadian recording industry to imitate U.S. file-sharing lawsuits." December 16, 2003. http://www.cbc.ca/arts/stories/CRIAtosue161203. (Accessed March 20 2004). "Dutch court throws out Kazaa case." December 19, 2003. Associated Press Wired News. http://www. wired.com/news/digiwood/0,1412,61672,00.html. (Accessed March 21, 2004). Janet McFarland. "Ruling deals blow to music industry." *The Globe and Mail*. April 1, 2004, Pg. B3; John Borland, "Supreme Court rules against file swapping," CNET News.com. June 27, 2005. http://news.com.com/; "IFPI Press Release: Kazaa settles with record industry and goes legitimate." July 27, 2006. http://www.cria.ca/news/270706_n. php; Macleans.ca staff. "Students at 36 US colleges sued for illegal downloading." April 4, 2007. http:// www.macleans.ca/ education/universities/article.jsp?content=20070404_101813_11500; "Piracy: online and on the Street." Recording Industry Association of America. http://www.riaa.com/physicalpiracy.php; "Copyright bill introduction applauded by Canadian record labels." Press Release. Canadian Recording Industry Association. June 2, 2010. http://www.cria.ca/news.php/. "Canada's recording industry welcomes US federal court ruling against LimeWire." Press Release. Canadian Recording Industry Association. May 13, 2010.http://www.cria.ca/news.php.

10.5 The Regulation of a Natural Monopoly

You will recall from our discussion of barriers to entry that whenever a single firm has the ability to produce all of the industry's output at a lower per-unit cost than other firms attempting to produce less than total industry output, a natural monopoly arises. Natural gas and electric utilities are examples. Long-run average costs for those firms typically fall as output increases. In a natural monopoly, economies of large-scale production dominate, leading to a single-firm industry.

The Pricing and Output Decision of the Natural Monopolist

We show data for a hypothetical natural monopoly in part (a) of Figure 10–10. Demand data is in columns 1 and 2, with marginal revenue in column 3. Total cost is in column 4. Notice that marginal cost in column 5 is constant over the range of demand provided. This might be typical of a hydroelectric utility—once the necessary dams are constructed, electricity can be produced at a relatively constant cost. Average total cost is in column 6.

FIGURE 10–10

Profit Maximization and Regulation Through Marginal Cost Pricing

The profit-maximizing monopolist here would produce at the point in part (b) where marginal cost equals marginal revenue, which means production of 5000 units of output. The price charged would be $8. If a regulatory commission attempted to regulate natural monopolies so that price equalled long-run marginal cost, the commission would make the monopolist set production at the point where the marginal cost curve intersects the demand curve. This is shown in part (c). The quantity produced would be 9000 units, and the price would be $4. However, average costs at 9000 units are equal to $5.56. Losses would ensue, equal to the shaded area. It would be self-defeating for a regulatory commission to force a natural monopoly to produce at an output rate at which MC = P without subsidizing some of its costs because losses would eventually drive the natural monopolist out of business.

Part (a)

(1)	(2)	(3)	(4)	(5)	(6)
		Marginal	Long-Run Total	Long-Run Marginal	Long-Run Average
Output (units)	Price per Unit	Revenue (MR)	Cost (TC)	Cost (MC)	Cost (ATC)
0	$13.00		$14 000		—
1 000	12.00	$12.00	18 000	$4.00	$18.00
2 000	11.00	10.00	22 000	4.00	11.00
3 000	10.00	8.00	26 000	4.00	8.67
4 000	9.00	6.00	30 000	4.00	7.50
5 000	8.00	4.00	34 000	4.00	6.80
6 000	7.00	2.00	38 000	4.00	6.33
7 000	6.00	0	42 000	4.00	6.00
8 000	5.00	−2.00	46 000	4.00	5.75
9 000	4.00	−4.00	50 000	4.00	5.56
10 000	3.00	−6.00	54 000	4.00	5.40
11 000	2.00	−8.00	58 000	4.00	5.27
12 000	1.00	−10.00	62 000	4.00	5.17

Part (b)

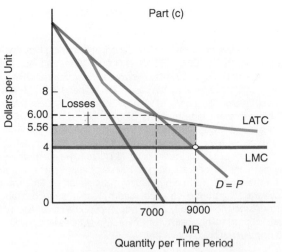

Part (c)

Columns 1, 2, 3, 5, and 6 are graphed in part (b). The intersection of MR and MC is at $4. The monopolist will, therefore, produce 5000 units and charge a price of $8 per unit.

What do we know about a monopolist's solution to the price–quantity question? When compared with a competitive situation, we know that consumers end up paying more for the product, and consequently they purchase less of it than they would purchase under competition. The monopoly solution is economically inefficient from society's point of view; the price charged for the product is higher than the opportunity cost to society, and consequently there is a misallocation of resources. That is, the price does not equal the true marginal cost of producing the good because the true marginal cost is at the intersection *A*, not at $8.

Regulation Using Marginal Cost Pricing

Assume that the government wants the natural monopolist to produce at an output at which price equals marginal cost, so that the value of the satisfaction that individuals receive from the marginal unit purchased is just equal to the marginal cost to society. **Marginal cost pricing** occurs when the monopoly firm is forced to set price equal to marginal cost. Where is that solution in part (c) of Figure 10–10? It is at the intersection of the marginal cost curve and the demand curve, where price equals $4. If a regulatory commission forces the natural monopolist to engage in *marginal cost pricing*, and hence to produce 9000 units to sell for $4 each, how large will the monopolist's profits be? Profits, of course, are the *positive* difference between total revenues and total costs. Total revenues equal price times output, and total costs equal average costs times output. At 9000 units, average cost is equal to $5.56, higher than the price that the regulatory commission forces our natural monopolist to charge. Profits turn out to be losses and are equal to the shaded area in part (c) of Figure 10–10. Thus, regulation that forces a natural monopolist to produce and price as if it were in a competitive situation would also force that monopolist into negative profits, or losses. Obviously, the monopolist would rather go out of business than be subject to such regulation.

Marginal cost pricing Pricing that occurs when the monopoly firm is forced to set price equal to marginal cost.

Regulation Using Average Cost Pricing

As a practical matter, then, regulators cannot force a natural monopolist to engage in marginal cost pricing. Consequently, regulation of natural monopolies has often taken the form of allowing the regulated natural monopolist to set price where LAC intersects *D*, at 7000 units of output, in part (c) of Figure 10–10. This is called **average cost pricing**—when the monopoly firm is forced to set price equal to average total cost. Average cost includes what the regulators deem a "fair" rate of return on investment.

Average cost pricing Pricing that occurs when the monopoly firm is forced to set price equal to average total cost.

While average cost pricing is not socially optimal—at 7000 units of output, price is still $2 above marginal cost—it does result in more output being produced at a lower cost to consumers. Regulators must beware, however, of problems associated with average cost pricing. Unless there are safeguards in place to ensure that the monopoly is cost efficient, the firm has no incentive to keep average costs low. It is easier for the firm to condone inefficiencies in the form of very generous fringe benefits and large expense accounts for executives, all of which inflate average costs. In the extreme, the monopoly could allow its average costs, and hence its regulated price, to rise to the profit-maximizing level of $8.

ISSUES AND APPLICATIONS

Is It Fair to Practise Price Discrimination in Higher Education?

Concepts Applied: Price Discrimination, Elasticity, Allocative Inefficiency, Equity

Students from across Ontario protest the ever-increasing costs of post-secondary tuition fees.

On March 18, 2010, scores of university students from across Alberta boarded chartered buses and braved the icy prairie winds to march on the government legislature grounds to protest proposed fee and tuition hikes. For example, the Alberta Minister of Advanced Education and Technology accepted proposals from the University of Alberta and University of Calgary to impose tuition hikes ranging from $800 to $3300 for programs such as Engineering, Pharmacy, Bachelor of Commerce, and Master of Business Administration, to be effective in 2011. This was in addition to a 4.1 percent tuition increase that happened in the 2009–2010 academic year.

The Alberta protests follow massive student demonstrations in Ontario, just three years earlier, where the common chant was: "Liar, liar, pants on fire! You said fees would go no higher!" In the previous fall (2006), the Ontario government let post-secondary institutions raise tuition by up to 5 percent overall, including 8 percent more for professional programs such as law and medicine.

To pay for their tuition, Canadian post-secondary students have accumulated a staggering debt of $13 billion, with 20 percent of Canadian students unable to repay what they owe. In other words, one in five college-bound students begins his or her adult career bankrupt!

Tuition Fees: Selected Canadian Universities

Table 10–2 describes the annual tuition and fees for the 2010–2011 academic year for selected universities and programs for different groups of students.

TABLE 10–2

Tuition and Fees Combined: Programs at Selected Canadian University

University/Program	In-Province Students	Out-of-Province Canadian Students	International Students
McGill (Quebec)			
Undergraduate Arts	$ 3597.90	$ 7197.60	$ 16 496.40
Medicine (year 1)	$ 7563.05	$ 15 908.15	$ 40 948.05
University of Toronto			
Undergraduate Arts	$ 6262.88	$ 6262.88	$ 25 262.68
Medicine (year 1)	$ 19 478.22	$ 19 478.22	$ 52 825.22
University of Alberta			
Undergraduate Arts	$ 6674.16	$ 6674.16	$ 19 422.56
Medicine (year 1)	$ 13 140.92	$ 13 140.92	$ 24 797.72
University of B.C.			
Undergraduate Arts	$ 5260.00	$ 5260.00	$ 22 060.00
Medicine (year 1)	$ 16 244.00	$ 16 244.00	Not offered

Sources: "Undergraduate fees 2010–2011." Student Information. McGill University website. http://www.mcgill.ca/student-accounts/fees/undergrad/; "Fee and refund schedules." Student Accounts. University of Toronto website. http://www.fees.utoronto.ca/session/fallwinter1011/fees_rfd_sch.htm; "Costs, tuition and fees." Office of the Registrar. University of Alberta website. http://www.registrar.ualberta.ca/ro.cfm?id=1. (Accessed September 5, 2010.); "Calculate your financial plan." University of British Columbia website. http://www.students.ubc.ca/youbc/va/costs.cfm?page. (Accessed September 5, 2010.)

Tuition Fee Structure and Monopoly Pricing Practices

Recall that price discrimination refers to the practice of pricing different amounts of the same product based on differences in "willingness to pay," not on cost differences. Table 10–2 suggests that price discrimination exists in the setting of various tuition fees by any one of the three universities examined. As an example, at McGill University in Quebec, in-province, out-of-province, and out-of-country (international) students pay different tuition fees for the same university program. To study in the first year of McGill's Arts program costs $3597.90, $7197.60, and $16 496.40, respectively, for a Quebec student, an out-of-province Canadian student, and an international student.

It is reasonable to explain the price discrimination noted above in terms of the fact that the elasticity of demand for the same education program likely differs among the different groups of students. The international students who attend Canadian universities typically come from wealthy families who can afford to send their children to other countries to study. This implies that the demand for the same educational program is more inelastic for international students when compared to typical Canadian students.

To the extent that the higher fees charged to study in medical programs are not fully explained by the higher costs of offering medical education compared to an arts education, this fee differential (between programs) constitutes another example of price discrimination in the tuition fee structure. In this case, one can hypothesize that a Canadian student's demand for the medical program is more inelastic than the Canadian student's demand for an Arts program. One reason for this would be that the medical graduate can expect to earn a significantly higher income over his or her lifetime than the typical arts graduate. Another reason might be that the Canadian medical student is more apt to come from a wealthier family than the typical Canadian arts student.

Evaluation of Price Discrimination in the Setting of Tuition Fees

At first glance, one might conclude that the significantly higher tuition fees paid by out-of-province or out-of-country students is a gross inequity and smacks of discrimination against "outsiders." However, one has to remember that tuition fees typically cover less than half the cost of a university student's education in Canada. The provincial taxpayer pays a significant amount of this education. Under this situation, many would argue that it would be inequitable to charge the same tuition fee to both the in-province student and the international student. This would result in a situation where the provincial taxpayer would pay for a significant portion of the education of a wealthy student coming from another country.

Why are taxpayers subsidizing university education? Why not charge all students the same higher tuition fee that covers the full cost of a university education? To the extent that a university education contributes to the economic growth of the province, the provincial community as a whole benefits and so should be willing to pay for some of the student's education. As well, if there were no subsidy, then tuition fees would increase significantly, reducing the ability of lower-income individuals to obtain a university degree. The provincial community as a whole would be losers to the extent that many of these lower-income individuals have the ability to be top performers in fields such as education, law, medicine, engineering, and business. A conflict with allocative efficiency occurs when limited educational resources are allocated to richer students as opposed to the students with the greatest ability and potential. This conflict may already be present, considering the high tuition fees for professional programs such as medicine.

For critical analysis:

1. How does the price discrimination practice noted in the tuition fee structure affect the university's total tuition revenue collected? Briefly explain with the aid of the appropriate diagrams.
2. Would one expect to see a larger or smaller degree of price discrimination in prestigious universities that have a very high level of global recognition? How might this type of pricing policy promote equity?
3. What would be the advantages and disadvantages of a government policy that eliminated tuition fees so that all university costs were paid by the taxpayer?

Sources: Louise Brown, "Students say McGuinty 'lied' about tuition hikes; Nationwide protests call for lower fees; counter-protest blasts 'truant hippies'," *Toronto Star*, February 8, 2007, MET edition, Pg. A14; "Universities receive approval to address market anomalies." Ministry of Advanced Education and Technology. April 7, 2010. http://www.alberta.ca/acn/201004/28100D99E32E1-0FD0-D9A9-E5A61C11A9A97679.html.

SUMMARY

Here is what you should know after reading this chapter. MyEconLab will help you identify what you know, and where to go when you need to practise. We suggest that as soon as you review one of the Learning Objective sections below, you then proceed to go through the related section in MyEconLab.

myeconlab

LEARNING OBJECTIVES	KEY TERMS	MYECONLAB PRACTICE
10.1 The Characteristics of Monopoly. A monopolist is a single seller of a product or a service for which there is no close substitute. To maintain a monopoly, there must be barriers to entry, which may include: (1) ownership of resources needed to enter the industry, (2) large capital outlays required for entry into the industry, (3) economies of scale, (4) legally required licences and public franchises, (5) patents, (6) tariffs, (7) safety and quality regulations, and (8) predatory behaviour. The monopoly firm is a price searcher, which means that it faces a downward-sloping demand curve, where marginal revenue is below the price, at each quantity level.	monopolist, 245 price searcher, 245 natural monopoly, 246 tariffs, 248	• **MyEconLab** Study Plan 10.1
10.2 Determining Output, Price, and Profit in Monopoly. The monopolist chooses the profit-maximizing price–output combination— the output at which marginal revenue equals marginal cost, and the highest price possible at this output level, as determined by the demand curve. Total maximum profit equals the monopolist's maximum profit quantity level multiplied by the difference between the firm's price and its average total cost, at the maximum profit quantity level. If, at the quantity where marginal revenue equals marginal cost, price is below average total cost, the firm will incur an economic loss.		• **MyEconLab** Study Plan 10.2
10.3 On Making Higher Profits: Price Discrimination. Price discrimination refers to the sale of the same product at different prices based on differences in willingness to pay. By price discriminating, the monopolist can increase its revenue and profit. Under perfect price discrimination, the firm charges the maximum amount that consumers are willing to pay for each unit sold. In this case, the demand or price curve equals the marginal revenue curve. The monopoly firm can increase its profit by charging a higher price in the market segment that is price inelastic	price discrimination, 255	• **MyEconLab** Study Plan 10.3

LEARNING OBJECTIVES	KEY TERMS	MYECONLAB PRACTICE
and a lower price in the market segment that is price elastic. Four conditions are necessary for price discrimination: (1) The firm faces a downward-sloping demand curve. (2) The firm must be able to separate different units sold or different customer groups at a reasonable cost. (3) Different groups of customers exhibit differing price elasticities of demand. (4) The resale of the product or service must be preventable.		
10.4 Social Evaluation of Monopoly. The social costs of monopoly include: (1) The firm is allocatively inefficient, to the extent that price exceeds marginal cost. (2) Due to the lack of competition, the monopoly firm may be productively inefficient to the extent that it does not produce at minimum long-run average total cost. (3) Due to barriers to entry, monopoly firms can charge excessive prices so as to enjoy positive economic profits in the long run. This can conflict with an equitable distribution of income to the extent that the excessive prices transfer real income from poorer consumers to already rich shareholders. The social benefits of monopoly may include: (1) In natural monopoly situations, a monopoly firm can be more productively efficient than a competitive firm. (2) The lure of long-run excess profits under monopoly may provide the incentive to invent or develop new products or services.		• **MyEconLab** Study Plan 10.4
10.5 The Regulation of a Natural Monopoly. Under marginal cost pricing, the monopoly firm is forced to produce at the output level where price just equals marginal cost. While this promotes allocative efficiency, this will result in perpetual losses in a natural monopoly situation, as marginal cost is below average total cost. With average cost pricing, the monopoly firm is forced to operate at a quantity level where price just equals average total cost. Compared to unregulated monopoly, average cost pricing will result in a lower price to consumers. As well, average cost pricing promotes an equitable distribution of income as the monopolist just earns a normal profit.	marginal cost pricing, 265 average cost pricing, 265	• **MyEconLab** Study Plan 10.5

PROBLEMS

(Answers to the odd-numbered problems appear at the back of the book.)

LO 10.1 Identify and explain the characteristics of a monopoly market structure.

1. For each of the following monopoly situations, state whether the barrier to entry is due to *economies of scale*, *predatory behaviour*, or *legal (government) restrictions*.
    a. A large supermarket maintains its monopoly position in a city subdivision by temporarily reducing prices every time a new competitor attempts to enter this market.
    b. A multinational drug company patents one of its new prescription drugs.
    c. The first company to bring cable television to a Canadian community eventually establishes itself as a natural monopoly in this market area.

2. Suppose that a monopolist faces the following demand schedule. Compute marginal revenue.

Price	Quantity Demanded	Marginal Revenue
$1000	1	$_____
920	2	$_____
840	3	$_____
760	4	$_____
680	5	$_____
600	6	$_____
520	7	$_____
440	8	$_____
350	9	$_____
260	10	$_____

In general, at each quantity level marginal revenue is _____ than price.

3. Explain the differences in the price elasticity of demand for an individual firm in a perfectly competitive industry as compared with a monopolist. Explain why the price elasticities differ.

4. A monopoly firm, being the sole supplier of its product, can charge any price it wants for the quantity level it decides to sell. Critically evaluate this statement.

LO 10.2 Using revenue and cost information, determine the monopolist's profit-maximizing or loss-minimizing level of output, price, and profit.

5. Use the graph to answer the questions.
    a. Suppose that a monopolist faces ATC_1. Define the rectangle that shows the monopolist's total costs at output rate Q. Also define the rectangle showing total revenue. Is the monopolist showing an economic loss, breakeven (normal profit), or an economic

profit? What is the significance of the MC = MR output?

b. Suppose that the monopolist faces ATC_2. Define the rectangle that shows the monopolist's total costs at output rate Q. Also define the rectangle showing total revenue. Is the monopolist showing an economic loss, breakeven (normal profit), or an economic profit? What is the significance of the MC = MR output?
c. Suppose that the monopolist faces ATC_3. Define the rectangle that shows the monopolist's total costs at output rate Q. Also define the rectangle showing total revenue. Is the monopolist showing an economic loss, breakeven (normal profit), or an economic profit? What is the significance of the MC = MR output?

6. In the text, we indicated that a monopolist will produce at the rate of output at which MR = MC and will then charge the highest price consistent with that output level. What conditions would exist if the monopolist charged a lower price? A higher price?

7. Examine the revenue and cost figures for a monopoly firm in the table below. For parts (a), (b), (c), and (d), assume a single-price monopoly.

Price	Quantity Demanded	Total Revenue	Marginal Revenue	Average Total Cost	Marginal Cost
$20	0	$_____			
16	1	$_____	$_____	$ 8.00	$ 5.00
12	2	$_____	$_____	7.50	7.00
10	3	$_____	$_____	8.00	9.00
7	4	$_____	$_____	9.25	13.00
4	5	$_____	$_____	11.00	18.00
0	6	$_____	$_____	13.16	24.00

a. Fill in all the blank columns in the table.
b. At what rate of output would the firm maximize profits?
c. What will be the profit-maximizing price?
d. What would be the amount of the maximum profits?

8. Explain why a monopolist will never set a price (and produce the corresponding output) at which the demand is price-inelastic.

9. Answer the questions based on the accompanying graph for a monopolist.

a. If this firm is a profit maximizer, how much output will it produce?
b. At what price will the firm sell its output?
c. How much profit or loss will this firm realize?

10. Pro-Golf Inc. has a monopoly over the manufacture and sale of the very popular Umph golf ball. The graph below describes Pro-Golf's per unit (per ball) daily costs and daily revenues in manufacturing the Umph golf ball.

a. How many balls per day should Pro-Golf manufacture in order to maximize its profits?
b. At the profit-maximizing level, what price will be charged per ball sold?

c. At the profit-maximizing level, what is the average total cost per ball?
d. At the profit-maximizing level, what is the daily profit per unit (per ball)?
e. At the profit-maximizing level, what is the daily total profits earned?

11. Due to a patent, RX Med Inc. has a monopoly on the manufacture and sale of the new anti-cold drug called Colds-Away. The graph below describes the per-unit (per bottle) monthly costs and monthly revenues in manufacturing Colds-Away.

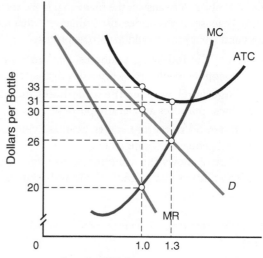

a. What is the profit-maximizing (or loss-minimizing) monthly production level?
b. What is the total dollar amount of the monthly maximum profits (or minimum losses)?

LO 10.3 Explain why a monopoly firm engages in price discrimination.

12. State the necessary conditions for price discrimination. Then, discuss how they might apply to the medical services of a doctor.

13. The accompanying table depicts the daily output, price, and costs of the only dry cleaner located near the campus of a small college town in a remote location. How much additional maximum profit can the monopoly dry cleaning firm earn by practising perfect price discrimination as opposed to charging a single price?

Output (suits cleaned)	Price per Suit	Total Cost	Marginal Cost
0	$8.00	$3.00	
1	7.50	6.00	$3.00
2	7.00	8.50	2.50
3	6.50	10.50	2.00
4	6.00	11.50	1.00
5	5.50	13.50	2.00
6	5.00	16.00	2.50
7	4.50	19.00	3.00
8	4.00	23.00	4.00

14. Explain how the four conditions necessary for price discrimination apply to Example 10–2, "Pricing Internet Service to Maximize Profit."

15. Refer to Problem 7 to answer the following:
    a. If the monopoly firm practises perfect price discrimination, the new marginal revenue column would be the same as the _____ column.
    b. Under perfect price discrimination, what rate of output would maximize profits?
    c. What would be the amount of the maximum profit under perfect price discrimination?

16. Refer to Problem 9 to answer the following. If the monopoly firm practises perfect price discrimination, what rate of output and what price would maximize profits?

17. For each of the following examples, explain how and why a monopoly would try to price discriminate:
    a. A large hotel supplies the same hotel rooms for business purposes and leisure purposes.
    b. A fast-food restaurant serves business people and retired people the same menu.
    c. A theatre shows the same movie to large families with children and to individuals and couples who have no children.

LO 10.4 Evaluate the long-run behaviour in monopoly from a social viewpoint.

18. Refer to Problem 9 to answer the following. Assume that the monopoly firm does not price discriminate.
    a. At the profit-maximizing output level, is the firm being productively efficient? Explain.
    b. At the profit-maximizing output level, is the firm being allocatively efficient? Explain.
    c. Explain how the profit behaviour of this monopoly firm can conflict with the goal of promoting a more equitable distribution of income.

19. What type of monopoly situation can
    a. promote productive efficiency?
    b. promote allocative efficiency?

20. Refer to Policy Example 10-4, "Swapping Songs on the Internet: Is It Really Free?" When is the practice of using the Internet to freely share files considered illegal? Who seems to be legally responsible for this practice? Explain how copyright can benefit society at large.

LO 10.5 Compare and contrast the use of marginal cost pricing versus average cost pricing in the regulation of a natural monopoly.

21. Unwired, Inc., has just obtained a patent on a satellite dish it invented that transmits TV programs and Internet services to homeowners. The table below describes the daily price and cost data for the satellite dishes it supplies, as a monopolist, to homeowners in the city of Digiton.

Quantity # dishes per day	Price per dish	Daily Total Revenue	Daily Marginal Revenue	Average Total Cost (per dish)	Marginal Cost (per dish)
1	$500		_____	$500	_____
2	450			350	$200
3	395			300	200
4	350			275	200
5	300			260	200
6	250			250	200
7	200			243	200

a. Assuming that Unwired, Inc., supplies the satellite dishes to Digiton residents without any government regulation, what would be Unwired's daily maximum profit quantity level? What would be Unwired's profit-maximizing price, assuming a single price monopoly? What would be the daily maximum profit?

b. If Unwired were forced by regulators to use marginal cost pricing, what daily quantity would Unwired supply to Digiton residents? What price would Unwired charge? What would be Unwired's daily profit (or loss) under marginal cost pricing?

c. If Unwired were forced by regulators to use average cost pricing, what daily quantity would Unwired supply to Digiton residents? What price would Unwired charge? What would be Unwired's daily profit (or loss) under average cost pricing?

d. From a social viewpoint, identify two reasons why average cost regulation would be preferred over unregulated monopoly.

22. The accompanying graph depicts a situation for a monopolist.

a. Under marginal cost pricing regulation, what would be the monopolist's quantity and price?

b. Under marginal cost pricing regulation, which rectangle in the graph would describe the firm's total losses?

c. Under average cost pricing regulation, what would be the monopolist's quantity and price?

d. What amount of profit (or loss) would the monopolist earn under average cost pricing?

e. In general, does average cost pricing encourage productive efficiency? Explain.

BUSINESS APPLICATION

LO 10.3 and 10.5 Explain why a monopoly firm engages in price discrimination; compare and contrast the use of marginal cost pricing versus average cost pricing in the regulation of a natural monopoly.

Accounting: Production, Pricing, and Profit Under Different Monopoly Situations

By obtaining a patent on a new acupuncture treatment that provides long-lasting relief for back pain, Dr. Kildare has achieved a monopoly situation. The following table describes the demand and cost behaviour associated with providing this treatment. The quantity in the first column of the table refers to the number of treatments provided per day. The $300 marginal cost showing in the table refers to the extra cost of providing the first treatment of the day. Since the doctor finds each treatment physically demanding, there is a point where diminishing returns set in and thus marginal cost eventually increases.

Quantity: # treatments per day	Price per treatment ($)	Total Revenue ($)	Marginal Revenue ($)	Average Total Cost ($)	Marginal Cost ($)
0					
1	720			420	300
2	660			350	280
3	580			300	200
4	500			350	500
5	420			420	700
6	340			510	960
7	260			620	1280
8	180			750	1660

Business Application Problems

1. Complete the Total Revenue and Marginal Revenue columns in the table.
2. Assume that the monopoly firm (Dr. Kildare) is not regulated and does not price discriminate.
   a. Find the profit-maximizing quantity level. Explain.
   b. Calculate the total dollar profit earned at the profit-maximizing level.
3. Assume that the monopoly firm practices perfect price discrimination.
   a. Determine the profit-maximizing quantity level.
   b. Calculate the total daily dollar profit at the profit-maximizing level.
4. Assume that the monopoly firm is regulated so as to receive a "fair profit."
   a. Find the "fair profit" quantity (imposed by the government). Explain.
   b. What would be the amount of economic profit earned under the "fair profit" form of regulation? Briefly explain.

The Deadweight Loss Due to Monopoly

We have just studied how a monopoly situation can conflict with the goal of allocative efficiency. That is, when compared with perfect competition, monopoly misallocates society's resources by restricting output. In this appendix, we examine some concepts that will allow us to estimate the total loss in economic well-being resulting from the allocative inefficiency that occurs in a monopoly industry.

Consumer Surplus

If you think about what made you feel good about a recent purchase, it is likely that you ended up paying less than the price at which you valued the product or service. When considering a specific market situation, **consumer surplus** refers to the difference between the maximum amount that consumers are willing to pay and the actual amount paid for all units of a product consumed.

Consumer surplus The difference between the maximum amount that consumers are willing to pay and the actual amount paid for all units of a product consumed.

For any given market situation, the consumer surplus can be determined once the market demand curve and the market price and quantity are known. For example, Figure E–1 describes the market for frying chickens in a Canadian province. If we assume that this is a perfectly competitive market, the market price and quantity will be $5 per kilogram and 3 million kilograms, respectively.

We can compute the consumer surplus in Figure E–1, as follows. The maximum that a consumer is willing to pay for the very first unit of chicken consumed is given by the height of the demand curve at a quantity of one kilogram, which is close to $8 (note that since the scale is in millions, the very first kilogram is close to zero kilograms on the x-axis). Since the price actually paid for the first kilogram is $5, the consumer derives a "surplus" of $8 − $5 = $3. This $3 "surplus" is described by the vertical distance between the demand curve and the $5 price line at the quantity of one kilogram (the height of the line AC in Figure E–1). The consumer surplus for all 3 million kilograms of chicken consumed would be equal to the area of the triangle ABC in Figure E–1. Since the area of a triangle is $(1/2 \times base \times height)$ the consumer surplus in this chicken market is $(1/2 \times 3 \times \$3) = \$4.5$ million. In general, the consumer surplus is the area of the region below the demand curve and above the price line. This surplus stems from a negatively sloped demand curve, which implies that there exists different willingness to pay for different units of the same product.

FIGURE E–1

Consumer Surplus in the Chicken Market

Given the market price of $5 per kilogram. and the market quantity of 3 million kilograms, the consumer surplus is the area of the region below the demand curve and above the price over the 3 million kilograms consumed. This is the shaded area of triangle ABC, which equals (½ × base × height), which equals (½ × 3 × 3) = $ 4.5 million.

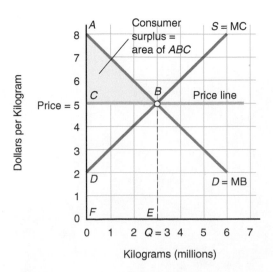

Another way of determining the consumer surplus from Figure E–1 is to subtract the total amount that consumers paid from the total consumer value derived from consuming the 3 million kilograms of chicken. The total consumer value equals the total area under the demand curve, over the 3 million kilogram quantity level, which equals the area of the region *ABEF*. The total amount paid by the consumers equals the area of region *BEFC*. The difference between the total consumer value (*ABEF*) and the total amount paid (*BEFC*) is the area of triangle ABC, which we now know is the consumer surplus.

Viewed in this way, we can see that the $4.5 million consumer surplus represents the additional consumer value or net benefit derived from consuming chicken as opposed to alternative products. In this way, we can say that consumer surplus measures the net benefit (well being) to buyers of participating in a specific market.

Producer Surplus

We now turn to examine the well-being of producers or suppliers in a specific market. **Producer surplus** refers to the difference between the actual amount that producers receive for a product and the lowest amount that they would be prepared to accept for it, which is equal to the marginal cost.

For any given market situation, the producer surplus can be determined once the market supply curve and the market price and quantity are known. In the chicken market, in Figure E-2, with the market price and quantity being $5 per kilogram and 3 million kilograms, respectively, we can compute the producer surplus as follows.

In order to produce the first kilogram of chicken, a producer must receive a minimum amount equal to its marginal cost, which is $2 (the height of the supply curve at a quantity of one kilogram). Since the price actually paid to a supplier for the first kilogram is $5, the supplier derives a "surplus" of $5 − $2 = $3. This $3 "surplus" is described by the vertical distance between the supply curve and the $5 price line at the quantity of one kilogram. The producer surplus related to all 3 million kilograms of chicken produced would be equal to the area of the triangle *BCD* in Figure E–2. Since the area of a triangle is (½ × base × height), the producer surplus in this chicken market is (½ × 3 × $3) = $4.5 million. In general, the producer surplus is the area of the region above the supply curve and below the price line. This surplus stems from a positively sloped supply curve, which implies that there exists a different marginal cost for different units of the same product. The producer surplus measures the benefit (well-being) to suppliers of participating in a specific market.

Producer surplus The difference between the actual amount that producers receive for a product and the lowest amount that they would be prepared to accept for it.

FIGURE E-2

Producer Surplus in the Chicken Market

Given the market price of $5 per kilogram, and the market quantity of 3 million kilograms, the producer surplus is the area of the region above the supply curve and below the price over the 3 million kilograms produced. This is the shaded area of triangle *BCD*, which equals (1/2 × base × height), which equals (1/2 × 3 × 3) = $ 4.5 million.

Allocative Efficiency and Perfect Competition

As was noted in Chapter 9, perfect competition establishes an equilibrium price and quantity where industry demand equals industry supply. This means that perfect competition promotes *allocative efficiency* as production takes place to the point where the marginal benefit of the last unit produced equals its marginal cost. At this allocatively efficient quantity, it can be shown that the sum of consumer and producer surpluses is maximized.

Allocative efficiency occurs when the sum of consumer and producer surpluses is maximized.

Figure E–3 describes a perfectly competitive chicken market, where the equilibrium price is \$5 (P_{pc}) and the equilibrium quantity is 3 million (Q_{pc}). At this equilibrium, the sum of consumer and producer surplus is maximized at (\$4.5 million + \$4.5 million) = \$9 million. Try as you might, you will not find a better quantity, in terms of maximizing consumer and producer surpluses. As you can see from Figure E–3, if the quantity is set at a level below 3 million kilograms, say, at 2 million kilograms, consumer surplus and producer surplus will be reduced by areas M and N, respectively. Similarly, if production is increased beyond 3 million kilograms, say, to 4 million, consumer and producer surpluses will be reduced by areas S and R, respectively.

Allocative Inefficiency and Monopoly

Suppose that all of the chicken producers in the province decide to form a marketing board that establishes a monopoly in terms of the sale of chicken. While marginal costs (the supply curve) stay the same, the monopoly's marginal revenue now lies below the demand curve, as shown in Figure E–4. In order to maximize profits, the chicken monopoly produces where marginal revenue equals marginal cost, which is at a quantity level of 2 million kilograms (Q_m) and at a price of \$6 per kilogram (Pm). Note that the monopoly quantity level is 1 million kilograms less than in perfect competition, and the monopoly price is \$1 higher than the competitive price.

FIGURE E–3

Perfect Competition and Allocative Efficiency

In this perfectly competitive chicken industry, the equilibrium price is P_{pc} = \$5 and the equilibrium quantity = Q_{pc} = 3 million kilograms. At this quantity, the sum of consumer and producer surpluses is maximized, which implies allocative efficiency. If the quantity is reduced to 2 million kilograms, consumer surplus and producer surpluses will be reduced by areas M and N, respectively. If production is increased to 4 million kilograms, consumer and producer surplus will be reduced by areas S and R, respectively.

The allocative efficiency loss due to monopoly is the loss in consumer and producer surpluses due to the reduction in quantity from 3 million to 2 million kilograms. The consumer surplus lost due to this reduction in quantity is the area of the triangle M, which equals $\frac{1}{2} \times 1 \times 1 = \$0.5$ million. Similarly, the loss in producer surplus due to the

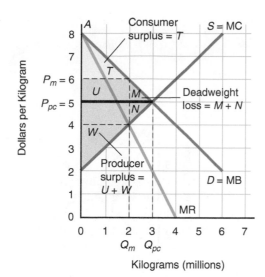

FIGURE E–4

Monopoly and Allocative Inefficiency

When the chicken industry is monopolized, the quantity drops from 3 million to 2 million kilograms and the price increases from $5 to $6 per kilogram. The reduction in quantity causes a reduction in consumer and producer surplus equal to the area of regions M and N combined, which equals $(\frac{1}{2} \times 2 \times 1) = \$1$ million. This is the deadweight loss due to allocative inefficiency in monopoly. The increase in price, under monopoly, results in a transfer in surplus from consumers to producers equal to the area of rectangle U, which equals $2 million.

reduction in quantity is the area of the triangle N, which equals $\frac{1}{2} \times 1 \times 1 = \$0.5$ million. The allocative efficiency loss resulting from this monopoly equals the combined loss in consumer and producer surplus, which equals $\$0.5 + \$0.5 = \$1$ million (area of regions M and N). We call this loss the **deadweight loss**—the combined loss in producer and consumer surplus resulting from the reduction in quantity under monopoly. The deadweight loss of $1 million is not recouped elsewhere in the economy, and so it is a loss to society as a whole.

Deadweight loss The combined loss in producer and consumer surplus resulting from the reduction in quantity under monopoly.

If you carefully examine Figure E–4, you will notice that under monopoly there is a loss in consumer surplus, in addition to the area of region M. The additional loss in consumer surplus is the area of rectangle U, which equals (height × length) = $1 \times 2 = \$2$ million. This $2 million loss is due to the higher price charged, which translates to a $2 million gain for the monopolist in the form of additional producer surplus. Note that this $2 million loss in consumer surplus is not a deadweight loss, as it is recouped by another group in the economy—the chicken producers.

APPENDIX SUMMARY

1. Consumer surplus refers to the difference between the maximum amount that consumers are willing to pay and the actual amount paid for all units of a product consumed. It is described as the area under the demand curve and above the price line over the quantity of the product consumed. It exists due to a negatively sloped demand curve, which reflects the differences in willingness to pay for different units of the same product. Consumer surplus refers to the net benefit that consumers get in participating in a market—a benefit that they do not pay for.

2. Producer surplus refers to the difference between the actual amount that producers receive for a product and the lowest amount that they would be prepared to accept for it. It is described as the area over the supply curve and below the price line over the quantity of the product produced. It exists due to a positively sloped supply curve, which reflects the differences in marginal cost incurred when producing different units of the same product. Producer surplus refers to the net benefit that suppliers get in participating in a market—a benefit that they do not pay for.

3. A perfectly competitive industry is allocatively efficient as it sets a price and quantity that maximizes the sum of consumer and producer surplus.

4. A monopoly industry restricts quantity and charges a higher price, when compared with perfect competition. The deadweight loss refers to the loss in producer and consumer surplus resulting from the reduction in quantity supplied, under monopoly. This deadweight loss is used to measure the cost of allocative inefficiency in monopoly.

5. The higher price in monopoly causes a transfer in surplus from consumers to producers.

APPENDIX PROBLEMS

E-1. Refer to the data in Figure 10–4 in Chapter 10 on page 252. Assume that the monopoly firm in Figure 10–4 operates at the profit-maximizing output level, and charges a single price for all units sold.

   a.   Compute the total consumer surplus.

   b.   Compute the total producer surplus.

   c.   Is this monopoly firm maximizing the sum of producer and consumer surpluses? Explain.

E-2. What happens to the consumer surplus in a market where a monopoly firm practises perfect price discrimination? Explain.

E-3. The following diagram describes the whole-wheat bagel market in a mid-size Canadian city.

   a.   If the whole-wheat bagels are supplied under perfect competition, compute the sum of the consumer and producer surpluses.

   b.   If the whole-wheat bagels are supplied under monopoly, compute the total dollar loss due to allocative inefficiency.

Monopolistic Competition and Oligopoly

For most of this century, two firms have dominated the Canadian market for beer—John Labatt Ltd. and Molson Brewing Co. Ltd. Molson, Canada's largest brewer, contributed to 42 percent of all Canadian beer sales in 2009. The two companies combined accounted for 82 percent of national beer sales. Labatt Blue is the best-selling Canadian beer in the world. Over the past two decades, the big two breweries have increasingly been challenged by imported beers, and by the entry of small microbreweries offering high-quality "craft" beers. Labatt and Molson appear to have decided not to fight the entry of these competitors. To understand this strategic behaviour, you need to learn more about markets that are not perfectly competitive but, at the same time, are not pure monopolies.

LEARNING OBJECTIVES

After reading this chapter, you should be able to:

11.1 Identify and explain the characteristics of monopolistic competition.

11.2 Using revenue and cost information, determine the price, output, and profit for a firm in monopolistic competition in the short run.

11.3 Describe long-run equilibrium in monopolistic competition.

11.4 Identify and explain the characteristics of oligopoly.

11.5 Identify and explain the types of pricing behaviour that can occur in oligopoly.

11.6 Identify, explain, and evaluate the various nonprice forms of competition in oligopoly.

11.7 Evaluate the behaviour in oligopoly from a social viewpoint.

MyEconLab helps you master each objective and study more efficiently. See end of chapter for details.

DID YOU KNOW THAT...?

The so-called father of the modern department store, John Wanamaker, once said, "Half the money I spend on advertising is wasted. The trouble is, I don't know which half." Obviously, Canadian businesses do not know either, for they continue to advertise more each year. Total annual advertising expenditures in Canada amount to billions of dollars. The number of ads popping up on the Internet shows that Canadian businesses will leave no stone unturned in their quest to let people know about their existence, what they have to sell, how they sell it, where it can be bought, and at what price.

Advertising did not show up in our analysis of perfect competition and monopoly. Nonetheless, it plays a large role in industries that lie somewhere between these two extreme types of market structures. A combination of consumers' preferences for variety and competition among producers has led to similar but differentiated products in the marketplace. This situation has been described as monopolistic competition, the subject of the first part of this chapter. In the second part of the chapter, we look at how firms in industries with a few major competitors make strategic decisions. Such decisions do not exist for pure monopolists, who do not have to worry about actual competitors. And clearly, perfect competitors cannot make any strategic decisions, for they must take the market price as given. We call firms that have the ability to make strategic decisions oligopolies, which we will define more formally later in this chapter.

11.1 The Characteristics of Monopolistic Competition

In the 1920s and 1930s, economists became increasingly aware that there were many industries for which both the perfectly competitive model and the pure monopoly model did not apply and did not seem to yield very accurate predictions. Theoretical and empirical research was instituted to develop some sort of middle ground. Two separately developed models of *monopolistic competition* resulted. American economist Edward Chamberlin published *The Theory of Monopolistic Competition* in 1933. The same year, Britain's Joan Robinson published *The Economics of Imperfect Competition*. In this chapter, we will outline the theory as presented by Chamberlin.

Chamberlin defined **monopolistic competition** as a market structure in which there is a relatively large number of firms offering similar but differentiated products. Monopolistic competition, therefore, has the following features:

Monopolistic competition
A market structure in which there is a relatively large number of firms offering similar but differentiated products.

1.   Large numbers of sellers in a highly competitive market
2.   Easy entry of new firms in the long run
3.   Product differentiation

Even a cursory look at the Canadian economy leads to the conclusion that monopolistic competition is the dominant form of market structure in Canada. Indeed, that is true of all developed economies.

Number of Firms

In a perfectly competitive situation, there is an extremely large number of firms; in pure monopoly, there is only one. In monopolistic competition, there is a large number of firms, but not as many as in perfect competition. This fact has several important implications for a monopolistically competitive industry.

1.   *Small share of market.* With so many firms, each firm has a relatively small share of the total market. Thus, it has only a very small amount of control over the market clearing price.
2.   *Lack of collusion.* With so many firms, it is very difficult for all of them to get together to collude—to cooperate in setting a pure monopoly price (and output). Price fixing in a monopolistically competitive industry is virtually impossible. Also, barriers to entry

are minor, and the flow of new firms into the industry makes collusive agreements less likely. The large number of firms makes the monitoring and detection of cheating very costly and extremely difficult. This difficulty is compounded by differentiated products and high rates of innovation; collusive agreements are easier for a homogeneous product than for heterogeneous ones.

3. *Independence.* Because there are so many firms, each one acts independently of the others. No firm attempts to take into account the reaction of all of its rival firms—that would be impossible with so many rivals. Rivals' reactions to output and price changes are largely ignored.

Easy Entry

For any current monopolistic competitor, potential competitors are always lurking in the background. Substantial barriers to entry, such as economies of scale, patents, and large initial capital costs, do not exist in monopolistic competition.

Product Differentiation

Perhaps the most important feature of monopolistic competition is **product differentiation**, which refers to the ways that the firm distinguishes its product, in a positive manner, from similar products or services offered by competitors. The firm's product can be positively distinguished by consumers on the basis of its physical attributes; the bundle of services offered with the product; the product's superior location or accessibility; sales promotion and advertising; and by other qualities associated with the product, real or imagined.

> **Product differentiation** The ways that the firm distinguishes its product, in a positive manner, from similar products or services offered by competitors.

Product differentiation means that the firm has some control over the price it charges. Unlike the perfectly competitive firm, the monopolistic competitive firm faces a downward-sloping demand curve, as shown in Figure 11–1. This means that the monopolistically competitive firm can increase the price of its product and still manage to attract loyal customers, due to product differentiation. For example, suppose that the typical daily rate charged to stay in a motel in a Canadian city is $75. One motel owner may decide to charge $100 per day. While this firm may end up renting fewer rooms per day than its competitors, some customers will still stay at this motel due to the motel's superior fitness facilities, convenient parking, and central location.

The elasticity of the monopolistically competitive firm's demand curve will depend on the degree to which the firm can positively differentiate its product in the eyes of the consumers in the industry. If the firm is very successful in establishing customer loyalty based on nonprice factors, then the firm's demand curve will be less elastic. Keep in mind, however, that the demand curve of the monopolistically competitive firm will still be relatively elastic compared with a monopoly situation, due to the presence of close substitutes.

A good example of a monopolistically competitive industry is the restaurant industry (excluding fast-food restaurants) in a Canadian city. Many small firms compete in the restaurant industry. Since the initial capital investment is not significant, it is relatively easy to enter this type of industry. Product differentiation in the restaurant industry can be established in a variety of ways. Any firm may choose to establish customer loyalty on the basis of the ethnic origin of the menu offerings, the superior service offered to patrons, the consistency of the quality of the meal established, the ease of parking at a convenient location, and the type of clientele attracted by the firm's advertising and brand image.

Monopolistically competitive industries are commonly found in the following sectors of the economy: retail apparel and gifts, personal services, entertainment and amusements, and hospitality. Example 11–1 describes a popular Canadian retail firm operating under conditions of monopolistic competition.

FIGURE 11–1

Short-Run and Long-Run Equilibrium with Monopolistic Competition

In part (a), the typical monopolistic competitor is shown making economic profits. If that were the situation, there would be entry into the industry, forcing the demand curve for the individual firm to decrease and shift leftward. Eventually, firms would find themselves in the situation depicted in part (c), where zero economic profits are being made. In part (b), the typical firm is in a monopolistically competitive industry making economic losses. If that were the case, firms would leave the industry. Each remaining firm's demand curve would shift outward to the right. Eventually, the typical firm would find itself in the situation depicted in part (c).

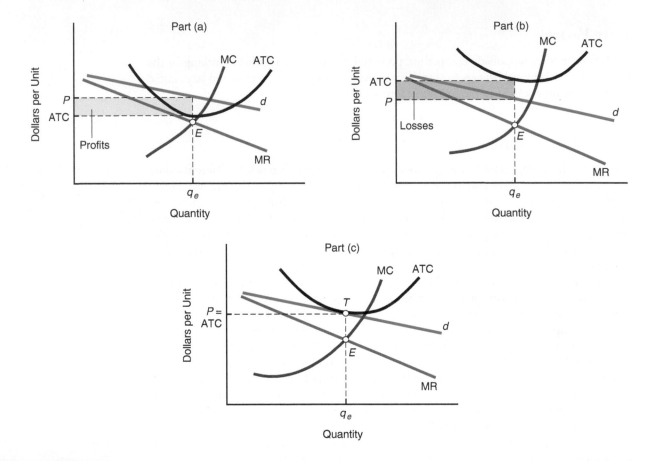

EXAMPLE 11–1   A Canadian Retail Success: Twenty-Seven Years Running

What types of product differentiation is The Running Room focusing on?

Did you know that John Stanton, the founder of our nation's renowned Running Room Canada Inc., used to be an overweight food industry executive who smoked two packs of cigarettes a day? After struggling through a 3-kilometre fun run with his sons in 1981, Stanton realized that he had to change his lifestyle. He started to run secretly before dawn so his neighbours did not notice just how out of shape he was. Recognizing the need to sell quality running shoes by staff knowledgeable about running, in 1984 Stanton opened a store and meeting place for runners in an old house in Edmonton. Initially, he shared this location with a hairdresser shop.

On May 6, 2010, the *Montreal Gazette* announced that the Running Room would open its 103rd store in Canada in downtown Montreal in August 2010. It is estimated that the company's 2010 annual sales of running and walking shoes, related equipment and apparel, and related services will amount to approximately $100 million. The family-owned company is reported to be the largest specialty running and walking products business in Canada.

In the Montreal area, the Yellow Pages list hundreds of separately owned stores selling retail footwear and related products and services. Some of these stores are small, independent

continued

retailers that target a specific market niche, such as work-related footwear, children's shoes, golf shoes, western footwear, and shoes for customers with specific foot problems. Others are focused on providing footwear at a discounted price, such as Payless Shoes and Shoe Ware-house. Yet others are in the form of shoe departments in conveniently located department stores that offer brand name shoes at regular as well as discounted prices. Sporting goods stores have also become popular sellers of all sorts of sport-related footwear.

Running Room has successfully focused on providing high-quality products and services for customers who want a healthy and fit lifestyle that includes running and walking routines. Based on knowledgeable staff, all of whom are runners and fitness walkers, Running Room provides top brand-name footwear that meets the individual needs of customers in terms of gender, level of running/walking experience, and foot strike. To complement its products, the company offers a variety of services, which include clinics in Fitness Walking, Learn to Run, Marathon, Half Marathon, 10K Training, Personal Best, and For Women Only Running, and a free Running Room Club, which encourages runners of all levels to run in a group twice weekly. Each year, the Running Room sponsors, organizes, and promotes numerous walks, runs, and charity events.

For critical analysis: Based on this example, would the Canadian retail footwear industry be classified as perfect competition or monopolistic competition? Explain.

Sources: "Running Room opens eighth store in Quebec." *The Gazette* (Montreal). May 6, 2010. Pg. B3; "Our history." Running Room. http://www.runningroom.com.

11.2 Short-Run Price, Output, and Profit in Monopolistic Competition

Now that we are aware of the assumptions underlying the monopolistic competition model, we can analyze the price and output behaviour of each firm in a monopolistically competitive industry. We assume in the analysis that follows that the desired product type and quality have been chosen. We further assume that the budget and the type of promotional activity have already been chosen and do not change.

The Individual Firm's Demand and Cost Curves

Because the individual firm is not a perfect competitor, its demand curve slopes downward, as is shown in all three parts of Figure 11–1. Hence, it faces a marginal revenue curve that is also downward sloping and below the demand curve. To find the profit-maximizing rate of output and the profit-maximizing price, we go to the output where the marginal cost curve intersects the marginal revenue curve from below. That gives us the profit-maximizing output rate. Then, we draw a vertical line up to the demand curve. That gives us the price that can be charged to sell exactly that quantity produced. This is what we have done in Figure 11–1. In each part, a marginal cost curve intersects the marginal revenue curve at E. The profit-maximizing rate of output is q_e, and the profit-maximizing price is P.

Short-Run Equilibrium

In the short run, it is possible for a monopolistic competitor to make economic profits—profits over and above the normal rate of return or beyond what is necessary to keep that firm in that industry. We show such a situation in part (a) of Figure 11–1. The average total cost curve is drawn in below the demand curve, d, at the profit-maximizing rate of output, q_e. Economic profits are shown by the shaded rectangle in that part.

Losses in the short run are clearly also possible. They are presented in part (b) of Figure 11–1. Here, the average total cost curve lies everywhere above the individual firm's demand curve, d. The losses are marked as the shaded rectangle.

Just as with any market structure or any firm, in the short run, it is possible to observe either economic profits or economic losses. In either case, the price does not equal marginal cost but, rather, is above it. Therefore, there is some misallocation of resources, a topic that we will discuss later in this chapter.

11.3 Long-Run Equilibrium in Monopolistic Competition

What can we expect of the typical firm in monopolistic competition in the long run? Economic profits will be reduced to zero—either through the entry of new firms that see a chance to make a higher rate of return than elsewhere, or by changes in the product quality and advertising outlays of existing firms in the industry. (Profitable products will be imitated by other firms.) As for economic losses in the short run, they will disappear in the long run because the firms that suffer them will leave the industry. They will go into another business where the expected rate of return is at least normal. Parts (a) and (b) of Figure 11–1, therefore, represent only short-run situations for a monopolistically competitive firm. In the long run, the average total cost curve will just touch the individual firm's demand curve d at the particular price that is profit-maximizing for that particular firm. This is shown in part (c) of Figure 11–1. This situation is called long-run equilibrium in monopolistic competition.

A word of warning: This is an idealized, long-run equilibrium situation for each firm in the industry. It does not mean that even in the long run we will observe every single firm in a monopolistically competitive industry making exactly zero economic profits or just a normal rate of return. We live in a dynamic world. All we are saying is that if this model is correct, the rate of return will tend toward normal—economic profits will tend toward zero.

Comparing Monopolistic Competition with Perfect Competition

In the long run, there are similarities and differences between perfect competition and monopolistic competition.

LONG-RUN PROFITS? Due to easy entry, the typical firm operating in either perfect competition or monopolistic competition can expect to earn zero economic profit or just a normal profit. In Figure 11–2, we can see that at the profit-maximizing output level for both perfect competition and monopolistic competition, price equals average total cost. Some economists would view these normal profits as being consistent with the goal of an equitable distribution of income.

PRODUCTIVE EFFICIENCY? Figure 11–2 part (a) reminds us that, at the profit-maximizing level of output, q_1, the typical perfectly competitive firm operates at minimum average total cost. That is, productive efficiency is being achieved in perfect competition, assuming the absence of economies of scale.

An examination of Figure 11–2 part (b) shows that at the profit-maximizing output level, q_2, the monopolistically competitive firm is operating at a quantity level that is less than the productively efficient level. Figure 11–2 part (b) should help you understand that because the demand curve is downward sloping in monopolistic competition, the long-run normal profit situation must occur to the left of the quantity where average total cost is at a minimum. This situation is one of **excess capacity**—a situation where the firm is operating at an output level below that required to achieve minimum average total cost. Such characteristics as easy entry and product differentiation result in a long-run situation where there are too many competitors, each saddled with excess capacity. As an example, the typical motel will have vacancy signs at frequent times of the year or the typical restaurant will have empty tables during many hours of each day. In other words, society's limited resources are being wasted!

Excess capacity A situation where the firm is operating at an output level below that required to achieve minimum average total cost.

FIGURE 11–2

Comparison of the Perfect Competitor with the Monopolistic Competitor

In part (a), the perfectly competitive firm has zero economic profits in the long run. The price is set equal to marginal cost, and the price is P_1. The firm's demand curve is just tangent to the minimum point on its average total cost curve, which means that the firm is operating at an optimum rate of production. With the monopolistically

competitive firm in part (b), there are also zero economic profits in the long run. The price is greater than marginal cost; the monopolistically competitive firm does not find itself at the minimum point on its average total cost curve. It is operating at a rate of output to the left of the minimum point on the ATC curve.

Part (a)
Perfect Competition

Part (b)
Monopolistic Competition

CONSUMER CHOICE? Chamberlin contended that the higher average total cost typical in monopolistic competition, when compared with the perfectly competitive firm, represents what he called the cost of producing "differentness." Chamberlin argued that it is rational for consumers to be willing to pay more for a product in an industry that offers a variety of close, but not identical, substitutes. Put differently, a range of consumer choices adds value to consumers.

11.4 The Characteristics of Oligopoly

There is another important market structure that we have yet to discuss. It involves a situation in which a few large firms dominate an entire industry. They are not competitive in the sense that we have used the term; they are not even monopolistically competitive. And because there are a few of them, a pure monopoly does not exist. We call such a situation an **oligopoly**, which consists of a small number of interdependent sellers. Each firm in the industry knows that other firms will react to its changes in prices, quantities, and qualities. An oligopoly market structure can exist for either a homogeneous or a differentiated product.

Oligopoly A market situation that consists of a small number of interdependent sellers.

Small Number of Firms

How many is "a small number of firms"? More than two but less than 100? The question is not easy to answer. Basically, though, oligopoly exists when a handful of firms dominate the industry enough to set prices. The top few firms in the industry account for an overwhelming percentage of total industry output.

Oligopolies usually involve three to five big companies dominating the industry. The Canadian banking industry is dominated by five large firms: the Royal Bank of Canada (RBC), TD Canada Trust, the Canadian Imperial Bank of Commerce (CIBC), the Bank of Montreal (BMO), and the Bank of Nova Scotia (Scotiabank). From World War II until the 1970s, the automobile industry was dominated by three large firms: General Motors (GM), Chrysler, and Ford.

Interdependence

Strategic dependence A situation in which one firm's actions with respect to price, quality, advertising, and related changes may be strategically countered by the reactions of one or more other firms in the industry.

All markets and all firms are, in a sense, interdependent. When a few large firms dominate an industry, they become strategically dependent on each others' actions. **Strategic dependence** is a situation in which one firm's actions with respect to price, quality, advertising, and related changes may be strategically countered by the reactions of one or more other firms in the industry. Such dependence can exist only when there are a limited number of major firms in an industry. The firms must recognize that they are interdependent. Any action on the part of one firm with respect to output, price, quality, or product differentiation will cause a reaction on the part of other firms. A model of such mutual interdependence is difficult to build, but examples are not hard to find in the real world. Oligopolists in the supermarket industry, for example, are constantly reacting to each other.

Recall that in the model of perfect competition, each firm ignores the reactions of other firms because each is able to sell all that it wants at the going market price. At the other extreme, the pure monopolist does not have to worry about the reaction of current rivals because there are none. In an oligopolistic market structure, the managers of firms are like generals in a war: They must attempt to predict the reaction of rival firms. It is a strategic game.

Barriers to Entry

Why are some industries dominated by a few large firms? Since new businesses are formed on a daily basis, some type of barrier to entry must be preventing these new firms from entering oligopoly industries.

ECONOMIES OF SCALE. In some industries, economies of scale prevent the entry of new firms. Recall that, when economies of scale exist, the firm's long-run average total cost declines as the firm increases its size of operation. Consequently, larger firms have a cost advantage over smaller firms. Given a limited total market demand, this cost disadvantage may prevent smaller new firms from entering the industry. Due to the high fixed costs related to acquiring and maintaining airplanes, as well as expensive reservation systems, economies of scale have been a factor in explaining why we have oligopoly (and, in some cases, monopoly) situations in the provision of domestic flights to Canadian cities.

LEGAL BARRIERS. Legal barriers to entry such as patents and government regulation may explain why a few firms dominate a market. In Canada, many new prescription drugs are protected by patents. In these cases, the company owning the patent may permit other competitors to sell similar substitutes of the new drug in return for payment of royalties, resulting in an oligopoly situation. The Canadian Radio-television and Telecommunications Commission (CRTC) is the regulatory agency of the federal government, in charge of licensing certain industries, including television and radio broadcasting, cable distribution, and Direct-to-Home. For many years, the commission's licensing practices have helped maintain oligopolies in such industries as cable TV distribution and national television network broadcasting.

FIRM-CREATED BARRIERS. The existing firms in an oligopoly industry frequently engage in behaviours that serve as barriers to entry for potential new firms. In some cases, existing oligopoly firms significantly lower the prices of their products, which makes it difficult for potential firms to earn a profit if they decide to enter the industry. Many oligopoly firms engage heavily in product differentiation, advertising, and brand proliferation, making it very costly for new entrants to gain a foothold in the market. In yet other oligopoly situations, the existing firms may practise exclusionary tactics that make it difficult for consumers to switch to the products that new firms offer. These firm-created barriers to entry will be discussed in more depth in later sections of this chapter.

Primarily, we have been talking about oligopoly in theoretical terms. It is time to look at the actual picture of oligopolies in Canada.

Measuring Industry Concentration

As we have stated, oligopoly is a situation where a few interdependent firms control a large part of the total output in an industry. In an attempt to identify the prevalence of oligopoly in Canadian industries, economists compute the **concentration ratio**—the percentage of total industry sales contributed by the four largest firms—for each industry.

Table 11–1 provides four-firm domestic concentration ratios for selected Canadian industries. In this table, you will notice that the concentration ratio for the beer industry is 90 percent. This means that the four largest Canadian breweries account for 90 percent of all annual Canadian beer sales. When an industry has a high concentration ratio, we refer to this industry as a highly concentrated industry.

Concentration ratio The percentage of total industry sales contributed by the four largest firms.

	Percentage of Value of Total Domestic Shipments Accounted for by the Top Four Firms
Tobacco products	99
Beer	90
Petroleum and coal products	75
Storage	72
Nonalcoholic beverages	69
Transportation equipment	68
Communications	65
Primary metals	63
Metal mining	59

Source: Adapted from Statistics Canada.

TABLE 11–1

Four-Firm Domestic Concentration Ratios for Selected Canadian Industries

In general, for a given industry, the higher the level of concentration, the lower the level of industry competition. However, one must realize in computing concentration ratios that competing firms are identified assuming national market boundaries. In some cases, this may not accurately reflect the true state of competition in an industry. As an example, for a number of years the "Big Three" North American automakers—GM, Chrysler, and Ford—were the dominant firms actually manufacturing vehicles on Canadian soil. This situation would result in a relatively high domestic concentration ratio, suggesting a high level of concentration and a very low level of competition in the Canadian auto industry. However, to the extent that Canadian consumers were purchasing cars produced in other countries, then the industry definition used to compute the concentration ratio is inaccurate. In fact, if we expand the size of the industry to include foreign automakers, the level of concentration would be reduced.

What industries in Canada are oligopolistic in nature? If we recognize that some industries are local in nature while others can be defined at the national or international level, we can identify quite a few oligopoly industries. Some examples include motor vehicles, petroleum-refining products, tobacco products, beer products, soft drinks, pet foods, cereals, airline services, banking services, long-distance service, TV distribution services, credit card services, car rentals in airports, daily newspapers in a city, cement manufacturers in a city, and computer manufacturers.

11.5 Price Behaviour in Oligopoly

At this point, we should be able to show oligopoly price and output determination in the way we showed it for perfect competition, pure monopoly, and monopolistic competition, but we cannot. Whenever there are relatively few firms competing in an industry, each can and does react to the price, quantity, quality, and product innovations that the others undertake. The manner in which each firm reacts to its rival is called the oligopolist's **best response function**.

Best response function The manner in which one oligopolist reacts to a change in price, output, or quality made by another competitor in the industry.

Oligopolistic competitors are interdependent. Consequently, the decision makers in such firms must employ strategies. And we must be able to model their strategic behaviour if we wish to predict how prices and outputs are determined in oligopolistic market structures. In general, we can think of the reactions of other firms to one firm's actions as part of a game that is played by all firms in the industry. Not surprisingly, economists have developed *game theory* models to describe firms' rational interactions. **Game theory** is the analytical framework in which two or more individuals, companies, or nations compete for certain payoffs that depend on the strategy that the others employ.

Some Basic Notions about Game Theory

Games can be either cooperative or noncooperative. If firms get together to collude or fix prices, that is considered a **cooperative game**. Whenever it is too costly for firms to negotiate such collusive agreements and to enforce them, they are in a **noncooperative game** situation. Most strategic behaviour in the marketplace would be described as a noncooperative game.

Games can be classified by whether the payoffs are negative, zero, or positive. A **zero-sum game** is one in which one player's losses are offset by another player's gains; at any time, sum totals are zero. If two retailers have an absolutely fixed total number of customers, the customers that one retailer wins over are exactly equal to the customers that the other retailer loses. A **negative-sum game** is one in which players as a group lose at the end of the game (although one perhaps by more than the other, and it's possible for one or more players to win). A **positive-sum game** is one in which players as a group end up better off. Some economists describe all voluntary exchanges as positive-sum games. After an exchange, both the buyer and the seller are better off than they were prior to the exchange.

Noncooperative Price Behaviour

Because oligopoly firms are mutually interdependent, each competitor (decision maker) has to devise a **strategy**, which is defined as a rule used to make a choice. The goal of the decision maker is, of course, to devise a strategy that is more successful than alternative strategies. Whenever a firm's decision makers can come up with certain strategies that are generally successful no matter what actions competitors take, these are called **dominant strategies**. The dominant strategy always yields the unique best action for the decision maker no matter what action the other "players" undertake. To better understand a noncooperative game and the notion of a dominant strategy, consider Example 11–2, "The Prisoners' Dilemma."

Game theory The analytical framework in which two or more individuals, companies, or nations compete for certain payoffs that depend on the strategy that the others employ.

Cooperative game A game in which firms get together to collude or fix prices.

Noncooperative game A game in which it is too costly for firms to negotiate collusive agreements and to enforce them.

Zero-sum game A game in which one player's losses are offset by another player's gains; at any time, sum totals are zero.

Negative-sum game A game in which players as a group lose at the end of the game.

Positive-sum game A game in which players as a group end up better off.

Strategy A rule used to make a choice.

Dominant strategies Strategies that are generally successful no matter what actions competitors take.

Payoff matrix A matrix of outcomes, or consequences, of the strategies available to the players in a game.

EXAMPLE 11–2 The Prisoners' Dilemma

One real-world example of simple game theory involves what happens when two people, both involved in a bank robbery, are later caught. What should they do when questioned by police? The result has been called the prisoners' dilemma. The two suspects, Sam and Carol, are interrogated separately and confronted with alternative potential periods of imprisonment. The interrogator indirectly indicates to Sam and Carol the following:

1. If both confess to the bank robbery, they will both go to jail for five years.
2. If neither confesses, they will each be given a sentence of two years on a lesser charge.
3. If one prisoner confesses, that prisoner goes free and the other one, who did not confess, will serve 10 years on bank robbery charges.

You can see the prisoners' alternatives in the **payoff matrix**—a matrix of outcomes, or consequences, of the strategies available to the players in a game—in Figure 11–3.

The two options for each prisoner are "confess" and "don't confess." There are four possibilities:

1. Both confess.
2. Neither confesses.
3. Sam confesses, but Carol does not.
4. Carol confesses, but Sam does not.

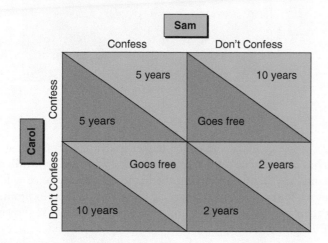

FIGURE 11–3

The Prisoners' Dilemma Payoff Matrix

Regardless of what the other prisoner does, each person is better off if he or she confesses. So, confessing is the dominant strategy and each ends up behind bars for five years.

In Figure 11–3, all of Sam's possible outcomes are shown on the upper half of each rectangle, and all of Carol's possible outcomes are shown on the lower half.

By looking at the payoff matrix, you can see that if Carol confesses, Sam's best strategy is to confess also—he will get only five years instead of 10. Conversely, if Sam confesses, Carol's best strategy is also to confess—she will get five years instead of 10. Now let us say that Sam is being interrogated and Carol does not confess. Sam's best strategy is still to confess because then he goes free instead of serving two years. Conversely, if Carol is being interrogated, her best strategy is still to confess even if Sam does not. She will go free instead of serving 2 years. To confess is a dominant strategy for Sam. To confess is also a dominant strategy for Carol. The situation is exactly symmetrical. So, this is the **prisoners' dilemma**—the strategic game in which two prisoners have a choice between confessing and not confessing to a crime; the game is used to understand why oligopoly firms may decide to engage in noncooperative pricing behaviour, even though it results in a negative-sum game. The prisoners know that both prisoners will be better off if neither confesses. Yet, it is in each individual prisoner's interest to confess, even though the collective outcome of each prisoner's pursuing his or her own interest is inferior for both.

For critical analysis: Can you apply the prisoners' dilemma to the firms in a two-firm industry that agree to split the market by charging the same (high) price? (*Hint*: Think about the payoff to cheating on the market-splitting agreement.) Is there a dominant strategy?

Prisoners' dilemma The strategic game in which two prisoners have a choice between confessing and not confessing to a crime.

Consider an oligopoly consisting of two firms with identical cost and demand curves. It can be shown that if each of these firms cooperates with the other to collectively produce the monopoly output and charges the *same* monopoly price, these two firms will maximize their joint profits. In Figure 11–4, this situation is displayed in the upper left hand portion of the payoff matrix, with both firms charging a *high* price resulting in each firm earning a profit of $6 million. The joint profit of $12 million is maximized with this cooperative pricing strategy.

The upper right (or lower left) portion of the payoff table shows that if one of the firms decides not to cooperate and, instead, lowers its price slightly below its competitor's,

FIGURE 11–4

Game Theory and Pricing
Strategies

This payoff matrix shows that if
both oligopolists choose a high
price, each makes $6 million. If
they both choose a low price,
each makes $4 million. If one
chooses a low price and the other
does not, the low-priced firm will
make $8 million. Unless they col-
lude, however, they will end up
at the low-priced solution.

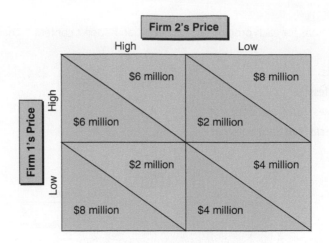

it is able to sell a larger quantity and earn a higher individual profit equal to $8 million.
While this firm has increased its profit, the joint profit of the two firms will now have been
reduced to $10 million. The firm charging the higher monopoly price will clearly be the
loser, selling a much lower quantity and earning a mere $2 million in profit. If both firms
decide to lower their price, each of their profits will be $4 million, as shown on the lower
right portion of the payoff table.

Given the payoff matrix in Figure 11–4, what would be the dominant strategy for Firm 2? If
Firm 1 were to charge the high monopoly price, the best thing for Firm 2 to do is to charge
the low price and earn a profit of $8 million. If, instead, Firm 1 were to charge the low price,
the best action for Firm 2 is to also charge the low price and earn a profit of $4 million. You
can see that the dominant strategy for Firm 2 is to charge the low price. Using similar reasoning, you will conclude that the dominant strategy for Firm 1 is also to charge a low price.

If the game described in Figure 11–4 is played once, we can see that it is in each firm's
individual self-interest to engage in noncooperative price behaviour and charge the low
price even though, collectively, the firms would be better off if they charged the high price
and earned a profit of $6 million each. Noncooperative pricing constitutes a negative sum
game. As with the prisoners' dilemma, oligopoly firms face a dilemma between cooperat-
ing to maximize joint profits and competing to maximize individual profit.

REPEATED GAMES. Let us expand our game theory analysis to more realistic situations
where the same pricing game is repeated over a period of years. If we examine Figure 11–4
more closely, we can see that both Firm 1 and Firm 2 would increase their annual profits
from $4 million to $6 million if they colluded and decided to each charge the high price—
the upper left portion of the payoff matrix in Figure 11–4. When competing firms collude,
this is classed as a form of cooperative pricing behaviour.

Let us assume that Firm 1 and Firm 2 decide to collude and keep prices high, repeatedly,
over a period of years. Again, if we refer to Figure 11–4, we can see that there is a strong
incentive for one of the two firms, say, Firm 1, to eventually "cheat" and lower the price, hop-
ing that the other firm, Firm 2, continues to keep the price high. If this occurs the cheating
firm will increase profit from $6 million to $8 million per year! This type of cheating is
referred to as **opportunistic behaviour** as it focuses solely on short-run gains and ignores
the benefits of cooperation in the long run.

As you might expect, if Firm 1 engages in opportunistic behaviour in one year, the
competing firm, Firm 2, is likely to respond by punishing the cheater. One common oligopoly response to cheating is called the **tit-for-tat strategy**, in which a firm cheats in the
current period if the rival firm cheated in the previous period but cooperates in the current
period if the rival firm cooperated in the previous period. If both firms follow the tit-for-
tat strategy, Firm 2 will respond to Firm 1's cheating by lowering the price in the next year,
while Firm 1 goes back to raising the price. Figure 11–4 indicates that this will lower
Firm 1's profits to $2 million, the worst possible result for Firm 1. Over the two-year

Opportunistic behaviour Actions
that focus solely on short-run
gains and ignore the benefits of
cooperation in the long run.

Tit-for-tat strategy A strategy in
which a firm cheats in the current period if the rival firm
cheated in the previous period
but cooperates in the current
period if the rival firm cooperated in the previous period.

period, Firm 1 achieves an average annual profit of (8 + 2) ÷ 2 = $5 million. This is lower than the annual $6 million profit resulting from the cooperative pricing situation.

Where does the tit-for-tat strategy lead in the long run? Suppose that both Firm 1 and Firm 2 pursue the tit-for-tat strategy, over a 10-year period. Assuming that the payoff matrix in Figure 11–4 applies to each of these 10 years, the average profit per year achieved by each firm will be $5 million (the simple average of the worst and best profits). Alternatively, if each firm had cooperated for each of the 10 years, the average yearly profit would be $6 million, a larger amount. In the long run, firms who experience the tit-for-tat strategy will likely see the benefits of pursuing some form of cooperative strategy. In other words, cooperative pricing is a positive-sum game.

Cooperative Price Behaviour

In the previous section, we noted that the largest industry payoffs accrue to oligopoly firms in cases where the competitors collude or pursue cooperative price behaviour. Cooperative price behaviour can take many forms. One example would be a formal price-fixing agreement among the oligopoly firms operating in the same industry.

PRICE FIXING. The most lucrative price-fixing situation would be where the oligopoly firms agree to raise the price of the product to the level where a monopolist would maximize profits. If all the firms agree to raise prices, the consumers have little choice but to buy the product at the higher price. From the oligopoly firms' viewpoint, this would be an example of a positive-sum game, where all the firms as a group end up achieving higher total profits. In Canada, formal agreements to fix prices are frequently deemed to be illegal, as the following Policy Example 11–1 illustrates.

POLICY EXAMPLE 11–1 Sweet Deal Between Canadian Chocolate Bar Makers?

On June 11, 2010, the B.C. Supreme Court ruled that a settlement worth close to $6 million offered by Cadbury Adams would be allowed to be part of a class action lawsuit against Canada's major manufacturers of chocolate bars: Nestlé Canada, Hershey Canada Inc., Mars Canada Inc., and Cadbury Adams Canada Inc.

The class action alleges that these four major manufacturers conspired to fix and artificially inflate the prices of chocolate products such as Caramilk bars, Smarties, M&M's and Oh Henry! bars in Canada. The lawsuit claims that representatives of the large chocolate manufacturers held secret meetings to discuss prices. The action also asserts that retail stores that attempted to undercut the retail prices suggested by the manufacturers would be penalized by having their supply of the popular chocolate bars restricted.

In February 2010, Cadbury agreed to pay $5.7 million and provide information against the other companies to have itself removed as a defendant in the lawsuit.

While an investigation by Canada's Competition Bureau asserts that a conspiracy among the manufacturers artificially inflated the price of chocolate bars sold between 2001 and 2008, no decision has been rendered to date.

It should be noted that Hershey is currently appealing the settlement agreement by Cadbury Adams and the Crown.

For critical analysis:

1. According to this example, is the alleged price-fixing agreement an example of a zero-sum, negative-sum, or positive-sum game?

2. Based on the allegations in the lawsuit, how does the agreement among the chocolate manufacturers attempt to keep chocolate bar prices inflated at the retail level?

Sources: "Chocolate conspiracy charge prompts deal." *CBC News.* June 12, 2010. http://www.cbc.ca/canada/british-columbia/story/2010/06/11/bc-chocolate-conspiracy-allegation-settlement.html; "Most candy buyers part of class action suit." *Waterloo Region Record* (Kitchener, Ontario). February 19, 2010. Pg. E6.

Cartel An association of suppliers in an industry that agree to set common prices and output quotas to prevent competition.

CARTEL. Perhaps the most comprehensive form of cooperative pricing occurs when the oligopoly firms in an industry join a cartel. A **cartel** is an association of suppliers in an industry that agree to set common prices and output quotas to prevent competition. The purpose of a cartel is to raise prices to monopoly levels in order to increase the total profits received by cartel members. Since cartels engage in a form of price fixing, they are generally illegal in Canada.

One of the most successful international cartels ever is the Organization of Petroleum Exporting Countries (OPEC), an association of the world's largest oil-producing countries. It is estimated that the eleven OPEC members, in total, possess about 78 percent of the world's total proven crude oil reserves. All of the members of OPEC meet regularly to establish daily production quotas. The long-term strategy of OPEC has been to restrict the daily production of oil in order to keep the price of oil significantly above competitive levels, as Example 11–3 describes.

EXAMPLE 11–3   OPEC Continues to Rule the World Oil Market

On November 1, 2006, the Organization of Petroleum Exporting Countries (OPEC) announced that they would cooperatively reduce their combined daily crude oil production by 1.2 million barrels. Just a few months later, in February 2007, OPEC announced another production cut of 500 000 barrels per day, bringing total OPEC production to a level of just over 30 million barrels per day in March 2007. In order to ensure this daily production target, each OPEC member has been allocated a daily production quota (in barrels), as follows: Saudi Arabia, 8 510 000; Iran, 3 740 000; Venezuela, 2 411 000; United Arab Emirates, 2 466 000; Nigeria, 2 170 000; Iraq, 2 054 000; Kuwait, 2 400 000; Libya, 1 683 000; Angola, 1 602 000; Indonesia, 855 000; Algeria, 1 340 000; and Qatar, 795 000.

The OPEC production cut took place despite the fact that oil prices have quadrupled since November 2001, reaching $78.65 per barrel in August 2006.

Why did OPEC cut production when oil prices are already high? Industry analysts contend that Saudi Arabia enforced the decrease in quotas in response to the falling U.S. dollar, as oil is priced globally in U.S. dollars. The decline in the value of the U.S. dollar has the effect of reducing the real income of the OPEC nations, as oil is their key trading commodity.

Oil prices continued to increase to record levels, peaking at over $140 per barrel in July 2008. Then, the great global recession caused oil prices to plummet to just over $30 per barrel in December 2008. Effective January 2009, OPEC implemented a record quota reduction totalling 4.2 million barrels per day.

Did all OPEC nations abide by the decreased production quotas, given the incentive to cheat in the midst of a global recession? As of March 2009, there was 80 percent compliance to the quota cuts, and industry observers expected to see more producers comply in the following months, in light of the strategic behaviour taken by Saudi Arabia in the past. Repeatedly, Saudi Arabia has effectively said to other members of OPEC, "If you stick to your agreed-on production limits, so shall we; but if you expand production beyond those limits, so shall we."

OPEC members have seen Saudi Arabia follow through on its threats of retaliation. In the 1980s, when Iran and Iraq were selling in excess of their quotas to finance their war, Saudi Arabia responded by significantly increasing its oil production. Oil prices collapsed. In just one year (1985 to 1986), crude oil prices plunged from US$24.10 to US$12.50 per barrel.

For critical analysis: What game theory strategy is being employed by the OPEC cartel? Why is Saudi Arabia so effective in enforcing this strategy?

Sources: Javier Blas, "Falling US dollar puts pressure on the buying power of OPEC nations. *Financial Times*, London, UK, July 24, 2007, p. 1; *OPEC Monthly Oil Market Report*. April 2007, p. 31. http://www.opec.org/home/Monthly%20Oil%20Market%20Reports/2007/pdf/mr042007.pdf; Stanley Reed. "OPEC sees good reasons to maintain production." *Bloomberg Business Week*. March 15, 2009. http://www.businessweek.com/globalbiz/content/mar2009/gb20090315_745055.htm?campaign_id=rss_daily.

PRICE LEADERSHIP. What if oligopolists do not actually collude to raise prices and share markets but do so implicitly? There are no formal cartel arrangements and no formal meetings. Nonetheless, there is tacit collusion. One example of this is the model of **price leadership**—a practice in many oligopolistic industries, in which the largest firm publishes its price list ahead of its competitors, which then match those announced prices.

In this model, the basic assumption is that the dominant firm, usually the biggest, sets the price and allows other firms to sell all they can at that price. The dominant firm then sells the rest. The dominant firm always makes the first move in a price leadership model. By definition, price leadership requires that one firm be the leader. Because of laws against collusion, firms in an industry cannot communicate this directly. That is why it is often natural for the largest firm to become the price leader. In the automobile industry, during the period of GM's dominance (until the 1980s), that company was traditionally the price leader. At various times in the breakfast-food industry, Kellogg was the price leader. In the banking industry, the Bank of Montreal has been the price leader in announcing changes in its prime rate, the interest rate charged on loans offered to the best credit risks. Typically, five or six hours after the Bank of Montreal would increase or decrease its prime rate, the other major banks would announce the same change in their prime rates.

> **Price leadership** A practice in many oligopolistic industries in which the largest firm publishes its price list ahead of its competitors, who then match those announced prices. Also called parallel pricing.

Factors Conducive to Cooperative Price Behaviour

What factors are likely to prompt cooperative price behaviour, as opposed to noncooperative price behaviour, in oligopoly? Economic research does point to various industry characteristics as being important in determining whether cooperation or competition will ensue in an oligopoly situation.

There will be a greater tendency for cooperation the *smaller the number of firms* in the industry. In this situation, if one firm attempts to cheat, it can expect significant retaliation, as this cheating will have a very large negative effect on the remaining competitors. Moreover, it is easier to identify a cheater with just a few large firms in the industry.

Cooperative price behaviour is more likely to be sustained in a *growing industry* than in a shrinking market. When demand is increasing, firms can easily increase sales without resorting to noncooperative pricing practices that steal customers away from their rivals. Conversely, in recessions, price agreements frequently break down as firms facing declining sales react in desperation by cutting prices.

The tendency toward joint pricing behaviour is greater for oligopoly firms supplying *identical* products as opposed to differentiated products. As an example, one would expect to see a greater degree of price cooperation in such industries as oil and steel refining, where competitors' products are relatively homogeneous. In these cases, rival firms can quickly and easily punish a cheating firm through reciprocal price cuts.

Forms of cooperative pricing, such as price fixing and cartels, are more likely to occur in countries where *legal sanctions preventing this activity are largely absent*. It has already been noted that in such countries as Canada and the United States, many types of cooperative pricing strategies are deemed to be illegal and can result in significant fines being imposed.

Example 11–4 describes how DeBeers, the dominant supplier of the world's rough diamonds, has made recent moves away from price cooperation, partly due to industry trends and partly due to its desire to sell more finished diamond products in the United States.

EXAMPLE 11–4 De Beers Diamond Cartel: A Thing of The Past?

"Diamonds Are Forever." For decades, that expression has applied not just to diamonds but also to South Africa's De Beers diamond cartel. At the centre of the cartel's operations is De Beers' marketing subsidiary, the Central Selling Organization (CSO). By restricting diamond sales each year, the CSO has aimed to maximize profits earned by De Beers and other members of a global cartel of diamond producers.

What type for oligopoly pricing behaviour is typical of the diamond industry?

continued

The CSO attempted to purchase most of the world's rough diamonds, even those that were not produced by the cartel firms. Using this strategy, the CSO controlled the diamond supply to the ultimate consumers. Each year, the CSO withheld from the marketplace stockpiles of $4 billion to $5 billion in uncut diamonds. Between 1986 and 1998, diamond prices increased by 50 percent!

Since 1998, things have not been going so smoothly for the cartel. Russia, Canada, and Australia have emerged as significant diamond producers, gradually loosening the De Beers cartel's grip on global diamond supply and pricing. Better techniques for making artificial diamonds have also played a role in bringing new competition to the industry.

De Beers has recently pledged to relinquish some of its practices intended to control the supply of rough diamonds. With diamond prices declining at the wholesale level, De Beers is making efforts to establish premium brand-name jewellery products at the retail level. Based on unresolved charges of price fixing, De Beers has been banned from competing in the lucrative U.S. retail diamond jewellery industry. In 2004, the South African company was reportedly in secret negotiations to end its exile from the United States. In July 2005, De Beers pleaded guilty in a U.S. court to fixing prices of industrial diamonds and agreed to a US$10 million fine.

Several class-action lawsuits were filed against De Beers asking for money damages on behalf of diamond purchasers. The lawsuits claim that De Beers monopolized diamond supplies and conspired to fix and inflate diamond prices, violating antitrust and consumer-protection laws. On May 27, 2008, a U.S. court approved a settlement whereby De Beers would pay $295 million to the various diamond purchasers that claimed damages in the class-action suits. As of spring 2010, the settlement was in the process of being appealed.

For critical analysis: What factors help to explain why there has been a tendency away from the practice of cooperative pricing in the rough diamond industry?

Sources: David Finlayson. "Return of De Beers may boost industry: Guilty plea to price fixing will open U.S. market." *Edmonton Journal.* March 3, 2004. Pg. G3; Eric Onstad. "De Beers quits chasing carats; Diamond giant likely to drop Russia's Alrosa." *Calgary Herald.* July 21, 2007. Final edition. Pg. C10; Matthew Craze and David Voreacos. "De Beers to pay US$250M to settle U.S. lawsuits: Price fixing alleged." *National Post.* December 1, 2005. National edition. Pg. FP5; "Commonly asked questions and answers." Diamond Class Action Settlement website. https://diamondsclassaction.com/FAQ.htm#14.

Pricing to Deter Entry into an Industry

Some economists believe that all decision making by existing firms in a stable industry involves some type of game playing. As noted above, one important part of game playing has to do with how existing competitors might react to a decision by other existing rivals. Another type of strategic decision making requires that existing firms in an oligopoly industry come up with strategies to deter entry of new competitors. An example would be when existing firms(s) adopt pricing and investment tactics to deter entry.

PREDATORY PRICING. New companies are more likely deterred from entering an oligopoly industry if they expect economic losses over a protracted period of time. Existing oligopoly firms can create this expectation by engaging in predatory pricing behaviour. **Predatory pricing** is a strategy in which existing firms cut the prices of their products below costs in order to discourage the entry of new firms. To enhance the effectiveness of predatory pricing, the existing firm(s) might invest in excess capacity so that they can expand output for a prolonged period of time.

Predatory pricing A strategy where existing firms cut the prices of their products below costs in order to discourage the entry of new firms.

For example, an existing supermarket might build a mega-store with lots of excess capacity in a brand new subdivision. If a new rival food retailer announces future plans to enter this subdivision, the existing supermarket may engage in predatory pricing over a protracted period of time due its excess capacity. The new potential rival, faced with having to meet the low prices for an extended period of time, may be scared off by the prospect of prolonged economic losses.

Policy Example 11–2 explains how investigations conducted by the Competition Bureau (the federal government agency in charge of maintaining fair competition in Canada) support the view that Air Canada has engaged in predatory pricing strategies at the expense of smaller regional airlines.

POLICY EXAMPLE 11–2 Turbulence in the Canadian Airline Industry

For many years, Canada was served by two national airlines—Air Canada and Canadian Airlines International. In January 2000, Air Canada purchased the financially plagued Canadian Airlines International, making Air Canada the dominant firm in the Canadian airline industry.

After Air Canada, a number of regional airlines, such as WestJet and CanJet, have attempted to expand their services on a broader national scale. Both regional airlines have filed complaints with the Canadian government's Competition Bureau, claiming that Air Canada has been pursuing anti-competitive practices aimed at deterring entry into Eastern Canadian markets.

In March 2001, the Competition Bureau completed an investigation of Air Canada's response to the entry of WestJet Airlines and CanJet Airlines into seven Eastern Canadian routes—Halifax–Montreal, Halifax–Ottawa, Halifax–St. John's, Toronto–Moncton, Toronto–Saint John, Toronto–Fredericton, and Toronto–Charlottetown. The Bureau concluded that in these seven markets, Air Canada was engaged in entry-deterring predatory behaviour that included adding capacity and pricing below "avoidable cost." If these anti-competitive practices were to continue, they could cause WestJet and CanJet to abandon these routes, which would lead to higher airfares in the long run.

The Competition Bureau asked the federal government's Competition Tribunal for a legal court order prohibiting Air Canada from engaging in various entry deterrence strategies. At one point in 2003, Air Canada was offering one-way fares between Toronto and Ottawa for $12! In July 2003, the Competition Tribunal filed a preliminary report that concluded that Air Canada did engage in predatory pricing behaviour in at least two of the seven routes investigated. Air Canada subsequently appealed the findings of this report.

In January 2009, the Competition Bureau clarified its enforcement approach related to anti-competitive acts such as predatory pricing. In essence, for a dominant firm (such as Air Canada) to be found guilty, the investigation would have to show that the dominant airline was reducing prices below its avoidable costs and that this conduct was likely to result in a substantial lessening or prevention of competition.

No enforcement action has been taken against Air Canada (to date), perhaps because the competition from WestJet has been increasing, not lessening. In 2000, Air Canada commanded a 77 percent share of the Canadian market, while WestJet held 7 percent. As of December 2009, Air Canada's market share had declined to 55 percent, and WestJet's share had increased to 38 percent. The CEO of WestJet has publically stated that he expects WestJet to have the same domestic market share as Air Canada by 2014. It is interesting to note that in 2009, while WestJet earned a $98.2 million profit, Air Canada lost $24 million.

For critical analysis: Using this example, identify and explain two entry-deterring strategies likely pursued by Air Canada.

Sources: Competition Bureau. "Competition bureau seeks order against anti-competitive practices by Air Canada." March 5, 2001. http://strategis.ic.gc.ca/epic/internet/incb-bc.nsf/en/ct02136e.html; The Canadian Press. "Airline flew for less than cost, tribunal decides." *Daily News*. Halifax, N.S., July 23, 2003, p. 23; Nicolas Van Praet. "Beddoe says Air Canada pursuing 'scorched earth policy' price war." *Edmonton Journal*. October 21, 2003. Pg. F3; Competition Bureau. "Competition bureau clarifies enforcement approach in the airline industry." September 23, 2004. http://www.competitionbureau.gc.ca/internet/index.cfm?itemID=247&lg=e; Brent Jang. "WestJet closing gap with Air Canada" *The Globe and Mail*. February 18, 2010. Pg. B9.

This chapter's Issues and Applications describes how game theory can be used in explaining entry-deterring behaviour (or the lack of it) in Canada's oligopolic brewing industry. As the Issues and Applications explains, strategic behaviour by the existing breweries can help explain the growth of the smaller microbreweries.

Price Wars

Sporadic price wars frequently break out in oligopoly situations. A **price war** is a situation where competing firms respond to a rival's price cut with even larger price cuts. Many of us have witnessed price wars involving closely located supermarkets or gas price wars among

Price war A situation where competing firms respond to a rival's price out with even larger price cuts.

gas retailers in a Canadian city. While most wars last for only a few days, some can drag into months and possibly even years.

Price wars are characteristic of oligopolies, due to the presence of interdependence, where one firm's price cut can significantly reduce the market share of a rival firm.

A price war can be caused by a variety of factors. It may be due to competing firms responding to opportunistic behaviour (cheating) on the part of one rival attempting to steal market share. Or this practice may be part of an overall strategy to deter new firms from successfully entering the oligopoly industry, as Example 11–5 suggests.

EXAMPLE 11–5   Wind Blows Down Canadian Wireless Prices

In Canada, what is likely to happen to cellphone prices? Why?

According to a recent study conducted by the OECD, Canada's cellphone market is one of the most expensive among the developed nations. Of the 30 developed nations surveyed, Canada ranked twenty-eighth in terms of affordability. Many attribute Canada's high cellphone plan prices to the lack of competition in the wireless carrier market, which is dominated by the "Big Three" oligopoly firms: Telus, Bell, and Rogers.

In 2009, the Canadian government began to encourage competition in the Canadian wireless market by allowing the new firm Wind Mobile to enter the industry, despite concerns that this firm was foreign owned. In the latter part of 2009, a price war emerged. It started with each of the Big Three firms dropping prices to the point of offering stripped-down, no-frills plans, including talk and text packages for as little as $15 per month. Telus's Koodo, Rogers's Fido, and Bell's Solo Mobile have been used to front this price war. These three firms were hoping to lock down as many customers as possible ahead of Wind Mobile's entry into the market. In December 2009, Wind Mobile countered the Big Three's price cuts by offering stripped-down cellphone plans for as low as $10 per month.

For critical analysis: According to this Example, what two tactics aimed at deterring entry have been employed by the Big Three? Explain.

Sources: Grant Robertson. "Globalive wades into wireless price battle." Report on Business. *The Globe and Mail.* December 13, 2009. http://www.theglobeandmail.com/report-on-business/globalive-wades-into-wireless-price-battle/article1398967/; Rick Eglinton. "Wind launches with cheaper phone rates." *Toronto Star.* December 16, 2009. http://www.thestar.com/business/article/739543—wind-launches-with-cheaper-cellphone-rates.

11.6 Nonprice Forms of Competition in Oligopoly

Since price wars are costly and collusion can be illegal, many oligopoly firms have channeled their competitive energies into nonprice forms of competition. We will examine the following forms of nonprice competition: product differentiation, mergers, exclusive dealing, increasing switching costs, exploiting network effects, and innovation.

There are several reasons why oligopoly firms prefer nonprice forms of competition over price competition. Successful forms of nonprice competition cannot be duplicated as quickly and easily by rival firms as price reductions. For example, compared with price-cutting opportunistic behaviour, successful product differentiation or product improvements can often achieve more permanent gains in market share. In addition, nonprice competition can often increase total industry sales and so can be viewed by the firms as positive-sum games.

Product Differentiation

Recall that product differentiation refers to the distinguishing of products by physical attributes, bundling of services, location and accessibility, sales promotion and advertising, and other qualities, real or imagined.

To appreciate the degree of product differentiation that can exist in oligopoly, consider the motor vehicle manufacturing industry and the "Big Three"—GM, Chrysler, and Ford. For each type of motor vehicle product line, there are many differences in styling features, options, financing plans, sales promotion and advertising campaigns, warranties, sponsorship of entertainment and sporting events, and so on.

ADVERTISING. Perhaps the most socially contentious form of product differentiation is advertising. Those critical of the advertising activities undertaken by large oligopoly firms have frequently put forth the following arguments. While advertising adds to the cost of the product(s) to consumers, much of the advertising conveys little or no valuable information. Does a TV commercial featuring a new Jeep in the middle of the desert or on the top of a cliff really convey valuable consumer information?

When oligopoly firms engage in expensive advertising campaigns, this can serve as a barrier to entry to entrepreneurs considering the prospect of entering the industry. If a new firm were to consider entering the national beer industry in Canada, the extensive amount of advertising and sales promotion that would be required to keep up with Molson and Labatt may well be a discouraging factor.

To the extent that a firm's advertising efforts are successful in establishing substantial brand-name loyalty, the consumer faces disadvantages similar to monopolized markets. The price charged on the brand name product might significantly exceed marginal and average total cost, thus resulting in allocative inefficiency and excess profits.

Finally, some advertisements and sales promotions deliberately mislead consumers. One of the most common violations of the *Canadian Competition Act* relates to firms' misrepresenting the regular or ordinary price of a product or service in an advertised sale or in-store sales promotion. In recent years, national Canadian retailers have been fined hundreds of thousands of dollars for tagging merchandise with percentage discounts off a misleading regular price. In other words, the original price indicated on the tagged merchandise did not represent the regular price, since the sale item was never sold for this amount. In some cases, the articles of merchandise were already tagged "Special" before even entering the store.

What are the social benefits of advertising? To the extent that media advertisements contain objective information about product characteristics and prices, the consumer can make a rational purchase decision without having to spend several days visiting competing stores. One way new firms can make consumers aware of their new products is through advertising.

Individual companies can use advertising to engage in signalling behaviour that can benefit consumers. By establishing a strong brand name or trademark, a firm is sending a signal to consumers that it plans to stay in business for a long time. Moreover, the strong brand name is used to indicate that the firm undertakes to provide a consistently high level of product quality. This type of signalling behaviour is especially important to those consumers who prefer to buy products through the Internet.

Example 11–6 suggests that, in some cases, advertising can actually lower per-unit costs and thereby promote productive efficiency.

EXAMPLE 11–6   Can Advertising Lead to Efficiency?

Advertising budgets by major retailers may just seem like an added expense, not a step on the road to economic efficiency. According to research by economists Kyle Bagwell and Garey Ramey, just the opposite is true. When retailers advertise heavily, they increase the number of shoppers that come to their store. Such increased traffic allows retailers to offer a wider selection of goods, to invest in cost-reduction technology (such as computerized inventory and satellite communications), and to exploit manufacturers' quantity discounts. Such cost reductions can help explain the success of Walmart, Zellers, Canadian Tire, and Home Depot. Consequently, Bagwell and Ramey conclude that advertising can help promote efficiency. Advertising that provides price information signals to consumers where they can find big-company, low-priced, high-variety stores.

For critical analysis: Which is true: "We are bigger because we are better," or "We are better because we are bigger"?

Mergers

Merger The joining of two or more firms under single ownership or control.

Horizontal merger The joining of firms that are producing or selling a similar product.

Vertical merger The joining of a firm with another to which it sells an output or from which it buys an input.

Conglomerate merger The joining of two firms from unrelated industries.

One way an oligopoly firm can significantly increase its share of industry sales is through a merger. A **merger** is the joining of two or more firms under single ownership or control. There are three types of mergers: horizontal, vertical, and conglomerate. A **horizontal merger** involves the joining of firms that are producing or selling a similar product. If two daily newspapers in the same city merge, this is a horizontal merger. A horizontal merger reduces competition and so increases the level of concentration in an industry.

A **vertical merger** is the joining of a firm with another to which it sells an output or from which it buys an input. When an oil refining company, such as Shell, purchases retail gas stations, this is a vertical merger. A **conglomerate merger** is the joining of two firms from unrelated industries. If an automobile manufacturer purchases a chain of restaurants, this is a conglomerate merger. In situations where mergers result in a few large, dominant corporations operating in one market, other firms, faced with the prospect of raising large amounts of capital to compete successfully, are deterred from entering the industry.

Exclusive Dealing

Exclusive Dealing A situation where the firm supplies its product to a customer on condition that the customer not buy similar products from rival firms supplying a similar product.

Exclusive dealing refers to a situation where a firm supplies its product to a customer on condition that the customer not buy similar products from rival firms supplying a similar product. Typically, the customer is another firm that plans to re-sell the product. If an oligopoly petroleum-refining company agreed to sell its gasoline to a Canadian gas retailer only if the gas station owner promised not to buy any gasoline from a rival refiner, this would be an example of an exclusive dealing agreement. This practice reduces price competition in that it prevents the gas retailer from contacting competing refiners to secure a lower price per litre. In turn, this makes the demand for each refiner's gasoline more inelastic so that refiners can charge higher prices.

It should be noted that in many countries, the practice of exclusive dealing is an illegal act and can result in a very large penalty, as Example 11–7 illustrates.

EXAMPLE 11–7 **Intel Bags Record Fine**

On May 12, 2009, the European Union fined Intel Corporation a record EUR1.06 billion (US$1.45 billion) and ordered the world's biggest maker of computer chips to stop exclusive dealing practices that severely restrained the chip sales of its major rival, Advanced Micro Devices (AMD), for a five-year period. The EU charged Intel with giving rebates to computer manufacturers such as Acer Inc., Dell Inc., Hewlett-Packard, Lenovo Group and NEC Corp. for buying all or most of their chips for their new computers from Intel. As well, EU claimed that Intel paid computer manufacturers to stop or delay the launch of new computers based on AMD chips.

At the time the record fine was assessed, the computer chip industry was dominated by the two firms—Intel and AMD—and that Intel supplied about 80 percent of the world's computer chips. On November 12, 2009, Intel agreed to pay $1.25 billion to AMD on the condition that AMD drop all of its lawsuits against Intel worldwide.

For critical analysis: Based on this example, who else has likely been significantly harmed by the exclusive practices of Intel, besides its rival chip makers?

Sources: Roger Parloff. "Intel settles with AMD. What's next?" *Fortune Magazine*. November 13, 2009. http://money.cnn.com/2009/11/13/technology/intel_amd_settlement.fortune/index.htm; Aoife White. "EU fines Intel $1.45 billion for sales tactics." *Daily Gleaner* (Fredericton, N.B.). May 14, 2009. Pg. D1.

Raising Customers' Switching Costs

If an existing firm can make it more costly for customers to switch from its product or service to a competitor's, the existing firm can better insulate itself from price competition as well as deter the entry of new firms. In other words, the oligopolistic firm can make the demand for its product or service more inelastic and by doing so can command a higher price.

There are a host of ways in which existing firms can raise customers' switching costs. In the past, makers of computer equipment produced operating systems and software that would not run on competitors' computers. Any customer wanting to change from one computer system to another faced a high switching cost. In the oligopolistic cellphone industry, customers who lock into cellphone contracts face increased switching costs in the form of cancellation penalties.

The Canadian banking industry provides a good illustration of high switching costs, as shown below in Example 11–8

EXAMPLE 11-8 High Switching Costs in the Credit World

One way banks keep their customers is by raising the cost of switching to a different bank. RBC offers RBC Rewards to its Visa credit card holders. This incentive enables its Visa users to accumulate reward points on all credit card purchases. Once sufficient reward points have accumulated, the credit card user can redeem these points for free travel services or free merchandise. A Royal Bank Visa holder who has accumulated a significant number of reward points will be reluctant to switch to another credit card, as this would entail a switching cost equal to the loss in reward points.

Similarly, CIBC offers mortgages that enable customers to accumulate Aeroplan Miles for every dollar of mortgage interest paid. If a CIBC customer decides to renew a mortgage with CIBC, the customer receives a significant number of bonus Aeroplan Miles. Due to these incentives, a CIBC customer faces switching costs if he or she decides to renew a mortgage with another bank.

For critical analysis: Can you think of switching cost examples in other oligopolistic industries, besides banking?

Network Effects

A common source of switching costs is a shared understanding among consumers about how to use a particular product, service, or brand. Such a shared understanding can sometimes generate **network effects**—situations where a customer's willingness to use an item depends on how other people use it. Common examples are telephones and fax machines. Ownership of a phone or fax machine is not very useful if no one else has one; but once a number of people own a phone or fax machine, the benefits that others gain from consuming these devices increases.

Network effect A situation where a customer's willingness to use an item depends on how many others use it.

In some industries, a few firms can reap most of the benefits of the network effect. Suppose that firms in an industry sell differentiated products or services that are subject to network effects. If the products or services of one, two, or a few firms catch on, these firms will capture the bulk of industry sales, and an oligopoly, or possibly even a near monopoly, will emerge.

People who tend to work on joint projects within a network of fellow employees, consultants, clients, suppliers, students, or professors naturally find it useful to share computer files. Trading computer files is much easier if all use the same word processing, spreadsheet, database, and presentation software. Clearly, the network effect has contributed to Microsoft's dominance in these office productivity software products. Any individual who contemplates switching to use a word processor other than MS Word is aware that he or she faces significant switching costs in terms of the time that will be required to convert files sent in Word to the rival word processor.

In the market for online auction services, an individual is more likely to use the services of an auction site if there is a significant likelihood that many other potential buyers or sellers also trade items on that site. Hence there is a network effect in the online auction industryso that eBay, Amazon, and Yahoo! account for more than 80 percent of total sales.

Online social networking has become one of the fastest-growing industries worldwide, with over 100 online social networking websites available in June 2010. Each social networking site provides a multitude of ways for its users to interact, such as chats, messaging, e-mail, photos, videos, voice chats, file sharing, blogging, wikis, discussion groups, and social applications. As Example 11–9 illustrates, the network effect is quickly changing the Internet social networking industry into an oligopoly situation that is particularly attractive to advertisers worldwide.

EXAMPLE 11–9 Facebook Frenzy

Because of the network effect, the online social networking industry is quickly becoming dominated by a few large websites. As of the first quarter of 2010, the major sites listed according to registered members were as follows: Facebook (400 000 000), Qzone (200 000 000) MySpace (180 000 000), Habbo (162 000 000), Windows Live Spaces (120 000 000), and orkut (100 000 000). It is interesting to note how fast a company can grow due to the network effect. Facebook added 370 000 000 new members in a period of less than three years! Indeed, Barack Obama benefited from this growth by using Facebook to gain voter support in the 2008 U.S. presidential election.

Facebook provides free membership to any individual who provides an e-mail address. Once a new member logs into the site, he or she typically fills out a personal profile, which can consist of personal demographics, interests, beliefs, and activities. Facebook provides simple navigation tools that allow individuals to easily join and interact with friends, family, colleagues, classmates, employees, and customers in a variety of networks and groups, based on their personal profiles. One key way that Facebook encourages the network effect is through its "Facebook Platform," which invites any software developer to create social networking applications that can be launched within Facebook. As more applications are developed, more users are attracted, which in turn attracts even more software applications.

In order for a Facebook user to gain permission to launch and use these applications, he or she may be asked to disclose additional personal information, such as his or her name, profile picture, gender, birthday, hometown, current residence, political views, activities, interests, musical preferences, favourite television shows, movie preferences, book preferences, favourite quotes, relationship status, dating interests, relationship interests, summer plans, Facebook user-network affiliations, education history, work history, course information, photo albums, and so on.

Advertisers are keenly interested in sites such as Facebook because they provide the opportunity to efficiently promote specific products and services to their target markets, based on the rich array of personal information that individual users provide in their profiles, interactions, and through the download of applications. It is estimated that in 2009, Facebook's annual revenue was approximately $800 million based on brand ads, ad deals with Microsoft, self service ads, and virtual goods.

On May 26, 2010, Facebook responded to world-wide privacy concerns by announcing plans to allow its individual users to more easily adjust privacy settings that limit access to users' personal information. At this time, the default settings still favour sharing of personal information.

For critical analysis: Explain why the network effect applies to the online social networking industry.

Sources: "List of social networking sites." Wikipedia. http://en.wikipedia.org/wiki/List_of_social_networking_websites. (Accessed June 14, 2010.); Nicholas Carlson. "Everything you wanted to know about Facebook's revenue but didn't know who to ask. July 2, 2009. *Business Insider*. SAI. http://www.businessinsider.com/breaking-down-facebooks-revenues-2009-7; Matt Hartley. "Has Facebook finally got privacy right?" May 26, 2010. *Financial Post*. http://www.financialpost.com/story.html?id=3074979.

Innovation

Oligopoly firms can promote their own self-interest as well as public interest by engaging in the innovative activities of research and development that result in the adoption of more efficient methods of production or the creation of new and improved products. A number of theoretical arguments can be put forth to suggest that an oligopoly market structure can be conducive to technological innovation. The large size of many oligopoly firms enables them to undertake expensive research and development activities. As well, due to barriers to entry and the lure of long-run excess profits, oligopoly firms have the incentive to innovate. Finally, interdependent oligopoly firms may prefer to channel their competitive energies into constructive product innovation as opposed to destructive price competition.

According to the evidence, what type of firms and industries tend to account for most of the innovative activity in North America? Data presented by the OECD in 2009 indicated that the majority of research and development is conducted by large firms, rather than small and medium-sized businesses. The percentage of business innovation activity undertaken by large companies, many of which operate in high concentration industries, is 85 percent in the U.S. and 64 percent in Canada.

High technology industries conduct the majority of research and development in the manufacturing sector in both the U.S. (67 percent) and Canada (59 percent). The high tech industries supply the following types products and services: computer hardware and software; communications; audio, video and television; and medical and pharmaceuticals. Canadian examples of innovative high tech companies include Nortel (computer networks) and Research In Motion (the BlackBerry).

Apple Inc. is a good example of how an oligopoly firm can use innovation, as well as other forms of nonprice competition already discussed, to effectively compete in high technology industries, as illustrated in Example 11–10.

EXAMPLE 11–10   Apple's iMania

On May 26, 2010, the $222.12 billion market value of Apple Inc. surpassed that of Microsoft Corporation ($219.18 billion) to make Apple the second most valued corporation in North America. This is a remarkable feat considering that just over a decade ago the chief technology officer of Microsoft declared Apple to be an "already dead" corporation. From a relatively broad viewpoint, one can attribute Apple's rapid growth to its focus on high-quality product innovation in high growth and high technology industries.

Apple's creation of the iPod in conjunction with its innovative iTunes software allowed it to challenge Sony and gain a prominent position in the music media and music distribution industries.

In the first quarter of 2010, Apple sold 8.75 million iPhones, double the number sold in the same period a year before. With this rapid growth in sales, the iPhone now ranks third in the global smartphone market, with a 14 percent share, behind the products of Nokia Corporation (47 percent) and Research In Motion (20 percent). In June 2010, the iPhone 4 was released, offering yet another set of innovative features, including video calling.

In 2010, Apple also created the iPad, a unique tablet computer that has the potential to create a new category of computers. The iPad provides its user with new ways to interact with the web, photos, music, videos, podcasts, HD movies, eBooks, TV shows, and thousands of software applications made especially for the device.

As consumers build their lives around the iPhone and its 200 000 software applications, they're potentially locked into buying newer versions of the iPhone as well as other Apple devices. The smartphones supplied by competitors cannot connect to iTunes, which manages iPhone owners' music, video, photos, and other files. Nor can rival phones run the vast array of

continued

iPhone software applications that its users have become dependent on. As more and more apps are developed for the iPhone, more consumers are encouraged to switch to the iPhone, which attracts even more software applications. Apple requires its third-party software developers to use only Apple's programming tools, excluding all programming tools provided by competitors such as Adobe.

For critical analysis: Identify and explain three nonprice forms of competition effectively used by Apple.

Sources: Jessica Mintz. "iPhone's sales outshine more advanced phones." *Waterloo Region Record* (Kitchener, Ont.). May 22, 2010. Pg. D14; Jenna Wortham. "Apple places new limits on app developers. *New York Times.* April 12, 2010. http://www.nytimes.com/2010/04/13/technology/companies/13apple.html?_r=1&scp=1&sq=apple%20places%20new%20limits%20on%20app%20developers&st=Search; Miguel Helft and Ashlee Vance. "Apple passes Microsoft as no. 1 in technology." *New York Times.* May 26, 2010. http://www.nytimes.com/2010/05/27/technology/27apple.html

As the OECD study indicates, Canadian businesses spend less on research and development as a percentage of their economy (1.5 percent) than the average OECD nation (2.4 percent). Economists attribute this relatively low level of innovative activity to two major factors. First, the high tech industries that typically focus on research and development activities are not as important in the resource-driven Canadian economy as in other developed nations. In addition, a significant number of large firms operating in Canada are owned by global multinational corporations where the research and development activities are conducted in the head offices located in other countries.

11.7 Social Evaluation of Oligopoly

Since in oligopoly just a few major firms supply a similar product, there is a danger that the lack of competitive pressure, coupled with the tendency to employ resources in unproductive types of nonprice competition, can result in productive inefficiency. Moreover, due to barriers to entry, the existing oligopolistic firms can continue to enjoy excess profits in the long run. To the extent that an oligopolistic industry engages in cooperative behaviour and acts like a monopoly, the industry will tend to restrict output and drive up the price compared with a competitive industry.

Depending on the specific situation, an oligopolistic market structure may be socially preferred over a more competitive environment. If significant economies of scale exist, cost efficiencies may be realized with just a few firms supplying the product or service. As well, there are both theoretical arguments as well as empirical evidence to suggest that an oligopolistic market structure can be conducive to innovation. The challenge lies in ensuring that the positive aspects of an oligopolistic market structure end up benefiting the consumer and not just the shareholders and executives of large corporations.

ISSUES AND APPLICATIONS

Game Theory: Opening Up the Brewing Industry

Concepts Applied: Game Theory, Strategic Behaviour, Entry Deterrence

Craft beers with exotic names like Warthog Cream Ale or Blanche de Chambly are slowly gaining a share of the beer market. The Labatt and Molson beer companies have found it more profitable not to fight their entry.

In 2009, Canadians consumed about 2.3 billion litres of beer, an increase of .9 percent over 2008. Beer remains the most popular alcoholic beverage in Canada, comprising 46 percent of the alcoholic beverage market, followed by wine at 29 percent. Together, Molson Coors (42 percent) and Labatt (40 percent) produce the lion's share of Canadian beer—82 percent of it. However, premium imports and small microbreweries have grown from virtually no sales in 1985 to capturing approximately 17 percent of the Canadian beer market in 2009. There are now over 50 microbreweries in Canada, producing craft beers with exotic names like Warthog Cream Ale, Moosehead Premium Dry, Blanche de Chambly, Brewmasters Black Lager, Rig Pig Pale Ale, Clancy's Amber Ale, Heroica Oatmeal Stout, Razzykat Raspberry Ale, and Black Oak Pale Ale. Part of the reason for the success of microbreweries is that many of these brands are unpasteurized specialty beers brewed without preservatives. As Canadians have aged, they have begun to drink less and discriminate more, turning from the old standards—Labatt Blue and Molson Canadian—to the high-quality craft beers.

Industry analysts suggest that a 1 percent share of the beer market is worth about $16 million in profits. So, why have Molson and Labatt not fought the entry into the industry by the microbreweries and the import beers? We can use game theory to help us answer this question.

Constructing the Game

The two players in this game are: (1) Molson and Labatt, which currently dominate the market for beer; and (2) a representative microbrewery that wants to enter the market. Molson and

Labatt can fight its entry or acquiesce. Fighting entry would cost each firm $1 million. The microbrewery's strategies are to enter the industry—which requires a $1 million fixed cost investment—or to stay out. If the firm successfully enters the market, it will capture a 1 percent market share worth $16 million. If it encounters a fight from the major breweries, however, it will lose the $1 million earmarked for setup costs.

The Solution

Molson and Labatt know that if the microbrewery wants to enter the market, fighting will cost them $18 million, while acquiescing will cost $16 million in lost profits. If the microbrewery decides to stay out of the market, then fighting will cost them $2 million, while acquiescing will cost nothing. In either case, the two breweries choose to acquiesce.

The microbrewery knows that if Labatt and Molson want to fight entry, it is better off staying out of the market and not losing its $1 million. If, however, Labatt and Molson want to acquiesce, the microbrewery is better off entering. Since Molson and Labatt's dominant strategy is to acquiesce, the microbrewery enters the market.

No Symmetrical Solution

This game is not symmetrical, since the microbrewery has no dominant strategy. If the major brewers decided to fight, the microbrewery would not enter the market. Nevertheless, Molson and Labatt choose not to fight, since fighting is an expensive undertaking. By behaving strategically, Molson and Labatt face increasing competition from small, high-quality brands.

The Payoffs

Figure 11–5 shows the payoff matrix for this game. If Molson and Labatt fight entry but are unsuccessful, they spend $2 million on the fight and lose $16 million in profits to the successful microbrewery, so they lose $18 million in total. If they fight and win, they spend $2 million fighting but retain the market share. If Molson and Labatt acquiesce, they lose a 1 percent market share to the microbrewery, for a payoff of negative $16 million. If they acquiesce and the microbrewery stays out, they spend nothing and lose nothing.

If the microbrewery chooses to enter the market and the major breweries fight, the firm spends $1 million on fighting off the two companies. If the microbrewery enters but Molson and Labatt acquiesce, the microbrewery earns a $16 million profit less the $1 million setup costs. If the microbrewery stays out, there are no profits and no costs involved.

FIGURE 11–5

Payoff Matrix

This payoff matrix shows that if the microbrewery enters the market, the best strategy for Molson and Labatt is to acquiesce. By acquiescing, the two dominant brewers lose $16 million, which is $2 million better than the $18 million loss that would occur if Molson and Labatt had fought the entry. If the microbrewery decides to stay out of the market, the best strategy of Molson and Labatt is also to acquiesce, as they would lose $0 compared to $2 million if they had fought the entry. Therefore the dominant strategy for Molson and Labatt is to acquiesce. Once Molson and Labatt decide to acquiesce, the best strategy for the microbrewery is to enter the market and earn $15 million in profit.

For critical analysis:

1. Is this game a positive-sum, zero-sum, or negative-sum game? How do you know?
2. What strategies, besides fighting, could Labatt and Molson use to deter entry by the microbreweries?

Sources: *Molson Coors 2006 Annual Report.* pp. 17, 20. http://media.corporate-ir.net/media_files/irol/10/101929/reports/2006AnnualReportEN.pdf. (Accessed July 24, 2007.); *2006 Annual Statistical Bulletin.* Brewers Association Of Canada. p. 5. http://www.brewers.ca/UserFiles/Documents/dfs/eng/statistics/asb/Keystone%20ASB%20(E)%20Final%202006.pdf. The Canadian Press. "Beer's market share dwindling as wine, spirits take hold: CP24. April 20, 2009. http://www.cp24.com/servlet/an/local/CTVNews/20100420/100420_beer/20100420/?hub=CP24Home; *2009 Annual Report.* Investor Relations. Molson Coors.http://phx.corporate-ir.net/phoenix.zhtml?c=101929&p=irol-reportsannual; 2009 Annual Report Anheuser-Busch. http://www.anheuser-busch.com/AnnualReports.html.

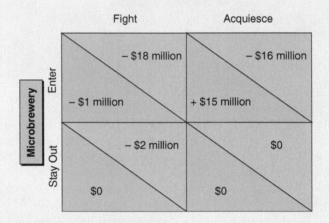

SUMMARY

Here is what you should know after reading this chapter. MyEconLab will help you identify what you know, and where to go when you need to practise. We suggest that as soon as you review one of the Learning Objective sections below, you then proceed to go through the related section in MyEconLab.

LEARNING OBJECTIVES	KEY TERMS	MYECONLAB PRACTICE
11.1 The Characteristics of Monopolistic Competition. Monopolistic competition, a market structure that lies between pure monopoly and perfect competition, has the following features: (1) a large number of sellers, (2) differentiated products, and (3) easy entry of firms in the long run. Each firm acts independently, as collusion is virtually impossible with a large number of competitors.	monopolistic competition, 280 product differentiation, 281	• **MyEconLab** Study Plan 11.1

LEARNING OBJECTIVES	KEY TERMS	MYECONLAB PRACTICE
11.2 Short-Run Price, Output, and Profit in Monopolistic Competition. Due to product differentiation, the demand curve for a firm in monopolistic competition is downward sloping, with marginal revenue below price. The firm chooses the profit-maximizing price-output combination—the output at which marginal revenue equals marginal cost, and the highest price possible at this output level, as determined by the demand curve. Total maximum profit equals the firm's maximum profit quantity level multiplied by the difference between the firm's price and average total cost, at the maximum profit quantity level. In the short run, the firm can be making a positive, negative, or zero economic profit.		• **MyEconLab** Study Plan 11.2
11.3 Long-Run Equilibrium in Monopolistic Competition. Similar to perfect competition, a monopolistically competitive firm will make a normal profit in the long run. The monopolistically competitive firm will operate at "excess capacity," which is at a quantity level that is less than the productively efficient, perfectly competitive, quantity level in the long run. Chamberlin argued that the difference between the average cost of production for a monopolistically competitive firm and a perfectly competitive firm is the cost of "differentness."	excess capacity, 284	• **MyEconLab** Study Plan 11.3
11.4 The Characteristics of Oligopoly. An oligopoly is a market situation dominated by a few interdependent sellers. An oligopoly market structure can exist for a homogeneous or a differentiated product. Oligopolies develop in the long run due to some type of barrier to entry such as economies of scale, legal restrictions, or firm-created barriers. Oligopoly industries exhibit high concentration ratios, which means that the top four or top eight firms account for a high percentage of industry sales.	oligopoly, 285 strategic dependence, 286 concentration ratio, 287	• **MyEconLab** Study Plan 11.4

LEARNING OBJECTIVES	KEY TERMS	MYECONLAB PRACTICE
11.5 Pricing Behaviour in Oligopoly. Since rival oligopoly firms are very interdependent, each firm must engage in strategic behaviour when determining its pricing strategy. One way to model this behaviour is to use game theory. The prisoners' dilemma game can be used to explain how an oligopoly firm, acting in its own individual self-interest, might engage in *noncooperative pricing behaviour*, even though this can reduce the joint profits of all the firms in the industry. In repeated games, the tit-for-tat strategy can result in *cooperative pricing behaviour.* Cooperative pricing strategies can include overt collusion tactics such as price fixing and cartels, or forms of tacit collusion such as price leadership. To the extent that oligopoly firms can cooperate and charge the monopoly price, joint profits will be maximized. There will be a greater tendency toward price cooperation (1) the smaller the number of rival firms, (2) in a growing industry situation, (3) the more identical the product supplied by all rivals, and (4) the lower the legal penalty attached to cooperative pricing behaviour. In some oligopoly situations the existing firms might engage in *price wars* or in order to deter new firms from entering the industry.	best response function, 287 game theory, 288 cooperative game, 288 noncooperative game, 288 zero-sum game, 288 negative-sum game, 288 positive-sum game, 288 strategy, 288 dominant strategies, 288 payoff matrix, 288 prisoners' dilemma, 289 opportunistic behaviour, 290 tit-for-tat strategy, 290 cartel, 292 price leadership, 293 predatory pricing, 294 price war, 296	• **MyEconLab** Study Plan 11.5
11.6 The Nonprice Forms of Competition in Oligopoly. Oligopoly firms often engage in nonprice forms of competition, including product differentiation, mergers, exclusive dealing, increasing switching costs, exploiting network effects, and innovation. Types of product differentiation include differences in product features, consumer incentives, financing options, sales promotions, and advertising. These nonprice forms of competition can achieve more permanent gains in market share, when compared to price-cutting, opportunistic behaviour. Advertising creates some social disadvantages: (1) it can increase the cost of production without adding valuable consumer information; (2) it can act as a barrier to entry; (3) it can result in greater monopoly power; and (4) it can seriously mislead the	merger, 298 horizontal merger, 298 vertical merger, 298 conglomerate merger, 298 exclusive dealing, 298 network effects, 299	• **MyEconLab** Study Plan 11.6

LEARNING OBJECTIVES	KEY TERMS	MYECONLAB PRACTICE

consumer. Advertising also creates some social benefits: (1) it can provide valuable technical and price information about a product; (2) it can serve as a valuable signalling device; and (3) it can promote productive efficiency in cases where it increases the sales volume so that economies of scale can be achieved.

Oligopoly firms can increase market share quickly through horizontal mergers. Exclusive dealing refers to a situation where the firm supplies its product to a customer on condition that the customer not buy similar products from rival firms supplying a similar product. By increasing switching costs, an existing oligopoly firm can better insulate itself from price competition as well as deter the entry of new firms. If an oligopoly firm can exploit the network effect, it can gain market share very quickly, as Facebook had found.

Theoretical arguments suggest that an oligopoly market structure can be conducive to technological innovation. The large size of many oligopoly firms enables them to undertake expensive research and development activities. As well, due to barriers to entry and the lure of long-run excess profits, oligopoly firms have the incentive to innovate. Finally, interdependent oligopoly firms may prefer to channel their competitive energies in constructive product innovation as opposed to destructive price competition.

11.7 Social Evaluation of Oligopoly. The social cost of oligopoly can include productive inefficiency, allocative inefficiency, and excess profits. Oligopoly can benefit society if it results from economies of scale or if it contributes to innovation.

• **MyEconLab** Study Plan 11.7

PROBLEMS

(Answers to the odd-numbered problems appear at the back of the book.)

LO 11.1 Identify and explain the characteristics of monopolistic competition.

1. Local night clubs in a large city typically operate under what type of market structure? Explain.

2. Compare and contrast the characteristics of monopolistic competition with perfect competition.

3. Explain why it is not rational for a perfectly competitive firm to incur significant advertising expenditures.

4. Referring to Example 11-1, "A Canadian Retail Success: Twenty-Seven Years Running," identify the various ways that Running Room has engaged in product differentiation.

LO 11.2 Using revenue and cost information, determine the price, output, and profit for a firm in monopolistic competition in the short run.

5. Sue Willows, a preschool teacher, created and now sells a mail-order kids' basic interactive math game in a CD format that features a popular cartoon character. She competes with numerous other similar games that are sold in a hard copy book format or as board games sold by toy retailers as well as children's online math games that can be downloaded from the Internet for a fee. Sue promotes this game regularly on commercials that run on a popular children's TV channel. The accompanying graph describes the per-unit price, revenue, and cost data associated with selling the CD.

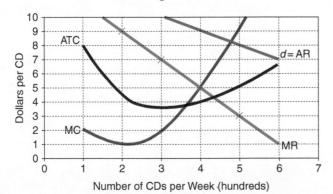

Based on this graph, complete the following.

a. Find the weekly profit-maximizing quantity.
b. Find the profit-maximizing price.
c. Find the total maximum weekly profit.
d. Which industry model best applies to Sue's game CD—perfect competition or monopolistic competition? Explain.

6. Tommy Soprano runs a take-out pizza outlet called The Healthy Alternative, which is located in a strip mall where there is a lot of parking available. Tommy sells only one type of pizza—a Loaded Vegetarian Pizza. The monthly fixed costs related to making and selling this pizza are: advertising $500; space and machine rental $1500; and salary and other costs $2000.

The variable costs involved in making and selling each pizza is $4 per pizza, regardless of the monthly quantity produced or sold.

Tommy directly competes with a children's pizza place, a meat lover's pizza parlour, as well as other takeout businesses selling hamburgers, subs, and Chinese food, all located within a three-block radius. Based on past experience, Tommy estimates the monthly demand for the Loaded Vegetarian Pizza as follows, depending on the pizza price.

Price per Pizza (P)	Pizzas Sold Per Month (Q)	Total Revenue (TR)	Marginal Revenue (MR)	Marginal Cost (MC)
$18	3200	_____	_____	_____
17	3600	_____	_____	_____
16	4000	_____	_____	_____
15	4400	_____	_____	_____
14	4800	_____	_____	_____

a. Fill in the blanks in the table. Note: To find marginal revenue, use the formula:

$$MR = (\text{Change in TR}) / (\text{Change in } Q)$$

b. Find the profit-maximizing quantity.
c. Find the profit-maximizing price.
d. Find the total maximum monthly profit.
e. Which industry model best suits Tommy's pizza firm—perfect competition or monopolistic competition? Explain.

LO 11.3 Describe long-run equilibrium in monopolistic competition.

7. The table at the top of the next page describes the price, revenue, and cost information for a small motel firm that rents rooms on a daily basis under monopolistic competition. Note that the quantity level refers to the number of rooms rented per night. The price refers to the nightly rental rate charged per room. Recall that marginal revenue is the extra revenue per room received, or the change in total revenue divided by the change in quantity.

a. Fill in the blanks in the table.
b. How many rooms must be rented per night in order to maximize profits?
c. What is the profit-maximizing price?
d. What is the amount of the total maximum profit?
e. Can this motel firm expect to earn these profits in the long run? Explain.
f. Identify the different ways motels and hotels can differentiate their "product."

Quantity (# rooms)	Price (per room)	Total Revenue	Marginal Revenue	Marginal Cost	Average Total Cost
0	$95	$____			
4	90	____	$____	$36	$86.00
8	85	____	____	34	60.00
12	80	____	____	33	51.00
16	75	____	____	34	46.75
20	70	____	____	36	44.60
24	65	____	____	39	43.67
28	60	____	____	43	43.57
32	55	____	____	48	44.13

8. The graph below depicts long-run equilibrium for a monopolistic competitor.
   a. Which output rate represents equilibrium?
   b. Which price represents equilibrium?
   c. Which labelled point indicates that economic profits are zero?
   d. Which labelled point indicates minimum ATC?
   e. Is ATC at the equilibrium output rate above or at minimum ATC?
   f. Is the equilibrium price greater than, less than, or equal to the marginal cost of producing at the equilibrium output rate?
   g. At what quantity would a perfectly competitive firm operate in the long run? Explain. What would be the perfectly competitive firm's level of economic profit in the long run?

Quantity per Time Period

9. The following table depicts the hourly quantity sold, prices, and costs for a popular used bookstore located close to a university campus. This store competes with numerous rival used bookstores but capitalizes on its location and the word-of-mouth reputation of the coffee it serves to its customers.

Quantity Sold (# Books)	Price ($)	Marginal Cost ($)	Average Total Cost ($)
0	6.00		
1	5.75	3.25	5.25
2	5.5	2.25	3.75
3	5.25	2.10	3.20
4	5.00	2.50	3.03
5	4.75	3.70	3.16
6	4.50	4.20	3.33
7	4.00	4.75	3.54

a. Why would this bookstore be classed as a firm in monopolistic competition?
b. In the short run, what would be the profit-maximizing hourly quantity, price, and total profit?
c. Suppose that after long-run equilibrium were achieved, the bookstore ended up selling two books per hour. What would be the long-run price and economic profit?
d. If this bookstore were operating in a perfectly competitive market, what would be the approximate price and economic profit, in the long run?

LO 11.4 Identify and explain the characteristics of oligopoly.

10. The following table indicates some information for industry A.

Firm	Annual Sales ($ millions)
1	200
2	150
3	100
4	75
5–30	300

a. What is the four-firm concentration ratio for this industry (with just 30 firms)?
b. Assume that industry A is the steel industry. What would happen to the concentration index if we redefined industry A as the cold rolled-steel industry? As the metals industry?

11. Classify each of the following as either a homogeneous product oligopoly or a differentiated product oligopoly.
    a. Cement manufacturing
    b. Auto manufacturing
    c. Oil refining
    d. Fast-food industry
    e. Soft drink manufacturing

12. Identify three types of barriers to entry characteristic of oligopoly.

LO 11.5 Identify and explain the types of pricing behaviour that can occur in oligopoly.

13. Suppose there are only two equal-sized firms—Firm A and Firm B—competing in an oligopoly industry. Each firm can decide either to raise or to lower the price of

the product. Each firm knows that the following outcomes will occur for each pricing decision, depending on how its rival reacts.

i. If both firms raise the price, each firm earns $5 million in annual profit.

ii. If both firms lower the price, each firm earns $3 million in annual profit.

iii. If one of the firms lowers the price while its rival raises the price, the firm with the low price will earn $7 million per year while the high-price firm will earn $1 million per year.

a. Construct a payoff matrix for these two oligopoly firms for all possible price decisions.

b. Assuming no collusion, what would be the dominant pricing strategy for each firm?

c. Suppose, in year 1, each firm decides to pursue cooperative pricing through collusion. What will be Firm A's annual profit?

d. Suppose, in year 2, Firm A decides to pursue opportunistic behaviour, while Firm B pursues a tit-for-tat strategy. What will be Firm A's profit in year 2?

e. If in year 3 both firms pursue a tit-for-tat strategy, what profit will Firm A earn in year 3?

f. In the long run, what would be the most profitable pricing strategy for each of these two firms?

14. Suppose two identical-sized oil refining firms, Apex and Petro, supply all the gasoline to a large city. If each firm agrees to limit its daily quantity to 20 000 litres per day, they will maximize their joint economic profits, with each firm earning $50 000 per day. If one of the firms increases its quantity to 40 000 litres, while the other firm supplies 20 000 litres, the economic profit earned by the firm with the larger quantity will increase to $75 000 per day, but the rival firm will be faced with an economic loss of $10 000 per day. If both companies increase their quantity so that each firm supplies 40 000 litres per day, zero economic profit will be earned by each competitor.

a. Construct a payoff matrix.

b. Assuming no collusion, in the short run, what would be the dominant quantity strategy for each firm?

c. If the tit-for-tat strategy is repeatedly used, in the long run, what quantity strategy would each firm employ?

15. Explain whether each of the following will increase or decrease the tendency toward cooperative pricing in an oligopoly.

a. The number of firms competing in the industry increases.

b. All the firms produce an identical product.

c. The industry sales are declining due to an economy wide recession.

16. On the basis of the information provided in Example 11–3, "OPEC Continues to Rule the World Oil Market," explain why Saudi Arabia is the key oil supplier responsible for the cooperative pricing behaviour displayed in OPEC.

17. Referring to Example 11–4, "De Beers Diamond Cartel: A Thing of the Past?", explain why diamonds are an attractive product to supply under a cartel arrangement.

LO 11.6 Identify, explain, and evaluate the various nonprice forms of competition in oligopoly.

18. Identify and explain three reasons why oligopolistic firms would favour nonprice competition over price competition.

19. According to Example 11–8, "Facebook Frenzy," social networking sites do not charge membership fees. Critically evaluate the idea that these online social networking sites are "free" to their members.

20. Identify and explain two arguments why an oligopoly industry environment might be very conducive to innovation.

21. When Coca-Cola increases its annual advertising expenses, it is likely that PepsiCo will do the same. Can you explain how this apparent self-cancelling behaviour can actually result in a positive-sum game for both companies?

LO 11.7 Evaluate the behaviour in oligopoly from a social viewpoint.

22. According to Example 11–6, "Can Advertising Lead to Efficiency?", advertising can actually contribute to productive efficiency. Explain the argument used in this example.

BUSINESS APPLICATION

LO 11.6 Identify, explain, and evaluate the various nonprice forms of competition in oligopoly.

Marketing: The Marketing Mix: The Four Ps

In order to enhance revenue and profit, firms operating under monopolistic competition and oligopoly may engage in product differentiation as well as price competition. In marketing terms, these firms attempt to create an effective *marketing mix* based on the needs and wants of their target market(s).

The *marketing mix* refers to the development of appropriate strategies for each of the "Four Ps"—*product, place, promotion*, and *price. Product* focuses on attributes such as design features, quality, types of services offered, guarantees, warranties, packaging, and style. *Place* refers to the selection and management of marketing channels and the physical distribution of products. In short, *place* is concerned with getting the product or service to the customer conveniently. *Promotion* refers to the methods the firm uses to enhance the target market's awareness and knowledge of the product or service being offered. These methods can include advertising, sales promotion, personal selling, and public relations. *Price* not only refers to the regular price of the product or service but also includes discounts, allowances, credit terms, and methods of payment accepted.

Business Application Problem

Steve Boyd has just started a business called InfoMutual that will provide monthly Canadian mutual fund information to sophisticated investors and to firms that sell mutual funds such as brokers, banks, and other financial advisors. Indicate which one of the Four Ps best relates to each of the following.

a. After considering other alternatives such as mail and fax, Steve decides to distribute his mutual fund information through a website.

b. In addition to providing the latest information relating to each Canadian mutual fund's performance, Steve plans to conduct sophisticated statistical analysis measuring the risk related to each type of fund. His analysis will also relate each mutual fund's performance with other mutual funds and with economywide factors.

c. In order to make his service known to prospective customers, Steve decides to register InfoMutual with major Internet search engines such as Google and Bing, as well as Facebook.

d. Steve rejects the idea of charging a monthly fee. Instead, customers can access his monthly information by paying a six-month or a one-year subscription fee.

e. Every quarter, Steve plans to provide detailed research reports to paid subscribers. These reports will profile a specific family of funds.

f. Steve plans to offer a cheaper educational subscription rate for business schools in colleges and universities that purchase a "site licence" for his services.

g. InfoMutual will regularly participate in popular investor blog and wiki discussions on the Internet in order to increase consumer awareness of the new company.

h. In order to make it convenient to pay for InfoMutual's subscription fee, each new customer will be provided with a free one-month temporary password. This free month of full service should provide ample time for the customer to arrange for the secure payment of the subscription fee.

i. Steve plans to have animated ads for InfoMutual appear on popular news and sports websites.

Answers to Odd-Numbered Problems

Chapter 1: The Nature of Economics

1. a. human capital
   b. land
   c. entrepreneurship
   d. physical capital
   e. labour

3. a. Macroeconomic, as the unemployment rate is national or economywide.
   b. Microeconomic, as wage increases of specific occupations, such as nurses and doctors, relate to specific parts of the economy.
   c. Microeconomic, as prices of a specific part of the economy—cigarettes—are being studied.
   d. Macroeconomic, as the inflation rate tracks the average price of all goods, which is an economy-wide measure.
   e. Macroeconomic, as the nation's total annual production is an economywide measure.
   f. Microeconomic, as an individual firm's situation, such as Eaton's bankruptcy, focuses on a specific part of the economy.

5. Jon's marginal cost of enrolling in the two-month computer course equals the cost of tuition, books, and fees plus the two months of earnings he sacrifices. This amounts to: $4500 + (2 \times $3000) = $10\,500$

7. No, your cash withdrawals are not free as there is an opportunity cost equal to the interest sacrificed by not putting your $5000 in an account (or another investment) giving you a higher rate of interest.

9. The decision based on availability of funds is not a rational one. In order to allocate resources in a manner that maximizes the satisfaction of the city's wants, the mayor should compare the marginal (extra) benefit of constructing the city hall with the marginal (extra) cost, including alternatives sacrificed. If the extra benefit to the city of constructing the city hall is less than the value of some other alternative that has to be sacrificed, such as paving of city roads, the mayor's decision is not rational.

11. a. We should observe younger drivers to be more frequently involved in traffic accidents than older persons.
    b. Slower monetary expansion should be associated with lower inflation.
    c. Professional basketball players receiving smaller salaries should be observed to have done less well in their high-school studies.

d. Employees being promoted rapidly should have lower rates of absenteeism than those being promoted more slowly.

13. a. Positive, for it is a statement that can be tested by the facts.
    b. Normative, involving a value judgment about what should be.
    c. Normative, involving a value judgment about what should be.
    d. Positive, for it is a statement that can be tested by the facts.

Appendix A: Reading and Working with Graphs

A-1. a. Price is independent, number of notebooks is dependent.
    b. Work-study hours is independent, credit hours is dependent.
    c. Hours studied is independent, and grade is dependent.

A-3.

x	y
4	12
3	9
2	6
1	3
0	0
−1	−3
−2	−6
−3	−9
−4	−12

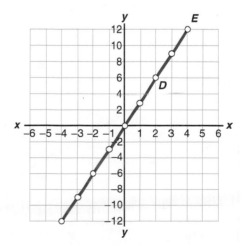

A-5. If you move along the line in Problem A-3 from point D to point E, the slope equals the change in the y-values divided by the change in the x-values, which is:

$$(12 - 6)/(4 - 2) = 6/2 = 3.$$

A-7. For the ordered pair $(4, 16)$ the tangent line is upward sloping, slope is positive.

For the ordered pair $(0, 0)$ the tangent line is horizontal, slope is zero.

For the ordered pair $(-4, 16)$ the tangent line is downward sloping, slope is negative.

Chapter 2: Production Possibilities and Economic Systems

1. a. The maximum amount of factories will be 2000 as shown by the production possibilities curve.

    b. The maximum number of factories would be 5000, as shown by combination A.

    c. A fixed amount of resources and technology prevents Epica from being able to produce combination J in 2008.

    d. If Epica is at point I, this could conflict with the goals of productive efficiency and full employment.

    e. i. The opportunity cost of an additional factory when moving from point E to D would be 2 yachts.

        ii. The opportunity cost of an additional factory when moving from point C to B would be 4 yachts.

    f. i. The opportunity cost of an additional yacht when moving from point A to B would be $\frac{1}{5}$ of a factory.

        ii. The opportunity cost of an additional yacht when moving from point E to F would be 1 factory.

    g. The Law of Increasing Relative Cost

    h. This situation conflicts with allocative efficiency.

    i. Economic growth will shift the production possibilities curve outward.

3. The plot of the product possibilities curve is displayed in the graph below.

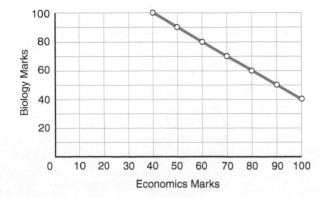

The PPC exhibits constant opportunity costs. That is, the cost of earning an additional mark in economics is always the same, in terms of additional biology marks sacrificed. In this case, the PPC is a straight line with the opportunity cost of earning an additional mark in economics always being 1 mark in biology.

5.

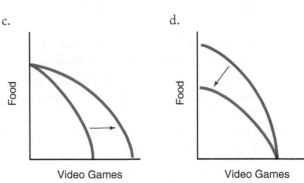

7. If we assume that a two-year college diploma consists of four 15-week semesters, this amounts to committing 60 weeks to college studies. The opportunity cost is: 60 wks × 35 h × $7 = $14 700. The incentive for incurring this cost is that, upon graduating, you will be earning an amount significantly in excess of $7 per hour. You are sacrificing current consumption to obtain a greater amount of future consumption.

9. Yes, you and your roommate should specialize. Since your opportunity cost of completing a basket of laundry (two meals) is lower than your roommate's (three meals), you should specialize in the laundry completion, while your roommate should specialize in the meal preparation. As an example, if you complete an extra basket of laundry, you give up only two meals. However, you free up an additional three hours of your roommate's time, which allows your roommate to produce an additional three meals. Overall, one extra meal is gained.

11. a. Toby has the absolute advantage in pizzas.

    b. Tony has the lower opportunity cost in producing one lasagne supreme (gives up one pizza versus two pizzas for Toby) so Tony has a comparative advantage in lasagne.

    c. Toby has the comparative advantage in pizza and Tony in lasagne. For each hour of specializing in the area of comparative advantage, there is a net gain of five pizzas (Toby: +10 pizzas and 5 lasagne; Tony +5 lasagne and −5 pizzas).

13. The invisible hand of self-interest and competition help to ensure that firms serve the consumer, without the heavy hand of government.

15. a. In the market system, the techniques that yield the highest (positive) profits will be used.

   b. Profit equals total revenue minus total cost. Because revenue from 100 units is fixed (at $100), if the firm wishes to maximize profit, this is equivalent to minimizing costs. To find total costs, simply multiply the price of each input by the amount of the input that must be used for each technique.

   Costs of A = ($10)(6) + ($8)(5) = $100

   Costs of B = ($10)(5) + ($8)(6) = $98

   Costs of C = ($10)(4) + ($8)(7) = $96

   Because technique C has the lowest costs, it also yields the highest profits ($100 − $96 = $4).

   c. Following the same methods yields these costs: A = $98, B = $100, and C = $102. Technique A will be used because it is the most profitable.

   d. The profits from using technique A to produce 100 units of X are $100 $98 = $2.

Appendix B: The Production Possibilities Curve and Comparative Advantage

B-1 a. The Richard family has the absolute advantage in each product, assuming that both families use the same amount of labour input, each day.

   b. For the Martin family the opportunity cost of one litre of beer is one litre of wine. For the Richard family the opportunity cost of one litre of beer is three litres of wine.

   c. The Martin family has the comparative advantage (lower opportunity cost) in beer and the Richard family has the comparative advantage in wine.

   d. Total combined beer production increases from three litres to four litres per day, a gain of one litre. Total combined wine production increases from 17 litres to 18 litres per day, a gain of one litre.

   e. For both families to share the gains from specialization, one litre of beer should trade for somewhere between one and three litres of wine (between each family's opportunity cost for beer).

Chapter 3: Demand and Supply

1. The absolute prices of heating oil and natural gas have both increased. The relative price of heating oil

decreased as it went from $1.00/$0.80 = 1.25 to $2.00/$3.20 = 0.63. This implies that the relative price of natural gas increased. Yes, consumers will increase their purchases of heating oil relative to natural gas, as heating oil's relative price has declined. This assumes that the prices shown in the table are per constant-quality unit.

3. a. Since the price of a substitute decreases, there will be a decrease in demand for Canadian beef and the demand curve will shift leftward.

   b. An increase in demand will occur, where the demand curve shifts rightward.

   c. An increase in quantity demanded will occur, which can be described as a movement along (down) the same demand curve.

   d. A decrease in demand will occur, where the demand curve will shift leftward.

   e. A decrease in quantity demanded will occur, which can be described as a movement along (up) the same demand curve.

5. a. P_e = $11 and Q_e = 80 million CDs.

   b. At a price of $13, there would be a surplus equal to (120 − 60) = 60 million CDs. The surplus will drive down the price.

   c. At a price of $10, there would be a shortage equal to (90 − 60) = 30 million CDs. The shortage will drive up the price.

7. The graph below illustrates a shift to the right in the demand curve, which indicates an *increase in demand*. The new equilibrium price and quantity are $12 and 100 million CDs. A change in any factor other than the price of CDs will cause an increase in demand, such as an increase in income or an increase in the popularity of rock music.

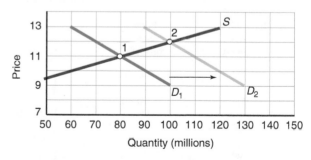

9. a. Increase in quantity demanded $Pe \downarrow$, $Qe \uparrow$ as a result of an increase in supply.

   b. Increase in demand $Pe \uparrow$, $Qe \uparrow$

   c. Increase in demand $Pe \uparrow$, $Qe \uparrow$

   d. Increase in demand $Pe \uparrow$, $Qe \uparrow$

   e. Decrease in demand $Pe \downarrow$, $Qe \downarrow$

11. a. At a price of $1.40, there would be a surplus equal to (5 − 3) or 2000 dozen eggs. This will drive down the price.

b. At a price of $0.80, there would be a shortage equal to (6 − 2) or 4000 dozen eggs. This will drive up the price.

c. The equilibrium price and quantity is $1.20 and 4000 dozen eggs.

d. i.   Increase in demand, $Pe \uparrow$, $Qe \uparrow$
    ii. Decrease in supply, $Pe \uparrow$, $Qe \downarrow$
    iii. Decrease in demand, $Pe \downarrow$, $Qe \downarrow$
    iv. Increase in supply, $Pe \downarrow$, $Qe \uparrow$

13. a. The equilibrium rent and quantity are $400 and 4000 units per month.

    b. There will be a shortage equal to (6 − 2) or 4000 units per month.

    c. In the short run, by keeping the price of a substitute (one-bedroom units) lower, there will be a decrease in demand for two-bedroom units, causing a decrease in equilibrium rent and quantity of two-bedroom units. In the longer run, due to the shortage of one-bedroom units, there will be an increase in demand for two-bedroom units, causing equilibrium price and quantity to increase.

15. a. Increase in demand and increase in supply. While the equilibrium quantity will increase, the combined effect on equilibrium price is indeterminate.

    b. Decrease in supply and increase in demand. While the equilibrium price will increase, the combined effect on equilibrium quantity is indeterminate.

    c. Increase in supply and decrease in demand. While the equilibrium price will decrease, the combined effect on equilibrium quantity is indeterminate.

Chapter 4: Elasticity

1. a.

Quantity Demanded per Week (kilograms)	Price per Kilogram	Elasticity
1000	$ 5	
800	10	$\frac{1}{3}$, or 0.33
600	15	$\frac{5}{7}$, or 0.714
400	20	$\frac{7}{5}$, or 1.4
200	25	$\frac{9}{3}$, or 3

b. This would depend on a person's preferences, one of the determinants of demand.

c. A person's preferences and income would determine whether tea is a luxury or necessity.

3. The problem is with the denominator, in calculating the percentage change in P. Because the initial price was zero, any increase in price is of infinite percentage.

However, if we take the average elasticity over a segment, there will be no problem. P will become the average of $P_1 (= 0)$ and $P_2 (= 10)$, or $(P_1 + P_2)/2 = 5$.

5. a. The price elasticity of demand for cars is elastic.

    b. The dealer's total revenue will increase.

7. a. Salt has few substitutes but is a very small portion of the total budget, and so it would be more inelastic.

    b. There are many suppliers of ski boats, and so you would probably shop around for the best deal, so it would be more elastic.

    c. A guitar pick takes up a very small portion of the total budget for a major rock band, and so it would be very inelastic.

7. No demand curve can possibly be perfectly inelastic, regardless of the price, because perfect inelasticity means absolutely no price responsiveness, no matter what the price, the quantity demanded remains unchanged.

9.

$$\frac{(2000 - 1000)/1500}{(20\,000 - 15\,000)/17\,500} = 0.67/0.286 = 2.34$$

a. The demand is elastic; as people's income increases, the demand for DVDs also increases.

b. Because the number is positive this would be considered a normal or luxury good.

11. a. $(525 - 600)/(525 + 600)/ 2/(15 - 17)/ (15 + 17)/2 = 1200/1125 = 1.07$

    b. The supply of salt is price elastic, the elasticity coefficient of supply is greater than 1.

Chapter 6: Extensions of Demand, Supply, and Elasticity

1. Ticket scalpers are middlemen who ensure that the scarce tickets get sold to those consumers who value the tickets the most. In other words, scalpers use the price system to ensure an efficient allocation of tickets.

3. a. The equilibrium price and quantity of $4 and 7 million crates would result.

    b. A shortage of (8 − 4) or 4 million crates would occur. This is an example of a price ceiling policy.

    c. The maximum black market price is that price associated with a quantity demanded of 4 million crates, which is $6 per crate.

    d. A surplus of (8 − 6) or 2 million crates would occur. This is an example of a price floor policy.

5. a. The equilibrium price and quantity of $1 and 40 million litres would result.

    b. At a maximum price of $0.80, a shortage of (50 − 30) or 20 million litres will result. This would be called a price ceiling policy.

    c. The black market price would be $1.20.

d. At a minimum price of $1.40, a surplus of $(60 - 20)$ or 40 million litres will result. This would be called a price floor policy.

7. a. Total revenue received is $4 per crate $\times$ 7 million crates = $28 million.

   b. A surplus of $(8 - 6)$ or 2 million crates would occur. Total revenue received is $5 $\times$ 8 million crates = $40 million. The total taxpayer cost would be (Support price $\times$ Surplus) or ($5 $\times$ 2 million) or $10 million.

   c. At a restricted quantity of 6 million crates, the quantity demanded schedule indicates that consumers would pay a price of $5. With the marketing board, the total revenue would be ($5 $\times$ 6 million) or 30 million. When the price is increased from the equilibrium price of $4 to the marketing board price of $5, the total revenue increases from $28 million to $30 million. This implies that the demand is inelastic.

9. a. Total revenue received is $1 per litre 40 million litres, or $40 million.

   b. An Offer to Purchase price policy of $1.20 would result in a surplus equal to $(50 - 30)$ or 20 million litres. Total revenue received is $1.20 $\times$ 50 million litres or $60 million. The total taxpayer cost equals ($1.20 $\times$ 20 million) or $24 million.

   c. If a marketing board restricts the quantity sold to 30 million litres, the price would be $1.20. The total revenue would be $1.20 $\times$ 30 = $36 million. When the price is increased from $1 to $1.20 the total revenue decreases from $40 million to $36 million, indicating that demand is elastic—the marketing board policy does not support the farmer!

11. As illustrated in problem 10, the import quota would increase the price of California wines to Canadian consumers. If demand is inelastic, the higher price will result in Canadians spending a greater total revenue on California wines.

13. a. At the price of $0.70 per litre, the gas suppliers will receive $0.50 per litre in their pockets, after paying the $0.20 per litre tax to the government. According to the before-tax supply table, if the firms receive $0.50 per litre in their pockets, they will supply 60 million litres per day. Therefore, the after-tax market quantity supplied is 60 million litres when the price is $0.70 per litre. The other market supplies (in millions of litres) starting with a price of $0.60 per litre are: 50, 40, 30, 20, 10.

   b. The after-tax equilibrium price and quantity is $0.50 per litre and 40 million litres per day, respectively.

   c. Since the equilibrium price went up from $0.40 per litre to $0.50 per litre, the buyer's portion of the tax

burden equals $0.10 per litre, which is the price increase. The seller's portion of the tax burden is the tax minus the buyer's portion, which is $0.20 − $0.10 = $0.10 per litre.

   d. The total tax revenue equals the tax per unit multiplied by the after-tax equilibrium quantity, which equals $0.20 per litre $\times$ 40 million litres = $8 million per day.

   e. The daily tax revenue will increase when demand becomes less elastic.

   f. The tax will more effectively reduce gas consumption when the demand becomes more elastic.

15. a. The before-tax equilibrium price and quantity are $0.60 per CD and 50 million CDs per month.

   b. The excise tax equals $0.20 per CD, which is the vertical distance between the S_1 and S_2 supply curves.

   c. The after-tax equilibrium price and quantity are $0.70 per CD and 40 million CDs.

   d. The buyers' portion of the tax burden equals the increase in equilibrium price, which is $0.10 per CD. The seller's portion is equal to the tax per CD minus the buyer's tax burden, which is $0.20 − $0.10 = $0.10 per CD.

   e. The total monthly tax revenue equals the after-tax equilibrium quantity multiplied by the per-unit tax, which equals 40 million CDs $\times$ $0.20 per CD equals $8 million.

   f. The tax revenue will increase when supply becomes less elastic.

   g. The excise tax will more effectively discourage the use of CDs when supply becomes more elastic.

APPENDIX C: THE DEADWEIGHT LOSS DUE TO GOVERNMENT PRICE CONTROLS

C-1 a. Under a laissez-faire policy, the equilibrium price of $1.20 per litre and equilibrium quantity of 3 million litres will prevail. The consumer surplus that relates to a quantity of 3 million litres equals to the area under the demand curve but over the price line. This area equals (.5 $\times$ base $\times$ height) = (.5 $\times$ 3 million $\times$ $.80 per litre) − $1.2 million. The producer surplus that relates to a quantity of 3 million litres equals to the area over the supply curve but under the price line. This area equals (.5 $\times$ base $\times$ height) = (.5 $\times$ 3 million $\times$ $1.20 per litre) = $1.8 million. The sum of the consumer and producer surplus equals $1.2 + $1.8 = $ 3 million.

   b. Under a price ceiling of $90 per litre, the quantity supplied will decrease from 3 million litres to 2 million litres per week. This will reduce the consumer surplus by (.5 $\times$ base $\times$ height) = .5 $\times$

1 million × $.40 = $.2 million. The producer surplus will be reduced by (.5 × base × height) = .5 × 1 million × $.30 = $.15 million. The total allocative efficiency loss would be $.2 + $.15 = $.35 million. Since this policy reduces the sum of consumer and producer surplus, this causes an allocatively inefficient situation.

c. The price ceiling policy results in an under production of gasoline as the marginal benefit of the last litre consumed ($1.60) exceeds its marginal cost ($.90).

Chapter 7: Consumer Choice

1. For you, the marginal utility of the fifth kilogram of oranges is equal to the marginal utility of the third ear of corn. Apparently, your friend's tastes differ from yours—for her, the marginal utilities are not equal. For her, corn's marginal utility is too low, while that of oranges is too high—that's why she wants you to get rid of some of the corn (raising its marginal utility). She would have you do this until marginal utilities, for her, were equal. If you follow her suggestions, you will end up with a market basket that maximizes her utility subject to the constraint of your income. Is it any wonder that shopping from someone else's list is a frustrating task?

3. Her marginal utility is 100 at $1. It is 200 at 50 cents, and 50 at $2. To calculate marginal utility per dollar, divide marginal utility by price per unit.

5. The utility-maximizing combination of cheeseburgers and french fries would be two cheeseburgers at 36 total

7. A fall in the price of the goods leads to more of that good being consumed, meaning that the satisfaction level has not been reached or diminishing marginal utility has not set in.

9. All that can be known for certain is that marginal utility is positive.
beef lover (your indifference curves are relatively flat),

11.

Number of Cheeseburgers	Total Utility of Cheeseburgers	Marginal Utility of Cheeseburgers	Boxes of French Fries	Total Utility of French Fries	Marginal Utility of French Fries
0	0	0	0	0	0
1	20	20	1	8	8
2	36	16	2	14	6
3	48	12	3	18	4
4	56	8	4	20	2
5	60	4	5	20	0

13. If there was no diminishing marginal utility of potatoes, people would take all the potatoes they could, and leave no money. They would be unable to sell those potatoes because people can buy them directly from the farmers.

Appendix D: More Advanced Consumer Choice Theory

D-1. The problem here is that such preferences are inconsistent (*intransitive* is the word that economists use). If this consumer's tastes really are this way, then when confronted with a choice among *A*, *B*, and *C*, she will be horribly confused because *A* is preferred to *B*, Which is preferred to *C*, which is preferred to *A*, which is preferred to *B*, which is preferred to *C*, and so on forever. Economists generally assume that preferences are consistent (or *transitive*): If *A* is preferred to *C*. Regardless of what people may say about their preferences, the assumption of transitivity seems to do quite well in predicting what people actually do.

D-3. With an income of $100 and the original prices, you could have consumed *either* 50 kilograms of beef *or* 5 units of shelter or any linear combination shown by the budget line labelled "Original" on the graph below. With the same income but the new prices, you can now consume 25 kilograms of beef or 10 units of shelter or any linear combination shown by the line labelled "New budget." Without information about your preferences, there is no way to tell whether you are better off or worse off. Draw a few indifference curves on the diagram. You will find that if you are a "shelter lover" (your indifference curves are relatively steep), the decline in the relative price of shelter will tend to make you better off. Conversely, if you are a beef lover (your indifference curves are relatively flat), the rise in the relative price of beef will make you worse off.

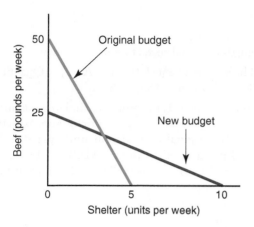

D-5. The first burrito is substituted at a rate of 10 servings of yogurt per burrito; the second burrito is substituted at a rate of 4:1; the third at a rate of 3:1; and the fourth at a rate of 2:1.

D-7. a. This person is simply indifferent between going or staying, an attitude that is perfectly consistent with our assumptions about consumer preferences.

   b. This statement denies the law of substitution and so is inconsistent with our assumptions about preferences.

   c. If we interpret "if I had my way" to mean "if I had an unlimited budget," this statement simply says that there is nonsatiation for these goods for this consumer—which is perfectly consistent with our assumptions about preferences.

Chapter 8: The Firm: Cost and Output Determination

1. Explicit costs = $12\,000 + $1000 + $20\,000 + $4000 = $37\,000

   Implicit costs = $40\,000 + (5000 \times 5\%) = $40\,250

3. Accounting profit = $200\,000 - $20\,000 - ($30\,000 \times 2) - $12\,000 - $40\,000 = $68\,000

   Economic profit = $200\,000 - $20\,000 ($30\,000 \times 2) - $12\,000 - $40\,000 - $40\,000 - $1000 = $27\,000

5.

Input of Labour	Total Output	Marginal Physical Product
0	0	----
1	25	25
2	60	35
3	85	25
4	105	20
5	115	10
6	120	5

7. a. Marginal performance was 5 out of 10, or 0.5.

   b. Since marginal performance was below average performance, average performance fell.

   c. Marginal performance would rise from 0.5 to 0.6, but average performance would still fall because 0.6 is less than the average, which was 0.8.

9. Total variable costs are equal to total costs of $5 million, less total fixed costs of $2 million, which equals $3 million. Average variable costs are equal to total variable costs divided by the number of units produced. Average variable costs, therefore, equal $3 million divided by 10 000, or $300.

11. Average total costs will fall until marginal costs are equal to the average total costs.

13. a. Q_3 c. Q_2 e. Q_4
    b. Q_4 d. Q_3

15. a. Experiencing economies of scale, costs are still decreasing.
    b. Plant Size E.

Chapter 9: Perfect Competition

1. a. Since there is one firm that can affect the market price, this is not perfect competition.

   b. This is not perfect competition, as each firm's product is not identical (not homogeneous) due to the differences in quality.

   c. Since government restricts entry through licensing, the easy-entry feature of perfect competition is violated.

3. a.

b. The industry's demand curve is typically downward sloping, while the firm's demand curve is perfectly elastic (horizontal). The firm's demand curve is perfectly elastic due to the assumption of having many firms supplying the identical product. If a firm were to raise its price just above the going price, it would lose all its sales.

5. In the table below, Total Profit is calculated by the formula:

Total Revenue − Total Cost:

Hourly Quantity (# of pizzas)	0	1	2	3	4	5	6	7	8	9	10
Total Profit (Price = $10)	−3	1	9	18	26	32	36	38	37	33	26
Total Profit (Price = $3)	−3	−6	−5	−3	−2	−3	−6	−11	−19	−30	−44
Total Profit (Price = $2)	−3	−7	−7	−6	−6	−8	−12	−18	−27	−39	−54

a. The profit at a price of $10 is based on the total revenue formula: $TR = 10 \times Q$. The profit-maximizing quantity is seven pizzas per hour with a total positive economic profit of $38 per hour.

b. The profit at a price of $3 is based on the total revenue formula: $TR = 3 \times Q$. The loss-minimizing quantity is four pizzas per hour with a total negative economic profit (loss) of $2 per hour. Note that by operating at four pizzas per hour, the firm minimizes its losses to be $2. If it shuts down, its total losses would be its total fixed cost of $3. The reason it should operate at four pizzas is that its total revenue of $12 exceeds its total variable cost of $11. By operating, it is able to contribute $1 toward covering its total fixed costs.

c. The profit at a price of $2 is based on the total revenue formula: $TR = 2 \times Q$. The loss-minimizing quantity is zero pizzas per hour with a total negative economic profit (loss) of $3 per hour, equal to total fixed cost. Since, at all quantities, total revenue is less than total variable cost, the firm should shut down.

7.

Output (units per hour)	Average Fixed Cost (AFC)	Average Variable Cost (AVC)	Average Total Cost (ATC)	Marginal Cost (MC)
1	$102.00	$40	$142.00	
2	51.00	35	86.00	$30
3	34.00	40	74.00	50
4	25.50	45	70.50	60
5	20.40	50	70.40	70
6	17.00	55	72.00	80
7	14.57	60	74.57	90

a. At a price of $81, the profit-maximizing quantity is where marginal revenue (price) approximately equals marginal cost, at six units per day.

The total profit equals (Price − ATC) × Quantity = (81 − 72) × 6 = $54 per hour.

b. At a price of $61, the profit-maximizing quantity is where marginal revenue (price) approximately equals marginal cost, at four units per day. The total profit equals (Price − ATC) × Quantity = (61 − 70.50) × 4 = −$38 per hour (minimum loss). No, if the firm were to shut down, it would face a larger loss equal to its total fixed cost of $102 per hour.

c. At a price of $31, the price is below minimum average variable cost, which is approximately $35, and so the firm should shut down. Its minimum loss equals its total fixed cost of $102.

d. The short-run breakeven point occurs at minimum average total cost, which is approximately $70.40 per unit.

e. The short-run shutdown point occurs at minimum average variable cost, which is just below $35.

9. a. At the price of $50, firm J will sell 81 units, where price or marginal revenue equals marginal cost.

b. Total profit equals (P − ATC) × Q = ($50 − $43) × 81 = $567.

c. Firm J will shut down when the price drops just below $20, which is minimum average variable cost.

d. Long-run price = $42 = minimum ATC

11. a. At $5 per chair, the profit-maximizing quantity would be 400 chairs per day, where Price = MC. The daily maximum profit would be:

(Price − ATC) × Q = ($5 − $4) × 400 = $400 per day

b. At $3, at best, the firm would be making negative economic profits as the price will be below ATC.

c. At a price of $3 per chair, the firm should NOT shut down as the price can exceed AVC.

d. At a price of $1 per chair, the firm should shut down as the price cannot exceed AVC.

13.

Price per Unit	Individual Quantity Supplied	Industry Supply (1000 firms)	Industry Demand
$91	7	7000	5000
81	6	6000	6000
51	3	3000	8000
31	0	0	9000

a. The short-run equilibrium price will be $81 per unit.

b. Short-run equilibrium is at six units, where marginal revenue (price) equals marginal cost. The total profit equals (Price − ATC) × Quantity = (81 − 72) × 6 = $54 per hour.

15. a. No, $81 will not be the long-run equilibrium price, as each firm is making a positive economic profit of $54 per hour. In the long run, new firms will enter the industry, attracted by the positive profits. As new firms enter, the industry price will fall below $81 and will keep falling until no more economic profit is being earned.

b. The long-run equilibrium price will just equal minimum long-run average total cost, which is approximately $70.40. At this price, each firm will earn zero economic profit so that there will be no incentive for new firms to continue to enter the industry.

17. a. Since per-unit costs increase as the industry expands, this is an increasing-cost industry with an upward-sloping long-run supply curve.

b. Since per-unit costs decrease as the industry expands, this is a decreasing-cost industry with a downward-sloping long-run supply curve.

19. a. Since this competitive industry is producing a product that entails external benefits, it will under-allocate resources to its product.

b. Since this competitive industry is producing a product that entails external costs, it will over-allocate resources to its product.

Chapter 10: Monopoly

1. a. Predatory behaviour
   b. Legal restriction
   c. Economies of scale

3. The perfectly competitive firm faces a perfectly elastic (horizontal) demand curve—it is a price-taker. This is because it competes with many firms in supplying the identical product. If the competitive firm were to increase its price just above the going price, it would lose all of its sales. The monopoly firm faces a downward-sloping demand curve, where the elasticity is neither perfectly elastic nor perfectly inelastic—it is a price-searcher. This is because the firm is the industry, and, as industry sales increase significantly, the price will decline.

5. a. The rectangle that shows total costs under ATC_1 is $OWCQ$. Total revenue is shown by $OXBQ$. This monopolist is in an economic profit situation. MC = MR is the output at which profit—the difference between total cost and total revenue—is maximized.

b. With ATC_2, the rectangle showing total costs is $OXBQ$. The same rectangle, $OXBQ$, gives total revenue. This monopolist is breaking even. MC = MR shows the only quantity that does not cause losses.

c. Under ATC_3, total costs are represented by rectangle $OYAQ$, total revenue by $OXBQ$. Here the monopolist is operating at an economic loss, which is minimized by producing where MC = MR.

7. a. The filled-in table should look as follows:

Price	Quantity Demanded	Total Revenue	Marginal Revenue	Average Total Cost	Marginal Cost
$20	0	$ 0	$ −	−	−
16	1	16	16	$ 8.00	$ 5.00
12	2	24	8	7.50	7.00
10	3	30	6	8.00	9.00
7	4	28	−2	9.25	13.00
4	5	20	−8	11.00	18.00
0	6	0	−20	13.16	24.00

b. The maximum profit output would be 2 units where marginal revenue is close to, but exceeds, marginal cost.

c. The profit-maximizing price would be $12.00.

d. The amount of maximum profit would be

$(P − ATC) × Q$ or $(12 − 7.5) × 2$ or $9.00.

9. a. The profit-maximizing output is 200, where MR equals MC.

b. The profit-maximizing price is $14.00, derived from the demand curve.

c. The amount of maximum profit is equal to $(P − ATC) × Q$ or $(14 − 12) × 200$ or $400.00.

11. a. The loss-minimizing level is 1 million bottles per month, where MR = MC.

b. At 1 million bottles per month, losses will be minimized at: $(P − ATC)(Q) = (30 − 33)(1$ million bottles$) = −$3 million per month

13. If the monopolist charges a single price for all suits cleaned, it will earn a maximum profit of $14 per day (where MR = MC). If the monopolist practises perfect price discrimination, it will clean eight suits per day (where P = MC) and earn a maximum profit of $23. Therefore, it will increase profits by $9 per day.

15. a. Under perfect price discrimination, the marginal revenue column would be the same as the price column.

    b. The maximum profit output would be where price approximately equals marginal cost or at three units.

    c. The maximum profit is calculated by taking total revenue minus total cost or (16 + 12 + 10) minus (3 × 8), which equals (38 − 24) = $14 profit.

17. a. The business people's demand for hotels would be more inelastic than the leisured people's demand for the same hotel. Therefore, the monopolist could enhance its profit by charging a higher price for those who use the hotel for business purposes. That is why you often see lower hotel rates offered on weekends than during the week.

    b. Business people do not have time to shop around for their fast-food meal, while retired people do have the time. Also, business people are likely to have a greater amount of income than retired people. These considerations would make the business people's demand for fast food more inelastic than the retired people's demand. The monopolist could increase profit by charging higher fast food prices to business people.

    c. The cost of a movie for a family of four is a larger part of the family budget than for a couple only. The family's demand for movies will be more elastic than the couple's demand. The monopolist can increase profit by charging the family less, per person. This is often done by charging children a lower admission fee than adults.

19. a. A natural monopoly can promote productive efficiency. That is, because of economies of scale, one large monopoly firm could produce the product at a lower average total cost than a smaller competitive firm.

    b. A perfectly discriminating monopoly can promote allocative efficiency to the extent that it produces at a quantity level where price (marginal benefit) just equals marginal cost.

21. The daily total revenue and marginal revenue are shown below.

Quantity	Price	TR	MR	ATC	MC
1	$500	$ 500	$ 500	$500	–
2	450	900	400	350	$200
3	395	1185	285	300	200
4	350	1400	215	275	200
5	300	1500	100	260	200
6	250	1500	0	250	200
7	200	1400	(100)	243	200

   a. The maximum profit quantity (MR = MC) is 4 dishes per day, with a price of $350 and a daily profit of $300.00.

   b. Under marginal cost pricing (P = MC), the daily quantity would be 7 dishes per day, with a price of $200 and a daily profit of −$301.

   c. Under average cost pricing (P = ATC), the daily quantity would be 6 dishes per day, with a price of $250 and a daily profit of $0 or normal profit.

   d. An unregulated monopolist tends to restrict output in order to drive up the price so as to make excess profits. Average cost pricing regulation provides a higher daily quantity at a lower price. The profit earned by the company is no more than a normal profit.

Appendix E: The Deadweight Loss Due to Monopoly

E-1 a. Use the table in part (a) of Figure 10–4 to compute the consumer surplus assuming that the monopoly firm maximizes profit and produces at nine units of output and charges $5.75 per unit. As shown in the table below, you can add up the surplus derived by the consumers for each of the nine units of output produced. The total consumer surplus is $9. (See Table E-1a.)

    b. Use the table in part (a) of Figure 10–4 to compute the producer surplus assuming that the monopoly firm maximizes profit and produces at nine units of output and charges $5.75 per unit. As shown in the table below, you can add up the surplus derived by the producer for each of the nine units of output produced. The total producer surplus is $22.50. (See Table E-1b.)

    c. No, the monopoly firm is not maximizing the sum of consumer and producer surpluses. Both surpluses would be maximized where price equals marginal cost (allocative efficiency level) at approximately 11 units of output, with price being close to $5.25.

Table E-1A

Quantity	1	2	3	4	5	6	7	8	9	Total Surplus
Maximum willing to pay (see price column)	$7.75	$7.50	$7.25	$7.00	$6.75	$6.50	$6.25	$6.00	$5.75	
Price actually paid	5.75	5.75	5.75	5.75	5.75	5.75	5.75	5.75	5.75	
Surplus	$2.00	$1.75	$1.50	$1.25	$1.00	$0.75	$0.50	$0.25	$0.00	$9.00

Table E-1B

Quantity	1	2	3	4	5	6	7	8	9	Total Surplus
Minimum prepared to accept (see marginal cost table)	$4.00	$3.50	$3.25	$3.05	$2.90	$2.80	$2.90	$3.15	$3.70	
Price actually received	5.75	5.75	5.75	5.75	5.75	5.75	5.75	5.75	5.75	
Surplus	$1.75	$2.25	$2.50	$2.70	$2.85	$2.95	$2.85	$2.60	$2.05	$22.50

E-3 a. Under perfect competition, the price and quantity would be $4 and 3000 bagels, respectively, where demand equals supply. The total consumer surplus would be the area under the demand curve and above the price line, which would be ($\frac{1}{2}$) ($3 × 3000 bagels) = $4500. The total producer surplus would be the area under the price line and above the supply curve, which would be ($\frac{1}{2}$) ($3 × 3000 bagels) = $4500. The sum of both surpluses would be $9000.

   b. Under monopoly, the price and quantity would be $5 and 2000 bagels respectively. The loss due to allocative inefficiency would be the deadweight loss equal to: ($\frac{1}{2}$)($2 × 1000 bagels) = $1000.

Chapter 11: Monopolistic Competition and Oligopoly

1. Local night clubs would be classed as monopolistically competitive firms. This is because each night club sells a differentiated product in terms of the physical facilities and decor; the type of music played; the type of entertainment and food offered; and, finally, the type of clientele that regularly visits the establishment. Note that there are typically numerous night clubs competing with each other and that entry into this type of business is relatively easy.

3. It is not rational for a perfectly competitive firm to advertise, as it can sell all it wants at the given price (perfectly elastic demand).

5. a. The profit-maximizing quantity is 400 CDs per week, where MR = MC.

   b. The profit-maximizing quantity is $9 per CD, which is the vertical distance up to the demand curve, at a quantity of 400 CDs

   c. Maximum weekly profit = (Price − ATC) × 400 CDs = ($9 − $4) × 400 = $2000 per week.

   d. Monopolistic competition best applies to Sue's CD game for the following reasons. Since the firm's demand curve is downward sloping, this indicates that Sue has some control over the price per CD. There is product differentiation in the form of advertising and physical differences (CD, online, hard copy, board games) in the products available to teach kids math. Finally, entry into this industry is relatively easy, if one has the skills to create an interactive math game on a CD or online.

7. a. The filled-in table should look as follows:

Quantity (# rooms)	Price (per room)	Total Revenue	Marginal Revenue	Marginal Cost	Average Total Cost
0	$95	$ 0			
4	90	360	$90	$36	$86.00
8	85	680	80	34	60.00
12	80	960	70	33	51.00
16	75	1200	60	34	46.75
20	70	1400	50	36	44.60
24	65	1560	40	39	43.67
28	60	1680	30	43	43.57
32	55	1760	20	48	44.13

   b. The maximum profit output is 24 rooms per night.

   c. The profit-maximizing price is $65 per room per night.

   d. The total amount of maximum profit is (P − ATC) × Q or ($65 − $43.67) × 24 or $511.92.

   e. No, due to easy entry the long-run profit will decline to zero economic profits.

   f. Product differentiation may include: spa facilities, pool, good food, different style of rooms, free parking, computer facilities, good entertainment, in-room movies, continental breakfast.

9. a.   This bookstore operates in monopolistic competition. It competes with numerous rivals, it differentiates its product in terms of location and its coffee, it sells books that will differ from its competitors', and, finally, it is relatively easy to enter this type of business.

    b.   The profit-maximizing quantity is at five books per hour, where the marginal revenue of $3.75 is approximately equal to the marginal cost of $3.70. The profit-maximizing price is $4.75 and the total profit is ($4.75 − $3.16) × 5 = $7.95 per hour.

    c.   At a quantity of two books per hour, the long-run equilibrium price will be $3.75, which just equals average total cost so that zero economic profits are earned.

    d.   If this were a perfectly competitive firm, it would have its price just equal minimum average total cost, which is somewhere between $3.03 and $3.16. At this price, zero economic profits would be earned.

11. a.   Homogeneous oligopoly

     b.   Differentiated oligopoly

     c.   Homogeneous oligopoly

     d.   Differentiated oligopoly.

     e.   Differentiated oligopoly

13. a.   The payoff matrix is described below. Firm A's payoffs are in the shaded areas.

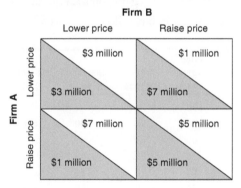

     b.   The dominant strategy is for each firm to lower the price.

     c.   Firm A's annual profit would be $5 million.

    d.   Firm A's annual profit would be $7 million.

    e.   Firm A's annual profit would be $1 million.

    f.   The most profitable long-run strategy would be for each firm to raise the price, where the long-run average annual profit would be $5 million.

15. a.   Decrease

     b.   Increase

     c.   Decrease

17. Diamonds are a great candidate for the cartel strategy of restricting quantity produced and sold, as that simply adds to the "rarity" or "scarcity" of this stone, enhancing its appeal to the consumer (especially the richer customers). Put another way, the price elasticity of demand for diamonds is inelastic, so that when quantity is restricted, total revenue increases, enhancing profits of the cartel firms, such as De Beer.

19. One could reasonably argue that social networking sites such as Facebook are far from being "free" from the members' viewpoint. To the extent that advertisers pay out monies to promote through Facebook, this adds costs to the products being sold, and at least some of these promotional costs will be passed on to consumers through increased product prices. As well, to the extent that members' personal information gets into the hands of third parties, this can cost various members in different ways. As an example, if in Facebook a member discloses specific information regarding his or her health problems, this information could be used by insurance companies to reject future applications for insurance coverage. Alternatively, dishonest individuals could use the personal information received through Facebook to commit various forms of identity theft.

21. When Pepsi quickly responds to Coke's ads, this can result in a positive-sum game for both firms in a number of ways. First, the heavy advertising can help both firms build significant barriers to entry and therefore prevent other firms from competing in a major way. Second, heavy advertising by both firms may cause the industry demand for their types of products (soft drinks, bottled water, and so on) to increase, thus benefiting all the firms in the industry.

Answers to Business Applications

Chapter 1: The Nature of Economics

a. i. Macroeconomic event, as the decline in the Canadian dollar is a broad national trend.

   ii. Increase the stock price, as Timber Corp's sales will increase, resulting in an increased profit.

b. i. Microeconomic event, as the tax focuses on a specific industry: cigarette manufacturing.

   ii. Decrease the price of the stock. A tax increase will raise the costs of production and reduce the annual profit.

c. i. Macroeconomic event, as the inflation is a broad global factor.

   ii. Increase the stock price. When inflation is out of control, investors often purchase gold, as it has historically been popular in times of economic crisis. As gold prices rise, the profits of gold mines increase.

d. i. Microeconomic event, as this is a factor that affects the specific firm in question.

   ii. Increase the stock price. When sales stay the same but operating costs decrease, the annual profit will increase.

e. i. Macroeconomic event, as interest rate trends tend to be a nationwide phenomenon.

   ii. Decrease the stock price. Since investors are selling stocks across all industries, this reduces stock prices, which, in turn, reduces the profit of Morgan Mutual Fund.

Chapter 2: Production Possibilities and Economics Systems

a. A Bachelor of Commerce Degree is a capital good from an individual's view, to the extent that it increases the individual's future earning power. It is therefore better suited to deficit financing.

b. A civic convention center would be considered to be a capital item from a city's viewpoint, and therefore better suited to deficit financing. One of the primary uses of this type of government resource is to generate revenues for the city in future years by bringing in visitors or convention delegates who will spend money on the city's hotels, restaurants, shops, and entertainment venues. Also, new business can be generated for firms in the cities who showcase their products and services through events such as trade shows.

c. The exercise gym can be viewed as a capital item from the employer's view, to the extent that it contributes towards healthier, more productive employees with better work attendance. It is therefore better suited to deficit financing.

d. The season's pass would more likely be a capital good for the insurance salesman to the extent that he meets potential clients on the golf course. It is therefore better suited to deficit financing.

e. From a city's view, it would seem that a sports team would more likely enhance future revenues as opposed to a city hall. The sports team would bring in players and fans from outside the city. As a result, more money would be spent in the city's hotels, restaurants, shops, and entertainment spots. The sports team is therefore better suited to deficit financing.

Chapter 3: Demand and Supply

a. Decrease in demand for tennis, increase in demand for golf (because it is less strenuous)

b. Increase in demand for Diet Coke (healthier), decrease in demand for Pepsi (because it appeals to a younger generation)

c. Increase in demand for urban condominiums, decrease in demand for suburban homes (for accessibility)

d. Decrease in demand for minivans, increase in demand for recreational vehicles (for retirement)

e. Decrease in demand for red meat, increase in demand for chicken (for health reasons)

Chapter 4: Elasticity

The demand for pharmaceutical drugs is very inelastic for at least two reasons. The consumer (patient) perceives pharmaceutical drugs to be necessity items. As well, many of the prescription drugs sold by a pharmaceutical company are sold in a monopoly environment, protected by patents. If the demand is very inelastic, the company will tend to charge high prices relative to the cost of producing the products, resulting in high profit margins. Based on the notion of fundamental stock analysis, the higher profit margins can account for higher stock price performance.

Chapter 6: Extensions of Demand, Supply, and Elasticity

1. a. Decrease in demand, fee will decrease
   b. Decrease in demand, fee will decrease
   c. Decrease in demand, fee will decrease
   d. Decrease in demand, fee will decrease
   e. Increase in supply, fee will decrease

2. Negative outlook, as all the events are putting downward pressure on the fees that dentists can charge. In turn, this will translate into decreased profit.

3. a. Decrease in supply, fee will increase
   b. Decrease in supply, fee will increase
   c. Increase in demand, fee will increase
   d. Increase in demand, fee will increase
   e. Increase in demand, fee will increase

4. a. Equilibrium price = $600 per crown, where market demand equals market supply
   b. Total revenue = $P_e \times Q_e$ = $600 × 12 000 = $7200.
   c. With the marketing board policy, there is a new vertical supply curve fixed at 11 000 crowns per year. This new supply curve intersects the demand curve at $800 per crown. The annual total revenue equals $800 × 11 000 = $8 800 000.
   d. The demand is inelastic, since as we have just seen, when the price increases from $600 to $800, total revenue increased. In general, when the price increases and total revenue increases, demand is inelastic.

Chapter 7: Consumer Choice

Yes. If just $1 is re-allocated away from hiring a beat police officer in order to spend an extra dollar on fighting crime with a vehicle, there would be an extra $4 contribution towards reducing theft. This extra contribution would be achieved without increasing the total budgetary expense!

Chapter 8: The Firm: Cost and Output Determination

a. Average fuel cost = 1074.60 ÷ 18 000 = $.0597 per km; total gas cost = $.0597 × 500 km = $29.85
b. Average variable cost = 1728 ÷ 18 000 = $.096 per km; total variable cost = $.096 × 500 = $48
c. Average total cost = 7469.61 ÷ 18 000 = $.41497 per km; total cost = $.41497 × 500 = $207.49
d. Average variable cost, as this includes all additional costs attributable to the business trip.

Chapter 9: Perfect Competition

a. AVC: 124, 120, 125, 135, 150, 170
   MC: 124, 116, 135, 165, 210, 270
   ATC: 374.00, 245.00, 208.33, 197.50, 200.00, 211.67
b. Profit maximizing quantity = 5000 tonnes per month; total profit = $150 000 per month.
c. Loss minimizing quantity = 3000 tonnes per month; total loss = $204 990 per month.
d. Loss minimizing quantity = 0 tonnes per month (shutdown); total loss = $250 000 per month.
e. No. As the example above shows, as prices change in the short run, profit maximization criteria will dictate varying optimal production levels. As an example, in part b above, the profit maximizing level is at q = 5000 tonnes. The minimum cost per unit occurs at q = 4000 tonnes.
f. No. As part c above illustrates, if Monique's operates at 3000 tonnes per month, the loss per month is $204 990, compared to a loss of $250 000 per month if the firm shut down. In this case, staying in operation creates a savings of $45 010.

Chapter 10: Monopoly

1. TR: 0   720   1320   1740   2000
        2100   2040   1820   1440
   MR: 720   600   420   260   100
        (60)   (220) (380)

2. a. $Q = 3$; b. Total maximum profit = $840
3. a. $Q = 5$; b. Economic profit = 0, so the doctor just earns a normal profit.
4. a. $Q = 4$; b. Total maximum profit = $1060

Chapter 11: Monopolistic Competition and Oligopoly

a. place
b. product
c. promotion
d. price
e. product
f. price
g. promotion
h. price
i. promotion

Answers to "For Critical Analysis" Questions

Chapter 1: The Nature of Economics

Example 1–1: The Economics of Web Page Design

The web designer of a frequently visited web page, such as Yahoo!'s home page, has "unlimited wants" that include such goals as: provide maximum exposure to all of Yahoo!'s own products and services; maximize revenue from selling advertising space to other companies; present high-quality images and animations; and prevent the web page from becoming too cluttered. The "limited resources" include a limited screen space size (that one views without scrolling) and limited time to hold the web surfer's attention.

Example 1–2: Is the Opportunity Cost of Finding a Mate Lower on the Internet?

There is a smaller selection of available people who match very specific characteristics. Therefore, the desire by persons to find people with very specific characteristics will involve higher search costs, in terms of the time spent dating, than would be the case with less picky requirements. In other words, the opportunity cost of dating in person is higher, which implies that people would be willing to pay more to avoid this by using the Internet alternative. This example shows how understanding opportunity cost can help the Internet firm decide on the appropriate price to charge for its different matching services.

Example 1–3: What Does a Year at College Really Cost?

Jane did not correctly determine the cost related to the decision to enroll in college full-time for eight months. She should add only the *extra* or *marginal* costs, which would be the tuition, books, college fees, and the income she sacrifices from not working full-time for eight months. This implies that the total costs of going to college would be $3600 + (8 months) × ($2000 per month) = $19 600 for the eight months spent at college. The other expenses, such as rent, food, transportation, personal care, and entertainment, can be viewed as unavoidable expenses she decided to incur before making any education decision that we would class as sunk costs. Sunk costs should not be included in computing the marginal or extra cost relating to her education decision. In order to make a rational decision, the marginal cost should be compared to the marginal benefit of enrolling in the business college program.

Policy Example 1–1: International Smuggling and Counterfeiting

Policies aimed at increasing the marginal cost of smuggling and counterfeiting include increasing the level of enforcement to increase the chances that criminals get caught (e.g., employing 50 000 special agents) as well as increasing the level of fines and other penalties for those criminals found guilty of crimes. Policies aimed at lowering the marginal benefits related to smuggling and counterfeiting include the lowering of taxes on the legal sale of cigarettes. This lowers the price of legal cigarettes relative to illegal cigarettes, and lowers the potential profits earned from smuggling and counterfeiting.

Example 1–4: Nice Guys Can Finish First

The findings of the study in this Example suggest that if a person engages in generous behaviour, he or she will be rewarded in terms of being attractive to the opposite sex, especially for long-term relationships.

Example 1–5: The Science Behind COLD-fX

The study examines the relationship between COLD-fX medication and the frequency of contracting colds and their duration and severity. The study attempts to apply the *ceteris paribus* assumption by holding constant other factors that might affect the frequency, duration, and severity, such as having just had a flu vaccination, taking other cold medication at the same time, the placebo effect, researcher's bias in favour of finding that COLD-fX is effective, and the general health of the subjects in the study.

Example 1–6: An Economic Model of Crime

An increase in the unemployment rate reduces the opportunity cost related to the time spent planning and committing the crime and the time spent evading being caught or, if caught, time spent in jail. This reduces the marginal cost of engaging in a criminal act so we would predict that an increase in the unemployment rate would increase the crime rate. A decrease in conviction rates reduces the expected punishment costs related to committing a crime. In turn, this reduces the marginal cost of engaging in a criminal act so we would predict that this would increase the crime rate.

Issues and Applications: Bottled Water: The Hummer of Beverages?

1. Scarcity brings home the point that resources are limited in the face of unlimited wants. Knowing this makes

one concerned about whether the $100 billion bottled water industry is effectively allocating our limited resources, as there are many other wants yet to be satisfied. Opportunity cost refers to the value of the best alternative that must be given up because a choice was made. By allocating $100 billion of resources to the bottled water industry we give up the opportunity to satisfy other wants such as promoting a pollution-free environment and increasing global access to safe water. Economics is the social science that is concerned with how our limited resources are being allocated to satisfy unlimited wants. The fact that the bottled water industry uses up a significant amount of limited resources makes it an economic issue.

2. Since this issue focuses on one industry or product area, the bottled water industry, it entails a microeconomic focus. A macroeconomic focus would relate to the level or growth of production or consumption in all Canadian industries.

3. In order to create the incentives necessary to reduce the amount of resources used to produce bottled water, the government would have to reduce the marginal benefit that firms derive from supplying bottled water. One way to do this would be to ban all exclusivity agreements, which would increase competition and reduce the prices that Coca-Cola and PepsiCo could charge for bottled water.

   Another way of reducing the marginal benefit would be to mount a major educational campaign that publicized the opportunity costs related to bottled water. If the campaign could get people to reduce their demand for bottled water, it would reduce the marginal benefit derived from supplying this product.

4. Policy analysis refers to the important process of relating a proposed policy to various socio-economic goals. In this example, the Toronto City Council's proposed policy of levying a tax on the sale of bottled water was related to equity and employment. That is, the beverage companies, in arguing against the tax, noted that it would be unfair to single out just one commodity, especially a healthier product, for taxation. Also, the beverage companies projected that if the tax was implemented it would cause people to buy less bottled water (and possibly other groceries) in Toronto, which could conflict with the employment goal. On a broader level, one could look at leaving the bottled water industry alone (status quo) as another possible policy. As this issue suggests, this status quo policy can conflict with other goals such as a cleaner, healthier environment, less global warming, and providing aid to poorer nations.

Chapter 2: Production Possibilities and Economic Systems

Example 2–1: Beware of "Free" Lecture Podcasts

1. The example notes that if you skip class, you give up the opportunity to ask questions during the lecture, as well as to interact with other class members. You may also end up scoring low on class participation marks. Other costs that you might incur include the cost of having to take the full responsibility of pacing yourself appropriately through all the course material in all your courses. It becomes too easy to postpone viewing the online lectures, so that you eventually get far behind in your course studies. By not getting to know your instructor, you might incur the cost of not being able to use your instructor as a reference for a future job opportunity.

2. Students who do attend class bear some of the opportunity cost of your absenteeism, as they have may not be able to complete the work that requires teamwork or group discussion. If there is a peer evaluation portion of a group mark, you would likely score low on this.

Example 2–2: One Laptop per Child

One Laptop per Child promotes productive efficiency in that it seeks to deliver education to poorer nations at a much lower cost than traditional bricks-and-mortar education. As noted in the example, traditional bricks-and-mortar education is simply too expensive (thousands of dollars per student) for poorer nations to afford. With One Laptop per Child, the major education cost is the $100 laptop per student.

Policy Example 2–1: The Multibillion Dollar Park

Production Possibilities Curve: Wilderness Area Goods and Oil and Gas Goods

The opportunity cost of moving from E to F is the wilderness area goods sacrificed to produce more oil and gas goods, as shown by the arrows in the graph. Since E is the allocatively efficient point, the marginal cost of moving from E to F exceeds the marginal benefit of doing so, when viewing this from society's viewpoint.

Example 2–3: Canadian Post-secondary Education Pays Off Big Time!

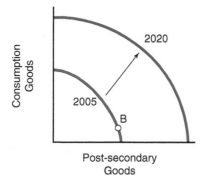

Example 2–4: Specializing in Providing Baggage-Free Business Trips

1. The new company FlyLite allows Steve Zilinek (the owner) to specialize in baggage handling, where he has a comparative advantage. At the same time, the business traveller can specialize in his or her business (as opposed to spending time on packing, baggage handling, etc.). Both of these people will make more money by spending more time on activities where they have a comparative advantage. This is a "win-win" situation.

2. If the trend is to take more time handling personal baggage at airports, this increases the opportunity cost related to the business traveller doing this activity as opposed to spending more time on his or her business. In turn, this will cause more business travellers to use FlyLite's services.

Policy Example 2–2: Canadian Politics: Right, Left, and Centre

Policy A: Waiting time for surgeries is reduced through the expansion of government-funded surgical units located in government-run hospitals. This is more consistent with the New Democrats as this involves providing more services through the government. Policy B: Waiting time for surgeries is reduced through the provision of new surgical services through privately owned health-care clinics. This is more consistent with the Conservatives as this involves providing more services through the private sector.

Example 2–5: India Has More Cellphones Than Toilets

In this Example, the way in which India has answered its "for whom" question is to create a very inequitable or uneven distribution of income: a small proportion of the population is very rich and own lots of cellphones, and a significant proportion is very poor and cannot afford toilet facilities. In other words, the uneven distribution of income affects "what and how much will be produced" in that more cellphones are produced than toilets.

One policy would be to more heavily tax the rich and use these tax dollars to produce more toilets. This will pay off in the long run with reduced government spending on health and support for those living in poverty.

Issues and Applications: Private or Public Auto Insurance: What Is Best for Canada?

1. Due to its no-fault feature, the pure command system does not have to employ the expensive legal and court-related resources to establish fault and the amount of damages experienced by injured parties. Since the government is the sole insurance provider in the province, it does not have to employ resources to market its services to the customer. Moreover, a government monopoly is able to avoid the duplication in administrative resources that typically occurs when numerous private car insurance companies compete with each other in the same province. Because the public system can offer the same insurance coverage with minimal use of resources, it is productively efficient.

2. By charging higher premiums for those individuals falling into high-risk classes, such as younger males, the private system helps to keep the riskier drivers off the road. Also, the fault system can provide an incentive to be more careful and avoid accidents. In a fault system, the injured party's right to sue for damages helps to ensure that the dollar value of the compensation resulting from an accident claim (marginal benefit) is sufficient to cover the full marginal cost related to the individual injuries and losses sustained from the accident. In this way, a fault system allocates the claim benefits (marginal benefits) in a way that matches the marginal accident costs of each individual, promoting allocative efficiency.

3. When a pure command system does not charge higher premiums based on age and gender, an equity trade-off may occur. On the one hand, equity is promoted when younger drivers with clean driving records pay lower premiums than older people who have accident histories. On the other hand, equity is compromised if the "no discrimination" practice increases collisions by encouraging riskier drivers to take to the road. In this case, older, female, safe drivers end up in more accidents caused by the riskier drivers and end up paying higher premiums.

4. With a rate freeze, the revenue from premiums stays the same but the expenses for paying out claims could increase with inflation, causing financial losses. In this situation, the private insurance companies may refuse to provide insurance in the province operating this type of mixed system. As a result, the only option would be for the government to provide the insurance.

Chapter 3: Demand and Supply

Example 3–1: Why RFID Tags are Catching On Fast

The law of demand explains the increased use of RFID tags. As this example explains, the price of RFID tags has been declining at a significant rate. As well the cost savings that companies achieve also amount to a reduced price of using the RFID technology.

Example 3–2: A Recession Tale of Two Macs

1. In the recession, as incomes decreased, the demand for Mac computers also decreased. Since there is a direct relation between income and demand, Mac computers is a normal good.

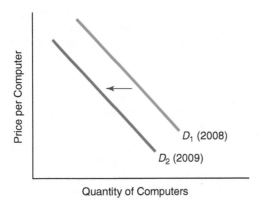

2. In the recession, as incomes decreased, the demand for McDonald's meals increased. Since there is an inverse relation between income and demand, McDonald's meals is an inferior good.

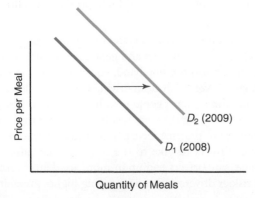

Example 3–3: Brunettes Now Have More Fun

Taste-related factors have increased the demand for brunette hair dyes. Graphically, this is reflected in a rightward shift in the demand curve for brunette hair dyes as shown below. The specific taste-related factors include: prominent female movie stars who are brunette; ethnic groups that are becoming more prominent in Canada have natural brunette hair shades; an aging population that prefers to use brunette hair dyes to cover gray hair.

Example 3–4: Garth Brooks, Used CDs, and the Law of Demand

According to this example, a used-CD market lowers the net price of a CD from $15 to $10, which would result in "an increase in quantity demanded" and a movement along the demand curve from point A to point B. At the same time, used CDs serve as a cheaper substitute for new music CDs. This second effect will decrease the demand for new music CDs and shift the demand curve to the left. If this decrease in demand exceeds the increase in quantity demanded, as shown in the accompanying diagram, Garth Brooks' fear of the used-CD market is justified.

Example 3–5: Surge in Electronics Sales Follow Dramatic Drop in LCD Prices

The market supply for LCD flat screen TVs has been increasing or shifting to the right, as indicated by the accompanying diagram. The determinants responsible for this shift in supply include falling prices (costs) of a key input—LCD panels, and increased technology devoted to LCD flat screen TVs.

The example predicts that, in the future, the market supply for plasma TVs will start to decline or shift left, as described in the diagrams above.

Example 3–6: Chocoholics Beware

1. Factors that are causing an increase in demand and thus an increase in equilibrium price of chocolate bars include an increase in average household income in China and the perceived cancer-fighting antioxidant health benefits of eating dark chocolate. Graphically, there will be a rightward shift in the demand curve for chocolate bars, causing an increase in equilibrium price.

2. Factors that are causing a decrease in supply and thus an increase in equilibrium price of chocolate bars include increased oil prices that increase transportation costs related to supplying chocolate bars; increase in sugar and corn prices due to the additional demand for these commodities for the production of ethanol; export tax put on cocoa by the government of Indonesia, which reduces the suppy of cocoa for the use of making chocolate bars. Graphically, there will be a leftward shift in the supply curve for chocolate bars, causing an increase in equilibrium price.

Example 3–7: Shale Natural Gas: A Game Changer for Alberta?

The factors causing a steep decline in natural gas prices include:

1. Global recession causing a decrease in demand
2. Warm winter causing a decrease in demand
3. New, cost-efficient source of natural gas in the U.S. causing an increase in supply

Issues and Applications: A Canadian Housing Bubble?

1. Three factors causing a temporary surge in Canadian home prices in early 2010 were

   a. The announcements that more stringent mortgage lending rules were to take place in April 2010. These had the effect of increasing demand for homes in the period just before the new rules were implemented.

   b. Record low mortgage interest rates and the announcements of higher rates to take place in mid 2010. These had the effect of increasing demand for homes before the rate increases took place.

   c. Announcements that the new Harmonized Sales Tax would take effect in B.C. and Ontario in July 2010. These had the effect of increasing demand before this period, since homebuyers wanted to take advantage of lower home-buying transaction costs.

      The effects of the increases in demand are shown in the following graph:

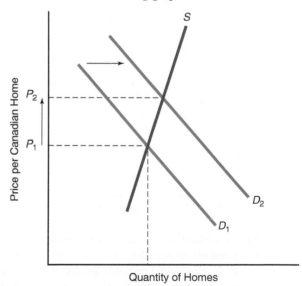

2. Three factors that have the potential to burst the Canadian housing bubble by reducing the demand for

Canadian owner-occupied homes include higher interest rates, high debt-to-asset and debt-to-income ratios, an aging population, implementation of tighter lending rules, and HST. The graph is presented below.

3. Two factors noted that will increase the supply of Canadian homes are the increase in housing starts and the increase in resale listings. The graph is shown below.

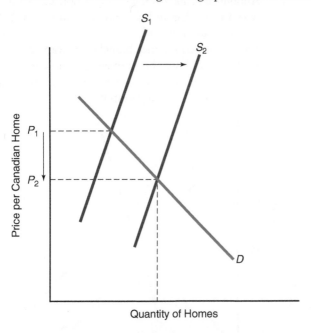

4. One can rationally purchase a home even if it turns out to be a bad investment based on the consumption benefits one derives from the home purchase: privacy; pride of ownership; tenure of home ownership—nobody can ask you to leave once your home is paid for; freedom to have pets; and freedom to renovate and landscape to suit your own preferences. Owning your own home can also enhance the enjoyment you derive from shopping for home-related items such as home furnishings, tools, and art.

Chapter 4: Elasticity

Example 4–1: "If They Doubled the Price, We'd Still Drink Coffee"

As we have all experienced, when the price of gas rises, because there are few substitutes, we usually do not change the amount we drive. Some will perhaps take the bus or start to carpool, but most will go on as before.

Example 4–2: The Price Elasticity of Demand for Gasoline

If we had not used the average-values formula, we would not have taken into account the change over a range. It makes a difference where we start the analysis when we deal with a range.

Policy Example 4–1: Who Pays Higher Cigarette Taxes?

As stated in the example, the price elasticity of demand for cigarettes is relatively low, between 0.2 to 0.4, so an increase in excise taxes of 10 percent would lead to a decline in cigarette purchases of 2 percent to 4 percent.

Example 4–3: What Do Real-World Price Elasticities of Demand Look Like?

In the short run, only minor adjustments to buying habits can be made; in the long run, major adjustments can be made.

Policy Example 4–2: Do People Substitute Wireless Phone Services for Wired Services?

As younger people switch more toward cellphones, the use of land-line phones will decrease.

Example 4–4: Frequent Flyer Miles as Income

The demand for travel will decrease because people will not perceive the flights as "free" anymore.

Issues and Applications: To Combat Cigarette Consumption, Should the Government Raise Taxes on Beer?

1. Cigarette consumers pay the bulk of the taxes imposed on cigarettes.

2. Cigarette consumers would need a large price change before they changed their habits, while beer drinkers could substitute some other alcoholic beverage for beer, so the beer producers would be more likely to see a decrease in their total revenues.

Chapter 6: Extensions of Demand, Supply, and Elasticity

Example 6–1: Booking Your Airline Flight—An Agent or the Web?

As the Example notes, studies over the past five years suggest that it is cheaper, on average, to book flights through professional agents. As well, since intermediaries are independent of the airlines, travel agents can reduce the transaction costs of finding the lowest-cost carrier(s) for customers to reach and return from a given destination. Online services do indeed allow airline customers the advantage of making their own reservations for relatively uncomplicated flights to their destinations. The cost of time spent searching for the best deal for more complicated routes could be quite high for someone who only occasionally flies and is thus unlikely to be familiar with the timetables, or for someone who has a high opportunity cost of time. Travel agents would be valuable to such persons. Using an agent can really help in cases where travel plans fail to materialize as planned. If problems should occur during your trip, help is a phone call away. It is up to your travel agent to provide a solution. If you purchase a ticket online, you are on your own. Most web fares are nonrefundable and nonchangeable; many have restrictions that travellers may be unaware of. A professional travel agent can frequently work behind the scenes on the traveller's behalf. Finally, since there are often a lot of alternative forms of lodging, each with quite different bundles of services and amenities, a consumer can derive a significant benefit by dealing with a knowledgeable agent who specializes in the destination region. In the end, the peace of mind travellers get when booking through professional travel agents is priceless.

Example 6–2 Is Ticketmaster in Cahoots with Scalpers?

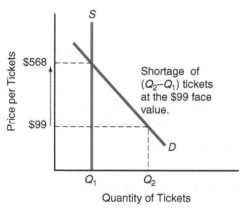

Policy Example 6–1: Assisted Human Reproduction Not for Sale in Canada?

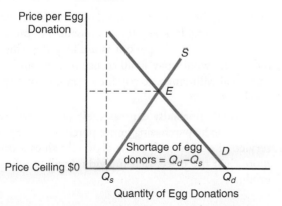

Policy Example 6–2: Do Minimum Wage Rates Benefit Canadian Workers?

If the B.C. minimum wage is increased from $8 to $10, the quantity of workers demanded by B.C. firms will decrease from B to A, while the quantity of workers who want to supply their labour increases from B to C. Overall, this policy will cause surplus of labour (unemployment) equal to distance AC. The study estimates this unemployment to be between 10 898 and 52 200 jobs lost.

Policy Example 6–3: The Beginning of the End for the Canadian Wheat Board?

In the accompanying demand and supply diagram, P_m stands for the marketing board price. Assuming that the wheat board is effective in negotiating a higher price for barley farmers, the price of barley would be at P_m if all sales are through the wheat board. As more and more farmers bypass the wheat board, the price will move toward equilibrium at P_e. If demand is inelastic, this would cause the farmers' total revenue to decline.

Policy Example 6–4: Could Legalizing Marijuana Reduce Mexican Drug Violence?

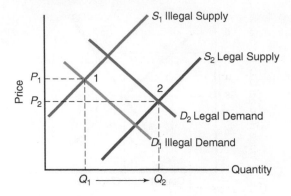

With an outright ban on marijuana, the supply is relatively small (far left) at S_1 due to the higher costs related to the risks of getting caught and convicted of supplying the banned drug. Also, D_1 reflects a lower demand at each price due to the consumers' risks of getting caught and convicted for possession. If marijuana is legalized, both the demand and supply will increase (shift right) to D_2 and S_2 due to the elimination of the risks. While the equilibrium quantity will increase, the effect on equilibrium price is indeterminate. If the increase in supply exceeds the increase in demand, as shown in the graph, the price will decrease under legalization.

Policy Example 6–5: An Excise Tax on Music Piracy?

The more inelastic the demand for or supply of blank media, the greater are the proceeds collected from the private copying levies. These levies will be relatively effective in discouraging the copying of music, the more elastic the demand and/or supply. Consumers who use blank media, such as CDs, to back up non-copyrighted material unfairly pay the private copying levies.

Issues and Applications: For-Profit Health Care in Canada?

1. Medicare's zero price ceiling policy for visits to the doctors and the hospitals prevents prices from efficiently allocating the limited health-care resources. Since the Canadian patient does not pay an additional charge for each additional hospital or doctor's visit, there is the danger that the limited health-care resources do not get allocated to the highest-value uses. Inefficient nonprice forms of rationing health-care resources, such as queuing, result from this price ceiling policy.

2. a. Features of the American system, such as insurance co-payments (user fees) and experience ratings serve as allocatively efficient forms of price rationing. In other words, only the patients who value the medical visits the most will be willing to pay the additional user fees or experience rating premiums. These user fees will discourage frivolous use of the limited health-care resources.

    b. The private for-profit health maintenance organizations are faced with incentives to provide a given level of health care with minimal use of resources and thus promote productive efficiency. These incentives include the profit motive and competition from other private health corporations.

3. User fees paid by the patients will not promote allocative efficiency, as consumers (patients) do not possess the expertise necessary to judge the true value of a contemplated visit to the doctor or hospital due to a health problem. Also, in many cases, the doctors act on behalf of the patient in decisions relating to the additional consumption of health-care resources.

4. User fees will reduce the access that poorer consumers have to health-care resources. In addition, the chronically ill are the ones who will pay the most out of their pockets, with user fees. The chronically ill end up paying twice—once because they are ill and a second time when they pay the user fee.

5. In the United States, there are a number of private for-profit corporations (HMOs) providing health insurance and hospital services. As a result, a much larger portion of every dollar spent on health care in the United States is spent on activities not directly related to patient health care, such as administration, marketing, and earning corporate profits. In other words, it costs more for the United States to provide the same patient care, which is productively inefficient.

Chapter 7: Consumer Choice

Example 7–1: Newspaper Vending Machines versus Candy Vending Machines

There are certain events that would make people want more than one paper, such as disasters, sports (winning the Stanley Cup), major celebrations, and so on.

Example 7–2: The Price of Water in Saudi Arabia

Some of the effects on human behaviour would be: fewer baths/showers, less waste of water, and the purchase of more perfume.

Issues and Applications: Contingent Valuation: Pricing the "Priceless"

1. Opinion polls ask people to value something they are not purchasing. It is easy for an individual to put a $500 value on the use of a park; it is unlikely that this same individual would pay $500 to use it. Demand curves show real willingness to pay for a quantity of a specific good or service.

2. Individuals normally express their perceived level of satisfaction by purchasing or not purchasing the good or service in question. If the individual values a product more than the price, that individual will purchase the product.

Chapter 8: The Firm: Cost and Output Determination

Policy Example 8–1: Nonprofit Firms Join in the Quest for Profits

A normal rate of return is the amount that must be paid to an investor to induce investment in a business, and so non-profit organizations still need some way to entice people to contribute to their organization.

Example 8–1: China's Increasing Labour Costs

Labour is one of the most important costs that a company has to consider when trying to determine where to build a factory. But other costs are also relevant, such as business taxes, raw material availability, cost of land, and even stability of the country's present government.

Example 8–2: The Cost of Driving a Car

Variable costs are the per-kilometre costs, while the fixed costs are the annual costs. The average total costs are the $19.40 per day, and the marginal costs are dependent on the kilometres driven.

Example 8–3: Economies of Scale at Dell

Dell's short-run average cost curves have decreased, making Dell more cost-efficient.

Issues and Applications: Business Look toward Costs to Determine Viability

Student answers will vary.

Chapter 9: Perfect Competition

Example 9–1: When Blogging Becomes a Competitive Business

Entry into the blogging business is not entirely free, as there are costs involved in setting up this business. The biggest cost is the opportunity cost of the blogger's time used in the business. Other costs would include the monthly cost of the Internet service provider.

Policy Example 9–1: Quelling Fears of "Mad Cow Disease" in Asia

According to this Example, the marginal revenue of selling an additional cow carcass to Europe is $200. On the basis of marginal analysis, beef producers would be willing to incur a marginal cost of up to $200 to test all animals destined for Asian consumption.

Example 9–2: High Sunk Costs Can Mean Deep Discounts

Moments before take-off, virtually all the costs related to filling an additional seat on the flight are fixed. These fixed costs would include the expenses related to the capital costs of the plane, airport landing fees, making the reservations and issu-ing tickets for this flight, hiring the flight's pilot and crew, and paying for the fuel for the flight. Since the marginal cost of filling an additional seat is very close to zero, the airline would be getting a contribution toward its fixed costs, as long as the standby fee were a positive amount (deep discount).

Example 9–3: U.S. Recession Takes Its Toll on Canadian Lumber Firms

In the global lumber market, there has been both a decrease in demand and increase in supply, causing the equilibrium price to fall to US$140 per 1000 board feet. In the Canfor sawmill diagram, we see how the price of US$140 is below average total cost, causing economic losses. In fact, the price is also below average variable cost, causing the sawmill to shut down in the short run. The shaded area represents Canfor's total economic losses.

Example 9–4: The Big Rush to Provide Digital Snaps in a Snap

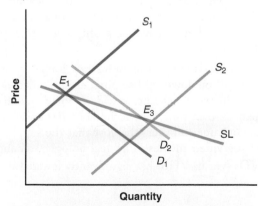

The long-run supply, SL, is formed by joining the points E_1 and E_2. As you can see, SL is downward sloping, indicating a decreasing-cost industry. As the industry expands, each firm's average total costs curve is shifting down (per-unit costs are declining).

Issues and Applications: Does Your Local Video Store Have a Future?

1. The new-release and best-seller home-video movie industry in Canada possesses a number of characteristics that conform to perfect competition. In a typical Canadian city, such as Toronto, there are a large number of buyers and sellers for the rental services relating to new-release and best-seller video movies. The large number of sellers include the many bricks-and-mortar stores renting videos in the same market area, as well as competition from close substitutes, including online video rentals, and purchases of videos from mass retailers. Each of the video rental firms competing with each other rents a homogeneous or identical service—the same new-release videos and best-sellers. There is easy entry in the video movie rental industry. That is evident from the fact that there are numerous small independent firms competing in this industry. As well, new close substitutes have entered the industry, such as renting videos online and buying DVDs supplied by mass retailers.

2. According to the theory covered in this chapter, the selling of a DVD at a price below average total cost could still contribute to fixed costs and possibly profit from other operations, as long as the price exceeds the average variable cost of selling the DVD—the shutdown price. If we assume that the average variable cost of each DVD is equal to the cost of goods sold of $25 per DVD, then, as long as the price exceeds $25, the DVD sale will contribute to fixed costs and possibly profit from the sale of other company products. Also, it was noted in this Issues and Applications that selling DVDs at low prices can attract additional customer traffic to the store. Once more customers enter the store, there is a greater chance that some of these customers will purchase other items, besides DVDs.

3. The typical firm renting new-release and best-seller video movies operates in an industry that new firms can easily enter. This being the case, new firms will continue to enter until zero economic profit, or a normal profit, will be earned.

4. The home-video movie industry's long-run supply curve will be downward sloping, as it is a decreasing-cost industry. As the home-video movie industry has expanded over time, new technology has lowered (and will continue to lower) the cost that the supplier will pay for video movies. The technological change to DVDs (versus VHS) has significantly lowered the cost

of goods sold to the video retailer. In the future, when movies are typically downloaded over the Internet, the cost of distributing each DVD will be significantly lower (no shipping costs etc.).

Chapter 10: Monopoly

Example 10–1: Microsoft's Abuse of Monopoly

According to this example, Microsoft engaged in predatory behaviour in a number of ways. It significantly eliminated competition in the browser market by giving Internet Explorer away, by integrating Explorer into its operating system, and by entering into agreements with computer manufacturers and Internet providers that restricted the distribution of competing software, such as Netscape Navigator. Similarly, by closely bundling Microsoft Media Player with its Windows operating system, it puts its rivals, such as RealNetworks, at an unfair disadvantage.

Policy Example 10–1: Should Canada Post Remain a Monopoly—Or Does It Matter?

1. The price elasticity of demand for Canada Post's letter mail service has become more elastic due to the increased competition from faxes and e-mail. Similarly, the price elasticity of demand for Canada Post's parcel delivery service has become more elastic due to the increased competition from large private courier companies. Since the emerging e-commerce industries involve the delivery of goods to one's home by courier, Canada Post could increase its presence in e-commerce and the package courier service.

2. If Canada Post loses its legal monopoly it will have to lower prices on the postal service it provides on the lucrative high population routes. This means that it will likely not have the profit from these routes to subsidize postal service on the remote rural routes. Either these routes will lose postal service or pay very high rates for postal delivery.

Policy Example 10–2: Forcing Individuals to Reveal How Much They Are Willing to Pay

1. By auctioning off each licence plate to the highest bidder, the maximum price that consumers are willing to pay for each licence plate is extracted. As an example, the first plate may go for $4000, the second plate for $3998, etc. This is a good approximation of perfect price discrimination under a monopoly situation. One reason the government pursues this practice is to maximize profit from the sale of licence plates.

2. By restricting the distribution of licence plates, the government is encouraging the citizens to use public transit, which reduces pollution and traffic congestion.

Example 10–2: Pricing Internet Service to Maximize Profit

1. Market 1 is the business market as it has relatively inelastic demand.

2. Reasons why the demand for Internet services is more inelastic for business users compared to personal users include: the Internet is more of a necessity to business users, and business users can write off Internet expenses as a tax deduction. Therefore, business users are willing to pay more for the same service.

3. The Internet service provider can enhance its profits by charging a higher price in the inelastic market, which increases total revenue. By lowering the price in the elastic market (personal user market) this will also increase total revenue. Another way to explain this is to set the price where marginal revenue equals marginal cost in each graph. You will see that this implies having the price set higher in Market 1, the business market, as shown in the graph below.

Example 10–3: The High Cost of Staying Alive

This Example suggests that Celgene, the monopoly supplier of thalidomide, charges an extremely high price, restricts the availability of the drug, and makes an above-normal profit, all of which are consistent with monopoly behaviour. Since thalidomide is now being used to prevent the return of a life threatening cancer, the demand for the drug would be extremely inelastic, thus allowing Celgene to charge exorbitant prices.

Policy Example 10–3: Monopolies are Milking Canadian Food Consumers

According to this Example, the social costs of farm marketing boards (monopolies) include the following. Like any typical monopoly, the boards restrict output and raise the price (relative to competitive levels), causing allocative inefficiency. The boards typically earn excess or above-normal profits in the long run. The boards conflict with productive efficiency by unnecessarily raising costs due to lobbying activities and resources being spent on enforcing trade barriers. Finally, the boards conflict with economic growth by slowing down the process of developing and expanding new food product areas

Policy Example 10–3: Swapping Songs on the Internet: Is it Really Free?

There are many individuals and companies that "pay" for the actions of those who freely download music files over the Internet. Because of the infringement of copyright, the music artists and recording companies suffer a loss of income due to the decline in legitimate music sales noted in the example. Other parties that lose out include the industries that distribute music legally, such as the manufacturers of music CDs, the companies that supply music downloads over the Internet for a fee, and the bricks-and-mortar music stores. Users who are successfully sued for their practice of freely downloading music files will also pay a price. Finally, we all lose out when copyright is infringed, to the extent that artists and recording companies lose the incentive to create high-quality musical productions that contribute to the enrichment and diversity of our culture and our freedom of expression.

Issues and Applications: Is It Fair to Practise Price Discrimination in Higher Education?

1. According to this Issue and Applications, universities charge a higher tuition fee in inelastic markets and lower fees in elastic markets. This is consistent with the practice of price discrimination under a monopoly (or near-monopoly) situation, which we know increases total tuition revenue and profit collected from tuitions. This can be shown graphically as follows below, where "profit maximization at MR = MC" implies a higher tuition fee in the inelastic market—international students and medical students.

2. For very prestigious universities, there is a very strong monopoly situation, which means that for those who can afford to attend the university, the demand is very inelastic. This would have the effect of leading to very high tuition fees for those student groups in the inelastic market. Often these prestigious universities have a large amount of money for student financial aid, so that poorer students can get access at a very low cost. In other words, charging rich students very high tuition fees provides the funds for financial aid to poorer students.

3. The advantages are:

    1. Tuition fees would no longer serve a barrier for low-income students to enroll in the university. This may help ensure that poor individuals who have a high level of ability are able to get the appropriate university education to reach their potential.

        In this way, society will get the best doctors, lawyers, engineers, and business people.

    2. The "free" university price will increase the enrollments at the universities and, to the extent that this results in increased graduates, this can enhance economic growth.

    The disadvantages are:

    1. If access to university is "free," students may not value their education, and so this policy attracts a lot of registrations but much fewer graduates. This would lead to a very inefficient use of educational resources. The quality of education would decline due to the entry of students who are not very serious about their studies.

    2. When there are no tuition fees, this reduces the revenue available to the university to hire resources including paying high salaries to attract top notch professors and researchers. This may impede economic growth in the future.

Chapter 11: Monopolistic Competition and Oligopoly

Example 11–1: A Canadian Retail Success: Twenty-Seven Years Running

The Canadian retail footwear industry would be classed as monopolistic competition. There are many firms competing in the same market area, and there is product differentiation. The Example indicates there can be physical differences in the product sold by different suppliers, such as western footwear, children's shoes, or quality running shoes. As Running Room illustrates, firms can compete on the basis of complementary services provided, such as running clinics; running clubs; and the sponsorship of running, walking and charity events. Also, different retail firms can offer different price levels, which conflicts with perfect competition where only one standardized price is charged.

Example 11–2: The Prisoners' Dilemma

Yes. Assume that two firms, A and B, agree to share the market and charge a high monopoly profit-maximizing price. Assume that there are now four possibilities:

(1) Both stick to the price agreement and each makes $100 in profits; (2) both ignore the agreement and charge lower prices, and each makes $40 in profits; (3) A sticks to the agreement, while B ignores and lowers the price. A makes a profit of $30 and B makes a profit of $120; and (4) B sticks to the agreement, while A ignores and lowers the price. B makes a profit of $30 and A makes a profit of $120. The dominant strategy is for neither to stick to the agreement, if it cannot be enforced.

Policy Example 11–1: Sweet Deal between Canadian Chocolate Bar Makers?

a. The price fixing agreement alleged that the major chocolate manufacturers secretly met to agree to artificially inflate prices from 2001 to 2008. This alleged behaviour is consistent with a positive-sum cooperative pricing model, where all parties to the agreement, as a group, are better off compared to a non-cooperative pricing situation.

b. The manufacturers are alleged to have sold the bars to the various retailers with the understanding that all the retailers would make sure that they maintained the retail prices at levels suggested by the manufacturers. If the retailers undercut the suggested retail prices, they would face the possibility of not being able to purchase the popular bars from the manufacturers.

Example 11–3: OPEC Continues to Rule the World Oil Market

Saudi Arabia, as the largest oil producer, can have the largest impact on oil production and prices. Since all OPEC members know this, they will be less likely to cheat when it is clear that Saudi Arabia will practise a tit-for-tat strategy and flood the market for oil if it finds one or more members of the cartel cheating.

Example 11–4: De Beers Diamond Cartel: A Thing of the Past?

The increased competition due to the greater presence of Russia, Canada, and Australia and due to better quality artificial diamonds moves the industry away from cooperative pricing tactics, such as cartels.

Policy Example 11–2: Turbulence in the Canadian Airline Industry

According to this example, Air Canada is being charged with two entry-deterring strategies—excess capacity and pricing below "avoidable costs," which we would call variable costs. The excess capacity allows Air Canada to add flights to any route that is challenged by WestJet or CanJet. Even without the excess capacity, a strategy of pricing below average variable cost would deter entry by WestJet or CanJet.

Example 11–5: Wind Blows Down Canadian Wireless Prices

The Big Three wireless firms—Telus, Bell, and Rogers—employed two tactics to prevent the successful entry of Wind Mobile. First, they dropped the prices of their plans. This meant that Wind Mobile had to enter the industry charging quite low plan prices, thus reducing the profits earned by Wind Mobile (or increasing its losses). Second, the Big Three sold plans that had lock-in clauses, where a penalty would have to be paid by any consumer wanting to switch to Wind Mobile's plans.

Example 11–6: Can Advertising Lead to Efficiency?

According to this example, both can be true. "We are better because we are bigger" is really the theme of this example, in that advertising allows a firm to get bigger, and this, in turn, can make the firm more efficient. To the extent that the firm gets more efficient, it can get even bigger (as it steals market share from rivals), so the phrase "We are bigger because we are better" can also hold true.

Example 11–7: Intel Bags Record Fine

Consumers who have purchased new computers worldwide have likely been harmed by the exclusive sales practices of Intel. That is because these practice result in less competition in the computer chip market and higher computer chip prices, which translate to higher computer prices. That is why there were about 80 consumer class-action lawsuits filed against Intel at the time that Intel offered to settle with AMD.

Example 11–8: High Switching Costs in the Credit World

In the auto industry, such firms as General Motors offer customers GM credit cards that accumulate reward points toward a discount for the purchase of a new vehicle, if purchased from General Motors. Gas stations, such as Petro-Canada, offer cards (i.e., Petro Points) that accumulate gas discounts based on volume usage.

Example 11–9: Facebook Frenzy

To explain how the network effect applies to the online social networking industry, let us first review the definition of "networking effect," which is a situation where a customer's willingness to use an item depends on how many others use it. In the case of social networking sites, a potential member is more likely to choose a site with a larger membership. The potential user is more likely to connect with long-lost friends or friends from other geographical regions if the user joins a large social network membership site. Other potential users (such as people running for political office) are more likely to join a site where they can more easily pick up large blocks of supporters, which would be the larger website. Also, advertisers are more likely to pay advertising dollars to larger websites as each advertising dollar will more likely reach a larger target audience.

Example 11–10: Apple's iMania

The forms of nonprice competition used by Apple include the following. Apple has effectively focused on innovation as a way to increase its market share. Examples include the novel hardware and software related to the iPod, iPhone, and iPad. Apple engages in exclusive dealing when it only allows software developers to develop applications for its "i-products" if the developers use Apple's programming tools and not competitors' tools. Apple has created significant "switching costs" in that iPod, or iPhone or iPad users would have to abandon their existing set of music and video playlists, photo albums, and software applications if they were to switch to a competitor's phone. Finally, Apple has effectively encouraged the network effect by encouraging third-party developers to develop apps that exclusively work with the iPhone. As well, iPhone 4's new video calling feature will encourage the network effect.

Issues and Applications: Game Theory: Opening Up the Brewing Industry

1. This game is a negative-sum game. Although the microbrewery gains $15 million, Labatt and Molson together lose $16 million.

2. Labatt and Molson could use other entry-deterring strategies. They could substantially increase their already high annual advertising expenditures as a barrier to entry. They could also reduce the price of their beer to average total cost. They would not earn economic profits, but the competing breweries would no longer have an incentive to enter the industry. Labatt and Molson could also introduce switching costs. For example, they could offer frequent flyer miles so that customers have a vested interest in staying with one company. In fact, Molson has offered Air Miles with the purchase of 15-can cases of its Canadian brand.

Glossary

Absolute advantage The ability to perform a task using the fewest number of labour hours.

Accounting profit Total revenue minus total explicit costs.

Age–earnings cycle The regular earnings profile of an individual throughout that person's lifetime.

Aggregates Economywide measures.

Allocative efficiency Producing the mix of goods and services most valued by consumers.

Anticombines legislation Laws that make illegal certain economic activies that might restrain trade.

Asymmetric information Exchange situations where one party directly participating in the market possesses special knowledge that is not available to the other party.

Average cost pricing Pricing that occurs when the monopoly firm is forced to set price equal to average total cost.

Average fixed costs Total fixed costs divided by the number of units produced.

Average physical product The total product divided by the number of workers expressed in output per hour.

Average tax rate The total taxes due divided by total taxable income.

Average total costs Total costs divided by the number of units produced; sometimes called per-unit total costs.

Average variable costs Total variable costs divided by the number of units produced.

Best response function The manner in which one oligopolist reacts to a change in price, output, or quality made by another competitor in the industry.

Bilateral monopoly A market structure in which a single buyer faces a single seller.

Black market A market in which the price-controlled good is sold at an illegally high price through various under-the-table methods.

Breakeven The output that a firm must produce to reach the point where its profits are zero.

Bureaucracy An administrative system run by a large staff following rules and procedures set down by government.

Bureaucrats Nonelected government officials.

Capital gain The positive difference between the buying and selling prices of an asset.

Capital loss The negative difference between the purchase price and the sale price of an asset.

Capture hypothesis A theory of regulatory behaviour that predicts that the regulators will eventually be captured by the special interests of the industry being regulated.

Cartel An association of suppliers in an industry that agree to set common prices and output quotas to prevent competition.

Ceteris paribus [KAY-ter-us PEAR-uh-bus] assumption The assumption that nothing changes except the factor or factors being studied; "other things being constant," or "other things being equal."

Collective decision making How voters, politicians, and other interested parties act and how these actions influence nonmarket decisions.

Common property Nonexclusive property that is owned by everyone and therefore by no one.

Common property resources Goods or resources that are nonexcludable but are rivalrous.

Comparable-worth doctrine The belief that women should receive the same wages as men if the levels of skill and responsibility in their jobs are equivalent.

Comparative advantage The ability to perform an activity at the lowest opportunity cost.

Complements Two goods are complements if both are used together for consumption or enjoyment.

Concentration ratio The percentage of total industry sales contributed by the four largest firms.

Conglomerate merger The joining of two firms from unrelated industries.

Constant returns to scale No change in long-run average costs when output increases.

Constant-cost industry An industry that can increase its output in the long run, without affecting input prices.

Consumer optimum Reached when the consumer has attained an optimum consumption set of goods and services.

Consumer surplus The difference between the maximum amount that consumers are willing to pay and the actual amount paid for all units of a product consumed.

Consumption The use of goods and services for direct personal satisfaction.

Cooperative game A game in which firms get together to collude or fix prices.

Cost-of-service regulation Regulation that allows the regulated companies to charge prices that reflect the actual average cost of providing the services, with a normal profit included in the assessment of these costs.

Creative response A response that conforms to the letter of the law but undermines its spirit.

Cross-elasticity of demand (*Exy*) The percentage change in the quantity demanded of one good (holding its price constant) divided by the percentage change in the price of a related good.

Deadweight loss The decrease in consumer and producer surplus that results from a situation of allocative inefficiency.

Decreasing-cost industry A situation where input prices decrease as the industry expands in the long run.

Demand The quantities of a specific good or service that individuals are willing to purchase at various possible prices, other things being constant.

Demand curve A graphical representation of the law of demand.

Demerit good Any good that the political process has deemed socially undesirable.

Dependent variable A variable whose value changes according to changes in the value of one or more independent variables.

Deregulation The elimination of regulations on economic activity.

Derived demand Input factor demand derived from demand for the final product being produced.

Diminishing marginal utility The principle that as an individual consumes more of a particular commodity, the total level of utility, or satisfaction, derived from that consumption usually increases. Eventually, however, the rate at which it increases diminishes as more is consumed.

Diseconomies of scale Increases in long-run average costs that occur as output increases.

Distribution of income The way income is allocated among the population.

Division of labour Individuals specializing in a subset of tasks related to a specific product.

Dominant strategies Strategies that are generally successful no matter what actions competitors take.

Economic profits Total revenues minus total opportunity costs of all inputs used, or total revenues minus the total of all implicit and explicit costs.

Economic regulation Regulation that controls the prices that firms are allowed to charge.

Economic system The social arrangements or institutional means through which resources are used to satisfy human wants.

Economic way of thinking Assumes that the typical response to an economic problem of scarcity is rational behaviour.

Economics A social science that studies how people allocate their limited resources to satisfy their wants.

Economies of scale Decreases in long-run average costs resulting from increases in output.

Elastic demand A demand relationship in which a given percentage change in price will result in a larger percentage change in quantity demanded.

Empirical Using real-world data to test the usefulness of a model.

Entrepreneurship Human resources that perform the functions of risk taking, organizing, managing, and assembling other factors of production to make business ventures.

Equilibrium A point from which there tends to be no movement unless demand or supply changes.

Excess capacity A situation where the firm is operating at an output level below that required to achieve minimum average total cost.

Excise tax A tax imposed on a particular commodity or service.

Exclusion principle The principle that no one can be denied the benefits of a public good for failing to pay for it.

Exclusive dealing A situation where the firm supplies its product to a customer on condition that the customer not buy similar products from rival firms supplying a similar product.

Explicit costs Expenses that business managers must take account of because they must actually be paid out by the firm.

External benefits A situation where the marginal social benefits from producing a product exceed the marginal private benefits.

External costs Situations where the marginal social costs of producing a product exceed the marginal private costs of production.

Externality A situation in which a private cost diverges from a social cost; a situation in which the costs of an action are not fully borne by the two parties engaged in exchange.

Featherbedding Unions' tendency to bargain for excessive use of workers.

Firm An organization that brings together factors of production—labour, land, physical capital, human capital, and entrepreneurial skill—to produce a product or service that it hopes can be sold at a profit.

Fixed costs All costs that do not vary—that is, all costs that do not depend on the rate of production.

Free-rider problem A situation in which some individuals take advantage of the fact that others will shoulder the burden of paying for public goods.

Game theory The analytical framework in which two or more individuals, companies, or nations compete for certain payoffs that depend on the strategy that the others employ.

Goods The physical items that consumers are willing to pay for.

Government, or political, goods Goods (and services) provided by the public sector; they can be either private or public goods.

Horizontal merger The joining of firms that are producing or selling a similar product.

Human capital The education and training of workers.

Implicit costs Expenses that business managers do not have to pay out of pocket.

Import quota A supply restriction that prohibits the importation of more than a specified quantity of a particular good in a one-year period.

Incentive Inducement to take a particular action.

Incentive structure The system of rewards and punishments individuals face with respect to their own actions.

Income elasticity of demand A horizontal shift in the demand curve in response to changes in income.

Income in kind Income received in the form of goods and services.

Increasing-cost industry A situation where input prices increase as the industry expands in the long run.

Independent variable A variable whose value is determined independently of, or outside, the equation under study.

Industry supply curve The locus of points showing the minimum prices at which given quantities will be forthcoming from the industry; also called the market supply curve.

Inelastic demand A demand relationship in which a given percentage change in price will result in a less than proportionate percentage change in the quantity demanded.

Inferior goods Goods for which demand falls as income rises.

Interest Income earned by capital.

Labour market signalling The theory that even if higher education does not change productivity, it acts as an effective signal of greater individual abilities.

Labour Productive contributions made by individuals who work.

Laissez-faire French term for "leave it alone"; the government should leave it (the economy) alone or "let it be."

Land Nonhuman gifts of nature.

Law of demand The observation that there is an inverse relationship between the price of any good and its quantity demanded, holding other factors equal.

Law of diminishing (marginal) returns The observation that after some point, successive equal-sized increases in a variable factor of production, such as labour, added to fixed factors of production, will result in smaller increases in output.

Law of increasing relative cost When society takes more resources and applies them to the production of any specific good, the opportunity cost increases for each additional unit produced.

Law of supply The observation that there is a direct relationship between the price of any good and its quantity supplied, holding other factors constant.

Long run The period of time in which all inputs can be varied.

Long-run average cost curve The locus (path) of points representing the minimum unit cost of producing any given rate of output, given current technology and resource prices.

Long-run industry supply curve A market supply curve showing the relationship between quantities supplied by the entire industry and prices, after sufficient time has passed to allow firms to change plant sizes and enter or exit the industry.

Lorenz curve A geometric representation of the distribution of income.

Macroeconomics The study of the behaviour of the economy as a whole.

Majority rule A collective decision-making system in which group decisions are made on the basis of 50.1 percent of the vote.

Marginal benefit The maximum amount that consumers are willing to pay for a specified unit of quantity. It is the height of the demand curve at the specified unit of quantity.

Marginal cost The minimum amount that firms must receive in order to supply a specified unit of quantity. It is the height of the supply curve at the specified unit of quantity.

Marginal costs Costs that result from a one-unit change in the production rate.

Marginal cost pricing A system where the price charged to the consumer is equal to the opportunity cost to society of producing the last unit of the good in question.

Marginal factor cost (MFC) The cost of using an additional unit of an input.

Marginal physical product The change in output caused by a one-unit change in the labour input.

Marginal physical product (MPP) of labour The change in output resulting from the addition of one more worker.

Marginal revenue The change in total revenues attributable to changing production by one unit of the product in question.

Marginal revenue product (MRP) The marginal physical product (MPP) times marginal revenue.

Marginal tax rate The change in taxes due divided by the change in taxable income.

Marginal utility The change in total utility divided by the change in the number of units consumed.

Market All of the arrangements that individuals have for exchanging with one another.

Market clearing price or **equilibrium price** The price at which market quantity demanded equals market quantity supplied.

Market demand Determined by adding the individual demand at each price for all the consumers in the market.

Market failure A situation in which perfect competition either overallocates or underallocates resources to a good or service.

Market structure Characteristics of an industry—such as the number of sellers, the ease of entry of new firms, each firm's ability to set the price, and the degree to which each firm's product differs from its competitor's.

Marketing boards A policy that allows producers to band together to restrict total quantity supplied by using quotas.

Merger The joining of two or more firms under single ownership or control.

Merit good Any good that the political process has deemed socially desirable.

Microeconomics The study of decision making undertaken by individuals and by firms in specific parts of the economy.

Minimum efficient scale (MES) The output rate when economies of scale end and constant economies of scale start.

Minimum wage The lowest hourly wage rate that firms may legally pay their workers.

Mixed economy An economic system in which decisions about how resources are used are made partly by the private sector and partly by the public sector.

Models or theories Simplified representations of the real world used to understand and predict economic phenomena.

Money price The actual price that you pay in dollars and cents for any good or service at any point in time.

Monopolist A single supplier of a good or service for which there are no close substitutes.

Monopolistic competition A market structure in which there is a relatively large number of firms offering similar but differentiated products.

Monopoly A firm that has great control over the price of a good it sells.

Monopsonist The single buyer of a factor of production.

Monopsonistic exploitation Monopsonistic exploitation is the difference between marginal revenue product and the wage rate.

Moral hazard A situation where one party to a transaction has both the ability and incentive to shift costs to other parties.

Natural monopoly The firm that first takes advantage of economies of scale in order to establish a monopoly position.

Negative-sum game A game in which players as a group lose at the end of the game.

Network effect A situation where a customer's willingness to use an item depends on how many others use it.

Noncooperative game A game in which it is too costly for firms to negotiate collusive agreements and to enforce them.

Nonprice-rationing devices Methods used to ration scarce goods that are price controlled.

Normal goods Goods for which demand rises as income rises.

Normal rate of return The amount that must be paid to an investor to induce investment in a business.

Normative economics Analysis based on value judgments made about what ought to be.

Offer-to-purchase policy A price floor policy reinforced by the purchase of surplus output by the government.

Oligopoly A market situation that consists of a small number of interdependent sellers.

Opportunistic behaviour Actions that focus solely on short-run gains and ignore the benefits of cooperation in the long run.

Opportunity cost The value of the best alternative that must be given up because a choice was made.

Opportunity cost of capital The amount of income, or yield, that could have been earned by investing in the next-best alternative.

Optimal quantity of pollution The level of pollution at which the marginal benefit equals the marginal cost of obtaining clean air.

Payoff matrix A matrix of outcomes, or consequences, of the strategies available to the players in a game.

Perfect competition A market structure in which each firm is such a small part of the industry that it cannot affect the price of the product in question.

Perfectly elastic demand A demand that has the characteristic that even the slightest increase in price will lead to zero quantity demanded.

Perfectly elastic supply When the slightest reduction in price will cause quantity supplied to fall to zero.

Perfectly inelastic demand A demand that exhibits zero responsiveness to price changes.

Perfectly inelastic supply When no matter what the price, the quantity supplied remains the same.

Physical capital Factories and equipment used in production.

Planning curve The curve that represents the various average costs attainable at the planning stage of the firm's decision making.

Planning horizon The long run, during which all inputs are variable.

Plant size The physical size of the factories that a firm owns and operates to produce its output.

Policies Action plans designed to achieve goals.

Positive economics Analysis that can be tested by observing the facts.

Positive-sum game A game in which players as a group end up better off.

Predatory pricing A strategy where existing firms cut the prices of their products below costs in order to discourage the entry of new firms.

Price ceiling The maximum price that may be allowed in an exchange.

Price controls Government-mandated minimum or maximum prices that may be charged for goods and services.

Price discrimination The practice of charging different prices for units of the same product, not justified by cost differences.

Price elasticity of demand (Ep) The relative amount by which the quantity demanded will change in response to a change in the price of a particular good.

Price elasticity of supply (Es) The responsiveness of the quantity supplied of a commodity to a change in its price.

Price floor A minimum price below which a good or service may not be sold.

Price leadership A practice in many oligopolistic industries in which the largest firm publishes its price list ahead of its competitors, who then match those announced prices. Also called parallel pricing.

Price searcher A firm that must determine the price–output combination that maximizes profit because it faces a downward-sloping demand curve.

Price support policies Policies that aim to help the farmers by enhancing the prices they receive for the farm products they supply.

Price system An economic system in which relative prices are constantly changing to reflect changes in supply and demand for different commodities.

Price taker A competitive firm that takes price as a given, something determined outside the individual firm.

Price war A situation where competing firms respond to a rival's price out with even larger price cuts.

Principle of rival consumption The principle that one person's consumption reduces the amount of private goods available for others to consume.

Prisoners' dilemma The strategic game in which two prisoners have a choice between confessing and not confessing to a crime.

Private costs Costs borne solely by the individuals who incur them; also called *internal costs*.

Private goods Goods and services that are both excludable and rivalrous.

Private marginal benefits The marginal benefits that accrue to the direct consumers of the product or service.

Private marginal costs The extra costs that the firms supplying the market must pay for.

Private property rights Exclusive rights of ownership.

Producer surplus The difference between the actual amount that producers receive for a product and the lowest amount that they would be prepared to accept for it.

Product differentiation The ways that the firm distinguishes its product, in a positive manner, from similar products or services offered by competitors.

Production Any activity that results in the conversion of resources into goods and services.

Production function The relationship between the amount of physical output the firm can produce and the quantity of capital and labour used to produce it.

Production possibilities curve (PPC) A curve that represents all possible production combinations of two goods that can be produced.

Productive efficiency Occurs when a given output level is produced at minimal cost.

Productively inefficient point Any point below the production possibilities curve, assuming resources are fully employed.

Profit Income earned by the entrepreneur.

Profit-maximizing rate of production The rate of production that maximizes total profits, or the difference between total revenues and total costs; also, the rate of production at which marginal revenue equals marginal cost.

Progressive taxation As taxable income increases, the percentage of income paid in taxes also increases.

Property rights The rights of an owner to use and to exchange that property.

Proportional rule A decision-making system in which actions are based on the proportion of the "votes" cast and are in proportion to them.

Proportional taxation A tax system in which regardless of an individual's income, the tax bill comprises exactly the same proportion. Also called a flat-rate tax.

Public goods Goods that are neither excludable nor rivalrous. They can be consumed jointly by many individuals simultaneously at no additional cost and with no reduction in quality or quantity.

Pure capitalist economy An economic system characterized by private ownership of all property resources.

Pure command economy An economic system characterized by public ownership of all property resources.

Rate-of-return regulation Regulation that allows regulated companies to set prices that ensure a normal, or competitive, rate of return on the investment in the business.

Rationality assumption An individual makes decisions based on maximizing his or her own self-interest.

Recycling The reuse of raw materials derived from manufactured products.

Regressive taxation A smaller percentage of taxable income is taken in taxes as taxable income increases.

Relative price Any commodity's price in terms of another commodity.

Rent Income earned by land.

Rent control The placement of a price ceiling or maximum price on rents.

Retained earnings Profits not given out to shareholders.

Scarcity The condition that arises because wants always exceed what can be produced with limited resources.

Services The tasks performed by others that consumers are willing to pay for.

Share-the-gains, share-the-pains theory A theory of regulatory behaviour in which the regulators must take account of the demands of three groups: legislators, members of the regulated industry, and consumers of the regulated industry's products or services.

Shortage A situation in which the quantity demanded exceeds the quantity supplied at a price below the market clearing price.

Short run Any time period that is so short that there is at least one input that the firm cannot alter.

Short-run breakeven price The price at which a firm's total revenues equal its total costs.

Short-run shutdown price The price that just equals minimum average variable cost.

Shutdown A short-run situation where the firm stays in business but temporarily produces at a zero quantity level.

Social costs The full costs borne by society whenever a resource use occurs.

Social marginal benefits Private marginal benefits plus external benefits.

Social marginal costs Private marginal costs plus external costs.

Social regulation Regulation that reflects concern for public welfare across all industries.

Specialization Working at a relatively well-defined, limited endeavour; individuals, regions, and nations producing a narrow range of products.

Strategic dependence A situation in which one firm's actions with respect to price, quality, advertising, and related changes may be strategically countered by the reactions of one or more other firms in the industry.

Strategy A rule used to make a choice.

Strikebreakers Temporary or permanent workers hired by a company to replace union members who are on strike.

Substitutes Two goods are substitutes when either one can be used to satisfy a similar want.

Sunk costs Irreversible costs incurred prior to your decision.

Supply The quantities of a specific good or service that firms are willing to sell at various possible prices, other things being constant.

Supply curve An upward-sloping curve that shows the typically direct relationship between price and quantity supplied.

Surplus A situation in which quantity supplied is greater than quantity demanded at a price above the market clearing price.

Tariffs Special taxes that are imposed on certain imported goods.

Tax bracket A specified level of taxable income to which a specific and unique marginal tax rate is applied.

Tax incidence The distribution of tax burdens among various groups in society.

Technology Society's pool of applied knowledge concerning how goods and services can be produced.

Terms of exchange The prices we pay for the desired items.

Terms of trade The amount of one product that must be traded in order to obtain an additional unit of another product.

Theory of contestable markets A hypothesis that most of the outcomes predicted by the theory of perfect competition will occur in certain industries with relatively few firms, due to easy entry.

Theory of public choice The analysis of collective decision making.

Three Ps Private property, Profits, and Prices inherent in capitalism.

Tit-for-tat strategy A strategy in which a firm cheats in the current period if the rival firm cheated in the previous period but cooperates in the current period if the rival firm cooperated in the previous period.

Total costs The sum of all costs incurred.

Total revenues The quantity sold multiplied by the price.

Transaction costs The costs associated with finding out exactly what is being exchanged as well as the cost of enforcing contracts.

Transfer payments. Payments made to individuals for which no services or goods are concurrently rendered in return.

Transfers in kind Payments that are in the form of actual goods and services for which no goods or services are rendered concurrently in return.

Unit elasticity of demand A demand relationship in which the quantity demanded changes exactly in proportion to the changes in price.

Util A representative unit by which utility is measured.

Utility The want-satisfying power of a good or service.

Utility analysis The analysis of consumer decision making based on utility maximization.

Variable costs Costs whose magnitude varies with the rate of production.

Vertical merger The joining of a firm with another to which it sells an output or from which it buys an input.

Voluntary exchange Acts of trading between individuals that make both parties to the trade subjectively better off.

Wages Income earned by labour.

x-axis The horizontal axis in a graph.

y-axis The vertical axis in a graph.

Zero-sum game A game in which one player's losses are offset by another player's gains; at any time, sum totals are zero.

Index

and competition, 398
government goods at zero price, 399
incentive structure, 398
influence on economy, 398
rational ignorance, 400–401
scarcity constraint, 398
similarities with market decision
    making, 398–399
size of, 405
use of force, 399
voting *vs.* spending, 399–400
public welfare, 316–317
pure capitalist economy, 43
    see also capitalism
pure command economy, 43, 49, 50

Q
Qatar, 292
quantity restrictions, 146–147, 158
Quebec Pension Plan (QPP), 371
Quebecor Inc., 316, 328

R
rate of return, 189
rate-of-return regulation, 314–315
rational decision making
    incentives, 7–8
    at the margin, 7
    and opportunity cost, 5–6
    rationality assumption, 5
    self-interest, 9
rational ignorance, 400–401
rationality assumption, 5, 173
rationing by queues, 135
rationing function of prices, 134–137
raw materials, availability of, 106
re-sale listings, 86
real GDP, 125
recession, 67, 85, 125, 227–228
Recording Association of America
    (RIAA), 263
recover, 379
recycling, 379, 385–387
reduce, 379
refusal to supply, 325
regressive taxation, 402
regulation
    anticombines legislation, 322–324
    auto safety regulation, 318
    capture hypothesis, 318
    cost-benefit analysis, 321–322
    cost-of-service regulation, 313–314
    creative response, 317
    deregulation, 315, 319, 321
    economic regulation, 313–315
    explanations of regulators' behaviour,
        318–319

federal regulatory agencies, 317*t*
feedback effects, 317
and monopoly, 313
natural monopolies, 315
and profit maximization, 314
rate-of-return regulation, 314–315
results of regulation, 317
share-the-gains, share-the-pains
    theory, 319
short-run *vs.* long-run effects,
    319–322
social regulation, 316–317
theory of contestable markets, 321
types of government regulation,
    313–318
relative price, 62–63, 63*t*
rent, 3
rent controls, 137–139, 137*f*, 161–162,
    161*f*, 161*f*, 162*f*
rent *vs.* own, 84–85, 84*t*
repeated games, 290–291
reproductive technologies, 140
resale price maintenance, 325
Research in Motion, 301
resource allocation, 149
resource management, 178
restrictive trade practices, 333
retained earnings, 404
reuse, 379
revenue
    marginal revenue, 217
    under monopoly, 248–249
    tax revenues, 150
    total revenues. *See* total revenues
reviewable matters, 323
RFID tags, 66
rivalrous goods, 122
Robinson, Joan, 280
Rolling Stones, 325–326
Romanow Report, 153
Running Room Canada Inc., 282–283

S
Saudi Arabia, 173, 292
scarcity
    competition, 135
    defined, 2
    market and public-sector decision
        making, 398
    and price, 134
    production possibilities curve (PPC)
        and trade-offs, 31–32
    and resources, 2–3
    scarce resources, 386–387
    specialization and self-interest, 41
    three basic economic questions, 43
    and wants, 2

scientific method
    assumptions, 10–11
    behavioural models, *vs.* thought
        processes, 12
    crime, economic model of, 12–13
    models or theories, 9–10
    testing models, 11–12
self-interest, 9, 41, 44
services, 2
shale natural gas, 82
Shanghai, 255
share-the-gains, share-the-pains
    theory, 319
Shaw Communications, 329
short run
    costs. *See* short-run costs
    defined, 192
    equilibrium, in perfect competition,
        226–228
    industry supply curve, 224–225, 225*f*
    vs. long run, 191–196
    loss minimization, 220–221, 220*f*
    management planning terms, 192
    output and profit, in perfect
        competition, 215–228
    regulation, effects of, 319–322
    supply, in perfect competition,
        224–225
short-run analysis in accounting, 243
short-run average cost curves, 197
short-run breakeven price,
    222, 222*f*
short-run cost curves, 201
short-run costs
    average and marginal costs,
        relationship between, 199–200
    average fixed costs, 197
    average total costs, 197
    average variable cost, 197
    fixed costs, 196
    marginal costs, 199
    minimum cost points, 200
    short-run average cost curves, 197
    total costs, 196
    variable costs, 197
short-run price elasticity of demand,
    102, 102*f*
short-run price elasticity of supply,
    105–106*f*
short-run shutdown price, 222–223,
    222*f*, 223*t*
shortage
    defined, 76
    and demand and supply, 77
shutdown, 221
signalling, 133
Simon, Julian, 387

Photo Credits

Chapter 1 Pages 1 and 15 Huguette Roe/Shutterstock; page 4 Comstock/Thinkstock; page 6 Sakala/Shutterstock; page 12 Monkey Business Images/Shutterstock; **Chapter 2** pages 29 and 47 Charlie Hutton/Shutterstock; page 32 Pixland/Thinkstock; page 33 iStockphoto/Thinkstock; page 46 Paul Prescott/Shutterstock; **Chapter 3** pages 61 and 83 Hemere/Thinkstock; page 69 AP Wideworld Photos; page 74 Yuri Arcurs/Shutterstock; page 79 R. Gino Santa Maria/ Shutterstock; **Chapter 4** pages 92 and 107 © Steve Manson/Getty Images; page 93 Jirka Bursik/ Shutterstock; page 101 Shutterstock; page 102 Shutterstock; **Chapter 6** pages 132 and 151 CP/Ryan Remiorz; pages 135 aceshot1/Shutterstock; page 139 Hemera/Thinkstock; page 146 Desiree Walstra/Shutterstock; **Chapter 7** pages 164 and 174 The Slide Farm/Al Harvey; page 165 Getty Images Entertainment; page 168 AP Wideworld Photos; page 173 Yuri Arcurs/ Shutterstock; **Chapter 8** pages 188 and 207 Yuri Arcurs/Shutterstock; page 193 Christophe Testi/Shutterstock; page 199 Shutterstock; **Chapter 9** pages 212 and 235 Dick Hemingway; page 214 Sean Buck/Shutterstock; page 221 iStockphoto/Thinkstock; page 228 Comstock/ Thinkstock; **Chapter 10** pages 244 and 266 CP/Tom Hanson; page 247 Photodisc/ Thinkstock; page 255 Brian Tan/Shutterstock; page 263 Pixland/Thinkstock; **Chapter 11** pages 279 and 303 Courtesy of Moosehead; page 282 Brendan Howard/Shutterstock; page 293 Boris 15/Shutterstock; page 296 Stockbyte/Thinkstock.